National Party Conventions 1831-1980

Congressional Quarterly Inc.
1414 22nd Street, N.W.
Washington, D.C. 20037

UNITED STATES

Congressional Quarterly Inc.

Congressional Quarterly Inc., an editorial research service and publishing company, serves clients in the fields of news, education, business and government. It combines Congressional Quarterly's coverage of Congress, government and politics with the more general subject range of an affiliated service, Editorial Research Reports.

Congressional Quarterly, founded in 1945 by Henrietta and Nelson Poynter, publishes the *Congressional Quarterly Weekly Report* and a variety of books, including college political science textbooks under the CQ Press imprint and public affairs paperbacks designed as timely reports to keep journalists, scholars and the public abreast of developing issues, events and trends. Recent public affairs titles include *Presidential Elections Since 1789, Third Edition, Employment in America* and *Defense Policy, Third Edition.* New CQ Press texts include *Interest Group Politics, Change and Continuity in the 1980 Elections, Revised Edition,* and *The Presidency and the American Political System.*

CQ also publishes information directories and reference volumes on the federal government, national elections and politics. They include the *Guide to Congress,* the *Guide to the Supreme Court,* the *Guide to U.S. Elections* and *Politics in America.* The *CQ Almanac,* a compendium of legislation for one session of Congress, is published each year. *Congress and the Nation,* a record of government for a presidential term, is published every four years.

CQ publishes *The Congressional Monitor,* a daily report on current and future activities of congressional committees, and several newsletters, including *Congressional Insight,* a weekly analysis of congressional action, and *Campaign Practices Reports,* a semimonthly update on campaign laws.

CQ conducts seminars and conferences on Congress, the legislative process, the federal budget, national elections and politics, and other current issues. CQ Direct Research performs contract research and maintains a reference library and query desk for clients.

Editorial Research Reports covers subjects beyond the specialized scope of Congressional Quarterly. It publishes reference material on foreign affairs, business, education, cultural affairs, national security, science and other topics of news interest. Founded in 1923, the service merged with Congressional Quarterly in 1956.

Printed in the United States of America

Library of Congress Cataloging in Publication Data

Main entry under title:

National party conventions, 1831-1980.

Includes bibliographies and index.
1. Political conventions — History.   2. Presidents — United States — Nomination — History.   I. Congressional Quarterly, inc.
JK2255.N37   1983   324.5´6´0973   83-14426
ISBN 0-87187-275-7

Editor: Patricia M. Russotto
Major Contributor: Rhodes Cook
Contributors: Irwin B. Arieff, Christopher Buchanan, John Felton, Kathryn Waters Gest, Larry Light, John L. Moore, Margaret C. Thompson, Elizabeth Wehr, Richard Whittle
Cover Design: Richard A. Pottern
Indexer: Janet E. Hoffman

Contents

Editor's Note. *National Party Conventions, 1831-1980* updates the first and second editions to cover the dramatic 1980 conventions that pitted Democratic incumbent Jimmy Carter against Republican challenger and eventual winner Ronald Reagan in a race for the White House. It also includes information on John B. Anderson's run for the presidency under the banner of his newly created National Unity Campaign. First published in 1975, the book contains data on U.S. nominating conventions that previously had been scattered among numerous sources not readily available to the general reader or researcher. The book begins by detailing the pre-convention nominating process from 1789 to 1828. The next section traces the development of the national nominating convention from its earliest days to the present, including discussions of the delegate selection process, convention party rules, credentials disputes, party platforms, and communications and the media. The third section, the heart of the book, provides descriptions of all major party conventions and excerpts from party platforms. Charts listing state-by-state breakdowns of key convention votes on rules and procedures disputes, as well as the balloting for presidential nominees, appear in the following section. An appendix includes historical profiles of American political parties, political party nominees from 1832 through 1980, and a biographical directory of presidential and vice presidential candidates. The general index provides quick access to information contained throughout the book.

Introduction

Since the 1830s, America's major political parties and most of the prominent third parties have met in conventions to nominate their presidential and vice presidential candidates. The convention is a uniquely American institution, never mentioned in the Constitution, nor was it the subject of congressional legislation until the Federal Election Campaign Act of 1974. But through its adaptability and multiplicity of functions, the convention has nonetheless been an enduring feature of the political landscape.

This third edition of *National Party Conventions* is being published at the beginning of the 1984 presidential primary season to provide readers with an up-to-date, comprehensive history of the nation's presidential nominating process in the nearly two centuries that have preceded. The volume begins with a discussion of the origins of the American party system, followed by a concentrated look at the convention system and each major and prominent third party convention ever held.

The convention system, although in continuous use for nearly 150 years, was never envisioned by the Founding Fathers. They established the electoral college as the lone mechanism to select the President. But the Founding Fathers also did not foresee the rise of political parties; and when competing parties developed in the formative years of the Republic, a nominating method had to be found. In the early 19th century, party leaders first employed congressional caucuses to nominate presidential candidates. But as the desire for increased democracy swept the nation, the exclusive caucuses proved unsatisfactory and a new method had to be found to involve mass citizen participation.

The new method turned out to be the convention and was initiated by the Anti-Masonic Party in September 1831. Their convention was small by modern standards, attracting 116 delegates from 13 states. The delegates adopted an address to the people (a forerunner of the modern platform) and nominated William Wirt for the presidency. Although Wirt fared poorly in the general election and the Anti-Masonic Party failed to survive the decade, the success of the convention as a nominating mechanism led to its adoption by other parties.

The Democrats held their first convention the following year, 1832, and without interruption have held a national convention every four years since then. The party's gathering in July 1984 in San Francisco would be the Democrats' 39th. The Republicans held their first convention in 1856, two years after the party's formation, and the August 1984 convention in Dallas would be the GOP's 33rd.

Through a century of massive political, social and technological changes, the survival of the convention is a tribute to both its adaptability and importance in the presidential nominating process. Throughout its history, the convention has had a number of functions — foremost, the selection of a national ticket, the adoption of a platform, the discussion of party affairs and the building of party unity. While the conduct and setting of the convention has changed dramatically over the years, the major functions have remained unchanged.

Before the Civil War, conventions were held in relative obscurity. At most, several hundred delegates attended. Delegate selection was often informal, and participation was open to anyone with the motivation to chance the nation's uncertain transportation system.

Improved transportation and communication have provided conventions in recent decades with greater national attention and placed them under closer scrutiny. Delegate selection has been formalized and the drive for increased democratization produced the presidential primary, now the major method of delegate selection.

Advances in television and radio have enabled conventions in the post-World War II years to become media spectaculars, with all the privacy of a fish bowl. The thousands of delegates, spectators and media representatives that would attend the Democratic and Republican conventions of 1984 offer a marked contract to the relatively informal conventions of the 1830s.

About This Book

The first section of this book describes the presidential nominating process in the pre-convention years, from 1789 to 1828. It discusses the origins of the American party system and the use of the congressional caucus in the period as the principal nominating method. The decline of

---

Photographs

Most of the photographs and engravings appearing in this book were obtained from the collection of the Library of Congress. The Smithsonian Institution provided the cover photograph of the 1868 Republican Convention (Smithsonian Photo No. 71146) and the photograph of Alton S. Parker on page 60. The photographs of Thomas E. Dewey, page 89, and Richard M. Nixon, page 99, were obtained from Wide World Photos Inc. The Dewey photograph, page 86, was obtained from Harris & Ewing photographers. The photographs of Jimmy Carter on pages 119 and 128 and the photograph of Ronald Reagan on page 128 were provided by the White House.

---

the caucus and rise of the convention system is discussed at the end of the section. *(p. 1)*

The second section provides an overview of the functions and development of the national convention. This section focuses on various aspects of the convention-delegate selection, credentials disputes, rules, the platform and convention officers — as well as basic changes in the conduct of conventions. The section concludes with chronological highlights of national party conventions, 1831 to 1980. *(p. 7)*

The third section is the heart of the volume, a description of the conventions of all parties that received at least two per cent of the popular vote in any presidential election since 1831. Included are all Democratic, Republican and Whig conventions, as well as those of leading third parties. Within each convention segment is a discussion of the contest for the presidential and vice presidential nominations, all significant roll calls, and an overview of the party platform. Each segment concludes with excerpts from the platform on leading issues of the campaign. The convention chronology is augmented by a section of charts entitled key convention ballots, showing the vote of each state and territory on major roll calls at all Democratic, Whig and Republican conventions. *(pp. 19, 139)*

The fourth section offers profiles of the parties whose conventions were described in the convention chronology, as well as other parties, such as the Communist, Socialist Labor and Socialist Workers, which are active today. *(p. 197)*

The fifth section is a biographical directory of all the candidates who received electoral votes, coupled with a comprehensive list of major and minor party nominees for President and Vice President since 1831. *(pp. 213, 221)*

The last section of the book is a bibliography that lists by chapter leading works relating to the subjects discussed. Interspersed throughout the book are valuable boxes that highlight material discussed in the text. Subjects of the boxes include notable credentials and platform fights, the Democrats' two-thirds rule, and convention sites and dates.

Pre-Convention Politics: 1789-1828

For nearly a century and a half, the United States has had an established two-party system. Yet such a system was never envisioned by the Founding Fathers, who viewed the existence of political parties with suspicion.

In his Farewell Address, written in 1796, President George Washington warned the American people of "the danger of parties," and went on to state: "There is an opinion that parties in free countries are useful checks upon the administration of the government, and serve to keep alive the spirit of liberty. This within certain limits is probably true; and in governments of a monarchical cast patriotism may look with indulgence, if not with favor, upon the spirit of party. But in those of the popular character, in governments purely elective, it is a spirit not to be encouraged.... A fire not to be quenched, it demands a uniform vigilance to prevent its bursting into a flame, lest, instead of warming, it should consume."

Washington's suspicion of parties was not unusual for the period and was shared by other early American leaders. Thomas Jefferson, writing in 1789, declared: "If I could not go to heaven but with a party, I would not go there at all." Even a generation later, after the establishment of an American party system, two early 19th century presidents continued to speak out against the existence of political parties. Andrew Jackson, 12 years before he was elected president, wrote in 1816: "Now is the time to exterminate the monster called party spirit." In 1822, after his unopposed 1820 election victory, President James Monroe characterized parties as "the curse of the country."

Early American leaders were heavily influenced in their attitude by a dominant anti-party theme in European political philosophy, which equated parties with factions and viewed both negatively. Thomas Hobbes (1588-1679), David Hume (1711-1776) and Jean Jacques Rousseau (1712-1778)—three European philosophers whose views strongly influenced the Founding Fathers—regarded parties as threats to state government.[1] In England there was no formal party system until the 1820s, several decades after the formation of parties in the United States. In colonial America there were no parties, and there were none in the Continental Congress or under the Articles of Confederation. (Footnotes, p. 6)

The Constitution did not provide either authority for or prohibitions against political parties. Historians have pointed out that most of the Founding Fathers had only a dim understanding of the function of political parties and thus were ambivalent, if not hostile, toward parties when they laid down the framework of the new government. Nevertheless, the delegates to the Constitutional Convention and their successors in Congress ensured a role for parties in the government when they gave protection to civil rights and the right to organize. The founders set up what they regarded as safeguards against excesses of party activity by providing an elaborate governmental system of checks and balances. The prevailing attitude of the convention on this matter was summed up by James Madison, who wrote in *The Federalist* that the "great object" of the new government was "to secure the public good and private rights against the danger of such a faction [party], and at the same time to preserve the spirit and the form of popular government."

Madison's greatest fear was that a party would become a tyrannical majority. This could be avoided, he believed, through the republican form of government which the proponents of the Constitution advocated. A republic, as understood by Madison, was an elected body of wise, patriotic citizens, while a democracy was equated with mob rule. In *The Federalist*, Madison dismissed the democratic form of government as a spectacle of "turbulence and contention."

Ironically, in this setting two competing parties grew up quickly. They developed as a result of public sentiment for and against adoption of the Constitution. The Federalist Party—a loose coalition of merchants, shippers, financiers and other business interests—favored the strong central government provided by the Constitution, while their opponents (at first called Anti-Federalists) were intent upon preservation of sovereignty of the states. Underlying the controversy was the desire of the interests represented by the Federalists to create a government with power to guarantee the value of the currency (and thus protect the position of creditors) and the desire of the agrarians and frontiersmen who made up the Anti-Federalists to maintain easy credit conditions and the power of state

"[N]othing could be more illjudged than that intolerant spirit which has at all times characterized political parties."

—Alexander Hamilton, 1787

legislatures to fend off encroachments by a remote federal government.

Unlike the Federalist Party, which was never more than a loose alliance of particular interests, the Anti-Federalists achieved a high degree of organization. The Federalists, in fact, never considered themselves a political party but rather a gentlemanly coalition of interests representing respectable society. What party management there was, they kept clandestine, a reflection of their own fundamental suspicion of parties.

There is no precise date for the beginning of parties, although both Thomas Jefferson and Alexander Hamilton (a Federalist) referred to the existence of a Jeffersonian republican "faction" in Congress as early as 1792.[2]

While party organization became more formalized in the 1790s and early 1800s, particularly among the Jeffersonians, they never acquired a nationally accepted name. The Jeffersonians most commonly referred to themselves as Republicans. Their opponents labeled the Republicans as Anti-Federalists, disorganizers, Jacobins and Democrats—the latter an unflattering term in the early years of the Republic. To many Americans in the late 18th century, a democrat was considered a supporter of mob rule and revolution and often ideologically identified with the bloody French Revolution. The designation Democrat-Republican was used by the Jeffersonians in several states, but was never widely accepted as a party label. However, historians often refer to the Jeffersonians as the Democratic-Republicans, to avoid confusion with the later and unrelated Republican Party, founded in 1854.[3]

Although the early American political leaders acknowledged the development of parties, they did not foresee the emergence of a two-party system. Rather, they often justified the existence of their own party as a reaction to an unacceptable opposition. Jefferson defended his party involvement as a struggle between good and evil: "[When] the principle of difference is as substantial and as strongly pronounced as between the republicans and the Monocrats of our country, I hold it as honorable to take a firm and decided part, and as immoral to pursue a middle line, as between the parties of Honest men, and Rogues, into which every country is divided."

Presidential Politics

The rise of parties forced an alteration in the presidential selection method envisioned by the creators of the Constitution. Delegates to the Constitutional Convention of 1787 had sought a presidential selection method in which the "spirit of party" would play no part. The electoral college system they finally settled on was a compromise born of the diversity of the states—the slavery in the South, the big-state versus small-state rivalries, complex-ities of the separation of powers system and a basic distrust in the political abilities of the populace.

Rather than having the people vote directly for president, the choice was to be entrusted to presidential "electors"—men the Founding Fathers hoped would be wise leaders in the separate states, able to choose the one man best qualified to be president.

Caucus System

But strong political parties soon developed and quickly removed the presidential nomination from the hands of state electors. The parties created the first informal nominating device for choosing a president: a caucus of each party's members in Congress. From 1796 until 1824, congressional caucuses—when a party had enough representatives to form one—chose almost all the candidates for president; the electors then chose from the party nominees. Only twice—in 1800 and 1824—as a result of a failure of any candidate to receive a majority of electoral votes, were presidential elections decided by the House of Representatives, and even in those two cases political parties were instrumental in the election of the president.

Election of 1789

In the United States' first presidential election, held in 1789 shortly after the ratification of the Constitution, the nominating and electing process centered in the electoral college. Electors chosen in the various states were, under the Constitution, entitled to cast two votes, and required to cast each vote for a different person. The individual receiving votes of a majority of the electors was named president and the person receiving the second highest total was named vice president. There were no formal nominations in 1789, but public opinion centered on George Washington of Virginia for president. He received 69 electoral votes, the maximum possible. John Adams of Massachusetts was the leading second choice, although he did not enjoy the degree of unanimity that surrounded Washington. Adams easily won the vice presidency, receiving 34 electoral votes.

Election of 1792

The Federalists and Democratic-Republicans were emerging as competitive parties by the election of 1792, and as a result the Republic experienced the first modification in the presidential nominating process. No attempt was made to displace President Washington, but the Democratic-Republicans mounted a challenge to Vice President Adams. Meeting in Philadelphia in October 1792, a group of Democratic-Republican leaders from the Middle Atlantic states and South Carolina endorsed New York Governor George Clinton over New York Senator Aaron Burr for the vice presidency. While Adams emerged victorious in the electoral college, the endorsement of Clinton by a meeting of party politicians was a milestone in the evolution of the presidential nominating process and a step away from the original electoral college system.

Election of 1796

The election of 1796 brought further modifications in the nominating method, evidenced by the appearance of the congressional caucus.

There was no opposition to Thomas Jefferson as the Democratic-Republican presidential candidate, and he was considered the party's standard-bearer by a consensus of party leaders. However, a caucus of Democratic-

Presidents, 1789-1829

Term	President	Vice President
1789-93	George Washington (Fed.)	John Adams (Fed.)
1793-97	George Washington (Fed.)	John Adams (Fed.)
1797-1801	John Adams (Fed.)	Thomas Jefferson (D-R)
1801-05	Thomas Jefferson (D-R)	Aaron Burr (D-R)
1805-09	Thomas Jefferson (D-R)	George Clinton (D-R)
1809-13	James Madison (D-R)	George Clinton (D-R)
1813-17	James Madison (D-R)	Elbridge Gerry (D-R)
1817-21	James Monroe (D-R)	Daniel D. Tompkins (D-R)
1821-25	James Monroe (D-R)	Daniel D. Tompkins (D-R)
1825-29	John Q. Adams (D-R)	John C. Calhoun (D-R)

Fed. - Federalist; D-R - Democratic-Republican

Republican senators was unable to agree on a running mate, producing a tie vote between New York Senator Aaron Burr and South Carolina Senator Pierce Butler that ended with a walk-out by Butler's supporters. As a result, there was no formal Democratic-Republican candidate to run with Jefferson.

The Federalists held what historian Roy F. Nichols described as a "quasi caucus" of the party's members of Congress in Philadelphia in May 1796.[4] The gathering chose Vice President Adams and Minister to Great Britain Thomas Pinckney of South Carolina as the Federalist candidates.

Election of 1800

In the election of 1800 the congressional caucus for the first time was used as the nominating body by both parties. Neither party, however, desired much publicity for its meeting, gathering in secret to deliberate. The proceedings of their caucuses were sketchily described by private correspondence and occasionally referred to in newspapers of the day. Unlike the public national conventions of later years, privacy was a hallmark of the early caucuses.[5]

Although the actual dates of the 1800 caucuses are hazy, it is believed that both were held in May.[6] The Democratic-Republican caucus was held in Marache's boardinghouse in Philadelphia, where 43 of the party's members of Congress selected Aaron Burr to run with Thomas Jefferson, the latter again the presidential candidate by consensus and not formally nominated by the caucus.

Federalist members of Congress met in the Senate chamber in Philadelphia and nominated President Adams and General Charles Cotesworth Pinckney of South Carolina. Pinckney, the older brother of the Federalist vice presidential candidate in 1796, was placed on the ticket at the insistence of Alexander Hamilton, who believed one of the South Carolina Pinckneys could win. Although the deliberations of the Federalist caucus were secret, the existence of the meeting was not. It was described by the local Democratic-Republican paper, the *Philadelphia Aurora*, as a "Jacobinical conclave." Further denunciations by the paper's author, Benjamin F. Bache, earned him a personal rebuke from the United States Senate.[7]

Election of 1804

The election of 1804 was the first to be held after ratification of the 12th Amendment to the Constitution, in September 1804. The amendment altered the electoral college system by requiring the electors to cast separate votes for president and vice president. The amendment was designed to avoid the unwieldy situation which had developed in 1800, when the leading two Democratic-Republican candidates, Jefferson and Burr, both received the same number of electoral votes. The unexpected tie vote threw the presidential election into the House of Representatives, where it took 36 ballots before Jefferson finally won. With ratification of the amendment, parties in 1804 and thereafter specifically designated their presidential and vice presidential candidates.

The Democratic-Republicans retained the caucus system of nomination in 1804, as they did for the next two decades, and for the first time publicly reported their deliberations. The party caucus was held in February and attracted 108 of the party's senators and representatives. President Jefferson was renominated by acclamation, but Vice President Burr was not considered for a second term. On the first nominating roll call publicly reported in American political history, Governor George Clinton of New York was chosen to run for vice president. He received 67 votes to easily defeat Senator John Breckinridge of Kentucky, who collected 20 votes. "To avoid unpleasant discussions" no names were placed in nomination, and the vote was taken by written ballot.[8]

Before adjourning, the caucus appointed a 13-member committee to conduct the campaign. A forerunner of party national committees, the new campaign group included members of both the House and Senate, but with no two individuals from the same state.

The Federalists dropped the congressional caucus as their nominating method. Federalist leaders in 1804 informally chose Charles Cotesworth Pinckney for president and Rufus King of New York for vice president. However, exactly how they formulated this ticket is unknown. There is no record in 1804 of any Federalist meeting to nominate candidates.[9]

Election of 1808

The Democratic-Republican caucus was held in January 1808. For the first time there was a formal call issued. Vermont Senator Stephen R. Bradley, the chairman of the 1804 caucus, issued the call to all 146 Democratic-Republicans in Congress and several Federalists sympathetic to the Democratic-Republican cause. His authority to call the caucus was questioned by several party leaders, but various reports indicate that 89 to 94 members of Congress attended.[10]

As in 1804 the balloting was done without the formal placing of names in nomination. For president, Jefferson's hand-picked successor, Secretary of State James Madison of Virginia, was an easy winner with 83 votes. Vice President Clinton and James Monroe of Virginia each received

"Among the numerous advantages promised by a well-constructed Union, none deserves to be more accurately developed than its tendency to break and control the violence of faction [party]."

—James Madison, 1787

"If I could not go to heaven but with a party, I would not go there at all."

—Thomas Jefferson, 1789

three votes. For vice president the caucus overwhelmingly renominated Clinton. He received 79 votes, while runner-up John Langdon of New Hampshire collected five. Despite his nomination, supporters of Clinton hoped that their man would be nominated by the Federalists later in the year. But their hopes were dashed when the nomination ultimately went to Pinckney.

As in 1804 the Democratic-Republican caucus appointed a campaign committee that was entrusted with the conduct of the campaign. Membership on the committee was expanded to 15 House and Senate members and it was formally called the "committee of correspondence and arrangement."[11] The committee was authorized to fill any vacancies on the national ticket, should any occur.

Before adjournment a resolution was passed defending the caucus system as "the most practicable mode of consulting and respecting the interest and wishes of all." A similar resolution was passed by later caucuses throughout the history of the system.

The resolution was meant to stem the rumblings of opposition to the caucus system. Seventeen Democratic-Republican members of Congress signed a protest against Madison's selection and questioned the authority of the caucus as a nominating body. Vice President Clinton, himself selected by the caucus, wrote of his disapproval of the caucus system.

The Federalists in 1808 again altered their presidential selection process, holding a secret meeting of party leaders in August of that year to choose the ticket. The meeting, held in New York City, was initially called by the Federalist members of the Massachusetts legislature. Twenty-five to thirty party leaders from seven states, all but South Carolina north of the Potomac River, attended the national meeting. There was some discussion of choosing Vice President George Clinton, a dissident Democratic-Republican, for the presidency, but the meeting ultimately selected the Federalist candidates of 1804: Charles Cotesworth Pinckney and Rufus King.

Election of 1812

The Democratic-Republicans held their quadrennial nominating caucus in May 1812. Eighty-three of the party's 138 members of Congress attended, with the New England and New York delegations poorly represented. The New York delegation was sympathetic to the candidacy of the state's lieutenant governor, De Witt Clinton, who was maneuvering for the Federalist nomination, while New England was noticeably upset with President Madison's foreign policy that was leading to war with England. President Madison was renominated with a near-unanimous total, receiving 82 votes. John Langdon of New Hampshire was chosen for vice president by a wide margin, collecting

64 votes to 16 for Governor Elbridge Gerry of Massachusetts. But Langdon declined the nomination, citing his age (70) as the reason. In a second caucus held in June, Gerry was a runaway winner, receiving 74 votes.

In 1812, as four years earlier, the Federalists held a secret meeting in New York City. It was over twice the size of the 1808 gathering, with 70 representatives from 11 states attending the three-day meeting in September. Delegates were sent to the conference by Federalist general committees, with all but nine of the delegates from the New England and Middle Atlantic states.

Debate centered on whether to run a separate Federalist ticket or to endorse the candidacy of DeWitt Clinton, the nephew of George Clinton. The younger Clinton had already been nominated for the presidency by the New York Democratic-Republican caucus, and the Federalists ultimately passed a resolution approving his candidacy and that of Jared Ingersoll. Ingersoll was a Pennsylvania Federalist who was initially nominated for vice president by a party legislative caucus in that state.

Election of 1816

The Federalist Party was nearly extinct by 1816 and did not hold any type of meeting to nominate candidates for president and vice president. As a result, nomination by the Democratic-Republican caucus was tantamount to election. Only 58 members of Congress attended the first caucus in the House chamber. With the expectation of better attendance, a second caucus was held several days later in mid-March, 1816, and drew 119 senators and representatives. By a vote of 65 to 54, Secretary of State James Monroe was nominated for president, defeating Secretary of War William H. Crawford of Georgia. Forty of Crawford's votes came from five states: Georgia, Kentucky, New Jersey, New York and North Carolina. The vice presidential nomination went to New York Governor Daniel D. Tompkins, who easily outdistanced Pennsylvania Governor Simon Snyder, 85 to 30. The nominations of Monroe and Tompkins revived a Virginia-New York alliance which extended back to the late 18th century. With the lone exception of 1812, every Democratic-Republican ticket since 1800 was composed of a presidential candidate from Virginia and a vice presidential candidate from New York.

While the collapse of the Federalists assured Democratic-Republican rule, it also increased intraparty friction and spurred further attacks on the caucus system. Twenty-two Democratic-Republican members of Congress were absent from the second party caucus, and at least 15 were known to be opposed to the system. Historian Edward Stanwood wrote that there were mass meetings around the country in protest to the caucus system.[12] Opponents claimed that the caucus was not envisioned by the writers of the Constitution, that presidential nominating should not be a function of Congress and that the caucus system encouraged presidential candidates to curry the favor of Congress.

Election of 1820

The 1820 election came during the "Era of Good Feelings," a phrase coined by a Boston publication, the *Columbian Centinel,* to describe a brief period of virtual one-party rule in the United States. With only one candidate, President James Monroe, there was no need for a caucus. One was called, but fewer than 50 of the Democratic-Republican's 191 members of Congress attended. The caucus voted unanimously to make no nominations and passed a resolution explaining that it was inexpedient to do so. Despite the fact that Monroe and Tompkins were not formally renominated, electoral slates were filed on their behalf. They both received nearly unanimous electoral college victories.

Demise of the Caucus

Election of 1824

In 1824 there was still only one party, but within this party there was an abundance of candidates for the presidency: Secretary of State John Quincy Adams of Massachusetts; Senator Andrew Jackson of Tennessee; Secretary of War John C. Calhoun of South Carolina; House Speaker Henry Clay of Kentucky; and Secretary of the Treasury William H. Crawford. It was generally assumed that Crawford was the strongest candidate among members of Congress and would win a caucus if one were held; therefore, Crawford's opponents joined the growing list of caucus opponents.

In early February, 1824, 11 Democratic-Republican members of Congress issued a call for a caucus to be held in the middle of the month. Their call was countered by 24 other members of Congress from 15 states who deemed it "inexpedient under existing circumstances" to hold a caucus. They claimed that 181 members of Congress were resolved not to attend if a caucus were held.

When the caucus convened in mid-February, only 66 members of Congress were present, with three-quarters of those attending from just four states—Georgia, New York, North Carolina and Virginia. As expected, Crawford won the presidential nomination, receiving 64 votes. Selected for vice president was Albert Gallatin of Pennsylvania, who received 57 votes. The caucus passed a resolution defending their actions as "the best means of collecting and concentrating the feelings and wishes of the people of the Union upon this important subject." A committee was appointed to write an address to the people. As written, the text of the address viewed with alarm the "dismemberment" of the Democratic-Republican Party.

The caucus nomination proved to be an albatross for Crawford as his opponents denounced him as the candidate of "King Caucus." Reflecting the increasing democratization of American politics, other presidential candidates relied on nominations by state legislatures to legitimize their presidential ambitions. However, in an attempt to narrow the field, the candidates had to negotiate among themselves. Calhoun alone withdrew to become the vice presidential candidate of all the anti-caucus entries. Adams offered the vice presidency to Jackson as "an easy and dignified retirement to his old age."[13] Jackson refused. Other maneuvers were equally unsuccessful, so that four presidential candidates remained in the field to collect electoral votes, subsequently throwing the election into the House of Representatives, where Adams won.

Election of 1828

The election of 1828 proved to be a transitional one in the development of the presidential nominating process. The caucus was dead, but the national nominating convention was not yet born. Jackson was nominated by his native Tennessee legislature and in October, 1825, three years before the election, accepted the nomination in a speech before the legislature. He accepted Vice President Calhoun as his running-mate, after it was proposed in January 1827, by the *United States Telegraph*, a pro-Jackson paper in Washington. A Pennsylvania state convention paired President Adams with Secretary of the Treasury Richard Rush of Pennsylvania, a ticket that Adams' supporters in other states accepted. Both Jackson and Adams were endorsed by other state legislatures, state conventions and mass meetings.

Trend Toward Conventions

The birth of the national convention system came in 1831, seven years after the death of the caucus. The caucus system collapsed when a field of candidates appeared who would not acquiesce to the choice of one caucus-approved candidate. But other factors were present to undermine the caucus system. These included changes in voting procedures and an expansion of suffrage. Between 1800 and 1824, the number of states in which the electors were chosen by popular vote rather than by the state legislature increased from four out of 16 to 18 out of 24. In 1824 the popular vote reached 1.1 million, compared with fewer than 400,000 in 1800. A broader base of support than the congressional caucus became essential for presidential aspirants.

State legislatures, state conventions and mass meetings all emerged in the 1820s to challenge the caucus. The trend to democratization of the presidential nominating process, as evidenced by the expansion of suffrage and increased importance of the popular vote for President, led shortly to creation of the national nominating convention. The convention system was initiated by the Anti-Masons in 1831, and subsequently was adopted by the major parties before the end of the decade. *(Anti-Masons, p. 200)*

The birth of the national nominating convention was a milestone in the evolution of the presidential nominating process. Political Scientist V. O. Key Jr. summarized some of the major forces that brought about the rise of the convention system: "The destruction of the caucus represented more than a mere change in the method of nomination. Its replacement by the convention was regarded as the removal from power of self-appointed oligarchies that had usurped the right to nominate. The new system, the convention, gave, or so it was supposed, the mass of party members an opportunity to participate in nominations. These events occurred as the domestic winds blew in from the growing West, as the suffrage was being broadened, and as the last vestiges of the early aristocratic leadership were disappearing. Sharp alterations in the distribution of power were taking place, and they were paralleled by the shifts in methods of nomination."[14]

"We must always have party distinctions."
—Martin Van Buren, 1827

With the establishment of the national convention came the re-emergence of the two-party system. Unlike the Founding Fathers, who were suspicious of competitive parties, some political leaders in the late 1820s and 1830s favorably viewed the existence of opposing parties. One of the most prominent of these men, Martin Van Buren, a leading organizer of Jackson's 1828 election victory and himself President after Jackson, had written in 1827: "We must always have party distinctions...."

—By Rhodes Cook

Footnotes

1. Arthur M. Schlesinger Jr., ed., *History of U.S. Political Parties*, volume 1 (1973), p. xxxiv.
2. *Ibid.*, p. 241; William N. Chambers, *Political Parties in a New Nation: The American Experience, 1776-1809* (1963), p. 57.
3. Schlesinger, *op. cit.*, p. 240; Roy F. Nichols, *The Invention of the American Political Parties* (1967), p. 176.
4. Nichols, *ibid.*, p. 192.
5. Schlesinger, *op. cit.*, p. 263.
6. Nichols, *op. cit.*, p. 207. Schlesinger, *op. cit.*, p. 252. George W. Stimpson, *A Book about American Politics* (1952), p. 42.
7. Nichols, *op. cit.*, p. 206; Edward Stanwood, *A History of the Presidency from 1788 to 1897* (1898), p. 59.
8. Nichols, *ibid.*, p. 226.
9. Stanwood, *op. cit.*, p. 83.
10. Nichols, *op. cit.*, p. 235.
11. Schlesinger, *op. cit.*, p. 264.
12. Stanwood, *op. cit.*, p. 110.
13. Eugene H. Roseboom, *A History of Presidential Elections* (1959), p. 83.
14. V. O. Key Jr., *Politics, Parties and Pressure Groups* (1964), p. 372.

Nominating Conventions

Although the presidential nominating convention has been a target of criticism throughout its existence, it has survived to become a traditional fixture of American politics. The longevity and general acceptance of the convention is in large part due to its multiplicity of functions — functions that the convention uniquely combines.

The convention is a nominating body, used by the Democrats, Republicans and most of the principal third parties over the past 150 years. The convention writes a platform, presenting the positions of the party on issues of the campaign. The convention serves as the supreme governing body of the political party, making major decisions on party affairs that in the interim between the conventions are made by the national committee with the guidance of the party chairman. The convention also serves as the ultimate campaign rally, gathering together thousands of party leaders and rank and file members from across the country in an atmosphere that varies widely, sometimes encouraging sober discussion but often resembling a carnival. And the convention serves as a forum for compromise among the diverse elements within a party, allowing the discussion and often the satisfactory solution of differing points of view. There have been many critics of the convention process, but because it successfully combines a multiplicity of functions, the convention has endured.

The convention is an outgrowth of the American political experience. Nowhere is it mentioned in the Constitution, nor has the authority of the convention ever been a subject of congressional legislation. Rather, the convention is the evolutionary result of the American presidential selection process. The convention has been the accepted nominating method of the major political parties since the election of 1832, but internal changes within the convention system have been massive since the early, formative years.

Convention Sites

In the pre-Civil-War period, conventions were frequently held in small buildings, even churches, and attracted only several hundred delegates and a minimum of spectators. Transportation and communications were slow, so most conventions were held in the late spring in a city centrally located geographically. Baltimore, Md., was the most popular convention city in the pre-Civil-War period, hosting the first six Democratic conventions (1832 through 1852), two Whig conventions, one National Republican convention, and the 1831 Anti-Masonic gathering — America's first national nominating convention.

With the nation's westward expansion, Chicago, Ill., in the heartland of America, emerged as the most frequent convention center. Since hosting its first convention in 1860, Chicago has been the site of 24 major party conventions (14 Republican, 10 Democratic). But in recent years, other factors have emerged to be considered along with geographic centrality in the choice of a convention city. The pledge of a financial contribution by the convention city to the party is a major consideration in site selection. The contribution, made in cash and goods and services, in recent years has often been in the vicinity of $1 million and is used to help defray expenses of the party in running the convention. Adequate hotel and convention hall facilities are also of prime importance, as modern-day conventions attract thousands of delegates, party officials, spectators and media representatives. In the last decade convention security has become an increasingly important factor in site selection. A reason given for the choice of Miami Beach, Florida, by the Republicans in 1968 and by both major parties in 1972 was the city's island location, believed to be a strategic advantage in the control of any disruptive protest demonstrations. For the party that controls the White House, often the overriding factor in any site selection decision is the personal preference of the incumbent president. His choice often carries great weight in the final selection of a convention city.

The choice of the convention site is made by the national committees of the two parties about one year before the convention is to take place and is the first major step in the quadrennial convention process. It is followed several months later by announcement of the convention call, the establishment of the major convention committees — credentials, rules, and platform (resolutions), the appointment of convention officers and finally the holding of the convention itself. While these basic steps in the quadrennial process have undergone little change over the past 150 years, there have been major alterations within the nominating convention system.

The call to the convention sets the date and site of the meeting, and is issued early in each election year, if not before. The call to the first Democratic convention, held in 1832, was issued by the New Hampshire Legislature. Early Whig conventions were called by party members in Congress. With the establishment of national committees later in the 19th century, the function of issuing the convention

Democratic Conventions, 1832–1980

Year	City	Dates	Presidential Nominee	Vice Presidential Nominee	No. of Pres. Ballots
1832	Baltimore	May 21-23	Andrew Jackson	Martin Van Buren	1
1835	Baltimore	May 20-22	Martin Van Buren	Richard M. Johnson	1
1840	Baltimore	May 5-6	Martin Van Buren	—[1]	1
1844	Baltimore	May 27-29	James K. Polk	George M. Dallas	9
1848	Baltimore	May 22-25	Lewis Cass	William O. Butler	4
1852	Baltimore	June 1-5	Franklin Pierce	William R. King	49
1856	Cincinnati	June 2-6	James Buchanan	John C. Breckinridge	17
1860	Charleston	April 23-May 3	Deadlocked		57
	Baltimore	June 18-23	Stephen A. Douglas	Benjamin Fitzpatrick Herschel V. Johnson[2]	2
1864	Chicago	August 29-31	George B. McClellan	George H. Pendleton	1
1868	New York	July 4-9	Horatio Seymour	Francis P. Blair	22
1872	Baltimore	July 9-10	Horace Greeley	Benjamin G. Brown	1
1876	St. Louis	June 27-29	Samuel J. Tilden	Thomas A. Hendricks	2
1880	Cincinnati	June 22-24	Winfield S. Hancock	William H. English	2
1884	Chicago	July 8-11	Grover Cleveland	Thomas A. Hendricks	2
1888	St. Louis	June 5-7	Grover Cleveland	Allen G. Thurman	1
1892	Chicago	June 21-23	Grover Cleveland	Adlai E. Stevenson	1
1896	Chicago	July 7-11	William J. Bryan	Arthur Sewall	5
1900	Kansas City	July 4-6	William J. Bryan	Adlai E. Stevenson	1
1904	St. Louis	July 6-9	Alton S. Parker	Henry G. Davis	1
1908	Denver	July 7-10	William J. Bryan	John W. Kern	1
1912	Baltimore	June 25-July 2	Woodrow Wilson	Thomas R. Marshall	46
1916	St. Louis	June 14-16	Woodrow Wilson	Thomas R. Marshall	1
1920	San Francisco	June 28-July 6	James M. Cox	Franklin D. Roosevelt	43
1924	New York	June 24-July 9	John W. Davis	Charles W. Bryan	103
1928	Houston	June 26-29	Alfred E. Smith	Joseph T. Robinson	1
1932	Chicago	June 27-July 2	Franklin D. Roosevelt	John N. Garner	4
1936	Philadelphia	June 23-27	Franklin D. Roosevelt	John N. Garner	Acclamation
1940	Chicago	July 15-18	Franklin D. Roosevelt	Henry A. Wallace	1
1944	Chicago	July 19-21	Franklin D. Roosevelt	Harry S Truman	1
1948	Philadelphia	July 12-14	Harry S Truman	Alben W. Barkley	1
1952	Chicago	July 21-26	Adlai E. Stevenson	John J. Sparkman	3
1956	Chicago	Aug. 13-17	Adlai E. Stevenson	Estes Kefauver	1
1960	Los Angeles	July 11-15	John F. Kennedy	Lyndon B. Johnson	1
1964	Atlantic City	Aug. 24-27	Lyndon B. Johnson	Hubert H. Humphrey	Acclamation
1968	Chicago	Aug. 26-29	Hubert H. Humphrey	Edmund S. Muskie	1
1972	Miami Beach	July 10-13	George McGovern	Thomas F. Eagleton R. Sargent Shriver[3]	1
1976	New York	July 12-15	Jimmy Carter	Walter F. Mondale	1
1980	New York	Aug. 11-14	Jimmy Carter	Walter F. Mondale	1

1. The 1840 Democratic convention did not nominate a candidate for vice president.
2. The 1860 Democratic convention nominated Benjamin Fitzpatrick, who declined the nomination shortly after the convention adjourned. On June 25 the Democratic National Committee selected Herschel V. Johnson as the party's candidate for vice president.

3. The 1972 Democratic convention nominated Thomas F. Eagleton, who withdrew from the ticket on July 31. On Aug. 8 the Democratic National Committee selected R. Sargent Shriver as the party's candidate for vice president.

call fell to these new party organizations. Each national committee presently has the responsibility for allocating delegates to each state.

Delegate Selection

The method of allocating delegates to the individual states and territories has been modified by both parties in the 20th century. Throughout the existence of the convention system in the 19th century, both the Democrats and Republicans distributed votes to the states based on their Electoral College strength. The first deviation from this procedure was made by the Republicans after their divisive 1912 convention, in which President William Howard Taft won renomination over former President Theodore Roosevelt, due largely to nearly solid support from the South — a region vastly over-represented in relation to its number of

Republican Conventions, 1856-1980

Year	City	Dates	Presidential Nominee	Vice Presidential Nominee	No. of Pres. Ballots
1856	Philadelphia	June 17-19	John C. Fremont	William L. Dayton	2
1860	Chicago	May 16-18	Abraham Lincoln	Hannibal Hamlin	3
1864	Baltimore	June 7-8	Abraham Lincoln	Andrew Johnson	1
1868	Chicago	May 20-21	Ulysses S. Grant	Schuyler Colfax	1
1872	Philadelphia	June 5-6	Ulysses S. Grant	Henry Wilson	1
1876	Cincinnati	June 14-16	Rutherford B. Hayes	William A. Wheeler	7
1880	Chicago	June 2-8	James A. Garfield	Chester A. Arthur	36
1884	Chicago	June 3-6	James G. Blaine	John A. Logan	4
1888	Chicago	June 19-25	Benjamin Harrison	Levi P. Morton	8
1892	Minneapolis	June 7-10	Benjamin Harrison	Whitelaw Reid	1
1896	St. Louis	June 16-18	William McKinley	Garret A. Hobart	1
1900	Philadelphia	June 19-21	William McKinley	Theodore Roosevelt	1
1904	Chicago	June 21-23	Theodore Roosevelt	Charles W. Fairbanks	1
1908	Chicago	June 16-19	William H. Taft	James S. Sherman	1
1912	Chicago	June 18-22	William H. Taft	James S. Sherman Nicholas Murray Butler[1]	1
1916	Chicago	June 7-10	Charles E. Hughes	Charles W. Fairbanks	3
1920	Chicago	June 8-12	Warren G. Harding	Calvin Coolidge	10
1924	Cleveland	June 10-12	Calvin Coolidge	Charles G. Dawes	1
1928	Kansas City	June 12-15	Herbert Hoover	Charles Curtis	1
1932	Chicago	June 14-16	Herbert Hoover	Charles Curtis	1
1936	Cleveland	June 9-12	Alfred M. Landon	Frank Knox	1
1940	Philadelphia	June 24-28	Wendell L. Willkie	Charles L. McNary	6
1944	Chicago	June 26-28	Thomas E. Dewey	John W. Bricker	1
1948	Philadelphia	June 21-25	Thomas E. Dewey	Earl Warren	3
1952	Chicago	July 7-11	Dwight D. Eisenhower	Richard M. Nixon	1
1956	San Francisco	Aug. 20-23	Dwight D. Eisenhower	Richard M. Nixon	1
1960	Chicago	July 25-28	Richard M. Nixon	Henry Cabot Lodge	1
1964	San Francisco	July 13-16	Barry Goldwater	William E. Miller	1
1968	Miami Beach	Aug. 5-8	Richard M. Nixon	Spiro T. Agnew	1
1972	Miami Beach	Aug. 21-23	Richard M. Nixon	Spiro T. Agnew	1
1976	Kansas City	Aug. 16-19	Gerald R. Ford	Robert Dole	1
1980	Detroit	July 14-17	Ronald Reagan	George Bush	1

1. The 1912 Republican convention nominated James S. Sherman, who died on Oct. 30. The Republican National Committee subsequently selected Nicholas Murray Butler to receive the Republican electoral votes for vice president.

Source for Data on Conventions: Bain, Richard C. and Parris, Judith H. *Convention Decisions and Voting Records*, Brookings Institution, Washington, D.C. 1973.

Republican voters. Before their 1916 convention the Republicans reduced the allocation of votes to the Southern states, marking the first major move by either party in modifying its delegate allocation method. At their 1924 convention the Republicans applied the first bonus system, by which states were awarded extra votes for supporting the Republican presidential candidate in the previous election. The concept of bonus votes, applied as a reward to the states for supporting the party ticket, has been used and expanded by both parties since that time.

The Democrats first used a bonus system in 1944, completing a compromise arrangement with Southern states for abolishing the party's controversial two-thirds nominating rule. Since then, both parties have used various delegate allocation formulas. At their 1972 convention the Republicans revised the method used in allocating delegates and added more than 900 new delegate slots. The Ripon Society, an organization of liberal Republicans, sued to have the new rules overturned. They argued that, because of the extra delegates awarded to states that voted Republican in the previous presidential election, small Southern and Western states were favored at the expense of the more populous but less Republican Eastern states. The challenge failed when the Supreme Court in February 1976 refused to hear the case and thus let stand a U.S. Court of Appeals decision upholding the rules.

Only 116 delegates from 13 states attended the initial national nominating convention held by the Anti-Masons in 1831, but with the addition of more states and the adoption of increasingly complex voting allocation formulas by the major parties, the size of conventions spiraled. The 1976 Republican convention had 2,259 delegates, while the Democrats in the same year had 3,075 delegates (casting 3,008 votes). The expanded size in part reflected the democratization of the conventions, with less command by a few party leaders and the dramatic growth of youth, women and minority delegates. Increased representation by such groups was one of the major reasons given by the

1984 Delegate Selection Rules

The rules governing delegate selection adopted by the Republicans and the Democrats differ on several key points. Following is a summary of the major differences in party delegate selection rules for 1984:

● Democrats require states to hold their primaries or the first stage of their caucus process between March 13 and June 12, 1984. Republicans leave the choice of delegate selection dates up to the state parties.

● Democrats require primary states to set filing deadlines 30 to 90 days before the election. Republicans leave any restrictions up to state statute or state party rules.

● The Democratic Party allows only Democrats to participate in its primaries and caucuses. Republicans allow cross-overs where state law permits.

● Democrats require delegates to declare presidential preference or uncommitted status. Republican delegates are not required to declare preference unless mandated by state law or state party regulations.

● Democratic delegates are bound for one ballot. Republicans require delegates bound to a candidate by state law in primary states to vote for that candidate.

● Democrats require states to elect an equal number of men and women delegates. Republicans request states to elect an equal number.

Republicans for the 60 percent increase in delegate strength authorized by the 1972 convention (and effective for the 1976 gathering). The Democrats adopted new rules in June 1978 expanding the number of delegates by 10 percent to provide extra representation for state and local officials. The new rules also required that women account for at least 50 percent of the delegates to the 1980 convention.

With the increased size of conventions has come a formalization in the method of delegate selection. In the formative years of the convention system, delegate selection was often haphazard and informal. At the Democratic convention in 1835, the state of Maryland had 188 delegates to cast the state's 10 votes. On the other hand, the 15 votes for the state of Tennessee were cast by a traveling businessman, who inadvertently happened to be in the convention city at the time of the convention. While the number of delegates and the number of votes allocated tended to be equal or nearly so later in the 19th century, domination of national conventions was frequently exercised by a few party bosses.

Two basic methods of delegate selection were employed in the 19th century and continued to be used into the 20th: the caucus method, by which delegates were chosen by meetings at the local or state level; and the appointment method, by which delegates were appointed by the governor or a powerful state leader.

Presidential Primaries

A revolutionary new mechanism for delegate selection emerged during the early 1900s: the presidential primary election in which delegates were elected directly by the voters.

Initiated in Florida in 1904, the presidential primary by 1912 was used by 13 states. In his first annual message to Congress the following year, President Woodrow Wilson advocated the establishment of a national primary to select presidential candidates: "I feel confident that I do not misinterpret the wishes or the expectations of the country when I urge the prompt enactment of legislation which will provide for primary elections throughout the country at which the voters of the several parties may choose their nominees for the presidency without the intervention of nominating conventions." Wilson went on to suggest the retention of conventions for the purpose of declaring the results of the primaries and formulating the parties' platforms.

Before any action was taken on Wilson's proposal, the progressive spirit that spurred the growth of presidential primaries died out. Not until after World War II, when widespread pressures for change touched both parties, especially the Democratic, was there a rapid growth in presidential primaries. By 1980 there were a record 37 presidential primaries.

Presently in most states that use it, participation in the presidential primary is restricted to voters belonging to the party holding the primary. In some states, however, participation by voters outside the party is allowed. New rules adopted by the Democrats in 1978 prohibited this practice in Democratic primaries.

1984 Democratic Rules

In June 1982, the Democratic National Committee (DNC) adopted several changes in the presidential nominating process recommended by the party's Commission on Presidential Nominations, chaired by North Carolina Governor James B. Hunt, Jr. The Hunt Commission, as it came to be known, suggested revisions in the nominating process designed to increase the power of party regulars and give the convention more freedom to act on its own. It was the fourth time in 12 years that the Democrats, struggling to repair their nominating process without repudiating earlier reforms, had rewritten their party rules.

One major change in the Democrats' rules was the creation of a new group of "superdelegates," party and elected officials who would go to the 1984 convention uncommitted and would cast about 14 percent of the ballots. The DNC also adopted a Hunt Commission proposal to weaken the rule binding delegates to vote for their original presidential preference on the first convention ballot. The new rule allowed a presidential candidate to replace any disloyal delegate with a more faithful one.

One of the most significant revisions was the Democrats' decision to relax proportional representation at the convention and end the ban on the "loophole" primary. Proportional representation is the distribution of delegates among candidates to reflect their share of the primary or caucus vote. Mandated by party rules in 1980, it was blamed by some Democrats for the protracted primary fight between President Jimmy Carter and Massachusetts Sen. Edward M. Kennedy. Because candidates needed only about 20 percent of the vote in most places to qualify for a share of the delegates, Kennedy was able to remain in contention. But while the system kept Kennedy going, it did nothing to help his chances of winning the nomination.

Although the Democrats' 1984 rules permitted states to retain proportional representation, they also allowed states to take advantage of two options that could help a front-running candidate build the momentum to wrap up the nomination early in the year.

One was a winner-take-more system. States could elect to keep proportional representation but adopt a winner bonus plan that would award the top vote-getter in each district one extra delegate.

The other option was a return to the loophole primary — winner take all by district. This system was outlawed by party rules in 1980, although Illinois and West Virginia were granted special exemptions to maintain their loophole voting systems.

In the loophole states, voters ballot directly for delegates, with each delegate candidate identified by presidential preference. Sometimes several presidential contenders win at least a fraction of the delegates in a given district, but the most common result is a sweep by the presidential front-runner, even if he has less than an absolute majority. Loophole primaries aid the building of a consensus behind the front-runner, while still giving other candidates a chance to inject themselves back into the race by winning decisively a major loophole state.

The DNC retained the delegate selection season adopted in 1978, a three month period stretching from the second Tuesday in March to the second Tuesday in June. But, in an effort to reduce the growing influence of early states in the nominating process, the Democrats required Iowa and New Hampshire to move their highly publicized elections to late winter. Party rules maintained the privileged status of Iowa and New Hampshire before other states, but mandated that their initial nominating rounds be held only eight days apart in 1984. Five weeks intervened between the Iowa caucuses and New Hampshire primary in 1980.

The DNC also retained rules requiring primary states to set candidate filing deadlines 30 to 90 days before the election and limiting participation in the delegate selection process to Democrats only. This last rule eliminated crossover primaries where voters could participate in the Democratic primary without designating their party affiliation. Blacks and Hispanics won continued endorsement of affirmative action in the new party rules. Women gained renewed support for the equal division rule, which required state delegations at the national convention to be divided equally between men and women.

Credentials Disputes

Before the opening of a convention, the national committee compiles a temporary roll of delegates. The roll is referred to the convention's credentials committee, which holds hearings on the challenges and makes recommendations to the convention, the final arbiter of all disputes.

Some of the most bitter convention battles have concerned the seating of contested delegations. In the 20th century most of the heated credentials fights have concerned delegations from the South. In the Republican Party the challenges focused on the power of the Republican state organizations to dictate the selection of convention delegates. The issue was hottest in 1912 and 1952, when the party throughout most of the South was a skeletal structure whose power was largely restricted to selection of convention delegates. Within the Democratic Party the question of Southern credentials emerged after World War II on the volatile issues of civil rights and party loyalty. Important credentials challenges on these issues occurred at the 1948, 1952, 1964 and 1968 Democratic conventions.

There were numerous credentials challenges at the 1972 Democratic convention, but unlike its immediate predecessors the challenges involved delegations from across the nation and focused on violations of the party's newly adopted guidelines.

After their 1952 credentials battle, the Republicans established a contest committee within the national committee to review credentials challenges before the convention. After their divisive 1968 convention the Democrats also created a formal credentials procedure within the national committee to review all challenges before the opening of the convention.

Equally important to the settlement of credentials challenges are the rules under which the convention operates. The Republican Party adopts a completely new set of rules at every convention. Although large portions of the existing rules are enacted each time, general revision is always possible.

After its 1968 convention the Democratic Party set out to reform itself and the convention system. The Commission on Rules and the Commission on Party Structure and Delegate Selection, both created by the 1968 convention, proposed many changes that were accepted by the national committee. As a result, a formal set of rules was adopted for the first time at the party's 1972 convention.

Two-Thirds and Unit Rules

Although not having a formal set of rules before 1972, the Democratic Party throughout the bulk of its history operated with two critical and controversial rules never used by the Republicans: the unit rule and the two-thirds nominating rule. The unit rule enabled the majority of a delegation, if authorized by its state party, to cast the entire vote of the delegation for one candidate or position. In use since the earliest Democratic conventions, the unit rule was abolished by the 1968 convention.

From its first convention in 1832 until its elimination over a century later at the 1936 convention, the Democrats employed the two-thirds nominating rule, which required

---

Democrats' Two-Thirds Rule

At their first convention in 1832, the Democrats adopted a rule requiring a two-thirds majority for nomination. Two presidential candidates — Martin Van Buren in 1844 and Champ Clark in 1912 — received majorities but failed to attain the two-thirds requirement.

In 1844, on the first ballot Van Buren received 146 of the 266 convention votes, 54.9 percent of the total. His total fell under a simple majority on succeeding roll calls and on the ninth ballot the nomination went to a dark horse candidate, former Gov. James K. Polk of Tennessee.

In 1912, from the 10th through the 16th ballots, Clark recorded a simple majority. He reached his peak on the 10th ballot, receiving 556 of the 1,094 convention votes, 50.8 percent of the total. The nomination, however, ultimately went to New Jersey Gov. Woodrow Wilson, who was selected on the 46th ballot.

At their 1936 convention, the Democrats voted to end the requirement for a two-thirds majority for nomination.

Notable Credentials Fights

1848, Democratic. Two rival New York state factions, known as the Barnburners and the Hunkers, sent separate delegations. By a vote of 126 to 125, the convention decided to seat both delegations and split New York's vote between them. This compromise suited neither faction: the Barnburners bolted the convention; the Hunkers remained but refused to vote.

1860, Democratic. Dissatisfaction with the slavery plank in the party platform spurred a walkout by several dozen southern delegates from the Charleston convention. When the tumultuous convention reconvened in Baltimore six weeks later, a credentials controversy developed on the status of the bolting delegates. The majority report of the credentials committee recommended that the delegates in question, except those from Alabama and Louisiana, be reseated. The minority report recommended that a larger majority of the withdrawing Charleston delegates be allowed to return. The minority report was defeated, 100-1/2 to 150, prompting a walkout by the majority of delegates from nine states.

1880, Republican. Factions for and against the candidacy of former President Ulysses S. Grant clashed on the credentials of the Illinois delegation. By a margin of 353 to 387, the convention rejected a minority report that proposed seating pro-Grant delegates elected at the state convention over other delegates elected at a congressional district caucus. Three other votes were taken on disputed credentials from different Illinois districts, but all were decided in favor of the anti-Grant forces by a similar margin. The votes indicated the weakness of the Grant candidacy. The nomination went to a dark horse candidate on the 36th ballot, Rep. James A. Garfield of Ohio.

1912, Republican. The furious struggle between President William Howard Taft and Theodore Roosevelt for the presidential nomination centered on credentials. The Roosevelt forces brought 72 delegate challenges to the floor of the convention, but the test of strength between the two candidates came on a procedural motion. By a vote of 567 to 507, the convention tabled a motion presented by the Roosevelt forces barring any of the delegates under challenge from voting on any of the credentials contests. This procedural vote clearly indicated Taft's control of the convention. All the credentials cases were settled in favor of the Taft delegates and the presidential nomination ultimately went to the incumbent president.

1932, Democratic. Two delegations favorable to the front runner for the presidential nomination, Franklin D. Roosevelt, came under challenge. However, in a show of strength, the Roosevelt forces won both contests: seating a Louisiana delegation headed by Sen. Huey P. Long by a vote of 638-3/4 to 514-1/4, and a Roosevelt delegation from Minnesota by an even wider margin, 658-1/4 to 492-3/4. Roosevelt won the nomination on the fourth ballot.

1952, Democratic. The refusal of three southern states — Louisiana, South Carolina and Virginia — to agree to a party loyalty pledge, brought their credentials into question. The Virginia delegation argued that the problem prompting the loyalty pledge was covered by state law. By a vote of 650-1/2 to 518, the convention approved the seating of the Virginia delegation. After Louisiana and South Carolina took positions similar to that of Virginia, they were seated by a voice vote.

1952, Republican. Sixty-eight delegates from three southern states (Georgia, Louisiana, and Texas) were the focal point of the fight for the presidential nomination between Gen. Dwight D. Eisenhower and Ohio Sen. Robert A. Taft. The national committee, controlled by forces favorable to Taft, had voted to seat delegations friendly to the Ohio Senator from these three states. But by a vote of 607 to 531 the convention seated the Georgia delegation favorable to Eisenhower and without roll calls seated the Eisenhower delegates from Louisiana and Texas. The General went on to win the presidential nomination on the first ballot.

1968, Democratic. A struggle between the anti-Vietnam war forces, led by Minnesota Sen. Eugene J. McCarthy, and the party regulars, headed by Vice President Hubert Humphrey, dominated the 17 credentials cases considered by the credentials committee. Three of the cases, involving the Texas, Georgia and Alabama delegations, required roll calls on the convention floor. All were won by the Humphrey forces. By a vote of 1,368-1/4 to 956-3/4, the regular Texas delegation headed by Gov. John B. Connally was seated. A minority report to seat the entire Georgia delegation led by black leader Julian Bond was defeated, 1,043.55 to 1,415.45. And a minority report to seat a McCarthy-backed, largely black delegation from Alabama was also rejected, 880-3/4 to 1,607. Humphrey, having shown his strength during the credentials contests, went on to an easy first ballot nomination.

1972, Democratic. The first test of strength at the convention between South Dakota Sen. George McGovern's delegates and party regulars came over credentials. Key challenges brought to the convention floor concerned the South Carolina, California and Illinois delegations. The South Carolina challenge was brought by the National Women's Political Caucus in response to alleged underrepresentation of women in the delegation. Although their position was supposedly supported by the McGovern camp, votes were withheld in order not to jeopardize McGovern's chances of winning the important California contest. The women's challenge lost 1,429.05 to 1,555.75. The California challenge was of crucial importance to McGovern, since it involved 151 delegates initially won by the South Dakota senator in the state's winner-take-all primary, but stripped from him by the credentials committee. By a vote of 1,618.28 to 1,238.22, McGovern regained the contested delegates, and thereby nailed down his nomination. With victory in hand, the dominant McGovern camp sought a compromise on the Illinois case, which pitted a delegation headed by Chicago's powerful Mayor Richard Daley against an insurgent delegation composed of party reformers. Compromise was unattainable and with the bulk of McGovern delegates voting for the reformers, a minority report to seat the Daley delegates was rejected.

any candidate for president or vice president to win not just a simple majority but a two-thirds majority. Viewed as a boon to the South since it allowed that region a virtual veto power over any possible nominee, the rule was abolished with the stipulation that the South would receive an increased vote allocation at later conventions.

In its century of use the two-thirds rule frequently produced protracted, multi-ballot conventions, often giving the Democrats a degree of turbulence the Republicans, requiring only a simple majority, did not have. Between 1832 and 1932, seven Democratic conventions took more than 10 ballots to select a presidential candidate. In contrast, in their entire convention history (1856 through 1976), the Republicans have had just one convention that required more than 10 ballots to select a presidential candidate.

One controversy that surfaced during the 1980 Democratic Party convention concerned a convention rule that bound delegates to vote on the first ballot for the candidates under whose banner they had been elected. Supporters of Sen. Edward M. Kennedy, D-Mass., had devoted their initial energies to prying the nomination from incumbent President Jimmy Carter by trying unsuccessfully to open the convention by defeating that rule. The final tally on the rule showed 1,936.42 delegates favoring the binding rule and 1,390.580 opposing it. Passage of the binding rule assured Carter's renomination, and shortly after the vote, Kennedy ended his nine-month challenge to the president by announcing that his name would not be placed in nomination Aug. 13.

Convention Officers

Credentials, rules and platform are the major convention committees, but each party has additional committees including one in charge of convention arrangements. Within the Republican Party the arrangements committee recommends a slate of convention officers to the national committee, which in turn refers the names to the committee on permanent organization for confirmation. The people the committee chooses are subject to the approval of the convention. In the Democratic Party, this function is performed by the rules committee.

Both in the Democratic and Republican parties, the presiding officer during the bulk of the convention is the permanent chairman. Over the past quarter century the position has usually gone to the party's leader in the House of Representatives. However, this loose precedent was broken in the Democratic Party by a rule adopted at the 1972 convention requiring that the position alternate every four years between the sexes.

Party Platforms

The adoption of a party platform is one of the principal functions of a convention. The platform committee is charged with the responsibility of writing a party platform to be presented to the convention for its approval.

The main problem of a platform committee is to write a platform all party candidates can use in their campaigns. For this reason, platforms often fit the description given them by the late Wendell L. Willkie, Republican presidential candidate in 1940: "fusions of ambiguity."

Despite the best efforts of platform-builders to compromise their differences in the comparative privacy of the committee room, they sometimes encounter so controver-

Notable Platform Fights

1860, Democratic. A minority report on the slavery plank, stating that the decision on allowing slavery in the territories should be left to the Supreme Court, was approved, 165 to 138. The majority report (favored by the South) declared that no government — local, state or federal — could outlaw slavery in the territories. The acceptance of the minority report precipitated a walkout by several dozen southern delegates and the eventual sectional split in the party.

1896, Democratic. The monetary plank of the platform committee, favoring free and unlimited coinage of silver at a ratio of 16 to 1 with gold, was accepted by the convention, which defeated a proposed gold plank, 303 to 626. During debate, William Jennings Bryan made his famous "Cross of Gold" speech supporting the platform committee plank, bringing him to the attention of the convention and resulting in his nomination for president.

1908, Republican. A minority report, proposing a substitute platform, was presented by Sen. Robert M. LaFollette (Wis.). Minority proposals included increased antitrust activities, enactment of a law requiring publication of campaign expenditures, and popular election of senators. All the proposed planks were defeated by wide margins; the closest vote, on direct election of senators, was 114 for, 866 against.

1924, Democratic. A minority plank was presented that condemned the activities of the Ku Klux Klan, then enjoying a resurgence in the South and some states in the Midwest. The plank was defeated 542-7/20 to 543-3/20, the closest vote in Democratic convention history.

1932, Republican. A minority plank favoring repeal of the 18th Amendment (Prohibition) in favor of a state-option arrangement was defeated, 460-2/9 to 690-19/36.

1948, Democratic. An amendment to the platform, strengthening the civil rights plank by guaranteeing full and equal political participation, equal employment opportunity, personal security and equal treatment in the military service, was accepted, 651-1/2 to 582-1/2.

1964, Republican. An amendment offered by Sen. Hugh Scott (Pa.) to strengthen the civil rights plank by including voting guarantees in state as well as in federal elections and by eliminating job bias was defeated, 409 to 897.

1968, Democratic. A minority report on Vietnam called for cessation of the bombing of North Vietnam, halting of offensive and search-and-destroy missions by American combat units, a negotiated withdrawal of American troops and establishment of a coalition government in South Vietnam. It was defeated, 1,041-1/4 to 1,567-3/4.

1972, Democratic. By a vote of 999.34 to 1,852.86, the convention rejected a minority report proposing a government guaranteed annual income of $6,500 for a family of four. By a vote of 1,101.37 to 1,572.80, a women's rights plank focusing on the issue of abortion was defeated.

sial a subject that it cannot be compromised. Under these conditions, dissident committee members often submit a minority report to the convention floor. Open floor fights are not unusual and like credentials battles, often serve as an indicator of the strength of the various candidates.

When the party has an incumbent president, the platform is often drafted in the White House, or at least approved by the president. Rarely is a platform adopted by a party that criticizes its incumbent president.

The first platform was adopted by the Democrats in 1840. It was a short document less than 1,000 words long. Since then the platforms with few exceptions have grown longer and longer, covering more issues and making an appeal to more interest groups. The platform adopted by the Republicans in 1976 was nearly 20,000 words long. The Democrats, however, bucked the trend toward longer platforms by adopting one in 1976 that was about half the length of their 25,000-word 1972 document. However, the Democrats' 1980 platform contained a record 40,000 words, and the Republicans' was almost as long.

The Republicans' 1980 platform mirrored the convention's emphasis on party unity and generally followed front-runner Ronald Reagan's wishes, in contrast to 1976, when platform deliberations had been marked by discord between the Reagan faction and incumbent President Gerald R. Ford. The 1980 platform was more a blueprint for victory in November than a definitive statement of party views. Rather than slug it out over specifics, the party's moderate and conservative wings agreed to blur their differences in order to appear united, to broaden the party's appeal and to smooth the way to the White House for their nominee. On a few issues, platform writers veered from traditional Republican positions. On others, they went out of their way to embrace policies that meshed with Reagan's views more than their own. But for the most part, they managed to fashion a policy statement that pleased no party faction entirely but with which all could live reasonably.

In contrast to the Republicans' harmony, the 1980 Democratic convention was marked by bitter contests over the party platform that was adopted Aug. 13 after two days of prolonged and sometimes raucus debate that pitted Carter against Kennedy and a coalition of special interest groups. The final document was filled with so many concessions to the Kennedy forces that it won only a halfhearted endorsement from the president.

In many key areas the platform bore little resemblance to the document that Carter operatives took to the first platform drafting meeting June 17. During that session numerous minor changes proposed by Kennedy backers were accepted. Then, two weeks before the convention, Carter began to yield on more substantive issues. By the time the platform debate started, Carter had accepted eight of Kennedy's minority reports. During the debate, six other minority planks were adopted either with Carter's acquiescence or in spite of his opposition.

Third Party Platforms

Throughout American history, many daring and controversial political platforms adopted by third parties have been rejected as too radical in their own time by the major parties. Yet these proposals have later won popular acceptance, made their way into the major party platforms — and into law.

Ideas such as the graduated income tax, popular elec-

tion of senators, women's suffrage, minimum wages, social security, day-care centers and the 18-year-old vote were advocated by Populists, Progressives and other independents long before they were finally accepted by the nation as a whole.

The radical third parties and their platforms have been anathema to the established wisdom of the day, denounced as impractical, dangerous, destructive of moral virtues and even traitorous. They have been anti-establishment and more far-reaching in their proposed solutions to problems than the major parties have dared to be.

In contrast to the third parties, Democrats and Republicans traditionally have been much more chary of adopting radical platform planks. Trying to appeal to a broad range of voters, the two major parties have tended to compromise differences or to turn down controversial planks.

The Democratic Party has been more ready than the Republicans to adopt once-radical ideas, but there is usually a considerable time lag between their origin in third parties and their eventual adoption in Democratic platforms. For example, while the Democrats by 1912 had adopted many of the Populist planks of the 1890s, the Bull Moose Progressives of that year were already way ahead of them in proposals for social legislation. Not until 1932 were many of the 1912 Progressive planks adopted by the Democrats. Similarly, not until the 1960s did Democratic platforms incorporate many of the more far-reaching proposals put forward by the 1948 Progressives.

Communications and the Media

Major changes in the national nominating convention have resulted from the massive advances in transportation and communication particularly evident in the 20th century.

A major impact of the revolution in transportation has affected the scheduling of conventions. In the 19th century, conventions were sometimes held a year or more before the election and at the latest were completed by late spring of the election year. With the ability of people to assemble quickly, conventions in recent years have been held later in the election year, usually in July or August. Advances in transportation have also affected site location. Geographic centrality is no longer the primary consideration in the selection of a convention city. Increasingly, coastal cities have been chosen as convention hosts.

The invention of new means of communication, particularly television, have had a further impact on the convention system. The changes spurred by the media have primarily been cosmetic ones, designed to give the convention a look of efficiency that was not so necessary in earlier days. As the conduct of the convention has undergone closer scrutiny by the American electorate, both parties have made major efforts to cut back the frivolity and hoopla, and to accentuate the more sober aspects of the convention process.

Radio coverage of conventions began in 1924; television coverage was initiated 16 years later. One of the first changes inspired by the media age was the termination of the custom that a presidential candidate not appear at the convention, but accept his nomination in a ceremony several weeks later. Franklin D. Roosevelt was the first major party candidate to break this tradition, when, in 1932, he delivered his acceptance speech in person before the Democratic convention. Thomas E. Dewey 12 years later became

Selection By Caucus Method

Although about three-fourths of the delegates to the 1980 nominating conventions were chosen in presidential primaries, party caucuses also had a share of the limelight. In 1980 15 states used the caucus method to select delegates to the nominating conventions, while 27 states used the primary method and 8 states employed a hybrid method of primaries and caucuses. Indeed, the Jan. 21, 1980, Iowa precinct caucuses assumed an importance that rivaled the traditionally important New Hampshire primary. In the process, the Iowa caucuses raised public consciousness of a delegate selection method that had been on the decline throughout the last decade.

The impact of caucuses in the 1970s decreased as the number of primaries grew dramatically. During the 1960s, a candidate sought to run well in primary states mainly to have a bargaining chip with which to deal with powerful leaders in the caucus states. Republicans Barry Goldwater in 1964 and Richard Nixon in 1968 and Democrat Hubert H. Humphrey in 1968 all built up solid majorities among caucus state delegates that carried them to their parties' nominations. Humphrey did not even enter a primary in 1968.

But since 1968 candidates have placed their principal emphasis on primary campaigning. First George McGovern, D-S.D. — and then incumbent Republican President Gerald R. Ford and Democratic challenger Jimmy Carter in 1976 — all won their parties' nominations by winning a large majority of the primary state delegates. Neither McGovern nor Ford won a majority of the caucus state delegates. Carter was able to win a majority only after his opponents' campaigns collapsed.

Complex Method

Compared to a primary, the caucus system is relatively complex. Instead of focusing on a single primary election ballot, the caucus presents a multi-tiered system that involves meetings scheduled over several weeks, sometimes even months. While there is mass participation at the first level only, meetings at this step often last several hours and attract only the most enthusiastic and dedicated party members.

The operation of the caucus varies from state to state, and each party has its own set of rules. But most use a process that begins with precinct caucuses or some other type of local mass meeting open to all party voters. Participants, often publicly declaring their votes, elect delegates to the next stage in the process.

In smaller states such as Delaware and Hawaii, delegates are elected directly to a state convention, where the national convention delegates are chosen.

In larger states like Iowa, there is at least one more step. Most frequently, delegates are elected at the precinct caucuses to county conventions, where the national convention delegates are chosen. In Iowa, Democrats hold their district conventions in April and their state convention in mid-June. Iowa Republicans hold district caucuses during the state convention in early June.

Participation, even at the first level of the caucus process, is usually much lower than in primary states. In few states did caucus turnout exceed 10 percent of those eligible to participate in 1976. Caucus participants usually are local party leaders and activists, not newcomers to the process. Many rank-and-file voters find a caucus complex and confusing; others find it intimidating.

In a caucus state the focus is on one-on-one campaigning. Time, not money, is the most valuable resource. Because organization and personal campaigning are so important, an early start is far more crucial in a caucus state than a primary. And because only a small segment of the electorate is targeted in most caucus states, candidates usually use media advertising sparingly. On the average, candidates in 1976 spent about $5 in every primary state for every $1 they spent in a caucus state.

Although the basic steps in the caucus process are the same for both parties, the rules that govern them are vastly different. Democratic rules have been revamped substantially since 1968, establishing national standards for grass-roots participation. Republican rules have remained largely unchanged with the states given wide latitude in drawing up their delegate selection plans. Democratic caucuses are open to Democrats only. Republicans allow crossovers where state law permits, creating a wide range of variations. The first step of the Democratic caucus process must be open, well-publicized mass meetings. In most states Republicans do the same. Generally, voters may only participate in the election of local party officials, who meet to begin the caucus process.

Caucus Revival

The most tangible evidence of a revival of the caucus process is found in the percentage of delegates elected from caucus states. For both parties this figure was on a sharp decline throughout the 1970s. But Democrats broke the downward trend and actually elected more delegates by the caucus process in 1980 than in 1976. The principal reason for the upward swing was that two of the largest delegations — Texas and Michigan — switched from primaries to caucuses to choose delegates. Those two switches more than offset the moves of the Democratic parties in Connecticut, Kansas, Louisiana, New Mexico and Puerto Rico from caucuses to primaries.

Throughout the 1970s, Republicans elected a larger proportion of their delegates from caucus states than did the Democrats. But that changed in 1980, with only 24 percent of the GOP convention coming from caucus states (compared to 31 percent in 1976 and 53 percent in 1968).

During the 1980 presidential campaign both Carter and Reagan reaped the harvest of early organization and grass-roots strength by garnering substantial leads in the caucus states. Carter won 64 percent of Democratic delegates in caucus states compared to 58 percent in primary states, while Reagan won 83 percent of caucus-selected delegates and 78 percent of the delegates elected in primaries.

the first Republican nominee to give his acceptance speech to the convention. Since then the final activity of both the Democratic and Republican conventions has been the delivery of the acceptance speeches by the vice presidential and presidential nominees.

In addition to curbing the circus-like aspects of the convention, party leaders in recent years have streamlined the schedule, with the assumption that the interest level of most of the viewing public for politics is limited. The result has been shorter speeches and generally fewer roll calls than at those conventions in the pre-television era.

Showmanship

Party leaders desire to put on a good show for the viewing public with the hope of winning votes for their party in November. The convention is a showcase, designed to show the party as both a model of democracy and an efficient, harmonious body. The schedule of convention activities is drawn up with an eye on the peak evening television viewing hours. There is an attempt to put the party's major selling points — the highly partisan keynote speech, the nominating ballots, and the candidates' acceptance speeches — on in prime time. As well, with an equal awareness of the television audience, party leaders often try to keep evidence of bitter party factionalism — such as explosive credentials and platform battles — out of the peak viewing period.

In the media age, the appearance of fairness is impor-

tant, and in a sense, this need to look fair and open has assisted the movement in recent years for party reform. Some influential party leaders, skeptical of reform of the convention, have found resistance difficult in the glare of television.

Before the revolution in the means of transportation and communication, conventions met in relative anonymity. Today, the convention is held in all the privacy of a fishbowl, with every action and every rumor closely scrutinized. It has become a media event, and as such has become a target for political demonstrations that can be not only an embarrassment to the party but a security problem as well.

But in spite of its difficulties, the convention system has survived. As the nation has grown over the past century and a half, the convention has evolved as well, changing its form but retaining its variety of functions which accounts for the remarkable longevity of the convention system. Criticism has been leveled at the convention, but no substitute has yet been offered that would nominate a presidential ticket, adopt a party platform, act as the supreme governing body of the party and serve as a massive campaign rally and propaganda forum. In addition to these functions, a convention is a place where compromise can take place — compromise often mandatory in a major political party that combines viewpoints that stretch across the political spectrum.

—By Rhodes Cook

Highlights of National Party Conventions, 1831-1980

1831   First national political convention was held in Baltimore by Anti-Masonic Party. Second such convention was held several months later by National Republican Party (no relation to modern Republicans).

1832   Democratic Party met in Baltimore for its first national political convention and nominated Andrew Jackson. The rule requiring a two-thirds majority for nominations was initiated.

1835   President Jackson called his party's convention more than a year before the election in order to prevent build-up of opposition to his choice of successor, Martin Van Buren.

1839   Whig Party held its first convention and chose the winning slate of William Henry Harrison and John Tyler. Party adopted unit rule for casting state delegations' votes.

1840   To avoid bitter battle over vice presidential nomination, Democratic Party set up a committee to select nominees, subject to approval of convention. In accordance with committee recommendations, Van Buren was nominated for President and no one for vice president.

1844   Democrats nominated James K. Polk — first "dark horse" or compromise candidate — after nine ballots. Silas Wright, convention's choice for vice president, declined the nomination. First time a convention nominee refused nomination. Convention subsequently nominated George M. Dallas.

1848   Democratic convention voted to establish continuing committee, known as "Democratic National Committee."

1852   Democrats and Whigs both adopted platforms before nominating candidates for president, setting precedent almost uniformly followed ever since.

1854   First Republican state convention held in Jackson, Mich., to nominate candidate slate. Platform denounced slavery.

1856   First Republican national convention held at Philadelphia. Kentucky sent only southern delegation. Nominated John C. Fremont for President.

1860   One of longest, most turbulent and mobile conventions in Democratic history. Democrats met in Charleston, S.C., April 23. After 10 days and no agreement on a presidential nominee, delegates adjourned and reconvened in Baltimore in mid-July, for what turned out to be another disorderly meeting. Delegates finally nominated Stephen A. Douglas for president.

Benjamin Fitzpatrick, the convention's choice for vice president, became the first candidate to withdraw after convention adjournment and be replaced by a selection of the national committee. Delegates who bolted the original convention later joined Baltimore dissidents to nominate Vice President John C. Breckinridge for President.

Republicans nominated Abraham Lincoln for the presidency. First Republican credentials dispute took place over seating delegates from slave states and over voting strength of delegates from states where party was comparatively weak. Party rejected unit rule for first time.

Constitutional Union Party running on a platform of national unity nominated John Bell for president.

1864   Civil War led to bitter debate within Democratic Party over candidates, including Gen. George B. McClellan, presidential nominee.

In attempt to close ranks during war, Republicans used the name "Union Party" at convention. Renominated Lincoln. Platform called for constitutional amendment outlawing slavery.

1868   Susan B. Anthony urged Democratic support for women's suffrage.

For the first time, Republicans gave a candidate (Ulysses S. Grant) 100 percent of vote on first ballot. Incumbent Andrew Johnson, who succeeded assassinated Lincoln, sought nomination unsuccessfully. First Republican convention with full southern representation.

1872   Republicans renominated Grant at Philadelphia. Dissident Liberal Republicans nominated Horace Greeley in Cincinnati. Democrats also nominated Greeley. Victoria Clafin Woodhull, nominated by the Equal Rights Party, was first woman presidential candidate. Black leader Frederick Douglass was her running mate.

1876   First time either party nominated incumbent governor for President; both major parties did so that year, with Rutherford B. Hayes (R Ohio) and Samuel J. Tilden (D N.Y.). Republican convention rejected unit rule for second time.

1880   Republicans nominated James A. Garfield for President on 36th ballot — party's all-time record number of ballots. Unit rule was rejected for the third and final time. Republican convention passed loyalty pledge for nominee, binding each delegate to his support.

1884   Democrats turned back Tammany Hall challenge to unit rule.

Republicans nominated James G. Blaine (Maine) for president and John Logan (Illinois) for vice president, reversing 24-year pattern of seeking presidential candidate from the Midwest and vice presidential candidate from the East. John Roy Lynch, three-term U.S. representative from Mississippi, became first black elected temporary chairman of national nominating convention.

1888   Frederick Douglass was first black to receive a vote in presidential balloting at political convention. He received one vote on fourth ballot at Republican convention. Nineteen names were entered into Republican balloting. Benjamin Harrison won nomination on eighth ballot.

1892   Democrat Grover Cleveland broke convention system tradition by receiving third presidential nomination. People's Party (the Populists) hold first national nominating convention in Omaha, Neb., and adopt first platform.

1896   Democrats, divided over silver-gold question, repudiated Cleveland administration and nominated William J. Bryan.

Thirty-four Republican delegates against free silver walked out of convention.

1900   Each party had one woman delegate.

1904   Florida Democrats elected national convention delegates in public primary, under the first legislation permitting any recognized party to hold general primary elections.

Republicans nominated Theodore Roosevelt, first time a vice president who had succeeded a deceased president went on to be nominated in his own right.

1908   Democrats, calling for legislation terminating what they called "partnership" between Republicans and corporations, pledged to refuse campaign contributions from corporations.

Call to Republican convention provided for election of delegates by primary method introduced in some states for the first time.

1912   Increasing numbers of delegates were selected in primaries held in 13 states.

First time Republicans renominated entire ticket — William H. Taft and James S. Sherman. Malapportionment of convention seats as result of Republican decline in South killed Theodore Roosevelt's chances of nomination. Taft renominated but 349 delegates protested his nomination by refusing to vote. Roosevelt nominated for President on Progressive ticket at separate convention.

1916   Democrats renominated entire ticket — Woodrow Wilson and Thomas R. Marshall — for first time.

Hopes of reuniting Republicans diminished when Roosevelt could not secure their nomination and refused Progressive renomination.

1920   For the first time, women attended conventions in significant numbers.

1924   Republicans adopted bonus votes for first time — three bonus delegates at large allotted to each state carried by party in last preceding presidential election. Republican convention was first to be broadcast on radio.

John W. Davis was nominated by Democrats on record 103rd ballot.

Three Democratic women received one or more votes for presidential nomination.

1928   Democrat Alfred E. Smith, governor of New York was first Roman Catholic nominated for President by a major party.

1932   Republicans began tradition of appointing party leader from House of Representatives as permanent convention chairman.

Franklin D. Roosevelt appeared before Democratic convention to accept presidential nomination, the first major party candidate to do so.

1936   Democratic Party voted to end requirement of two-thirds delegate majority for nomination, a rule adopted at party's first convention and one that sometimes had led to lengthy balloting and selection of dark horse slates.

Republicans nominated Alfred M. Landon and Frank Knox in vain effort to break new Democratic coalition.

1940   Franklin D. Roosevelt was nominated for unprecedented third term. He then wrote out a refusal of his renomination because of opposition to his vice presidential choice, Henry A. Wallace. Opposition deferred and Wallace was nominated.

Republicans held first political convention to be televised.

1944   Franklin D. Roosevelt, already having broken tradition by winning third term, was nominated for fourth time. Democrats put system of bonus votes into effect for states that voted Democratic in previous presidential election.

Thomas E. Dewey became first Republican candidate to accept nomination in appearance before the convention.

1948   After Democratic convention adopted strong civil rights plank, entire Mississippi delegation and 13 of Alabama's 26 delegates walked out.

Dissidents from 13 southern states met several days later and nominated South Carolina Gov. Strom Thurmond for President.

Democrats began appointing speaker of the House as permanent chairman. Practice followed, with exception of 1960 when Sam Rayburn declined, through 1968. Since 1948 conventions, presidential nominees of both parties have appeared at their conventions.

Republicans renominated Thomas E. Dewey — first time party renominated a defeated presidential candidate.

1952   Adlai E. Stevenson, who did not seek the nomination, was chosen as Democratic nominee in one of few genuine "drafts" in history of either political party.

Republican women delegates wanted to nominate Sen. Margaret Chase Smith (Maine) for vice president, but Smith requested her name not be put in nomination.

1956   Democratic nominee Stevenson left choice of running mate to convention. Winner of open race was Sen. Estes Kefauver (Tenn.). First time a party loyalty provision was put into effect during delegate selection.

Dwight D. Eisenhower renominated unanimously on first ballot at Republican convention.

1960   Democrats adopted civil rights plank that was strongest in party history. Presidential nominee John F. Kennedy was second Catholic to receive presidential nomination of major party.

Republican nominee Richard M. Nixon was party's first vice president nominated for President at completion of his term.

1964   Democratic President Johnson was nominated for second term by acclamation. Fight over credentials of Alabama and Mississippi delegations was overriding issue first two days of convention.

Sen. Margaret Chase Smith's name was placed in nomination for presidency at Republican convention — first time a woman placed in nomination by a major party. Sen. Barry Goldwater (Ariz.) won the nomination.

1968   Democratic delegates voted to end unit rule and to eliminate it from all levels of party politics for 1972 convention.

Republicans nominated Richard Nixon, who had made one of most remarkable political comebacks in American history.

1972   With newly adopted party reform guidelines, the Democratic convention included a record number of women, youth and minorities. Open debate on many issues occurred with an unprecedented 23 credentials challenges brought to the floor. George McGovern, who built up following as an antiwar candidate, nominated for president on first ballot. His choice for vice president, Thomas Eagleton, became the second candidate in American history to withdraw from the ticket and be replaced by a selection of the national committee, R. Sargent Shriver.

In a harmonious convention Republicans renominated Richard Nixon and Spiro Agnew with nearly unanimous votes.

1976   The Democrats in a unified convention nominated Jimmy Carter. The gathering was notable for the lack of bitter floor fights and credentials challenges that had characterized some of the recent conventions.

Incumbent President Gerald R. Ford received the Republican nomination, narrowly surviving a challenge from Ronald Reagan.

1980   The Democrats renominated incumbent President Jimmy Carter in a convention marked by bitter contests over the party platform and rules binding delegates to vote on the first ballot for the candidates under whose banner they were elected. The struggle pitted Carter forces against supporters of Sen. Edward M. Kennedy, D-Mass., who were trying to pry the nomination away from the president and alter the party platform. While the Carter camp prevailed on the delegate binding rule, Kennedy managed to force major concessions in the Democratic platform.

In contrast, a harmonious and unified Republican convention nominated former California Gov. Ronald Reagan. Rumors abounded during the convention that former President Gerald R. Ford would serve as Reagan's vice-presidential candidate. After it became obvious that efforts to persuade Ford to join the ticket had failed, Reagan chose George Bush as his running mate.

CONVENTION CHRONOLOGY, 1831–1980

Convention Chronology: Sources

This section (pages 21 to 138) contains brief descriptions of all presidential nominating conventions of major American political parties and excerpts from party platforms. The chronology begins in 1831, when the Anti-Masonic Party held the first nominating convention in American history, and concludes with the Democratic and Republican Party conventions of 1980.

The narrative includes conventions for all parties receiving at least 2 percent of the popular vote in the presidential election. Thus, conventions for the Socialist Party, which received at least 2 percent of the presidential popular vote in 1904, 1908, 1912, 1920 and 1932, are included. Socialist Party conventions for other presidential election years when the party received less than 2 percent of the popular vote do not appear.

The source most frequently consulted in preparing the narrative was *Convention Decisions and Voting Records,* Brookings Institution, Washington, D.C., 1973, by Richard C. Bain and Judith H. Parris. Other works consulted appear in the bibliographies beginning on p. 229.

Ballot Vote Totals

Throughout the narrative, vote totals appear for significant ballots on platform disputes and procedural issues and for presidential and vice presidential balloting. The source used for 1835-1972 vote totals was *Convention Decisions and Voting Records.* The sources for the 1976 and 1980 vote totals were *The Official Proceedings of the Democratic National Convention* and the Republican National Committee. Charts showing state-by-state voting on selected ballots appear in a separate section, "Key Convention Ballots," pages 131 to 196. *(See p. 140 for details on these charts.)*

Platform Excerpts

The source for the party platform excerpts which appear in the convention chronology was *National Party Platforms, 1840-1968,* University of Illinois Press, 1972, compiled by Kirk H. Porter and Donald Bruce Johnson. For the 1972, 1976 and 1980 Democratic and Republican platforms, the official texts of the platforms adopted by the two parties were used.

In adopting the material from *National Party Platforms, 1840-1968,* Congressional Quarterly has added boldface subheadings to highlight the organization of the texts. For example, excerpts from the 1844 Democratic Party platform appear on page 26. The boldface headings — **Appeal to the Masses, Strict Construction, Internal Improvements,** etc. — do not appear in the text of the party platform as it was published in *National Party Platforms, 1840 - 1968.* In all other respects, Congressional Quarterly has followed the style and typography of the platform texts appearing in *National Party Platforms, 1840 - 1968.*

1831-32 Conventions

Presidential Candidates

William Wirt
Anti-Mason

Henry Clay
National Republican

Andrew Jackson
Democrat

Anti-Masons

In September 1831, the Anti-Masonic Party held the first national nominating convention in American history. One hundred sixteen delegates from 13 states, none south of Maryland, gathered in Baltimore. They selected the party's presidential and vice presidential candidates, adopted an address to the people (a precursor of the party platform) and established a national corresponding committee that created the framework for a national campaign organization.

Ironically, the Anti-Masons, whose keystone was opposition to Masonry, nominated a former Mason, William Wirt of Maryland, as their presidential standard-bearer. In spite of a rule requiring a three-fourths nominating majority, Wirt was an easy first-ballot winner and the nearly unanimous nominee of the convention.

He was not, however, the first choice of party leaders, who had been rebuffed in their earlier efforts to persuade Henry Clay and later Supreme Court Justice John McLean to take the presidential nomination. Wirt himself was not an enthusiastic candidate, stating that he saw nothing repugnant about Masonry and that if his views did not suit the convention, he would willingly withdraw from the ticket. The delegates supported Wirt and chose Amos Ellmaker of Pennsylvania as his vice presidential running mate.

National Republicans

In December 1831, the National Republicans held their national convention in Baltimore. The National Republicans were united primarily in their opposition to incumbent President Jackson. The idea of a convention had been proposed by an anti-Jackson committee in New York City and approved by the leading National Republican newspaper, the *National Intelligencer.* There was no uniform method of delegate selection, with state conventions, legislative caucuses and local meetings all being used.

One hundred sixty-eight delegates from 18 states attended the National Republican convention, although nearly one-quarter were late in arriving due to inclement winter weather. Without any pre-established rules, it was agreed that the roll calls would be taken by announcing each delegate's name. Henry Clay of Kentucky was the convention's unanimous choice for president, and former Rep. John Sergeant of Pennsylvania was selected without opposition for vice president. Letters accepting their nominations were received from both candidates.

There was no formal platform, although the convention adopted an address to the people that criticized Jackson for dividing a previously harmonious country.

In May 1832, a convention of young National Republicans met in Washington, D.C., and passed a series of resolutions calling for a protective tariff, federal support of internal improvements and recognition of the Supreme Court as the ultimate authority on constitutional questions. The last was a rebuke of Jackson for disregarding Supreme Court decisions concerning the Cherokee Indians. Other resolutions criticized Jackson's use of the spoils system in distributing patronage and his handling of foreign policy with Great Britain. Although not a formal platform, the resolutions adopted by the convention of young National Republicans were the most definitive discussion of issues during the 1832 campaign.

Democrats

The Democrats held their first national convention in Baltimore in late May 1832. Representatives from 23 states attended. The call for a Democratic national convention had been made by Jacksonian members of the New Hampshire Legislature, and their proposal was approved by prominent members of President Andrew Jackson's administration. The convention was called to order by a member of the New Hampshire Legislature, who explained the intent of the gathering in these words:

> "...[The] object of the people of New Hampshire who called this convention was, not to impose on the people, as candidates for either of the two first offices of the government, any local favorite; but to concentrate the opinions of all the states.... They believed that the example of this convention would operate favorably in future elec-

tions; that the people would be disposed, after seeing the good effects of this convention in conciliating, the different and distant sections of the country, to continue this mode of nomination." *(Reprinted from* Convention Decisions and Voting Records, *by Richard C. Bain, p. 17.)*

The convention adopted two rules which were retained by Democratic conventions well into the 20th century. One based each state's convention vote on its electoral vote, an apportionment method unchanged until 1940.

A second rule established a two-thirds nominating majority, a controversial measure that remained a feature of Democratic conventions until 1936. The 1832 convention also adopted the procedure of having one person from each delegation announce the vote of his state.

The delegates did not formally nominate Jackson for the presidency, instead they concurred in the various nominations he had received earlier from state legislatures. Jackson's choice for vice president, Martin Van Buren of New York, was easily nominated on the first ballot, receiving 208 of the 283 votes cast.

Instead of adopting a platform or address to the people, the convention decided that each state delegation should write its own report to its constituents. The convention also determined to establish general corresponding committees in each state, which would provide a nationwide organization for the campaign.

1835-36 Conventions

Presidential Candidates

Martin Van Buren
Democrat

William Henry Harrison
Whig

Daniel Webster
Whig

Hugh L. White
Whig

Democrats

The Democrats held their second national convention in Baltimore in May 1835. The early date had been set by President Jackson to prevent the emergence of opposition to his hand-picked successor, Vice President Martin Van Buren. Delegates from 22 states and two territories attended, and the size of the delegations was generally related to their distance from Baltimore. One hundred eighty-eight individuals were on hand from Maryland to cast the state's 10 votes, but only one person attended from Tennessee—a visiting businessman who cast 15 votes. Alabama, Illinois and South Carolina were unrepresented.

Two rival Pennsylvania delegations arrived, precipitating the first credentials dispute in convention history. It was decided to seat both delegations and let them share the Pennsylvania vote.

An effort to eliminate the rule requiring a two-thirds nominating majority initially passed by a margin of 231 to 210 (apparently counting individual delegates instead of state convention votes), but the two-thirds rule was reimposed by a voice vote. A question developed whether the nominating majority should be based on only the states represented or on all the states in the union. It was decided to base the majority on only those present.

Martin Van Buren won the presidential nomination, winning all 265 votes. Richard M. Johnson of Kentucky barely reached the necessary two-thirds majority on the first vice presidential ballot, receiving 178 votes, just one vote more than the required minimum. *(Chart, p. 141)*

Johnson, famous as the alleged slayer of the Indian chief Tecumseh, had aroused some disapproval because of his personal life. Johnson had lived with a mulatto mistress by whom he had two daughters.

Once again the Democrats did not write a formal platform, although an address to the people was published in the party newspaper, *The Washington Globe.* Van Buren wrote a letter of acceptance in which he promised to "tread generally in the footsteps of President Jackson."

Whigs

During Jackson's second term, a new party, the Whigs, emerged as the Democrats' primary opposition. It con-tained remnants of the short-lived National Republican Party, as well as anti-Jackson elements in the Democratic and Anti-Masonic Parties. Although the Whigs were a ris-ing political force, the party lacked national cohesion in 1836. Instead of holding a convention and nominating national candidates, the Whigs ran regional candidates nominated by state legislatures. It was the hope of Whig strategists that the regional candidates would receive enough electoral votes to throw the election into the House of Representatives, where the party could unite behind the leading prospect.

Sen. Daniel Webster of New Hampshire ran as the Whig candidate in Massachusetts; Sen. Hugh L. White of Tennessee was the party standard-bearer in the South; Gen. William Henry Harrison of Ohio was the Whig can-didates in the rest of the country. The Whigs chose Francis Granger of New York as Harrison and Webster's running mate and John Tyler of Virginia to run with White.

1839-40 Conventions

Presidential Candidates

William Henry Harrison
Whig

Martin Van Buren
Democrat

Whigs

By 1839, the Whigs had established themselves as a powerful opposition party, unified enough to run a national candidate against the Democratic President, Martin Van Buren. The call for the Whigs' first national convention was issued by a group of party members in Congress. Nearly 250 delegates responded, gathering in Harrisburg, Pa., in December 1839.

Three candidates were in contention for the presiden-tial nomination: Generals William Henry Harrison of Ohio and Winfield Scott of Virginia and Sen. Henry Clay of Ken-tucky. After long debate, it was decided that each state would ballot separately, then select representatives who would meet and discuss the views and results of their delegation meetings with representatives of the other states. The unit rule would be in effect, binding the entire vote of each state to the candidate who received a majority of the state's delegates.

The nominating rules agreed to by the convention strongly favored the forces opposed to Clay. First, they negated substantial Clay strength in state delegations in which he did not hold a majority of the vote. Second, they permitted balloting in relative anonymity, so that delegates would be more likely to defect from the popular Kentuckian than they would if the balloting were public.

Clay led on the first ballot, but switches by Scott delegates on subsequent roll calls gave the nomination to Harrison. On the final ballot, Harrison received 148 votes to 90 for Clay and 16 for Scott. Harrison's vote was short of a two-thirds majority, but under Whig rules, only a simple majority was needed to nominate.

To give the ticket factional and geographic balance, a friend of Clay, former Democrat John Tyler of Virginia, was the unanimous selection for vice president. The con-vention did not risk destruction of the tenuous unity of its anti-Democratic coalition by adopting a party platform or statement of principles.

Democrats

In May 1840, the Democrats held their national con-vention in Baltimore. The call once again was initiated by members of the New Hampshire Legislature. Delegates from 21 states attended, while five states were unrepresented. Again, the size of the state delegations was largely determined by their distance from Baltimore. New Jersey sent 59 people to cast the state's eight votes, while only one delegate came from Massachusetts to decide that state's 14 votes.

To avoid a bitter dispute over the vice presidential nomination, the convention appointed a committee to recommend nominees for both spots on the ticket. The committee's recommendation that Van Buren be renominated for president was passed by acclamation. On the touchier problem of the vice presidency, the committee recommended that no nomination be made, a suggestion that was also agreed to by the convention. Dissatisfaction with the personal life of Vice President Johnson had increased, leading to the decision that state Democratic leaders determine who would run as the vice presidential candidate in their own states.

Before the nominating process had begun, the convention had approved the first party platform in American history. A platform committee was appointed "to prepare resolutions declaratory of the principles of the...party." The committee report was approved without discussion.

The first Democratic platform was a short document, less than 1,000 words long. Although brief by modern standards, the platform clearly emphasized the party's belief in a strict reading of the Constitution. It began by stating "that the federal government is one of limited powers" and spelled out in detail what the federal government could not do. The platform stated that the federal government did not have the power to finance internal improvements, assume state debts, charter a national bank or interfere with the rights of the states, especially relating to slavery. The platform criticized the abolitionists for stirring up the explosive slavery question. The Democrats urged the government to practice economy, supported President Van Buren's independent treasury plan and affirmed their belief in the principles expressed in the Declaration of Independence.

In addition to the platform, the convention adopted an address to the people, which was written by a separate committee. Much longer than the platform, the address discussed party principles, lauded Van Buren and Jackson for following these principles and warned of dire consequences if the opposition should be elected.

Following are excerpts from the Democratic platform of 1840:

Strict Construction. *Resolved,* That the federal government is one of limited powers, derived solely from the constitution, and the grants of power shown therein, ought to be strictly construed by all the departments and agents of the government, and that it is inexpedient and dangerous to exercise doubtful constitutional powers.

Internal Improvements. *Resolved,* That the constitution does not confer upon the general government the power to commence and carry on, a general system of internal improvements.

State Debts. *Resolved,* That the constitution does not confer authority upon the federal government, directly or indirectly, to assume the debts of the several states, contracted for local internal improvements, or other state purposes; nor would such assumption be just or expedient.

Equality of Rights. *Resolved,* That justice and sound policy forbid the federal government to foster one branch of industry to the detriment of another, or to cherish the interests of one portion to the injury of another portion of our common country—that every citizen and every section of the country, has a right to demand and insist upon an equality of rights and privileges, and to complete and ample protection of person and property from domestic violence, or foreign aggression.

Government Spending. *Resolved,* That it is the duty of every branch of the government, to enforce and practice the most rigid economy, in conducting our public affairs, and that no more revenue ought to be raised, than is required to defray the necessary expenses of the government.

National Bank. *Resolved,* That congress has no power to charter a national bank; that we believe such an institution one of deadly hostility to the best interests of the country, dangerous to our republican institutions and the liberties of the people, and calculated to place the business of the country within the control of a concentrated money power, and above the laws and the will of the people.

States' Rights, Slavery. *Resolved,* That congress has no power, under the constitution, to interfere with or control the domestic institutions of the several states, and that such states are the sole and proper judges of everything appertaining to their own affairs, not prohibited by the constitution; that all efforts by abolitionists or others, made to induce congress to interfere with questions of slavery, or to take incipient steps in relation thereto, are calculated to lead to the most alarming and dangerous consequences, and that all such efforts have an inevitable tendency to diminish the happiness of the people, and endanger the stability and permanency of the union, and ought not to be countenanced by any friend to our political institutions.

Independent Treasury. *Resolved,* That the separation of the moneys of the government from banking institutions, is indispensable for the safety of the funds of the government, and the rights of the people.

Democratic Principles. *Resolved,* That the liberal principles embodied by Jefferson in the Declaration of Independence, and sanctioned in the constitution, which makes ours the land of liberty, and the asylum of the oppressed of every nation, have ever been cardinal principles in the democratic faith; and every attempt to abridge the present privilege of becoming citizens, and the owners of soil among us, ought to be resisted with the same spirit which swept the alien and sedition laws from our statutebook.

1843-44 Conventions

Presidential Candidates

James G. Birney
Liberty

Henry Clay
Whig

James K. Polk
Democrat

Liberty Party

The Liberty Party held its second national convention in Buffalo, N.Y., in August 1843. The party, born of the failure of the Whigs and the Democrats to make a strong appeal to abolitionist voters, had held its first national convention in April 1840 in Albany, N.Y. James G. Birney of Michigan, a former slave owner, was nominated for president and Thomas Earle of Ohio was chosen as his running mate. In the 1840 election the party polled 0.29 per cent of the national popular vote.

At the 1843 convention, 148 delegates from 12 states assembled in Buffalo and renominated Birney for the presidency and chose Thomas Morris of Ohio as his running mate. The party platform was more than 3,000 words long, the lengthiest platform written by any party in the 19th century. In spite of its length, the platform discussed only one issue, slavery. In the 1844 election, the party received 2.3 per cent of the national popular vote, its highest total in any presidential election. By 1848, most members of the party joined the newly-formed Free Soil Party.

Following are excerpts from the Liberty Party platform of 1844:

Resolved. That the Liberty party...will demand the absolute and unqualified divorce of the General Government from Slavery, and also the restoration of equality of rights, among men, in every State where the party exists, or may exist.

Therefore, Resolved, That we hereby give it to be distinctly understood, by this nation and the world, that, as abolitionists, considering that the strength of our cause lies in its righteousness—and our hope for it in our conformity to the LAWS OF GOD, and our respect for the RIGHTS OF MAN, we owe it to the Sovereign Ruler of the Universe, as a proof of our allegiance to Him, in all our civil relations and offices, whether as private citizens, or as public functionaries sworn to support the Constitution of the United States, to regard and to treat the third clause of the second section of the fourth article of that instrument, whenever applied to the case of a fugitive slave, as utterly null and void, and consequently as forming no part of the Constitution of the United States, whenever we are called upon, or sworn, to support it.

Whigs

In a harmonious one-day session, the Whigs' national convention nominated for the presidency the party's former leader in Congress, Henry Clay. It was a final rebuff for President John Tyler from the party that had nominated him for the second spot on its ticket in 1840. Three years of bickering between the White House and Whig leaders in Congress had made Tyler, former Democrat, *persona non grata* in the Whig Party.

Delegates from every state were represented at the Whig convention, held in Baltimore on May 1, 1844. Clay was the unanimous nominee, and it was proposed that he be invited to address the convention the next day. However, the Kentuckian declined this opportunity to make the first acceptance speech in American political history, stating in a letter that he was unable to reconcile an appearance with his "sense of delicacy and propriety." *(Chart, p. 142)*

Three potential candidates for the vice presidency sent letters of withdrawal before balloting for second place on the ticket began. Unlike the convention four years earlier, the Whigs abandoned their relatively secret state caucus method of voting and adopted a public roll call, with the chair calling the name of each delegate. Theodore Frelinghuysen of New Jersey won a plurality of the convention vote for vice president on the first ballot and went on to gain, on the third ballot, the required majority.

After the nominations, a series of resolutions was adopted, including one that defined Whig principles and served as the party's first platform. It was a brief document, fewer than 100 words long, and the only clear difference between it and the platform adopted later by the Democratic convention was on the issue of distributing proceeds from the sale of public land. The Whigs favored distribution of these revenues to the states; the Democrats opposed it, believing the proceeds should be retained by the federal government. In a continued reaction to the Jackson administration, the Whigs criticized "executive usurpations" and proposed a single-term presidency. The rest of the Whig platform called for government efficiency, "a well-regulated currency" and a tariff for revenue and the protection of American labor.

Westward territorial expansion, particularly the annexation of Texas, was not mentioned in the Whig platform, but it was an explosive issue by 1844 which made a significant impact on the Democratic convention.

Following are excerpts from the Whig platform of 1844:

Resolved, That these principles may be summed as comprising, a well-regulated currency; a tariff for revenue to defray the necessary expenses of the government, and discriminating with special reference to the protection of the domestic labor of the country; the distribution of proceeds of the sales of the public lands; a single term for the presidency; a reform of executive usurpations; —and, generally—such an administration of the affairs of the country as shall impart to every branch of the public service the greatest practicable efficiency, controlled by a well regulated and wise economy.

Democrats

Delegates from every state except South Carolina assembled in Baltimore in late May 1844 for the Democratic convention. The front-runner for the presidential nomination was Martin Van Buren, whose status was threatened on the eve of the convention by his statement against the annexation of Texas. Van Buren's position jeopardized his support in the South, and with a two-thirds majority apparently necessary, dimmed his chances of obtaining the presidential nomination. The question of requiring a two-thirds nominating majority was debated in the early sessions of the convention, and by a vote of 148 to 118, the two-thirds majority rule, initially adopted by the party in 1832, was ratified. *(Chart, p. 141)*

Van Buren led the early presidential balloting, actually receiving a simple majority of the vote on the first ballot. On succeeding roll calls, however, his principal opponent, Lewis Cass of Michigan, gained strength and took the lead. But neither candidate approached the 178 votes needed for nomination.

With a deadlock developing, sentiment for a compromise candidate appeared. James K. Polk, former speaker of the Tennessee House and former governor of Tennessee, emerged as an acceptable choice and won the nomination on the ninth ballot. It marked the first time in American history that a dark horse candidate won a presidential nomination. *(Chart, p. 141)*

A friend of Van Buren, Sen. Silas Wright of New York, was the nearly unanimous nominee of the convention for vice president. But Wright refused the nomination, quickly notifying the delegates by way of Samuel Morse's new invention, the telegraph. After two more ballots, George M. Dallas of Pennsylvania was chosen as Polk's running mate.

Among its final actions, the convention appointed a central committee and recommended that a nationwide party organization be established—a forerunner of the national committee. The delegates did not adopt a platform, but appointed a committee to draft resolutions.

The resulting document contained the same resolutions included in the party's 1840 platform, plus several new planks. The Democrats opposed the distribution of the proceeds from the sale of public lands; were against placing any restrictions on the executive veto power; and, to alleviate the sectional bitterness aroused by the prospect of western expansion, recommended the annexation of both Texas and Oregon.

President Tyler, although abandoned by the major parties, wanted to remain in office. Friends and federal officeholders gathered in Baltimore at the same time as the Democrats and nominated Tyler. However, it became apparent that the President's national vote-getting appeal was limited, and he withdrew from the race in favor of the Democrat, Polk.

Following are excerpts from the Democratic platform of 1844:

Appeal to the Masses. *Resolved,* That the American Democracy place their trust, not in factitious symbols, not in displays and appeals insulting to the judgment and subversive of the intellect of the people, but in a clear reliance upon the intelligence, patriotism, and the discriminating justice of the American masses.

That we regard this as a distinctive feature of our political creed, which we are proud to maintain before the world, as the great moral element in a form of government springing from and upheld by the popular will; and we contrast it with the creed and practice of Federalism, under whatever name or form, which seeks to palsy the will of the constituent, and which conceives no imposture too monstrous for the popular credulity.

Strict Construction. That the Federal Government is one of limited powers, derived solely from the Constitution.

Internal Improvements. That the Constitution does not confer upon the General Government the power to commence or carry on a general system of internal improvements.

State Debts. That the Constitution does not confer authority upon the Federal Government, directly or indirectly, to assume the debts of the several states.

Government Spending. That it is the duty of every branch of the government to enforce and practice the most rigid economy in conducting our public affairs, and that no more revenue ought to be raised than is required to defray the necessary expenses of the government.

National Bank. That Congress has no power to charter a United States Bank, that we believe such an institution one of deadly hostility to the best interests of the country, dangerous to our republican institutions and the liberties of the people.

States' Rights. That Congress has no power, under the Constitution, to interfere with or control the domestic institutions of the several States; and that such States are the sole and proper judges of everything pertaining to their own affairs, not prohibited by the Constitution; that all efforts, by abolitionists or others, made to induce Congress to interfere with questions of slavery, or to take incipient steps in relation thereto, are calculated to lead to the most alarming and dangerous consequences.

Public Lands. *Resolved,* That the proceeds of the Public Lands ought to be sacredly applied to the national objects specified in the Constitution, and that we are opposed to the laws lately adopted, and to any law for the distribution of such proceeds among the States, as alike inexpedient in policy and repugnant to the Constitution.

Executive Veto Power. *Resolved,* That we are decidedly opposed to taking from the President the qualified veto power by which he is enabled, under restrictions and responsibilities amply sufficient to guard the public interest.

Western Expansion. *Resolved,* That our title to the whole of the Territory of Oregon is clear and unquestionable; that no portion of the same ought to be ceded to England or any other power, and that the reoccupation of Oregon and the re-annexation of Texas at the earliest practicable period are great American measures, which this Convention recommends to the cordial support of the Democracy of the Union.

1848 Conventions

Presidential Candidates

Lewis Cass
Democrat

Zachary Taylor
Whig

Martin Van Buren
Free Soil

Democrats

Delegates from every state gathered in Baltimore in May 1848, for the Democratic Party's fifth national convention. A seating dispute between two rival New York delegations enlivened the early convention sessions. The conflict reflected a factional fight in the state Democratic Party between a more liberal anti-slavery faction, known as the Barnburners and a more conservative faction, known as the Hunkers. By a vote of 126 to 125, the convention adopted a compromise by which both delegations were seated and shared New York's vote. However, this compromise satisfied neither of the contesting delegations. The Barnburners bolted the convention. The Hunkers remained, but refused to vote. *(Chart, p. 142)*

Before the presidential balloting could begin, the convention had to decide whether or not to use the controversial two-thirds rule. Consideration of the rule preceded the credentials controversy, which brought an objection from New York delegates who wanted their seating dispute settled first. But by a vote of 133 to 121, the convention refused to table the issue. A second vote on adoption of the two-thirds rule was approved, 176 to 78. *(Chart, p. 142)*

The front-runner for the presidential nomination was Sen. Lewis Cass of Michigan. Although Cass was from the North, his view that the existence of slavery in the territories should be determined by their inhabitants (a forerunner of Stephen Douglas' "popular sovereignty") was a position acceptable to the South.

Cass received 125 votes on the first ballot, more than double the total of his two principal rivals, James Buchanan of Pennsylvania and Levi Woodbury of New Hampshire. Cass' vote total steadily increased during the next three roll calls, and on the fourth ballot he received 179 votes and was nominated. His vote was actually short of a two-thirds majority of the allotted convention votes, but the chair ruled that with New York not voting, the required majority was reduced. *(Chart, p. 142)*

The vice presidential nomination went on the second ballot to Gen. William O. Butler of Kentucky, who had 169 of the 253 votes cast. As in the earlier presidential balloting,

Butler's two-thirds majority was based on votes cast rather than votes allotted. Butler's primary rival for the nomination was a military colleague, Gen. John A. Quitman of Mississippi.

One of the most significant acts of the convention was the formation of a national committee, with one member from each state, that would handle party affairs until the next convention four years later.

As in 1840 and 1844, the heart of the Democratic platform was a series of resolutions describing the party's concept of a federal government with limited powers. New resolutions emphasized Democratic opposition to a national bank and the distribution of land sales to the states, while applauding the independent treasury plan, the lower tariff bill passed in 1846 and the successful war against Mexico. An effort by William L. Yancey of Alabama to insert in the platform a plank on slavery that would prevent interference with the rights of slaveholders in states or territories was defeated, 216 to 36. The slavery plank written in the platform had the same wording as earlier versions in the 1840 and 1844 Democratic platforms. The plank was milder than Yancey's proposal, stating simply that Congress did not have the power to interfere with slavery in the states. The convention adopted the complete platform by a vote of 247 to 0.

Following are excerpts from the 1848 Democratic platform:

> **Mexican War.** *Resolved,* That the war with Mexico, provoked on her part by years of insult and injury, was commenced by her army crossing the Rio Grande, attacking the American troops, and invading our sister State of Texas; and that, upon all the principles of patriotism and laws of nations, it is a just and necessary war on our part, in which every American citizen should have shown himself on the side of his country, and neither morally nor physically, by word or by deed, have given "aid and comfort to the enemy."
>
> **Democratic Accomplishments.** *Resolved,* That the fruits of the great political triumph of 1844, which elected James K. Polk and George M. Dallas President and Vice-President of the United States, have fulfilled the hopes of the Democracy of the Union—in defeating the declared pur-

poses of their opponents to create a national bank; in preventing the corrupt and unconstitutional distribution of the land proceeds, from the common treasury of the Union, for local purposes; in protecting the currency and the labor of the country from ruinous fluctuations, and guarding the money of the people for the use of the people, by the establishment of the constitutional treasury; in the noble impulse given to the cause of free trade, by the repeal of the tariff in 1842 and the creation of the more equal, honest, and productive tariff of 1846.

Whigs

Whig delegates from every state except Texas gathered in Philadelphia in June 1848. Although the Lone Star state was unrepresented, a Texas Whig state convention had earlier given a proxy for their votes to the Louisiana delegates. There was debate in the convention about the legality of the proxy, but it was ultimately accepted by the delegates.

The battle for the Whig's presidential nomination involved three major contenders, the party's respected aging statesman, Henry Clay of Kentucky; and two generals—Zachary Taylor and Winfield Scott, both of Virginia—whose political appeal was significantly increased by their military exploits in the recently completed Mexican War. Taylor led throughout the balloting, taking the lead on the first ballot with 111 votes, compared with 97 for Clay and 43 for Scott. Taylor increased his lead on subsequent roll calls, winning the nomination on the fourth ballot with 171 of the 280 votes cast. *(Chart, p. 143)*

Millard Fillmore of New York and Abbott Lawrence of Massachusetts were the prime contenders for the vice presidential nomination. Fillmore led Lawrence, 115 to 109, on the first ballot and pulled away to win on the second ballot with 173 of the 266 votes cast.

A motion to make the presidential and vice presidential nominations unanimous failed when several delegates objected, doubting Taylor's support of Whig principles.

The Whig convention did not formally adopt a party platform, although a ratification meeting held in Philadelphia after the convention adopted a series of resolutions. The resolutions avoided a discussion of issues, instead lauding the party's presidential nominee, Zachary Taylor, and affirming his faithfulness to the tenets of the party.

Free Soilers

Anti-slavery Whigs, New York Barnburners and members of the Liberty Party gathered in Buffalo, N.Y., in August 1848 to form a new third party, the Free Soilers. While opposition to slavery was a common denominator of the various elements in the new party, the dissident Democrats and Whigs also were attracted to the Free Soil Party by the lack of influence they exerted in their former parties. The call for a free soil convention was made by the New York Barnburners at their state conclave in June 1848 and by a nonpartisan gathering in Columbus, Ohio, the same month. The latter assembly, organized by Salmon P. Chase, was entitled a People's Convention of Friends of Free Territory and was designed to set the stage for a national free soil convention.

Four hundred sixty-five delegates from 18 states (including representatives from the slave states of Delaware, Maryland and Virginia) assembled in Buffalo for the birth of the Free Soil Party. Because of the large number of delegates, convention leaders determined that delegates from each state would select several members to form a Committee on Conference, which would conduct convention business. The rest of the delegates would sit in a large tent and listen to campaign oratory.

Martin Van Buren, the former Democratic president and a favorite of the Barnburners, was chosen as the new party's standard-bearer on the first ballot. Van Buren received 244 votes to defeat John P. Hale of New Hampshire, who had 181 votes. Hale had been nominated by the Liberty Party in October 1847, but with Van Buren's nomination, he withdrew from the race. The vice presidential nomination went to a former Whig, Charles Francis Adams of Massachusetts.

The platform adopted by the Free Soil Party focused on the slavery issue, but its opposition to slavery was milder than earlier Liberty Party platforms. The Free Soilers also declared themselves on other issues besides slavery, further distinguishing themselves from the single-minded Liberty Party.

While the Free Soilers opposed the extension of slavery into the territories, they did not feel the federal government had the power to interfere with slavery in the states. Although this position was significantly stronger than the position adopted by the Democrats, it was milder than the all-out opposition to slavery expressed by the Liberty Party four years earlier.

The Free Soilers also adopted positions on a variety of other issues, supporting free land for settlers, a tariff for revenue purposes, cheap postage and federal spending for river and harbor improvements. Basically, the Free Soil platform expressed belief in a federal government with broader powers than that conceived by the Democrats.

Following are excerpts from the 1848 Free Soil Party platform:

Slavery. *Resolved*, That Slavery in the several States of this Union which recognize its existence, depends upon the State laws alone, which cannot be repealed or modified by the Federal Government, and for which laws that Government is not responsible. We therefore propose no interference by Congress with Slavery within the limits of any State.

Resolved, THAT IT IS THE DUTY OF THE FEDERAL GOVERNMENT TO RELIEVE ITSELF FROM ALL RESPONSIBILITY FOR THE EXISTENCE OR CONTINUANCE OF SLAVERY WHEREVER THAT GOVERNMENT POSSESS CONSTITUTIONAL POWER TO LEGISLATE ON THAT SUBJECT, AND IS THUS RESPONSIBILE FOR ITS EXISTENCE.

Resolved, That the true, and, in the judgment of this Convention, the *only* safe means of preventing the extension of Slavery into territory now free, is to prohibit its existence in all such territory by *an act of Congress*.

Government Administration. *Resolved*, That we demand CHEAP POSTAGE for the people; a retrenchment of the expenses and patronage of the Federal Government; the *abolition* of all *unnecessary* offices and salaries; and the election by the People of all civil officers in the service of the Government, so far as the same may be practicable.

Internal Improvements. *Resolved*, That *river and harbor improvements*, when demanded by the safety and convenience of commerce with foreign nations, or among the several States, are objects of *national concern;* and that it is the duty of Congress, in the exercise of its constitutional powers, to provide therefor.

Homesteading. *Resolved*, That the FREE GRANT TO ACTUAL SETTLERS, in consideration of the expenses they incur in making settlements in the wilderness, which are usually fully equal to their actual cost, and of the public benefits resulting therefrom, of reasonable portions of the public lands, under suitable limitations, is a wise and just measure of public policy, which will promote, in various ways, the interest of all the States of this Union; and we therefore recommend it to the favorable consideration of the American People.

Tariff. *Resolved,* That the obligations of honor and patriotism require the earliest practical payment of the

national debt, and we are therefore in favor of such a tariff of duties as will raise revenue adequate to defray the necessary expenses of the Federal Government, and to pay annual installments of our debt and the interest thereon.

Party Motto. *Resolved,* That we inscribe on our banner, "FREE SOIL, FREE SPEECH, FREE LABOR, AND FREE MEN."

1852 Conventions

Presidential Candidates

Franklin Pierce
Democrat

Winfield Scott
Whig

John P. Hale
Free Soil

Democrats

In spite of the efforts of the major politicians of both parties, the explosive slavery question was fast becoming the dominant issue in American politics and was threatening the tenuous intersectional alliances that held together both the Democratic and Whig parties. Under the cloud of this volatile issue, the Democratic convention convened in Baltimore in June 1852.

The delegates were called to order by the party's first national chairman, Benjamin F. Hallett of Massachusetts. Hallett's first action was to limit the size of each state delegation to its electoral vote, dispatching members of oversized delegations to the rear of the hall. Retention of the two-thirds rule provoked little opposition, unlike the disputes at the 1844 and 1848 conventions, and an effort to table the rule was soundly beaten, 269 to 13.

With a degree of orderliness, the convention disposed of procedural matters, clearing the way for the presidential balloting. There were four major contenders for the nomination: Sen. Lewis Cass of Michigan, James Buchanan of Pennsylvania and William L. Marcy of New York—all three over 60 years old—and the rising young senator from Illinois, Stephen A. Douglas, 39. All four challengers led at one point during the numerous ballots that followed.

Cass jumped in front initially, receiving 116 votes on the first ballot. Buchanan trailed with 93, while Marcy and Douglas were far back with 27 and 20 votes, respectively. Cass' vote dropped after the first few roll calls, but he was able to hold the lead until the 20th ballot, when Buchanan moved in front. Buchanan led for several roll calls, followed by Douglas, who edged into the lead on the 30th ballot, only to be quickly displaced by Cass on the 32nd ballot. Marcy made his spurt between the 36th and 46th ballots, and took

the lead on the 45th and 46th ballots. But in spite of the quick changes in fortune, none of the four contenders could win a simple majority of the votes, let alone the two-thirds required. *(Chart, p. 144)*

With a deadlock developing, on the 35th ballot the Virginia delegation introduced a new name, Franklin Pierce of New Hampshire. Although formerly a member of both houses of Congress, Pierce was little known nationally and not identified with any party faction. Pierce's relative anonymity made him an acceptable alternative in the volatile convention. Pierce received 15 votes on the 35th ballot and gradually gained strength on subsequent ballots, with the big break coming on the 49th roll call. Nearly unanimous votes for Pierce in the New England states created a bandwagon effect that resulted in his nomination on this ballot with 279 of the 288 votes cast. The 49 ballots took two days.

Beginning the vice presidential roll call, a spokesman for the Maine delegation suggested that second place on the ticket go to a representative of the South, specifically mentioning Sen. William R. King of Alabama. King moved into a strong lead on the first ballot with 125 votes and easily won nomination on the second roll call with 277 of the 288 votes cast.

The platform adopted by the Democratic convention contained the same nine resolutions that had been in all party platforms since 1840, detailing the Democratic concept of a limited federal government. The platform included a plank supporting the Compromise of 1850, the congressional solution to the slavery question. Actually, both the Whigs and Democrats endorsed the Compromise of 1850. The major point of dispute between the two parties was over the issue of internal improvements, with the

Whigs taking a broader view of federal power in this sphere.

Following are excerpts from the Democratic platform of 1852:

> **Compromise of 1850.** *Resolved,* ...the democratic party of the Union, standing on this national platform, will abide by and adhere to a faithful execution of the acts known as the compromise measures settled by the last Congress—"the act for reclaiming fugitives from service or labor" included; which act, being designed to carry out an express provision of the constitution, cannot, with fidelity thereto be repealed nor so changed as to destroy or impair its efficiency.
>
> *Resolved,* That the democratic party will resist all attempts at renewing, in congress or out of it, the agitation of the slavery question, under whatever shape or color the attempt may be made.
>
> **Democratic Principles.** *Resolved,* That, in view of the condition of popular institutions in the Old World, a high and sacred duty is devolved, with increased responsibility upon the democratic party of this country, as the party of the people, to uphold and maintain the rights of every State, and thereby the Union of the States, and to sustain and advance among us constitutional liberty, by continuing to resist all monopolies and exclusive legislation for the benefit of the few at the expense of the many, and by a vigilant and constant adherence to those principles and compromises of the constitution, which are broad enough and strong enough to embrace and uphold the Union as it was, the Union as it is, and the Union as it shall be, in the full expansion of the energies and capacity of this great and progressive people.

Whigs

Although in control of the White House, the Whigs were more sharply divided by the Compromise of 1850 than were the Democrats. The majority of northern Whigs in Congress opposed the Compromise, while most southern members of the party favored it. Faced with widening division in their ranks, Whig delegates convened in Baltimore in June 1852. The call for this national convention had been issued by Whig members of Congress, and delegates from all 31 states attended.

The convention sessions were often lively and sometimes raucous. When asked to present its report the first day, the credentials committee responded that it was not ready to report and "didn't know when—maybe for days." A minister, invited to the hall to deliver a prayer to the convention, never had his chance. The delegates debated when the prayer should be delivered and finally decided to omit it.

A heated debate occurred on how many votes each state would be apportioned on the platform committee. By a vote of 149 to 144, the delegates adopted a plan whereby each state's vote on the committee would reflect its strength in the electoral college. Strong protests from southern and small northern states, however, brought a reversal of this decision, and although no formal vote was recorded, representation on the platform committee was changed so that each state received one vote.

The northern and southern wings of the Whig Party were nearly equally represented at the Baltimore convention, and the close split produced a prolonged battle for the party's presidential nomination. The two major rivals for the nomination, President Millard Fillmore and Winfield Scott, had nearly equal strength. Ironically, the basic appeal of Fillmore of New York was among southern delegates, who appreciated his support of the Compromise of 1850.

Although a native of Virginia, Scott was not popular in the South because of his ambivalence on the Compromise and the active support given him by a leading anti-slavery northerner, Sen. William H. Seward of New York. Scott's strength was in the northern and western states. A third candidate in the field was Daniel Webster, the party's elder statesman, whose appeal was centered in his native New England.

On the first ballot, Fillmore received 133 votes, Scott had 132 and Webster collected 29. This nearly equal distribution of the vote between Fillmore and Scott continued with little fluctuation through the first two days of balloting. Midway through the second day, after the 34th ballot, a motion was made to adjourn. Although defeated by a vote of 126 to 76, other motions were made to adjourn throughout the rest of the session. Finally, amid increasing confusion, after the 46th ballot, delegates voted by a margin of 176 to 116 to adjourn. *(Chart, p. 145)*

Commotion continued the next day, with southern delegates trying unsuccessfully to expel Henry J. Raymond, the editor of *The New York Times,* who was also a delegate by proxy. In an article, Raymond had charged collusion between party managers and southern delegates, with the South getting its way on the platform while Scott received the presidential nomination.

Amid this uproar, the leaders of the Fillmore and Webster forces were negotiating. Fillmore was willing to release his delegates to Webster, if Webster could muster 41 votes on his own. As the balloting continued, it was apparent that Webster could not; and enough delegates defected to Scott to give the Mexican War hero a simple majority and the nomination on the 53rd ballot. On the final roll call, Scott received 159 votes, compared with 112 for Fillmore and 21 for Webster.

Several individuals placed in nomination for the vice presidency refused it immediately. The chairman of the convention finally declared Secretary of the Navy William A. Graham of North Carolina to be the unanimous selection. No formal roll call vote was recorded.

For only the second time in their history, the Whigs adopted a party platform. Like their Democratic adversaries, the Whigs supported the Compromise of 1850 and perceived the federal government as having limited powers. Additional planks called for a tariff on imports to raise revenue and for an isolationist foreign policy that avoided "entangling alliances." The platform was adopted by a vote of 227 to 66, with all the dissenting votes cast by delegates from the North and West.

Following are excerpts from the Whig platform of 1852:

> **Strict Construction.** The Government of the United States is of a limited character, and it is confined to the exercise of powers expressly granted by the Constitution, and such as may be necessary and proper for carrying the granted powers into full execution, and that all powers not granted or necessarily implied are expressly reserved to the States respectively and to the people.
>
> **Foreign Policy.** That while struggling freedom everywhere enlists the warmest sympathy of the Whig party, we still adhere to the doctrines of the Father of his Country, as announced in his Farewell Address, of keeping ourselves free from all entangling alliances with foreign countries, and of never quitting our own to stand upon foreign ground, that our mission as a republic is not to propagate our opinions, or impose on other countries our form of government by artifice or force; but to teach, by example, and show by our success, moderation and justice, the

blessings of self-government, and the advantages of free institutions.

Tariff. Revenue sufficient for the expenses of an economical administration of the Government in time of peace ought to be derived from a duty on imports, and not from direct taxation.

Internal Improvements. The Constitution vests in Congress the power to open and repair harbors, and remove obstructions from navigable rivers, whenever such improvements are necessary for the common defense, and for the protection and facility of commerce with foreign nations, or among the States, said improvements being, in every instance, national and general in their character.

Compromise of 1850. That the series of acts of the Thirty-first Congress,—the act known as the Fugitive Slave Law, included—are received and acquiesced in by the Whig Party of the United States as a settlement in principle and substance, of the dangerous and exciting question which they embrace; and, so far as they are concerned, we will maintain them, and insist upon their strict enforcement, until time and experience shall demonstrate the necessity of further legislation.

Free Democrats (Free Soilers)

After the 1848 election, the New York Barnburners returned to the Democratic Party, and the rest of the Free Soilers were ready to coalesce with either the Democrats or the Whigs. But the process of absorption was delayed by the Compromise of 1850. It was viewed as a solution to the slavery question by the two major parties but was regarded as a sellout by most anti-slavery groups.

Responding to a call for a national convention issued by a Cleveland, Ohio, anti-slavery meeting, delegates gathered in Pittsburgh in August 1852. Anti-slavery Whigs and remnants of the Liberty Party were in attendance at what was termed the Free Soil Democratic Convention.

John P. Hale of New Hampshire unanimously won the presidential nomination, and George W. Julian of Indiana was selected as his running mate.

Although the platform covered a number of issues, the document focused on the slavery question. The Free Soil Democrats opposed the Compromise of 1850 and called for the abolition of slavery. Like both major parties, the plat-

form expressed the concept of a limited federal government, but agreed with the Whigs that the government should undertake certain river and harbor improvements. The Free Democrats went beyond the other parties in advocating a homestead policy, extending a welcome to immigrants and voicing support for new republican governments in Europe and the Caribbean.

Following are excerpts from the Free Democratic platform of 1852:

Strict Construction. That the Federal Government is one of limited powers, derived solely from the Constitution, and the grants of power therein ought to be strictly construed by all the departments and agents of the Government, and it is inexpedient and dangerous to exercise doubtful constitutional powers.

Compromise of 1850. That, to the persevering and importunate demands of the slave power for more slave States, new slave Territories, and the nationalization of slavery, our distinct and final answer is—no more slave States, no slave Territory, no nationalized slavery, and no national legislation for the extradition of slaves.

That slavery is a sin against God and a crime against man, which no human enactment nor usage can make right; and that Christianity, humanity, and patriotism, alike demand its abolition.

That the Fugitive Slave Act of 1850 is repugnant to the Constitution, to the principles of the common law, to the spirit of Christianity, and to the sentiments of the civilized world. We therefore deny its binding force upon the American People, and demand its immediate and total repeal.

Homesteading. That the public lands of the United States belong to the people, and should not be sold to individuals nor granted to corporations, but should be held as a sacred trust for the benefit of the people, and should be granted in limited quantities, free of cost, to landless settlers.

Internal Improvements. That river and harbor improvements, when necessary to the safety and convenience of commerce with foreign nations or among the several States, are objects of national concern, and it is the duty of Congress in the exercise of its constitutional powers to provide for the same.

1856 Conventions

Presidential Candidates

John C. Fremont
Republican

Millard Fillmore
Know Nothing

James Buchanan
Democrat

Republicans

With the decline of the Whigs and the increasing importance of the slavery issue, there was room for a new political party. Officially born in 1854, the new Republican Party moved to fill the vacuum.

The party's first meeting was held in Pittsburgh in February 1856, with delegates from 24 states attending. United in their opposition to the extension of slavery and the policies of the Pierce administration, the gathering selected a national committee (with one representative from each state), which was empowered to call the party's first national convention.

The subsequent call was addressed not to Republicans but "to the people of the United States" who were opposed to the Pierce administration and the congressional compromises on slavery. Each state was allocated six delegates at the forthcoming convention, with three additional delegates for each congressional district.

When the first Republican national convention assembled in Philadelphia in June 1856, the gathering was clearly sectional. There were nearly 600 delegates present, representing all the northern states, the border slave states of Delaware, Maryland, Virginia and Kentucky, and the District of Columbia. The territory of Kansas, symbolically important in the slavery struggle, was treated as a state and given full representation. There were no delegations from the remaining southern slave states.

Under convention rules, the roll call was to proceed in alphabetical order, with each state allocated three times its electoral vote. In response to a question, the chair decided that a simple majority would be required and not the two-thirds majority mandated by the Democratic convention. This was an important rule that distinguished the conventions of the two major parties well into the 20th century.

Two major contenders for the Republican presidential nomination, Salmon P. Chase of Ohio and William H. Seward of New York, both withdrew before the balloting began. Another contender, Supreme Court Justice John McLean of Ohio, withdrew briefly, but then re-entered the race. However, McLean could not catch the front-runner, John C. Fremont of California. Although briefly a U.S.

senator, Fremont was most famous as an explorer, and he benefited from being free of any ideological identification.

The other contenders were all identified with one of the factions that had come to make up the new party. Fremont won a preliminary, informal ballot, receiving 359 votes to 190 for McLean. On the formal roll call, Fremont won easily, winning 520 of the 567 votes. *(Chart, p. 146)*

A preliminary, informal ballot was taken for the vice presidency as well. William L. Dayton, a former senator from New Jersey, led with 253 votes, more than twice the total received by an Illinois lawyer, Abraham Lincoln, who had served in the House of Representatives 1846-48. On the formal ballot, Dayton swept to victory with 523 votes. His nomination was quickly made unanimous.

The Republican platform was approved by a voice vote. It was a document with sectional appeal, written by northern delegates for the North. Unlike the Democrats, the Republicans opposed the concept of popular sovereignty and believed that slavery should be prohibited in the territories. Specifically, the platform called for the admission of Kansas as a free state.

The Republicans also differed with the Democrats on the question of internal improvements, supporting the view that Congress should undertake river and harbor improvements. The Republican platform denounced the Ostend Manifesto, a document secretly drawn up by three of Pierce's ambassadors in Europe, that suggested the United States either buy or take Cuba from Spain. The Republicans termed the manifesto a "highwayman's plea, that 'might makes right.' "

Both parties advocated the building of a transcontinental transportation system, with the Republicans supporting the construction of a railroad.

Following are excerpts from the Republican platform of 1856:

Slavery. This Convention of Delegates, assembled in pursuance of a call addressed to the people of the United States, without regard to past political differences or divisions, who are opposed to the repeal of the Missouri Compromise; to the policy of the present Administration; to the extension of Slavery into Free Territory; in favor of the admission of Kansas as a Free State; of restoring the action of the Federal Government to the principles of Washington and Jefferson....

That the Constitution confers upon Congress sovereign powers over the Territories of the United States for their government; and that in the exercise of this power, it is both the right and the imperative duty of Congress to prohibit in the Territories those twin relics of barbarism—Polygamy, and Slavery.

Cuba. That the highwayman's plea, that "might makes right," embodied in the Ostend Circular, was in every respect unworthy of American diplomacy, and would bring shame and dishonor upon any Government or people that gave it their sanction.

Transcontinental Railroad. That a railroad to the Pacific Ocean by the most central and practicable route is imperatively demanded by the interests of the whole country.

Internal Improvements. That appropriations by Congress for the improvement of rivers and harbors, of a national character, required for the accommodation and security of our existing commerce, are authorized by the Constitution, and justified by the obligation of the Government to protect the lives and property of its citizens.

American (Know-Nothings)

In addition to the Republicans, the American Party or Know-Nothings aspired to replace the Whigs as the nation's second major party. However, unlike the Republicans, the Know-Nothings were a national political organization, and the slavery issue that helped unite the Republicans, divided the Know-Nothings. The main Know-Nothing concern was to place restrictions on the large number of European immigrants who arrived in the 1840s and 1850s.

The party held its first and only national convention in Philadelphia in February 1856. Several days before the convention began, the American Party's national council met and drew up the party platform. When the convention assembled, anti-slavery delegates objected to the platform, with its espousal of popular sovereignty, and called for the nomination of candidates who would outlaw slavery in the new territories. When their resolution was defeated, 141 to 59, these anti-slavery delegates—mainly from New England and Ohio—bolted the convention.

The remaining delegates nominated former President Millard Fillmore (1850-53) of New York for president. Fillmore was popular in the South for his support of compromise slavery measures during his administration, and was nominated on the second ballot. Andrew Jackson Donelson of Tennessee was chosen as the vice presidential candidate.

In June 1856, several days before the Republican convention was scheduled to begin, the anti-slavery Know-Nothings assembled in New York and nominated Speaker of the House Nathaniel P. Banks of Massachusetts for the presidency and former Governor William F. Johnston of Pennsylvania as his running-mate. Banks, who actually favored Fremont's nomination, withdrew from the race when Fremont was chosen as the Republican candidate. Johnston bowed out in favor of Fremont's running mate, William L. Dayton, later in the campaign.

The Know-Nothing convention that had met earlier in Philadelphia adopted a platform similar to that of the Democrats on the slavery question. The document advocated non-interference in the affairs of the states and the concept of popular sovereignty for deciding slavery in the territories. Although also calling for economy in government spending, the bulk of the Know-Nothing platform dealt with restricting immigrants. Among the nativistic planks were proposals that native-born citizens be given the first chance for all government offices, that the naturalization period for immigrants be extended to 21 years and that paupers and convicted criminals be kept from entering the United States.

Following are excerpts from the Know-Nothing platform of 1856:

Slavery, States' Rights. The unequalled recognition and maintenance of the reserved rights of the several states, and the cultivation of harmony and fraternal good-will between the citizens of the several states, and to this end, non-interference by Congress with questions appertaining solely to the individual states, and non-intervention by each state with the affairs of any other state.

The recognition of the right of the native-born and naturalized citizens of the United States, permanently residing in any territory thereof, to frame their constitutions and laws, and to regulate their domestic and social affairs in their own mode, subject only to the provisions of the federal Constitution, with the right of admission into the Union whenever they have the requisite population for one representative in Congress.

Nativism. *Americans must rule America;* and to this end, *native*-born citizens should be selected for all state, federal, or municipal offices of government employment, in preference to naturalized citizens....

No person should be selected for political station (whether of native or foreign birth), who recognizes any alliance or obligation of any description to any foreign prince, potentate or power, who refuses to recognize the federal and state constitutions (each within its own sphere), as paramount to all other laws, as rules of particular [political] action.

A change in the laws of naturalization, making a continued residence of twenty-one years, of all not heretofore provided for, an indispensable requisite for citizenship hereafter, and excluding all paupers or persons convicted of crime from landing upon our shores.

Democrats

In June 1856, delegates from all 31 states gathered in Cincinnati, Ohio, for the party's seventh quadrennial convention. It was the first Democratic convention to be held outside Baltimore.

Roll-call votes were taken during the first two days on the establishment of a platform committee and on the method of ticket allocation for the galleries. The first close vote came on the credentials committee report concerning the seating of two contesting New York delegations. By a vote of 136 to 123, the convention agreed to a minority report seating both contending factions and splitting the state's vote between them.

Three men were in contention for the party's presidential nomination: President Franklin Pierce of New Hampshire, James Buchanan of Pennsylvania and Sen. Stephen A. Douglas of Illinois. All three had actively sought the nomination before. Ironically, Buchanan, who had spent the previous three years as ambassador to Great Britain, was in the most enviable position. Having been abroad, Buchanan had largely avoided the increasing slavery controversy that bedeviled his major rivals.

Buchanan led on the first ballot with 135½ votes, with Pierce receiving 122½ and Douglas 33. As the balloting continued, Pierce lost strength, while both Buchanan and Douglas gained. After the 15th roll call, the vote stood: Buchanan, 168½, Douglas, 118½. Pierce 3½. *(Chart, p. 146)*

While the two front-runners had substantial strength, neither of them was a sectional candidate. Both received votes from northern and southern delegations. With the possibility of a stalemate looming, Douglas withdrew after the 16th ballot. On the 17th roll call, Buchanan received all 296 votes, and the nomination.

On the first ballot for the vice presidency, 11 different individuals received votes. Rep. John A. Quitman of Mississippi led with 59 votes, followed by Rep. John C. Breckinridge of Kentucky, with 50. At the beginning of the second ballot, the New England delegations cast a nearly unanimous vote for Breckinridge, creating a bandwagon effect that resulted in the nomination of the Kentuckian. Ironically, before the vice presidential balloting began, Breckinridge had asked that his name be withdrawn from consideration. Believing himself too young (he was 35), Breckinridge stated that "promotion should follow seniority."

In spite of his earlier demurrer, Breckinridge was in the convention hall and announced his acceptance of the nomination. It marked one of the few times in American political history that a candidate was present for his own nomination.

The party platform was considered in two segments, with the domestic and foreign policy sections debated separately. The theme of the domestic section, as in past platforms, was the Democrats' concept of a limited federal government. The unconstitutionality of a national bank, federal support for internal improvements and distribution of proceeds from the sale of public land were again mentioned.

Nearly one-third of the entire platform was devoted to the slavery question, with support for the various congressional compromise measures stressed. The Democratic position was underscored in a passage that was capitalized in the convention *Proceedings*: "non-interference by Congress with slavery in state and territory, or in the District of Columbia."

In another domestic area, the Democrats denounced the Know-Nothings for being un-American. The convention approved the domestic policy section of the platform by a vote of 261 to 35, with only the New York delegation voting in opposition.

The foreign policy section of the platform expressed a nationalistic and expansionist spirit that was absent from previous Democratic platforms. There were six different foreign policy planks, each voted on separately. The first plank, calling for free trade, passed 210 to 29. The second, favoring implementation of the Monroe Doctrine, passed 240 to 21. The third plank, backing westward continental expansion, was approved 203 to 56. The fourth plank, which expressed sympathy with the people of Central America, grew out of the United States' dispute with Great Britain over control of that area. The plank was approved, 221 to 38. The fifth plank, calling for United States "ascendancy in the Gulf of Mexico," passed 229 to 33. A final resolution, presented separately, called for the construction of roads to the Pacific Ocean. The resolution was at first tabled by a vote of 154 to 120, and a second vote to reconsider failed, 175 to 121. But when the resolution was raised a third time after the presidential nomination, it passed, 205 to 87.

Following are excerpts from the Democratic platform of 1856:

Slavery. *Resolved*, That claiming fellowship with, and desiring the co-operation of all who regard the preservation of the Union under the Constitution as the paramount issue—and repudiating all sectional parties and platforms concerning domestic slavery, which seek to embroil the States and incite to treason and armed resistance to law in the Territories; and whose avowed purposes, if consummated, must end in civil war and disunion, the American Democracy recognize and adopt the principles contained in the organic laws establishing the Territories of Kansas and Nebraska as embodying the only sound and safe solution of the "slavery question" upon which the great national idea of the people of this whole country can repose in its determined conservatism of the Union—NON-INTERFERENCE BY CONGRESS WITH SLAVERY IN STATE AND TERRITORY, OR IN THE DISTRICT OF COLUMBIA.

Know-Nothings. ...the liberal principles embodied in the Declaration of Independence...makes ours the land of liberty and the asylum of the oppressed....every attempt to abridge the privilege of becoming citizens...ought to be resisted....

Since the foregoing declaration was uniformly adopted by our predecessors in National Conventions, an adverse political and religious test has been secretly organized by a party claiming to be exclusively American, it is proper that the American Democracy should clearly define its relation thereto, and declare its determined opposition to all secret political societies, by whatever name they may be called.

Free Trade. *Resolved*, That there are questions connected with the foreign policy of this country, which are inferior to no domestic question whatever. The time has come for the people of the United States to declare themselves in favor of free seas and progressive free trade....

Latin America. [W]e should hold as sacred the principles involved in the Monroe Doctrine: their bearing and import admit of no misconstruction; they should be applied with unbending rigidity.

Gulf of Mexico. *Resolved*, That the Democratic party will expect of the next Administration that every proper effort be made to insure our ascendency in the Gulf of Mexico.

Transcontinental Roads. *Resolved*, That the Democratic party recognizes the great importance, in a political and commercial point of view, of a safe and speedy communication, by military and postal roads, through our own territory, between the Atlantic and Pacific coasts of this Union, and that it is the duty of the Federal Government to exercise promptly all its constitutional power to the attainment of that object.

Whigs

On the verge of extinction, the Whig Party held its last national convention in September 1856. Delegates assembled in Baltimore from 21 states and endorsed the Know-Nothing ticket of Fillmore and Donelson.

However, the Whigs adopted their own platform. It avoided specific issues, instead calling for preservation of the union. The platform criticized both the Democrats and Republicans for appealing to sectional passions and argued for the presidential candidacy of the former Whig, Millard Fillmore.

Following are excerpts from the Whig platform of 1856:

Resolved, That the Whigs of the United States are assembled here by reverence for the Constitution, and unalterable attachment to the National Union, and a fixed determination to do all in their power to preserve it for themselves and posterity. They have no new principles to announce—no new platform to establish, but are content broadly to rest where their fathers have rested upon the Constitution of the United States, wishing no safer guide, no higher law.

1860 Conventions

Presidential Candidates

Stephen A. Douglas
Democrat

John C. Breckinridge
Southern Democrat

Abraham Lincoln
Republican

John Bell
Constitutional Union

Democrats

Rarely in American history has there been a convention as tumultuous as the one that assembled in Charleston, S.C., in April 1860. The Democrats met at a time when their party was threatened by sectional division, caused by the explosive slavery question. The issue had grown increasingly inflammatory during the 1850s, and because of rising emotions, the chances of a successful compromise solution decreased.

From the outset of the convention, there was little visible effort to obtain party unity. Parliamentary squabbling with frequent appeals to the chair marked the early sessions. Before the presidential balloting even began, 27 separate roll calls on procedural and platform matters were taken.

A bitter dispute between northern and southern delegates over the wording of the platform's slavery plank precipitated a walkout by several dozen southern delegates. Both the majority and minority reports submitted to the convention called for a reaffirmation of the Democratic platform of 1856. In addition, however, the majority report (favored by the South) declared that no government—local, state or federal—could outlaw slavery in the territories. The minority report took a more moderate position, stating that the decision on allowing slavery in the territories should be left to the Supreme Court.

After a day of debate, the convention agreed, by a vote of 152 to 151, to recommit both reports to the platform committee. Basically, the vote followed sectional lines, with southern delegates approving recommittal. However, the revised majority and minority reports subsequently presented to the convention were similar to the originals.

An amendment by Benjamin F. Butler of Massachusetts, to endorse the 1856 platform without any mention of slavery, was defeated, 198 to 105. After two procedural roll calls, the delegates voted, 165 to 138, to accept the minority report. The vote followed sectional lines, with the northern delegates victorious. *(Chart, p. 147)*

Unhappy with the platform and unwilling to accept it, 45 delegates from nine states bolted the convention. The majority of six southern delegations withdrew (Alabama,

Mississippi, Florida, Texas, South Carolina and Louisiana), and scattered delegates from three other states (Arkansas, Delaware and North Carolina).

With the size of the convention reduced, chairman Caleb Cushing of Massachusetts made an important decision. He ruled that the two-thirds nominating majority would be based on the total votes allocated (303) rather than the number of delegates present and voting. Although Cushing's ruling was approved by a vote of 141 to 112, it countered precedents established at the 1840 and 1848 Democratic conventions, when the nominating majority was based on those present and voting.

Cushing's ruling made it nearly impossible for any candidate to amass the necessary two-thirds majority. Particularly affected was the front-runner, Sen. Stephen A. Douglas of Illinois, whose standing in the South had diminished with his continued support of popular sovereignty. Douglas moved into a big lead on the first ballot, receiving 145½ votes to 42 for Sen. Robert M. T. Hunter of Virginia and 35½ for James Guthrie of Kentucky. Despite his large lead over the rest of the field, Douglas was well short of the 202 votes needed for nomination, and with his sectional appeal, had little chance of gaining the needed delegates.

After three days of balloting and 57 presidential roll calls, the standing of the three candidates had undergone little change. Douglas led with 151½ votes, followed by Guthrie with 65½ and Hunter with 16. The delegates, in session for 10 days and wearied by the presidential deadlock, voted 194½ to 55½ to recess for six weeks and reconvene in Baltimore. This marked the first and only time that a major party adjourned its convention and moved it from one city to another.

Reconvening in Baltimore in June, the delegates were faced with another sticky question: whether or not to seat the delegates who had bolted the Charleston convention. The majority report presented by the credentials committee reviewed each case individually, and recommended that the bolting southern delegates, except those from Alabama and Louisiana, be reseated. The minority report recommended that a larger majority of the withdrawing

Charleston delegates be reseated. The minority report was defeated, 150 to 100½. Ten more roll calls followed on various aspects of the credentials dispute, but they did not change the result of the first vote. (Chart, p. 147)

The convention vote on credentials produced a new walkout, involving the majority of delegates from Virginia, North Carolina, Tennessee, Maryland, Kentucky, Missouri, Arkansas, California and Oregon, and anti-Douglas delegates from Massachusetts. With the presidential balloting ready to resume, less than two-thirds of the original convention was present.

On the first ballot, Douglas received 173½ of the 190½ votes cast. On the second ballot, his total increased to 190½, but it was obviously impossible for him to gain two-thirds (202) of the votes allocated (303). After the second roll call, a delegate moved that Douglas, having obtained a two-thirds majority of the votes cast, be declared the Democratic presidential nominee. The motion passed unanimously on a voice vote. (Chart, p. 147)

The convention left the selection of the vice presidential candidate to a caucus of the remaining southern delegates. They chose Sen. Benjamin Fitzpatrick of Alabama, who received all 198½ votes cast on the vice presidential roll call.

Shortly after the convention adjourned, Fitzpatrick declined the nomination. For the first time in American history, a national committee was called upon to fill a vacancy on the ticket. By a unanimous vote of committee members, the former governor of Georgia, Herschel V. Johnson, was chosen to be Douglas' running mate.

The Democratic platform, in addition to the controversial slavery plank, provided a reaffirmation of the 1856 platform, with its proposals for a limited federal government but an expansionist foreign policy. The 1860 platform added planks that continued the expansionist spirit, calling for the construction of a transcontinental railroad and acquisition of the island of Cuba.

Following are excerpts from the 1860 Democratic platform:

> **Slavery.** Inasmuch as difference of opinion exists in the Democratic party as to the nature and extent of the powers of a Territorial Legislature, and as to the powers and duties of Congress, under the Constitution of the United States, over the institution of slavery within the Territories,
>
> Resolved, That the Democratic party will abide by the decision of the Supreme Court of the United States upon these questions of Constitutional law.
>
> **Transcontinental Railroad.** Resolved, That one of the necessities of the age, in a military, commercial, and postal point of view, is speedy communication between the Atlantic and Pacific States; and the Democratic party pledge such Constitutional Government aid as will insure the construction of a Railroad to the Pacific coast, at the earliest practicable period.
>
> **Cuba.** Resolved, That the Democratic party are in favor of the acquisition of the Island of Cuba on such terms as shall be honorable to ourselves and just to Spain.

Southern Democrats (Breckinridge Faction)

A small group of southern delegates that bolted the Charleston convention met in Richmond, Va., in early June. They decided to delay action until after the resumed Democratic convention had concluded. In late June, they met in Baltimore with bolters from the regular Democratic convention. There were representatives from 19 states among the more than 200 delegates attending, but most of the 58 northern delegates were officeholders in the

Buchanan administration. Vice President John C. Breckinridge of Kentucky won the presidential nomination, and Sen. Joseph Lane of Oregon was chosen as his running mate.

The platform adopted by the southern Democrats was similar to the one approved by the Democratic convention at Charleston. The bolters reaffirmed the Democrats' 1856 platform, called for the construction of a transcontinental railroad and acquisition of Cuba. But on the controversial slavery issue, the rump assemblage adopted the minority plank defeated at the Charleston convention. The failure to reach agreement on this one issue, the most disruptive sectional split in the history of American political parties, presaged the Civil War.

Following are excerpts from the platform adopted by the southern (or Breckinridge faction) Democrats in 1860:

> Resolved, that the platform adopted by the Democratic party at Cincinnati be affirmed, with the following explanatory resolutions:
>
> 1. That the Government of a Territory organized by an act of Congress is provisional and temporary, and during its existence all citizens of the United States have an equal right to settle with their property in the Territory, without their rights, either of person or property, being destroyed or impaired by Congressional or Territorial legislation.
>
> 2. That it is the duty of the Federal Government, in all its departments, to protect, when necessary, the rights of persons and property in the Territories, and wherever else its constitutional authority extends.

Republicans

With their major opposition split along sectional lines, the Republicans gathered for their convention in Chicago in a mood of optimism. The Democrats had already broken up at Charleston before the Republican delegates convened in May 1860.

The call for the convention was addressed not only to faithful party members but to other groups that shared the Republicans' dissatisfaction with the policies of the Buchanan administration. The call to the convention particularly emphasized the party's opposition to any extension of slavery into the territories.

Delegates from all the northern states and the territories of Kansas and Nebraska, the District of Columbia, and the slave states of Maryland, Delaware, Virginia, Kentucky, Missouri and Texas assembled at Chicago's new 10,000-seat convention hall, known as the Wigwam. A carnival-like atmosphere enveloped Chicago, with bands marching through the streets and thousands of enthusiastic Republicans ringing the overcrowded convention hall.

Inside, the delegates' first debate concerned the credentials report. The question was raised whether the represented southern states should be allocated votes reflecting their electoral college strength, when there were very few Republicans in these states. By a vote of 275½ to 171½, the convention recommitted the credentials report for the purpose of scaling down the vote allocation of the southern states.

A second debate arose over what constituted a nominating majority. The rules committee recommended that the nominating majority reflect the total electoral vote of all the states in the Union. The minority report argued that, since all the states were not represented, the nominating majority suggested by the rules committee would in fact require nearly a two-thirds majority. The minority report recommended instead that nominations be based on a simple majority of votes allocated for the states represented. The minority report passed, 349½ to 88½.

Sen. William H. Seward of New York was the front-runner for the presidential nomination and led on the first ballot. Seward received 173½ votes to lead runner-up Abraham Lincoln of Illinois, who had 102. Sen. Simon Cameron of Pennsylvania followed with 50½ votes, Salmon P. Chase of Ohio with 49 and Edward Bates of Missouri with 48. *(Chart, p. 148)*

With the packed galleries cheering their native son, Lincoln closed the gap on the second roll call. After two ballots, the voting stood: Seward, 184½; Lincoln, 181; Chase, 42½; Bates, 35. Lincoln, who had gained national prominence two years earlier as a result of his debates on slavery with Democrat Stephen A. Douglas in the 1858 campaign for the U.S. Senate, emerged as the candidate of the anti-Seward forces. On the third ballot, he won the nomination. When the third roll call was completed, Lincoln's vote total stood at 231½, 1½ votes short of a majority. But Ohio quickly shifted four votes to Lincoln, giving him the nomination. After changes by other states, the final vote was Lincoln, 340; Seward, 121½.

The primary contenders for the vice presidential nomination were Sen. Hannibal Hamlin of Maine and Cassius M. Clay of Kentucky. Hamlin assumed a strong lead on the first ballot, receiving 194 votes to 100½ for Clay. On the second roll call, an increased vote for Hamlin from states in his native New England created a bandwagon for the Maine senator. Hamlin won the nomination on the second ballot with 367 votes, far outdistancing Clay, who received 86. After the roll call was completed, Hamlin's nomination was declared unanimous.

About half of the platform adopted by the Republican convention dealt with the slavery question. Unlike the Democrats, the Republicans clearly opposed the extension of slavery into the territories. However, the Republican platform also expressed support for states' rights, which served as a rebuke to radical abolitionism.

The Republican and Democratic platforms again were opposed on the question of internal improvements. The Republicans supported river and harbor improvements, while the Democrats, by reaffirming their 1856 platform, opposed any federal support for internal improvements. Both parties favored construction of a transcontinental railroad and opposed restrictions on immigration.

However, on two major issues, the Republicans went beyond the Democrats, advocating a protective tariff and homestead legislation.

Following are excerpts from the 1860 Republican platform:

Slavery. That the new dogma that the Constitution, of its own force, carries slavery into any or all of the territories of the United States, is a dangerous political heresy, at variance with the explicit provisions of that instrument itself, with contemporaneous exposition, and with legislative and judicial precedent; is revolutionary in its tendency, and subversive of the peace and harmony of the country.

That the normal condition of all the territory of the United States is that of freedom.... we deny the authority of Congress, of a territorial legislature, or of any individuals, to give legal existence to slavery in any territory of the United States.

States' Rights. That the maintenance inviolate of the rights of the states, and especially the right of each state to order and control its own domestic institutions according to its own judgment exclusively, is essential to that balance of powers on which the perfection and endurance of our political fabric depends; and we denounce the lawless invasion by armed force of the soil of any state or territory, no matter under what pretext, as among the gravest of crimes.

Tariff. That, while providing revenue for the support of the general government by duties upon imports, sound policy requires such an adjustment of these imports as to encourage the development of the industrial interests of the whole country.

Transcontinental Railroad. That a railroad to the Pacific Ocean is imperatively demanded by the interests of the whole country; that the federal government ought to render immediate and efficient aid in its construction; and that, as preliminary thereto, a daily overland mail should be promptly established.

Constitutional Union

At the invitation of a group of southern Know-Nothing congressmen, the remnants of the 1856 Fillmore campaign, conservative Whigs and Know-Nothings, met in Baltimore in May 1860 to form the Constitutional Union Party.

The chief rivals for the presidential nomination were former Sen. John Bell of Tennessee and Gov. Sam Houston of Texas. Bell won on the second ballot, and Edward Everett of Massachusetts was selected as his running mate.

The Constitutional Union Party saw itself as a national unifying force in a time of crisis. The brief platform did not discuss issues, instead denouncing the sectionalism of the existing parties and calling for national unity.

Following are excerpts from the 1860 Constitutional Union platform:

Whereas, Experience has demonstrated that Platforms adopted by the partisan Conventions of the country have had the effect to mislead and deceive the people, and at the same time to widen the political divisions of the country, by the creation and encouragement of geographical and sectional parties; therefore

Resolved, that it is both the part of patriotism and of duty to *recognize* no political principle other than THE CONSTITUTION OF THE COUNTRY, THE UNION OF THE STATES, AND THE ENFORCEMENT OF THE LAWS.

1864 Conventions

Presidential Candidates

Abraham Lincoln
Republican

George McClellan
Democrat

Republicans (Union Party)

Although elements in the Republican Party were dissatisfied with the conduct of the Civil War, President Lincoln was in firm control of his party's convention, which met in Baltimore in June 1864. As with previous Republican conventions, the call was not limited to the party faithful. Democrats in support of the Lincoln war policy were encouraged to attend, and the name "Union Party" was used to describe the wartime coalition.

Delegates were present from all the northern states, the territories, the District of Columbia and the slave states of Arkansas, Florida, Louisiana, Tennessee, South Carolina and Virginia. Credentials disputes occupied the early sessions. The credentials committee recommended that all the southern states except South Carolina be admitted, but denied the right to vote. A minority report, advocating voting privileges for the Tennessee delegation, was passed, 310 to 151. A second minority report favoring voting privileges for Arkansas and Louisiana was approved, 307 to 167. However, the credentials committee recommendation that Florida and Virginia be denied voting rights, and South Carolina be excluded entirely, were accepted without a roll call.

Although dissatisfaction with the administration's war policy had spawned opposition to Lincoln, the boomlets for such presidential hopefuls as Treasury Secretary Salmon P. Chase had petered out by convention time. The Lincoln forces controlled the convention, and the President was easily renominated on the first ballot. Lincoln received 494 of the 516 votes cast, losing only Missouri's 22 votes, which were committed to Gen. Ulysses S. Grant. After the roll call, Missouri moved that the vote be made unanimous.

Lincoln did not publicly declare his preference for a vice presidential running mate, leaving the selection to the convention. The main contenders included the incumbent Vice President, Hannibal Hamlin of Maine; the former senator and military governor of Tennessee, Democrat Andrew Johnson; and former Sen. Daniel S. Dickinson of New York. Johnson led on the first ballot with 200 votes, followed by Hamlin with 150 and Dickinson with 108. After completion of the roll call, a switch to Johnson by the Ken-

tucky delegation ignited a surge to the Tennesseean that delivered him 492 votes and the nomination.

The Republican (Union) platform was approved without debate. Unlike the Democrats, who criticized the war effort and called for a quick, negotiated peace, the Republicans favored a vigorous prosecution of the war until the South surrendered unconditionally. The Republicans called for the eradication of slavery, with its elimination embodied in a constitutional amendment.

Although the Republican document focused on the Civil War, it also included planks encouraging immigration, urging the speedy construction of a transcontinental railroad and reaffirming the Monroe Doctrine.

Following are excerpts from the Republican (Union) platform of 1864:

> *Resolved*...we pledge ourselves, as Union men, animated by a common sentiment and aiming at a common object, to do everything in our power to aid the Government in quelling by force of arms the Rebellion now raging against its authority, and in bringing to the punishment due to their crimes the Rebels and traitors arrayed against it.
>
> *Resolved*, That we approve the determination of the Government of the United States not to compromise with Rebels, or to offer them any terms of peace, except such as may be based upon an unconditional surrender of their hostility and a return to their just allegiance to the Constitution and laws of the United States, and that we call upon the Government to maintain this position and to prosecute the war with the utmost possible vigor to the complete suppression of the Rebellion, in full reliance upon the self-sacrificing patriotism, the heroic valor and the undying devotion of the American people to the country and its free institutions.
>
> *Resolved*, That as slavery was the cause, and now constitutes the strength of this Rebellion, and as it must be, always and everywhere, hostile to the principles of Republican Government, justice and the National safety demand its utter and complete extirpation from the soil of the Republic...we are in favor, furthermore, of such an amendment to the Constitution, to be made by the people in conformity with its provisions, as shall terminate and forever prohibit the existence of Slavery within the limits of the jurisdiction of the United States.

Resolved, That the thanks of the American people are due to the soldiers and sailors of the Army and Navy, who have periled their lives in defense of the country and in vindication of the honor of its flag.

Democrats

The Democrats originally scheduled their convention for early summer, but postponed it until late August to gauge the significance of military developments.

The party, badly split during the 1860 campaign, no longer had the southern faction with which to contend. But while there was no longer a regional split, new divisions arose over the continuing war. There was a large peace faction, known as the Copperheads, that favored a quick, negotiated peace with the South. Another faction supported the war but criticized its handling by the Lincoln administration. A third faction supported Lincoln's conduct of the war and defected to support the Republican President.

Although factionalized, the Democratic delegates that assembled in Chicago were optimistic about their party's chances. The war-weary nation, they thought, was ready to vote out the Lincoln administration if there was not a quick change in northern military fortunes.

Although the border states were represented at the Democratic convention, the territories and seceded southern states were not. In spite of the party's internal divisions, there was little opposition to the presidential candidacy of Gen. George B. McClellan of New Jersey. The former commander of the Union Army won on the first ballot, receiving 174 of the 226 votes cast. Former Gov. Thomas H. Seymour of Connecticut trailed with 38 votes. A switch to McClellan by several Ohio delegates prompted shifts by other delegations and brought McClellan's total to 202½. It was moved by Clement Vallandigham, a leader of the Copperhead faction, that his nomination be made unanimous.

Eight candidates were placed in nomination for the vice presidency. James Guthrie of Kentucky led Rep. George H. Pendleton of Ohio, the favorite of the Copperheads, on the first ballot, 65½ to 55. However, shifts to Pendleton by Illinois, Kentucky and New York after completion of the roll call created a bandwagon that led quickly to his unanimous nomination. In the convention hall at the time of his selection, Pendleton made a short speech of acceptance.

The platform adopted by the Democrats reflected the views of the Copperhead faction. The Lincoln administration's conduct of the Civil War was denounced, with particular criticism of the use of martial law and the abridgement of state and civil rights. The platform called for an immediate end to hostilities and a negotiated peace. The "sympathy" of the party was extended to soldiers and sailors involved in the war. Besides a criticism of the war and its conduct by the Lincoln administration, there were no other issues discussed in the platform.

Following are excerpts from the Democratic platform of 1864:

Resolved, That this convention does explicitly declare, as the sense of the American people, that after four years of failure to restore the Union by the experiment of war, during which, under the pretense of a military necessity of war-power higher than the Constitution, the Constitution itself has been disregarded in every part, and public liberty and private right alike trodden down, and the material prosperity of the country essentially impaired, justice, humanity, liberty, and the public welfare demand that immediate efforts be made for a cessation of hostilities, with a view of an ultimate convention of the States, or other peaceable means, to the end that, at the earliest practicable moment, peace may be restored on the basis of the Federal Union of the States.

Resolved, That the sympathy of the Democratic party is heartily and earnestly extended to the soldiery of our army and sailors of our navy, who are and have been in the field and on the sea under the flag of our country, and, in the events of its attaining power, they will receive all the care, protection, and regard that the brave soldiers and sailors of the republic have so nobly earned.

1868 Conventions

Presidential Candidates

Ulysses S. Grant
Republican

Horatio Seymour
Democrat

Republicans

The "National Union Republican Party," as the political organization was termed in its platform, held its first postwar convention in Chicago in May 1868. Delegations from the states of the old Confederacy were accepted; several included blacks.

The turbulent nature of postwar politics was evident in the fact that Gen. Ulysses S. Grant, the clear front-runner for the Republican nomination, had been considered a possible contender for the Democratic nomination less than a year earlier. Basically apolitical, Grant had broken with President Johnson less than six months before the convention.

Grant was the only candidate placed in nomination, and on the ensuing roll call he received all 650 votes.

While the presidential race was cut and dried, the balloting for vice president was wide open, with 11 candidates receiving votes on the initial roll call. Sen. Benjamin F. Wade of Ohio led on the first ballot with 147 votes, followed by New York Gov. Reuben E. Fenton with 126, Massachusetts Sen. Henry Wilson with 119 and Speaker of the House Schuyler Colfax of Indiana with 115.

Over the next four ballots, Wade and Colfax were the front-runners, with Colfax finally moving ahead on the fifth ballot. His lead over Wade at this point was only 226 to 207, but numerous vote shifts after the roll call quickly pushed the Indiana representative over the top and gave him the nomination. After all the vote changes, Colfax's total stood at 541, followed by Fenton with 69 and Wade with 38.

Not surprisingly, the platform adopted by the Republicans differed sharply with the Democrats over reconstruction and the presidency of Andrew Johnson. The Republican platform applauded the Radical reconstruction program passed by Congress and denounced Johnson as "treacherous" and deserving of impeachment. The Republican platform approved of voting rights for black men in the South but determined that this was a subject for each state to decide in the rest of the nation.

The two parties also differed on their response to the currency question. While the Democrats favored a "soft money" policy, the Republicans supported a continued "hard money" approach, rejecting the Democratic proposal that the economic crisis could be eased by an increased supply of greenbacks.

Following are excerpts from the Republican platform of 1868:

Reconstruction. We congratulate the country on the assured success of the reconstruction policy of Congress, as evinced by the adoption, in the majority of the States lately in rebellion, of constitutions securing equal civil and political rights to all, and regard it as the duty of the Government to sustain those constitutions, and to prevent the people of such States from being remitted to a state of anarchy or military rule.

The guaranty by Congress of equal suffrage to all loyal men at the South was demanded by every consideration of public safety, of gratitude, and of justice, and must be maintained; while the question of suffrage in all the loyal States properly belongs to the people of those States.

President Andrew Johnson. We profoundly deplore the untimely and tragic death of Abraham Lincoln, and regret the accession of Andrew Johnson to the Presidency, who has acted treacherously to the people who elected him and the cause he was pledged to support; has usurped high legislative and judicial functions; has refused to execute the laws; has used his high office to induce other officers to ignore and violate the laws; has employed his executive powers to render insecure the property, the peace, the liberty, and life of the citizen; has abused the pardoning power; has denounced the National Legislature as unconstitutional; has persistently and corruptly resisted, by every means in his power, every proper attempt at the reconstruction of the States lately in rebellion; has perverted the public patronage into an engine of wholesale corruption; and has been justly impeached for high crimes and misdemeanors, and properly pronounced guilty thereof by the vote of thirty-five senators.

Currency. We denounce all forms of repudiation as a national crime; and national honor requires the payment of the public indebtedness in the utmost good faith to all creditors at home and abroad, not only according to the letter, but the spirit of the laws under which it was contracted.

Democrats

Reunited after the Civil War, the Democratic Party held its first postwar convention in New York's newly constructed Tammany Hall. It was no accident that convention proceedings began on July 4, 1868. The Democratic National Committee had set the date, and its chairman, August Belmont of New York, opened the first session with a harsh criticism of Republican reconstruction policy and the abridgement of civil rights.

Delegates from southern states were voting members of the convention, but an effort to extend representation to the territories was defeated, 184 to 106.

Before the presidential balloting began, the convention chairman ruled that, as at the 1860 Charleston assembly, a nominating majority would be based on two-thirds of the total votes allocated (317) and not votes cast. On the opening ballot, the party's vice presidential candidate four years earlier, George H. Pendleton of Ohio, took the lead. Pendleton, although popular in the economically depressed Midwest because of his plan to inflate the currency by printing more greenbacks, had little appeal in the eastern states. Nonetheless, he led on the first ballot with 105 votes. President Andrew Johnson was next, with 65 votes. Johnson's vote was largely complimentary and declined after the first roll call. Pendleton, however, showed increased strength, rising to a peak of 156½ votes on the eighth ballot. But Pendleton's total was well short of the 212 votes required to nominate, and his total steadily decreased after the eighth roll call. *(Chart, p. 150)*

The collapse of the Pendleton and Johnson candidacies produced a boom for Gen. Winfield Scott Hancock of Pennsylvania. Opponents of Hancock attempted to break his surge by calling for adjournment after the 16th ballot. Although the move for adjournment was defeated, 174½ to 142½, the Hancock boom began to lose momentum. The Civil War general peaked at 144½ votes on the 18th ballot, well short of a two-thirds majority.

With Hancock stymied, a new contender, Sen. Thomas A. Hendricks of Indiana, gained strength. Hendricks' vote rose to 132 on the 21st ballot, and the trend to the Indiana senator continued on the 22nd ballot until the roll call reached Ohio. However, Ohio shifted its entire vote to Horatio Seymour, the permanent chairman of the convention and a former governor of New York. Seymour declined to be a candidate, and so announced to the convention, but Ohio did not change its vote, and friends of Seymour hustled the reluctant candidate from the hall. The bandwagon had begun, and when the vote switches were completed, Seymour had received all 317 votes.

The vice presidential nomination went to Gen. Francis P. Blair Jr. of Missouri, a former Republican, who was unanimously selected on the first ballot. The names of several other candidates were placed in nomination, but the announcement of Blair's candidacy created a bandwagon that led to the withdrawal of the others.

The Democratic platform was accepted by a voice vote without debate. The platform began by declaring the questions of slavery and secession to be permanently settled by the Civil War. Several planks criticized the Republican reconstruction program, passed by the party's Radical wing in Congress. The Radicals themselves were scathingly denounced for their "unparalleled oppression and tyranny." The Democratic platform expressed its support for Andrew Johnson's conduct as president and decried the attempts to impeach him.

For the first time, the question of the coinage and printing of money was discussed in the party platform. Two planks were included that could be generally interpreted as supporting Pendleton's inflationary greenback plan.

On the tariff issue, the Democrats called for a tariff that would primarily raise revenue but also protect American industry.

Following are excerpts from the Democratic platform of 1868:

> **Reconstruction.** ...we arraign the Radical party for its disregard of right, and the unparalleled oppression and tyranny which have marked its career.
>
> Instead of restoring the Union, it has, so far as in its power, dissolved it, and subjected ten States, in time of profound peace, to military despotism and negro supremacy.
>
> **President Andrew Johnson.** That the President of the United States, Andrew Johnson, in exercising the power of his high office in resisting the aggressions of Congress upon the Constitutional rights of the States and the people, is entitled to the gratitude of the whole American people; and in behalf of the Democratic party, we tender him our thanks for his patriotic efforts in that regard.
>
> **Currency.** ...where the obligations of the government do not expressly state upon their face, or the law under which they were issued does not provide, that they shall be paid in coin, they ought, in right and in justice, to be paid in the lawful money of the United States.... One currency for the government and the people, the laborer and the officeholder, the pensioner and the soldier, the producer and the bond-holder.

1872 Conventions

Presidential Candidates

Horace Greeley
Liberal Republican, Democrat

Ulysses S. Grant
Republican

Liberal Republicans

The short-lived Liberal Republican Party grew out of grievances that elements in the Republican Party had with the policies of the Grant administration. There was particular dissatisfaction with the "carpetbag" governments in the South, support for extensive civil service reform and a general distaste for the corrupt administration of President Grant.

The idea for the Liberal Republican movement originated in Missouri, where, in the 1870 state elections, a coalition of reform Republicans and Democrats swept to victory. In January 1872, a state convention of this new coalition issued the call for a national convention to be held that May in Cincinnati, Ohio.

Without a formal, nationwide organization, the delegate selection process was haphazard. Some of the delegates were self-appointed, but generally the size of each delegation reflected twice a state's electoral vote.

Three separate groups—reformers, anti-Grant politicians and a coalition of four influential newspaper editors known as "the Quadrilateral"—vied for control of the convention. For the presidential nomination, the reformers favored either Charles Francis Adams of Massachusetts or Sen. Lyman Trumbull of Illinois. The professional politicians were inclined to Supreme Court Justice David Davis of Illinois or Horace Greeley of New York. The newspaper editors opposed Davis.

On the first ballot, Adams led with 203 votes, followed by Greeley with 147, Trumbull with 110, Gov. B. Gratz Brown of Missouri with 95 and Davis with 92½. After the roll call, Brown announced his withdrawal from the race and his support for Greeley. For the next five ballots, Greeley and Adams battled for the lead. But on the sixth ballot, the professional politicians were able to ignite a stampede for Greeley that resulted in his nomination.

Many of the reform-minded delegates, disgusted with the selection of the New York editor, left the convention. The vice presidential nomination went on the second ballot to a Greeley supporter, Gov. Brown of Missouri.

The platform adopted by the Liberal Republicans differed with the one later accepted by the Republicans on three main points: reconstruction, civil service reform and the tariff.

The Liberal Republicans called for an end to reconstruction with its "carpetbag" governments, a grant of universal amnesty to southern citizens and a return to home rule in the South. The Liberal Republicans sharply criticized the corruption of civil service under the Grant administration and labeled its reform one of the leading issues of the day. The civil service plank advocated a one-term limit on the presidency.

The presence of delegates supporting both protection and free trade led to a tariff plank that frankly stated the party's position on the issue should be left to local determination.

Following are excerpts from the Liberal Republican platform of 1872:

Reconstruction. We demand the immediate and absolute removal of all disabilities imposed on account of the Rebellion, which was finally subdued seven years ago, believing that universal amnesty will result in complete pacification in all sections of the country.

Local self-government, with impartial suffrage, will guard the rights of all citizens more securely than any centralized power. The public welfare requires the supremacy of the civil over the military authority, and freedom of person under the protection of the *habeas corpus*.

Civil Rights. We recognize the equality of all men before the law, and hold that it is the duty of Government in its dealings with the people to mete out equal and exact justice to all of whatever nativity, race, color, or persuasion, religious or political.

Civil Service Reform. The Civil Service of the Government has become a mere instrument of partisan tyranny and personal ambition and an object of selfish greed. It is a scandal and reproach upon free institutions and breeds a demoralization dangerous to the perpetuity of republican government. We therefore regard such thorough reforms of the Civil Service as one of the most pressing necessities of the hour; that honesty, capacity, and fidelity constitute the only valid claim to public employment; that the offices of the Government cease to be a matter of arbitrary favoritism and patronage, and that public station become again a post of honor. To this end it is imperatively required that no President shall be a candidate for re-election.

Tariff.... recognizing that there are in our midst honest but irreconcilable differences of opinion with regard to the respective systems of Protection and Free Trade, we remit the discussion of the subject to the people in their Congress Districts, and to the decision of Congress thereon, wholly free of Executive interference or dictation.

Homesteading. We are opposed to all further grants of lands to railroads or other corporations. The public domain should be held sacred to actual settlers.

Democrats

The Democratic convention that met in Baltimore in July 1872 was one of the most bizarre in American political history. In sessions totaling only six hours, the delegates endorsed the decisions on candidates and platform made at a convention one month earlier by the Liberal Republicans. The Democratic convention merely rubber-stamped the creation of a coalition of Liberal Republicans and the core of the Democratic Party. *(Chart, p. 151)*

This new coalition was established with little dissent at the Democratic convention. When it came time for the presidential balloting, nominating speeches were not allowed. On the subsequent roll call, Greeley, the nominee of the Liberal Republicans, received 686 of the allotted 732 votes. It was an ironic choice, because in earlier decades, Greeley, as editor of *The New York Tribune*, had been a frequent critic of the Democratic Party. More than anything else, however, Greeley's selection underscored the lack of strong leadership in the post-Civil-War Democratic Party.

In similar fashion, the convention endorsed the nomination of B. Gratz Brown for vice president. Brown, the the governor of Missouri and the choice of the Liberal Republicans, was the nearly unanimous nominee of the Democrats, with 713 votes.

By a vote of 574 to 158, the delegates agreed to limit debate on the platform to one hour. Except for a brief introduction, the Democrats approved the same platform that had been adopted by the Liberal Republicans a month earlier. Key planks called for an end to reconstruction and complete amnesty for southern citizens, a return to a federal government with limited powers, civil service reform and the halt of grants of public land to railroads and other corporations. Ironically, the platform also favored a hard-money policy, a reversal of the Democrats' soft-money stand in 1868. Although there was some objection to the point-by-point acceptance of the Liberal Republican platform, it was adopted by a vote of 671 to 62. *(For platform excerpts, see the Liberal Republican section, p. 42.)*

Republicans

With the reform wing of the Republican Party already having bolted, the remaining elements of the party gathered in relative harmony in Philadelphia in June 1872. President Ulysses S. Grant was renominated without opposition, receiving all 752 votes cast. *(Chart, p. 151)*

The only contest at the convention centered around the vice presidential nomination, with the incumbent, Schuyler Colfax of Indiana, and Sen. Henry Wilson of Massachusetts the two major rivals. Wilson took a slim plurality over Colfax on the first roll call, 364½ to 321½, but a vote shift by Virginia after completion of the roll gave Wilson the necessary majority with 399½ votes.

Without debate or opposition, the platform was adopted. It lauded the 11 years of Republican rule, noting the success of reconstruction, the hard-money policy and the homestead program. A tariff plank called for a duty on imports to raise revenue as well as to protect American business.

The platform also included several progressive planks, including a recommendation that the franking privilege be abolished, an extension of rights to women and a call for federal and state legislation that would ensure equal rights for all races throughout the nation. The last plank was a significant change from the 1868 platform, which called for black suffrage in the South but left the decision on black voting rights to the individual states elsewhere.

Following are excerpts from the Republican platform of 1872:

Reconstruction. We hold that Congress and the President have only fulfilled an imperative duty in their measures for the suppression of violent and treasonable organizations in certain lately rebellious regions, and for the protection of the ballot-box, and therefore they are entitled to the thanks of the nation.

Civil Rights. Complete liberty and exact equality in the enjoyment of all civil, political, and public rights should be established and effectually maintained throughout the Union, by efficient and appropriate State and Federal legislation. Neither the law nor its administration should admit any discrimination in respect of citizens by reason of race, creed, color, or previous condition of servitude.

Civil Service Reform. Any system of the civil service under which the subordinate positions of the government are considered rewards for mere party zeal is fatally demoralizing, and we therefore favor a reform of the system by laws which shall abolish the evils of patronage, and make honesty, efficiency, and fidelity the essential qualifications for public positions, without practically creating a life-tenure of office.

Tariff. ...revenue...should be raised by duties upon importations, the details of which should be so adjusted as to aid in securing remunerative wages to labor, and to promote the industries, prosperity, and growth of the whole country.

Homesteading. We are opposed to further grants of the public lands to corporations and monopolies, and demand that the national domain be set apart for free homes for the people.

Women's Rights. The Republican party is mindful of its obligations to the loyal women of America for their noble devotion to the cause of freedom. Their admission to wider fields of usefulness is viewed with satisfaction, and the honest demand of any class of citizens for additional rights should be treated with respectful consideration.

1876 Conventions

Presidential Candidates

Rutherford B. Hayes
Republican

Samuel J. Tilden
Democrat

Republicans

The Republican convention assembled in Cincinnati, Ohio, in mid-June 1876. The call to the convention extended the olive branch to the dissident Liberal Republicans, who in large measure had rejoined their original party.

One of the highlights of the early sessions was a speech by the prominent black leader, Frederick Douglass, who lambasted the Republicans for freeing the slaves but providing no means for their economic or physical security.

A dispute developed over the seating of two contesting Alabama delegations. It was a candidate-oriented dispute, with the majority report favoring a delegation strongly for House Speaker James G. Blaine of Maine. The minority report supported a delegation pledged to Sen. Oliver P. Morton of Indiana. In the subsequent roll call, the convention decided in favor of the Blaine delegation by a vote of 369 to 360.

The presidential race was contested by the champions of the three nearly equal wings of the party. The Radicals were led by Senators Roscoe Conkling of New York and Morton; the Half-Breeds, by Blaine, and the reformers by former Treasury Secretary Benjamin H. Bristow of Kentucky.

A fiery nominating speech for Blaine, delivered by Col. Robert G. Ingersoll, referred to the House speaker as the "plumed knight," an appellation that stuck with Blaine the rest of his political career. Although it was a compelling speech, its effect was reduced by a failure in the hall's lighting system, which forced an early adjournment.

Nonetheless, when balloting commenced the next morning, Blaine had a wide lead, receiving 285 votes on the first ballot, compared with 124 for Morton, 113 for Bristow and 99 for Conkling. *(Chart, p. 153)*

In the middle of the second ballot, a procedural dispute arose over the legality of the unit rule. Three delegates in the Pennsylvania delegation wished to vote for another candidate and appealed to the chair. The chair ruled that their votes should be counted, even though Pennsylvania was bound by the state convention to vote as a unit. The ruling of the chair was upheld on a voice vote, but subsequent debate brought a roll call on reconsidering the decision. The

motion to reconsider passed, 381 to 359. However, by a margin of 395 to 353, another roll call upheld the power of the convention chairman to abolish the unit rule.

Although the vote had long-range significance for future Republican conventions, in the short run it provided a slight boost for Blaine, who gained several delegates in Pennsylvania. On the next four ballots, Blaine retained his large lead, but could not come close to the necessary 379 votes needed for nomination. The only candidate to show increased strength was Gov. Rutherford B. Hayes of Ohio, who jumped from 68 votes on the fourth roll call to 104 on the fifth.

On the sixth ballot, however, Blaine showed renewed strength, rising to 308 votes, while Hayes assumed second place with 113. The House speaker continued to gain on the seventh ballot, but the anti-Blaine forces quickly and successfully united behind Hayes. The Ohio governor, a viable compromise choice who had not alienated any of the party factions, won the nomination with 384 votes to 351 for Blaine.

Five candidates were placed in nomination for the vice presidency. However, Rep. William A. Wheeler of New York was so far in the lead that the roll call was suspended after South Carolina voted, and Wheeler was declared the nominee by acclamation.

Platform debate centered on the party's immigration plank. A Massachusetts delegate proposed deletion of the plank, which called for a congressional investigation of oriental immigration. The delegate argued that the plank was inconsistent with the Republican principle that favored the equality of all races. However, by a vote of 518 to 229, the plank was retained as written.

The Republican platform included a scathing denunciation of the Democratic Party, but only on the issues of currency and tariff was it markedly different from the opposition. The Republicans, unlike the Democrats, favored complete payment of Civil War bonds in hard money as quickly as possible. While the Democrats supported a tariff for revenue purposes only, the Republicans implied that the tariff should protect American industry as well as raise revenue.

As in past platforms, the Republicans called for the extension of civil rights, civil service reform, increased rights for women, the abolition of polygamy and the distribution of public land to homesteaders. A new plank proposed that a constitutional amendment be passed forbidding the use of federal funds for non-public schools.

Following are excerpts from the Republican platform of 1876:

> **Currency.** In the first act of congress, signed by President Grant, the national government...solemnly pledged its faith "to make provisions at the earliest practicable period, for the redemption of the United States notes in coin." Commercial prosperity, public morals, and the national credit demand that this promise be fulfilled by a continuous and steady progress to specie payment.
>
> **Tariff.** The revenue necessary for current expenditures and the obligations of the public debt must be largely derived from duties upon importations, which, so far as possible, should be so adjusted as to promote the interests of American labor and advance the prosperity of the whole country.
>
> **Immigration.** It is the immediate duty of congress fully to investigate the effects of the immigration and importation of Mongolians on the moral and material interests of the country.
>
> **Education.** The public school system of the several states is the bulwark of the American republic; and, with a view to its security and permanence, we recommend an amendment to the constitution of the United States, forbidding the application of any public funds or property for the benefit of any school or institution under sectarian control.
>
> **Democratic Party.** We therefore note with deep solicitude that the Democratic party counts, as its chief hope of success, upon the electoral vote of a united South, secured through the efforts of those who were recently arrayed against the nation; and we invoke the earnest attention of the country to the grave truth, that a success thus achieved would reopen sectional strife and imperil national honor and human rights.
>
> We charge the Democratic party with being the same in character and spirit as when it sympathized with treason; with making its control of the house of representatives the triumph and opportunity of the nation's recent foes; with reasserting and applauding in the national capitol the sentiments of unrepentant rebellion; with sending Union soldiers to the rear, and promoting Confederate soldiers to the front; with deliberately proposing to repudiate the plighted faith of the government; with being equally false and imbecile upon the over-shadowing financial question; with thwarting the ends of justice, by its partisan mismanagements and obstruction of investigation; with proving itself, through the period of its ascendency in the lower house of congress, utterly incompetent to administer the government;—and we warn the country against trusting a party thus alike unworthy, recreant, and incapable.

Democrats

America's rapid westward expansion was typified by the site of the Democratic Party's 1876 convention—St. Louis, Mo. It marked the first time that a national convention was held west of the Mississippi River.

The Democratic delegates assembled in late June. The one procedural matter debated was a proposal that the two-thirds rule be abolished at the 1880 convention and that the Democratic National Committee include such a recommendation in its next convention call. A move to table the proposal was defeated, 379 to 359. However, the national committee took no action on the proposal.

Two governors, Samuel J. Tilden of New York and Thomas A. Hendricks of Indiana, were the principal contenders for the presidential nomination, with Tilden having a substantial lead in delegates as the convention opened. Ironically, Tilden's most vocal opposition came from his own New York delegation, where John Kelly of Tammany Hall spearheaded an effort to undermine Tilden's candidacy. Tilden's reform moves as governor had alienated Tammany Hall, and several times during the convention, Kelly took the floor to denounce Tilden.

Nonetheless, Tilden had a substantial lead on the first ballot, receiving 401½ votes to 140½ for Hendricks. Although short of the 492 votes needed to nominate, Tilden moved closer when Missouri switched its votes to him after the first roll call. The movement to Tilden continued on the second ballot, and he finished the roll call with 535 votes, more than enough to assure his nomination. *(Chart, p. 152)*

Hendricks, the runner-up for the presidential nomination, was the nearly unanimous choice of the delegates for the vice presidency. Hendricks received 730 votes, with the other eight votes not being cast.

The Democratic platform was an unusual one. Rather than being arranged in usual fashion with a series of numbered planks, it was written in paragraph form in language unusually powerful for a party platform. The theme of the document was the need for reform, and nearly half the paragraphs began with the phrase, "Reform is necessary...."

Debate focused on the party's stand on the currency issue. The majority report proposed repeal of the Resumption Act of 1875, a hard-money measure that called for the payment of Civil War bonds in coin. A minority report sponsored by delegates from five eastern states proposing deletion of this position was defeated, 550 to 219. A second minority report, introduced by midwestern delegates, favored a more strongly worded opposition to the Resumption Act. It too was defeated, 505 to 229, with midwestern delegations providing the bulk of the minority vote. The platform as a whole was approved, 651 to 83, again with most of the dissenting votes coming from the Midwest.

Besides the currency proposal, the platform called for extensive civil service reform, a tariff for revenue purposes only, restrictions on Chinese immigration and a new policy on the distribution of public land that would benefit the homesteaders and not the railroads. In addition to its reform theme, the platform was filled with sharp criticisms of Republican rule.

Following are excerpts from the Democratic platform of 1876:

> **Civil Service Reform.** Reform is necessary in the civil service. Experience proves that efficient economical conduct of the government is not possible if its civil service be subject to change at every election, be a prize fought for at the ballot-box, be an approved reward of party zeal instead of posts of honor assigned for proved competency and held for fidelity in the public employ; that the dispensing of patronage should neither be a tax upon the time of our public men nor an instrument of their ambition. Here again, profession falsified in the performance attest that the party in power can work out no practical or salutary reform. Reform is necessary even more in the higher grades of the public service. President, Vice-President, judges, senators, representatives, cabinet officers—these and all others in authority are the people's servants. Their offices are not a private perquisite; they are a public trust. When the annals of this Republic show disgrace and censure of a Vice-President; a late Speaker of the House of Representatives

marketing his rulings as a presiding officer; three Senators profiting secretly by their votes as law-makers; five chairmen of the leading committees of the late House of Representatives exposed in jobbery; a late Secretary of the Treasury forcing balances in the public accounts; a late Attorney-General misappropriating public funds; a Secretary of the Navy enriched and enriching friends by a percentage levied off the profits of contractors with his department; an Ambassador to England censured in a dishonorable speculation; the President's Private Secretary barely escaping conviction upon trial for guilty complicity in frauds upon the revenue; a Secretary of War impeached for high crimes and misdemeanors—the demonstration is complete, that the first step in reform must be the people's choice of honest men from another party, lest the disease of one political organization infect the body politic, and lest by making no change of men or parties, we get no change of measures and no real reform.

Currency. We denounce the improvidence which, in eleven years of peace, has taken from the people in Federal taxes thirteen times the whole amount of the legal-tender notes and squandered four times their sum in useless expense, without accumulating any reserve for their redemption. We denounce the financial imbecility and immorality of that party, which, during eleven years of peace, has made no advance toward resumption, no preparation for resump-

tion, but instead has obstructed resumption by wasting our resources and exhausting all our surplus income, and while annually professing to intend a speedy return to specie payments, has annually enacted fresh hindrances thereto. As such hindrance we denounce the resumption clause of the act of 1875 and we here demand its repeal.

Tariff. We denounce the present tariff levied upon nearly four thousand articles as a masterpiece of injustice, inequality and false pretense, which yields a dwindling and not a yearly rising revenue, has impoverished many industries to subsidize a few.... We demand that all customhouse taxation shall be only for revenue.

Homesteading. Reform is necessary to put a stop to the profligate waste of public lands and their diversion from actual settlers by the party in power, which has squandered two hundred millions of acres upon railroads alone, and out of more than thrice that aggregate has disposed of less than a sixth directly to the tillers of the soil.

Immigration. ...we denounce the policy which thus discards the liberty-loving German and tolerates the revival of the coolie-trade in Mongolian women for immoral purposes, and Mongolian men held to perform servile labor contracts, and demand such modification of the treaty with the Chinese Empire, or such legislation within constitutional limitations, as shall prevent further importation or immigration of the Mongolian race.

1880 Conventions

Presidential Candidates

James A. Garfield
Republican

James B. Weaver
Greenback

Winfield Hancock
Democrat

Republicans

The Republicans gathered in Chicago beginning June 2, 1880, for their seventh quadrennial nominating convention. For the first time, the convention call was addressed only to Republicans and not more broadly to others who sympathized with party principles.

The convention was divided into two factions. One, headed by Sen. Roscoe Conkling of New York, favored the nomination of former President Grant for a third term. The anti-Grant faction, although not united around one candidate, included the eventual nominee, Rep. James A. Garfield of Ohio, among its leaders.

Pre-convention skirmishing focused on the selection of a temporary chairman. The Grant forces desired one from their own ranks who would uphold the unit rule—a rule im-

portant to Grant, because he had the support of a majority of delegates in several large states. However, the Grant strategy was blocked, and a temporary chairman neutral to both sides was chosen by the Republican National Committee, leaving the ultimate decision on the unit rule to the convention.

A test of strength between the two factions came early in the convention on an amended motion by Conkling directing the credentials committee to report to the convention prior to the rules committee. Conkling's amended motion was defeated, 406 to 318.

In spite of the defeat of the amended motion, much time was spent debating delegate credentials. More than 50 cases were presented in committee, and seven of them came to the floor for a vote. Five of the cases featured seating disputes among delegates selected in district caucuses and those chosen for the same seats in state conventions. In each case—involving delegates from the states of Illinois, Kansas and West Virginia—the convention supported the claim of the delegates elected at the district level.

The Illinois credentials fight produced the only candidate-oriented division, with the Grant forces favoring the seating of the delegates selected at the state convention. But by a margin of 387 to 353, the convention voted to seat the delegates selected in the district caucuses. Three other votes were taken on disputed credentials from different Illinois districts, but all were decided in favor of the anti-Grant forces by a similar margin. *(Chart, p. 155)*

The majority report of the rules committee advocated that the controversial unit rule not be used. A motion by the Grant forces that the presidential nominations begin without passage of the rules committee report was defeated, 479 to 276. The vote was a key setback for the supporters of the former president, as the majority report was subsequently adopted by acclamation.

While the Grant forces suffered defeat on adoption of the unit rule, their candidate assumed the lead on the first ballot for president, with 304 votes. Maine Sen. James G. Blaine followed closely with 284, and Treasury Secretary John Sherman of Ohio, the candidate nominated by Rep. Garfield, trailed with 93 votes.

Ballot after ballot was taken throughout the day, but after the 28th roll call, the last of the night, there was little change in the vote totals of the leading candidates. Grant led with 307 votes; Blaine had 279, and Sherman, 91.

When balloting resumed the next morning, Sherman's vote total jumped to 116, the biggest gain among the contenders, but still well behind Grant and Blaine. Grant gained votes on the 34th ballot, rising to a new high of 312, but on the same roll call a boom for Garfield began, with the Ohio representative collecting 16 votes from Wisconsin. Garfield protested that he was not a candidate but was ruled out of order by the chairman.

The Ohio representative continued to gain on the 35th ballot, his vote total rising to 50. On the next ballot, Garfield won the nomination, receiving the votes of nearly all the anti-Grant delegates. At the end of the roll call, Garfield had 399 votes; Grant, 306, and Blaine, 42, with nine votes distributed among other candidates.

Four men were placed in nomination for the vice presidency, but Chester A. Arthur of New York was the easy winner on the first ballot. Arthur, the former collector of the port of New York, received 468 votes to 193 for former Rep. Elihu B. Washburne of Illinois. Most of Arthur's support came from delegates who had backed Grant.

The Republican platform was passed by a voice vote without debate. For the first time, the platform included planks that clearly called for the exercise of federal power, emphasizing that the Constitution was "a supreme law, and not a mere contract." This philosophy contrasted with the Democratic platform, which favored home rule and government decentralization.

The two parties also differed on the tariff issue. The Republicans favored a revenue tariff that would also protect American industry, while the Democrats explicitly called for a revenue tariff only.

In its original form, the Republican platform did not include a civil service plank. An amendment from the floor, however, calling for a "thorough, radical and complete" reform of the civil service, was passed by a voice vote.

Following are excerpts from the Republican platform of 1880:

Federal Power. The Constitution of the United States is a supreme law, and not a mere contract. Out of confederated States it made a sovereign nation. Some powers are denied to the Nation, while others are denied to the States; but the boundary between the powers delegated and those reserved is to be determined by the National and not by the State tribunal.

The work of popular education is one left to the care of the several States, but it is the duty of the National Government to aid that work to the extent of its constitutional power. The intelligence of the Nation is but the aggregate of the intelligence in the several States, and the destiny of the Nation must be guided, not by the genius of any one State, but by the aggregate genius of all.

Tariff. We affirm the belief, avowed in 1876, that the duties levied for the purpose of revenue should so discriminate as to favor American labor....

Civil Service Reform. The Republican party,...adopts the declaration of President Hayes that the reform of the civil service should be thorough, radical and complete.

Chinese Immigration.....the Republican party, regarding the unrestricted immigration of the Chinese as a matter of grave concernment...would limit and restrict that immigration by the enactment of such just, humane and reasonable laws and treaties as will produce that result.

Greenback Party

A coalition of farmer and labor groups met in Chicago beginning June 9, 1880, to hold the second national Greenback Party convention. The party's first convention was held four years earlier, but it was not until 1880 that the Greenback Party received over two per cent of the popular vote. The party held their third and final convention four years later, but was unable in 1884 to attain two per cent of the popular vote. *(Greenback Party profile, p. 203)*

The 1880 convention attracted representatives of the various Greenback Party factions, as well as 44 delegates from the Socialist Labor Party. Rep. James B. Weaver of Iowa was nominated for the presidency, and B. J. Chambers of Texas was chosen as his running mate.

The platform adopted was far broader than the one conceived by the Greenbacks at their first convention in 1876. That year they focused solely on the currency issue. For the agrarian interests, currency planks remained which called for the unlimited coinage of silver and gold and the issuance of currency by the federal government and not private banks. Also adopted for the farm elements were planks advocating increased public land for settlers, denouncing large monopolies and proposing that Congress control passenger and freight rates.

Included for the labor groups were proposals for an eight-hour day, the abolition of child labor, the improvement of working conditions and the curtailment of Chinese immigration.

The Greenback platform also included planks that favored a graduated income tax and women's suffrage.

Following are excerpts from the Greenback platform of 1880:

Currency. ...All money, whether metallic or paper, should be issued and its volume controlled by the Government, and not by or through banking corporations, and when so issued should be a full legal-tender for all debts, public and private.

That the bonds of the United States should not be refunded, but paid as rapidly as practicable, according to contract. To enable the Government to meet these obligations, legal-tender currency should be substituted for the notes of the National banks, the National banking system abolished, and the unlimited coinage of silver, as well as gold, established by law.

Labor. That labor should be so protected by National and State authority as to equalize the burdens and insure a just distribution of its results; the eight-hour law of Congress should be enforced, the sanitary condition of industrial establishments placed under rigid control; the competition of contract labor abolished, a bureau of labor statistics established, factories, mines, and workshops inspected, the employment of children under fourteen years of age forbidden, and wages paid in cash.

Chinese Immigration. Slavery being simply cheap labor, and cheap labor being simple slavery, the importation and presence of Chinese serfs necessarily tends to brutalize and degrade American labor.

Homesteading. Railroad land grants forfeited by reason of non-fulfillment of contract should be immediately reclaimed by the Government, and henceforth the public domain reserved exclusively as homes for actual settlers.

Regulation of Monopolies. It is the duty of Congress to regulate inter-state commerce. All lines of communication and transportation should be brought under such legislative control as shall secure moderate, fair and uniform rates for passenger and freight traffic.

We denounce as destructive to prosperity and dangerous to liberty, the action of the old parties in fostering and sustaining gigantic land, railroad, and money corporations and monopolies, invested with, and exercising powers belonging to the Government, and yet not responsible to it for the manner of their exercise.

Income Tax. All property should bear its just proportion of taxation, and we demand a graduated income tax.

Women's Suffrage. That every citizen of due age, sound mind, and not a felon, be fully enfranchised, and that this resolution be referred to the States, with recommendation for their favorable consideration.

Democrats

The Democrats held their 13th quadrennial nominating convention in Cincinnati, Ohio, in late June 1880. Credentials disputes enlivened the early sessions, with two competing New York delegations the focus of attention. The challenging group, controlled by Tammany Hall, requested 20 of New York's 70 votes. But by a margin of 457 to 205½, the convention refused their request.

Samuel J. Tilden, the Democratic standard-bearer in 1876 and the narrow loser in that controversial election, was not a candidate in 1880, although he did not officially notify his supporters of this fact until the presidential balloting had begun. Tilden's indecision, however, had long before opened the door for other prospective candidates.

On the first ballot, Gen. Winfield Scott Hancock of Pennsylvania, a candidate for the nomination in both 1868 and 1876, led with 171 votes, followed by Sen. Thomas F. Bayard of Delaware with 153½ and former Rep. Henry G. Payne of Ohio (who served as a stalking horse for the Tilden forces), with 81.

Tilden's declaration of non-candidacy was announced before the second ballot, and the Tilden forces shifted their strength to House Speaker Samuel J. Randall of Pennsylvania. Nonetheless, Hancock was the big gainer on the second ballot, his vote total jumping to 320. Randall followed with 128½, and Bayard slipped to third place with 112. Although Hancock was well short of the 492 votes needed for nomination, Wisconsin began a string of vote switches to Hancock that resulted in the military leader's selection. After all the changes, Hancock received 705 of the 738 votes cast.

The vice presidential nomination went by acclamation to former Rep. William H. English of Indiana, the only candidate.

The platform was accepted without debate or opposition. Its style of short, sharp phrases contrasted with the 1876 platform, which was written in flowing sentences built around the theme of the necessity of reform.

The 1880 platform called for decentralization of the federal government with increased local government, currency based on hard money, a tariff for revenue only, civil service reform and an end to Chinese immigration. The platform saved its harshest language to describe the party's reaction to the controversial election of 1876, which it labeled "the great fraud."

Following are excerpts from the Democratic platform of 1880:

Government Centralization. Opposition to centralization and to that dangerous spirit of encroachment which tends to consolidate the powers of all the departments in one, and thus to create whatever be the form of government, a real despotism. No sumptuary laws; separation of Church and State, for the good of each; common schools fostered and protected.

Currency. Home rule; honest money, consisting of gold and silver, and paper convertible into coin on demand.

Tariff.....a tariff for revenue only.

Civil Service Reform. We execrate the course of this administration in making places in the civil service a reward for political crime, and demand a reform by statute which shall make it forever impossible for a defeated candidate to bribe his way to the seat of the usurper by billeting villains upon the people.

Chinese Immigration. No more Chinese immigration, except for travel, education, and foreign commerce, and that even carefully guarded.

Election of 1876. The great fraud of 1876-77, by which, upon a false count of the electoral votes of two States, the candidate defeated at the polls was declared to be President, and for the first time in American history, the will of the people was set aside under a threat of military violence, struck a deadly blow at our system of representative government. The Democratic party, to preserve the country from the horrors of a civil war, submitted for the time in firm and patriotic faith that the people would punish this crime in 1880. This issue precedes and dwarfs every other. It imposes a more sacred duty upon the people of the Union than ever addressed the conscience of a nation of free men.

1884 Conventions

Presidential Candidates

James G. Blaine
Republican

Grover Cleveland
Democrat

Republicans

The Republicans gathered in Chicago in June 1884 for their convention. For the first time, the call to the convention prescribed how and when delegates should be selected, an effort to avoid the credentials disputes that had besieged the convention four years earlier.

The assassination of President Garfield had opened up the Republican presidential race, and the party war horse, James G. Blaine of Maine, emerged as the front-runner for the nomination. However, there was strong opposition to Blaine, including President Chester A. Arthur of New York.

The first test between the two sides was over the choice of a temporary chairman. The Blaine forces supported former Sen. Powell Clayton of Arkansas, while the anti-Blaine coalition favored a black delegate from Mississippi, John R. Lynch. Lynch won by a vote of 424 to 384.

A motion by the Blaine forces to adjourn after the presidential nominating speeches was also beaten, 412 to 391. But on the first ballot, Blaine assumed the lead with 334½ votes, followed by President Arthur with 278 and Sen. George F. Edmunds of Vermont with 93. Most of Arthur's strength was in the South, where the administration's patronage power had great effect.

Blaine gained votes on the next two ballots, his total rising to 375 on the third ballot, while Arthur dropped slightly to 274. After this roll call, the anti-Blaine forces attempted to force adjournment, but were defeated, 458 to 356. On the fourth ballot, Blaine received the nomination, winning 541 votes to 207 for Arthur and 41 for Edmunds.

Sen. John A. Logan of Illinois was the only person placed in nomination for vice president. Logan, who earlier had been in contention for the presidential nomination, received 779 of the 820 votes in the convention for second place on the ticket.

The party platform was adopted without dissent, and on major issues was little different from the planks presented by the Democrats. The Republicans proposed a tariff that would both protect American industry and raise revenue, called for civil service reform, advocated restrictions on Chinese immigration and favored increased availability of public lands for settlers. In addition, the

Republicans adopted features of the Greenback Party platform, calling for government regulation of railroads and an eight-hour work day.

Following are excerpts from the Republican platform of 1884:

> **Tariff.** We...demand that the imposition of duties on foreign imports shall be made, not "for revenue only," but that in raising the requisite revenues for the government, such duties shall be so levied as to afford security to our diversified industries and protection to the rights and wages of the laborer; to the end that active and intelligent labor, as well as capital, may have its just reward, and the laboring man his full share in the national prosperity.
>
> **Chinese Immigration.**....we denounce the importation of contract labor, whether from Europe or Asia, as an offense against the spirit of American institutions; and we pledge ourselves to sustain the present law restricting Chinese immigration, and to provide such further legislation as is necessary to carry out its purposes.
>
> **Labor.** We favor the establishment of a national bureau of labor; the enforcement of the eight hour law.
>
> **Regulation of Railroads.** The principle of public regulation of railway corporations is a wise and salutary one for the protection of all classes of the people; and we favor legislation that shall prevent unjust discrimination and excessive charges for transportation, and that shall secure to the people, and the railways alike, the fair and equal protection of the laws.

Democrats

The 1884 Democratic convention was held in Chicago in July. For the first time, the party extended delegate voting rights to the territories and the District of Columbia.

A debate over the unit rule highlighted the first day of the convention. Delegates from Tammany Hall, a minority of the New York delegation, presented an amendment to the temporary rules designed to abolish the unit rule. All the New York delegates were bound by their state convention to vote as a unit. However, the national convention defeated the amendment by a vote of 463 to 332, thus limiting the power of the Tammany delegates.

A resolution was passed opening the position of party chairman to individuals who were not members of the

Democratic National Committee. Another resolution, to eliminate the two-thirds rule at future conventions, was put to a vote, but the roll call was suspended when it became apparent the resolution would not pass.

Several peculiarities were evident during the presidential nominating speeches. Sen. Thomas A. Hendricks of Indiana, the favorite of the Hoosier delegation, nominated former Sen. Joseph E. McDonald as the state's favorite son in a speech listing attributes that easily could have described Hendricks. Two seconding speeches for Gov. Grover Cleveland of New York were delivered by Tammany delegates who actually used the time to denounce him.

In spite of the opposition within his own delegation, Cleveland was the front-runner for the nomination and had a big lead on the first ballot. Cleveland received 392 votes, easily outdistancing Sen. Thomas F. Bayard of Delaware, who had 170. Former Sen. Allen G. Thurman of Ohio was next, with 88. Hendricks received one vote, but protested to the convention that he was not a candidate.

A boom for Hendricks was undertaken on the second ballot, with the Indiana delegation shifting its support from McDonald to Hendricks. However, Cleveland also gained and continued to hold a large lead over the rest of the field. After two roll calls, these vote totals stood: Cleveland, 475; Bayard, 151½; Hendricks, 123½; Thurman, 60. With the New York governor holding a majority of the vote, North Carolina switched to Cleveland, and this started a bandwagon that gave him the required two-thirds majority. After the shifts, Cleveland received 683 of the 820 votes in the convention.

Over the objections of the Indiana delegation, Hendricks was nominated for the vice presidency. The Indiana leaders were a bit upset that Hendricks did not receive the presidential nomination, but did contribute to his nearly unanimous total for second place on the ticket. When the roll call was completed, Hendricks had received all but four votes.

The Democratic platform of 1884 was one of the longest documents adopted by the party in the 19th century. The platform was about 3,000 words long, with the first third devoted to a description of alleged Republican failures.

The platform straddled the increasingly important tariff issue. In 1880, the Democrats clearly favored a revenue tariff only, but the 1884 document called for both revenue and protection of American industry.

A minority report introduced by former Gov. Benjamin F. Butler of Massachusetts focused on the tariff issue.

Butler advocated a duty on imports that would hit harder at luxury items and less on necessities than the tariff favored by the majority report, and would also ensure more protection for American labor. The minority report was defeated, 721½ to 96½.

Butler, a former Republican and, earlier in 1884, nominated for president by the Greenback and Anti-Monopoly parties, also introduced substitute planks on labor, monopoly, public corporations, currency and civil service reform. These other planks were defeated by a voice vote, and the platform as written was adopted by acclamation.

Following are excerpts from the Democratic platform of 1884:

Tariff. Knowing full well,...that legislation affecting the operations of the people should be cautious and conservative in method, not in advance of public opinion, but responsive to its demands, the Democratic party is pledged to revise the tariff in a spirit of fairness to all interests.

But in making reduction in taxes, it is not proposed to injure any domestic industries, but rather to promote their healthy growth. From the foundation of this Government, taxes collected at the Custom House have been the chief source of Federal Revenue. Such they must continue to be. Moreover, many industries have come to rely upon legislation for successful continuance, so that any change of law must be at every step regardful of the labor and capital thus involved. The process of reform must be subject in the execution to this plain dictate of justice....

Sufficient revenue to pay all the expenses of the Federal Government...can be got, under our present system of taxation, from the custom house taxes on fewer imported articles, bearing heaviest on articles of luxury, and bearing lightest on articles of necessity.

Civil Liberties—Civil Service Reform. We oppose sumptuary laws which vex the citizen and interfere with individual liberty; we favor honest Civil Service Reform, and the compensation of all United States officers by fixed salaries; the separation of Church and State; and the diffusion of free education by common schools, so that every child in the land may be taught the rights and duties of citizenship.

Chinese Immigration. [W]e...do not sanction the importation of foreign labor, or the admission of servile races, unfitted by habits, training, religion, or kindred, for absorption into the great body of our people, or for the citizenship which our laws confer. American civilization demands that against the immigration or importation of Mongolians to these shores our gates be closed.

1888 Conventions

Presidential Candidates

Clinton B. Fisk
Prohibitionist

Grover Cleveland
Democrat

Benjamin Harrison
Republican

Prohibition

The Prohibition Party held their fifth national convention in Indianapolis in late May 1888. The party had held conventions since the 1872 campaign, but not until 1888 did the Prohibitionists receive at least two per cent of the popular vote. *(Prohibition Party, p. 207)*

The 1888 convention selected Clinton B. Fisk of New Jersey for president and John A. Brooks of Missouri as his running mate. While the platform focused on the need for prohibition, planks were included that covered other issues. The Prohibition Party favored a tariff that would both protect American industry and raise revenue, supported the extension of voting rights, favored immigration restrictions and proposed the abolition of polygamy.

Following are excerpts from the Prohibition Party platform of 1888:

> **Prohibition.** That the manufacture, importation, exportation, transportation and sale of alcoholic beverages should be made public crimes, and prohibited as such.

> **Tariff.** That an adequate public revenue being necessary, it may properly be raised by import duties; but import duties should be so reduced that no surplus shall be accumulated in the Treasury, and that the burdens of taxation shall be removed from foods, clothing and other comforts and necessaries of life, and imposed on such articles of import as will give protection both to the manufacturing employer and producing laborer against the competition of the world.

Democrats

When the Democratic convention assembled in St. Louis in early June 1888, the party, for the first time since the outset of the Civil War, was in control of the White House. There was no contest for the presidential nomination, with the incumbent, Grover Cleveland, renominated by acclamation. However, the death of Vice President Thomas A. Hendricks in 1885 left open the second place on the ticket.

Former Sen. Allen G. Thurman of Ohio was the favorite for the vice presidential nomination and won easily on the first ballot with 684 votes. Gov. Isaac P. Gray of Indiana had 101 votes, and Gen. John C. Black of Illinois trailed with 36. After the nomination of the 75-year-old Thurman, red bandannas were strung up around the hall. The bandanna was Thurman's political symbol, used extensively in his public habit of pinching snuff.

The platform was adopted by acclamation. It reaffirmed the Democratic platform written four years earlier, but in addition lauded the policies of President Cleveland and the achievements of Democratic rule, opposed the existing protective tariff and supported legislation to modify it and proposed a reformation of tax laws. A plank introduced from the floor favoring Irish home rule was included in the platform.

Following are excerpts from the Democratic platform of 1888:

> **Tariff.** The Democratic party of the United States, in National Convention assembled, renews the pledge of its fidelity to Democratic faith and reaffirms the platform adopted by its representatives in the Convention of 1884, and indorses the views expressed by President Cleveland in his last annual message to Congress as the correct interpretation of that platform upon the question of Tariff reduction; and also indorses the efforts of our Democratic Representatives in Congress to secure a reduction of excessive taxation....

> *Resolved,* That this convention hereby indorses and recommends the early passage of the bill for the reduction of the revenue now pending in the House of Representatives.

> **Tax Reform.** All unnecessary taxation is unjust taxation.... Every Democratic rule of governmental action is violated when through unnecessary taxation a vast sum of money, far beyond the needs of an economical administration, is drawn from the people and the channels of trade, and accumulated as a demoralizing surplus in the National Treasury.... The Democratic remedy is to enforce frugality in public expense and abolish needless taxation.

> **Federal Power.** Chief among its principles of party faith are the maintenance of an indissoluble Union of free and indestructible States, now about to enter upon its second century of unexampled progress and renown; devotion to a plan of government regulated by a written Constitution, strictly specifying every granted power and expressly

reserving to the States or people the entire ungranted residue of power.

Republicans

The Republicans assembled for their convention in Chicago in late June 1888. Not only was the party out of the White House for the first time since the Civil War, but a perennial contender for the presidential nomination, James G. Blaine, had taken himself out of the running. Although this encouraged a number of candidates to seek the nomination, none came near to mustering the needed majority as the balloting for president began.

The 832 convention votes were distributed among 14 candidates, with Sen. John Sherman of Ohio leading the field with 229 votes. Circuit Judge Walter Q. Gresham of Indiana followed with 107 votes, while four other candidates received more than 70 votes. During the rest of the day, two more ballots were taken, with little appreciable change in the strength of the candidates. After the third roll call, Sherman led with 244 votes, followed by Gresham with 123 and former Gov. Russell A. Alger of Michigan with 122.

The unexpected withdrawal from the race of Chauncey Depew of New York, the favorite of that state's delegation, prompted a call for adjournment after the third ballot. The motion passed, 531 to 287.

When balloting resumed the next morning, the biggest gainer was former Sen. Benjamin Harrison of Indiana. Although Sherman still held the lead with 235 votes on the fourth ballot, Harrison's vote total had leaped from 94 votes on the third to 216 on the fourth. There was little change on the fifth ballot, taken on a Saturday, and after the roll call the delegates approved, 492 to 320, a motion to adjourn until Monday. The motion was generally supported by delegates opposed to Harrison.

When the convention reconvened, both Sherman and Harrison showed small gains—Sherman rising to 244 votes and Harrison to 231. On the next roll call, the seventh, Harrison took the lead for the first time, thanks largely to a shift of votes from delegates previously holding out for Blaine. Harrison led, 279 to 230, and the trend to the Indianan accelerated to a bandwagon on the next ballot. Harrison easily achieved a majority on the eighth roll call, winning 544 votes to 118 for Sherman.

Three individuals were placed in nomination for vice president, but former Rep. Levi P. Morton of New York was the runaway winner on the first ballot. Morton received 592 votes to easily outdistance Rep. William Walter Phelps of New Jersey, who had 119 votes, and William O. Bradley of Kentucky, who had 103.

The platform sharply differed with that of the Democrats on the important tariff issue, strongly supporting the protective tariff and opposing the legislation favored by the Democrats. Like the Democrats, the Republicans called for a reduction in taxes, specifically recommending repeal of taxes on tobacco and on alcohol used in the arts and for mechanical purposes. In other areas, the Republicans favored the use of both gold and silver as currency, strongly opposed the Mormon practice of polygamy and called for veterans' pensions.

Following are excerpts from the Republican platform of 1888:

Tariff. We are uncompromisingly in favor of the American system of protection; we protest against its destruction as proposed by the President and his party. They serve the interests of Europe; we will support the interests of America.... The protective system must be maintained. Its abandonment has always been followed by general disaster to all interests, except those of the usurer and the sheriff. We denounce the Mills bill as destructive to the general business, the labor and the farming interests of the country, and we heartily indorse the consistent and patriotic action of the Republican Representatives in Congress in opposing its passage.

Tax Reform. The Republican party would effect all needed reduction of the National revenue by repealing the taxes upon tobacco, which are an annoyance and burden to agriculture, and the tax upon spirits used in the arts, and for mechanical purposes, and by such revision of the tariff laws as will tend to check imports of such articles as are produced by our people, the production of which gives employment to our labor, and releases from import duties those articles of foreign production (except luxuries), the like of which cannot be produced at home. If there shall remain a larger revenue than is requisite for the wants of the government we favor the entire repeal of internal taxes rather than the surrender of any part of our protective system at the joint behests of the whiskey trusts and the agents of foreign manufacturers.

Currency. The Republican party is in favor of the use of both gold and silver as money, and condemns the policy of the Democratic Administration in its efforts to demonetize silver.

Veterans' Benefits. The gratitude of the Nation to the defenders of the Union cannot be measured by laws.... We denounce the hostile spirit shown by President Cleveland in his numerous vetoes of measures for pension relief, and the action of the Democratic House of Representatives in refusing even a consideration of general pension legislation.

Polygamy. The political power of the Mormon Church in the Territories as exercised in the past is a menace to free institutions too dangerous to be longer suffered. Therefore we pledge the Republican party to appropriate legislation asserting the sovereignty of the Nation in all Territories where the same is questioned, and in furtherance of that end to place upon the statute books legislation stringent enough to divorce the political from the ecclesiastical power, and thus stamp out the attendant wickedness of polygamy.

1892 Conventions

Presidential Candidates

Benjamin Harrison
Republican

Grover Cleveland
Democrat

James B. Weaver
Populist

Republicans

Although President Harrison was unpopular with various elements in the Republican Party, administration forces were in control of the convention that assembled in early June 1892 in Minneapolis, Minn. A Harrison supporter, former Rep. William McKinley of Ohio, was elected without opposition as the convention's permanent chairman.

A question concerning the credentials of six Alabama delegates resulted in a protracted debate on whether the six delegates in question could vote on their own case. The situation was resolved when the Alabama delegates voluntarily abstained from voting. The minority report, which proposed seating the six Alabama delegates on the original roll, was defeated, 463 to 423½, and the majority report was subsequently adopted, 476 to 365½. The two votes were candidate-oriented, with the winning side in each case composed largely of Harrison voters.

Harrison's chances of renomination were so strong that two other possibilities, James G. Blaine and William McKinley, never publicly announced as candidates for the presidency. Harrison won easily on the first ballot, receiving 535-1/6 votes to 182-1/6 for Blaine and 182 for McKinley. McKinley was in the ironic position of presiding over the convention at the same time he was receiving votes on the presidential ballot. The Ohioan withdrew briefly as permanent chairman and moved that Harrison's nomination be made unanimous. The motion was withdrawn after objections but placed McKinley publicly on the Harrison bandwagon. *(Chart, p. 159)*

While the Republican Party had an incumbent vice president in Levi P. Morton, the New York delegation supported Whitelaw Reid, the former editor of *The New York Tribune* and ambassador to France. With Morton making little effort to retain his position, Reid was nominated by acclamation, the first time a Republican convention had dispensed with a roll call in choosing a member of its national ticket.

The platform was adopted by a voice vote, and on only two major issues did it differ from that of the Democrats. The Republicans supported a protective tariff, clearly different from the Democrats, who supported import duties for revenue only. The Republicans also included a plank that sympathized with the prohibition effort, while the Democrats announced their opposition "to all sumptuary laws."

Both parties favored a bimetallic currency, with gold and silver of equal value, and supported the construction of a canal across Nicaragua. In addition, the Republicans advocated an expansionist foreign policy.

Following are excerpts from the Republican platform of 1892:

Tariff. We reaffirm the American doctrine of protection. We call attention to its growth abroad. We maintain that the prosperous condition of our country is largely due to the wise revenue legislation of the Republican congress.

We believe that all articles which cannot be produced in the United States, except luxuries, should be admitted free of duty, and that on all imports coming into competition with the products of American labor, there should be levied duties equal to the difference between wages abroad and at home.

Currency. The American people, from tradition and interest, favor bi-metallism, and the Republican party demands the use of both gold and silver as standard money, with such restrictions and under such provisions, to be determined by legislation, as will secure the maintenance of the parity of values of the two metals so that the purchasing and debt-paying power of the dollar, whether of silver, gold, or paper, shall be at all times equal. The interests of the producers of the country, its farmers and its workingmen, demand that every dollar, paper or coin, issued by the government, shall be as good as any other.

Foreign Policy. We reaffirm our approval of the Monroe doctrine and believe in the achievement of the manifest destiny of the Republic in its broadest sense.

Central American Canal. The construction of the Nicaragua Canal is of the highest importance to the American people, both as a measure of National defense and to build up and maintain American commerce, and it should be controlled by the United States Government.

Prohibition. We sympathize with all wise and legitimate efforts to lessen and prevent the evils of intemperance and promote morality.

Democrats

One of the strangest conventions in party annals was held by the Democrats in Chicago in late June 1892. Much of the disturbance was due to stormy weather, with the accompanying noise and leaks in the roof frequently interrupting the proceedings. Inside the hall, the discomfort of the delegates was increased by the vocal opposition of 600 Tammany Hall workers to the renomination of former President Grover Cleveland of New York.

Although Cleveland was a solid favorite for renomination, he was opposed by his home state delegation. The Tammany forces engineered an early state convention that chose a delegation committed to Gov. David B. Hill. But in spite of the hostility of the New York delegation, Cleveland was able to win renomination on the first ballot, receiving 617-1/3 votes to 114 for Hill and 103 for Gov. Horace Boies of Iowa. *(Chart, p. 159)*

Four individuals were placed in nomination for the vice presidency, with Adlai E. Stevenson of Illinois assuming the lead on the first ballot. Stevenson, a former representative and later assistant postmaster general during Cleveland's first administration, led former Gov. Isaac P. Gray of Indiana, 402 to 343. After the first roll call was completed, Iowa switched to Stevenson, starting a bandwagon that led quickly to his nomination. After all the switches had been tallied, Stevenson was the winner with 652 votes, followed by Gray with 185.

The platform debate centered around the tariff plank. The plank, as originally written, straddled the issue. But a sharply worded substitute proposed from the floor, calling for a tariff for revenue only, passed easily, 564 to 342. The currency section of the platform called for stable money, with the coinage of both gold and silver in equal amounts. The platform also included a plank that called for the construction of a canal through Nicaragua.

Following are excerpts from the Democratic platform of 1892:

> **Tariff.** We denounce Republican protection as a fraud, a robbery of the great majority of the American people for the benefit of the few. We declare it to be a fundamental principle of the Democratic party that the Federal Government has no constitutional power to impose and collect tariff duties, except for the purpose of revenue only, and we demand that the collection of such taxes shall be limited to the necessities of the Government when honestly and economically administered.
>
> **Currency.** ...We hold to the use of both gold and silver as the standard money of the country, and to the coinage of both gold and silver without discriminating against either metal or charge for mintage, but the dollar unit of coinage of both metals must be of equal intrinsic and exchangeable value, or be adjusted through international agreement or by such safeguards of legislation as shall insure the maintenance of the parity of the two metals and the equal power of every dollar at all times in the markets and in the payment of debts; and we demand that all paper currency shall be kept at par with and redeemable in such coin.
>
> **Central American Canal.** For purposes of national defense and the promotion of commerce between the States, we recognize the early construction of the Nicaragua Canal and its protection against foreign control as of great importance to the United States.
>
> **Prohibition.** We are opposed to all sumptuary laws, as an interference with the individual rights of the citizen.
>
> **Federal Power.**...we solemnly declare that the need of a return to these fundamental principles of free popular government, based on home rule and individual liberty, was never more urgent than now, when the tendency to centralize all power at the Federal capital has become a menace to the reserved rights of the States that strikes at the very roots of our Government under the Constitution as framed by the fathers of the Republic.

Prohibition

The Prohibition Party's sixth convention was held in Cincinnati in late June 1892 and nominated John Bidwell of California for president and James B. Cranfill of Texas as his running mate. While the Prohibition Party continued to run a national ticket through the 1972 election, 1892 marked the last year that the party received over two per cent of the popular vote.

Although beginning and ending with calls for prohibition, the 1892 platform as a whole was a reform-minded document, favoring women's suffrage and equal wages for women, an inflated currency and the nationalization of railroad, telegraph, and other public corporations.

Following are excerpts from the Prohibition platform of 1892:

> **Prohibition.** ...We declare anew for the entire suppression of the manufacture, sale, importation, exportation and transportation of alcoholic liquors as a beverage by Federal and State legislation, and the full powers of Government should be exerted to secure this result. Any party that fails to recognize the dominant nature of this issue in American politics is undeserving of the support of the people.
>
> **Women's Rights.** No citizen should be denied the right to vote on account of sex, and equal labor should receive equal wages, without regard to sex.
>
> **Currency.** The money of the country should consist of gold, silver, and paper, and be issued by the General Government only, and in sufficient quantity to meet the demands of business and give full opportunity for the employment of labor. To this end an increase in the volume of money is demanded, and no individual or corporation should be allowed to make any profit through its issue. It should be made a legal tender for the payment of all debts, public and private. Its volume should be fixed at a definite sum per capita and made to increase with our increase in population.
>
> **Tariff.** Tariff should be levied only as a defense against foreign governments which levy tariff upon or bar out our products from their markets, revenue being incidental.
>
> **Government Nationalization.** Railroad, telegraph, and other public corporations should be controlled by the Government in the interest of the people.

People's Party (Populists)

The most successful of the 19th century farmer-labor coalitions was the People's Party, commonly known as the Populists, which formally organized as a political party at a convention in Cincinnati in May 1891. Further organization was accomplished at a convention in St. Louis the next February, from which emanated the call to the party's first national nominating convention, to be held that summer in Omaha, Neb. The election of 1892 was the only one in which the Populists received over two per cent of the national vote. Four years later the party endorsed the Democratic ticket, and from 1900 through 1908 the Populists ran separate tickets, but failed to receive two per cent of the popular vote. *(Populist Party profile, p. 206)*.

The call to the 1892 convention specified procedures for the selection of delegates and set the size of the convention at 1,776 delegates. Thirteen to fourteen hundred delegates actually assembled in Omaha for the Populist convention, which opened July 2. The field for the presidential nomination was reduced by the death early in 1892 of the southern agrarian leader, Leonidas L. Polk of North Carolina, and the refusal of Judge Walter Q. Gresham of Indiana to seek the nomination. First place on the ticket went to former Rep. James B. Weaver of Iowa, who defeated Sen. James H. Kyle of South Dakota, 995 to 275.

James G. Field of Virginia won the vice presidential nomination over Ben Terrell of Texas by a vote of 733 to 554. The ticket bridged any sectional division, pairing a former Union general (Weaver) with a former Confederate major (Field).

On July 4, the delegates enthusiastically adopted the platform. It contained few ideas that were not contained in the earlier platforms of other farmer-labor parties. But the document adopted by the Populists brought these proposals together into one forcefully written platform. More than half the platform was devoted to the preamble, which demanded widespread reform and sharply criticized the two major parties. It attacked the Democrats and Republicans for waging "a sham battle over the tariff," while ignoring more important issues.

The remainder of the platform was divided into three major parts that discussed finance, transportation and land policy. The Populists proposed that the currency be inflated, with the unlimited coinage of silver and a substantial increase in the circulating medium to at least $50 per capita. The Populists' currency plank was sharply different from those of the two major parties, which favored a stable, bimetallic currency.

The Populists also went well beyond the two major parties in advocating the nationalization of the railroads and telegraph and telephone companies. Both the Populists and Democrats advocated land reform, although the proposals received greater emphasis in the Populist platform.

The Populists included a call for a graduated income tax and expanded government power.

Although not considered part of the platform, supplementary resolutions were passed that favored the initiative and referendum, a limit of one term for the president, the direct election of senators, the secret ballot and additional labor-oriented proposals that called for improvement in working conditions.

Following are excerpts from the Populist platform of 1892:

Preamble. The conditions which surround us best justify our co-operation; we meet in the midst of a nation brought to the verge of moral, political, and material ruin. Corruption dominates the ballot-box, the Legislatures, the Congress, and touches even the ermine of the bench. The people are demoralized; most of the States have been compelled to isolate the voters at the polling places to prevent universal intimidation and bribery. The newspapers are largely subsidized or muzzled, public opinion silenced, business prostrated, homes covered with mortgages, labor impoverished, and the land concentrating in the hands of capitalists. The urban workmen are denied the right to organize for self-protection; imported pauperized labor beats down their wages, a hireling standing army, unrecognized by our laws, is established to shoot them down, and they are rapidly degenerating into European conditions.

The fruits of the toil of millions are boldly stolen to build up colossal fortunes for a few, unprecedented in the history of mankind; and the possessors of these, in turn despise the Republic and endanger liberty. From the same prolific womb of governmental injustice we breed the two great classes—tramps and millionaires....

We have witnessed for more than a quarter of a century the struggles of the two great political parties for power and plunder, while grievous wrongs have been inflicted upon the suffering people. We charge that the controlling influence dominating both these parties have permitted the existing dreadful conditions to develop without serious effort to prevent or restrain them. Neither do they now promise us any substantial reform. They have agreed together to ignore, in the coming campaign, every issue but one. They propose to drown the outcries of a plundered people with the uproar of a sham battle over the tariff, so that capitalists, corporations, national banks, rings, trusts, watered stock, the demonetization of silver and the oppressions of the usurers may all be lost sight of. They propose to sacrifice our homes, lives, and children on the altar of mammon; to destroy the multitude in order to secure corruption funds from the millionaires.

...We believe that the power of government—in other words, of the people—should be expanded (as in the case of the postal service) as rapidly and as far as the good sense of an intelligent people and the teachings of experience shall justify, to the end that oppression, injustice and poverty, shall eventually cease in the land.

While our sympathies as a party of reform are naturally upon the side of every proposition which will tend to make men intelligent, virtuous and temperate, we nevertheless regard these questions, important as they are, as secondary to the great issues now pressing for solution, and upon which not only our individual prosperity, but the very existence of free institutions depend; and we ask all men to first help us to determine whether we are to have a republic to administer, before we differ as to the conditions upon which it is to be administered, believing that the forces of reform this day organized with never cease to move forward, until every wrong is remedied, and equal rights and equal privileges securely established for all the men and women of this country.

Currency. We demand free and unlimited coinage of silver and gold at the present legal ratio of 16 to 1.

We demand that the amount of circulating medium be speedily increased to not less than $50 per capita.

We demand that postal savings banks be established by the government for the safe deposit of the earnings of the people and to facilitate exchange.

Transportation. Transportation being a means of exchange and a public necessity, the government should own and operate the railroads in the interest of the people. The telegraph and telephone, like the post office system, being a necessity for the transmission of news, should be owned and operated by the government in the interest of the people.

Land. The land, including all the natural sources of wealth, is the heritage of the people, and should not be monopolized for speculative purposes, and alien ownership of land should be prohibited. All land now held by railroads and other corporations in excess of their actual needs, and all lands now owned by aliens, should be reclaimed by the government and held for actual settlers only.

Explanatory Note

This section on the history of party nominating conventions includes party conventions for parties receiving at least two per cent of the popular vote in the presidential election. The Socialist Party, for example, received at least two per cent of the popular vote in 1904, 1908, 1912, 1916, 1920 and 1932; the Socialist Party conventions for these years are included in this section. The Socialist Party conventions for other years when the party received less than two per cent of the vote are not included. *(Additional details on this section, p. 20)*

1896 Conventions

Presidential Candidates

William McKinley
Republican

William J. Bryan
Democrat

Republicans

The currency issue, which spawned several third party efforts in the late 19th century, emerged as the dominant issue of contention between the Republican and Democratic parties in the campaign of 1896. The forces in favor of the gold standard were firmly in control of the Republican convention that was held in St. Louis in early June 1896.

Actually, the convention was less a forum for the discussion of issues than a showcase for the political acumen of Mark Hanna of Ohio. Hanna, William McKinley's campaign manager, had been intensely courting delegates across the country, especially in the South, for more than a year before the convention. Before the rap of the opening gavel, Hanna had amassed a majority of the delegates for the popular Ohio governor.

The first evidence of McKinley strength came on a credentials question. A minority report was introduced claiming the credentials committee had held hearings on only two of 160 cases and proposing that the committee resume hearings. A maneuver to squelch the minority report was made when a delegate moved to cut off debate. With the McKinley forces providing most of the majority, the motion passed, 551½ to 359½.

Four other candidates in addition to McKinley were in contention for the presidential nomination, but McKinley was the runaway winner on the first ballot. He received 661½ votes to 84½ for the runner-up, House Speaker Thomas B. Reed of Maine. *(Chart, p. 161)*

There were two serious contenders for the vice presidential nomination: Garret A. Hobart, a McKinley supporter and former state legislator from New Jersey, and Henry Clay Evans, a former candidate for governor of Tennessee. Hobart won, wining 523½ votes on the first ballot to 287½ for Evans.

As at the Democratic convention, the platform debate centered around the currency issue. The gold forces, firmly in control of the Republican convention, produced a majority report that called for maintenance of the gold standard until the time when bimetallism could be effected by an international agreement. This plank did not satisfy the silver minority. Led by Sen. Henry M. Teller of Colorado, a minority plank was introduced favoring the unlimited coinage of silver and gold at the ratio of 16 to 1. Teller's plank, similar to the currency plank adopted later by the Democrats, was defeated, 818½ to 105½. A second roll call on adoption of the majority plank resulted in another decisive defeat for the silver forces. The majority plank carried, 812½ to 110½.

With the decisive defeat of the minority plank, Teller led a walkout by 24 silver delegates, including the entire Colorado and Idaho delegations and members of the Montana, South Dakota and Utah delegations. The rest of the platform was adopted by a voice vote.

The currency plank that caused the commotion was buried deep in the middle of the Republican platform. The document began with a denunciation of Democratic rule and proceeded into a discussion of the merits of a protective tariff. A tariff for revenue purposes only was advocated in the Democratic platform, but the issue in the Republican document was clearly considered to be of secondary importance.

The Republican platform was also distinguishable from that of the Democrats in recommending a more expansionistic foreign policy, proposing stricter immigration restrictions and, for the first time, specifically denouncing the practice of lynching.

Following are excerpts from the Republican platform of 1896:

Currency. The Republican party is unreservedly for sound money.... We are unalterably opposed to every measure calculated to debase our currency or impair the credit of our country. We are therefore opposed to the free coinage of silver, except by international agreement with the leading commercial nations of the earth, which agreement we pledge ourselves to promote, and until such agreement can be obtained the existing gold standard must be maintained.

Tariff. We renew and emphasize our allegiance to the policy of protection, as the bulwark of American industrial independence, and the foundation of American development and prosperity.... Protection and Reciprocity are twin measures of American policy and go hand in hand. Democratic rule has recklessly struck down both, and both must be re-established. Protection for what we produce; free admission for the necessaries of life which we do not produce; reciprocal agreement of mutual interests, which gain open markets for us in return for our open markets for others. Protection builds up domestic industry and trade and secures our own market for ourselves; reciprocity builds up foreign trade and finds an outlet for our surplus.

Foreign Policy. Our foreign policy should be at all times firm, vigorous and dignified, and all our interests in the western hemisphere should be carefully watched and guarded.

The Hawaiian Islands should be controlled by the United States, and no foreign power should be permitted to interfere with them. The Nicaragua Canal should be built, owned and operated by the United States. And, by the purchase of the Danish Islands we should secure a much needed Naval station in the West Indies.... We therefore, favor the continued enlargement of the navy, and a complete system of harbor and sea-coast defenses.

Immigration. For the protection of the equality of our American citizenship and of the wages of our workingmen, against the fatal competition of low priced labor, we demand that the immigration laws be thoroughly enforced, and so extended as to exclude from entrance to the United States those who can neither read nor write.

Lynching. We proclaim our unqualified condemnation of the uncivilized and preposterous [barbarous] practice well known as lynching, and the killing of human beings suspected or charged with crime without process of law.

Democrats

The Democratic convention that assembled in Chicago in July 1896 was dominated by one issue—currency. A delegate's viewpoint on this single issue influenced his position on every vote taken. Generally, the party was split along regional lines, with eastern delegations favoring a hard-money policy with maintenance of the gold standard, and most southern and western delegations supporting a soft-money policy with the unlimited coinage of silver.

Division in the convention was apparent on the first day, when the silver forces challenged the national committee's selection of Gov. David B. Hill of New York as temporary chairman. The pro-silver delegates put up Sen. John W. Daniel of Virginia for the post, and Daniel won easily, 556 to 349. His victory indicated the dominance of the silver forces and presaged their ability to control the convention.

Two sets of credentials challenges were next on the agenda. By a voice vote, the convention agreed to seat a Nebraska delegation headed by a young silver supporter, William Jennings Bryan. And by a vote of 558 to 368, the convention defeated a recommendation to seat Michigan delegates supported by the hard-money-dominated national committee.

With their lack of strength apparent, the gold forces declined to run a candidate for president. However, the silver delegates could not initially coalesce behind one candidate, and 14 individuals received votes on the first ballot. Rep. Richard P. (Silver Dick) Bland of Missouri was the pacesetter, with 235 votes, followed by former Rep. Bryan of Nebraska with 137 and 97 for Robert E. Pattison, former Pennsylvania governor. Bryan, 36 years old, earlier had electrified the convention during the platform debate on currency, with his memorable "Cross of Gold" speech, which had elevated him to the position of a major contender. *(Chart, p. 160)*

On the next two roll calls, both candidates showed gains. Bland's total climbed to 291 on the third ballot and

Bryan's rose to 219. Bryan continued to gain on the next ballot and assumed the lead over Bland, 280 to 241. The movement to Bryan accelerated on the fifth ballot, and he won the nomination easily, receiving 652 of the 930 convention votes. Although Bryan was the nearly unanimous choice of the silver forces, 162 gold delegates indicated their dissatisfaction with the proceedings by refusing to vote.

With Bryan declining to indicate a preference for vice president, 16 candidates received votes for the office on the first ballot. The Nebraska delegation, following Bryan's example, declined to participate in the vice-presidential balloting.

Former Rep. John C. Sibley of Pennsylvania took the lead on the first ballot with 163 votes, followed by Ohio editor and publisher John R. McLean with 111, and Maine shipbuilder Arthur Sewall with 100.

Bland spurted into the lead on the second ballot with 294 votes, followed by McLean and Sibley. After the roll call, Sibley withdrew, and on the third ballot the race between Bland and McLean tightened. The Missourian led, 255 to 210, but he too withdrew after the roll call. Sewall emerged as McLean's major competitor on the fourth ballot, and with the withdrawal of the Ohio journalist from the race, the nomination was Sewall's on the fifth ballot. Actually, Sewall's vote total of 602 on the final roll call was less than two-thirds of the convention vote, but with 251 disgruntled gold delegates refusing to vote, the required majority was reduced to only those voting.

Not surprisingly, the platform debate centered around the currency plank. The eastern delegations proposed that until silver coinage could be arranged by international agreement, the gold standard should be maintained. The southern and western delegations countered by demanding that the unlimited coinage of silver should begin without requiring a delay to reach an international agreement. Bryan managed the platform debate for the silver forces and scheduled himself as the final speaker, an enviable position from which to make a deep impression on the emotion-packed convention.

Bryan made the most of his opportunity, ending his dramatic speech with the famous peroration: "You shall not press down upon the brow of labor this crown of thorns, you shall not crucify mankind upon a cross of gold." The gold plank was defeated, 626 to 303. Although the speech was a key factor in Bryan's nomination, it was not influential in defeating the gold plank, which was already doomed for defeat. *(Chart, p. 160)*

A resolution commending the Cleveland administration was also defeated, 564 to 357, and after several attempts to modify the currency plank were rejected by voice votes, the platform as a whole was adopted, 622 to 307.

Following are excerpts from the Democratic platform of 1896:

Currency. We demand the free and unlimited coinage of both silver and gold at the present legal ratio of 16 to 1 without waiting for the aid or consent of any other nation.

Railroads. The absorption of wealth by the few, the consolidation of our leading railroad systems, and the formation of trusts and pools require a stricter control by the Federal Government of those arteries of commerce. We demand the enlargement of the powers of the Interstate Commerce Commission and such restriction and guarantees in the control of railroads as will protect the people from robbery and oppression.

No Third Term. We declare it to be the unwritten law of this Republic, established by custom and usage of 100 years, and sanctioned by the examples of the greatest and wisest of those who founded and have maintained our

Government that no man should be eligible for a third term of the Presidential office.

Federal Power. During all these years the Democratic Party has resisted the tendency of selfish interests to the centralization of governmental power, and steadfastly maintained the integrity of the dual scheme of government established by the founders of this Republic of republics. Under its guidance and teachings the great principle of local self-government has found its best expression in the maintenance of the rights of the States and in its assertion of the necessity of confining the general government to the exercise of the powers granted by the Constitution of the United States.

1900 Conventions

Presidential Candidates

William McKinley
Republican

William J. Bryan
Democrat

Republicans

Surface harmony was the hallmark of the Republican conclave held in Philadelphia in June 1900. The Colorado delegation, which had walked out of the 1896 convention, was honored by having one of its members, Sen. Edward O. Wolcott, chosen as temporary chairman.

There was no opposition to President McKinley, and he won all 926 votes on the first roll call. However, the death of Vice President Hobart in 1899 had left the second spot on the ticket open. McKinley did not have a preference and asked his campaign manager, Mark Hanna, not to influence the convention. McKinley's hands-off policy worked to the advantage of the popular governor of New York and hero of the Spanish-American War, Theodore Roosevelt, whom Hanna disliked. *(Chart, p. 162)*

Roosevelt's popularity, coupled with the desire of New York boss Thomas C. Platt to eliminate a powerful state rival, enabled the 41-year-old governor to clinch the nomination before balloting began. On the vice presidential roll call, Roosevelt received all but one vote. The single uncast vote came from Roosevelt's New York delegation, which cast 71 of its 72 votes for Roosevelt.

The Republicans adopted a platform that applauded the four years of Republican rule and credited McKinley's policies with improving business conditions and winning the Spanish-American War. The platform defended postwar expansionism and called for increased foreign trade and the creation of a Department of Commerce.

As in 1896, the Republican platform opposed the unlimited coinage of silver and supported maintenance of the gold standard. On the tariff issue, the Republicans continued to laud the protective duty on imports.

Following are excerpts from the Republican platform of 1900:

Foreign Trade, Panama Canal. We favor the construction, ownership, control and protection of an Isthmian Canal by the Government of the United States. New markets are necessary for the increasing surplus of our farm products. Every effort should be made to open and obtain new markets, especially in the Orient, and the Administration is warmly to be commended for its successful efforts to commit all trading and colonizing nations to the policy of the open door in China.

International Expansion. In accepting by the Treaty of Paris the just responsibility of our victories in the Spanish war, the President and the Senate won the undoubted approval of the American people. No other course was possible than to destroy Spain's sovereignty throughout the West Indies and in the Philippine Islands. That course created our responsibility before the world, and with the unorganized population whom our intervention had freed from Spain, to provide for the maintenance of law and order, and for the establishment of good government and for the performance of international obligations. Our authority could not be less than our responsibility; and wherever sovereign rights were extended it became the high duty of the Government to maintain its authority, to put down armed insurrection and to confer the blessings of liberty and civilization upon all the rescued peoples.

Anti-trust. We recognize the necessity and propriety of the honest co-operation of capital to meet new business conditions and especially to extend our rapidly increasing foreign trade, but we condemn all conspiracies and combinations intended to restrict business, to create monopolies, to limit production, or to control prices; and favor such legislation as will effectively restrain and prevent all such abuses, protect and promote competition and secure the rights of producers, laborers, and all who are engaged in industry and commerce.

Currency. We renew our allegiance to the principle of the gold standard and declare our confidence in the wisdom of the legislation of the Fifty-sixth Congress, by which the parity of all our money and the stability of our currency upon a gold basis has been secured....

We declare our steadfast opposition to the free and unlimited coinage of silver.

Tariff. We renew our faith in the policy of Protection to American labor. In that policy our industries have been established, diversified and maintained. By protecting the home market competition has been stimulated and production cheapened.

Democrats

The Democrats opened their 1900 convention in Kansas City, Mo., on July 4, and showed a degree of party harmony not evident at their convention four years earlier. After the party factionalism of 1896, the delegates made a conscious effort to display a unified front—an effort aided by the decline of the controversial silver issue. The discovery of new gold deposits in North America and the subsequent increase in currency had lessened the divisive impact of the silver issue.

William Jennings Bryan, the Democratic standard-bearer in 1896, was renominated without opposition, receiving all 936 votes. The harmony in the convention was evident when former New York Sen. David B. Hill, a leader of the gold forces four years earlier, gave a seconding speech for Bryan. *(Chart, p. 162)*

Seven names were placed in nomination for the vice presidency. However, two withdrew before the balloting began. Adlai E. Stevenson of Illinois, vice president under Grover Cleveland, led on the first roll call with 559½ votes, followed by Hill, who received 200 votes in spite of withdrawing from the race before the voting started. After completion of the ballot, there were a series of vote switches that resulted in Stevenson's unanimous nomination.

The platform was adopted without floor debate. The major theme of the document was anti-imperialism, although an attack on trusts and a discussion of the currency question also were emphasized.

The anti-imperialism section was placed at the beginning of the platform and was labeled the most important issue of the campaign. The delegates enthusiastically accepted the plank, which forcefully criticized American international expansion after the Spanish-American War. The platform asserted "that no nation can long endure half republic and half empire," and denounced increasing U.S. militarism. The Democratic position sharply differed from the one advocated by the Republicans, whose platform defended post-war expansionism.

After the anti-imperialism section was a sharp attack on monopolies, the most detailed anti-trust section that had yet appeared in a Democratic platform. The plank called for more comprehensive anti-trust legislation and more rigid enforcement of the laws already enacted. Although the Republicans also condemned monopolies, the issue received a mere one-sentence mention in their platform.

With the decline of the silver issue, the necessity of a pro-silver plank was a matter of debate in the resolutions committee. However, Bryan threatened to withdraw his candidacy if a plank calling for the unlimited coinage of silver was not included in the platform. By a majority of one vote, the resolutions committee included the silver plank, and it was accepted without dissent by the convention. The Democratic position set up another distinction with the Republicans, who, as four years earlier, favored maintenance of the gold standard.

In addition to the anti-imperialism, anti-trust and currency sections of the platform, the Democrats proposed the creation of a Department of Labor, favored the direct election of senators and unlike the Republicans, supported the construction and ownership of a Nicaraguan canal. The Republican platform advocated construction and ownership of a canal across the Isthmus of Panama.

Following are excerpts from the Democratic platform of 1900:

Anti-imperialism.....We hold that the Constitution follows the flag, and denounce the doctrine that an Executive or Congress deriving their existence and their powers from the Constitution can exercise lawful authority beyond it or in violation of it. We assert that no nation can long endure half republic and half empire, and we warn the American people that imperialism abroad will lead quickly and inevitably to despotism at home....

We are not opposed to territorial expansion when it takes in desirable territory which can be erected into States in the Union, and whose people are willing and fit to become American citizens. We favor trade expansion by every peaceful and legitimate means. But we are unalterably opposed to seizing or purchasing distant islands to be governed outside the Constitution, and whose people can never become citizens....

The importance of other questions, now pending before the American people is no wise diminished and the Democratic party takes no backward step from its position on them, but the burning issue of imperialism growing out of the Spanish war involves the very existence of the Republic and the destruction of our free institutions. We regard it as the paramount issue of the campaign....

We oppose militarism. It means conquest abroad and intimidation and oppression at home. It means the strong arm which has ever been fatal to free institutions.... This republic has no place for a vast military establishment, a sure forerunner of compulsory military service and conscription. When the nation is in danger the volunteer soldier is his country's best defender.

Anti-trust. We pledge the Democratic party to an unceasing warfare in nation, State and city against private monopoly in every form. Existing laws against trusts must be enforced and more stringent ones must be enacted.... Tariff laws should be amended by putting the products of trusts upon the free list, to prevent monopoly under the plea of protection.

Currency. We reaffirm and indorse the principles of the National Democratic Platform adopted at Chicago in 1896, and we reiterate the demand of that platform for an American financial system made by the American people for themselves, and which shall restore and maintain a bi-metallic price-level, and as part of such system the immediate restoration of the free and unlimited coinage of silver and gold at the present legal ratio of 16 to 1, without waiting for the aid or consent of any other nation.

1904 Conventions

Presidential Candidates

Eugene V. Debs
Socialist

Theodore Roosevelt
Republican

Alton B. Parker
Democrat

Socialists

The Socialist Party held its first national nominating convention in Chicago in early May 1904, and nominated Eugene V. Debs of Indiana for president and Benjamin Hanford of New York as his running mate. Debs ran in 1900 as the presidential candidate of two socialist groups, the Social Democratic Party and a moderate faction of the Socialist Labor Party.

The bulk of the platform was devoted to the philosophy of the international Socialist movement, with its belief in the eventual demise of capitalism and the ultimate achievement of a classless, worker-oriented society. To hasten the creation of a Socialist society, the platform favored many reforms advocated by the Populists and earlier agrarian-labor movements: the initiative, referendum and recall; women's suffrage; tax reform, including the graduated income tax; the public ownership of transportation, communication and exchange; and various labor benefits, including higher wages and shorter hours.

Following are excerpts from the Socialist platform of 1904:

> To the end that the workers may seize every possible advantage that may strengthen them to gain complete control of the powers of government, and thereby the sooner establish the cooperative commonwealth, the Socialist Party pledges itself to watch and work, in both the economic and the political struggle, for each successive immediate interest of the working class; for shortened days of labor and increases of wages; for the insurance of the workers against accident, sickness and lack of employment; for pensions for aged and exhausted workers; for the public ownership of the means of transportation, communication and exchange; for the graduated taxation of incomes, inheritances, franchises and land values, the proceeds to be applied to the public employment and improvement of the conditions of the workers; for the complete education of children, and their freedom from the workshop; for the prevention of the use of the military against labor in the settlement of strikes; for the free administration of justice; for popular government, including initiative, referendum, proportional representation, equal suffrage of men and women, municipal home rule, and the recall of officers by their constituents; and for every gain or advantage for the workers that may be

wrested from the capitalist system, and that may relieve the suffering and strengthen the hands of labor. We lay upon every man elected to any executive or legislative office the first duty of striving to procure whatever is for the workers' most immediate interest, and for whatever will lessen the economic and political powers of the capitalist, and increase the like powers of the worker.

Republicans

President Theodore Roosevelt was totally in command of the Republican convention held in Chicago in June 1904. His most dangerous potential rival for the nomination, Sen. Mark Hanna of Ohio, had died in February, leaving the field clear for Roosevelt.

The rather trivial matter of most interest before the presidential balloting began was Hawaii's vote allocation. The rules committee recommended that the vote of the territory be reduced from six to two. A substitute amendment proposed that Hawaii retain its six votes for the 1904 convention but that its vote allocation be reviewed by the national committee for future conventions. The substitute was accepted by the narrow margin of 495 to 490.

Roosevelt's nomination caused less commotion. On the first ballot, he received all 994 votes. The party leadership favored Sen. Charles W. Fairbanks of Indiana for the vice presidency. Although the Georgia, Illinois, Missouri and Nebraska delegations noted that they preferred other candidates, Fairbanks was nominated by acclamation.

The party platform was adopted without dissent. In the document the Republicans charted little new ground, instead detailing the benefits of Republican rule and restating old positions. America's expansionistic foreign policy was praised, as was the protective tariff and the gold standard.

A display of Roosevelt theatrics followed the adoption of the platform. The convention chairman was instructed to read a message from the secretary of state to the American consul in Morocco: "We want either Perdicaris alive or Raisuli dead." The message referred to an alleged American citizen, Ion Perdicaris, who had been captured by the Moroccan chieftain, Raisuli. The American ultimatum read to the convention followed the dispatch of several ships to Morocco. The reading of the message roused the delegates, as it was no doubt intended to do.

Following are excerpts from the Republican platform of 1904:

Shipbuilding. We...favor legislation which will encourage and build up the American merchant marine, and we cordially approve the legislation of the last Congress which created the Merchant Marine Commission to investigate and report upon this subject.

Monopoly. Combinations of capital and of labor are the results of the economic movement of the age, but neither must be permitted to infringe upon the rights and interests of the people. Such combinations, when lawfully formed for lawful purposes, are alike entitled to the protection of the laws, but both are subject to the laws and neither can be permitted to break them.

Democrats

William Jennings Bryan, after two unsuccessful campaigns for the presidency, was not a candidate for the Democratic nomination in 1904. However, he was present at the party's convention in St. Louis that July and was a prominent factor in the proceedings.

Bryan's first appearance before the convention came during a credentials dispute, featuring a challenge by Bryan supporters in Illinois to the state delegation approved by the credentials committee. Bryan spoke in behalf of his supporters, but their minority report was beaten, 647 to 299.

Bryan appeared again to second the presidential nomination of Sen. Francis M. Cockrell of Missouri, one of eight candidates nominated. Much of his speech, however, was devoted to criticizing the conservative front-runner, Alton B. Parker, chief justice of the New York Court of Appeals, while boosting more progressive candidates. In spite of Bryan's opposition, Parker came within nine votes of receiving the necessary two-thirds majority on the first ballot. Parker had 658 votes, followed by Rep. William Randolph Hearst of New York, with 200, and Cockrell, who trailed with 42. Although Hearst had progressive credentials, Bryan hesitated to support him and jeopardize his own leadership of the progressive wing of the party.

With Parker so close to victory, Idaho shifted its votes to the New York judge, prompting enough switches by other states to give Parker 679 votes and the nomination. Hearst, with his strength in the Middle West and West, finished with 181 votes. *(Chart, p. 163)*

With the nomination in hand, Parker stunned the convention by sending a telegram to the New York delegation, announcing his support of the gold standard and advising the convention to select a new candidate if they found his position unacceptable. Parker supporters drafted a response stating that there was nothing to preclude his nomination, because the platform was silent on the currency issue.

Bryan, ill with a fever in his hotel but still a supporter of the silver cause, rose from his sickbed to join several southern leaders on the floor of the convention in denouncing Parker's telegram and the drafted response.

Nonetheless, the response recommended by the Parker forces was approved, 794 to 191, with opposition principally from the Middle West and West.

For vice president, the convention chose former West Virginia Sen. Henry G. Davis. He nearly achieved a two-thirds majority on the first ballot, receiving 654 votes. With Davis' nomination so near, a motion to declare him the vice presidential candidate was approved. Davis, at age 80, was the oldest candidate ever put on a national ticket by a major party. He was a man of great wealth, and the Democrats hoped that he would give freely to their campaign.

Although the platform was accepted without debate by a voice vote, there was maneuvering behind the scenes to meet the objections of Bryan. The initial platform draft before the resolutions committee included a plank that declared that recent gold discoveries had removed the currency question as a political issue. Bryan found this plank objectionable and successfully fought in the resolutions committee for its deletion. Bryan was less successful in having an income tax plank included but was able to get a more strongly worded anti-trust resolution.

Unlike the Democratic platform of 1900, which focused on anti-imperialism, anti-monopoly and currency, the 1904 platform covered about two dozen topics with nearly equal emphasis.

The Democrats and Republicans disagreed on one new issue: federal support for private shipping firms. The Democrats opposed government assistance; the Republicans favored it. But on other issues the platform of the Democrats, like that of the Republicans, broke little new ground, instead restating positions that had been included in earlier Democratic platforms. There was a continued attack on American imperialism and a call for a smaller Army. There were planks that urged less international involvement and more emphasis on domestic improvements. Again, there were denunciation of the protective tariff, support for increased anti-trust legislation and a call for the direct election of senators.

The Roosevelt administration was criticized as "spasmodic," "erratic," "headstrong," "arbitrary"—a new group of words to describe the Republican opposition.

Following are excerpts from the Democratic platform of 1904:

Roosevelt Administration. The existing Republican administration has been spasmodic, erratic, sensational, spectacular and arbitrary. It has made itself a satire upon the Congress, courts, and upon the settled practices and usages of national and international law....the necessity of reform and the rescue of the administration of Government from the headstrong, arbitrary and spasmodic methods which distract business by uncertainty, and pervade the public mind with dread, distrust and perturbation.

Shipbuilding. We denounce the ship subsidy bill recently passed by the United States Senate as an iniquitous appropriation of public funds for private purposes and a wasteful, illogical and useless attempt to overcome by subsidy the obstructions raised by Republican legislation to the growth and development of American commerce on the sea.

We favor the upbuilding of a merchant marine without new or additional burdens upon the people and without bounties from the public treasury.

1908 Conventions

Presidential Candidates

Eugene V. Debs
Socialist

William H. Taft
Republican

William J. Bryan
Democrat

Socialists

The Socialists met in Chicago in May 1908 and renominated the ticket that had represented the party four years earlier: Eugene V. Debs of Indiana for president and Benjamin Hanford of New York as his running mate.

The platform was divided into several major sections, including a discussion of principles, and topics entitled general demands, industrial demands and political demands. The Socialists' goal was the creation of a classless society, and in pursuance of this goal, the movement was identified as a party of the working class.

Among the general demands were proposals for public works programs to aid the unemployed and public ownership of land, means of transportation and communication and monopolies.

Industrial demands included calls for reduced working hours, the abolition of child labor and more effective inspections of working areas.

The section on political demands began with a restatement of earlier positions, with a call for tax reform, women's suffrage and the initiative, referendum and recall. However, the section also included more radical demands, such as the abolition of the Senate, the amendment of the Constitution by popular vote, the direct election of all judges and the removal of power from the Supreme Court to declare legislation passed by Congress unconstitutional.

Following are excerpts from the Socialist platform of 1908:

Public Works Projects. The immediate government relief for the unemployed workers by building schools, by reforesting of cutover and waste lands, by reclamation of arid tracts, and the building of canals, and by extending all other useful public works. All persons employed on such works shall be employed directly by the government under an eight hour work day and at the prevailing union wages. The government shall also loan money to states and municipalities without interest for the purpose of carrying on public works. It shall contribute to the funds of labor organizations for the purpose of assisting their unemployed members, and shall take such other measures within its power as will lessen the widespread misery of the workers caused by the misrule of the capitalist class.

Public Ownership. The collective ownership of railroads, telegraphs, telephones, steamship lines and all other means of social transportation and communication, and all land.

The collective ownership of all industries which are organized on a national scale and in which competition has virtually ceased to exist.

Labor. The improvement of the industrial condition of the workers,

(a) By shortening the workday in keeping with the increased productiveness of machinery.

(b) By securing to every worker a rest period of not less than a day and a half in each week.

(c) By securing a more effective inspection of workshops and factories.

(d) By forbidding the employment of children under sixteen years of age.

(e) By forbidding the interstate transportation of the products of child labor, of convict labor and of all uninspected factories.

(f) By abolishing official charity and substituting in its place compulsory insurance against unemployment, illness, accident, invalidism, old age and death.

Tax Reform. The extension of inheritance taxes, graduated in proportion to the amount of the bequests and the nearness of kin.

A graduated income tax.

Women's Suffrage. Unrestricted and equal suffrage for men and women,....

Senate. The abolition of the senate.

Constitutional and Judicial Reforms. The abolition of the power usurped by the supreme court of the United States to pass upon the constitutionality of legislation enacted by Congress. National laws to be repealed or abrogated only by act of Congress or by a referendum of the whole people.

That the constitution be made amendable by majority vote.

That all judges be elected by the people for short terms, and that the power to issue injunctions shall be curbed by immediate legislation.

Republicans

The Republicans held their convention in Chicago in June 1908. Although President Roosevelt declined to be a candidate for re-election, his choice for the presidency, Secretary of War William Howard Taft, was assured of nomination before the convention began.

Two hundred and twenty-three of the 980 seats at the convention were contested, but all the challenges were settled before the convention assembled. However, a dispute arose over the vote allocation formula for the next convention. An amendment to the rules committee report proposed that the vote allocation be based on population rather than the electoral vote, as was currently in effect. Essentially, the amendment would have reduced the power of the southern delegations. But a combination of southern delegates and Taft supporters from other states defeated the amendment, 506 to 471. *(Chart, p. 165)*

Seven names were placed in nomination for the presidency, but Taft was a landslide winner on the first ballot, receiving 702 votes. Sen. Philander C. Knox of Pennsylvania was a distant runner-up with 68 votes.

For vice president, the convention selected Rep. James S. Sherman, a conservative New Yorker. Sherman won 816 votes on the first ballot, easily outdistancing former New Jersey Gov. Franklin Murphy, who had 77 votes.

The Wisconsin delegation, led by Sen. Robert M. La Follette, introduced a detailed minority report to the party platform. The Wisconsin proposals were considered in several separate sections. The first section included proposals for the establishment of a permanent tariff commission, the creation of a Department of Labor and the limitation of an eight-hour day for government workers. It was defeated, 952 to 28.

The second section recommended legislation to require the publication of campaign contributions. It was defeated, 880 to 94. Further sections of the minority report proposed the physical valuation of railroad property in order to determine reasonable rates, and the direct election of senators. The railroad reform plank was beaten, 917 to 63, while the senatorial election plank was rejected, 866 to 114. After these votes, the majority report on the platform was adopted by a voice vote.

The platform approved by the delegates applauded the benefits of Republican rule, noting that under the party's guidance, the United States had become the wealthiest nation on earth. The principle of a protective tariff was applauded, as was the gold standard, an expansionist foreign policy and support for America's merchant marine.

Following are excerpts from the Republican platform of 1908:

Party Differences. In history, the difference between Democracy and Republicanism is that the one stood for debased currency, the other for honest currency; the one for free silver, the other for sound money; the one for free trade, the other for protection; the one for the contraction of American influence, the other for its expansion; the one has been forced to abandon every position taken on the great issues before the people, the other has held and vindicated all.

The present tendencies of the two parties are even more marked by inherent differences. The trend of Democracy is toward socialism, while the Republican party stands for a wise and regulated individualism.... Ultimately Democracy would have the nation own the people, while Republicanism would have the people own the nation.

Democrats

The Democratic convention of 1908 was held in July in Denver, Colo.—the first convention held by a major party in a western state. The convention was dominated by the Bryan forces, who regained control of the party after the conservative Alton B. Parker's landslide defeat in 1904.

Bryan's strength was evident on the first roll-call vote, concerning a Pennsylvania credentials dispute. The majority report claimed there were voting irregularities in five Philadelphia districts and urged the seating of Bryan delegates in place of those elected. By a vote of 604½ to 386½, the convention defeated the minority report, which argued for the delegates initially elected in the primary, and then passed the majority report by a voice vote.

Bryan's presidential nomination was never in doubt. He was an easy winner on the first ballot, receiving 888½ votes to 59½ for Judge George Gray of Delaware and 46 for Minnesota Gov. John A. Johnson. *(Chart, p. 164)*

Bryan left the choice of his running mate to the delegates. Although four names were placed in nomination, former Indiana gubernatorial candidate John W. Kern was chosen by acclamation. *The New York Times* sarcastically described the consistency of the Bryan-Kern ticket: "For a man twice defeated for the Presidency was at the head of it, and a man twice defeated for governor of his state was at the tail of it."

The platform adopted by the convention was tailored to Bryan's liking and had as its theme, "Shall the people rule?" The first portion of the document criticized Republican rule, specifically denouncing government overspending, a growing Republican-oriented bureaucracy and an unethical link between big business and the Republican Party characterized by large, unreported campaign contributions.

Meeting three weeks after the Republicans, the Democrats adopted most of the minority planks rejected earlier by the Republicans. Included in the Democratic platform were calls for the physical valuation of railroads, the creation of a Department of Labor, eight-hour work days for government employees, the direct election of senators and a prohibition against corporate campaign contributions and individual contributions over "a reasonable amount." The two parties continued to disagree on support of the American merchant marine, the nature of tariff revision and the direction of foreign policy, particularly regarding the lands acquired after the Spanish-American War.

The Democratic platform restated the party's support of a lower tariff, more extensive anti-trust legislation with more rigid enforcement, a graduated income tax, increased power for the Interstate Commerce Commission to regulate railroads, telephone and telegraph companies, and a recommendation of prompt independence for the Philippines.

The Democrats included a plank abhorring Roosevelt's attempt to create a "dynasty," a direct reference to the outgoing President's hand-picking his war secretary, William Howard Taft, as the next Republican presidential candidate.

Following are excerpts from the Democratic platform of 1908:

Appeal to the Masses. The conscience of the nation is now aroused to free the Government from the grip of those who have made it a business asset of the favor-seeking corporations. It must become again a people's government, and be administered in all its departments according to the Jeffersonian maxim, "equal rights to all; special privileges to none."

"Shall the people rule?" is the overshadowing issue which manifests itself in all the questions now under discussion.

Campaign Contributions. We demand Federal legislation forever terminating the partnership which has existed between corporations of the country and the Republican party under the expressed or implied agreement that in return for the contribution of great sums of money wherewith to purchase elections, they should be allowed to continue substantially unmolested in their efforts to encroach upon the rights of the people....

We pledge the Democratic party to the enactment of a law prohibiting any corporation from contributing to a campaign fund and any individual from contributing an amount above a reasonable maximum, and providing for the publication before election of all such contributions.

Labor. Questions of judicial practice have arisen especially in connection with industrial disputes. We deem that the parties to all judicial proceedings should be treated with rigid impartiality, and that injunctions should not be issued in any cases in which injunctions would not issue if no industrial dispute were involved....

We favor the eight hour day on all Government work.

We pledge the Democratic party to the enactment of a law by Congress, as far as the Federal jurisdiction extends, for a general employer's liability act covering injury to body or loss of life of employes.

We pledge the Democratic party to the enactment of a law creating a Department of Labor, represented separately in the President's Cabinet, in which Department shall be included the subject of mines and mining.

1912 Conventions

Presidential Candidates

Eugene V. Debs
Socialist

William H. Taft
Republican

Woodrow Wilson
Democrat

Theodore Roosevelt
Progressive

Socialists

Eugene V. Debs of Indiana was nominated by the Socialists in 1912 to make his fourth run for the presidency. The convention, which met in Indianapolis in May, chose Emil Seidel of Wisconsin as his running mate.

The platform adopted by the Socialists was similar to the one written four years earlier, with calls for increased worker benefits, public works jobs for the unemployed, public ownership of land and the means of transportation and communication, tax reform, widespread political reform and a social insurance program.

The Socialists also added new proposals, advocating public ownership of the banking and currency system, the introduction of minimum wage scales, the elimination of the profit system in government contracts, an increase in corporation taxes and the direct election of the president and vice president.

Following are excerpts from the Socialist platform of 1912:

Social Insurance. By abolishing official charity and substituting a non-contributory system of old age pensions, a general system of insurance by the State of all its members against unemployment and invalidism and a system of compulsory insurance by employers of their workers, without cost to the latter, against industrial diseases, accidents and death.

Government Contracts. By abolishing the profit system in government work and substituting either the direct hire of labor or the awarding of contracts to cooperative groups of workers.

Minimum Wage. By establishing minimum wage scales.

Tax Reform. The adoption of a graduated income tax, the increase of the rates of the present corporation tax and the extension of inheritance taxes, graduated in proportion to the value of the estate and to nearness of kin—the proceeds of these taxes to be employed in the socialization of industry.

Banking and Currency. The collective ownership and democratic management of the banking and currency system.

Direct Election of President. The election of the President and Vice-President by direct vote of the people.

Republicans

The 1912 Republican convention was one of the most tumultuous ever. It was held in Chicago in June, and served as a fiery culmination to the bitter contest between President Taft and former President Theodore Roosevelt for the party's presidential nomination.

Roosevelt had overwhelmed Taft in the presidential primaries, but Roosevelt's popular strength was more than offset by Taft's control of the national committee and southern delegations. Taft supporters held 37 of 53 seats on the national committee, an edge that the incumbent President's managers used to advantage in settling seating disputes. Two hundred and fifty-four of the 1,078 convention seats were contested before the national committee, and 235 were settled in favor of Taft delegates. Although a number of Roosevelt challenges were made with little justification, the dispensation of the challenges showed Taft's control of the convention organization.

With the conservative Republicans united behind Taft, Roosevelt faced the additional problem of sharing support from the progressive wing of the party with another candidate, Sen. Robert M. La Follette of Wisconsin. La Follette had only 41 delegates; but, angered by Roosevelt's bid to control the progressive forces, refused to withdraw as a candidate.

The first skirmish at the convention was over the choice of a temporary chairman. The Taft forces favored Sen. Elihu Root of New York, while the Roosevelt delegates supported Gov. Francis E. McGovern of Wisconsin. On a prolonged roll call, during which the vote of each delegate was taken individually, Root defeated McGovern, 558 to 501. *(Chart, p. 167)*

With the contest for the temporary chairmanship settled, the battle shifted to credentials. Virtually shut out in the settlement of credentials cases by the national committee, the Roosevelt forces brought 72 delegate challenges to the floor of the convention. Before consideration of the cases, the Roosevelt leaders moved that none of the challenged delegates (favorable to Taft) be allowed to vote on any of the credentials contests. However, a motion to table this proposal carried, 567 to 507, and the challenged delegates were allowed to vote on all cases except their own. Although the Taft forces were clearly in control of the convention, four credentials cases were presented for a vote, and all were decided in favor of the Taft delegates. The rest of the contests were settled by voice votes.

At this point, Roosevelt, who had dramatically come to Chicago to direct his forces, advised his delegates to abstain from voting but to remain in the convention as a silent protest to what he regarded as steam roller tactics. In the convention hall itself, the pro-Roosevelt galleries emphasized the feelings of their leader by rubbing sandpaper and blowing horns to imitate the sounds of a steam roller.

Only two names were placed in nomination for the presidency—Taft and La Follette. Taft was nominated by Warren G. Harding of Ohio, who himself would be president less than a decade later, but at the time was merely a former lieutenant governor. With most of the Roosevelt delegates abstaining, Taft won easily on the first ballot with 556 votes. Roosevelt received 107 votes and La Follette 41, while 348 delegates were present but did not vote.

Vice President James S. Sherman was easily renominated, collecting 596 votes to 21 for the runner-up, Sen. William E. Borah of Idaho. However, 352 delegates were present but refused to vote, and 72 others were absent. In recognition of Sherman's failing health, the convention passed a resolution empowering the national committee to fill any vacancy on the ticket that might occur.

Although the Roosevelt delegates had remained in the convention hall as a silent protest to the renomination of Taft and Sherman, the groundwork for the creation of a Roosevelt-led third party had begun as soon as the credentials contests were settled in favor of Taft. Before the Republican convention even began its presidential balloting, Roosevelt announced that he would accept the nomination of the "honestly elected majority" of the Republican convention or a new progressive party. The next day, June 22, after final adjournment of the Republican convention, many of the Roosevelt delegates assembled in a Chicago auditorium to hear their leader announce his availability as a candidate of an honestly elected progressive convention. Gov. Hiram Johnson of California was named temporary chairman of the new party, and planning was begun to hold a national convention later in the summer.

As in 1908, a progressive minority report to the platform was submitted. However, instead of taking individual votes on the various planks, the convention tabled the whole report by a voice vote. Subsequently, the majority report was accepted by a vote of 666 to 53, with 343 delegates present but not voting.

The platform lauded the accomplishments of the McKinley, Roosevelt and Taft administrations, but contained few major positions different from the Democrats'. The Republican platform included, however, new planks favoring judicial reform and legislation publicizing campaign contributions and outlawing corporate campaign donations.

Following are excerpts from the Republican platform of 1912:

Tariff.   The protective tariff is so woven into the fabric of our industrial and agricultural life that to substitute for it a tariff for revenue only would destroy many industries and throw millions of our people out of employment. The products of the farm and of the mine should receive the same measure of protection as other products of American labor.

Campaign Contributions.   We favor such additional legislation as may be necessary more effectually to prohibit corporations from contributing funds, directly or indirectly, to campaigns for the nomination or election of the President, the Vice-President, Senators, and Representatives in Congress.

We heartily approve the recent Act of Congress requiring the fullest publicity in regard to all campaign contributions, whether made in connection with primaries, conventions, or elections.

Judicial Reform.   That the Courts, both Federal and State, may bear the heavy burden laid upon them to the complete satisfaction of public opinion, we favor legislation to prevent long delays and the tedious and costly appeals which have so often amounted to a denial of justice in civil cases and to a failure to protect the public at large in criminal cases.

Democrats

For the first time since 1872, the Democratic convention was held in Baltimore. The delegates, who assembled in the Maryland city in June, one week after the Republicans began their convention in Chicago, had a number of presidential candidates to choose from, although House Speaker Champ Clark of Missouri and Gov. Woodrow Wilson of New Jersey were the major contenders.

Once again, William Jennings Bryan had a major impact on the proceedings of a Democratic convention. His first appearance came in opposition to the national committee's selection of Judge Alton B. Parker, the party's standard-bearer in 1904, as temporary chairman. Bryan nominated Sen. John W. Kern of Indiana for the post. In declining to be a candidate for temporary chairman, Kern recommended that Parker also withdraw as a candidate. But when Parker refused, Kern nominated Bryan for the post. Parker won on the roll call that followed, 579 to 508, with most of the Wilson delegates voting for Bryan, the Clark delegates splitting their support and delegates for other candidates favoring Parker. *(Chart, p. 166)*

The defeat of Bryan produced an avalanche of telegrams from across the country, with a contemporary estimate of more than 100,000 flooding the delegates in Baltimore. Most of the telegrams were written by progressives and served to weaken the candidacy of the more conservative Clark.

In an attempt to appease Bryan, Parker urged members of the platform committee to select the Nebraskan as their chairman. Bryan, however, refused this overture. Subsequently, the platform committee announced that, by a margin of 41 to 11, the committee had voted to delay presentation of the platform until after selection of the candidates.

The Wilson forces won their first key vote on a question involving the unit rule. The vote specifically concerned the Ohio delegation, where district delegates, elected for Wilson, were bound by the state convention to vote for Ohio Gov. Judson Harmon. By a vote of 565½ to 491-1/3, the convention approved the right of the district delegates to vote for Wilson.

The Wilson forces won another test on a credentials dispute concerning the South Dakota delegation. The credentials committee recommended seating a delegation pledged to Clark; but the convention, by a vote of 639½ to 437, supported the minority report, which called for seating delegates pledged to Wilson.

Bryan reappeared before the presidential balloting and introduced a resolution opposing the nomination of any candidate "who is the representative of or under obligation to J. Pierpont Morgan, Thomas F. Ryan, August Belmont, or any other member of the privilege-hunting and favor-seeking class." Bryan's resolution passed easily, 883 to 202½.

Six names were placed in nomination for the presidency. Clark led on the first ballot with 440½ votes, followed by Wilson with 324, Harmon with 148 and Rep. Oscar W. Underwood of Alabama with 117½. Seven hundred and twenty-six votes were needed to nominate. *(Chart, p. 166)*

For nine ballots, there was little change in the vote totals, but on the 10th roll call, New York shifted its 90 votes from Harmon to Clark. Expecting a quick triumph, the Clark forces unleashed an hour-long demonstration. However, their celebration was premature. While Clark had 556 votes, a majority, his total was well short of the two-thirds majority (730 votes) required by the rules.

The 10th ballot proved to be the high-water mark for Clark. On succeeding roll calls, he slowly began to lose strength. During the 14th ballot, Bryan received permission to address the convention again, this time to explain his vote. "The Great Commoner" announced that he could not support a candidate endorsed by the Tammany-controlled New York delegation and, although bound earlier by state primary results to support Clark, was now switching his vote to Wilson. Most of the Nebraska delegation followed Bryan in voting for Wilson. After the 14th ballot, the vote totals stood: Clark, 553; Wilson, 361; Underwood, 111.

There were long intervals between other major vote switches. On the 20th ballot, Kansas shifted 20 of its votes from Clark to Wilson. On the 28th ballot, after a weekend recess, Indiana's favorite son, Gov. Thomas R. Marshall, withdrew in favor of Wilson. The slow trend in favor of the New Jersey governor finally enabled Wilson to pass Clark on the 30th roll call, 460 to 455; Underwood remained a distant third with 121½ votes. *(Chart, p. 166)*

The convention adjourned for the evening after the 42nd ballot, but the Wilson momentum continued the next day. Illinois switched its 58 votes to Wilson on the 43rd ballot, giving him a simple majority with 602 votes. Clark continued to decline, slipping to 329 votes.

Wilson showed slight gains on the next two ballots, but the big break came on the 46th roll call, when Underwood withdrew. This was followed by the withdrawal of Clark and the other remaining candidates. Wilson received 990 votes on the 46th ballot, followed by Clark with 84.

The failure of Clark to win the nomination, marked the first occasion since 1844 that a candidate achieved a simple majority of the votes, without subsequently winning the necessary two-thirds majority. The 46 roll calls also represented the highest number of presidential ballots taken at any convention, Republican or Democratic, since 1860.

Wilson preferred Underwood as his running mate, but the Alabama representative was not interested in second place on the ticket. On the vice presidential roll call that followed, nine candidates received votes, led by Marshall with 389 votes and North Dakota Gov. John Burke with 304-2/3. Marshall lengthened his lead over Burke on the second ballot, 644½ to 386-1/3. After the roll call was completed, a New Jersey delegate moved that Marshall's nomination be made unanimous, and the motion passed.

The Democratic platform was approved without debate before selection of the vice presidential candidate. The platform restated a number of positions included in earlier party documents. It blamed the high cost of living on the protective tariff and the existence of trusts, and it called for a lower, revenue-only tariff and the passage of stronger anti-trust legislation. The tariff issue was one of the major areas on which there was a marked difference between the parties, as the Republicans continued to support a protective tariff.

As in 1908, planks were included favoring the publicizing of campaign contributions and calling for the prohibition of corporate contributions and a limit on individual contributions.

The Democrats' labor plank was also virtually a restatement of the party's position four years earlier, supporting creation of a Department of Labor, a more limited use of injunctions, the guaranteed right of workers to organize and passage of an employers' compensation law. In contrast to the Democrats' support of employers' liability, the Republicans advocated workmen's compensation legislation.

Unlike the Republicans, federal legislation was urged by the Democrats to regulate the rates of railroad, telegraph, telephone and express companies based on valuation by the Interstate Commerce Commission. A plank was also included in the Democratic platform calling for the ratification of constitutional amendments establishing a graduated income tax and the direct election of senators—issues on which the Republican platform was silent. Imperialism was again denounced, as it had been in every Democratic platform since 1900.

New planks advocated a single-term presidency, the extension of presidential primaries to all states, reform of the judicial system to eliminate delays and cut expenses in court proceedings, and the strengthening of the government's pure food and public health agencies.

Following are excerpts from the Democratic platform of 1912:

Single-term Presidency. We favor a single Presidential term, and to that end urge the adoption of an amendment to the Constitution making the President of the United States ineligible to reelection, and we pledge the candidates of this Convention to this principle.

Presidential Primaries. The movement toward more popular government should be promoted through legislation in each State which will permit the expression of the preference of the electors for national candidates at presidential primaries.

Judicial Reform. We recognize the urgent need of reform in the administration of civil and criminal law in the United States, and we recommend the enactment of such legislation and the promotion of such measures as will rid the present legal system of the delays, expense, and uncertainties incident to the system as now administered.

States' Rights. Believing that the most efficient results under our system of government are to be attained by the full exercise by the States of their reserved sovereign powers, we denounce as usurpation the efforts of our opponents to deprive the States of any of the rights reserved to them, and to enlarge and magnify by indirection the powers of the Federal government.

Progressives

Early in August 1912, the bolting Roosevelt forces assembled in Chicago and nominated their leader to guide a new party, the Progressives. More than 2,000 delegates, representing every state except South Carolina, gathered for the three-day convention. It was a diverse assembly that matched the Populists in crusading idealism, and included, for the first time, women as well as men politicians and social workers as well as businessmen.

While the delegates enthusiastically sang "Onward, Christian Soldiers" and "The Battle Hymn of the Republic" and cheered the appearance of Roosevelt before the convention, there was some dissension caused by the party's racial policy.

During the campaign for the Republican presidential nomination, Taft had the support of party organizations in the South, which included blacks. As a result, Roosevelt directed his appeal strictly to white leaders in the region. Describing southern black delegates as uneducated and purchasable, Roosevelt insisted that only "lily white" delegations from the South be seated at the Progressive convention, but allowed blacks to be included in delegations from other states. Although there was no floor debate on this policy, a number of liberal delegates were dissatisfied with Roosevelt's decision.

Both Roosevelt and his hand-picked choice for vice president, Gov. Hiram W. Johnson of California, were nominated by acclamation. Jane Addams, a Chicago social worker and leader in the women's rights movement, gave evidence of the role of women in the Progressive Party by delivering a seconding speech for Roosevelt.

Like the nominations of the Progressive standard-bearers, the party platform was adopted by acclamation. But the voice vote hid the dissatisfaction felt by midwestern and western Progressives over the anti-trust plank. Most of the Progressives from these regions favored the busting of trusts through enforcement of the Sherman Anti-trust Act. Roosevelt, however, favored government regulation rather than trust-busting.

The platform approved by the convention included the trust-busting position. However, Roosevelt and his close advisers deleted the section in the official report. While there was obvious disagreement in the party on this issue, there were no floor debate and no roll-call vote on the subject.

With the theme, "A Covenant with the People," the platform argued for increased democratization coupled with more people-oriented federal programs. The party favored nationwide presidential primaries, the direct election of senators, the initiative, referendum and recall and women's suffrage. Additionally, the Progressives proposed that state laws ruled unconstitutional be submitted to a vote of the state electorate.

The platform also advocated congressional reforms: the registration of lobbyists; the publicizing of committee hearings except in foreign affairs, and the recording of committee votes.

Like the Democrats, the Progressives favored creation of a Department of Labor and a more limited use of labor injunctions, but additionally the new party called for a prohibition of child labor and convict contract labor.

The Progressives went beyond both major parties in proposing the union of government health agencies into a single national health service and the creation of a social insurance system that would assist both the elderly and workers who were ill or unemployed.

To help support their proposed federal programs, the Progressives recommended passage of the income tax amendment and establishment of a graduated inheritance tax.

Having adopted their platform and selected their candidates, the delegates to the Progressive convention adjourned by singing the "Doxology."

Following are excerpts from the Progressive platform of 1912:

Electoral Reform. In particular, the party declares for direct primaries for the nomination of State and National officers, for nation-wide preferential primaries for candidates for the presidency; for the direct election of United States Senators by the people; and we urge on the States the policy of the short ballot, with responsibility to the people secured by the initiative, referendum and recall.

Women's Suffrage. The Progressive party, believing that no people can justly claim to be a true democracy which denies political rights on account of sex, pledges itself to the task of securing equal suffrage to men and women alike.

Judicial Reform. That when an Act, passed under the police power of the State, is held unconstitutional under the State Constitution, by the courts, the people, after an ample interval for deliberation, shall have an opportunity to vote on the question whether they desire the Act to become law, notwithstanding such decision.

Campaign Contributions. We pledge our party to legislation that will compel strict limitation of all campaign contributions and expenditures, and detailed publicity of both before as well as after primaries and elections.

Congressional Reform. We pledge our party to legislation compelling the registration of lobbyists; publicity of committee hearings except on foreign affairs, and recording of all votes in committee....

National Health Service. We favor the union of all the existing agencies of the Federal Government dealing with the public health into a single national health service without discrimination against or for any one set of therapeutic methods, school of medicine, or school of healing with such additional powers as may be necessary to enable it to perform efficiently such duties in the protection of the public from preventable diseases as may be properly undertaken by the Federal authorities, including the executing of existing laws regarding pure food, quarantine and cognate subjects, the promotion of vital statistics and the extension of the registration area of such statistics, and cooperation with the health activities of the various States and cities of the Nation.

Social Insurance. The protection of home life against the hazards of sickness, irregular employment and old age through the adoption of a system of social insurance adapted to American use...

Anti-trust Action. We therefore demand a strong National regulation of inter-State corporations...we urge the establishment of a strong Federal administrative commission of high standing, which shall maintain permanent active supervision over industrial corporations engaged in inter-State commerce, or such of them as are of public importance, doing for them what the Government now does for the National banks, and what is now done for the railroads by the Inter-State Commerce Commission.

Income and Inheritance Taxes. We believe in a graduated inheritance tax as a National means of equalizing the obligations of holders of property to Government, and we hereby pledge our party to enact such a Federal law as will tax large inheritances, returning to the States an equitable percentage of all amounts collected.

We favor the ratification of the pending amendment to the Constitution giving the Government power to levy an income tax.

Tariff. We demand tariff revision because the present tariff is unjust to the people of the United States. Fair dealing toward the people requires an immediate downward revision of those schedules wherein duties are shown to be unjust or excessive....

The Democratic party is committed to the destruction of the protective system through a tariff for revenue only—a policy which would inevitably produce widespread industrial and commercial disaster.

Republicans and Democrats. Political parties exist to secure responsible government and to execute the will of the people.

From these great tasks both of the old parties have turned aside. Instead of instruments to promote the general welfare, they have become the tools of corrupt interests which use them impartially to serve their selfish purposes. Behind the ostensible government sits enthroned an invisible government owing no allegiance and acknowledging no responsibility to the people.

To destroy this invisible government, to dissolve the unholy alliance between corrupt business and corrupt politics is the first task of the statesmanship of the day.

States' Rights. The extreme insistence on States' rights by the Democratic party in the Baltimore platform demonstrates anew its inability to understand the world into which it has survived or to administer the affairs of a union of States which have in all essential respects become one people.

1916 Conventions

Presidential Candidates

Charles E. Hughes
Republican

Woodrow Wilson
Democrat

Republicans

The Republicans and Progressives both held their conventions in Chicago in early June 1916. The leadership of both parties was ready to negotiate to heal the split that had divided the Republican Party in 1912.

Before the convention began, the Republican National Committee already had effected reform in the vote allocation formula. To meet the objection raised in 1912 that the South was over-represented, the national committee adopted a new method of vote allocation that considered a state's Republican voting strength as well as its electoral vote. Under the new formula, the southern states lost 78 delegate seats, or more than a third of their 1912 total.

But while the Republicans were willing to make some internal reforms, most party leaders were adamantly opposed to nominating the hero of the Progressives, Theodore Roosevelt. Before the presidential balloting began, the Republican convention approved by voice vote the selection of a five-man committee to meet jointly with representatives of the Progressive convention, with the hope of finding a course of action that would unify the two parties.

However, the Republican representatives reported back that while the Progressives desired unity with the Republicans, they firmly favored the nomination of Roosevelt. The Republican convention chairman, Sen. Warren G. Harding of Ohio, instructed the conferees to continue negotiations, but also allowed the presidential balloting to begin.

Charles Evans Hughes, a Supreme Court justice and former governor of New York, was the front-runner for the Republican nomination. Hughes did not actively seek the nomination and remained on the Supreme Court during the pre-convention period. But he was viewed by many party leaders as an ideal compromise candidate, because of his progressive credentials and lack of involvement in the divisive 1912 campaign.

However, some conservative party leaders felt Hughes was too progressive and sought other candidates. Seventeen men received votes on the first ballot, led by Hughes with 253½. Next were Sen. John W. Weeks of Massachusetts with 105 votes and former Sen. Elihu Root of New York with 103. Five of the other vote recipients had at least 65 votes each. The justice widened his lead on the second ballot, receiving 328½ votes to 98½ for Root. After the second roll call, the convention voted 694½ to 286½ to recess for the evening. Most of the votes for adjournment came from delegates outside the Hughes column. *(Chart, p. 169)*

While the Republican convention was in recess, the joint committee of Republicans and Progressives continued to negotiate. The Republican members proposed Hughes as a compromise candidate, but in a message from his home in Oyster Bay, N.Y., Roosevelt stunned both parties by suggesting the name of Henry Cabot Lodge, a conservative senator from Massachusetts.

The Progressive delegates reacted defiantly to this recommendation by nominating Roosevelt by acclamation and selecting John M. Parker of Louisiana as his running mate. Roosevelt, however, immediately scotched the enthusiasm of the Progressive delegates by conditionally declining the nomination. Roosevelt informed the convention that he would support Hughes if the latter's positions on major issues were acceptable.

When the Republican convention reconvened the next day, the opposition to Hughes had evaporated. The New Yorker received 949½ of the 987 convention votes on the third ballot, and his nomination was subsequently declared unanimous.

Charles W. Fairbanks of Indiana, vice president under Roosevelt, was the convention's choice to fill out the Republican ticket. Fairbanks won on the first ballot by 863 votes to 108 for former Nebraska Sen. Elmer E. Burkett.

The Wisconsin delegation again presented its own minority platform report, which included planks that denounced "dollar diplomacy" and called for women's suffrage, a referendum before any declaration of war and constitutional amendments to establish the initiative, referendum and recall. The minority report was defeated and the majority report was approved by voice votes.

The adopted platform harshly criticized the policies of the Wilson administration. In foreign policy, the Republicans denounced the Wilson government for "shifty expedients" and "phrase making" and promised "strict and honest neutrality." The platform condemned the administration for its intervention in Mexico and non-involvement in the Philippines. The Republicans also called for a stronger national defense.

The two parties continued to disagree on the tariff issue, with the Republicans criticizing the lower (Democratic-passed) Underwood tariff and arguing for a higher, protective tariff. The Republican platform lauded the party's efforts in passing anti-trust and transportation rate regulation, but criticized the Democrats for harassing business.

Following are excerpts from the Republican platform of 1916:

Foreign Policy. We desire peace, the peace of justice and right, and believe in maintaining a strict and honest neutrality between the belligerents in the great war in Europe. We must perform all our duties and insist upon all our rights as neutrals without fear and without favor. We believe that peace and neutrality, as well as the dignity and influence of the United States, cannot be preserved by shifty expedients, by phrase making, by performances in language, or by attitudes ever changing in an effort to secure votes or voters.

National Defense. We must have a Navy so strong and so well proportioned and equipped, so thoroughly ready and prepared, that no enemy can gain command of the sea and effect a landing in force on either our Western or our Eastern coast. To secure these results we must have a coherent continuous policy of national defence, which even in these perilous days the Democratic party has utterly failed to develop, but which we promise to give to the country.

Merchant Marine. We are utterly opposed to the Government ownership of vessels as proposed by the Democratic party, because Government-owned ships, while effectively preventing the development of the American Merchant Marine by private capital, will be entirely unable to provide for the vast volume of American freights and will leave us more helpless than ever in the hard grip of foreign syndicates.

Tariff. The Republican party stands now, as always, in the fullest sense for the policy of tariff protection to American industries and American labor.

Business. The Republican party firmly believes that all who violate the laws in regulation of business, should be individually punished. But prosecution is very different from persecution, and business success, no matter how honestly attained, is apparently regarded by the Democratic party as in itself a crime. Such doctrines and beliefs choke enterprise and stifle prosperity. The Republican party believes in encouraging American business as it believes in and will seek to advance all American interests.

Women's Suffrage. The Republican party, reaffirming its faith in government of the people, by the people, for the people, as a measure of justice to one-half the adult people of this country, favors the extension of the suffrage to women, but recognizes the right of each state to settle this question for itself.

Democrats

The Democratic convention of 1916 was held in St. Louis in mid-June. The delegates were nearly unanimous in their support for President Wilson, who was renominated by the vote of 1,092 to 1—the lone dissenting vote coming from an Illinois delegate who disapproved of a motion to nominate Wilson by acclamation. With Wilson's approval, Vice President Marshall was renominated by acclamation.

For the first time in more than two decades, William Jennings Bryan was not a major convention force. Bryan was defeated in his bid to be a delegate-at-large from Nebraska and attended the convention as a reporter. He was invited to address the delegates and echoed the theme stressed by other speakers, that Wilson would keep the nation out of war.

Wilson was the recognized leader of the Democratic Party, but the pacifistic theme, emphasized by Bryan and other convention orators, struck a responsive chord among the delegates that was mildly alarming to Wilson and his managers. They initially had planned to accent the theme of Americanism and national unity.

The wording of the national unity plank was a matter of debate within the platform committee. The Democratic senators from Missouri warned that Wilson's strongly worded plank might offend German-American citizens. Nonetheless, the Wilson plank was retained and placed prominently near the beginning of the platform.

The only section of the platform brought to a floor vote was the plank on women's suffrage. The majority plank favored extending the vote to women, while a minority plank advocated leaving the matter to the individual states. The minority plank was defeated, 888½ to 181½. The rest of the platform was then adopted by a voice vote. The Democratic position on women's suffrage contrasted with that of the Republicans who proposed leaving the matter up to the individual states. *(Chart, p. 168)*

The platform's inclusion of national unity and military preparedness planks was a contrast with earlier Democratic platforms around the turn of the century, which had consistently denounced imperialism and denied the need for a stronger military. Even though spurred by the war in Europe, the new planks were a notable change.

The rest of the platform focused on the progressive reforms of the Wilson administration, particularly in tariff, banking, labor and agriculture. Wilson himself was lauded as "the greatest American of his generation."

Noticeably absent from the platform were two planks in the party's document four years earlier: a call for a single-term presidency and a defense of states' rights.

Following are excerpts from the Democratic platform of 1916:

National Unity. In this day of test, America must show itself not a nation of partisans but a nation of patriots. There is gathered here in America the best of the blood, the industry and the genius of the whole world, the elements of a great race and a magnificent society to be welded into a mighty and splendid Nation. Whoever, actuated by the purpose to promote the interest of a foreign power, in disregard of our own country's welfare or to injure this government in its foreign relations or cripple or destroy its industries at home, and whoever by arousing prejudices of a racial, religious or other nature creates discord and strife among our people so as to obstruct the wholesome process of unification, is faithless to the trust which the privileges of citizenship respose in him and is disloyal to his country.

Military Preparedness. We therefore favor the maintenance of an army fully adequate to the requirements of order, of safety, and of the protection of the nation's rights, the fullest development of modern methods of seacoast defence and the maintenance of an adequate reserve of citizens trained to arms and prepared to safeguard the people and territory of the United States against any danger of hostile action which may unexpectedly arise; and a fixed policy for the continuous development of a navy, worthy to support the great naval traditions of the United States and fully equal to the international tasks which this Nation hopes and expects to take a part in performing.

Tariff. We reaffirm our belief in the doctrine of a tariff for the purpose of providing sufficient revenue for the operation of the government economically administered, and unreservedly endorse the Underwood tariff law as truly exemplifying that doctrine.

Women's Suffrage. We recommend the extension of the franchise to the women of the country by the States upon the same terms as to men.

Socialists

The Socialists did not hold a convention in 1916, but did nominate candidates and adopt a platform. The candidates were chosen in unique mail referendum. With Debs' refusal to run, the presidential nomination went to Allan L. Benson of New York. George R. Kirkpatrick of New Jersey was selected as his running mate.

More than half of the Socialist platform was devoted to criticizing the United States' preparations for war. The Socialists opposed the war in Europe and viewed the American drive for preparedness as an effort by ruling capitalists to protect the system and their profits.

The Socialist platform specifically advocated no increase in military appropriations, a national referendum on any declaration of war, the shifting of the power to make foreign policy from the president to Congress, the abandonment of the Monroe Doctrine and immediate independence for the Philippines.

The rest of the platform was divided into sections entitled political demands, industrial demands and collective ownership. The proposals in these sections paralleled earlier Socialist platforms, although there was a new plank, advocating lending by the federal government to local governments, which was an early expression of the concept of revenue-sharing.

Following are excerpts from the Socialist platform of 1916:

Militarism and Preparedness. The working class must recognize militarism as the greatest menace to all efforts toward industrial freedom, and regardless of political or industrial affiliations must present a united front in the fight against preparedness and militarism.... The war in Europe, which diminished and is still diminishing the remote possibility of European attack upon the United States, was nevertheless seized upon by capitalists and by unscrupulous politicians as a means of spreading fear throughout the country, to the end that, by false pretenses, great military establishments might be obtained. We denounce such "preparedness" as both false in principle, unnecessary in character and dangerous in its plain tendencies toward militarism.

Foreign Policy. We, therefore, demand that the power to fix foreign policies and conduct diplomatic negotiations shall be lodged in congress and shall be exercised publicly, the people reserving the right to order congress, at any time, to change its foreign policy.

Referendum on War. That no war shall be declared or waged by the United States without a referendum vote of the entire people, except for the purpose of repelling invasion.

Federal Loans to Local Governments. The government shall lend money on bonds to countries and municipalities at a nominal rate of interest for the purpose of taking over or establishing public utilities and for building or maintaining public roads or highways and public schools.

1920 Conventions

Presidential Candidates

Eugene V. Debs
Socialist

Warren G. Harding
Republican

James M. Cox
Democrat

Socialists

The Socialists held their convention in New York in May and for the fifth time nominated Eugene V. Debs of Indiana for president. It was one of the strangest candidacies in American political history, because at the time, Debs was serving a 10-year prison term in the Atlanta federal penitentiary for his outspoken opposition to the American war effort. Seymour Stedman of Ohio was chosen as his running mate.

The Socialist platform was again a distinctive document, going far beyond the platforms of the two major parties in the radical nature of the reforms proposed. The platform characterized the war policies and peace proposals of the Wilson administration as "despotism, reaction and oppression unsurpassed in the annals of the republic." It called for the replacement of the "mischievous" League of Nations with an international parliament. It favored recognition of both the newly established Irish Republic and the Soviet Union.

The Socialists continued to advocate extensive tax reform and included new calls for a tax on unused land and a progressive property tax on wartime profits that would help pay off government debts. The platform warned that the continuing militaristic mood of both major parties could lead to another war.

The Socialists continued to recommend extensive labor benefits, but for the first time they specifically mentioned migratory workers as needing government assistance.

Following are excerpts from the Socialist platform of 1920:

> **League of Nations.** The Government of the United States should initiate a movement to dissolve the mischievous organization called the "League of Nations" and to create an international parliament, composed of democratically elected representatives of all nations of the world based upon the recognition of their equal rights, the principles of self determination, the right to national existence of colonies and other dependencies, freedom of international trade and trade routes by land and sea, and universal disarmament, and be charged with revising the Treaty of Peace on the principles of justice and conciliation.

> **Labor.** Congress should enact effective laws to abolish child labor, to fix minimum wages, based on an ascertained cost of a decent standard of life, to protect migratory and unemployed workers from oppression, to abolish detective and strike-breaking agencies and to establish a shorter work-day in keeping with increased industrial productivity.

> **Blacks.** Congress should enforce the provisions of the Thirteenth, Fourteenth and Fifteenth Amendments with reference to the Negroes, and effective federal legislation should be enacted to secure to the Negroes full civil, political, industrial and educational rights.

Republicans

In mid-June, Republicans met for the fifth straight time in Chicago for their quadrennial convention. For the first time, women were on the floor in large numbers as delegates. With the constitutional amendment granting women the vote on the verge of passage, Republicans, especially in the Midwest and West, were quick to include women in their delegations.

The Republicans, like the Democrats two weeks later, entered their convention with no clear front-runner for the presidential nomination. Three candidates were at the top of the list, but two of them, Maj. Gen. Leonard Wood of New Hampshire and Sen. Hiram Johnson of California, split the party's progressive wing, while the third entry, Gov. Frank Lowden of Illinois, ran poorly in the presidential primaries and was accused of campaign spending irregularities.

Eleven names were placed in nomination for the presidency, but none came close during the first day of balloting to the 493 votes needed to nominate. Wood led on the initial roll call with 287½ votes, trailed by Lowden with 211½ and Johnson with 133½. Ohio Sen. Warren G. Harding, who had not campaigned for the nomination as extensively as the three pacesetters, placed sixth with 65½ votes. Wood, Lowden and Johnson all gained strength during the first three ballots. *(Chart, p. 171)*

After the third roll call, the Johnson delegates moved for adjournment, but were defeated, 701½ to 275½. On the fourth ballot, Wood's vote total rose to 314½, well short of a majority but the highest mark attained yet by any candidate. At this point, Harding stood in fifth place with 61½ votes. Although a motion to adjourn had been soundly defeated after the previous roll call, the permanent chairman, Sen. Henry Cabot Lodge of Massachusetts, entertained a new motion to adjourn and declared it passed on a closely divided voice vote.

The adjournment gave Republican leaders a chance to confer and discuss the various presidential possibilities. Much is made in history books about Harding's selection that night in the legendary "smoke-filled room," when Harding was allegedly interviewed at 2 o'clock by Republican leaders and, answering their questions satisfactorily, was chosen as the nominee. The authenticity of the meeting has been questioned, as has the power of the politicians who made the designation. But nonetheless, it was clear that Harding was a viable compromise choice who was both acceptable to the conservative party leadership and could be nominated by the delegates.

Harding's vote total rose slowly in the next day's balloting, until the ninth ballot, when a large shift, primarily of Lowden delegates, boosted the Ohio senator's vote from 133 to 374½. This was the highest total for any candidate to this point and started a bandwagon that produced Harding's nomination on the 10th ballot. After the various switches, the final vote stood: Harding, 692-1/5; Wood, 156, and Johnson, 80-4/5, with the rest of the vote scattered.

Immediately after Harding's nomination, the vice presidential balloting began. After the nomination of Wisconsin Sen. Irvine L. Lenroot, a delegate from Oregon rose and, standing on his chair, nominated Massachusetts Gov. Calvin Coolidge. An enthusiastic demonstration followed, showing the wide delegate support for Coolidge. The governor, who had risen to national prominence less than a year earlier with his handling of a Boston police strike, was a runaway winner on the one vice presidential ballot. Coolidge received 674½ votes to Lenroot's 146½.

The Wisconsin delegation again presented a detailed minority report to the platform. It included planks that opposed entry into the League of Nations under the terms of the proposed treaty, objected to compulsory military service, called for the quick conclusion of peace negotiations and normalization of foreign relations and recommended a bonus for servicemen to match the wages of wartime civilian workers.

In domestic reforms, the Wisconsin report advocated the election of federal judges and the passage of a constitutional amendment that would establish the initiative, referendum and recall. The entire minority report was rejected by a voice vote, and the platform as written was adopted in a similar manner.

The platform began by denouncing the Wilson administration for being completely unprepared for both war and peace. It went on to criticize Wilson for establishing an "executive autocracy" by arrogating to himself power that belonged to other branches of government.

The platform included a League of Nations plank that intentionally straddled the controversial issue, applauding the Republican-controlled Senate for defeating Wilson's League but pledging the party "to such agreements with the other nations of the world as shall meet the full duty of America to civilization and humanity...."

To help cut federal spending, the Republicans favored consolidating some departments and bureaus and establishing an executive budget.

Both parties continued to differ on the tariff, with the Democrats reiterating their belief in a revenue tariff and the Republicans restating their support of a protective tariff.

Following are excerpts from the Republican platform of 1920:

> **League of Nations.** The Republican party stands for agreement among the nations to preserve the peace of the world....
> The covenant signed by the President at Paris failed signally...and contains stipulations, not only intolerable for an independent people, but certain to produce the injustice, hostility and controversy among nations which it proposed to prevent.
> ...we pledge the coming Republican administration to such agreements with the other nations of the world as shall meet the full duty of America to civilization and humanity, in accordance with American ideals, and without surrendering the right of the American people to exercise its judgment and its power in favor of justice and peace.

Democrats

San Francisco was the host city for the 1920 Democratic convention, marking the first time a convention of one of the major parties was held west of the Rockies. Not only was the site a new one, but when the convention opened in late June, for the first time in a generation the Democratic Party had no recognized leader such as Cleveland, Bryan or Wilson.

President Wilson had some hope of a third nomination, but his failing health and skidding popularity made this an unrealistic prospect. But Wilson's refusal to endorse another candidate prevented the emergence of any presidential hopeful as a front-runner for the nomination. In all, 24 candidates received votes on the first presidential roll call, but none approached the 729 votes needed for nomination. William Gibbs McAdoo, Wilson's son-in-law and former treasury secretary, led with 266 votes, in spite of having withdrawn from the race several days before the convention began. Attorney General A. Mitchell Palmer, famed for his efforts during the "Red Scare," followed closely with 254 votes. Two governors, Ohio's James M. Cox and New York's Alfred E. Smith, trailed with 134 and 109 votes, respectively. *(Chart, p. 170)*

Another ballot was taken before evening adjournment, with the top four candidates retaining the same order and nearly the same vote.

During the next day's balloting, Cox gained steadily and passed both McAdoo and Palmer. When the majority of McAdoo and Palmer delegates successfully carried a motion to recess after the 16th ballot, Cox held the lead with 454½ votes. McAdoo was next with 337 votes and Palmer trailed with 164½.

Six more ballots were taken during the evening session, and although Cox's lead narrowed, he still led McAdoo after the 22nd ballot, 430 to 372½. In the next day's balloting, McAdoo gradually gained ground until he finally passed Cox on the 30th ballot, 403½ to 400½. After completion of the roll call, the motion was made to eliminate the lowest candidate on each succeeding ballot until a nominee had been selected. This drastic proposal to shorten the convention was defeated, 812½ to 264.

Balloting continued without interruption through the 36th roll call. McAdoo still led with 399 votes, but his margin over Cox was reduced to 22 votes, and Palmer with 241 votes achieved his highest total since the 11th ballot.

A candidate was finally nominated during the evening session of the convention's third day of presidential balloting. The Palmer revival fizzled quickly, with most of his delegates going to either McAdoo or Cox. The Ohio governor regained the lead on the 39th ballot, when the majority of the Indiana delegation shifted from McAdoo to Cox. After this roll call, Cox led McAdoo, 468½ to 440, Palmer having slipped to 74. Cox continued to gain, and a last-ditch effort by McAdoo delegates to force an adjournment failed, 637 to 406. Cox's vote total reached 699½ votes on the 44th ballot, and with victory imminent, a motion was adopted to declare the Ohio governor the unanimous nominee of the convention. *(Chart, p. 170)*

Cox's choice for the vice presidential nomination was Franklin Delano Roosevelt of New York, the 38-year-old assistant secretary of the Navy. Roosevelt was nominated by acclamation.

William Jennings Bryan attended the convention and proposed five planks as amendments to the platform. Only his plank endorsing prohibition, however, was submitted for a roll-call vote, and it was soundly beaten, 929½ to 155½. A counterproposal by a New York delegate, recognizing the legality of the prohibition amendment to the Constitution but favoring the manufacture of beer and light wines for home use, was also defeated, 724½ to 356. The platform finally adopted did not discuss the prohibition question.

Bryan's four other planks covered a wide range of issues. He favored establishing a national newspaper, reducing from two-thirds to a simple majority the vote needed to approve treaties in the Senate, expressed opposition to peacetime universal compulsory military training and recommended that interstate companies reveal the difference between the cost and selling price of their products. All four planks were defeated by voice votes.

One other amendment, calling for the recognition of Irish independence, came to the floor for a roll-call vote. It was beaten, 674 to 402½. Included instead was a milder plank sympathizing with the Irish struggle for in-dependence. Subsequently, the delegates approved by voice vote the entire platform as it was first written.

Although the delegates were unwilling to renominate Wilson, the platform was largely devoted to praise of his leadership and legislation passed during his presidency. The platform reflected Wilson's thinking by placing the League of Nations plank prominently at the beginning and supporting the President's call for American membership. The plank did allow for reservations to the treaty, but none that would prevent American participation in the League.

Following are excerpts from the Democratic platform of 1920:

League of Nations. The Democratic Party favors the League of Nations as the surest, if not the only, practicable means of maintaining the permanent peace of the world and terminating the insufferable burden of great military and naval establishments....

We commend the President for his courage and his high conception of good faith in steadfastly standing for the covenant agreed to by all the associated and allied nations at war with Germany, and we condemn the Republican Senate for its refusal to ratify the treaty merely because it was the product of Democratic statesmanship, thus interposing partisan envy and personal hatred in the way of the peace and renewed prosperity of the world....

We advocate the immediate ratification of the treaty without reservations which would impair its essential integrity, but do not oppose the acceptance of any reservations making clearer or more specific the obligations of the United States to the league associates.

Irish Independence. The great principle of national self-determination has received constant reiteration as one of the chief objectives for which this country entered the war and victory established this principle.

Within the limitations of international comity and usage, this Convention repeats the several previous expressions of the sympathy of the Democratic Party of the United States for the aspirations of Ireland for self-government.

1924 Conventions

Presidential Candidates

Calvin Coolidge
Republican

John W. Davis
Democrat

Robert M. La Follette
Progressive

Republicans

The Republicans gathered for their convention in Cleveland, Ohio, in June. For the first time, a convention was broadcast by radio. Also for the first time, Republican Party rules were changed to elect women to the national committee, with one man and one woman to be chosen from each state and territory.

Unlike the Democratic marathon which began two weeks later in New York, there was surface harmony at the Republican convention. President Coolidge's success in the spring primaries, and his ability to defuse the corruption issue, eliminated any major opposition. Coolidge was easily nominated on the first ballot, receiving 1,065 votes. Wisconsin Sen. Robert M. La Follette was a distant second with 34 votes, while California Sen. Hiram W. Johnson collected the remaining 10. *(Chart, p. 174)*

The vice presidential nomination was a confused matter. Eight candidates were nominated, and on the first ballot, former Illinois Gov. Frank O. Lowden led with 222 votes. Although Lowden publicly stated that he would not accept the nomination, he received a majority of the vote on the second roll call. A recess was taken to see if Lowden had changed his mind, but when it was certain that he had not, the delegates resumed balloting.

On the third roll call, former budget bureau director Charles G. Dawes received 682½ votes to win the nomination. Secretary of Commerce Herbert Hoover was second with 234½ votes.

As was its custom throughout the early 20th century, the Wisconsin delegation proposed a detailed minority report to the platform. Proposals included government ownership of railroads and water power, an increased excess profits tax and reduced taxes on individuals with low incomes. The Wisconsin platform was rejected without a roll-call vote.

The platform that was adopted lauded the economy in government shown by the Republican administration and promised a reduction in taxes.

The Democrats and Republicans continued to differ on the tariff issue, with the Republicans again defending the protective tariff. The Ku Klux Klan was not mentioned in the Republican platform, nor was it discussed on the floor. The controversial organization was the subject of a divisive floor fight at the Democratic convention.

The Republican platform criticized the corruption found to exist in the Harding administration, but also denounced efforts "to besmirch the names of the innocent and undermine the confidence of the people in the government under which they live."

In the area of foreign policy, the Republicans opposed membership in the League, although favoring participation in the World Court. While applauding the return of peace and reflecting the nation's increasing mood of isolationism, the Republicans opposed cutbacks in the Army and Navy.

Following are excerpts from the Republican platform of 1924:

Corruption. We demand the speedy, fearless and impartial prosecution of all wrong doers, without regard for political affiliations; but we declare no greater wrong can be committed against the people than the attempt to destroy their trust in the great body of their public servants. Admitting the deep humiliation which all good citizens share that our public life should have harbored some dishonest men, we assert that these undesirables do not represent the standard of our national integrity.

Taxes. We pledge ourselves to the progressive reduction of taxes of all the people as rapidly as may be done with due regard for the essential expenditures for the government administered with rigid economy and to place our tax system on a sound peace time basis.

League of Nations. This government has definitely refused membership in the league of nations or to assume any obligations under the covenant of the league. On this we stand.

Military. There must be no further weakening of our regular army and we advocate appropriations sufficient to provide for the training of all members of the national guard, the citizens' military training camps, the reserve officers' training camps and the reserves who may offer themselves for service. We pledge ourselves for service. We pledge ourselves to round out and maintain the navy to the full strength provided the United States by the letter and spirit of the limitation of armament conference.

War Profiteering. ...should the United States ever again be called upon to defend itself by arms the president be empowered to draft such material resources and such services as may be required, and to stabilize the prices of services and essential commodities, whether used in actual warfare or private activities.

Republican Philosophy. The prosperity of the American nation rests on the vigor of private initiative which has bred a spirit of independence and self-reliance. The republican party stands now, as always, against all attempts to put the government into business.

American industry should not be compelled to struggle against government competition. The right of the government to regulate, supervise and control public utilities and public interests, we believe, should be strengthened, but we are firmly opposed to the nationalization or government ownership of public utilities.

Democrats

The 1924 Democratic convention in New York's old Madison Square Garden was the longest in American history. From the opening gavel on June 24 through final adjournment on July 10, the convention spanned 17 days. The reason for the convention's unprecedented length was an almost unbreakable deadlock between the party's rural and urban factions that extended the presidential balloting for a record 103 roll calls. *(Chart, pp. 172-173)*

Gov. Alfred E. Smith of New York was the candidate of the urban delegates, while William Gibbs McAdoo of California led the rural forces. But beyond any ideological differences between the two candidates was a bitter struggle between the urban and rural wings for control of the party. Smith, a Roman Catholic of Irish ancestry and an opponent of prohibition and the Ku Klux Klan, embodied characteristics loathed by the rural leaders. McAdoo, a Protestant, a supporter of prohibition and tolerant of the Ku Klux Klan, was equally unacceptable to the urban forces. Without a strong leader to unite the two factions, and with the two-thirds rule in effect, a long deadlock was inevitable.

Besides Smith and McAdoo, 14 other candidates were nominated. The most memorable speech was delivered by Franklin Delano Roosevelt, who, in nominating Smith, referred to him as "the happy warrior," a description that remained with Smith the rest of his career.

Presidential balloting commenced on Monday, June 30. McAdoo led on the first roll call with 431½ votes, followed by Smith with 241, with 733 votes needed for nomination. Through the week, 77 ballots were taken, but none of the candidates approached the required two-thirds majority. At the end of the week, after the 77th ballot, McAdoo led with 513 votes; Smith had 367; John W. Davis of West Virginia, the eventual nominee, was a distant third with 76½, an improvement of 45½ votes over his first-ballot total. McAdoo had reached the highest total for any candidate, 530 votes, on the 69th ballot.

William Jennings Bryan, making his last appearance at a Democratic convention, as a delegate from Florida, was given permission to explain his opposition to Smith during the 38th ballot. But Bryan's final convention oration was lost in a chorus of boos from the urban forces who found his rural philosophy increasingly objectionable.

After the 66th ballot, the first of a series of proposals was introduced to break the deadlock. It was recommended that the convention meet in executive session and listen to each of the candidates. This received majority approval, 551 to 538, but a two-thirds majority was needed to change the rules. A second proposal, to invite Smith alone to address the convention, also fell short of the necessary two-thirds, although achieving a majority, 604½ to 473.

After the 73rd ballot, it was recommended that the lowest vote-getter be dropped after each roll call until only five candidates remained, a proposal to be in effect for one day only. This recommendation was defeated, 589½ to 496. A more drastic motion, to adjourn after the 75th ballot and reconvene two weeks later in Kansas City, was decisively beaten, 1,007.3 to 82.7. The delegates did agree, however, to have representatives of each candidate hold a conference over the weekend.

Balloting resumed on Monday, July 7, with the 78th roll call. After the 82nd ballot, a resolution was passed, 985 to 105, releasing all delegates from their commitments.

McAdoo's vote dropped sharply as the balloting progressed, and for the first time, on the 86th roll call, was passed by Smith's, 360 to 353½. A boom for Indiana Sen. Samuel M. Ralston, which had begun on the 84th ballot, petered out on the 93rd roll call, when Ralston quit the race. At the time of his withdrawal, Ralston was in third place with 196¼ votes.

After the ballot, Roosevelt announced that Smith was willing to withdraw from the race if McAdoo would also. McAdoo rejected this suggestion. McAdoo did regain the lead from Smith on the 94th ballot, 395 to 364½, but with victory beyond reach, released his delegates after the 99th ballot.

Davis was the principal beneficiary of the McAdoo withdrawal, moving into second place on the 100th ballot and gaining the lead on the next roll call with 316 votes. Most of Smith's strength moved to Alabama's anti-Klan, anti-prohibition senator, Oscar W. Underwood, who took second place on the 101st ballot with 229½ votes. Underwood, however, could not keep pace with Davis, who stretched his lead on the next two ballots. After the 103rd ballot, Davis' total stood at 575½ votes to 250½ for the Alabama senator.

Before the next ballot could begin, Iowa switched its vote to Davis, causing other shifts that brought Davis the nomination. After the changes had been recorded, Davis had 844 votes to 102½ for Underwood. The West Virginian's nomination was then declared unanimous.

The core of Davis' vote had come from the rural delegates; urban delegates gave him the necessary votes to win the nomination. After nine days of balloting, the Democrats had a presidential candidate.

The party leadership preferred Gov. Charles W. Bryan of Nebraska, William Jennings Bryan's younger brother, as Davis' running mate. Bryan trailed Tennessee labor leader George L. Berry on the first ballot, 263½ to 238, but vote switches begun by Illinois after the roll call brought Bryan the nomination. After the changes Bryan had 740 votes, barely beyond the two-thirds majority necessary.

The discord evident in the presidential and vice presidential balloting had its roots in the spirited platform battle that preceded the nominations. The first subject of debate was the League of Nations, with the majority report recommending that American entry be determined by a national referendum. The minority plank argued that this was an unwieldy solution that would put the issue aside. Instead, the minority report favored entry into the League of Nations and World Court without reservation. The minority position was rejected, 742½ to 353½. Nonetheless, the Democratic position differed markedly from the Republicans, who flatly opposed membership in the League, although favoring participation in the World Court.

The League of Nations debate proved to be merely a warmup for the controversial religious liberties plank. The focus of debate was the Ku Klux Klan, which was opposed by name in the minority report but was not mentioned in the majority report. In one of the closest votes in convention history, the minority plank was defeated, 543-3/20 to 542-7/20. The vote closely followed factional lines, with most rural delegates opposing condemnation of the Klan and urban delegates supporting the minority plank.

The rest of the platform stressed Democratic accomplishments during the Wilson presidency, in contrast to Republican corruption. Democratic links with the common man were emphasized, while the Republicans were denounced as the party of the rich. The Democratic platform advocated increased taxes on the wealthy in contrast to the Republicans, who promised a reduction in taxes.

The Democrats continued to advocate a low tariff that would encourage competition. A plank demanding states' rights appeared in the platform, but there were also calls for government regulation of the anthracite coal industry, federal support of the American merchant marine and legislation that would restrict and publicize individual campaign contributions.

There were planks favoring a cutback in the American military, a national referendum before any declaration of war (except outright aggression against the United States) and the drafting of resources as well as men during wartime. The anti-militaristic planks were a return to the position the party had held earlier in the 20th century.

Following are excerpts from the Democratic platform of 1924:

Republican Corruption. Such are the exigencies of partisan politics that republican leaders are teaching the strange doctrine that public censure should be directed against those who expose crime rather than against criminals who have committed the offenses. If only three cabinet officers out of ten are disgraced, the country is asked to marvel at how many are free from taint. Long boastful that it was the only party "fit to govern," the republican party has proven its inability to govern even itself. It is at war with itself. As an agency of government it has ceased to function.

Income Tax. The income tax was intended as a tax upon wealth. It was not intended to take from the poor any part of the necessities of life. We hold that the fairest tax with which to raise revenue for the federal government is the income tax. We favor a graduated tax upon incomes, so adjusted as to lay the burdens of government upon the taxpayers in proportion to the benefits they enjoy and their ability to pay.

Campaign Contributions. We favor the prohibition of individual contributions, direct and indirect, to the campaign funds of congressmen, senators or presidential candidates, beyond a reasonable sum to be fixed in the law, for both individual contributions and total expenditures, with requirements for full publicity.

States' Rights. We demand that the states of the union shall be preserved in all their vigor and power. They constitute a bulwark against the centralizing and destructive tendencies of the republican party.

Anti-militarism. We demand a strict and sweeping reduction of armaments by land and sea, so that there shall be no competitive military program or naval building. Until international agreements to this end have been made we advocate an army and navy adequate for our national safety....

War is a relic of barbarism and it is justifiable only as a measure of defense.

War Profiteering. In the event of war in which the man power of the nation is drafted, all other resources should likewise be drafted. This will tend to discourage war by depriving it of its profits.

Progressives

Under the sponsorship of the Conference for Progressive Political Action, representatives of various liberal, labor and agrarian groups met in Cleveland on July 4 to launch the Progressive Party and ratify the ticket of Wisconsin Sen. Robert M. La Follette for president and Montana Sen. Burton K. Wheeler for vice president. The conference earlier had designated La Follette as its presidential nominee and had given him the power to choose his running mate. The national ticket of the Progressives crossed party lines, joining a Republican, La Follette, with a Democrat, Wheeler. The ticket was endorsed by the Socialists, who supported the Progressive candidates rather than run a separate national ticket.

In large part, the Progressive platform advocated measures that had been proposed earlier by the Populists, Socialists and Progressives before World War I. The key issue, as viewed by the La Follette Progressives, was "the control of government and industry by private monopoly." The platform favored the government ownership of railroads and water power, rigid federal control over natural resources, the outlawing of injunctions in labor disputes, a cutback in military spending, tax reform and political reform—including the direct election of the president, a national referendum before a declaration of war (except in cases of invasion), election of federal judges and congressional power to override the Supreme Court.

Following are excerpts from the Progressive platform of 1924:

Anti-monopoly. The great issue before the American people today is the control of government and industry by private monopoly.

For a generation the people have struggled patiently, in the face of repeated betrayals by successive administrations, to free themselves from this intolerable power which has been undermining representative government.

Through control of government, monopoly has steadily extended its absolute dominion to every basic industry.

In violation of law, monopoly has crushed competition, stifled private initiative and independent enterprise....

The equality of opportunity proclaimed by the Declaration of Independence and asserted and defended by Jefferson and Lincoln as the heritage of every American citizen has been displaced by special privilege for the few, wrested from the government of the many.

Tax Reform. We...favor a taxation policy providing for immediate reductions upon moderate incomes, large increases in the inheritance tax rates upon large estates to prevent the indefinite accumulation by inheritance of great fortunes in a few hands, taxes upon excess profits to penalize profiteering, and complete publicity, under proper safeguards, of all Federal tax returns.

Court Reform. We favor submitting to the people, for their considerate judgment, a constitutional amendment providing that Congress may by enacting a statute make it effective over a judicial veto.

We favor such amendment to the constitution as may be necessary to provide for the election of all Federal Judges, without party designation, for fixed terms not exceeding ten years, by direct vote of the people.

National Referendums. Over and above constitutions and statutes and greater than all is the supreme sovereignty of the people, and with them should rest the final decision of all great questions of national policy. We favor such amendments to the Federal Constitution as may be necessary to provide for the direct nomination and election of the President, to extend the initiative and referendum to the federal government, and to insure a popular referendum for or against war except in cases of actual invasion.

1928 Conventions

Presidential Candidates

Herbert Hoover
Republican

Alfred E. Smith
Democrat

Republicans

In mid-June 1928, the Republicans held their convention in Kansas City, Mo. Nearly a year earlier, President Coolidge had declared his intention not to seek re-election with a typically brief statement: "I do not choose to run for President in 1928." While some business leaders hoped that Coolidge would be open to a draft, the taciturn incumbent made no effort to encourage them. The vacuum caused by Coolidge's absence was quickly filled by Commerce Secretary Herbert Hoover of California, whose success in the spring primaries solidified his position as the front-runner.

Hoover's strength was evident on the first roll call of the convention, a credentials challenge to 18 Hoover delegates from Texas. In a vote that revealed candidate strength, the move to unseat the Hoover delegates was defeated, by a 659½ to 399½ vote. In the presidential balloting that followed, he gained more votes to win the nomination easily on the first ballot. Hoover's vote total was swelled before the balloting began by the withdrawal of his principal opponent, former Illinois Gov. Frank O. Lowden, who declared in a letter that he could not accept the party platform's stand on agriculture. Six names were placed in nomination, but Hoover was a landslide winner, receiving 837 of the 1,089 convention votes. Lowden finished second with 74 votes. *(Chart, p. 175)*

Sen. Charles Curtis of Kansas was virtually unopposed for the vice presidential nomination, receiving 1,052 votes.

Although Wisconsin's prominent progressive leader, Robert M. La Follette, had died in 1925, the Wisconsin delegation again presented a minority platform. The report was presented by Sen. Robert M. La Follette Jr., who had taken over his father's Senate seat. Among the planks of the Wisconsin report were proposals favoring enactment of the McNary-Haugen farm bill, government operation of major water power projects, increased income taxes on the rich and liberalization of prohibition. No vote was taken on the Wisconsin proposals.

A resolution favoring repeal of prohibition was tabled by a voice vote.

A separate agricultural resolution was proposed that advocated the basic provisions of the McNary-Haugen bill (twice vetoed by Coolidge), without mentioning the controversial bill by name. On a roll-call vote, the resolution was defeated, 807 to 277, with support centered in the farm states but with most Hoover delegates voting against it.

The platform as originally written was adopted by a voice vote. The platform promised continued prosperity and government economy. The belief in a protective tariff was reiterated. The document concluded with a plank entitled "home rule," which expressed the party's belief in self-reliance and strong local government.

Following are excerpts from the Republican platform of 1928:

Tariff. We reaffirm our belief in the protective tariff as a fundamental and essential principle of the economic life of this nation.... However, we realize that there are certain industries which cannot now successfully compete with foreign producers because of lower foreign wages and a lower cost of living abroad, and we pledge the next Republican Congress to an examination and where necessary a revision of these schedules to the end that American labor in these industries may again command the home market, may maintain its standard of living, and may count upon steady employment in its accustomed field.

Outlaw War. We endorse the proposal of the Secretary of State for a multilateral treaty proposed to the principal powers of the world and open to the signatures of all nations, to renounce war as an instrument of national policy and declaring in favor of pacific settlement of international disputes, the first step in outlawing war.

Agriculture. We promise every assistance in the reorganization of the marketing system on sounder and more economical lines and, where diversification is needed, Government financial assistance during the period of transition.

The Republican Party pledges itself to the enactment of legislation creating a Federal Farm Board clothed with the necessary powers to promote the establishment of a farm marketing system of farmer-owned and controlled stabilization corporations or associations to prevent and control surpluses through orderly distribution....

We favor, without putting the Government into business, the establishment of a Federal system of organization for co-operative and orderly marketing of farm products.

Prohibition. The people through the method provided by the Constitution have written the Eighteenth Amendment into the Constitution. The Republican Party pledges itself and its nominees to the observance and vigorous enforcement of this provision of the Constitution.

Republican Philosophy. There is a real need of restoring the individual and local sense of responsibility and self-reliance; there is a real need for the people once more to grasp the fundamental fact that under our system of government they are expected to solve many problems themselves through their municipal and State governments, and to combat the tendency that is all too common to turn to the Federal Government as the easiest and least burdensome method of lightening their own responsibilities.

Democrats

The Democratic convention was held in late June in Houston, Texas, the first time since 1860 that the party's nominating convention had been conducted in a southern city. The rural and urban wings of the party, which had produced the fiasco in Madison Square Garden four years earlier, wanted no more bloodletting. This explained the acceptance of Houston as the convention site by the urban forces, whose presidential candidate, Gov. Alfred E. Smith of New York, was the front-runner for the nomination. Smith's path to the nomination was largely unobstructed, thanks to the decision of William Gibbs McAdoo not to run. McAdoo, the rural favorite in 1924, feared the possibility of another bitter deadlock that would destroy party unity.

The convention broke with tradition by bypassing politicians and selecting Claude G. Bowers of Indiana, a historian and an editorial writer for *The New York World*, as temporary chairman.

When it came time for the selection of a presidential candidate, Franklin Delano Roosevelt once again placed Smith's name in nomination. On the roll call that followed, the New York governor came within 10 votes of the required two-thirds. Ohio quickly switched 44 of its votes to Smith, and the switch pushed "the happy warrior" over the top. When the vote switches were completed, Smith had received 849-1/6 of the 1,100 convention votes. No other candidate's vote had totaled more than 100. *(Chart, p. 175)*

Senate Minority Leader Joseph T. Robinson of Arkansas had little opposition for the vice presidency and was nominated on the first ballot with 914-1/6 votes. Sen. Alben W. Barkley of Kentucky finished a distant second with 77 votes. After a vote switch, Robinson had 1,035-1/6 votes. As a "dry" Protestant from the South, Robinson balanced the ticket. He was the first southerner to be nominated for national office by either major party since the Civil War.

For the first time since 1912, there were no roll-call votes on amendments to the Democratic platform. A minority plank was introduced calling for the party's complete support of prohibition, but there was no effort to force a roll-call vote. The platform included a milder prohibition plank that promised "an honest effort to enforce the 18th Amendment (prohibition)." On the surface there was little difference from the Republican plank, which pledged "vigorous enforcement" of prohibition. But in a telegram read to the convention shortly before its final adjournment, Smith negated the effect of the milder plank by declaring there should be "fundamental changes in the present provisions for national prohibition." Smith's statement was

disappointing to many "dry" delegates and lessened whatever enthusiasm they felt for the New York governor. No other issues were discussed, and the platform as written was approved by a voice vote.

Agriculture, the most depressed part of the economy in the 1920s, received more space in the platform than any other issue. The Democrats opposed federal subsidies to farmers, but advocated government loans to cooperatives and the creation of a federal farm board that would operate similarly to the Federal Reserve Board. While the Republican platform also favored creation of a farm board, as a whole it called for more initiative by the farmers themselves and less direct government help than did the Democratic platform.

Since the late 19th century, Democratic platforms had favored a low tariff. The 1928 tariff plank represented a change, expressing as much interest in ensuring competition and protecting the American wage-earner as in raising revenue. Instead of being consistently low, tariff rates were to be based on the difference between the cost of production in the United States and abroad. As a result of the Democrats' altered stand on the tariff, the positions of the two parties on this issue were the closest they had been in a generation.

The Democrats' 1928 platform did not mention the League of Nations, in contrast to the Republicans, who restated their opposition to the League. Both parties called for maintenance of American military strength until international disarmament agreements could be reached. A section of the Democratic foreign policy plank questioned the extent of presidential power in the area of international affairs. President Coolidge was specifically criticized for authorizing American military intervention in Nicaragua without congressional approval.

An unemployment plank was included in the Democratic platform that proposed the creation of public works jobs in times of economic hardship.

As was the case with most Democratic platforms since the early 19th century, there was a defense of states' rights and a plank that recognized education as an area of state responsibility. The Democrats made no mention of civil rights in contrast to the Republicans, who, as in 1920, proposed federal anti-lynching legislation.

Following are excerpts from the Democratic platform of 1928:

Prohibition. Speaking for the national Democracy, this convention pledges the party and its nominees to an honest effort to enforce the eighteenth amendment.

Agriculture. Farm relief must rest on the basis of an economic equality of agriculture with other industries. To give this equality a remedy must be found which will include among other things:

(a) Credit aid by loans to co-operatives on at least as favorable a basis as the government aid to the merchant marine.

(b) Creation of a federal farm board to assist the farmer and stock raiser in the marketing of their products, as the Federal Reserve Board has done for the banker and business man.

Presidential War Power. Abolition of the practice of the President of entering into and carrying out agreements with a foreign government, either de facto or de jure, for the protection of such government against revolution or foreign attack, or for the supervision of its internal affairs, when such agreements have not been advised and consented to by the Senate, as provided in the Constitution of the United States, and we condemn the administration for carrying out such an unratified agreement that requires us to use our armed forces in Nicaragua.

Tariff. Duties that will permit effective competition, insure against monopoly and at the same time produce a fair revenue for the support of government. Actual difference between the cost of production at home and abroad, with adequate safeguard for the wage of the American laborer must be the extreme measure of every tariff rate.

Unemployment and Public Works. We favor the adoption by the government, after a study of this subject, of a scientific plan whereby during periods of unemployment appropriations shall be made available for the construction of necessary public works and the lessening, as far as consistent with public interests, of government construction work when labor is generally and satisfactorily employed in private enterprise.

Education. We believe with Jefferson and other founders of the Republic that ignorance is the enemy of freedom and that each state, being responsible for the intellectual and moral qualifications of its citizens and for the expenditure of the moneys collected by taxation for the support of its schools, shall use its sovereign right in all matters pertaining to education.

1932 Conventions

Presidential Candidates

Norman Thomas
Socialist

Herbert Hoover
Republican

Franklin D. Roosevelt
Democrat

Socialists

The Socialist Party held its convention in Milwaukee, Wis., in May and renominated the same ticket that had represented the party in 1928: Norman Thomas of New York for president and James H. Maurer of Pennsylvania for vice president. Aided by the deepening economic depression, the Socialists received over two per cent of the popular vote for the first time since 1920. The party continued to run a national ticket until 1956, but 1932 was the last election in which the Socialists received at least two per cent of the vote.

By a vote of 117 to 64, the convention adopted a resolution supporting the efforts of the Soviet Union to create a Socialist society. An attempt to oust Morris Hillquit as national chairman of the party was beaten, 108 to 81.

The Socialist platform of 1932 included a number of proposals that were included in earlier party platforms, such as public ownership of natural resources and the means of transportation and communication, increased taxes on the wealthy, an end to the Supreme Court's power to rule congressional legislation unconstitutional and a reduction in the size and expenditures of the military.

The platform also advocated United States recognition of the Soviet Union and American entry into the League of Nations. Repeal of prohibition was recommended, as was the creation of a federal marketing system that would buy and market farm commodities.

To meet the hardship of the Depression, the Socialists listed a series of proposals, which included the expenditure of $10-billion for unemployment relief and public works projects.

Following are excerpts from the Socialist platform of 1932:

Unemployment Relief. 1. A Federal appropriation of $5,000,000,000 for immediate relief for those in need to supplement State and local appropriations.

2. A Federal appropriation of $5,000,000,000 for public works and roads, reforestation, slum clearance, and decent homes for the workers, by Federal Government, States and cities.

3. Legislation providing for the acquisition of land, buildings, and equipment necessary to put the unemployed to work producing food, fuel, and clothing and for the erection of houses for their own use.

4. The 6-hour day and the 5-day week without reduction of wages.

5. A comprehensive and efficient system of free public employment agencies.

6. A compulsory system of unemployment compensation with adequate benefits, based on contributions by the Government and by employers.

7. Old-age pensions for men and women 60 years of age and over.

8. Health and maternity insurance.

Republicans

As the incumbent party during the outset of the Depression, the Republicans bore the major political blame for the worsening economy. In a subdued mood, the party gathered in Chicago in June 1932 for its national convention. Republican leaders did not view their electoral prospects optimistically for the fall election, but saw no realistic alternative to President Hoover.

Hoover was easily if unenthusiastically renominated, receiving 1,126½ of the 1,154 convention votes. The highlight of the presidential balloting was the attempt by former Maryland Sen. Joseph I. France, who ran in several spring primaries, to gain the rostrum and nominate former President Coolidge. France's dramatic plan, however, was foiled by convention managers, who refused him permission to speak and had him escorted from the hall. (p. 177)

Vice President Charles Curtis had stiff opposition in his bid for renomination. The incumbent was seriously challenged by Maj. Gen. James G. Harbord of New York and the national commander of the American Legion, Hanford MacNider of Iowa. Curtis was short of a majority after the first ballot, but Pennsylvania quickly shifted its 75 votes to the Vice President, and this pushed him over the top. With the vote standing at Curtis, 634¼; MacNider, 182¾, and Harbord, 161¾, Curtis' renomination was made unanimous.

The major platform controversy surrounded the prohibition plank. The majority plank, supported by Hoover, was ambiguous. It called for the enforcement of prohibition but advocated a national referendum that would permit each state to determine whether or not it wanted prohibition. A more clear-cut minority plank favored repeal of prohibition. The minority proposal was defeated, however, 690-19/36 to 460-2/9. Following this roll call, the rest of the platform was approved by a voice vote.

The document approved by the Republicans was the longest in the party's history—nearly 9,000 words. It blamed the United States' continued economic problems on a worldwide depression, but lauded Hoover's leadership in meeting the crisis. The Republicans saw reduced government spending and a balanced budget as keys to ending the Depression. The party platform viewed unemployment relief as a matter for private agencies and local governments to handle.

The Republicans continued their support of a protective tariff. On the agricultural issue, the party proposed acreage controls to help balance supply and demand.

The final plank of the Republican platform urged party members in Congress to demonstrate party loyalty by supporting the Republican program. The plank warned that the party's strength was jeopardized by internal dissent.

Following are excerpts from the Republican platform of 1932:

Unemployment Relief. The people themselves, by their own courage, their own patient and resolute effort in the readjustments of their own affairs, can and will work out the cure. It is our task as a party, by leadership and a wise determination of policy, to assist that recovery....

True to American traditions and principles of government, the administration has regarded the relief problem as one of State and local responsibility. The work of local agencies, public and private has been coordinated and enlarged on a nation-wide scale under the leadership of the President.

Government Spending. We urge prompt and drastic reduction of public expenditure and resistance to every appropriation not demonstrably necessary to the performance of government, national or local.

Agriculture. The fundamental problem of American agriculture is the control of production to such volume as will balance supply with demand. In the solution of this problem the cooperative organization of farmers to plan production, and the tariff, to hold the home market for American farmers, are vital elements. A third element equally as vital is the control of the acreage of land under cultivation, as an aid to the efforts of the farmer to balance production.

Prohibition. We...believe that the people should have an opportunity to pass upon a proposed amendment the provision of which, while retaining in the Federal Government power to preserve the gains already made in dealing with the evils inherent in the liquor traffic, shall allow the States to deal with the problem as their citizens may determine, but subject always to the power of the Federal Government to protect those States where prohibition may exist and safeguard our citizens everywhere from the return of the saloon and attendant abuses.

Democrats

With the nation in the midst of the Great Depression, the Democratic Party had its best chance for victory since 1912. The delegates assembled in Chicago in late June 1932, confident that the convention's nominee would defeat President Hoover.

Gov. Franklin D. Roosevelt of New York entered the convention with a majority of the votes, but was well short of the two-thirds majority needed for nomination. Ironically, his principal opponent was the man he had nominated for the presidency three times, former New York Gov. Alfred E. Smith.

Roosevelt's strength was tested on several key roll calls before the presidential balloting began. Two of the votes involved credentials challenges to Roosevelt delegations from Louisiana and Minnesota. By a vote of 638¾ to 514¼, the delegates seated the Roosevelt forces from Louisiana, headed by Sen. Huey P. Long. And by a wider margin of 658¼ to 492¾, the convention seated the Roosevelt delegates from Minnesota. *(Chart, p. 176)*

After settlement of the credentials cases, the battleground shifted to the selection of the permanent convention chairman. The Roosevelt forces backed Montana Sen. Thomas J. Walsh, who was recommended by the committee on permanent organization. The Smith and other anti-Roosevelt factions coalesced behind Jouett Shouse of Kansas, chairman of the executive committee of the Democratic National Committee, who was recommended for permanent chairman by the national committee. But by a vote of 626 to 528, the Roosevelt forces won again, and Walsh assumed the gavel as permanent chairman.

The Roosevelt managers considered challenging the two-thirds rule; but, realizing that a bruising fight could alienate some of their own delegates, particularly in the South, they dropped the idea. Instead, the report of the rules committee recommended that a change in the two-thirds rule be delayed until the 1936 convention.

The presidential balloting began in the middle of an all-night session. After a motion to adjourn was defeated, 863½ to 281½, the first roll call began at 4:30 a.m. Roosevelt received a clear majority of 666¼ votes on the first ballot, compared with 201¾ for Smith and 90¼ for House Speaker John Nance Garner of Texas. Seven hundred and seventy votes were necessary for nomination. *(Chart, p. 176)*

Roosevelt gained slightly on the second ballot, advancing to 677¾ votes, while Smith dropped to 194¼ and Garner remained constant. Of side interest was the shift of Oklahoma's votes from its governor to Will Rogers, the state's famous humorist.

There were few changes on the next roll call, and at 9:15 a.m., the delegates agreed to adjourn. The vote totals after three ballots: Roosevelt, 682.79; Smith, 190¼; Garner, 101¼.

When balloting resumed the next evening, William Gibbs McAdoo of California quickly launched the bandwagon for Roosevelt by announcing that his state's 44 votes were switching from Garner to the New York governor. Other states followed California's lead, and when the fourth ballot was complete, Roosevelt had 945 votes and the nomination. With the Smith vote holding at 190½, no effort was made to make the nomination unanimous.

Although it is not clear whether there was a formal deal struck before the fourth ballot between the Garner and Roosevelt forces, the Texas representative was the unanimous choice of the convention for vice president. Forty states seconded his nomination, and no roll call was taken.

In an effort to break what he described as "absurd traditions," Roosevelt flew from Albany to Chicago to accept the presidential nomination personally. (Previously, a major party candidate would be formally notified of his nomination in a ceremony several weeks after the convention.) In his speech of acceptance, Roosevelt struck a liberal tone and issued his memorable pledge of "a new deal for the American people."

The platform adopted by the convention was not a blueprint for the New Deal to follow. It was less than 2,000 words long, the party's shortest platform since 1888, and less than one-fourth as long as the document adopted by the Republicans. It blamed the Depression on the "disastrous policies" practiced by the Republicans, but made few new proposals, instead forcefully restating positions that had appeared in earlier party platforms.

The Democrats advocated a balanced budget and a cut of at least 25 per cent in federal spending, and called for the removal of the federal government from competition with private enterprise in all areas except public works and natural resources.

The Democratic platform, unlike its Republican counterpart, advocated extensive unemployment relief and public works projects, regulation of holding companies and securities exchanges, "a competitive tariff for revenue" and the extension of farm cooperatives.

The plank which sparked the most enthusiasm among the delegates was the call for the repeal of prohibition. A milder plank favored by "dry" delegates was resoundingly defeated, 934¾ to 213¾.

The only measure added from the floor of the convention favored "continuous responsibility of government for human welfare, especially for the protection of children." It was approved by a standing vote.

Following are excerpts from the Democratic platform of 1932:

Government Spending. We advocate an immediate and drastic reduction of governmental expenditures by abolishing useless commissions and offices, consolidating departments and bureaus, and eliminating extravagance to accomplish a saving of not less than twenty-five per cent in the cost of the Federal Government. And we call upon the Democratic Party in the states to make a zealous effort to achieve a proportionate result.

We favor maintenance of the national credit by a federal budget annually balanced on the basis of accurate executive estimates within revenues, raised by a system of taxation levied on the principle of ability to pay.

Unemployment Relief, Public Works Projects. We advocate the extension of federal credit to the states to provide unemployment relief wherever the diminishing resources of the states makes it impossible for them to provide for the needy; expansion of the federal program of necessary and useful construction effected *[sic]* with a public interest, such as adequate flood control and waterways.

We advocate the spread of employment by a substantial reduction in the hours of labor, the encouragement of the shorter week by applying that principle in government service; we advocate advance planning of public works.

We advocate unemployment and old-age insurance under state laws.

Prohibition. We advocate the repeal of the Eighteenth Amendment. To effect such repeal we demand that the Congress immediately propose a Constitutional Amendment to truly represent *[sic]* the conventions in the states called to act solely on that proposal; we urge the enactment of such measures by the several states as will actually promote temperance, effectively prevent the return of the saloon, and bring the liquor traffic into the open under complete supervision and control by the states.

Agriculture. Extension and development of the Farm Cooperative movement and effective control of crop surpluses so that our farmers may have the full benefit of the domestic market.

The enactment of every constitutional measure that will aid the farmers to receive for their basic farm commodities prices in excess of cost.

Explanatory Note

This section on the history of party nominating conventions includes party conventions for parties receiving at least two per cent of the popular vote in the presidential election. The Socialist Party, for example, received at least two per cent of the popular vote in 1904, 1908, 1912, 1916, 1920 and 1932; the Socialist Party conventions for these years are included in this section. The Socialist Party conventions for other years when the party received less than two per cent of the vote are not included. *(Additional details on this section, p. 20)*

1936 Conventions

Presidential Candidates

Alfred M. Landon
Republican

Franklin D. Roosevelt
Democrat

William Lemke
Union

Republicans

The Republican convention, held in Cleveland in early June, was an unusually harmonious gathering for a party out of power. There were only two roll-call votes on the convention floor, for president and vice president, and they were both one-sided.

The only matter of debate was the vote allocation for Alaska, Hawaii and the District of Columbia. By a voice vote, the convention approved the minority report of the rules committee, which sliced the vote for these three from six to three votes apiece.

Former President Hoover received an enthusiastic reception when he spoke, but by that time Kansas Gov. Alfred M. Landon had the presidential nomination sewed up. Landon, one of the few Republican governors to be re-elected during the Depression, received 984 votes on the first ballot, compared with 19 for Sen. William E. Borah of **Idaho.** *(Chart, p. 178)*

Before the balloting began, Landon had sent a telegram to the convention that expressed his agreement with the "word and spirit" of the party platform, but elaborated his position on several points. The Kansan advocated the passage of a constitutional amendment to ensure women and children safe working conditions and to establish guidelines for wages and hours in the event that legislation passed by Congress was ruled unconstitutional. Landon's message also proposed extending the civil service to include all workers in federal departments and agencies below the rank of assistant secretary, and defined "sound currency" as currency that could be exchanged for gold. Landon's pronouncements were met with 30 minutes of cheering.

For vice president, the convention selected Col. Frank Knox of Illinois, publisher of *The Chicago Daily News.* Knox, who had earlier campaigned energetically, if not successfully, for the presidential nomination, received all 1,003 votes on the first ballot.

The Republican platform, which began with the sentence, "America is in peril," focused on the alleged threat of New Deal policies to American constitutional government. The platform assailed the Roosevelt administration for "dishonoring American traditions" and promised to protect local self-government and the power of the Supreme Court.

The Republicans promised a balanced budget, reduced federal expenditures, a "sound currency," a more discriminating public works program and the administration of unemployment relief by "non-political local agencies" that would be financed jointly by the various states and the federal government.

The Republicans shared with the Democrats the belief in an isolationist foreign policy and the concepts of social security, unemployment insurance and crop control.

Following are excerpts from the Republican platform of 1936:

Roosevelt's "New Deal." America is in peril. The welfare of American men and women and the future of our youth are at stake. We dedicate ourselves to the preservation of their political liberty, their individual opportunity and their character as free citizens, which today for the first time are threatened by Government itself....

The powers of Congress have been usurped by the President.

The integrity and authority of the Supreme Court have been flouted.

The rights and liberties of American citizens have been violated.

Regulated monopoly has displaced free enterprise.

The New Deal Administration constantly seeks to usurp the rights reserved to the States and to the people.

Unemployment Relief. The return of responsibility for relief administration to nonpolitical local agencies familiar with community problems....

Undertaking of Federal public works only on their merits and separate from the administration of relief.

Government Spending, Currency. Balance the budget—not by increasing taxes but by cutting expenditures, drastically and immediately....

We advocate a sound currency to be preserved at all hazards.

The first requisite to a sound and stable currency is a balanced budget.

Foreign Policy. We pledge ourselves to promote and maintain peace by all honorable means not leading to foreign alliances or political commitments.

Obedient to the traditional foreign policy of America and to the repeatedly expressed will of the American people, we pledge that America shall not become a member of the League of Nations nor of the World Court nor shall America take on any entangling alliances in foreign affairs.

Democrats

The 1936 Democratic convention, held in Philadelphia in late June, was one of the most harmonious in party history. There were no floor debates, and, for the first time since 1840, there were no roll-call votes.

The only matter that required discussion—elimination of the century-old two-thirds rule—was settled in the rules committee. There, by a vote of 36 to 13, the committee agreed to abrogate the rule, which had been a controversial part of Democratic conventions since 1832. To mollify the South, which was particularly threatened by elimination of the two-thirds rule, the rules committee added a provision that would include consideration of a state's Democratic voting strength in determining its future convention vote allocation. The rules committee report was approved by a voice vote.

Both President Roosevelt and Vice President Garner were renominated by acclamation, but more than a full day of oratory was expended in eulogizing the Democratic standard-bearers. Roosevelt was seconded by delegates from each of the states and territories—more than 50 separate speakers. Seventeen delegates spoke on behalf of Garner.

Both Roosevelt and Garner personally accepted their nominations in ceremonies at the University of Pennsylvania's Franklin Field. Before a crowd estimated as large as 100,000, Roosevelt electrified his listeners with a speech that blasted his adversaries among the rich as "economic royalists" and included the sentence: "This generation of Americans has a rendezvous with destiny."

As in 1932, the platform adopted by the Democrats was a short one, about 3,000 words. The document paid lip service to the concept of a balanced budget and reduced government spending, but it supported continuation of the extensive federal programs undertaken by the Roosevelt administration.

The platform did not, as many in past years had, mention states' rights; this reflected the party's changing view toward federal power. To counter what was viewed as obstructionism by the Supreme Court, the Democrats suggested the possibility of passing a "clarifying amendment" to the Constitution which would enable Congress and state legislatures to enact bills without the fear of an unfavorable decision from the Supreme Court.

The foreign policy plank recognized the isolationist mood of the period, calling for neutrality in foreign disputes and the avoidance of international commitments that would draw the United States into war.

Following are excerpts from the Democratic platform of 1936:

Federal Power. The Republican platform proposes to meet many pressing national problems solely by action of the separate States. We know that drought, dust storms, floods, minimum wages, maximum hours, child labor, and working conditions in industry, monopolistic and unfair business practices cannot be adequately handled exclusively by 48 separate State legislatures, 48 separate State administrations, and 48 separate State courts. Transactions

and activities which inevitably overflow State boundaries call for both State and Federal treatment.

We have sought and will continue to seek to meet these problems through legislation within the Constitution.

If these problems cannot be effectively solved by legislation within the Constitution, we shall seek such clarifying amendment as will assure to the legislatures of the several States and to the Congress of the United States, each within its proper jurisdiction, the power to enact those laws which the State and Federal legislatures, within their respective spheres, shall find necessary, in order adequately to regulate commerce, protect public health and safety and safeguard economic security. Thus we propose to maintain the letter and spirit of the Constitution.

Government Spending. We are determined to reduce the expenses of government. We are being aided therein by the recession in unemployment. As the requirements of relief decline and national income advances, an increasing percentage of Federal expenditures can and will be met from current revenues, secured from taxes levied in accordance with ability to pay. Our retrenchment, tax and recovery programs thus reflect our firm determination to achieve a balanced budget and the reduction of the national debt at the earliest possible moment.

Foreign Policy. We reaffirm our opposition to war as an instrument of national policy, and declare that disputes between nations should be settled by peaceful means. We shall continue to observe a true neutrality in the disputes of others; to be prepared, resolutely to resist aggression against ourselves; to work for peace and to take the profits out of war; to guard against being drawn, by political commitments, international banking or private trading, into any war which may develop anywhere.

Union Party

With the support of Father Charles E. Coughlin and his National Union for Social Justice, on June 19, 1936, Rep. William Lemke of North Dakota, a Republican, declared his presidential candidacy on the newly formed Union Party ticket. Thomas O'Brien, a Boston railroad union lawyer, was announced as Lemke's running mate. The fledgling political organization had a brief existence, running a national ticket only in the 1936 election *(Union Party profile, p. 210)*

The Union Party was basically an extension of Coughlin's organization, and the Lemke-O'Brien ticket was endorsed at the National Union for Social Justice convention in August by a vote of 8,152 to 1.

The Union Party platform was reportedly written by Coughlin, Lemke and O'Brien at the Roman Catholic priest's church in Royal Oak, Mich. It was a brief document, less than 1,000 words, that contained 15 points similar to the 16-point program favored by Coughlin's National Union. The primary distinctions between the Union Party and the two major parties were in currency expansion, civil service reform and restrictions on wealth. The Union Party called for the creation of a central bank, regulated by Congress, that would issue currency to help pay off the federal debt and refinance agricultural and home mortgage indebtedness. The Union Party platform also proposed extending the civil service to all levels of the federal government and advocated placing restrictions on annual individual income coupled with a ceiling on gifts and inheritances. The new party differed from the Socialists by emphasizing that private property should not be confiscated.

Following are excerpts from the Union Party platform of 1936:

Currency Expansion. Congress and Congress alone shall coin and issue the currency and regulate the value of all money and credit in the United States through a central bank of issue.

Immediately following the establishment of the central bank of issue Congress shall provide for the retirement of all tax-exempt, interest-bearing bonds and certificates of indebtedness of the Federal Government and shall refinance all the present agricultural mortgage indebtedness for the farmer and all the home mortgage indebtedness for the farmer and all the home mortgage indebtedness for the city owner by the use of its money and credit which it now gives to the private bankers.

Civil Service Reform. Congress shall so legislate that all Federal offices and positions of every nature shall be distributed through civil-service qualifications and not through a system of party spoils and corrupt patronage.

Restrictions on Wealth. Congress shall set a limitation upon the net income of any individual in any one year and a limitation of the amount that such an individual may receive as a gift or as an inheritance, which limitation shall be executed through taxation.

Foreign Policy. Congress shall establish an adequate and perfect defense for our country from foreign aggression either by air, by land, or by sea, but with the understanding that our naval, air, and military forces must not be used under any consideration in foreign fields or in foreign waters either alone or in conjunction with any foreign power. If there must be conscription, there shall be a conscription of wealth as well as a conscription of men.

1940 Conventions

Presidential Candidates

Wendell L. Willkie
Republican

Franklin D. Roosevelt
Democrat

Republicans

The Republican convention was held in Philadelphia in late June, and it culminated one of the most successful of all campaign blitzes. Wendell L. Willkie, an Indiana native who had never before run for public office, was nominated by the Republicans to run for president. A Democrat until 1938, Willkie had gained fame as a defender of private enterprise in opposition to Roosevelt's public power projects. Although Willkie had broad personal appeal, he and his well-financed group of political "amateurs" did not launch their presidential bid until late spring and missed the presidential primaries. Willkie's momentum came from his rapid rise in the Republican preference polls, as he soared from only 3 per cent in early May to 29 per cent six weeks later.

At the Republican convention, 10 names were placed in nomination for the presidency. Willkie's principal rivals were Manhattan District Attorney Thomas E. Dewey, making his first presidential bid at age 38, and Ohio Sen. Robert A. Taft. On the first ballot, Dewey led with 360 votes, followed by Taft with 189 and Willkie with 105. Five hundred and one votes were needed for nomination. (p. 179)

After the first roll call, Dewey steadily lost strength, while Willkie and Taft gained. Willkie assumed the lead on the fourth ballot, passing both Dewey and Taft. Willkie's vote was 306, while Taft moved into second place with 254. Dewey dropped to third with 250.

On the fifth ballot, the contest narrowed to just Willkie and Taft, as both candidates continued to gain—Willkie jumping to 429 votes and Taft to 377. The shift of Michigan's votes to Willkie on the sixth ballot started a bandwagon for the Indianan which pushed him over the top. When the roll call was completed, Willkie was nominated with 655 votes, and a motion to make his nomination unanimous was adopted. (Chart, p. 179)

As his running mate, Willkie favored Senate Minority Leader Charles L. McNary of Oregon. McNary, a supporter of some New Deal measures, was opposed by Rep. Dewey Short of Missouri, a vocal anti-New Dealer. McNary, however, was able to win easily on a single ballot, receiving 890 votes to 108 for Short.

The Republican platform was adopted without debate, although an Illinois member of the platform committee commented that his state would have preferred a stronger anti-war plank. As it was, the Republican foreign policy plank sharply criticized the Roosevelt administration for not adequately preparing the nation's defense. However, the rest of the plank was similar to the one adopted three weeks later by the Democrats at their convention: opposing involvement in war but stressing national defense, and advocating aid to the Allies that would not be "inconsistent with the requirements of our own national defense."

In domestic affairs, the Republicans lambasted the extension of federal power under the New Deal and promised cuts in government spending and the reduction of federal competition with private enterprise. The Republican platform agreed with the concept of unemployment relief and social security initiated by the Roosevelt administration, but proposed the administration of these programs by the states and not the federal government.

The Republicans attacked Roosevelt's monetary measures and advocated currency reforms that included congressional control.

The platform also proposed new amendments to the Constitution that would provide equal rights for men and women and would limit a president to two terms in office.

Following are excerpts from the Republican platform of 1940:

> **Foreign Policy.** The Republican Party is firmly opposed to involving this Nation in foreign war....

> The Republican Party stands for Americanism, preparedness and peace. We accordingly fasten upon the New Deal full responsibility for our unpreparedness and for the consequent danger of involvement in war....

> Our sympathies have been profoundly stirred by invasion of unoffending countries and by disaster to nations whole [whose] ideals most closely resemble our own. We favor the extension to all peoples fighting for liberty, or whose liberty is threatened, of such aid as shall not be in violation of international law or inconsistent with the requirements of our own national defense.

> **Unemployment Relief.** We shall remove waste, discrimination, and politics from relief—through administration by the States with federal grants-in-aid on a fair and nonpolitical basis, thus giving the man and woman on relief a larger share of the funds appropriated.

> **Currency.** The Congress should reclaim its constitutional powers over money, and withdraw the President's arbitrary authority to manipulate the currency, establish bimetallism, issue irredeemable paper money, and debase the gold and silver coinage. We shall repeal the Thomas Inflation Amendment of 1933 and the (foreign) Silver Purchase Act of 1934, and take all possible steps to preserve the value of the Government's huge holdings of gold and re-introduce gold into circulation.

> **Women's Rights.** We favor submission by Congress to the States of an amendment to the Constitution providing for equal rights for men and women.

> **No Third Term.** To insure against the overthrow of our American system of government we favor an amendment to the Constitution providing that no person shall be President of the United States for more than two terms.

Democrats

At the time of both major party conventions in the summer of 1940, Hitler's forces were moving quickly and relentlessly across western Europe. International events assumed a major importance in political decisions. President Roosevelt, who gave evidence before 1940 that he would not seek a third term, became increasingly receptive to the idea of a draft as the Democratic convention drew nearer. The threat to American security caused by the awesomely successful Nazi military machine, coupled with Roosevelt's inability to find an adequate New Deal-style successor, seemed to spur F.D.R.'s decision to accept renomination.

The Democratic convention was held in Chicago in mid-July. On the second night of the convention, a message from Roosevelt was read stating that he did not desire to run for re-election and urged the delegates to vote for any candidate they wished. Although worded in a negative way, the message did not shut the door on a draft. The delegates reacted, however, by sitting in stunned silence until a Chicago city official began shouting over the public address system, "We want Roosevelt." The cheerleading galvanized the delegates into an hour-long demonstration.

Presidential balloting was held the next day. Roosevelt won easily on the first roll call, although two members of his administration, Vice President Garner and Postmaster General James A. Farley of New York, ran against him. Roosevelt received 946-13/30 of the 1,100 votes. Farley had 72-9/10 and Garner had 61. *(Chart, p. 178)*

While the delegates were satisfied to have Roosevelt at the top of the ticket again, many balked at his choice for vice president, Agriculture Secretary Henry A. Wallace of Iowa. Wallace, a leading liberal in the administration and a former Republican, was particularly distasteful to conservative Democrats. Many delegates were expecting Roosevelt to leave the vice presidential choice to the convention and were unhappy to have the candidate dictated to them.

It took a personal appearance at the convention by the President's wife, Eleanor Roosevelt, and a threat by F.D.R. that he would not accept the presidential nomination without his hand-picked running mate, that steered the delegates toward Wallace. In spite of the pressure by the Roosevelt forces, the vote was scattered among 13 candidates on the vice presidential ballot. Wallace, though, was able to obtain a slim majority, 626-11/30 votes to 329-3/5 for the runner-up, House Speaker William B. Bankhead of Alabama. Because of the displeasure of many of the delegates, Wallace was asked not to address the convention.

The convention closed by hearing a radio address by Roosevelt, who stated that he had not wanted the nomination but accepted it because the existing world crisis called for personal sacrifice.

The party platform was adopted without a roll call, although there was an amendment presented by a Minnesota representative that opposed any violation of the two-term tradition. It was rejected by a voice vote. The platform as adopted was divided into three sections. The first discussed American military preparedness and foreign policy; the second detailed the New Deal's benefits for various segments of the economy (agriculture, labor, business); the third listed New Deal welfare measures, ranging from unemployment relief to low-cost housing.

As a concession to the party's isolationist wing, the first section contained the administration's promise not to participate in foreign wars or fight in foreign lands, except in case of an attack on the United States. The plank stressed the need of a strong national defense to discourage aggression, but also pledged to provide to free nations (such as Great Britain) material aid "not inconsistent with the interests of our own national self-defense."

An electric power plank was included in the second section of the platform as a direct result of the Republicans' selection of Wendell L. Willkie, a former utilities executive, as their presidential candidate. The Democrats argued in favor of the massive public power projects constructed during the New Deal and criticized private utilities such as the one formerly headed by Willkie.

The third section of the platform drew a sharp distinction with the Republicans on the issue of unemployment relief, opposing any efforts to turn the administration of relief over to the states or local governments.

Following are excerpts from the Democratic platform of 1940:

Democratic Achievements. Toward the modern fulfillment of the American ideal, the Democratic Party, during the last seven years, has labored successfully:

1. *To strengthen democracy by defensive preparedness against aggression, whether by open attack or secret infiltration;*
2. *To strengthen democracy by increasing our economic efficiency; and*
3. *To strengthen democracy by improving the welfare of the people.*

Foreign Policy. We will not participate in foreign wars, and we will not send our army, naval or air forces to fight in foreign lands outside of the Americas, except in case of attack....

Weakness and unpreparedness invite aggression. We must be so strong that no possible combination of powers would dare to attack us. We propose to provide America with an invincible air force, a navy strong enough to protect all our seacoasts and our national interests, and a fully-equipped and mechanized army.

Unemployment Relief. We shall continue to recognize the obligation of Government to provide work for deserving workers who cannot be absorbed by private industry.

We are opposed to vesting in the states and local authorities the control of Federally-financed work relief. We believe that this Republican proposal is a thinly disguised plan to put the unemployed back on the dole.

Electric Power. The nomination of a utility executive by the Republican Party as its presidential candidate raises squarely the issue, whether the nation's water power shall be used for all the people or for the selfish interests of a few. We accept that issue.

1944 Conventions

Presidential Candidates

Thomas E. Dewey
Republican

Franklin D. Roosevelt
Democrat

Republicans

For the first time since 1864, the nation was at war during a presidential election year. The Republicans held their convention first, meeting in Chicago in late June 1944. With a minimum of discord, the delegates selected a national ticket and adopted a platform. New York Gov. Thomas E. Dewey, the front-runner for the presidential nomination, was the nearly unanimous selection when his last two rivals, Gov. John W. Bricker of Ohio and former Minnesota Gov. Harold E. Stassen, both withdrew from the race before the roll call. On the single ballot, Dewey received 1,056 of the 1,057 votes cast. The one dissenting vote was cast by a Wisconsin delegate for Gen. Douglas MacArthur. *(Chart, p. 180)*

As Dewey's running mate, the delegates unanimously selected Gov. Bricker, an isolationist and party regular, who received all 1,057 votes cast. During the nominating speeches, Rep. Charles A. Halleck of Indiana made the unusual move of recommending his state's first choice for vice president, William L. Hutcheson, for secretary of labor.

Dewey came to Chicago personally to accept the nomination, becoming the first Republican presidential candidate to break the tradition of waiting to accept the nomination in a formal notification ceremony. The thrust of Dewey's speech was an attack on the Roosevelt administration, which he referred to as "stubborn men grown old and tired and quarrelsome in office."

The platform was approved without dissent. The international section was written in a guarded tone. It favored "responsible participation by the United States in post-war cooperative organization," but declared that any agreement must be approved by a two-thirds vote of the Senate. The Republicans favored the establishment of a postwar Jewish state in Palestine.

The domestic section of the platform denounced the New Deal's centralization of power in the federal government, with its increased government spending and deficits. The Republicans proposed to stabilize the economy through the encouragement of private enterprise.

The platform restated several of the planks included four years earlier, among which were the call for an equal rights amendment, a two-term limitation on the president and the return of control over currency matters from the president to Congress.

The Republicans included a civil rights plank which called for a congressional investigation of the treatment of blacks in the military, passage of a constitutional amendment to eliminate the poll tax and legislation that permanently would establish a Fair Employment Practice Commission and outlaw lynching.

Following are excerpts from the Republican platform of 1944:

Postwar International Organization. We favor responsible participation by the United States in post-war cooperative organization among sovereign nations to prevent military aggression and to attain permanent peace with organized justice in a free world.

Such organization should develop effective cooperative means to direct peace forces to prevent or repel military aggression. Pending this, we pledge continuing collaboration with the United Nations to assure these ultimate objectives....

We shall sustain the Constitution of the United States in the attainment of our international aims; and pursuant to the Constitution of the United States any treaty or agreement to attain such aims made on behalf of the United States with any other nation or any association of nations, shall be made only by and with the advice and consent of the Senate of the United States provided two-thirds of the Senators present concur.

Israel. In order to give refuge to millions of distressed Jewish men, women and children driven from their homes by tyranny, we call for the opening of Palestine to their unrestricted immigration and land ownership, so that in accordance with the full intent and purpose of the Balfour Declaration of 1917 and the Resolution of a Republican Congress in 1922, Palestine may be constituted as a free and democratic Commonwealth. We condemn the failure of the President to insist that the mandatory of Palestine carry out the provision of the Balfour Declaration and of the mandate while he pretends to support them.

New Deal. Four more years of New Deal policy would centralize all power in the President, and would daily subject every act of every citizen to regulation by his henchmen; and this country could remain a Republic only in name. No problem exists which cannot be solved by American methods. We have no need of either the communistic or the fascist technique.

...The National Administration has become a sprawling, overlapping bueaucracy. It is undermined by executive abuse of power, confused lines of authority, duplication of effort, inadequate fiscal controls, loose personnel practices and an attitude of arrogance previously unknown in our history.

Economy. We reject the theory of restoring prosperity through government spending and deficit financing.

We shall promote the fullest stable employment through private enterprise.

Civil Rights. We pledge an immediate Congressional inquiry to ascertain the extent to which mistreatment, segregation and discrimination against Negroes who are in our armed forces are impairing morale and efficiency, and the adoption of corrective legislation.

We pledge the establishment by Federal legislation of a permanent Fair Employment Practice Commission.

The payment of any poll tax should not be a condition of voting in Federal elections and we favor immediate submission of a Constitutional amendment for its abolition.

We favor legislation against lynching and pledge our sincere efforts in behalf of its early enactment.

Agriculture. An American market price to the American farmer and the protection of such price by means of support prices, commodity loans, or a combination thereof, together with such other economic means as will assure an income to agriculture that is fair and equitable in comparison with labor, business and industry. We oppose subsidies as a substitute for fair markets.

Serious study of and search for a sound program of crop insurance with emphasis upon establishing a self-supporting program.

Democrats

President Franklin Delano Roosevelt, who four years earlier did not make a final decision about accepting a third nomination until the last moment, clearly stated his intention to run for a fourth term a week before the 1944 convention was to open in Chicago. In a message to Democratic National Chairman Robert E. Hannegan of Missouri released July 11, Roosevelt declared that while he did not desire to run, he would accept renomination reluctantly as a "good soldier."

The early sessions of the convention were highlighted by approval of the rules committee report and settlement of a credentials challenge. The rules committee mandated the national committee to revamp the convention's vote allocation formula in a way that would take into account Democratic voting strength. This measure was adopted to appease southern delegates, who in 1936 were promised an increased proportion of the convention vote in return for elimination of the two-thirds rule. No action had been taken to implement the pledge in the intervening eight years.

The credentials dispute involved the Texas delegation, which was represented by two competing groups. By a voice vote, the convention agreed to seat both groups.

Vice President Wallace enlivened the presidential nominations by appearing before the convention to urge Roosevelt's renomination. Wallace termed the President the "greatest liberal in the history of the U.S." In the balloting that followed, Roosevelt easily defeated Virginia Sen. Harry F. Byrd, who was supported by some conservative southern delegates unhappy with the domestic legislation favored by the New Deal. The final tally: Roosevelt, 1,086; Byrd, 89; former Postmaster General James A. Farley, 1. *(Chart, p. 180)*

After his selection, Roosevelt accepted the nomination in a radio address delivered from the San Diego Naval Base, where he had stopped off en route to a wartime conference.

The real drama of the convention, the selection of the vice presidential nominee, came next. Roosevelt had been ambivalent about the choice of his running mate, encouraging several people to run but not publicly endorsing any of them. The President wrote an ambiguous letter to the convention chairman, which was read to the delegates. In the message, Roosevelt stated that if he were a delegate himself he would vote for Wallace's renomination, but that the ultimate choice was the convention's and it must consider the pros and cons of its selection.

In another message, written privately for National Chairman Hannegan, Roosevelt declared that he would be happy to run with either Missouri Sen. Harry S Truman or Supreme Court Justice William O. Douglas. Most of the party bosses preferred Truman to the more liberal alternatives, Wallace and Douglas. Truman was originally slated to nominate former South Carolina Sen. and Supreme Court Justice James F. Byrnes for vice president. But, spurred by his political advisers, Roosevelt telephoned Truman in Chicago and urged him to accept the nomination. Truman reluctantly agreed.

Roosevelt's final preference for Truman was not publicly announced, and 12 names were placed before the convention. Wallace led on the first roll call with 429½ votes, followed by Truman with 319½. Favorite sons and other hopefuls shared the remaining votes cast.

Truman passed Wallace on the second ballot, 477½ to 473, and immediately after completion of the roll call, Alabama began the bandwagon for the Missouri senator by switching its votes to him. When all the shifts had been made, Truman was an easy winner with 1,031 votes, while Wallace finished with 105.

The platform adopted by the convention was a short one, only 1,360 words. The first third of the platform lauded the accomplishments of Roosevelt's first three terms. The rest of the document outlined the party's proposals for the future. In foreign affairs, the Democrats advocated the creation of a postwar international organization that would have adequate forces available to prevent future wars. The party also called for American membership in an international court of justice. The Democrats joined their Republican opponents in favoring the establishment of an independent Jewish state in Palestine.

The domestic section of the platform proposed a continuation of New Deal liberalism, with passage of an equal rights amendment for women, price guarantees and crop insurance for farmers and the establishment of federal aid to education that would be administered by the states.

A minority report concerning foreign policy was presented which proposed that an international air force be established to help keep peace. The proposal was rejected, however, when the platform committee chairman indicated that the existence of an air force was included in the majority report's call for "adequate forces" to be at the disposal of the proposed international organization.

Following are excerpts from the Democratic platform of 1944:

Postwar International Organizations. That the world may not again be drenched in blood by international outlaws and criminals, we pledge:

To join with the other United Nations in the establishment of an international organization based on the principle of the sovereign equality of all peace-loving states, open to membership by all such states, large and small, for the prevention of aggression and the maintenance of international peace and security.

To make all necessary and effective agreements and arrangements through which the nations would maintain adequate forces to meet the needs of preventing war and of making impossible the preparation for war and which would have such forces available for joint action when necessary.

Such organization must be endowed with power to employ armed forces when necessary to prevent aggression and preserve peace.

Israel. We favor the opening of Palestine to unrestricted Jewish immigration and colonization, and such a policy as to result in the establishment there of a free and democratic Jewish commonwealth.

Women's Rights. We favor legislation assuring equal pay for equal work, regardless of sex.

We recommend to Congress the submission of a Constitutional amendment on equal rights for women.

Education. We favor Federal aid to education administered by the states without interference by the Federal Government.

Agriculture. Price guarantees and crop insurance to farmers with all practical steps:

To keep agriculture on a parity with industry and labor.

To foster the success of the small independent farmer.

To aid the home ownership of family-sized farms.

To extend rural electrification and develop broader domestic and foreign markets for agricultural products.

Civil Rights. We believe that racial and religious minorities have the right to live, develop and vote equally with all citizens and share the rights that are guaranteed by our Constitution. Congress should exert its full constitutional powers to protect those rights.

1948 Conventions

Presidential Candidates

| **Thomas E. Dewey**
Republican | **Harry S Truman**
Democrat | **J. Strom Thurmond**
States' Rights | **Henry A. Wallace**
Progressive |

Republicans

The Republican convention was held in Philadelphia in late June. As in 1944, New York Gov. Thomas E. Dewey entered the convention as the front-runner for the nomination. But unlike four years earlier, when he was virtually handed the nomination, Dewey was contested by several candidates, including Ohio Sen. Robert A. Taft and former Minnesota Gov. Harold E. Stassen.

In all, seven names were placed in nomination, with 548 votes needed to determine a winner. Dewey led on the first roll call with 434 votes, followed by Taft with 224 and Stassen with 157. The other candidates were each well below 100 votes. *(Chart, p. 182)*

On the second roll call, Dewey moved closer to the nomination, receiving 515 votes. Taft and Stassen continued to trail, with 274 and 149 votes respectively. At this point, the anti-Dewey forces requested a recess, which was agreed to by the confident Dewey organization.

Unable to form a coalition that could stop Dewey, all his opponents withdrew before the third ballot. On the subsequent roll call, the former New York governor was the unanimous choice of the convention, receiving all 1,094 votes.

Dewey's choice for vice president was California Gov. Earl Warren, who was nominated by acclamation. Warren had been a favorite son candidate for the presidency, and agreed to take second place on the ticket only after receiving assurances that the responsibilities of the vice presidency would be increased if Dewey were elected.

The Republican platform was adopted without dissent. The wording of the platform was unusually positive for a party out of the White House. The failures of the Truman administration were dismissed in a short paragraph, with the rest of the document praising the accomplishments of the Republican 80th Congress and detailing the party's proposals for the future.

One of the major issues of the 1948 campaign was the controversial Taft-Hartley labor law, a measure supported by the Republicans, but which most Democratic leaders felt should be repealed. The Republicans were silent on national health insurance, and the party's housing position stressed private initiative rather than federal legislation. As in 1944, the Republicans opposed the poll tax and segregation in the military and favored legislation to outlaw lynching.

The Republican platform had a states' rights tinge to it by declaring for state control of tidelands, tributary waters, lakes and streams.

On the increasingly controversial issue of internal security, the Republicans included a sharply worded plank proposing more legislation "to expose the treasonable activities of Communists."

The Republican platform accepted the concept of a bipartisan foreign policy. Paragraphs were included that supported the Marshall Plan for European recovery, the United Nations and recognition of Israel.

Following are excerpts from the Republican platform of 1948:

Civil Rights. This right of equal opportunity to work and to advance in life should never be limited in any individual because of race, religion, color, or country of origin. We favor the enactment and just enforcement of such Federal legislation as may be necessary to maintain this right at all times in every part of this Republic....

Lynching or any other form of mob violence anywhere is a disgrace to any civilized state, and we favor the prompt enactment of legislation to end this infamy....

We favor the abolition of the poll tax as a requisite to voting.

We are opposed to the idea of racial segregation in the armed services of the United States.

Housing. Housing can best be supplied and financed by private enterprise; but government can and should encourage the building of better homes at less cost. We recommend Federal aid to the States for local slum clearance and low-rental housing programs only where there is a need that cannot be met either by private enterprise or by the States and localities.

Labor. Here are some of the accomplishments of this Republican Congress: a sensible reform of the labor law, protecting all rights of Labor while safeguarding the entire community against those breakdowns in essential industries which endanger the health and livelihood of all....

We pledge continuing study to improve labor-management legislation in the light of experience and changing conditions....

We favor equal pay for equal work regardless of sex.

Internal Security. We pledge a vigorous enforcement of existing laws against Communists and enactment of such new legislation as may be necessary to expose the treasonable activities of Communists and defeat their objective of establishing here a godless dictatorship controlled from abroad.

Foreign Policy. We are proud of the part that Republicans have taken in those limited areas of foreign policy in which they have been permitted to participate. We shall invite the Minority Party to join us under the next Republican Administration in stopping partisan politics at the water's edge.

United Nations. We believe in collective security against aggression and in behalf of justice and freedom. We shall support the United Nations as the world's best hope in this direction, striving to strengthen it and promote its effective evolution and use. The United Nations should progressively establish international law, be freed of any veto in the peaceful settlement of international disputes, and be provided with the armed forces contemplated by the Charter.

Israel. We welcome Israel into the family of nations and take pride in the fact that the Republican Party was the first to call for the establishment of a free and independent Jewish Commonwealth.

Democrats

The Democratic delegates were in a melancholy mood when they gathered in Philadelphia in mid-July 1948. Roosevelt was dead; the Republicans had regained control of Congress in 1946; Roosevelt's successor, Harry S Truman, appeared unable to stem massive defections of liberals and southern conservatives from the New Deal coalition.

The dissatisfaction of southern delegates with policies of the national party was a prominent feature of the 1948 convention. Although the national committee had been mandated by the 1944 convention to devise a new vote allocation procedure that would appease the South, the redistribution of votes for the 1948 convention merely added two votes to each of the 36 states that backed Roosevelt in the 1944 election. This did not appreciably bolster southern strength.

As the convention progressed, southern displeasure focused on the civil rights issue. The Mississippi delegation included in its credentials anti-civil-rights resolutions which bound the delegation to bolt the convention if a states' rights plank were not included in the platform. The Mississippi resolutions also denied the power of the national convention to require the Democratic Party of Mississippi to support any candidate who favored President Truman's civil rights program or any candidate who failed to denounce that program.

A minority report was introduced that recommended the Mississippi delegation not be seated. This proposal was defeated by a voice vote, and in the interest of party harmony, no roll-call vote was taken. However, in an unusual move, several delegations, including those of California and New York, asked that they be recorded in favor of the minority report.

Joined by several other southern states, Texas presented a minority proposal to the rules committee report, which favored re-establishment of the two-thirds rule. The minority proposal, however, was beaten by a voice vote.

When the presidential balloting began, the entire Mississippi delegation and 13 members of the Alabama delegation withdrew in opposition to the convention's stand on civil rights. However, their withdrawal in no way jeopardized the nomination of Truman. Some party leaders had earlier flirted with the possibility of drafting Gen. Dwight D. Eisenhower or even Supreme Court Justice William O. Douglas. But the lack of interest of these two men in the Democratic nomination left the field clear for Truman.

The incumbent won a clear majority on the first ballot, receiving 926 votes to 266 for Georgia Sen. Richard B. Russell, who received the votes of more than 90 per cent of the remaining southern delegates. Among the states of the Old Confederacy, Truman received only 13 votes, all from North Carolina. After several small vote switches, the final tally stood: Truman, 947½; Russell, 263. *(Chart, p. 181)*

Veteran Kentucky Sen. Alben W. Barkley, the convention's keynoter, was nominated by acclamation for vice president.

Truman appeared before the convention to accept the nomination and aroused the dispirited delegates with a lively speech attacking the Republican Congress. Referring to it as the "worst 80th Congress," Truman announced that he would call a special session so that the Republicans could pass the legislation they said they favored in their platform.

The Democratic platform was adopted by a voice vote, but there was heated discussion of the civil rights section that preceded final acceptance. The civil rights plank, as presented to the convention by the platform committee, favored equal rights for all citizens but was couched in generalities such as those in the 1944 plank. Southern delegates, however, wanted a weaker commitment to civil rights, and three different amendments were offered by various southern delegations.

One, presented by former Gov. Dan Moody of Texas and signed by 15 members of the platform committee, was a broadly worded statement that emphasized the powers of the states. A second amendment, sponsored by two Tennessee members of the platform committee, was a brief, emphatic statement declaring the rights of the states. The third amendment, introduced by the Mississippi delegation as a substitute for the Moody amendment, specifically listed the powers of the states to maintain segregation. The Moody amendment was beaten, 924 to 310, with nearly all the support limited to the South. The other two amendments were rejected by voice vote. *(p. 181)*

With the introduction of these weakening amendments by the southern delegations, northern liberals countered by proposing an amendment designed to strengthen the civil rights plank. Introduced by former Rep. Andrew J. Biemiller of Wisconsin and championed by Minneapolis Mayor Hubert H. Humphrey, the amendment commended Truman's civil rights program and called for congressional action to guarantee equal rights in voting participation, employment opportunity, personal security and military service. The Biemiller amendment was passed, 651½ to 582½, with delegations from the larger northern states supporting it. Delegations from the South were in solid opposition and were joined by delegates from border and small northern states. *(p. 181)*

The rest of the platform lauded Truman's legislative program and blamed the Republican Congress for obstructing beneficial legislation. In the New Deal tradition, the platform advocated the extension of social security, raising of the minimum wage, establishment of national health insurance and the creation of a permanent flexible price support system for farmers. The Congress was blamed for obstructing passage of federal aid to education, comprehensive housing legislation and funding for the Marshall Plan to help rebuild Europe. The Republicans were also criticized for crippling reciprocal trade agreements, passage of the Taft-Hartley Act and even the rising rate of inflation.

The development of the cold war with the Communist world produced a new issue, internal security, on which the two major parties differed sharply. While the Republican position stressed the pursuit of subversives, the Democrats placed more emphasis on the protection of individual rights.

In foreign affairs, the Democratic platform called for the establishment of a United Nations military force, international control of the atomic bomb and recognition of the state of Israel.

Following are excerpts from the Democratic platform of 1948:

Civil Rights. We highly commend President Harry S Truman for his courageous stand on the issue of civil rights.

We call upon the Congress to support our President in guaranteeing these basic and fundamental American Principles: (1) the right of full and equal political participation; (2) the right to equal opportunity of employment; (3) the right of security of person; (4) and the right of equal treatment in the service and defense of our nation.

Housing. We shall enact comprehensive housing legislation, including provisions for slum clearance and low-rent housing projects initiated by local agencies. This nation is shamed by the failure of the Republican 80th Congress to pass the vitally needed general housing legislation as recommended by the President. Adequate housing will end the need for rent control. Until then, it must be continued.

Social Security, Health Insurance. We favor the extension of the Social Security program established under Democratic leadership, to provide additional protection against the hazards of old age, disability, disease or death. We believe that this program should include:

Increases in old-age and survivors' insurance benefits by at least 50 per cent, and reduction of the eligibility age for women from 65 to 60 years; extension of old-age and survivors' and unemployment insurance to all workers not now covered; insurance against loss of earnings on account of illness or disability; improved public assistance for the needy.

Labor. We advocate the repeal of the Taft-Hartley Act. It was enacted by the Republican 80th Congress over the President's veto....

We favor the extension of the coverage of the Fair Labor Standards Act as recommended by President Truman, and the adoption of a minimum wage of at least 75 cents an hour in place of the present obsolete and inadequate minimum of 40 cents an hour.

We favor legislation assuring that the workers of our nation receive equal pay for equal work, regardless of sex.

United Nations. We will continue to lead the way toward curtailment of the use of the veto. We shall favor such amendments and modifications of the charter as experience may justify. We will continue our efforts toward the establishment of an international armed force to aid its authority. We advocate the grant of a loan to the United Nations recommended by the President, but denied by the Republican Congress, for the construction of the United Nations headquarters in this country.

Disarmament. We advocate the effective international control of weapons of mass destruction, including the atomic bomb, and we approve continued and vigorous ef-

forts within the United Nations to bring about the successful consummation of the proposals which our Government has advanced.

Israel. We pledge full recognition to the State of Israel. We affirm our pride that the United States under the leadership of President Truman played a leading role in the adoption of the resolution of November 29, 1947, by the United Nations General Assembly for the creation of a Jewish State.

Internal Security. We shall continue vigorously to enforce the laws against subversive activities, observing at all times the constitutional guarantees which protect free speech, the free press and honest political activity. We shall strengthen our laws against subversion to the full extent necessary, protecting at all times our traditional individual freedoms.

States' Rights (Dixiecrats)

Provoked by the Democratic convention's adoption of a strong civil rights plank, Gov. Fielding L. Wright of Mississippi invited other disgruntled southern Democrats to meet in Birmingham, Ala., on July 17 to select a regional ticket that would reflect southern views.

It was a disgruntled group that gathered in Birmingham, just three days after the close of the Democratic convention. Placards on the floor of the convention hall identified 13 states, yet there were no delegates from Georgia, Kentucky or North Carolina, and Virginia was represented by four University of Virginia students and an Alexandria woman who was returning home from a trip south. Most major southern politicians shied away from the bolters, fearing that involvement would jeopardize their standing with the national party and their seniority in Congress.

Former Alabama Gov. Frank M. Dixon vocalized the anti-civil-rights mood of the gathering with a keynote address charging that Truman's civil rights program would "reduce us to the status of a mongrel, inferior race, mixed in blood, our Anglo-Saxon heritage a mockery."

As its standard-bearers, the convention chose South Carolina Gov. J. Strom Thurmond for president and Gov. Wright for vice president. Thurmond's acceptance speech touched on another grievance of bolting southern Democrats: their decreasing power within the Democratic Party. Thurmond warned: "If the South should vote for Truman this year, we might just as well petition the Government to give us colonial status."

The platform adopted by the Dixiecrats was barely 1,000 words long, but it forcefully presented the case for states' rights. The platform warned that the tendency toward greater federal power ultimately would establish a totalitarian police state.

The Dixiecrats saved their most vitriolic passages to describe the civil rights plank adopted by the Democratic convention. They declared their support for segregation and charged that the plank adopted by the Democrats was meant "to embarrass and humiliate the South."

The platform also charged the national Democratic Party with ingratitude, claiming that the South had supported the Democratic ticket with "clock-like regularity" for nearly 100 years, but that now the national party was being dominated by states controlled by the Republicans.

Following are excerpts from the States' Rights platform of 1948:

States' Rights. We believe that the protection of the American people against the onward march of totalitarian government requires a faithful observance of Article X of the American Bill of Rights which provides that: "The powers not delegated to the United States by the Constitution, nor prohibited by it to the states, are reserved to the states respectively, or to the people."

Civil Rights. We stand for the segregation of the races and the racial integrity of each race; the constitutional right to choose one's associates; to accept private employment without governmental interference, and to earn one's living in any lawful way. We oppose the elimination of segregation employment by Federal bureaucrats called for by the misnamed civil rights program. We favor home rule, local self-government and a minimum interference with individual rights.

We oppose and condemn the action of the Democratic convention in sponsoring a civil rights program calling for the elimination of segregation, social equality by Federal fiat, regulation of private employment practices, voting and local law enforcement.

We affirm that the effective enforcement of such a program would be utterly destructive of the social, economic and political life of the Southern people, and of other localities in which there may be differences in race, creed or national origin in appreciable numbers.

Progressives

On Dec. 29, 1947, former Vice President Henry A. Wallace announced his presidential candidacy at the head of a new liberal party. Officially named the Progressive Party at its convention in Philadelphia in late July 1948, the new party was composed of some liberal Democrats as well as more radical groups and individuals that included some Communists.

Nearly 3,200 delegates nominated Wallace for the presidency and Democratic Sen. Glen H. Taylor of Idaho as his running mate. The colorful Taylor and his family regaled the delegates with their rendition of "When You Were Sweet Sixteen."

On the final night of the convention, 32,000 spectators assembled to hear Wallace deliver his acceptance speech at Shibe Park. The Progressive standard-bearer expressed his belief in "progressive capitalism," which would place "human rights above property rights," and envisioned "a new frontier...across the wilderness of poverty and sickness."

Former Roosevelt associate Rexford G. Tugwell chaired the 74-member platform committee that drafted a detailed platform, about 9,000 words in length, that was adopted by the convention. The platform denounced the two major parties as champions of big business and claimed the new party to be the true "political heirs of Jefferson, Jackson and Lincoln." However, many political observers and opponents of the Progressives dismissed the new party as a Communist-front organization.

Although numerous positions taken by the Progressives in 1948 were considered radical, many were later adopted or seriously considered by the major parties.

The foreign policy section of the platform advocated negotiations between the United States and the Soviet Union ultimately leading to a peace agreement, and sharply criticized the "anti-Soviet hysteria" of the period. The platform called for repeal of the draft; repudiation of the Marshall Plan; worldwide disarmament featuring abolition of the atomic bomb; amnesty for conscientious objectors imprisoned in World War II; recognition and aid to Israel; extension of United Nations humanitarian programs, and the establishment of a world legislature.

In the domestic area, the Progressives opposed internal security legislation, advocated the 18-year-old vote, favored the creation of a Department of Culture, called for

food stamp and school hot lunch programs and proposed a federal housing plan that would build 25 million homes in 10 years and subsidize low-income housing.

The Progressives also reiterated the proposals of earlier third parties by favoring the direct election of the president and vice president, extensive tax reform, stricter control of monopolies and the nationalization of the principal means of communication, transportation and finance.

The Progressives joined the Democrats and Republicans in proposing strong civil rights legislation and an equal rights amendment for women.

Following are excerpts from the Progressive platform of 1948:

Soviet Union. The Progressive Party...demands negotiation and discussion with the Soviet Union to find areas of agreement to win the peace.

Disarmament. The Progressive Party will work through the United Nations for a world disarmament agreement to outlaw the atomic bomb, bacteriological warfare, and all other instruments of mass destruction; to destroy existing stockpiles of atomic bombs and to establish United Nations controls, including inspection, over the production of atomic energy; and to reduce conventional armaments drastically in accordance with resolutions already passed by the United Nations General Assembly.

World Legislation. The only ultimate alternative to war is the abandonment of the principle of the coercion of sovereignties by sovereignties and the adoption of the principle of the just enforcement upon individuals of world federal law, enacted by a world federal legislature with limited but adequate powers to safeguard the common defense and the general welfare of all mankind.

Draft. The Progressive Party calls for the repeal of the peacetime draft and the rejection of Universal Military Training.

Amnesty. We demand amnesty for conscientious objectors imprisoned in World War II.

Internal Security. We denounce anti-Soviet hysteria as a mask for monopoly, militarism, and reaction....

The Progressive Party will fight for the constitutional rights of Communists and all other political groups to express their views as the first line in the defense of the liberties of a democratic people.

Civil Rights. The Progressive Party condemns segregation and discrimination in all its forms and in all places....

We call for a Presidential proclamation ending segregation and all forms of discrimination in the armed services and Federal employment.

We demand Federal anti-lynch, anti-discrimination, and fair-employment-practices legislation, and legislation abolishing segregation in interstate travel.

We call for immediate passage of anti-poll tax legislation, enactment of a universal suffrage law to permit all citizens to vote in Federal elections, and the full use of Federal enforcement powers to assure free exercise of the right to franchise.

Food Stamps, School Lunches. We also call for assistance to low-income consumers through such programs as the food stamp plan and the school hot-lunch program.

Housing. We pledge an attack on the chronic housing shortage and the slums through a long-range program to build 25 million new homes during the next ten years. This program will include public subsidized housing for low-income families.

Nationalization. As a first step, the largest banks, the railroads, the merchant marine, the electric power and gas industry, and industries primarily dependent on government funds or government purchases such as the aircraft, the synthetic rubber and synthetic oil industries must be placed under public ownership.

Youth Vote. We call for the right to vote at eighteen.

1952 Conventions

Presidential Candidates

Dwight D. Eisenhower
Republican

Adlai E. Stevenson
Democrat

Republicans

For the third straight time, both major parties held their conventions in the same city. In 1952, the site was Chicago; the Republicans met there in early July two weeks before the Democrats. The battle for the presidential nomination pitted the hero of the party's conservative wing, Sen. Robert A. Taft of Ohio, against the favorite of most moderate and liberal Republicans, Gen. Dwight D. Eisenhower. The general, a Texas native, had resigned as supreme commander of the North Atlantic Treaty Organization (NATO) less than six weeks before the convention in order to pursue the nomination actively.

As in 1912, when Taft's father had engaged in a bitter struggle with Theodore Roosevelt for the nomination, the outcome of the presidential race was determined in preliminary battles over convention rules and credentials.

The first confrontation came on the issue of the voting rights of challenged delegates. The Taft forces proposed adoption of the 1948 rules, which would have allowed contested delegates to vote on all cases except their own. The Eisenhower forces countered by proposing what they called a "fair play amendment," which would seat only those contested delegates who were approved by at least a two-thirds vote of the national committee. At stake were a total of 68 delegates from Georgia, Louisiana and Texas, with the large majority of the challenged delegates in favor of Taft. The Taft forces introduced a substitute to the "fair play amendment," designed to exempt seven delegates from Louisiana. On the first test of strength between the two candidates, the Eisenhower forces were victorious, as the substitute amendment was defeated, 658 to 548. The "fair play amendment" was subsequently approved by a voice vote. *(Chart, p. 184)*

The second confrontation developed with the report of the credentials committee. The Eisenhower forces presented a minority report concerning the contested Georgia, Louisiana and Texas seats. After a bitter debate, a roll-call vote was taken on the Georgia challenge, with the Eisenhower forces winning again, 607 to 531.

The Louisiana and Texas challenges were settled in favor of the Eisenhower forces without a roll-call vote. The favorable settlement of the credentials challenges increased the momentum behind the Eisenhower candidacy

Before the presidential balloting began, a nonpartisan debate was held on a proposal to add state chairmen to the national committee from states recording Republican electoral majorities and to remove the requirement that women hold one of each state's seats on the national committee. The proposal was primarily intended to decrease southern influence on the national committee. But the major opposition was raised by a number of women delegates who objected to the rule change; however, their effort to defeat it was rejected by voice vote.

Five men were nominated for the presidency, but on completion of the first roll call, Eisenhower had 595 votes and was within nine votes of victory. Taft was a strong second with 500 votes. However, before a second ballot could begin, Minnesota switched 19 votes from favorite son Harold E. Stassen to Eisenhower, giving the latter the nomination. After a series of vote changes, the final tally stood: Eisenhower, 845; Taft, 280; other candidates, 81. The general's nomination was subsequently made unanimous.

Eisenhower's choice as a running mate, 39-year-old Sen. Richard M. Nixon of California, was nominated by acclamation. After Nixon's selection, Eisenhower delivered his acceptance speech, promising to lead a "crusade" against "a party too long in power."

The 6,000-word platform was adopted by a voice vote. The document included a sharp attack on the Democrats, charging the Roosevelt and Truman administrations with "violating our liberties...by seizing powers never granted," "shielding traitors" and attempting to establish "national socialism." The foreign policy section, written by John Foster Dulles, supported the concept of collective security but denounced the Truman policy of containment and blamed the administration for the Communist takeover of China. The Republican platform advocated increased national preparedness.

As well as castigating the Democrats for an incompetent foreign policy, the Republicans denounced their opposition for laxness in maintaining internal security. A plank asserted: "There are no Communists in the Republican Party."

On most domestic issues the platform advocated a reduction in federal power. The civil rights plank proposed federal action to outlaw lynching, poll taxes and discriminatory employment practices. However, unlike the plank four years earlier, the Republican position included a paragraph that declared the individual states had primary responsibility for their own domestic institutions. On a related issue of states' rights, the Republicans, as in 1948, favored state control of tideland resources.

Following are excerpts from the Republican platform of 1952:

Democratic Failures. We charge that they have arrogantly deprived our citizens of precious liberties by seizing powers never granted.

We charge that they work unceasingly to achieve their goal of national socialism....

We charge that they have shielded traitors to the Nation in high places, and that they have created enemies abroad where we should have friends.

We charge that they have violated our liberties by turning loose upon the country a swarm of arrogant bureaucrats and their agents who meddle intolerably in the lives and occupations of our citizens.

We charge that there has been corruption in high places, and that examples of dishonesty and dishonor have shamed the moral standards of the American people.

We charge that they have plunged us into war in Korea without the consent of our citizens through their authorized representatives in the Congress, and have carried on that war without will to victory....

Tehran, Yalta and Potsdam were the scenes of those tragic blunders with others to follow. The leaders of the Administration in power acted without the knowledge or consent of Congress or of the American people. They traded our overwhelming victory for a new enemy and for new oppressions and new wars which were quick to come.

...And finally they denied the military aid that had been authorized by Congress and which was crucially needed if China were to be saved. Thus they substituted on our Pacific flank a murderous enemy for an ally and friend.

Internal Security. By the Administration's appeasement of Communism at home and abroad it has permitted Communists and their fellow travelers to serve in many key agencies and to infiltrate our American life....

There are no Communists in the Republican Party. We have always recognized Communism to be a world conspiracy against freedom and religion. We never compromised with Communism and we have fought to expose it and to eliminate it in government and American life.

Civil Rights. We believe that it is the primary responsibility of each State to order and control its own domestic institutions, and this power, reserved to the states, is essential to the maintenance of our Federal Republic. However, we believe that the Federal Government should take supplemental action within its constitutional jurisdiction to oppose discrimination against race, religion or national origin.

We will prove our good faith by:

Appointing qualified persons, without distinction of race, religion or national origin, to responsible positions in the Government.

Federal action toward the elimination of lynching.

Federal action toward the elimination of poll taxes as a prerequisite to voting.

Appropriate action to end segregation in the District of Columbia.

Enacting Federal legislation to further just and equitable treatment in the area of discriminatory employment practices. Federal action should not duplicate state efforts to end such practices; should not set up another huge bureaucracy.

Labor. We favor the retention of the Taft-Hartley Act.

...We urge the adoption of such amendments to the Taft-Hartley Act as time and experience show to be desirable, and which further protect the rights of labor, management and the public.

Democrats

The Democrats held their 1952 convention in Chicago in late July. The convention lasted six days, the longest by either party in the post-World-War-II years. The proceedings were enlivened by disputes over credentials and a party loyalty pledge and a wide-open race for the presidential nomination.

The legitimately selected Texas delegation, dominated by the Dixiecrat wing of the state party, was challenged by a delegation loyal to the national party, but chosen in a rump assembly. Without a roll-call vote, the convention approved the credentials of the Dixiecrat-oriented delegates, although their seating was protested by northern liberals.

The Dixiecrat bolt of 1948 resulted in the introduction of a party loyalty pledge at the 1952 convention. The resolution, introduced by Sen. Blair Moody of Michigan, proposed that no delegate be seated who would not assure the credentials committee that he would work to have the Democratic national ticket placed on the ballot in his state under the party's name. This resolution was aimed at several southern states which had listed the Thurmond-Wright ticket under the Democratic Party label on their state ballots in 1948.

Sen. Spessard L. Holland of Florida introduced a substitute resolution that simply declared it would be "honorable" for each delegate to adhere to the decisions reached in the convention. Holland's resolution, however, was defeated by a voice vote, and the Moody resolution was approved in a similar fashion.

The report of the credentials committee listed three southern states—Louisiana, South Carolina and Virginia—that declined to abide by the Moody resolution. The question of their seating rights came to a head during the roll call for presidential nominations, when Virginia questioned its status in the convention. A motion to seat the Virginia delegation in spite of its non-observance of the resolution was presented for a vote. Although not agreeing to the pledge, the chairman of the Virginia delegation indicated that the problem prompting the Moody resolution was covered by state law. After a long, confusing roll call, interrupted frequently by demands to poll individual delegates, the motion to seat the Virginia delegation passed, 650½ to 518. (Chart, p. 183)

After efforts to adjourn were defeated, the Louisiana and South Carolina delegations offered assurances similar to those presented by Virginia and were seated by a voice vote.

Eleven names were placed in nomination for the presidency, although the favorite of most party leaders, Illinois Gov. Adlai E. Stevenson, was a reluctant candidate. Stevenson expressed interest only in running for re-election as governor, but a draft-Stevenson movement developed and gained strength quickly as the convention proceeded.

Sen. Estes Kefauver of Tennessee, a powerful vote-getter in the primaries, was the leader on the first ballot, with 340 votes. He was followed by Stevenson with 273, Georgia Sen. Richard B. Russell, the southern favorite, with 268, and W. Averell Harriman of New York with 123½.

The second ballot saw gains by the three front-runners, with Kefauver's vote rising to 362½, Stevenson's to 324½ and Russell's to 294. A recess was taken during which Harriman and Massachusetts' favorite son, Gov. Paul A. Dever, both withdrew in favor of Stevenson.

The Illinois governor won a narrow majority on the third ballot, receiving 617½ of the 1,230 convention votes. Kefauver finished with 275½ and Russell with 261. The selection of Stevenson represented the first success for a presidential draft movement of a reluctant candidate since the nomination of James A. Garfield by the Republicans in 1880. *(Chart, p. 183)*

For vice president, Stevenson chose Alabama Sen. John J. Sparkman, who was nominated by acclamation.

Although a reluctant candidate, Stevenson promised the delegates a fighting campaign, but also warned: "Better we lose the election than mislead the people; and better we lose than misgovern the people."

The Democratic platform was adopted without the rancor that had accompanied consideration of the party platform four years earlier. The document was approved by a voice vote, although both the Georgia and Mississippi delegations asked that they be recorded in opposition.

The platform promised extension and improvement of New Deal and Fair Deal policies that had been proposed and enacted over the previous 20 years. The party's foremost goal was stated to be "peace with honor," which could be achieved by support for a strengthened United Nations, coupled with the policy of collective security in the form of American assistance for allies around the world. The peaceful use of atomic energy was pledged, as were efforts to establish an international control system. However, the platform also promised the use of atomic weapons, if needed, for national defense.

The civil rights section of the platform was nearly identical to the plank that appeared in the 1948 platform. Federal legislation was called for to guarantee equal rights in voting participation, employment opportunity and personal security.

The platform called for changes in the social security and tax systems. A plank favored the extension of social security and elimination of the work clause so that the elderly could collect benefits and still work. The closing of tax loopholes and a reduction of taxes were recommended, although the latter proposal would not be effected until national defense needs were met.

Political reform was recommended that would require the disclosure of campaign expenses in federal elections.

The Democrats and Republicans took different stands on several major domestic issues. The Democrats favored repeal of the Taft-Hartley Act; the Republicans proposed to retain the act but make modifications where necessary. The Democrats advocated closing tax loopholes and, after defense needs were met, reducing taxes. The Republicans called for tax reduction based on a cut in government spending. In education, the Democrats favored federal assistance to state and local units; the Republicans viewed education solely as the responsibility of local and state governments.

The Democrats favored continuation of federal power projects, while the Republicans opposed "all-powerful federal socialistic valley authorities."

Both parties favored a parity price program for farmers. The Democrats advocated a mandatory price support program for basic agricultural products at not less than 90 per cent of parity, and the Republicans proposing a program that would establish "full parity prices for all farm products."

Following are excerpts from the Democratic platform of 1952:

Atomic Energy. In the field of atomic energy, we pledge ourselves:

(1) to maintain vigorous and non-partisan civilian administrations, with adequate security safeguards;

(2) to promote the development of nuclear energy for peaceful purposes in the interests of America and mankind;

(3) to build all the atomic and hydrogen firepower needed to defend our country, deter aggression, and promote world peace;

(4) To exert every effort to bring about bona fide international control and inspection of all atomic weapons.

Civil Rights. We will continue our efforts to eradicate discrimination based on race, religion or national origin....

We are proud of the progress that has been made in securing equality of treatment and opportunity in the Nation's armed forces and the civil service and all areas under Federal jurisdiction....

At the same time, we favor Federal legislation effectively to secure these rights to everyone: (1) the right to equal opportunity for employment; (2) the right to security of persons; (3) the right to full and equal participation in the Nation's political life, free from arbitrary restraints.

Agriculture. We will continue to protect the producers of basic agricultural commodities under the terms of a mandatory price support program at not less than ninety per cent of parity. We continue to advocate practical methods for extending price supports to other storables and to the producers of perishable commodities, which account for three-fourths of all farm income.

Campaign Finance. We advocate new legislation to provide effective regulation and full disclosure of campaign expenditures in elections to Federal office, including political advertising from any source.

Labor. We strongly advocate the repeal of the Taft-Hartley Act.

Tax Reform. We believe in fair and equitable taxation. We oppose a Federal general sales tax. We adhere to the principle of ability to pay. We have enacted an emergency excess profits tax to prevent profiteering from the defense program and have vigorously attacked special tax privileges.... As rapidly as defense requirements permit, we favor reducing taxes, especially for people with lower incomes....

Justice requires the elimination of tax loopholes which favor special groups. We pledge continued efforts to the elimination of remaining loopholes.

Social Security. We favor the complete elimination of the work clause for the reason that those contributing to the Social Security program should be permitted to draw benefits, upon reaching the age of eligibility, and still continue to work.

Education. Local, State and Federal governments have shared responsibility to contribute appropriately to the pressing needs of our educational system. We urge that Federal contributions be made available to State and local units which adhere to basic minimum standards.

The Federal Government should not dictate nor control educational policy.

1956 Conventions

Presidential Candidates

Adlai E. Stevenson
Democrat

Dwight D. Eisenhower
Republican

Democrats

Both parties held their conventions in August, the latest date ever for the Republicans and the latest for the Democrats since the wartime convention of 1864. For the first time since 1888 the date of the Democratic convention preceded that of the Republicans. The Democrats met in mid-August in Chicago with an allotment of 1,372 votes, the largest in party history. The increased allotment was the result of a new distribution formula, which for the first time rewarded states for electing Democratic governors and senators in addition to supporting the party's presidential candidate.

A provision of the convention call handled the party loyalty question, a thorny issue at the 1952 convention, by assuming that in the absence of a challenge, any delegate would be understood to have the best interests of the party at heart. Another provision of the call threatened any national committeeman who did not support the party's national ticket with removal from the Democratic National Committee.

In an unusual occurrence, nominating speeches were delivered by a past and a future President for men who would not attain the office themselves. Sen. John F. Kennedy of Massachusetts placed Adlai E. Stevenson's name in nomination, while former President Truman seconded the nomination of New York Gov. W. Averell Harriman. Truman criticized Stevenson as a "defeatist," but was countered by Mrs. Eleanor Roosevelt, who appeared before the convention in support of the former Illinois governor.

In spite of the oratorical byplay, Stevenson was in good position to win the nomination before the convention even began, having eliminated his principal rival, Tennessee Sen. Estes Kefauver, in the primaries. Stevenson won a majority on the first ballot, receiving 905½ votes to easily defeat Harriman, who had 210. Sen. Lyndon B. Johnson of Texas finished third, with 80 votes. Upon completion of the roll call, a motion was approved to make Stevenson's nomination unanimous. *(Chart, p. 185)*

In an unusual move, Stevenson announced that he would not personally select his running mate but would leave the choice to the convention. Stevenson's desire for an open selection was designed to contrast with the expected cut-and-dried nature of the upcoming Republican convention. But the unusual move caught both delegates and prospective candidates off guard.

Numerous delegations passed on the first ballot, and upon completion of the roll call, votes were scattered among 13 different candidates. When the vote totals were announced at the end of the roll call, Kefauver led with 483½ votes, followed by Kennedy with 304, Tennessee Sen. Albert A. Gore with 178, Mayor Robert F. Wagner of New York City with 162½ and Minnesota Sen. Hubert H. Humphrey with 134½. Six hundred and eighty-seven votes were needed to nominate.

With a coalition that included the majority of southern and eastern delegates, Kennedy drew into the lead on the second ballot. After the roll call but before the chair recognized vote changes, the totals stood: Kennedy, 618; Kefauver, 551½; Gore, 110½. Kentucky, the first state to be recognized, shifted its 30 votes to Kennedy, leaving the 39-year-old senator fewer than 40 votes short of the nomination.

But Gore was recognized next and began a bandwagon for Kefauver by withdrawing in favor of his Tennessee colleague. Other states followed Gore's lead, and at the conclusion of the vote shifts, Kefauver had a clear majority. The final tally was Kefauver, 755½ and Kennedy, 589. Kennedy moved that his opponent's nomination be made unanimous.

Ironically, Kefauver won a majority of the votes in only two states in his home region, Tennessee and Florida. His strength lay in midwestern and western delegations.

As in 1948, platform debate focused on the civil rights issue. A Minnesota member of the platform committee introduced a minority report which advocated a civil rights plank stronger than that in the majority report. The plank presented by the platform committee pledged to carry out Supreme Court decisions on desegregation, but not through the use of force. The party promised to continue to work for equal rights in voting, employment, personal security and education. The Minnesota substitute was more specific, as it favored federal legislation to achieve equal voting rights and employment opportunities and to guarantee personal safety. The minority plank also favored more rigid enforcement of civil rights legislation. Although several states clamored for a roll-call vote, the chair took a voice vote, which went against the Minnesota substitute.

The entire platform was the longest yet approved by a Democratic convention, about 12,000 words. The document was divided into 11 sections, the first dealing with defense and foreign policy and the remainder with domestic issues.

The platform described President Eisenhower as a "political amateur...dominated...by special privilege." It applauded the legislative accomplishments of the Democratic Congress elected in 1954 and proposed a continuation of the social and economic legislation begun during the New Deal.

The foreign policy of the Eisenhower administration was criticized in a plank that accused the Republicans of cutting funds for the military in an attempt to balance the budget. The Democrats declared that the United States must have the strongest military in the world in order to discourage aggression by America's enemies. The foreign policy plank also pledged to strengthen the United Nations as a peacekeeping organization and promised to work diligently for worldwide disarmament.

The platform blamed the Republicans for allowing big business to dominate the economy and promised tax relief and other government assistance to help small business. The Democrats advocated repeal of the Taft-Hartley Act, as the party had done in every platform since 1948, and favored an increase in the minimum wage. Tax reductions were proposed for lower-income taxpayers, and an increase of at least $200 in the personal tax exemption was recommended.

For farmers, the Democrats proposed price supports at 90 per cent of parity on basic crops, as opposed to the Republican program of flexible price supports.

For the first time since the beginning of the New Deal, the Democratic platform mentioned the importance of states' rights. The party also reiterated its position on education, which advocated federal assistance, but stated that ultimate control of the schools lay in the hands of state and local governments.

In political reform, the platform proposed restrictions on government secrecy and repeated the party's call for the passage of an equal rights amendment.

Following are excerpts from the Democratic platform of 1956:

> **Foreign Policy.** *The Failure at Home.* Political considerations of budget balancing and tax reduction now come before the wants of our national security and the needs of our Allies. The Republicans have slashed our own armed strength, weakened our capacity to deal with military threats, stifled our air force, starved our army and weakened our capacity to deal with aggression of any sort save by retreat or by the alternatives, "massive retaliation" and global atomic war. Yet, while our troubles mount, they tell us our prestige was never higher, they tell us we were never more secure.

> **Disarmament.** To eliminate the danger of atomic war, a universal, effective and enforced disarmament system must be the goal of responsible men and women everywhere. So long as we lack enforceable international control of weapons, we must maintain armed strength to avoid war. But technological advances in the field of nuclear weapons make disarmament an ever more urgent problem. Time and distance can never again protect any nation of the world.

> **Labor.** We unequivocally advocate repeal of the Taft-Hartley Act. The Act must be repealed because State "right-to-work" laws have their genesis in its discriminatory anti-labor provisions....

> The Taft-Hartley Act has been proven to be inadequate, unworkable and unfair. It interferes in an arbitrary manner with collective bargaining, causing imbalance in the relationship between management and labor.

> **Agriculture.** Undertake immediately by appropriate action to endeavor to regain the full 100 per cent of parity the farmers received under the Democratic Administrations. We will achieve this by means of supports on basic commodities at 90 per cent of parity and by means of commodity loans, direct purchases, direct payments to producers, marketing agreements and orders, production adjustments, or a combination of these, including legislation, to bring order and stability into the relationship between the producer, the processor and the consumer.

> **Education.** We are now faced with shortages of educational facilities that threaten national security, economic prosperity and human well-being. The resources of our States and localities are already strained to the limit. Federal aid and action should be provided, within the traditional framework of State and local control.

> **Tax Reform.** We favor realistic tax adjustments, giving first consideration to small independent business and the small individual taxpayer. Lower-income families need tax relief; only a Democratic victory will assure this. We favor an increase in the present personal tax exemption of $600 to a minimum of at least $800.

> **Government Secrecy.** *Freedom of Information.* During recent years there has developed a practice on the part of Federal agencies to delay and withhold information which is needed by Congress and the general public to make important decisions affecting their lives and destinies. We believe that this trend toward secrecy in Government should be reversed and that the Federal Government should return to its basic tradition of exchanging and promoting the freest flow of information possible in those unclassified areas where secrets involving weapons development and bona fide national security are not involved.

> **States' Rights.** While we recognize the existence of honest differences of opinion as to the true location of the Constitutional line of demarcation between the Federal Government and the States, the Democratic Party expressly recognizes the vital importance of the respective States in our Federal Union. The Party of Jefferson and Jackson pledges itself to continued support of those sound principles of local government which will best serve the welfare of our people and the safety of our democratic rights.

> **Civil Rights.** We are proud of the record of the Democratic Party in securing equality of treatment and opportunity in the nation's armed forces, the Civil Service, and in all areas under Federal jurisdiction. The Democratic Party pledges itself to continue its efforts to eliminate illegal discriminations of all kinds, in relation to (1) full rights to vote, (2) full rights to engage in gainful occupations, (3) full rights to enjoy security of the person, and (4) full rights to education in all publicly supported institutions.

> Recent decisions of the Supreme Court of the United States relating to segregation in publicly supported schools and elsewhere have brought consequences of vast importance to our Nation as a whole and especially to communities directly affected. We reject all proposals for the use of force to interfere with the orderly determination of these matters by the courts.

Republicans

The Republicans opened their convention in San Francisco three days after the close of the Democratic convention in Chicago. In contrast to the turbulent convention of their adversaries, the Republicans' renomination of

Eisenhower and Nixon was a formality. The only possible obstacle to Eisenhower's candidacy was his health, but by August 1956 his recovery from a heart attack and an ileitis operation was complete enough to allow him to seek a second term. On the convention's single roll call for president, Eisenhower received all 1,323 votes.

What drama occurred at the Republican convention surrounded the vice presidential nomination. Several weeks before the opening of the convention, former Minnesota Gov. Harold Stassen, then disarmament adviser to Eisenhower, had begun a movement to replace Vice President Nixon with Massachusetts Gov. Christian A. Herter. However, with lack of interest from party leaders, this movement petered out. At the convention, both Herter and Stassen gave nominating speeches for Nixon. During the roll call, a commotion was caused by a Nebraska delegate, who attempted to nominate "Joe Smith." After some discussion, it was determined that "Joe Smith" was a fictitious individual, and the offending delegate was escorted from the hall. On the one ballot for vice president, a unanimous vote was recorded for Nixon.

While no opposition to the platform was expressed on the floor of the convention, several southern delegates were unhappy with the civil rights plank and withdrew from the convention. The plank in question listed advances in desegregation under the Republican administration, voiced acceptance of the Supreme Court ruling on school desegregation and pledged to enforce existing civil rights statutes.

The platform as a whole was slightly longer than the Democratic document and was dedicated to Eisenhower and "the youth of America." Unlike the Democratic platform, which began with a discussion of foreign policy and national defense, the first issue pursued by the Republicans was the economy.

The Eisenhower administration was praised for balancing the budget, reducing taxes and halting inflation. The platform promised continued balanced budgets, gradual reduction of the national debt and cuts in government spending consistent with the maintenance of a strong military. Two measures favored by the Democrats, tax relief for small businesses and tax reductions for low-income and middle-income families, were both mentioned as secondary economic goals in the Republican platform.

The labor plank advocated revision but not repeal of the Taft-Hartley Act. The agricultural section favored elimination of price-depressing surpluses and continuation of the flexible price-support program. As they had for the past quarter century, the Republicans joined the Democrats in recommending passage of an equal rights amendment.

The foreign policy section of the Republican platform praised the Eisenhower administration for ending the Korean War, stemming the worldwide advance of communism and entering new collective security agreements. The plank also emphasized the necessity of a bipartisan foreign policy. The "preservation" of Israel was viewed as an "important tenet of American foreign policy," a notable difference from the Democratic platform, which took a more even-handed approach toward both Israel and the Arab states.

The national defense section emphasized the United States' possession of "the strongest striking force in the world," a rebuttal to Democratic charges that the Republicans had jeopardized the efficiency of the armed forces in an effort to balance the budget.

Following are excerpts from the Republican platform of 1956:

Economy. We pledge to pursue the following objectives:

Further reductions in Government spending as recommended in the Hoover Commission Report, without weakening the support of a superior defense program or depreciating the quality of essential services of government to our people.

Continued balancing of the budget, to assure the financial strength of the country which is so vital to the struggle of the free world in its battle against Communism; and to maintain the purchasing power of a sound dollar, and the value of savings, pensions and insurance.

Gradual reduction of the national debt.

Then, insofar as consistent with a balanced budget, we pledge to work toward these additional objectives:

Further reductions in taxes with particular consideration for low and middle income families.

Initiation of a sound policy of tax reductions which will encourage small independent businesses to modernize and progress.

Labor. Revise and improve the Taft-Hartley Act so as to protect more effectively the rights of labor unions, management, the individual worker, and the public. The protection of the right of workers to organize into unions and to bargain collectively is the firm and permanent policy of the Eisenhower Administration.

Agriculture. This program must be versatile and flexible to meet effectively the impact of rapidly changing conditions. It does not envision making farmers dependent upon direct governmental payments for their incomes. Our objective is markets which return full parity to our farm and ranch people when they sell their products.

Civil Rights. The Republican Party accepts the decision of the U.S. Supreme Court that racial discrimination in publicly supported schools must be progressively eliminated. We concur in the conclusion of the Supreme Court that its decision directing school desegregation should be accomplished with "all deliberate speed" locally through Federal District Courts. The implementation order of the Supreme Court recognizes the complex and acutely emotional problems created by its decision in certain sections of our country where racial patterns have been developed in accordance with prior and longstanding decisions of the same tribunal.

We believe that true progress can be attained through intelligent study, understanding, education and good will. Use of force or violence by any group or agency will tend only to worsen the many problems inherent in the situation. This progress must be encouraged and the work of the courts supported in every legal manner by all branches of the Federal Government to the end that the constitutional ideal of equality before the law, regardless of race, creed or color, will be steadily achieved.

Foreign Policy. The advance of Communism has been checked, and, at key points, thrown back. The once-monolithic structure of International Communism, denied the stimulant of successive conquests, has shown hesitancy both internally and abroad.

National Defense. We *have* the strongest striking force in the world—in the air—on the sea—and a magnificent supporting land force in our Army and Marine Corps.

Israel. We regard the preservation of Israel as an important tenet of American foreign policy. We are determined that the integrity of an independent Jewish State shall be maintained. We shall support the independence of Israel against armed aggression. The best hope for peace in the Middle East lies in the United Nations. We pledge our continued efforts to eliminate the obstacles to a lasting peace in this area.

1960 Conventions

Presidential Candidates

John F. Kennedy
Democrat

Richard M. Nixon
Republican

Democrats

For the first time, a national political convention was held in Los Angeles. More than 4,000 delegates and alternates converged on the California metropolis in July to select the Democratic standard-bearers for 1960. The delegate allocation method had been changed since 1956 by the Democratic National Committee, from a formula that included Democratic voting strength to a system that emphasized population only. No states lost seats, but the new formula tended to strengthen populous northern states.

The early sessions of the convention dealt with rules and credentials. The convention rules, approved without debate, included the compromise loyalty pledge adopted by the 1956 convention. The only credentials dispute involved two contesting delegations from the Commonwealth of Puerto Rico. By a voice vote, the convention agreed to seat both delegations while splitting the vote of the Commonwealth.

The front-runner for the presidential nomination was Massachusetts Sen. John F. Kennedy, whose success in the primaries and support from many of the party's urban leaders put him on the verge of a nominating majority. His principal rival was Senate Majority Leader Lyndon B. Johnson of Texas, although the favorite of the convention galleries was Adlai E. Stevenson, the party's unsuccessful standard-bearer in 1952 and 1956. Johnson challenged Kennedy to a debate, which was held before a joint gathering of the Massachusetts and Texas delegations. Coming the day before the balloting, the debate had little effect on the ultimate outcome.

Nine men were nominated, but Kennedy received a clear majority on the first ballot. At the end of the roll call, the Massachusetts senator had 806 votes, to easily outdistance Johnson, who received 409. Missouri Sen. Stuart Symington was a distant third with 86 votes, and Stevenson followed with 79½. A motion to make Kennedy's nomination unanimous was approved by a voice vote. Kennedy's selection marked the first time since 1920 that a senator had been nominated for the presidency by Democrats or Republicans and the first time since 1928 that a Roman

Catholic had been represented on a national ticket of one of the two major parties. *(Chart, p. 186)*

Kennedy surprised some supporters and political observers by choosing his erstwhile adversary, Lyndon Johnson, as his running mate. A motion to nominate Johnson by acclamation was approved by a voice vote.

Kennedy delivered his acceptance speech to 80,000 spectators at the Los Angeles Coliseum. He envisioned the United States as "on the edge of a new frontier—the frontier of the 1960s—a frontier of unknown opportunities and perils—a frontier of unfulfilled hopes and threats," adding that this "new frontier...is not a set of promises—it is a set of challenges."

The Democratic platform was easily the longest yet written by the party, about 20,000 words. The platform itself was approved by a voice vote, although the civil rights and fiscal responsibility planks were debated on the convention floor, and roll-call votes had been taken in committee.

Regional hearings had been held by subcommittees of the 108-member platform committee in the spring, but votes on controversial issues were not taken by the full committee until the convention. A plank that urged elimination of the immigration quota system was approved, 66 to 28, with opposition led by Mississippi Sen. James O. Eastland. An agricultural plank recommending price supports at 90 per cent of parity was passed, 66 to 22, with opponents claiming that it was a restatement of the liberal program proposed by the National Farmers Union. A motion to reconsider the plank was defeated, 38 to 32. An Eastland motion to delete condemnation of "right to work" laws was defeated without a recorded vote.

The civil rights plank caused the greatest controversy. Sen. Sam J. Ervin Jr. of North Carolina introduced motions to delete portions that proposed establishing a Fair Employment Practices Commission, continuing the Civil Rights Commission as a permanent agency, granting the attorney general the power to file civil injunction suits to prevent desegregation, and setting 1963 as the deadline for the initiation of school desegregation plans. Ervin's motions were defeated by a voice vote, and the entire plank was approved, 66 to 24.

Delegates from nine southern states signed a statement that repudiated the civil rights plank. Led by Georgia Democratic Chairman James H. Gray and Ervin, these nine states introduced a minority report on the convention floor calling for elimination of the platform's civil rights plank. After an hour's debate, the minority report was rejected by a voice vote.

A minority amendment introduced by the Virginia delegation, proposing that the fiscal responsibility plank include a planned schedule for reduction of the national debt, also was rejected by a voice vote.

As approved by the convention, the platform began with a discussion of foreign policy. The Democrats blamed the Republican administration for allowing the United States military strength to deteriorate. The national defense plank declared there was a "missile gap, space gap, and limited-war gap," and promised to improve America's military position so that it would be second to none. The Democrats recommended creation of "a national peace agency for disarmament planning and research." The money saved by international disarmament, the plank stated, could be used to attack world poverty.

Foreign military aid was viewed as a short-range necessity that should be replaced by economic aid "as rapidly as security considerations permit." At the same time, the platform proposed that development programs be placed on a "long-term basis to permit more effective planning."

The Democrats' economic plank called for an average national growth rate of five per cent annually. Economic growth at this rate would create needed tax revenue, the Democrats believed, which—coupled with cuts in government waste, closing of tax loopholes and more extensive efforts to catch tax evaders—would help balance the budget. In times of recession or depression, the Democrats promised to use measures such as public works projects and temporary tax cuts.

The platform promised an increase in the minimum wage to $1.25 an hour and pledged to extend coverage to include more workers. There was a pledge to amend the social security program so the elderly could continue working without sacrificing basic benefits.

Equal rights legislation was favored, although the platform did not call for passage of a constitutional amendment as it did in 1956.

Following are excerpts from the Democratic platform of 1960:

National Defense. Our military position today is measured in terms of gaps—missile gap, space gap, limited-war gap....

This is the strength that must be erected:

1. Deterrent military power such that the Soviet and Chinese leaders will have no doubt that an attack on the United States would surely be followed by their own destruction.

2. Balanced conventional military forces which will permit a response graded to the intensity of any threats of aggressive force.

3. Continuous modernization of these forces through intensified research and development, including essential programs now slowed down, terminated, suspended, or neglected for lack of budgetary support.

Disarmament. This requires a national peace agency for disarmament planning and research to muster the scientific ingenuity, coordination, continuity, and seriousness of purpose which are now lacking in our arms control efforts....

As world-wide disarmament proceeds, it will free vast resources for a new international attack on the problem of world poverty.

Immigration. The national-origins quota system of limiting immigration contradicts the founding principles of this nation. It is inconsistent with our belief in the rights of man. This system was instituted after World War I as a policy of deliberate discrimination by a Republican Administration and Congress....

Foreign Aid. Where military assistance remains essential for the common defense, we shall see that the requirements are fully met. But as rapidly as security considerations permit, we will replace tanks with tractors, bombers with bulldozers, and tacticians with technicians.

Civil Rights. We believe that every school district affected by the Supreme Court's school desegregation decision should submit a plan providing for at least first-step compliance by 1963, the 100th anniversary of the Emancipation Proclamation....

For this and for the protection of all other Constitutional rights of Americans, the Attorney General should be empowered and directed to file civil injunction suits in Federal courts to prevent the denial of any civil right on grounds of race, creed or color.

Economy. We Democrats believe that our economy can and must grow at an average rate of 5% annually, almost twice as fast as our average annual rate since 1953. We pledge ourselves to policies that will achieve this goal without inflation....

The policies of a Democratic Administration to restore economic growth will reduce current unemployment to a minimum.

Tax Reform. We shall close the loopholes in the tax laws by which certain privileged groups legally escape their fair share of taxation.

Among the more conspicuous loopholes are depletion allowances which are inequitable, special consideration for recipients of dividend income, and deductions for extravagant "business expenses" which have reached scandalous proportions.

Labor. We pledge to raise the minimum wage to $1.25 an hour and to extend coverage to several million workers not now protected.

Agriculture. The Democratic Administration will work to bring about full parity income for farmers in all segments of agriculture by helping them to balance farm production with the expanding needs of the nation and the world.

Measures to this end include production and marketing quotas measured in terms of barrels, bushels and bales, loans on basic commodities at not less than 90% of parity, production payments, commodity purchases, and marketing orders and agreements.

Government Spending. The Democratic Party believes that state and local governments are strengthened—not weakened—by financial assistance from the Federal Government. We will extend such aid without impairing local administration through unnecessary Federal interference or red tape.

Republicans

On July 25, 10 days after the close of the Democratic convention, the Republican convention opened in Chicago. Although Vice President Nixon had a lock on the presidential nomination, the party's two major figures four years later, Arizona Sen. Barry Goldwater and New York Gov. Nelson A. Rockefeller, both had major roles in convention activities.

Both Goldwater and Rockefeller announced that they did not want their names placed in nomination, but the Arizona delegation disregarded Goldwater's request and nominated him anyway. In a convention speech, the Arizona senator withdrew his name and went on to advise conservative Republicans to work within the party: "Let's grow up conservatives.... If we want to take this party back—and I think we can someday—let's get to work."

On the roll call that followed, Nixon was a nearly unanimous choice, receiving 1,321 votes to 10 for Goldwater (all from Louisiana). On a voice vote, Nixon's nomination was made unanimous.

Nixon reportedly wanted Rockefeller as his running mate, but was unable to persuade the New Yorker to join the ticket. The Republican standard-bearer subsequently turned to United Nations Ambassador Henry Cabot Lodge Jr., a former senator from Massachusetts who had been beaten for re-election by John Kennedy in 1952. On the vice-presidential ballot, Lodge received all but one vote. The lone dissenter, a Texas delegate, initially abstained but switched his vote to Lodge at the end of the roll call.

In his acceptance speech, Nixon promised to campaign in all 50 states and rebutted a theme in Kennedy's acceptance speech. "Our primary aim must be not to help government, but to help people—to help people attain the life they deserve," said Nixon.

Much of the drama of the 1960 Republican convention surrounded the party platform. And the highlight of the platform maneuvering was a late-night meeting involving Nixon and Rockefeller, held at Rockefeller's New York City apartment two days before the opening of the convention. The meeting, a secret to most of Nixon's closest aides, resulted in a 14-point agreement between the two Republican leaders on major issues contained in the platform. The agreement, informally dubbed the "compact of Fifth Avenue," was issued by Rockefeller, who declared that the meeting was held at Nixon's insistence.

Half of the 14 points dealt with national security and foreign policy. The other half discussed domestic issues, including government reorganization, civil rights, agriculture, economic growth and medical care for the elderly. Although not markedly different in wording from the draft of the platform committee, the "compact" expressed a tone of urgency that was not evident in the draft.

The Nixon-Rockefeller agreement was made with the knowledge of the platform committee chairman, Charles H. Percy of Illinois, but was greeted with hostility by many members of the committee and by party conservatives. Goldwater termed the "compact" a "surrender" and the "Munich of the Republican Party" that would ensure the party's defeat that fall.

The two issues of greatest controversy were civil rights and national defense. The original civil rights plank, drafted by the platform committee, did not express support for civil rights demonstrations or promise federal efforts to gain job equality for blacks. The Nixon-Rockefeller agreement did both. Nixon threatened to wage a floor fight if the stronger civil rights plank was not inserted in the platform. By a vote of 50 to 35, the platform committee agreed to reconsider the original civil rights plank; by a margin of 56 to 28, the stronger plank was approved.

With the approval of both Rockefeller and President Eisenhower, several changes were made in the national security plank, that emphasized the necessity of quickly upgrading America's armed forces. The platform committee approved reconsideration of the original defense plank by a voice vote, and the whole platform was adopted unanimously.

With disagreements resolved in the committee, there were neither a minority report nor floor fights. The convention approved the platform by a voice vote.

In its final form, the Republican platform was shorter than its Democratic counterpart, although still nearly 15,-000 words in length. The foreign policy section asserted that the nation's greatest task was "to nullify the Soviet conspiracy." The platform claimed that America's military strength was second to none, but in line with the Nixon-Rockefeller "compact," indicated that improvements were needed in some parts of the armed forces.

The Republicans joined their Democratic opposition in favoring a workable disarmament program but did not advocate a phaseout of foreign military aid, as did the Democrats. However, the Republicans proposed a change in the funding of foreign aid that emphasized "the increasing use of private capital and government loans, rather than outright grants."

The Republicans agreed with the Democrats that the nation should experience more rapid economic growth, but did not adopt the five per cent annual growth rate favored by the Democrats. The Republicans stressed the virtues of a balanced budget and regarded free enterprise, rather than massive government programs, as the key to economic growth.

As in 1956, the two parties differed on farm price supports. The Republicans supported a program of flexible support payments, while the Democrats recommended setting price supports at 90 per cent of parity.

Both parties proposed allowing individuals to work beyond their mandatory retirement age, although the Democrats tied their proposal to amendment of the social security program.

The Republicans did not urge elimination of the immigration quota system, as did their opponents, but they favored overhaul of the system to allow an increase in immigration.

On the issue of equal rights, the Republicans continued to favor passage of a constitutional amendment. The Democrats had backed away from this position, which they had held in earlier platforms, instead proposing the passage of equal rights legislation in Congress.

As they had since the beginning of the New Deal, the Republican and Democratic platforms differed noticeably as to the extent and desirability of federal spending. The Democrats viewed federal assistance to state and local governments as beneficial. The Republicans believed the federal government could help meet the problems of urban growth, but that state and local governments should administer all the programs they could best handle.

Following are excerpts from the Republican platform of 1960:

National Defense. The future of freedom depends heavily upon America's military might and that of her allies. Under the Eisenhower-Nixon Administration, our military might has been forged into a power second to none....

The strategic imperatives of our national defense policy are these:

A second-strike capability, that is, a nuclear retaliatory power that can survive surprise attack, strike back, and destroy any possible enemy.

Highly mobile and versatile forces, including forces deployed, to deter or check local aggressions and "brush fire wars" which might bring on all-out nuclear war.

National determination to employ all necessary military capabilities so as to render any level of aggression unprofitable. Deterrence of war since Korea, specifically, has been the result of our firm statement that we will never again permit a potential aggressor to set the ground rules for his aggression; that we will respond to aggression with the full means and weapons best suited to the situation....

Disarmament. We are similarly ready to negotiate and to institute realistic methods and safeguards for disarmament, and for the suspension of nuclear tests. We advocate an early agreement by all nations to forego nuclear tests in the atmosphere, and the suspension of other tests as verification techniques permit.

Immigration. The annual number of immigrants we accept be at least doubled.

Obsolete immigration laws be amended by abandoning the outdated 1920 census data as a base and substituting the 1960 census.

The guidelines of our immigration policy be based upon judgment of the individual merit of each applicant for admission and citizenship.

Foreign Aid.   Agreeable to the developing nations, we would join with them in inviting countries with advanced economies to share with us a proportionate part of the capital and technical aid required. We would emphasize the increasing use of private capital and government loans, rather than outright grants, as a means of fostering independence and mutual respect.

Civil Rights. *Voting:* We pledge:

Continued vigorous enforcement of the civil rights laws to guarantee the right to vote to all citizens in all areas of the country....

Public Schools. We pledge:

The Department of Justice will continue its vigorous support of court orders for school desegregation....

We oppose the pretense of fixing a target date 3 years from now for the mere submission of plans for school desegregation. Slow-moving school districts would construe it as a three-year moratorium during which progress would cease, postponing until 1963 the legal process to enforce compliance. We believe that each of the pending court actions should proceed as the Supreme Court has directed and that in no district should there be any such delay.

Employment. We pledge:

Continued support for legislation to establish a Commission on Equal Job Opportunity to make permanent and to expand with legislative backing the excellent work being performed by the President's Committee on Government Contracts....

Housing. We pledge:

Action to prohibit discrimination in housing constructed with the aid of federal subsidies.

Public Facilities and Services. We pledge:

Removal of any vestige of discrimination in the operation of federal facilities or procedures which may at any time be found....

Economy. We reject the concept of artificial growth forced by massive new federal spending and loose money policies. The only effective way to accelerate economic growth is to increase the traditional strengths of our free economy—initiative and investment, productivity and efficiency....

Agriculture. Use of price supports at levels best fitted to specific commodities, in order to widen markets, ease production controls, and help achieve increased farm family income.

Government Reorganization. The President must continue to be able to reorganize and streamline executive operations to keep the executive branch capable of responding effectively to rapidly changing conditions in both foreign and domestic fields....

Two top positions should be established to assist the President in, (1) the entire field of National Security and International Affairs, and (2) Governmental Planning and Management, particularly in domestic affairs.

Government Spending. Vigorous state and local governments are a vital part of our federal union. The federal government should leave to state and local governments those programs and problems which they can best handle and tax sources adequate to finance them. We must continue to improve liaison between federal, state and local governments. We believe that the federal government, when appropriate, should render significant assistance in dealing with our urgent problems of urban growth and change. No vast new bureaucracy is needed to achieve this objective.

1964 Conventions

Presidential Candidates

Barry Goldwater
Republican

Lyndon B. Johnson
Democrat

Republicans

Division between the party's conservative and moderate wings, muted during the Eisenhower administration, exploded at the Republican's July convention in San Francisco.

Although Sen. Barry Goldwater of Arizona, the hero of Republican conservatives, had a commanding lead as the convention opened, he was vigorously challenged by Pennsylvania Gov. William W. Scranton, the belated leader of the moderate forces. Two days before the presidential balloting, a letter in Scranton's name was sent to Goldwater. It charged the Goldwater organization with regarding the delegates as "little more than a flock of chickens whose necks will be wrung at will." The message continued, describing Goldwater's political philosophy as a "crazy-quilt collection of absurd and dangerous positions." The letter concluded by challenging the Arizona senator to a debate before the convention. Although the message was written by Scranton's staff without his knowledge, the Pennsylvania governor supported the substance of the letter. Goldwater declined the invitation to debate.

Although seven names were placed in nomination for the presidency, the outcome was a foregone conclusion. Goldwater was an easy winner on the first ballot, receiving 883 of the 1,308 votes. Scranton was a distant second with 214 votes; New York Gov. Rockefeller followed with 114. Scranton moved that Goldwater's nomination be made unanimous, and his motion was approved by a voice vote. Support for the major moderate candidates, Scranton and Rockefeller, was centered in the Northeast. Goldwater had an overwhelming majority of the delegates from other regions. *(Chart, p. 187)*

As his running mate, Goldwater selected the Republican national chairman, Rep. William E. Miller of New York. On disclosing his choice of Miller, Goldwater stated that "one of the reasons I chose Miller is that he drives Johnson nuts." On the vice presidential roll call, the conservative New York representative received 1,305 votes, with three delegates from Tennessee abstaining. A Roman Catholic, Miller became the first member of that faith ever to run on a Republican national ticket.

Goldwater's acceptance speech was uncompromising and did not attempt to dilute his conservatism in an effort to gain votes: "Anyone who joins us in all sincerity we welcome. Those who do not care for our cause, we don't expect to enter our ranks in any case. And let our Republicanism so focused and so dedicated not be made fuzzy and futile by unthinking and stupid labels. I would remind you that extremism in the defense of liberty is no vice. And let me remind you also that moderation in the pursuit of justice is no virtue."

By a voice vote, the convention adopted the party platform, but not before the moderate forces waged floor fights on three issues—extremism, civil rights and control of nuclear weapons. Within the platform committee, 70 to 80 different amendments were presented, but when the platform reached the floor, the moderates concentrated on these three specific issues.

Extremism was the first issue considered, with Sen. Hugh Scott of Pennsylvania introducing an amendment that specifically denounced efforts of the John Birch Society, the Ku Klux Klan and the Communist Party to infiltrate the Republican Party. Rockefeller spoke on behalf of the amendment but was booed throughout his speech. Rockefeller argued that a "radical, high-financed, disciplined minority" was trying to take over the Republican Party, a minority "wholly alien to the middle course...the mainstream." The amendment was rejected on a standing vote, by a margin estimated at two to one.

A second amendment on extremism, proposed by Michigan Gov. George W. Romney, condemned extremist groups but not by name. The Romney amendment was similarly rejected on a standing vote by about the same margin.

Scott introduced a civil rights amendment adding additional pledges to the existing plank, including more manpower for the Justice Department's civil rights division; a statement of pride in Republican support of the 1964 Civil Rights Act; requirements for first-step compliance with school desegregation by all school districts in one year; voting guarantees to state as well as federal elections, and promises to eliminate job bias. The platform's brief plank on civil rights called for "full implementation and faithful execution" of the 1964 act, but also stated that "the elimination of any such discrimination is a matter of heart, conscience and education as well as of equal rights under law." On a roll-call vote, the Scott amendment was defeated, 897 to 409. The pattern of the vote closely followed the presidential ballot, with support for the amendment centered in the Northeast. *(Chart, p. 187)*

Romney offered a brief, alternative civil rights plank, which pledged action at the state, local and private levels to eliminate discrimination in all fields. It was defeated by a voice vote.

Scott proposed another amendment, declaring the president to have sole authority to control the use of nuclear weapons. This contrasted with Goldwater's position advocating that NATO commanders be given greater authority in the use of tactical nuclear weapons. The Scott amendment was rejected on a standing vote.

In its final form, the Republican platform was barely half as long as its Democratic counterpart. The Republican platform was divided into four sections, the first two enumerating Democratic failures in foreign policy and domestic affairs. The last two sections detailed Republican proposals.

The Republicans were suspicious of any detente with the Communist world, instead calling for "a dynamic strategy of victory...for freedom." The platform claimed American military strength was deteriorating and promised the establishment of a military force superior to the nation's enemies. The Republicans expressed distrust of the 1963 nuclear test ban treaty and vowed to "never unilaterally disarm America." The platform promised to revitalize the North Atlantic Treaty Organization (NATO), which was viewed as a keystone of Republican foreign policy.

Concerning specific trouble spots around the world, the platform demanded removal of the Berlin Wall, pledged to "move decisively to assure victory in South Vietnam" and promised to recognize a Cuban government in exile as well as to supply assistance to Cuban guerrilla freedom fighters.

Coupled with the anti-communism of the foreign policy sections was the central theme of the domestic sections—the need to trim the power of the federal government and to relocate it in state and local governments. This conservative philosophy was evident in various domestic planks.

The Republicans promised a reduction of at least $5-billion in federal spending and pledged to end budget deficits. A proposal was made to cut federal income taxes and to transfer the excise tax and several other federal tax sources from the federal government to state and local governments. The Republicans also recommended that state and local tax payments be credited against federal income tax :s.

The platform favored a reduction of federal involvement in school financing and advocated passage of a constitutional amendment to allow prayer in public schools. A plank was included that urged passage of legislation to curb the flow of obscene materials through the mails.

The "one man, one vote" ruling of the Supreme Court brought the recommendation by the Republicans that a constitutional amendment be passed to allow states with bicameral legislatures to use a measurement other than population.

Following are excerpts from the Republican platform of 1964:

Peace. This Administration has sought accommodations with Communism without adequate safeguards and compensating gains for freedom. It has alienated proven allies by opening a "hot line" first with a sworn enemy rather than with a proven friend, and in general pursued a risky path such as began at Munich a quarter century ago....

The supreme challenge to this policy is an atheistic imperialism—Communism.

Our nation's leadership must be judged by—indeed, American independence and even survival are dependent upon—the stand it takes toward Communism.

That stand must be: victory for freedom. There can be no peace, there can be no security, until this goal is won.

National Defense. This Administration has adopted policies which will lead to a potentially fatal parity of power with Communism instead of continued military superiority for the United States.

It has permitted disarmament negotiations to proceed without adequate consideration of military judgment—a procedure which tends to bring about, in effect, a unilateral curtailment of American arms rendered the more dangerous by the Administration's discounting known Soviet advances in nuclear weaponry.

It has failed to take minimum safeguards against possible consequences of the limited nuclear test ban treaty, including advanced underground tests where permissible and full readiness to test elsewhere should the need arise....

...we will regularly review the status of nuclear weaponry under the limited nuclear test ban to assure this nation's protection. We shall also provide sensible, continuing reviews of the treaty itself....

We will maintain a superior, not merely equal, military capability as long as the Communist drive for world domination continues. It will be a capability of balanced force, superior in all its arms, maintaining flexibility for effective performance in the rapidly changing science of war.

Republicans will never unilaterally disarm America.

Berlin. We will demand that the Berlin Wall be taken down prior to the resumption of any negotiations with the Soviet Union on the status of forces in, or treaties affecting, Germany.

Cuba. We Republicans will recognize a Cuban government in exile; we will support its efforts to regain the independence of its homeland; we will assist Cuban freedom fighters in carrying on guerrilla warfare against the Communist regime; we will work for an economic boycott by all nations of the free world in trade with Cuba; and we will encourage free elections in Cuba after liberty and stability are restored.

Vietnam. We will move decisively to assure victory in South Viet Nam. While confining the conflict as closely as possible, America must move to end the fighting in a reasonable time and provide guarantees against further aggression. We must make it clear to the Communist world that, when conflict is forced with America, it will end only in victory for freedom.

United Nations. This Administration has failed to provide forceful, effective leadership in the United Nations.

It has weakened the power and influence of this world organization by failing to demand basic improvements in its procedures and to guard against its becoming merely a form of anti-Western insult and abuse.

Federal Power. Humanity is tormented once again by an age-old issue—is man to live in dignity and freedom under God or be enslaved—are men in government to serve, or are they to master, their fellow men?...

1. Every person has the right to govern himself, to fix his own goals, and to make his own way with a minimum of governmental interference.

2. It is for government to foster and maintain an environment of freedom encouraging every individual to develop to the fullest his God-given powers of mind, heart and body; and, beyond this, government should undertake

only needful things, rightly of public concern, which the citizen cannot himself accomplish.

We Republicans hold that these two principles must regain their primacy in our government's relations, not only with the American people, but also with nations and peoples everywhere in the world.

Economy. In furtherance of our faith in the individual, we also pledge prudent, responsible management of the government's fiscal affairs to protect the individual against the evils of spendthrift government—protecting most of all the needy and fixed-income families against the cruelest tax, inflation—and protecting every citizen against the high taxes forced by excessive spending, in order that each individual may keep more of his earnings for his own and his family's use.

Tax Reform. In furtherance of our faith in limited, frugal and efficient government we also pledge: credit against Federal taxes for specified State and local taxes paid, and a transfer to the States of excise and other Federal tax sources, to reinforce the fiscal strength of State and local governments so that they may better meet rising school costs and other pressing urban and suburban problems such as transportation, housing water systems and juvenile delinquency....

Civil Rights. Full implementation and faithful execution of the Civil Rights Act of 1964, and all other civil rights statutes, to assure equal rights and opportunities guaranteed by the Constitution to every citizen;...continued opposition to discrimination based on race, creed, national origin or sex. We recognize that the elimination of any such discrimination is a matter of heart, conscience, and education, as well as of equal rights under law.

Education. To continue the advancement of education on all levels, through such programs as selective aid to higher education, strengthened State and local tax resources, including tax credits for college education, while resisting the Democratic efforts which endanger local control of schools; to help assure equal opportunity and a good education for all, while opposing Federally-sponsored "inverse discrimination," whether by the shifting of jobs, or the abandonment of neighborhood schools, for reasons of race;....

School Prayer. Support of a Constitutional amendment permitting those individual's and groups who choose to do so to exercise their religion freely in public places, provided religious exercises are not prepared or prescribed by the state or political subdivision thereof and no person's participation therein is coerced, thus preserving the traditional separation of church and state;....

Obscenity. Enactment of legislation, despite Democratic opposition, to curb the flow through the mails of obscene material which has flourished into a multimillion dollar obscenity racket;....

Medical Care for Elderly. Full coverage of all medical and hospital costs for the needy elderly people, financed by general revenues through broader implementation of Federal-State plans, rather than the compulsory Democratic scheme covering only a small percentage of such costs, for everyone regardless of need;....

Reapportionment. Support of a Constitutional amendment, as well as legislation, enabling States having bicameral legislatures to apportion one House on bases of their choosing, including factors other than population;....

Democrats

In late August in Atlantic City, N.J., the Democratic convention nominated President Lyndon B. Johnson for a full term in the White House. The proceedings were stage-managed by the President and were met with little visible dissent on the convention floor. The four-day event was a political triumph for the veteran politician from Texas, who less than a year earlier had been the assassinated John F. Kennedy's Vice President.

The Democratic convention was larger than any previous convention of an American political party, with 5,260 delegates and alternates. A new vote allocation formula was in effect which combined consideration of a state's electoral vote with its support for the Kennedy-Johnson ticket in 1960. While no states lost votes from four years earlier, many of the larger states gained significantly. As a result, there were 2,316 votes at the 1964 convention, compared with 1,521 in 1960.

With no controversy surrounding either the party nominee or platform, attention focused on the credentials challenge brought by the integrated Mississippi Freedom Democratic Party against the all-white delegation sent by the regular state party. By a voice vote, the convention approved a compromise negotiated by Minnesota Sen. Hubert H. Humphrey. The settlement called for seating of the Mississippi regulars, provided they signed a written pledge to back the national ticket and urged the state's presidential electors to do likewise. It also proposed the seating of two members of the Mississippi Freedom Democrats as delegates at large, and the remainder of the delegation as honored guests; and it stipulated that at future conventions, delegations would be barred from states that allowed racial discrimination in voting. Although the convention approved this solution, the Freedom Democrats rejected the compromise, and all but four members of the regular Mississippi delegation refused to sign the pledge and left the convention.

The convention also approved a recommendation requiring the Alabama delegation to sign a personal loyalty oath, the result of the state party's placing "unpledged" (anti-Johnson) electors on the Alabama ballot. Eleven Alabama members signed the loyalty oath; the remaining 42 delegates and alternates withdrew from the convention.

The roll-call vote for president was dispensed with, and Johnson was nominated by acclamation. Immediately after his selection, Johnson made the unprecedented move of appearing before the delegates to announce his choice for vice president, Humphrey. Johnson had tried to make his selection as suspenseful and dramatic as possible. Although most observers felt Humphrey would be the choice, earlier that day Johnson had called both the Minnesota senator and Connecticut Sen. Thomas J. Dodd to the White House. However, at this meeting Johnson invited Humphrey to be on the ticket, and later that night, the delegates nominated Humphrey by acclamation. (The 1964 Democratic convention was only the second in party history in which there were no roll-call votes—the other time was 1936.)

On the final day of the convention, the two nominees delivered their acceptance speeches. Humphrey frequently referred to the Republican candidate, Sen. Goldwater, as "the temporary Republican spokesman," and listed major legislation supported by a majority of both parties in the Senate, "but not Sen. Goldwater."

The emotional highlight of the convention was the appearance of Attorney General Robert F. Kennedy, who introduced a film about the presidency of his late brother.

By a voice vote, the convention approved the party platform. Following the trend toward longer and longer documents, the platform was 22,000 words in length. Although the document was adopted without debate on the convention floor, several roll-call votes were taken in the platform committee. By a vote of 53 to 16, the committee rejected a proposal by Sen. Joseph S. Clark of Pennsylvania to strengthen the disarmament plank. Clark's proposal called for further disarmament "under world law," wording the majority of the committee did not want to include.

By a margin of 39 to 38, the platform committee pledged to support a constitutional amendment giving the District of Columbia representation in Congress. On another roll-call vote (52 to 19), the committee promised to repeal the Taft-Hartley Act provision permitting state right-to-work laws.

Without a recorded vote, the committee adopted another provision by Sen. Clark proposing revision of congressional rules and procedures to "assure majority rule after reasonable debate and to guarantee that major legislative proposals of the President can be brought to a vote after reasonable consideration in committee." The proposal was a reference to the Senate cloture rule, requiring a two-thirds vote to cut off debate, and to the power of the House Rules Committee to keep legislation from the floor.

The entire platform was a wide-ranging document designed to appeal to as many segments of the electorate as possible. Self-described as a "covenant of unity," the platform was written in a moderate tone to contrast with the unqualified conservatism expressed in the Republican platform.

The latter three-quarters of the Democratic platform was a section entitled "An Accounting of Stewardship, 1961-1964," which described the accomplishments of the Kennedy-Johnson administration in 38 areas of public policy. The first quarter of the platform discussed the party's position on major issues of the day, from peace and national defense to civil rights, the economy, agriculture, natural resources, urban affairs, federal power and government reform, and extremism.

In view of the militant anti-communism of Sen. Goldwater and the Republican platform, the Democrats viewed peace and national defense as winning issues with a majority of the electorate. The Democrats claimed that the world was closer to peace than in 1960, due in part to the United States' overwhelming nuclear superiority and internal splits in the Communist world, as well as the success of international negotiations such as those resulting in the nuclear test ban treaty. But, in an allusion to Goldwater's stance, the platform warned that recklessness by a president in foreign policy could result in nuclear disaster. The Democratic platform included a provision rejected by the Republicans, insisting that control of nuclear weapons must be kept in the hands of the president.

While peace and national defense were stressed by the Democrats, the Republican platform concentrated on the need to limit the power of the federal government. On this issue, the Democratic platform included a recommendation to help state and local governments develop new revenue sources. But the Democratic plank also included an assertion that contradicted the Republicans' criticism of expanding federal power: "No government at any level can properly complain of violation of its power, if it fails to meet its responsibilities."

Neither party had a civil rights plank containing specifics. The difference was wording, with the Democrats promising "fair, effective enforcement" of the 1964 Civil Rights Act, but precluding the use of quotas in combating racial discrimination. The Republicans pledged "full implementation and faithful execution" of civil rights laws.

An effort at the Republican convention to have the party platform condemn specific "extremist" groups failed, although the issue was hotly debated on the convention floor. Without dissent, the Democratic platform included a provision that condemned extremism of the right and left, especially the Communist Party, the Ku Klux Klan and the John Birch Society.

The two parties differed in their opinion of the health of the economy. The Republicans blamed their opposition for inflation and continuing unemployment and promised a reduction of at least $5-billion in federal spending. The Democrats countered by claiming the Kennedy-Johnson administration had engineered "the longest and strongest peacetime prosperity in modern history."

Following are excerpts from the Democratic platform of 1964:

Peace. At the start of the third decade of the nuclear age, the preservation of peace requires the strength to wage war and the wisdom to avoid it. The search for peace requires the utmost intelligence, the clearest vision, and a strong sense of reality.... Battered by economic failures, challenged by recent American achievements in space, torn by the Chinese-Russian rift, and faced with American strength and courage—international Communism has lost its unity and momentum.

National Defense. Specifically, we must and we will:
—Continue the overwhelming supremacy of our Strategic Nuclear Forces.
—Strengthen further our forces for discouraging limited wars and fighting subversion.
—Maintain the world's largest research and development effort, which has initiated more than 200 new programs since 1961, to ensure continued American leadership in weapons systems and equipment....

Control of the use of nuclear weapons must remain solely with the highest elected official in the country—the President of the United States....

The complications and dangers in our restless, constantly changing world require of us consummate understanding and experience. One rash act, one thoughtless decision, one unchecked reaction—and cities could become smouldering ruins and farms parched wasteland.

Civil Rights. The Civil Rights Act of 1964 deserves and requires full observance by every American and fair, effective enforcement if there is any default....

True democracy of opportunity will not be served by establishing quotas based on the same false distinctions we seek to erase, nor can the effects of prejudice be neutralized by the expedient of preferential practices.

Extremism. We condemn extremism, whether from the Right or Left, including the extreme tactics of such organizations as the Communist Party, the Ku Klux Klan and the John Birch Society.

Federal Power. The Democratic Party holds to the belief that government in the United States—local, state and federal—was created in order to serve the people. Each level of government has appropriate powers and each has specific responsibilities. The first responsibility of government at every level is to protect the basic freedoms of the people. No government at any level can properly complain of violation of its power, if it fails to meet its responsibilities.

The federal government exists not to grow larger, but to enlarge the individual potential and achievement of the people.

The federal government exists not to subordinate the states, but to support them.

Economy. In 42 months of uninterrupted expansion under Presidents Kennedy and Johnson, we have achieved the longest and strongest peacetime prosperity in modern history....

It is the national purpose, and our commitment, that every man or woman who is willing and able to work is entitled to a job and to a fair wage for doing it.

1968 Conventions

Presidential Candidates

Richard M. Nixon
Republican

Hubert H. Humphrey
Democrat

George C. Wallace
American Independent

Republicans

The Republican convention, held in Miami Beach, Fla., in early August, had a surface tranquility that the later Democratic convention lacked. Only two roll-call votes were taken on the convention floor, to nominate presidential and vice presidential candidates.

There was only one credentials challenge seriously considered by the Republican credentials committee, and that involved a single delegate. By a 32-32 vote, the committee defeated an unexpectedly strong attempt to overturn the preconvention decision to seat Rep. H.R. Gross of Iowa rather than a Des Moines housewife. The full convention approved the report of the credentials committee without a roll-call vote.

The report of the rules committee was approved without comment. It included recommendations to prohibit discrimination in the selection of future convention delegates and to add the Republican state chairmen as members of the Republican National Committee.

Twelve names were placed in nomination for the presidency, although the contest was clearly among three candidates: the front-runner, former Vice President Richard M. Nixon, and two governors, Nelson A. Rockefeller of New York and Ronald Reagan of California. The ideological gulf between the more liberal Rockefeller and the more conservative Reagan made it difficult for them to agree on a common strategy to stop Nixon, even when Reagan abandoned his favorite-son status for active candidacy two days before the balloting.

In order to head off the defection to Reagan of his more conservative supporters, Nixon seemed to take a sharp tack to the right the day before the balloting. He told southern delegations that he would not run an administration which would "ram anything down your throats," that he opposed school busing, that he would appoint "strict constitutionalists" to the Supreme Court and that he was critical of federal intervention in local school board affairs.

Nixon won the nomination on the first ballot, receiving 692 votes (25 more than necessary) to easily outdistance Rockefeller, who had 277, and Reagan, who had 182. After

vote switches, the final totals were Nixon, 1,238, Rockefeller, 93, and Reagan, 2. In a brief speech to the convention, Reagan moved that Nixon's nomination be made unanimous, but his motion was never put to a vote. *(p. 189)*

In his selection of a running mate, Nixon surprised many observers by tapping Maryland Gov. Spiro T. Agnew. Agnew, who had delivered the major nominating speech for Nixon, had, ironically, been one of Rockefeller's earliest and strongest supporters. But the Maryland governor ceased his active support of Rockefeller in March, irked by the New York governor's indecision about entering the race, and, at the beginning of convention week, announced his support for Nixon.

In addition to Agnew, the name of Michigan Gov. George Romney also was placed in nomination for vice president. Agnew was an easy winner, receiving 1,119 votes to 186 for Romney who made no effort to withdraw his name. After completion of the roll call, a Romney motion to make Agnew's nomination unanimous was approved.

The delegates approved without debate the 1968 Republican platform, which steered a careful middle course between conservatives and liberals on domestic policy and between "doves" and "hawks" on the touchy Vietnam issue. The 11,500-word document was somewhat more liberal in tone than that of 1960 and was far removed from the militantly conservative tone of the 1964 document.

A major floor fight on the platform was averted when platform committee members, led by Senate Minority Leader Everett McKinley Dirksen of Illinois, substituted for the original hard-line war plank new language stressing the need for de-Americanization of both the military and civilian efforts in Vietnam. Both "hawks" and "doves" decided to go along with the revised version.

As originally written, the plank criticized the Johnson administration for not leaving key Vietnam decisions to the military and for the administration's policy of military gradualism. Both Nixon and Rockefeller backers opposed the strong language, and a compromise Vietnam plank was accepted. As well as advocating the de-Americanization of the war, it proposed concentrating on protection of the

South Vietnamese population rather than on capturing territory, and on efforts to strengthen local forces and responsibility.

While the platform endorsed continued negotiations with Hanoi, it remained silent on the important issues of a bombing pause and of a possible Saigon coalition that would include the Communists. During platform committee deliberations, Sen. Jacob K. Javits of New York offered a plank to bring the National Liberation Front into the negotiations, but the suggestion was rejected overwhelmingly.

In its discussion of national defense, the platform criticized the administration for failure to develop superior new weaponry. The document indicated that when the Vietnam war was over, a reduced defense budget might make possible increased federal spending on social welfare programs. But it neither suggested how much more spending nor recommended any substantial increases in the near future.

The platform treated rioting and crime in militant fashion: "We will not tolerate violence!" The crime plank criticized the Johnson administration for not taking effective action against crime and pledged "an all-out federal-state-local crusade."

It was in the cities plank that the party, in a short statement, mentioned civil rights legislation. The statement simply pledged: "Energetic, positive leadership to enforce statutory and constitutional protections to eliminate discrimination." It was seen as an endorsement of the recently enacted open housing law, in addition to other federal civil rights statutes. The platform did not endorse any new civil rights legislation. However, the Republicans endorsed high-priority objectives of civil rights groups, such as increased food for the poor and job-training programs.

In its youth plank, the Republicans made two specific proposals. First, the party urged the states to lower the voting age to 18 but did not endorse proposals for a constitutional amendment similarly to lower the federal voting age. Second, the plank advocated action to shorten the period in which young men were eligible for the draft and proposed to develop eventually a voluntary force.

Following are excerpts from the Republican platform of 1968:

Vietnam. The Administration's Vietnam policy has failed—militarily, politically, diplomatically, and with relation to our own people.

We condemn the Administration's breach of faith with the American people respecting our heavy involvement in Vietnam. Every citizen bitterly recalls the Democrat campaign oratory of 1964: "We are not about to send American boys 9-10,000 miles away from home to do what Asian boys ought to be doing for themselves." The Administration's failure to honor its own words has led millions of Americans to question its credibility.

The entire nation has been profoundly concerned by hastily-extemporized, undeclared land wars which embroil massive U.S. Army forces thousands of miles from our shores. It is time to realize that not every international conflict is susceptible of solution by American ground forces....

We pledge to adopt a strategy relevant to the real problems of the war, concentrating on the security of the population, on developing a greater sense of nationhood, and on strengthening the local forces. It will be a strategy permitting a progressive de-Americanization of the war, both military and civilian....

We pledge a program for peace in Vietnam—neither peace at any price nor a camouflaged surrender of legitimate United States or allied interests—but a positive program that will offer a fair and equitable settlement to all, based on the principle of self-determination, our national interests and the cause of long-range world peace.

We will sincerely and vigorously pursue peace negotiations as long as they offer any reasonable prospect for a just peace. We pledge to develop a clear and purposeful negotiating position.

National Defense. Grave errors, many now irretrievable, have characterized the direction of our nation's defense.

A singular notion—that salvation for America lies in standing still—has pervaded the entire effort. Not retention of American superiority but parity with the Soviet Union has been made the controlling doctrine in many critical areas. We have frittered away superior military capabilities, enabling the Soviets to narrow their defense gap, in some areas to outstrip us, and to move to cancel our lead entirely by the early Seventies.

China. Improved relations with Communist nations can come only when they cease to endanger other states by force or threat. Under existing conditions, we cannot favor recognition of Communist China or its admission to the United Nations.

Israel. The fact of a growing menace to Israel is undeniable. Her forces must be kept at a commensurate strength both for her protection and to help keep the peace of the area. The United States, therefore, will provide countervailing help to Israel, such as supersonic fighters, as necessary for these purposes.

Crime. Fire and looting, causing millions of dollars of property damage, have brought great suffering to home owners and small businessmen, particularly in black communities least able to absorb catastrophic losses. The Republican Party strongly advocates measures to alleviate and remove the frustrations that contribute to riots. We simultaneously support decisive action to quell civil disorder, relying primarily on state and local governments to deal with these conditions.

America has adequate peaceful and lawful means for achieving even fundamental social change if the people wish it. *We will not tolerate violence!*

Lawlessness is crumbling the foundations of American society....

We must re-establish the principle that men are accountable for what they do, that criminals are responsible for their crimes, that while the youth's environment may help to explain the man's crime, it does not excuse that crime.

The present Administration has:

—Refused to sanction the use of either the court-supervised wiretapping authority to combat organized crime or the revised rules of evidence, both made available by Congress.

—Failed to deal effectively with threats to the nation's internal security by not prosecuting identified subversives....

For the future, we pledge an all-out, federal-state-local crusade against crime, including:

—Leadership by an Attorney General who will restore stature and respect to that office:....

—Enactment of legislation to control indiscriminate availability of firearms, safeguarding the right of responsible citizens to collect, own and use firearms for legitimate purposes, retaining primary responsibility at the state level, with such federal laws as necessary to better enable the states to meet their responsibilities.

Economy. Under the Johnson-Humphrey Administration we have had economic mismanagement of the highest order....

Such funds as become available with the termination of the Vietnam war and upon recovery from its impact on our national defense will be applied in a balanced way to critical domestic needs and to reduce the heavy tax burden.

Democrats

While violence flared in the streets and thousands of police and guards imposed security precautions unprecedented at presidential nominating conventions, the 1968 Democratic convention met in late August in Chicago to nominate Hubert H. Humphrey of Minnesota for the presidency and to endorse the controversial Vietnam policies of the Johnson-Humphrey administration.

Twin themes—physical force to keep order and political force to overrule minority sentiment in the Democratic Party—were apparent throughout the convention.

The physical force, supplied by 11,900 Chicago police, 7,500 Army regulars, 7,500 Illinois National Guardsmen and 1,000 FBI and Secret Service agents, was exerted to keep vociferous Vietnam war critics away from the convention headquarters hotels and the International Amphitheatre where official sessions were held. A security ring several blocks wide guarded the amphitheatre, itself surrounded by a barbed wire fence and multiple security checkpoints for entering delegates, newsmen and guests. No violence erupted in the amphitheatre area, but there were days of bitter demonstrations in the area of the downtown hotels which ended with repeated police use of tear gas. At the end of convention week, the Chicago police announced that 589 persons had been arrested during the disturbances, with more than 119 police and 100 demonstrators injured.

The political force was exerted by the Johnson administration organization backing Vice President Humphrey, whose supporters enjoyed clear control of convention proceedings from start to end. In a distinct minority were the anti-war factions which rallied around the candidacies of Senators Eugene J. McCarthy of Minnesota and George McGovern of South Dakota. The McCarthy forces mounted a series of challenges to the Humphrey faction—on credentials, rules, the platform and finally the nomination itself.

In the first business of the convention, the Humphrey and McCarthy forces joined to ban the unit rule, rejecting by voice vote a motion by the Texas delegation to retain the rule through the 1968 convention.

However, as expected, the brief moments of unity between the opposing sides ended when the convention moved on to consider credentials challenges. The two sides split on the question of adjournment, with the Humphrey forces defeating by a vote of 1,701½ to 875, a motion to delay consideration of credentials until the second session.

The credentials committee had considered an unprecedented number of challenges, involving delegates from 15 states. Although McCarthy supported almost all the challenges, his candidacy was not always the paramount issue. In the case of the disputed southern delegations, racial imbalance, the party loyalty issue, or a combination of both, were more important. Of the 17 different challenges, McCarthy supported all but one (in Wisconsin); McGovern backed all the southern challenges; Humphrey supported only the Mississippi challenge publicly.

In a historic move, the convention by a voice vote seated a new loyalist Democratic faction from Mississippi and unseated the delegation of the traditionally segregationist, conservative regular party.

The credentials committee decided all other challenges in favor of the regular delegations, but minority reports were filed for the Alabama, Georgia, North Carolina and Texas challengers. The North Carolina case was decided by

a voice vote supporting the regular delegation, but the other three cases were settled by roll-call votes.

The first state to be considered was Texas, and by a vote of 1,368¼ to 956¾, the convention approved the seating of the regular delegation led by Gov. John B. Connally. The rival McCarthy-supported Texas faction was led by Sen. Ralph W. Yarborough. *(Chart, p. 188)*

The Georgia case was considered next, with the credentials committee recommending that both rival delegations be seated and the Georgia vote split evenly between them. However, both delegations found this to be an unsatisfactory solution and presented reports to have their entire delegation seated alone. A minority report to seat the challenging Loyal National Democrats, led by black state Rep. Julian Bond, was defeated 1,415.45 to 1,043.55. A minority report to seat the regular delegation, hand-picked by Gov. Lester G. Maddox and State Chairman James H. Gray, was rejected by a voice vote. The solution recommended by the credentials committee was subsequently approved by a voice vote. *(p. 188)*

The Alabama case involved three competing factions: the regulars, the largely black National Democratic Party of Alabama (NDPA) and the integrated Alabama Independent Democratic Party (AIDP), created solely to run a slate of presidential electors loyal to the national party against the third-party candidacy of Alabama Gov. George C. Wallace. The credentials committee proposed seating all members of the regular delegation who would sign a loyalty pledge and replacing those who would not sign with loyal members of the AIDP delegation. However, the McCarthy-backed NDPA introduced a minority report to seat its entire delegation. By a vote of 1,607 to 880¾, the convention rejected this minority report, and by a voice vote approved the recommendation of the credentials committee. *(p. 188)*

The remainder of the credentials committee report was approved, including a resolution instructing the Democratic National Committee to include, in the call for the 1972 convention, encouragement to state parties to ensure that all Democrats in each state have a "meaningful and timely" opportunity to participate in delegate selection.

McCarthy, McGovern and other liberal factions won their greatest breakthrough on convention rules, obtaining abolition of a mandatory unit rule for the 1968 convention, and, by a vote of 1,351¼ to 1,209, obtaining elimination of the unit rule at every level of party activity leading up to and including the 1972 convention. Many Humphrey-pledged delegates also backed the unit rule change. Also a part of this successful minority report was the requirement that the delegate selection process in 1972 be public and held within the calendar year of the convention. *(p. 188)*

A proposal to add state chairmen and state Young Democratic presidents to the Democratic National Committee was defeated, 1,349¼ to 1,125¾.

On Wednesday night, on the third day of the convention, while nominations and balloting for president took place at the amphitheatre, the worst violence of the convention broke out downtown, and television screens carried pictures of phalanxes of Chicago police advancing on demonstrators.

At the same time, hundreds of Chicago Mayor Richard J. Daley's workers were brought into the galleries with apparently improper credentials. Some delegates, apparently refusing to show their credentials to the omnipresent security guards, were physically ejected from the convention floor. The McCarthy and McGovern forces charged "atrocities" and tried to adjourn the convention for two weeks. House Majority Leader Carl Albert of Oklahoma, the convention chairman, refused to accept their motions.

In addition to Humphrey, McCarthy and McGovern, only two other candidates were placed in nomination—the Rev. Channing E. Phillips of the District of Columbia, who became the first black ever nominated for the presidency at a national convention, and North Carolina Gov. Dan K. Moore. Telegrams were read from President Johnson and Massachusetts Sen. Edward M. Kennedy, each stating that he did not choose to be nominated.

The emotional highlight of the session was provided by McGovern's nominator, Connecticut Sen. Abraham A. Ribicoff, who charged that "with George McGovern as president of the United States we wouldn't have to have Gestapo tactics in the streets of Chicago."

Humphrey was an easy winner on the first ballot, receiving 1,759¼ votes to 601 for McCarthy, 146½ for McGovern and 67½ for Phillips. Humphrey's winning majority included the bulk of party moderates, big-city organizations of the North (including Daley's) and southern conservatives. In a tumultuous ending to one of the wildest nights in American politics, Chairman Albert gaveled through a motion to make the nomination unanimous (despite major opposition on the floor) and adjourned the session. *(Chart, p. 188)*

As his running mate, Humphrey chose Maine Sen. Edmund S. Muskie. Julian Bond's name also was placed in nomination, but Bond, then 28, withdrew, explaining that he was under the "legal age" to be president (the constitutional minimum is 35). Before the end of the first ballot, Albert recognized Mayor Daley, who moved that Muskie be declared the nominee by acclamation. With the convention in a particularly unruly state, the Daley motion was quickly adopted. At the time the roll call was suspended, Muskie already had received 1,942½ votes, a majority. Bond was a distant second with 48½.

A filmed tribute to the late New York Sen. Robert F. Kennedy preceded the vice presidential nomination. Kennedy had been a presidential candidate until his assassination in June after winning the California primary. The tribute to Kennedy evoked a long, standing ovation and the singing of "The Battle Hymn of the Republic."

The 18,000-word platform, adopted by a voice vote, was a document that met the demands of the Democratic Party's liberals word for word in almost every section except that which dealt with United States policy in Vietnam. At one point during the platform-writing sessions, it appeared that Humphrey might assent to a plank calling for a halt in U.S. bombing of North Vietnam, but President Johnson reportedly sent personal instructions that the plank should support administration policy.

The administration plank, approved by a 62-35 vote in the platform committee, supported a bombing halt only when it "would not endanger the lives of our troops in the field," did not call for a reduction in search-and-destroy missions or a withdrawal of troops until the end of the war and advocated a new government in Saigon only after the war had ended. The minority plank, drafted by McCarthy and McGovern, called for an immediate halt to the bombing, reduction of offensive operations in the South Vietnamese countryside, a negotiated troop withdrawal and encouragement of the South Vietnamese government to negotiate with Communist insurgents.

The bitterness created by the Vietnam issue and Humphrey's march toward the nomination finally erupted when the convention managers attempted to force debate and voting on the Vietnam plank at 2 a.m., when most television viewers were already asleep. Albert, in violation of convention rules, refused to recognize a motion from a McCarthy backer to adjourn, but a few minutes later, when the convention could not be brought to order, recognized a similar motion from Mayor Daley.

Nearly three hours of debate were held the next afternoon. On the subsequent roll call, the minority plank was defeated, 1,567¾ to 1,041¼. After the result was announced, members of the New York delegation and others slipped on black armbands and sang "We Shall Overcome." *(Chart, p. 188)*

Unlike the Republican platform, which called for decreased United States involvement in Vietnam, Democrats adopted a plank which called for a continued strong American war effort. Although the Democrats agreed with Republicans that the South Vietnamese eventually should take over their nation's defense, they gave no indication that an expanded Vietnamese role could lead to U.S. troop reductions in the near future.

While promising to reduce waste in military spending, the Democrats stated that the nation "must and will maintain a strong and balanced defense establishment adequate to the task of security and peace." The platform said there "must be no doubt" about U.S. capability to meet either nuclear or more limited challenges.

Crime was one of the leading domestic issues. The platform contained a strongly worded but rather unspecific plank on crime, a plank containing fewer detailed proposals than its Republican counterpart. The Democratic crime plank was entitled "Justice and Law," in a deliberate effort to avoid use of such phrases as "law and order," which were in the Republican plank and which some observers felt had connotations of overly suppressive tactics, particularly in black ghettos.

The Democratic plank did not mention the role of the attorney general. The Republicans said they would seek an attorney general who would "restore stature and respect to that office." Nor did the Democrats, unlike the Republicans, mention implementation of the federal wiretapping authority granted by the Safe Streets Act, or prosecution of subversives.

Both parties pledged further efforts to control the indiscriminate sale of firearms, but neither party was specific. Democratic liberals had tried unsuccessfully within the platform committee to strengthen the gun control section.

The Democratic platform contained a more specific endorsement of open housing than did the Republican document. Both platforms urged better job opportunities, housing and food programs for the poor, and the Democrats also promised reforms in existing welfare programs.

The Democrats, like the Republicans, called for tax reform, but their goals were more pointed. The platform asked for a minimum income tax for wealthy persons based on total income regardless of source and committed the party to seeking decreased rates for lower-income families and an increase in the minimum standard deduction.

The Democrats supported a constitutional amendment to permit 18-year-old voting and recommended a draft lottery and better community representation on draft boards.

Reform of the electoral college was favored, so that it would accurately reflect the will of the voters.

Following are excerpts from the Democratic platform of 1968:

Vietnam. Recognizing that events in Vietnam and the negotiations in Paris may affect the timing and the actions we recommend we would support our Government in the following steps:

Bombing—Stop all bombing of North Vietnam when this action would not endanger the lives of our troops in the field; this action should take into account the response from Hanoi.

Troop Withdrawal—Negotiate with Hanoi an immediate end or limitation of hostilities and the withdrawal from South Vietnam of all foreign forces—both United States and allied forces, and forces infiltrated from North Vietnam.

Election of Postwar Government—Encourage all parties and interests to agree that the choice of the postwar government of South Vietnam should be determined by fair and safeguarded elections, open to all major political factions and parties prepared to accept peaceful political processes. We would favor an effective international presence to facilitate the transition from war to peace and to assure the protection of minorities against reprisal.

Interim Defense and Development Measures—Until the fighting stops, accelerate our efforts to train and equip the South Vietnamese army so that it can defend its own country and carry out cutbacks of U.S. military involvement as the South Vietnamese forces are able to take over their larger responsibilities. We should simultaneously do all in our power to support and encourage further economic, political and social development and reform in South Vietnam, including an extensive land reform program. We support President Johnson's repeated offer to provide a substantial U.S. contribution to the post-war reconstruction of South Vietnam as well as to the economic development of the entire region, including North Vietnam. Japan and the European industrial states should be urged to join in this post-war effort.

National Defense. We must and will maintain a strong and balanced defense establishment adequate to the task of security and peace. There must be no doubt about our strategic nuclear capacity, our capacity to meet limited challenges, and our willingness to act when our vital interests are threatened....

We face difficult and trying times in Asia and in Europe We have responsibilities and commitments we cannot escape with honor.

China. The immediate prospects that China will emerge from its self-imposed isolation are dim. But both Asians and Americans will have to coexist with the 750 million Chinese on the mainland. We shall continue to make it clear that we are prepared to cooperate with China whenever it is ready to become a responsible member of the international community. We would actively encourage economic, social and cultural exchange with mainland China as a means of freeing that nation and her people from their narrow isolation.

Israel. As long as Israel is threatened by hostile and well-armed neighbors, we will assist her with essential military equipment needed for her defense, including the most advanced types of combat aircraft.

Crime. In fighting crime we must not foster injustice. Lawlessness cannot be ended by curtailing the hard-won liberties of all Americans. The right of privacy must be safeguarded. Court procedures must be expedited. Justice delayed is justice denied.

A respect for civil peace requires also a proper respect for the legitimate means of expressing dissent. A democratic society welcomes criticism within the limits of the law. Freedom of speech, press, assembly and association, together with free exercise of the franchise, are among the legitimate means to achieve change in a democratic society. But when the dissenter resorts to violence, he erodes the institutions and values which are the underpinnings of our democratic society. We must not and will not tolerate violence.

Tax Reform. We support a proposal for a minimum income tax for persons of high income based on an individual's total income regardless of source, in order that wealthy persons will be required to make some kind of income tax contribution, no matter how many tax shelters they use to protect their incomes.

We also support a reduction of the tax burden on the poor by lowering the income tax rates at the bottom of the tax scale and increasing the minimum standard deduction. No person or family below the poverty level should be required to pay federal income taxes.

Electoral Reform. We fully recognize the principle of one man, one vote in all elections. We urge that due consideration be given to the question of Presidential primaries throughout the nation. We urge reform of the electoral college and election procedures to assure that the votes of the people are fully reflected.

American Independent Party

Former Alabama Gov. George C. Wallace declared his third-party presidential candidacy on Feb. 8, 1968. The vehicle for his candidacy was his personally created American Independent Party. No convention was held by the party to ratify his selection. (A descendant of the 1968 Wallace campaign, the American Party ran a national ticket in 1972 but received less than two per cent of the vote.)

On Feb. 14, Wallace announced the choice of former Georgia Gov. Marvin Griffin as his "interim" vice presidential running mate, but made clear that an official candidate would be chosen later in the campaign. Griffin's tentative candidacy was necessary to allow the American Independent Party to get on the ballot in several states.

On Oct. 3, Wallace announced his choice of retired Air Force Gen. Curtis E. LeMay, an Ohio native, as his official running mate.

Ten days later, Wallace released the text of his party's platform. The document generally took a harder line toward domestic and international problems than did the Democratic and Republican platforms.

Wallace favored termination of the Vietnam war through negotiations, but added that if negotiations failed, the United States should seek a military solution.

As expected, the emphasis of the platform on domestic issues centered on returning control of local affairs to the states and communities, with the federal government serving in an assisting role rather than an authoritarian manner.

To curb the interference of the federal government in local affairs, Wallace advocated adoption of a constitutional amendment under which federal district judges would stand for election periodically and higher judges, including Supreme Court Justices, were required to be periodically reconfirmed by the Senate. Wallace further proposed, in essence, repeal of the open housing provision of the 1968 Civil Rights Act and to "absolutely prohibit the agencies and agents of the Federal Government from intruding into and seeking to control the affairs of the local school systems of the states, counties and cities of the nation." He further pledged to "cooperate with the administrators of our institutions of higher learning now in the hands of revolutionaries. We must support these officials in the restoration of order on their campuses and we must assure that no assistance, financial or otherwise, from the federal level be given to those seeking to disrupt and destroy these great institutions."

In a section entitled "Crime and Disorder," Wallace pledged to give his full support to law enforcement agencies at every level of government, to "insist on fair and equal treatment for all persons before the bar of justice," to appoint an attorney general "interested in the enforcement rather than the disruption of the legal processes," and to oppose federal legislation requiring gun registration.

Wallace also promised to seek an immediate increase in social security benefits, to increase agricultural support prices to 90 per cent of parity and to seek legislation increasing maximum support to 100 per cent of parity.

Following are excerpts from the American Independent Party platform of 1968:

Vietnam. We earnestly desire that the conflict be terminated through peaceful negotiations and we will lend all aid, support, effort, sincerity and prayer to the efforts of our negotiators. Negotiation will be given every reasonable and logical chance for success and we will be patient to an extreme in seeking an end to the war through this means. If it becomes evident that the enemy does not desire to negotiate in good faith, that our hopes of termination of hostilities are not being realized and that the lives and safety of our committed troops are being further endangered, we must seek a military conclusion.

National Defense. We propose an intensive and immediate review of the policies, practices and capabilities of the Department of Defense with a view to reestablishing sound principles of logic and reasoning to the decisions and directives of that agency and to eliminating from its ranks all of those who have been party to the dissemination and promulgation of the false doctrines of security and the coercion, intimidation and punishment of all who would oppose or disagree with them.

Middle East. Should arms continue to be introduced ...by foreign powers to such an extent as to endanger the peace in this part of the world, we must take steps to assure that a balance of force is brought to exist. We will join with other nations of the free world in providing the means whereby this balance of force will continue and the threat of aggression of one nation against another is made less likely.

United Nations. We will not abandon the United Nations Organization unless it first abandons us. It should be given fair opportunity at resolving international disputes, however, we will not subordinate the interest of our nation to the interest of any international organization. We feel that in this organization, as in any other, participating members should bear proportionate shares of the cost of operation and we will insist on financial responsibility on the part of the member nations.

Crime. Lawlessness has become commonplace in our present society. The permissive attitude of the executive and judiciary at the national level sets the tone for this moral decay. The criminal and anarchist who preys on the decent law abiding citizen is rewarded for his misconduct through never ending justification and platitudes from those in high places who seem to have lost their concern for that vast segment of America that so strongly believes in law and order....

We will appoint as Attorney General a person interested in the enforcement rather than the disruption of legal processes and restore that office to the dignity and stature it deserves and requires.

Economy. We will review and propose revisions to our present tax structure so as to ease the load of the small income citizen and to place upon all their rightful share of the tax burden....

We will eliminate the favorable treatment now accorded the giant, non-tax paying foundations and institutions and require these organizations to assume their rightful responsibility as to the operation of our government....

We propose to rely heavily upon a competitive market structure rather than upon prices administered or fixed by bureaucratic procedures.

Federal Power. The Federal Government, in derogation and flagrant violation of this Article [X] of the Bill of Rights, has in the past three decades seized and usurped many powers not delegated to it, such as, among others: the operation and control of the public school system of the several states; the power to prescribe the eligibility and qualifications of those who would vote in our state and local elections; the power to intrude upon and control the farmer in the operation of his farm; the power to tell the property owner to whom he can and cannot sell or rent his property; and, many other rights and privileges of the individual citizen, which are properly subject to state or local control, as distinguished from federal control. The Federal Government has forced the states to reapportion their legislatures, a prerogative of the states alone. The Federal Government has attempted to take over and control the seniority and apprenticeship lists of the labor unions; the Federal Government has adopted so-called "Civil Rights Acts," particularly the one adopted in 1964, which have set race against race and class against class, all of which we condemn.

The Judiciary. In the period of the past three decades, we have seen the Federal judiciary, primarily the Supreme Court, transgress repeatedly upon the prerogatives of the Congress and exceed its authority by enacting judicial legislation, in the form of decisions based upon political and sociological considerations, which would never have been enacted by the Congress. We have seen them, in their solicitude for the criminal and lawless element of our society, shackle the police and other law enforcement agencies; and, as a result, they have made it increasingly difficult to protect the law-abiding citizen from crime and criminals. This is one of the principal reasons for the turmoil and the near revolutionary conditions which prevail in our country today, and particularly in our national capital. The Federal judiciary, feeling secure in their knowledge that their appointment is for life, have far exceeded their constitutional authority, which is limited to interpreting or construing the law.

It shall be our policy and our purpose, at the earliest possible time, to propose and advocate and urge the adoption of an amendment to the United States Constitution whereby members of the Federal judiciary at District level be required to face the electorate on his record at periodical intervals; and, in the event he receives a negative vote upon such election, his office shall thereupon become vacant, and a successor shall be appointed to succeed him.

With respect to the Supreme Court and the Courts of Appeals I would propose that this amendment require reconfirmation of the office holder by the United States Senate at reasonable intervals.

1972 Conventions

Presidential Candidates

George McGovern
Democrat

Richard M. Nixon
Republican

Democrats

Massive reforms in convention rules and delegate selection procedures made the Democratic convention held in Miami Beach, Fla., in July 1972 significantly different from the violence-plagued assembly in Chicago four years earlier.

Two special commissions, created by the 1968 convention, drafted the reforms. The Commission on Rules, chaired by Michigan Rep. James G. O'Hara, composed the first set of rules ever written on Democratic convention procedure. Among the reforms which were adopted by the Democratic National Committee were:

● A new vote allocation formula based nearly equally on electoral college strength and the Democratic vote in recent presidential elections.

● An expansion of the convention rules, platform and credentials committees so that their make-up would reflect state population differences rather than the previous method of allocating two seats to each state.

● The assurance that women and men be equally represented on committees and among convention officers.

● The requirement that the meetings and votes of all convention committees be open to the public.

● The requirement that the reports and minority views of all the committees be released at specified dates before the opening of the convention.

● The banning of floor demonstrations for candidates.

● The arrangement of the states and territories for roll calls in random sequence determined by lot rather than in the traditional alphabetical order.

The Commission on Party Structure and Delegate Selection, first chaired by South Dakota Sen. George McGovern and later by Minnesota Rep. Donald M. Fraser, formulated 18 guidelines to be met by the states in the delegate selection process. With the approval of these guidelines by the Democratic National Committee, they became part of the 1972 convention call, thus requiring the states to be in full compliance with the guidelines before they would be seated.

Among the important features of the 18 guidelines were the elimination of the unit rule; the restriction that no more than ten per cent of a state's delegation be named by its state committee; the requirement that all steps in the delegate selection process be publicly advertised and held in easily accessible public places within the calendar year of the convention, the requirement that women, youth and minority groups be included in delegations "in reasonable relationship" to their presence in the state's population, and the establishment of a detailed, public method of hearing delegate challenges.

The reforms encouraged an unprecedented number of challenges. The credentials committee opened hearings in Washington, D.C., two weeks before the start of the convention, faced with 82 challenges from 30 states and one territory. A total of 1,289 delegates were challenged, representing more than 40 per cent of the convention delegates. More than four-fifths of the challenges were filed on grounds of non-compliance with reform commission guidelines regarding adequate representation of women, youth and minorities.

The most controversial challenges involved the California delegation and the part of the Illinois delegation controlled by Chicago Mayor Richard J. Daley.

The credentials committee, in a move that caught supporters of McGovern, a candidate for the presidential nomination, by surprise, upheld a challenge of California's winner-take-all primary law, stripping McGovern of 151 of the 271 delegate votes he had won in the primary.

The committee voted 72 to 66 to award the 151 convention seats to Minnesota Sen. Hubert H. Humphrey and seven other candidates in proportion to their share of the popular ballots cast in the state's June primary. Although McGovern was clearly the front-runner for the nomination, the decision, if not overturned by the full convention, threatened his chances of being selected.

In a tense and dramatic balloting session the next day, the committee voted 71 to 61 to unseat Daley and 58 of his Chicago delegates. The committee decided to replace the 59 delegates on grounds that the procedures under which the Daley delegates had been selected violated five of the party's reform guidelines. Most of the Illinois delegates challenging Daley supported McGovern.

Although the losing sides in both the California and Illinois decisions took their cases to the courts, the courts ruled that the party conventions decide their claims.

The emotional credentials challenges were considered on the first night of the convention. Twenty-three challenges from 15 states were brought to the convention floor, but the spotlight was on the California and Illinois cases. A key preliminary vote took place on a challenge to the South Carolina delegation brought by the National Women's Political Caucus. The challenge, seeking to increase the number of women in the state delegation, was rejected by a vote of 1,555.75 to 1,429.05. *(Chart, p. 190)*

The outcome of the vote could have set an important precedent on what constituted a majority on subsequent challenges. Anti-McGovern forces had hoped to get a ruling from the chair allowing an absolute majority of 1,509 delegates to prevail rather than a simple majority of delegates actually voting.

Convention Chairman Lawrence F. O'Brien (also chairman of the Democratic National Committee) had announced earlier that a majority would consist of one-half plus one of the number of eligible voters. The rules provided that no delegates could vote on their own credentials challenges.

Because the winning total on the South Carolina vote exceeded by a wide margin both the eligible majority and the absolute majority of the convention's 3,016 votes, the anti-McGovern coalition was unable to force a test of what constituted a majority. Thus the vote, although it rejected the position of South Carolina challengers favorable to McGovern, set the stage for returning the 151 California delegates to McGovern. The McGovern forces subsequently won the crucial California challenge, 1,618.28 to 1,238.22. *(Chart, p. 190)*

Immediately after the vote on the California challenge, a Wallace delegate from Florida appealed the ruling of the chair that allowed 120 McGovern delegates from California to vote on their state's other 151 delegates. The appeal was rejected, 1,689.52 to 1,162.23.

Former Nebraska Gov. Frank B. Morrison, a McGovern supporter, proposed a compromise solution for the Illinois case that would seat both the Daley delegates and the insurgent challengers, while splitting the vote between them. The Morrison proposal asked for suspension of the rules—a parliamentary procedure requiring a two-thirds majority. The motion to suspend the rules was rejected by 1,473.08 nays to 1,411.05 yeas.

The minority report, which asked for seating of the Daley delegates alone, was defeated, 1,486.04 to 1,371.56. The vote seated a group, a majority of which supported McGovern, headed by Chicago Alderman William Singer and black activist Jesse Jackson. *(Chart, p. 190)*

No other roll-call votes were needed to resolve the remaining credentials challenges. After the settlement of all the delegate contests, the convention had a composition unlike that of any previous major party convention. The 1972 Democratic assembly was the largest in major party history, with 3,203 delegates casting 3,016 votes. Unlike 1968, the majority of delegates were chosen in state primary elections rather than in state conventions or caucuses. Nearly two-thirds of the delegates to the 1972 convention were selected in primaries, while only 41 per cent had been elected by the primary system four years earlier.

There were also large increases in the number of women, youth and racial minorities at the 1972 convention.

The proportion of women delegates rose from 13 per cent in 1968 to 40 per cent in 1972; the number of youth delegates (30 and under) dramatically jumped from 2.6 per cent in 1968 to 21 per cent four years later; and black delegates made up 15 per cent of the 1972 convention, compared with 5.5 per cent in 1968. But while women, youth and blacks were better represented than at earlier conventions, there was a lower level of participation by elected party officials. Only 30 of the 255 Democratic U.S. House members were present in Miami Beach.

The report of the rules committee was approved on the second day of the convention by a voice vote. The report proposed the abolition of winner-take-all primaries in 1976; the abolition of cross-over voting by Republicans in future Democratic presidential primaries; the selection of a woman as chairman of the 1976 convention, with the job rotating between the sexes thereafter; the creation of a special fund in the Democratic National Committee to subsidize the expenses of poor delegates at future national conventions and other party councils, and the appointment of a commission to make "appropriate revisions" in the reform guidelines.

Although the delegates overwhelmingly accepted these reforms, they balked at approving the party charter drafted by the rules committee. The new charter, the first ever written for a major party, was intended to free the national party of four-year presidential election cycles and to broaden public involvement in major national policy questions. But the charter was opposed by some party leaders, particularly members of Congress, who viewed the document as shifting power from elected politicians to the grass-roots level. By a vote of 2,408.45 to 195.10, the convention approved a compromise resolution to delay consideration of the charter until a proposed midterm policy conference in 1974. The compromise also enlarged the Democratic National Committee and revised its membership to reflect Democratic strength in the various states.

The settlement of the California challenge on the opening night of the convention in favor of the McGovern forces effectively locked up the presidential nomination for the South Dakota senator. The next day, two of his major rivals in the primaries, Senators Humphrey and Muskie, withdrew from the race. In the balloting on the third day of the convention, McGovern was an easy winner on the first roll call. Before switches, McGovern had received 1,728.35 votes to 525 for Sen. Henry M. Jackson of Washington, 381.7 for Gov. Wallace of Alabama and 151.95 for Rep. Shirley Chisholm of New York. After vote changes, McGovern's vote total rose to 1,864.95, but no attempt was made to make his nomination unanimous. *(Chart, p. 191)*

With McGovern's first choice for vice president, Sen. Edward M. Kennedy of Massachusetts, rebuffing all overtures, McGovern selected Missouri Sen. Thomas F. Eagleton. The vice presidential balloting was prolonged by the nomination of six other candidates, and by the time the roll call was suspended, votes were distributed among more than 70 different "candidates." Eagleton received 1,741.81 votes, a majority. He was followed by Frances T. ("Sissy") Farenthold, a women's rights leader from Texas, who had 404.04 votes, Sen. Mike Gravel of Alaska with 225.38 and former Massachusetts Gov. Endicott Peabody with 107.26. On the motion of Farenthold, the roll call was suspended and Eagleton was nominated by acclamation.

With the length of the vice presidential roll call, it was nearly 3 a.m. before McGovern was able to deliver his acceptance speech. In it he stressed the anti-war theme that was a basic part of his campaign and implored the nation to "come home" to its founding ideals.

Barely ten days after selection of the Democratic ticket, on July 25, Eagleton disclosed that he voluntarily had hospitalized himself three times between 1960 and 1966 for "nervous exhaustion and fatigue." McGovern strongly supported his running mate at the time, but in the following days, his support for the Missouri Senator began to wane. After a meeting with McGovern on July 31, Eagleton withdrew from the ticket. It marked the first time since 1860 that a major-party candidate had withdrawn from a national ticket after the convention had adjourned.

On Aug. 5, McGovern announced that his choice to replace Eagleton was R. Sargent Shriver of Maryland, U.S. ambassador to France and the former director of the Peace Corps and the Office of Economic Opportunity. The newly enlarged Democratic National Committee formally nominated Shriver in an Aug. 8 meeting in Washington. The new vice presidential candidate received 2,936 of the 3,013 votes cast, with the Missouri vote going to Eagleton and four of Oregon's votes to former Sen. Wayne Morse.

The 1972 Democratic platform was probably the most liberal and the longest (about 25,000 words) ever offered by a major political party. The platform was more a collection of independent reform proposals than a unified plan of action. Its recommendations, largely written by separate subject-area task forces, did not translate into a compact program for Congress to consider or for a president to propose. But the platform's common themes reflected the changes in the party since 1968 and set it off from all other Democratic platforms of the previous generation.

The convention made no concessions to the views of Wallace, even though he made a dramatic appearance at the podium in a wheelchair to urge adoption of minority planks his supporters had offered.

The planks called for a constitutional amendment to outlaw busing, tax reform, reintroduction of the death penalty, cutbacks in foreign aid, popular election of federal judges and Senate reconfirmation of Supreme Court justices, a school prayer amendment and support for the right to own guns. They were rejected by voice votes.

Twenty separate minority planks were considered by the convention, but only two were adopted, both by voice vote. One strengthened the American commitment to Israel by adding language promising "a military force in Europe and at sea in the Mediterranean ample to deter the Soviet Union from putting unbearable pressure on Israel." The second endorsed "allocation of federal surplus lands to American Indians on a priority basis."

Two roll-call votes were taken on other planks. The National Welfare Rights Organization sponsored a measure requiring the federal government to guarantee every family of four an annual income of $6,500. This proposal lost, 1,852.86 to 999.34. The other roll call was on a minority plank supporting the right of women to control their reproductive lives without legal interference. Offered by pro-abortion groups, it was defeated 1,572.80 to 1,101.37.

Two other significant minority planks were rejected by voice votes. One was a tax reform measure pushed by Oklahoma Sen. Fred Harris, which had the slogan, "Take the rich off welfare." The other was a "gay rights" plank endorsing the repeal of all laws regarding voluntary sex acts performed by adults in private.

The platform session demonstrated the firm control McGovern had over the proceedings of the convention. The two minority planks added to the platform were the only proposed additions that McGovern did not specifically oppose. He asked his delegates to support the pro-Israel plank and told them to vote their consciences on the Indian issue.

Planks dealing with domestic issues composed more than four-fifths of the platform. The domestic planks recommended little significant expansion of the size and scope of the federal government. With the major exception of health insurance, the platform sought to restructure society by shifting money and political power to the underprivileged, not by developing federal agencies to alter their lives.

The platform endorsed income redistribution through tax reforms and a guaranteed annual income. It sought expansion of minority-group rights in all political and federal government affairs. To solve the financial crisis at local levels, it endorsed general revenue sharing with local control over use of the money. All this represented a departure from the statist liberalism that had dominated Democratic platforms since the New Deal of the 1930s.

The foreign policy planks broke with the Cold War rhetoric of 1968 and previous years. While endorsing the concept of a strong national defense, the platform devoted more space to peace in Indochina, improved relations with the Communist world and less help for non-Communist totalitarian regimes. Only four years earlier, the Democrats had given considerable space to warnings against Soviet and Chinese expansion and to praise for the North Atlantic Treaty Organization. The 1968 platform called for scrutiny of wasteful defense spending practices, but the 1972 document made military cuts a major campaign promise and a source of financing for domestic programs.

The platform's position on the Vietnam war was blunt and unequivocal. As "the first order of business" of a Democratic administration, the platform pledged "immediate and complete withdrawal of all U.S. forces in Indochina." The plank also promised an end to military aid to the Saigon regime, but pledged economic assistance to Vietnam to help the nation emerge from the war. Amnesty for war resisters was recommended after the return of American prisoners of war.

Following are excerpts from the Democratic platform of 1972:

Foreign Policy. The next Democratic Administration should:

● End American participation in the war in Southeast Asia.

● Re-establish control over military activities and reduce military spending, where consistent with national security.

● Defend America's real interests and maintain our alliances, neither playing world policeman nor abandoning old and good friends.

● Not neglect America's relations with small third-world nations in placing reliance on great power relationships.

● Return to Congress, and to the people, a meaningful role in decisions on peace and war, and

● Make information public, except where real national defense interests are involved.

Vietnam. We believe that war is a waste of human life. We are determined to end forthwith a war which has cost 50,000 American lives, $150 billion of our resources, that has divided us from each other, drained our national will and inflicted incalculable damage to countless people. We will end that war by a simple plan that need not be kept secret: The immediate total withdrawal of all Americans from Southeast Asia.

Military Spending. Military strength remains an essential element of a responsible international policy. America must have the strength required for effective deterrence.

But military defense cannot be treated in isolation from other vital national concerns. Spending for military purposes is greater by far than federal spending for education, housing, environmental protection, unemployment insurance or welfare. Unneeded dollars for the military at once add to the tax burden and pre-empt funds from programs of direct and immediate benefit to our people. Moreover, too much that is now spent on defense not only adds nothing to our strength but makes us less secure by stimulating other countries to respond.

Vietnam Amnesty. To those who for reasons of conscience refused to serve in this war and were prosecuted or sought refuge abroad, we state our firm intention to declare an amnesty, on an appropriate basis, when the fighting has ceased and our troops and prisoners of war have returned.

Federal Power. The new Democratic Administration can begin a fundamental re-examination of all federal domestic social programs and the patterns of service delivery they support. Simply advocating the expenditure of more funds is not enough, although funds are needed, for billions already have been poured into federal government programs like urban renewal, current welfare and aid to education, with meager results. The control, structure and effectiveness of every institution and government grant system must be fully examined and these institutions must be made accountable to those they are supposed to serve.

Economy. The heart of a program of economic security based on earned income must be creating jobs and training people to fill them. Millions of jobs—real jobs, not make-work—need to be provided. Public service employment must be greatly expanded in order to make the government the employer of last resort and guarantee a job for all.

Tax Reform. The cost of government must be distributed more fairly among income classes. We reaffirm the long-established principle of progressive taxation—allocating the burden according to ability to pay—which is all but a dead letter in the present tax code.

Poverty. The next Democratic Administration must end the present welfare system and replace it with an income security program which places cash assistance in an appropriate context with all of the measures outlined above, adding up to an earned income approach to ensure each family an income substantially more than the poverty level ensuring standards of decency and health, as officially defined in the area. Federal income assistance will supplement the income of working poor people and assure an adequate income for those unable to work.

Crime. There must be laws to control the improper use of hand guns. Four years ago a candidate for the presidency was slain by a hand gun. Two months ago, another candidate for that office was gravely wounded. Three out of four police officers killed in the line of duty are slain with hand guns. Effective legislation must include a ban on sale of hand guns known as Saturday night specials which are unsuitable for sporting purposes.

Free Expression and Privacy. The new Democratic Administration should bring an end to the pattern of political persecution and investigation, the use of high office as a pulpit for unfair attack and intimidation and the blatant efforts to control the poor and to keep them from acquiring additional economic security or political power.

The epidemic of wiretapping and electronic surveillance engaged in by the Nixon Administration and the use of grand juries for purposes of political intimidation must be ended. The rule of law and the supremacy of the Constitution, as these concepts have traditionally been understood, must be restored.

Rights of Women. Women historically have been denied a full voice in the evolution of the political and social institutions of this country and are therefore allied with all underrepresented groups in a common desire to form a more humane and compassionate society. The Democratic Party pledges the following:

• A priority effort to ratify the Equal Rights Amendment....

• Appointment of women to positions of top responsibilities in all branches of the federal government, to achieve an equitable ratio of women and men.

School Busing. We support the goal of desegregation as a means to achieve equal access to quality education for all our children. There are many ways to desegregate schools: School attendance lines may be redrawn; schools may be paired; larger physical facilities may be built to serve larger, more diverse enrollments; magnet schools or educational parks may be used. Transportation of students is another tool to accomplish desegregation. It must continue to be available according to Supreme Court decisions to eliminate legally imposed segregation and improve the quality of education for all children.

Agriculture. We will resist a price ceiling on agriculture products until farm prices reach 110 percent of parity, based on the 1910-14 ratios, and we will conduct a consumer education program to inform all Americans of the relationship between the prices of raw commodities and retail prices;

We will end farm program benefits to farm units larger than family-size,...

Presidential Elections. We favor a Constitutional change to abolish the Electoral College and to give every voter a direct and equal voice in Presidential elections. The amendment should provide for a runoff election, if no candidate received more than 40 percent of the popular vote.

Republicans

Six weeks after the Democratic convention, the Republicans gathered in the same Miami Beach convention hall. The late August convention, precisely programmed to make the most of free prime time, was a gigantic television spectacular from start to finish. The main business of the convention, the nomination of President Nixon and Vice President Agnew to a second term, was a carefully planned ritual.

The selection of Miami Beach as the convention city provided as much drama as the convention itself. Initially the Republicans had chosen San Diego, Calif., as the host city, but the reluctance of that city to provide necessary facilities on schedule, coupled with the revelation that the International Telephone and Telegraph Corporation had pledged as much as $400,000 in local contributions, led the Republican National Committee to move the convention to Miami Beach.

Despite the preliminary organizational problems, the atmosphere of the convention itself was almost euphoric, and the sessions proceeded with dispatch. The five sessions lasted only 16 hours and 59 minutes, compared with the 32 hours and 18 minutes of the Democratic convention.

The one debate, which lasted only an hour, occurred over the adoption of new procedures for selecting national convention delegates. The Republican National Committee's preconvention rules committee approved a 1976 delegate allocation plan initiated by Texas Sen. John G. Tower and New York Rep. Jack F. Kemp. The plan emphasized a state's Republican presidential vote in awarding bonus delegates. It was viewed as especially beneficial to small southern and western states. The convention rules committee amended the Tower-Kemp plan to make it more palatable to larger states by adding some bonus delegates for states electing Republican governors and members of Congress.

However, Rep. William A. Steiger of Wisconsin introduced a different .plan, weighted more toward states electing Republican governors and members of Congress—a plan that would work to the advantage of the larger states. The debate on the contrasting plans focused on the question of whether states should be rewarded chiefly for delivering their electoral votes to a Republican presidential candidate or whether the bonus should be based to some extent on gubernatorial and congressional contests.

The dispute was in part a battle between liberals and conservatives. Final victory for the conservatives was achieved on a 910-to-434 roll-call vote that defeated the Steiger amendment. The reallocation formula adopted by the delegates would expand the 1976 convention to more than 2,000 delegates, compared with the 1,348 who came to Miami Beach in 1972.

The struggle over the delegate allocation formula was the only sign of party division at the convention. Nixon was renominated on the third night of the convention, receiving 1,347 of the 1,348 votes. The only opposing vote was cast reluctantly by a delegate from New Mexico for Rep. Paul N. McCloskey Jr. of California, whose anti-war challenge of the President had fizzled after the year's first primary in New Hampshire. *(Chart, p. 192)*

One measure of the unity that surrounded the festive proceedings was the appearance of New York Gov. Nelson A. Rockefeller to deliver Nixon's nominating speech. Rockefeller had become a loyal supporter of the President after having been his chief rival for the Republican nomination in 1960 and 1968.

Agnew was nominated the next night with 1,345 votes. There were two abstentions and one waggish vote for newscaster David Brinkley.

In his acceptance speech, Nixon combined a review of his first four years with promises for the next four and indirect but highly partisan attacks on his Democratic opponent, George McGovern. Nixon stressed that the choice in the upcoming election was "not between radical change and no change, the choice...is between change that works and change that won't work."

The Republican platform provoked little discussion on the convention floor and was approved by a voice vote. Two amendments were offered to the platform. The first, which would have pledged a prohibition on deficit federal spending, was defeated by voice vote. The second, advocating self-determination for American Indians, was approved by voice vote with the consent of the platform committee chairman, Rep. John J. Rhodes of Arizona.

The document, approximately 20,000 words long, was generally moderate in its proposals and conservative in language, in contrast to the Democrats' liberal platform.

The actual drafting of the Republican platform was heavily influenced by the White House, and platform committee sessions were held behind closed doors. In contrast, the Democrats held ten regional hearings around the country, drafted their platform in public and were required by party rules to produce a final version at least ten days before the convention opened.

The Republican platform was sharply critical not only of McGovern's new leadership of the Democratic Party but also of the Kennedy and Johnson administrations of the "nightmarish" 1960s.

The contrast with the Democratic platform on domestic affairs was stark. The Democrats advocated in-come redistribution through tax reform and a guaranteed annual income. The Republicans mentioned tax reform but did not include specifics. They rejected the guaranteed income plan.

Both parties called for a reduction in property taxes, although the Republicans made no mention of the value-added tax, a revenue measure the Nixon administration was said to be considering.

The Democrats advocated an immediate end to economic controls; the Republicans proposed to remove the controls "once the economic distortions spawned in the late 1960's are repaired."

The Democrats supported a federally financed and administered national health insurance system, while the Republicans supported a national health insurance plan financed by employers and employees as well as the federal government.

The Republicans opposed busing children to achieve racial balance in schools. The Democrats, however, viewed busing as "another tool" to bring about desegregation. The Republicans supported voluntary school prayer, an issue the Democrats did not mention.

The Republicans opposed legislation on gun control, while the Democrats endorsed a ban on the sale of handguns. The Republicans opposed the legalization of marijuana; the Democrats did not mention the subject in their platform.

Both parties took similar positions on several controversial social issues. The Republicans and Democrats both supported the equal rights amendment to the Constitution, but neither platform specifically mentioned abortion or the rights of homosexuals.

Major differences between the parties were evident in national defense and foreign affairs. The Republicans chided the Democrats for proposing "meat-ax slashes" in the defense budget and charged that their proposals were "worse than misguided; they are dangerous." The Republicans rejected what they described as "a whimpering 'come back America' retreat to isolationism."

The continuing Vietnam war highlighted the foreign policy section. The Republican platform took a swipe at the Democrats by promising that the Nixon administration would not abandon the South Vietnamese or "go begging to Hanoi." If negotiations with North Vietnam failed, the platform promised continuation of the administration's Vietnamization program, gradually phasing out American involvement in the war. But before the remaining United States troops would be withdrawn, the Republicans declared, there must be a return of prisoners of war and an accounting of those missing in action. The Republicans opposed any form of amnesty.

The Republicans pledged to maintain an adequate nuclear deterrent, to help other nations develop the capability to defend themselves, to honor treaty commitments and to defend American interests but limit involvement when American interests were not involved.

The Democrats had taken a stronger stand than in previous platforms against what they considered misguided American support for repressive regimes throughout the world. In addition, the Democrats argued for re-examination of the hostile United States policy toward Cuba.

Following are excerpts from the Republican platform of 1972:

Foreign Policy. Historians may well regard these years as a golden age of American diplomacy. Never before has our country negotiated with so many nations on so wide a range of subjects—and never with greater success.

Vietnam. We will continue to seek a settlement of the Vietnam war which will permit the people of Southeast Asia to live in peace under political arrangements of their own choosing. We take specific note of the remaining major obstacle to settlement—Hanoi's demand that the United States overthrow the Saigon government and impose a Communist-dominated government on the South Vietnamese. We stand unequivocally at the side of the President in his effort to negotiate honorable terms, and in his refusal to accept terms which would dishonor this country.

Military Spending. To the alarm of free nations everywhere, the New Democratic Left now would undercut our defenses and have America retreat into virtual isolation, leaving us weak in a world still not free of aggression and threats of aggression. We categorically reject this slash-now, beg-later approach to defense policy....

We draw a sharp distinction between prudent reductions in defense spending and the meat-ax slashes with which some Americans are not beguiled by the political opposition.

Vietnam Amnesty. We are proud of the men and women who wear our country's uniform, especially of those who have borne the burden of fighting a difficult and unpopular war. Here and now we reject all proposals to grant amnesty to those who have broken the law by evading military service. We reject the claim that those who fled are more deserving, or obeyed a higher morality, than those next in line who served in their places.

Economy. We have already removed some temporary controls on wages and prices and will remove them all once the economic distortions spawned in the late 1960's are repaired. We are determined to return to an unfettered economy at the earliest possible moment.

We affirm our support for the basic principles of capitalism which underline the private enterprise system of the United States. At a time when a small but dominant faction of the opposition Party is pressing for radical economic schemes which so often have failed around the world, we hold that nothing has done more to help the American people achieve their unmatched standard of living than the free enterprise system.

Tax Reform. We reject the deceitful tax "reform" cynically represented as one that would soak the rich, but in fact one that would sharply raise the taxes of millions of families in middle-income brackets as well. We reject as well the lavish spending promised by the opposition Party which would more than double the present budget of the United States Government. This, too, would cause runaway inflation or force heavy increases in personal taxes.

Gun Control. [We pledge to] safeguard the right of responsible citizens to collect, own and use firearms for legitimate purposes, including hunting, target shooting and self-defense. We will strongly support efforts of all law enforcement agencies to apprehend and prosecute to the limit of the law all those who use firearms in the commission of crimes.

Women's Rights. Continued...support of the Equal Rights Amendment to the Constitution, our Party being the first national party to back this Amendment.

School Busing. We are irrevocably opposed to busing for racial balance. Such busing fails its stated objective—improved learning opportunities—while it achieves results no one wants—division within communities and hostility between classes and races. We regard it as unnecessary, counter-productive and wrong.

School Prayer. We reaffirm our view that voluntary prayer should be freely permitted in public places—particularly, by school children while attending public schools—provided that such prayers are not prepared or prescribed by the state or any of its political subdivisions and that no person's participation is coerced, thus preserving the traditional separation of church and state.

Education. Our efforts to remedy ancient neglect of disadvantaged groups will continue in universities as well as in society at large, but we distinguish between such efforts and quotas. We believe the imposition of arbitrary quotas in the hiring of faculties or the enrollment of students has no place in our universities; we believe quotas strike at the essence of the university.

Health. To assure access to basic medical care for all our people, we support a program financed by employers, employees and the Federal Government to provide comprehensive health insurance coverage, including insurance against the cost of long-term and catastrophic illnesses and accidents and renal failure which necessitates dialysis, at a cost which all Americans can afford....

We oppose nationalized compulsory health insurance. This approach would at least triple in taxes the amount the average citizen now pays for health and would deny families the right to choose the kind of care they prefer. Ultimately it would lower the overall quality of health care for all Americans.

Welfare. Perhaps nowhere else is there a greater contrast in policy and philosophy than between the Administration's remedy for the welfare ills and the financial orgy proposed by our political opposition....

We flatly oppose programs or policies which embrace the principle of a government-guaranteed income. We reject as unconscionable the idea that all citizens have the right to be supported by the government, regardless of their ability or desire to support themselves and their families.

1976 Conventions

Presidential Candidates

Jimmy Carter
Democrat

Gerald R. Ford
Republican

Democrats

Jimmy Carter, whose presidential primary campaign flouted Democratic Party regulars, brought the party's diverse elements together July 12-15 in a show of unaccustomed unity.

The four-day convention in New York City was the party's most harmonious in 12 years and a stark contrast to the bitter and divisive conventions of 1968 and 1972.

The spirit of harmony was evident in the committee reports. No credentials challenges were carried to the convention floor and just one minority plank to the platform was offered. Only the Rules Committee report sparked much debate, and it was muted in comparison to the emotional struggles in the previous two conventions.

The lack of a spirited competition for the presidential nomination was an important factor in the absence of credentials challenges. However, the groundwork for the harmonious atmosphere had been established months earlier, when the Democratic National Committee adopted new delegate selection and convention rules.

The delegate selection rules abolished the implicit quota system that had been the basis of most challenges in 1972. The only basis for a challenge in 1976 was the violation of a state's delegate selection or affirmative action plan to assure the fair representation of minorities. Since all states had their plans approved by the Compliance Review Commission of the national committee, the Credentials Committee was not weighing the fairness of the plan, but merely whether the state party had implemented it. Unlike 1972, the burden of proof was on the challenging individual or group, not on the state parties.

The task of challengers was further impeded by the action of the national committee in October 1975, raising the petition requirement for convention minority reports from 10 per cent to 25 per cent of Credentials Committee members.

The stringent new rules had an effect on the demographic composition of the convention. A post-convention survey by the national committee indicated that 36 per cent of the delegates in 1976 were women, compared with 38 per cent in 1972; 7 per cent were black compared with 15 per cent four years earlier and 14 per cent were youths, compared with 21 per cent in 1972.

The first roll call of the convention came on a Rules Committee minority report that would have permitted extended debate on the platform. The measure was promoted by party liberals, who complained that the restrictive convention rules cut off their chance for full debate. They urged platform debate on a maximum of three issues for a total of one hour, if at least 300 delegates from 10 states signed a petition for such issues. The proposal called for debate only; no votes would have been taken.

Carter delegates, though, were nearly unanimous in their opposition, fearing that adoption of the minority report would unduly lengthen the proceedings. By a vote of 735 to 1,957½ the minority report was rejected.

Liberals had better luck when the rules relating to future conventions were considered. By voice votes, they won approval of majority reports to establish the party's new Judicial Council as an arbiter of party rules and to eliminate the controversial loophole primary.

A loophole primary is one that permits election of delegates on a winner-take-all basis at the congressional district level. Carter and national committee Chairman Robert S. Strauss both favored the minority report which called simply for review of the loophole primary by the newly established Commission on the Role and Future of Presidential Primaries, headed by Michigan State Chairman Morley Winograd.

Liberals argued that this was not enough. They claimed that the loophole primary violated the party charter, which requires proportional representation. Their position prevailed in the Rules Committee by a razor-thin margin of 58½ to 58¼.

Although Carter managers were unhappy with the majority report, they did not press for a roll call and it was approved by voice vote.

Liberal amendments, though, to mandate the size and agenda of the party's 1978 mid-term conference and to lower the minority report requirement at future conventions were defeated on roll-call votes.

The minority report on the 1978 conference would have required a prescribed agenda that included the discussion of policy matters. It would also have mandated a conference of at least 2,000 delegates, two-thirds of them elected at the congressional district level. On the roll call the proposal ran ahead, 1,240 to 1,128, but failed because of convention rules requiring a constitutional majority of 1,505 votes.

Another roll call came on the unsuccessful attempt by liberal delegates to have the minority report requirement at future conventions lowered from 25 per cent to 15 per cent of convention committee members. It was rejected, 1,249 to 1,354½.

Potentially the most explosive of the rules issues, regarding a "female quota" at future conventions, was settled in behind the scenes meetings between Carter and representatives of the women's caucus.

At the Rules Committee meeting in Washington, D.C., in late June, the women's caucus had demanded equal representation with men in state delegations at future conventions. The Carter forces balked at this. Carter's views prevailed in the Rules Committee, which urged each state to promote equal division between the sexes but left the implementation of the rule to each state party. The women's caucus filed a minority report.

But both sides expressed a willingness to compromise, and in New York City July 11 and 12, Carter met with representatives of the women's caucus. They reached a compromise that encouraged—but did not require—equal representation for women at the party's mid-term conference and at future conventions. Language was inserted calling for the national committee to "encourage and assist" state parties in achieving equal division.

The compromise also included agreements between Carter and the women on other questions. Carter promised to establish an independent women's division in the party outside the realm of the chairman and pledged full party representation for women.

The candidate promised to work for the ratification of the Equal Rights Amendment and pledged high government positions for women.

With acceptance of this compromise by the women's caucus, the minority report was withdrawn and the compromise language on equal division was worked into the majority report.

Balloting for President came on July 14, the third day of the convention, but it was merely a formality. Carter had locked up the nomination over a month earlier when he won the June 8 Ohio primary, a victory that prompted a cascade of endorsements and stymied his remaining opposition.

Besides Carter, three other names were placed in nomination: Arizona Rep. Morris K. Udall, Carter's most persistent primary challenger; California Gov. Edmund G. Brown Jr. and anti-abortion crusader Ellen McCormack. The proceedings, though, turned into a love-feast as Udall before the balloting and Brown afterwards appeared at the convention to declare their support for Carter.

On the presidential roll call, Carter received 2,238½ of the convention's 3,008 votes, topping the needed majority little more than halfway through the balloting with the vote from Ohio. Udall finished second with 329½ votes, followed by Brown with 300½, Alabama Gov. George C. Wallace with 57 and McCormack with 22. The rest of the vote was scattered. After completion of the roll call—and vote switches in California, Rhode Island and Louisiana—a motion to make the nomination unanimous was approved by voice vote. *(Chart p. 193)*

The following morning Carter announced that his choice for Vice President was Minnesota Sen. Walter F. Mondale. Carter noted that it was a difficult decision, admitting that he had changed his mind three times in the previous 30 days.

In explaining his choice, Carter cited Mondale's experience and political philosophy, his concept of the presidency and the preparation Mondale had made for his interview with Carter. Most of all, Carter emphasized compatibility, saying, "It's a very sure feeling that I have."

Mondale was one of seven prospective running mates Carter had personally interviewed. Sens. Edmund S. Muskie (Maine), John Glenn (Ohio) and Mondale were interviewed at Carter's home in Plains, Ga. Sens. Henry M. Jackson (Wash.), Frank Church (Idaho) and Adlai E. Stevenson III (Ill.) and Rep. Peter W. Rodino Jr. (N.J.) were interviewed by Carter at the convention in New York. Rodino withdrew his name from consideration shortly after his interview.

Like the presidential roll call the previous night, the balloting for Vice President July 15 was a formality. Mondale had only one declared opponent, Gary Benoit, a Massachusetts college student and a Wallace delegate. Two others were nominated but withdrew—Rep. Ronald V. Dellums (Calif.) and Vietnam war resister Fritz Efaw of Oklahoma.

Dellums, a black legislator from Berkeley, appeared personally to withdraw his name and used the opportunity to plead with Carter to pay attention to the needs of minorities at home and to Third-World aspirations abroad.

On the roll call, Mondale swamped his rivals, receiving 2,817 votes, more than 90 per cent of the convention total. Retiring House Speaker Carl Albert (Okla.) finished a distant second with 36 votes, all cast as a complimentary gesture by his home state delegation. Rep. Barbara C. Jordan (Texas), the black congresswoman from Houston, followed with 24½ votes, an apparent tribute to her dramatic keynote address.

Following the balloting, Mondale delivered his acceptance speech, and succeeded in arousing the delegates with a partisan oratorical style reminiscent of his Minnesota mentor, Sen. Hubert H. Humphrey.

"We have just lived through the worst scandal in American history," Mondale declared, "and are now led by a President who pardoned the person who did it." His reference to the Watergate affair and to the Nixon pardon brought the delegates to their feet.

Carter's acceptance speech, unlike Mondale's, was not a rousing one in the traditional sense. But Carter was able to begin his address before 11 p.m., in the prime television slot that Strauss had promised as a contrast to George McGovern's nearly unheard 3 a.m. acceptance speech in 1972.

Like less-heralded Carter addresses earlier in the campaign, the acceptance speech ranged across a variety of issues and featured at least a few lines for those at different ends of the political spectrum. For the right, there were criticisms of wasteful federal bureaucracy, a call for a balanced budget and praise for business competition with "minimal intrusion of government in our free economic system."

For the left, there were endorsements of national health insurance, reform of the tax structure and further efforts to end discrimination by race and sex.

There was populism, with partisan overtones: "I see no reason why big-shot crooks should go free and the poor ones go to jail."

There were appeals to humanism: "We should make major investments in people, not in buildings and weapons. The poor, the aged, the weak and the afflicted must be treated with respect and with compassion and with love."

Throughout the speech was Carter's familiar emphasis on competence—a competent American people, a need for competence in the federal bureaucracy and derision for an incompetent Republican administration. "We can have an American government," Carter said, "that has turned away from scandal and corruption and official cynicism and is once again as decent and competent as our people."

"Love must be translated into simple justice," Carter said at one point, dropping his voice almost to a velvety whisper and holding the attention of the audience. A few moments later, he called for "full involvement by those who know what it is to suffer from discrimination," raising his voice almost to a shout and drawing loud applause. Then he added quietly, "and they'll be in the government if I'm elected."

The 1976 platform was carefully constructed by the Carter forces at Platform Committee meetings in Washington, D.C., in June. The 90-page document was something of a throwback to earlier years—a broad statement of party goals rather than a list of legislative programs and controversial stands on issues.

The platform and the care with which it was written reflected the Democrats' determination to avoid the platform fights and issues which proved costly to the party in the previous two elections. The 1968 Vietnam plank approved on the convention floor split the party so badly that many anti-war Democrats refused to support nominee Hubert H. Humphrey.

The 1972 platform, probably the longest (about 25,000 words) and most liberal ever offered by a major party, covered too many issues in elaborate detail. It provided Republicans with free ammunition, such as the damaging charge that Democrats in 1972 favored "amnesty, acid and abortion."

Unlike 1972, when there was sharp, divisive debate on 20 minority planks, only one minority plank—on revising the Hatch Act—was presented to the delegates in Madison Square Garden. It was approved by the Carter forces and was adopted by a voice vote after minimal debate.

The minority plank called for revision of the 1939 Hatch Act "so as to extend to federal workers the same political rights enjoyed by other Americans as a birthright, while still protecting the Civil Service from political abuse." It was designed to allow federal employees to run for federal office and to participate in partisan election campaigns. President Ford had vetoed a bill April 12 that would have permitted such activity.

Major goals outlined in the rest of the platform:
- A target of 3 per cent unemployment within four years.
- A phased-in national health insurance system to be supported through payroll deductions and other federal tax revenues.
- Gradual replacement of federal-state welfare systems with a federal system of income maintenance for recipients who accepted jobs or job training.
- "Full and complete pardon" for Vietnam War resisters, and case-by-case judgment for military deserters.
- Prohibitions against control of multiple energy resources by major oil companies.
- Strategic arms limitation agreements with the Soviet Union "emphasizing mutual reductions."

Following are excerpts from the Democratic platform of 1976:

Economy. To meet our goals we must set annual targets for employment, production and price stability; the Federal Reserve must be made a full partner in national economic decisions and become responsive to the economic goals of Congress and the President; credit must be generally available at reasonable interest rates; tax, spending and credit policies must be carefully coordinated with our economic goals, and coordinated within the framework of national economic planning.

Full Employment. We have met the goals of full employment with stable prices in the past and can do it again. The Democratic Party is committed to the right of all adult Americans willing, able and seeking work to have opportunities for useful jobs at living wages. To make that commitment meaningful, we pledge ourselves to the support of legislation that will make every responsible effort to reduce adult unemployment to 3 per cent within 4 years.

Consistent and coherent economic policy requires federal anti-recession grant programs to state and local government, accompanied by public employment, public works projects and direct stimulus to the private sector. In each case, the programs should be phased in automatically when unemployment rises and phased out as it declines.

Inflation. At times, direct government involvement in wage and price decisions may be required to ensure price stability. But we do not believe that such involvement requires a comprehensive system of mandatory controls at this time.

Tax Reform. We pledge the Democratic Party to a complete overhaul of the present tax system, which will review all special tax provisions to ensure that they are justified and distributed equitably among our citizens. A responsible Democratic tax reform program could save over $5-billion in the first year with larger savings in the future.

We will strengthen the internal revenue tax code so that high income citizens pay a reasonable tax on all economic income.

We will reduce the use of unjustified tax shelters in such areas as oil and gas, tax-loss farming, real estate and movies.

We will seek and eliminate provisions that encourage uneconomic corporate mergers and acquisitions.

Government Reform. The Democratic Party is committed to the adoption of reforms such as zero-based budgeting, mandatory reorganization timetables, and sunset laws which do not jeopardize the implementation of basic human and political rights.

An Office of Citizen Advocacy should be established as part of the executive branch, independent of any agency, with full access to agency records and with both the power and the responsibility to investigate complaints.

We support the revision of the Hatch Act so as to extend to federal workers the same political rights enjoyed by other Americans as a birthright, while still protecting the Civil Service from political abuse.

We call for legislative action to provide for partial public financing on a matching basis of the congressional elections, and the exploration of further reforms to insure the integrity of the electoral process.

Health. We need a comprehensive national health insurance system with universal and mandatory coverage. Such a national health insurance system should be financed by a combination of employer-employee shared payroll taxes and general tax revenues. Consideration should be given to developing a means of support for national health insurance that taxes all forms of economic income.

Welfare Reform. We should move toward replacement of our existing inadequate and wasteful system with a simplified system of income maintenance, substantially financed by the federal government, which includes a requirement that those able to work be provided with appropriate available jobs or job training opportunities.

Those persons who are physically able to work (other than mothers with dependent children) should be required to accept appropriate available jobs or job training.

As an interim step, and as a means of providing immediate federal fiscal relief to state and local governments, local governments should no longer be required to bear the burden of welfare costs. Further, there should be a phased reduction in the states' share of welfare costs.

Civil Rights and Liberties. ...[W]e pledge vigorous federal programs and policies of compensatory opportunity to remedy for many Americans the generations of injustice and deprivation; and full funding of programs to secure the implementation and enforcement of civil rights.

We seek ratification of the Equal Rights Amendment, to insure that sex discrimination in all its forms will be ended, implementation of Title IX, and elimination of discrimination against women in all federal programs.

We pledge effective and vigorous action to protect citizens' privacy from bureaucratic and technological intrusions, such as wiretapping and bugging without judicial scrutiny and supervision; and a full and complete pardon for those who are in legal or financial jeopardy because of their peaceful opposition to the Vietnam War, with deserters to be considered on a case-by-case basis.

We fully recognize the religious and ethical nature of the concerns which many Americans have on the subject of abortion. We feel, however, that it is undesirable to attempt to amend the U.S. Constitution to overturn the Supreme Court decision in this area.

Education. Mandatory transportation of students beyond their neighborhoods for the purpose of desegregation remains a judicial tool of last resort for the purpose of achieving school desegregation. The Democratic Party will be an active ally of those communities which seek to enhance the quality as well as the integration of educational opportunities. We encourage a variety of other measures, including the redrawing of attendance lines, pairing of schools, use of the "magnet school" concept, strong fair housing enforcement, and other techniques for the achievement of racial and economic integration.

The Party reaffirms its support of public school education. The Party also renews its commitment to the support of a constitutionally acceptable method of providing tax aid for the education of all pupils in non-segregated schools in order to insure parental freedom in choosing the best education for their children.

Housing. We support direct federal subsidies and low interest loans to encourage the construction of low and moderate income housing.

Cities. Federal policies and programs have inadvertently exacerbated the urban crisis. Within the framework of a new partnership of federal, state and local governments, and the private sector, the Democratic Party is pledged to the development of America's first national urban policy.

The Democratic Party recognizes that a number of major, older cities—including the nation's largest city—have been forced to undertake even greater social responsibilities, which have resulted in unprecedented fiscal crises. There is a national interest in helping such cities in their present travail, and a new Democratic President and the Congress shall undertake a massive effort to do so.

Criminal Justice. [W]e support a major reform of the criminal justice system, but we oppose any legislative effort to introduce repressive and anti-civil libertarian measures in the guise of reform of the criminal code.

Gun Control. Handguns simplify and intensify violent crime. Ways must be found to curtail the availability of these weapons. The Democratic Party must provide the leadership for a coordinated federal and state effort to strengthen the presently inadequate controls over the manufacture, assembly, distribution and possession of handguns and to ban Saturday night specials.

Furthermore, since people and not guns commit crimes, we support mandatory sentencing for individuals convicted of committing a felony with a gun.

The Democratic Party, however, affirms the right of sportsmen to possess guns for purely hunting and target-shooting purposes.

Transportation. ...[W]e will work to expand substantially the discretion available to states and cities in the use of federal transportation money, for either operating expenses or capital programs on the modes of transportation which they choose. A greater share of Highway Trust Fund money should also be available on a flexible basis.

Energy. The Democratic energy platform begins with a recognition that the federal government has an important role to play in insuring the nation's energy future, and that it must be given the tools it needs to protect the economy and the nation's consumers from arbitrary and excessive energy price increases and help the nation embark on a massive domestic energy program focusing on conservation, coal conversion, exploration and development of new technologies to insure an adequate short-term and long-term supply of energy for the nation's needs.

The pricing of new natural gas is in need of reform. We should narrow the gap between oil and natural gas prices with new natural gas ceiling prices that maximize production and investment while protecting the economy and the consumer.

Strip mining legislation designed to protect and restore the environment, while ending the uncertainty over the rules governing future coal mining, must be enacted.

The huge reserves of oil, gas and coal on federal territory, including the outer continental shelf, belong to all the people. The Republicans have pursued leasing policies which give the public treasury the least benefit and the energy industry the most benefit from these public resources. Consistent with environmentally sound practices, new leasing procedures must be adopted to correct these policies, as well as insure the timely development of existing leases.

U.S. dependence on nuclear power should be kept to the minimum necessary to meet our needs. We should apply stronger safety standards as we regulate its use. And we must be honest with our people concerning its problems and dangers as well as its benefits.

When competition inadequate to insure free markets and maximum benefit to American consumers exists, we support effective restrictions on the right of major companies to own all phases of the oil industry.

We also support the legal prohibition against corporate ownership of competing types of energy, such as oil and coal. We believe such "horizontal" concentration of economic power to be dangerous both to the national interest and to the functioning of the competitive system.

Establishment of a more orderly system for setting energy goals and developing programs for reaching those goals should be undertaken. The current proliferation of energy jurisdictions among many executive agencies underscores the need for a more coordinated system. Such a system should be undertaken, and provide for centralization of overall energy planning in a specific executive agency and an assessment of the capital needs for all priority programs to increase production and conservation of energy.

Agriculture. Foremost attention must be directed to the establishment of a national food and fiber policy which will be fair to both producer and consumer....

Producers shall be encouraged to produce at full capacity within the limits of good conservation practices, including the use of recycled materials, if possible and desirable, to restore natural soil fertility. Any surplus production needed to protect the people of the world from famine shall be stored on the farm in such a manner as to isolate it from the market place.

Environment. The Democratic Party's strong commitment to environmental quality is based on its conviction that environmental protection is not simply an aesthetic goal, but is necessary to achieve a more just society. Cleaning up air and water supplies and controlling the proliferation of dangerous chemicals is a necessary part of a successful national health program. Protecting the worker from workplace hazards is a key element of our full employment program.

Federal environmental anti-pollution requirement programs should be as uniform as possible to eliminate economic discrimination. A vigorous program with national minimum environmental standards fully implemented, recognizing basic regional differences, will ensure that states and workers are not penalized by pursuing environmental programs.

Foreign Policy. Eight years of Nixon-Ford diplomacy have left our nation isolated abroad and divided at home. Policies have been developed and applied secretly and arbitrarily by the executive department from the time of secret bombing in Cambodia to recent covert assistance in Angola. They have been policies that relied on ad hoc, unilateral maneuvering, and a balance-of-power diplomacy suited better to the last century than to this one. They have disdained traditional American principles which once earned the respect of other peoples while inspiring our own. Instead of efforts to foster freedom and justice in the world, the Republican administration has built a sorry record of disregard for human rights, manipulative interference in the internal affairs of other nations, and, frequently, a greater concern for our relations with totalitarian adversaries than with our democratic allies. And its efforts to preserve, rather than reform, the international status quo betray a self-fulfilling pessimism that contradicts a traditional American belief in the possibility of human progress.

We will act on the premise that candor in policy-making with all its liabilities, is preferable to deceit. The Congress will be involved in the major international decisions of our government, and our foreign policies will be openly and consistently presented to the American people. We will support reform of the international monetary system to strengthen institutional means of coordinating national economic policies, especially with our European and Japanese allies....

We will give priority attention to the establishment of an international code of conduct for multinational corporations and host countries.

We will eliminate bribery and other corrupt practices.

We will also actively seek to limit the dangers inherent in the international development of atomic energy and in the proliferation of nuclear weapons.

The United States should not provide aid to any government—anywhere in the world—which uses secret police, detention without charges, and torture to enforce its powers. Exceptions to this policy should be rare, and the aid provided should be limited to that which is absolutely necessary. The United States should be open and unashamed in its exercise of diplomatic efforts to encourage the observance of human rights in countries which receive American aid.

National Defense. To this end, our strategic nuclear forces must provide a strong and credible deterrent to nuclear attack and nuclear blackmail. Our conventional forces must be strong enough to deter aggression in areas whose security is vital to our own. In a manner consistent with these objectives, we should seek those disarmament and arms control agreements which will contribute to mutual reductions in both nuclear and conventional arms.

...[W]ith the proper management, with the proper kind of investment of defense dollars, and with the proper choice of military programs, we believe we can reduce present defense spending by about $5-billion to $7-billion.

In order to provide for a comprehensive review of the B1 test and evaluation program, no decision regarding B-1 production should be made prior to February 1977.

Detente. Our task is to establish U.S.-U.S.S.R. relations on a stable basis, avoiding excesses of both hope and fear. Patience, a clear sense of our own priorities, and a willingness to negotiate specific firm agreements in areas of mutual interest can return balance to relations between the United States and the Soviet Union.

However, in the area of strategic arms limitation, the U.S. should accept only such agreements that would not over-all limit the U.S. to levels of intercontinental strategic forces inferior to the limits provided for the Soviet Union.

United Nations. The heat of debate at the General Assembly should not obscure the value of our supporting United Nations involvement in keeping the peace and in the increasingly complex technical and social problems—such as pollution, health, economic development and population growth—that challenge the world community.

Middle East. We shall continue to seek a just and lasting peace in the Middle East. The cornerstone of our policy is a firm commitment to the independence and security of the State of Israel.

We will continue our consistent support of Israel, including sufficient military and economic assistance to maintain Israel's deterrent strength in the region, and the maintenance of U.S. military forces in the Mediterranean adequate to deter military intervention by the Soviet Union.

We will avoid efforts to impose on the region an externally devised formula for settlement, and will provide support for initiatives toward settlement, based on direct face-to-face negotiation between the parties and normalization of relations and a full peace within secure and defensible boundaries.

Asia. We remain a Pacific power with important stakes and objectives in the region, but the Vietnam War has taught us the folly of becoming militarily involved where our vital interests were not at stake.

We reaffirm our commitment to the security of the Republic of Korea, both in itself and as a key to the security of Japan. However, on a prudent and carefully planned basis, we can redeploy, and gradually phase out, the U.S. ground forces, and can withdraw the nuclear weapons now stationed in Korea without endangering that support, as long as our tactical air and naval forces in the region remain strong.

Latin America. We must make clear our revulsion at the systematic violations of basic human rights that have occurred under some Latin American military regimes.

We pledge support for a new Panama Canal treaty, which insures the interests of the United States in that waterway, recognizes the principles already agreed upon, takes into account the interests of the Canal work force, and which will have wide hemispheric support.

Relations with Cuba can only be normalized if Cuba refrains from interference in the internal affairs of the United States, and releases all U.S. citizens currently detained in Cuban prisons and labor camps for political reasons. We can move towards such relations if Cuba abandons its provocative international actions and policies.

Africa. We must adopt policies that recognize the intrinsic importance of Africa and its development to the United States, and the inevitability of majority rule on that continent.

The next Democratic administration will work aggressively to involve black Americans in foreign policy positions, at home and abroad, and in decisions affecting African interests.

Republicans

After four boisterous, raucous and sometimes tearful days, Republicans ended their 1976 national convention on a positive note absent during most of a gathering characterized by strident attacks on the Democrats and the Congress they controlled.

The Republican delegates arrived in Kansas City for the Aug. 16-19 convention more evenly split than they had been since 1952, when Dwight D. Eisenhower edged Sen. Robert A. Taft (Ohio 1939-53) for the GOP nomination. Both President Gerald R. Ford, breaking with tradition, and former California Gov. Ronald Reagan arrived in town three days before the balloting to continue their pursuit of delegates.

Ford, relying heavily on the prestige of the presidency that sometimes had failed to produce results during the seven-month campaign, invited a number of wavering delegates to his hotel suite in the new Crown Center Hotel while Reagan also courted delegates personally.

Campaign strategists and conservative supporters pursued other maneuvers that either fizzled or could not break Ford's scanty but solid delegate margin. Early in the week, conservative House members tried unsuccessfully to convince Sen. James L. Buckley (Cons-R N.Y.) to seek the nomination in an effort to draw off enough votes to deny Ford a first-ballot victory.

By a margin of 111 votes on Aug. 17, the Reagan forces lost the first and probably the most important roll call of the convention. The vote came on a Reagan-sponsored amendment to the Rules Committee report that would have required all presidential candidates to name their running mates before the presidential balloting the next night.

The idea of a test vote on the vice presidential question was sprung by Reagan's campaign manager, John Sears, barely a week before the convention, when on Aug. 9 he appeared before the Rules Committee of the Republican National Committee and urged that the proposal be included as Section C of Rule 16. The amendment was clearly aimed at throwing Ford on the defensive, because Reagan had designated Pennsylvania Sen. Richard S. Schweiker as his running mate on July 26. Under the proposal, failure of a candidate to comply would have freed all delegates from any commitments to vote for him.

The Reagan proposal was handily defeated in the pre-convention Rules Committee, where Ford supporters predominated. But Sears was publicly confident that the Reagan forces could carry the issue on the convention floor. Victory on the rules question, he predicted, would be a stepping stone to Reagan's nomination.

The convention debate and vote on Rule 16 was the focal point of the Aug. 17 session and was treated as such by many in the gallery and on the floor, who interrupted the proceedings several times with loud chanting. Vociferous cheers and boos erupted from the Ford and Reagan sections of the hall as speeches were delivered for or against their positions.

Supporters of the proposals characterized it as a "right to know" amendment. "A presidential candidate must tell us who's on his team before we are expected to join him," argued former Missouri Rep. Thomas B. Curtis, the sponsor of the amendment. "The delegates have the right to be consulted for a day of decision that will have an impact for years to come."

Speakers against the amendment countered that it was solely a maneuver of the Reagan forces and that any vice presidential selection reform should be deliberately considered on its merits.

The roll call began with Alabama, solid for Reagan, casting all of its 37 votes for the amendment. The Reagan forces held the lead throughout the early going, losing the advantage about halfway through the roll call when New York went 20-134 against the amendment.

The deficit of the Reagan backers increased after Ohio went 7-90 against and Pennsylvania 14-89 against. The Pennsylvania result was a clear indication that state leaders in the Ford campaign remained in control of the delegation, despite Schweiker's effort to woo their support.

Reagan strength near the end of the roll call tightened the count, but Florida and Mississippi, which had passed when first called, cast heavy votes against the amendment. Florida's 28-38 vote against sealed the amendment's defeat. Mississippi, under the unit rule, cast its entire 30 votes against the Reagan proposal, padding the Ford margin.

The final count stood at 1,069 in favor of the amendment and 1,180 against, with 10 abstentions. The vote was the first tangible evidence of Ford strength at the convention and paved the way for his nomination. *(Chart, p. 194)*

None of the other parts of the Rules Committee report were debated, including the controversial "justice resolution" (Rule 18), which bound delegates elected in primary states according to state law. Fearing a defection of "closet" Reagan delegates in several primary-state delegations, Ford leaders had pushed for the amendment. In contrast to their attitude toward Rule 16, the Reagan forces did not order a fight on the "justice" resolution, although it was extensively debated in committee deliberations. After the roll-call vote on Rule 16, the Rules Committee report was adopted by a voice vote.

Whatever enthusiasm the Reagan supporters had lost after their defeat on the vice presidential rule had returned by presidential nominating night, Aug. 18.

Two and one-half hours of the six-hour session were consumed in demonstrations. Reagan's supporters were by far the most boisterous. But it was the Californian's last hurrah.

On the presidential roll call, Reagan, bolstered by the votes in California and some Deep South states, took a healthy lead. But, as everyone expected, Ford's strength in the big northeastern states—New York, New Jersey, Pennsylvania, Connecticut, Ohio—and others such as Minnesota and Illinois pushed Ford ahead.

There was a pause as the Virginia delegation was individually polled. Then West Virginia, voting 20 to 8 in favor of Ford, put the President over the top.

The final vote was 1,187 for Ford, 1,070 for Reagan, one vote from the New York delegation for Commerce Secretary Elliot L. Richardson and one abstention. *(Chart, p. 194)*

On a voice vote the convention made the nomination unanimous.

Ford added to the partisan style of the Republican ticket the next day by selecting Sen. Robert Dole of Kansas as his running mate after Reagan ruled out his acceptance of the second spot. While little mentioned during speculation about Ford's vice presidential choice, Dole, a former chairman of the Republican National Committee, was seen as an effective gut fighter against the Carter forces who would allow Ford to keep his campaign style presidential.

Vice President Nelson A. Rockefeller nominated his own potential successor, telling the crowd that the Kansas senator not only could stand the heat of political battle, but also could "really dole it out."

On the vice presidential roll call, Dole received 1,921 of the convention's 2,259 votes. North Carolina Sen. Jesse A. Helms, a hero of the conservatives, finished a distant second with 103 votes. The remaining votes were scattered among 29 other "candidates."

Ford's acceptance speech concentrated on his record since taking office in mid-1974 and his future goals. The President took credit for cutting inflation in half, increasing employment to a record level and bringing the country to peace.

He touched several times on the restoration of confidence in the White House and the return of personal integrity to the executive branch of government. His administration, Ford said, had been "open, candid and forthright" from the beginning.

Needling his opponent, Ford asserted to applause: "My record is one of specifics, not smiles."

For the future, Ford promised continued economic recovery, less "impudence" from bureaucracy and a balanced federal budget by 1978. He listed a host of other proposals ranging from tax reform to a sane nuclear policy.

"We will build on performance, not promises; experiences, not expediency; real progress instead of mysterious plans to be revealed in some dim and distant future," Ford said in another reference to Carter.

While primarily positive in tone, Ford's speech did rebuke the Democratic Congress for its passage of bills he had vetoed and its obstruction of his proposals to revise tax rules, restrict busing and overhaul criminal laws.

"My friends, Washington is not the problem—their Congress is the problem," he argued.

Ford diverged from his prepared text to issue a direct challenge to Carter.

"I'm ready, eager to go before the American people and debate the real issues face to face with Jimmy Carter," the President said. "The American people have the right to know first-hand exactly where both of us stand."

The 1976 Republican platform was a conservative document, combining restrained compliments toward the Ford administration with frequent and slashing attacks on the Democratic Congress.

Ford and Reagan both praised the platform. Although neither side was entirely happy with the final document, both sides were willing to compromise to avoid splitting the party.

By the time the convention got around to debating the platform the night of Aug. 17, an expected bitter struggle between Ford and Reagan forces had been deflated by the earlier vote on rules. The arena, which had been packed two hours earlier, held a somewhat smaller crowd after midnight. Many Ford delegates in particular, confident that they had won the main event, left while members of the Platform Committee presented the 65-page document.

Two minority planks were offered, in accordance with Platform Committee rules that required petitions signed by 25 per cent of the members. The first, sponsored by Ann F. Peckham of Wisconsin, called for deleting all platform references to abortion. The committee-approved section supported a constitutional amendment "to restore protection of the right to life of unborn children."

The 12-minute debate on the abortion plank did not split along Ford-Reagan lines. Supporters of the minority report argued that abortion was not a suitable topic for a party document. Opponents insisted that the anti-abortion language should be retained. The minority report was defeated clearly by voice vote, and the language stayed in.

The second minority report, a six-paragraph addition to the foreign policy section, was sponsored by 34 Reagan supporters on the Platform Committee. Without mentioning names, it criticized President Ford and Secretary of State Henry A. Kissinger for losing public confidence, making secret international agreements and discouraging the hope of freedom for those who do not have it—presumably captive nations.

Many of Ford's supporters, including Rep. John B. Anderson (Ill.) and Senate Minority Leader Hugh Scott (Pa.), earlier had expressed strong opposition to the "morality in foreign policy" plank, as it came to be called. Ford's floor leader, Sen. Robert P. Griffin (Mich.), and Rep. David C. Treen (La.) sought compromise language in informal negotiations on the floor. But the Reagan forces, led by Sen. Helms, were adamant.

Not wishing to offend the Reagan forces further, Ford's supporters decided not to fight. Sen. Roman L. Hruska (Neb.), chairman of the foreign policy subcommittee, announced from the podium that there would be no organized opposition to the plank. It was passed by voice vote. The convention then approved the platform, as amended.

The document reflected the nearly equal influence of President Ford and Ronald Reagan at the convention. It was a traditional Republican blueprint for limited government—a clear contrast with the Democratic platform.

Ordinarily, the platform of the party holding the White House heaps praise on the incumbent President and boasts of the way he has led the nation. The Republican platform did not go that far. With Ford embroiled in a contest for the nomination, the platform writers chose to mention him by name only a few times. Richard M. Nixon was never mentioned. There were only vague references to Watergate.

The platform's foreign policy planks, over which Ford and Reagan clashed most strongly, praised the record of "two Republican administrations." But they also repeated some of Reagan's campaign criticisms of current foreign policy. Kissinger, a favorite target of the party's conservative wing, was not mentioned.

The domestic planks boasted of reductions in inflation and steered clear of direct government initiatives to reduce unemployment. The President was commended for vetoes of 40 bills that would have increased federal spending.

The platform concentrated most of its fire on Congress. The Republicans barely acknowledged their opponent for national leadership, Jimmy Carter. The platform mentioned Carter only once, on the first page.

Following are excerpts from the Republican Party platform of 1976:

Republican Philosophy. —As a general rule we believe that government action should be taken first by the government that resides as close to you as possible. Governments tend to become less responsive to your needs the farther away they are from you. Thus, we prefer local and state government to national government, and decentralized national government wherever possible. The Democrats' Platform repeats the same thing on every page: More government, more spending, more inflation. Compare. This Republican Platform says exactly the opposite—less government, less spending, less inflation. In other words, we want you to retain more of your own money; money that represents the worth of your labors, to use as you see fit for the necessities and conveniences of life.

Economy. We believe it is of paramount importance that the American people understand that the number one destroyer of jobs is inflation.

Republicans hope every American realizes that if we are to permanently eliminate high unemployment, it is essential to protect the integrity of our money. That means putting an end to deficit spending.

Wage and price controls are not the solution to inflation. They attempt to treat only the symptom—rising prices—not the cause. Historically, controls have always been a dismal failure, and in the end they create only shortages, black markets and higher prices. For these reasons the Republican Party strongly opposes any reimposition of such controls, on a standby basis or otherwise.

Sound job creation can only be accomplished in the private sector of the economy. Americans must not be fooled into accepting government as the employer of last resort.

No nation can spend its way into prosperity; a nation can only spend its way into bankruptcy.

Tax Reform. Simplification should be a major goal of tax reform.

When balanced by expenditure reductions, the personal exemption should be raised to $1,000.

Agriculture. We oppose government-controlled grain reserves, just as we oppose federal regulations that are unrealistic in farm practices, such as those imposed by the Occupational Safety and Health Administration (OSHA) and the Environmental Protection Agency (EPA).

We firmly believe that when the nation asks our farmers to go all out to produce as much as possible for world-wide markets, the government should guarantee them unfettered access to those markets. Our farmers should not be singled out by export controls.

Government Reform. There must be functional realignment of government, instead of the current arrangement by subject areas or constituencies.

Revenue Sharing is an effort to reverse the trend toward centralization. Revenue Sharing must continue without unwarranted federal strictures and regulations.

Block grant programs should be extended to replace many existing categorical health, education, child nutrition and social programs.

While we oppose a uniform national primary, we encourage the concept of regional presidential primaries, which would group those states which voluntarily agree to have presidential primaries in a geographical area on a common date.

...[W]e oppose "federal post card registration." The possibilities could not only cheapen our ballot, but in fact threaten the entire electoral process.

We offer these proposals of far-reaching reform:

Public accountability demands that [congressmen] publicly vote on increases on the expenses of their office.

—Elimination of proxy voting which allows Members [of Congress] to record votes in committee without being present for the actual deliberations or vote on a measure.

—Full public disclosure of financial interests by Members [of Congress] and divestiture of those interests which present conflicts of interest.

—Improved lobby disclosure legislation so that the people will know how much money is being spent to influence public officials.

Criminal Justice. Each state should have the power to decide whether it wishes to impose the death penalty for certain crimes. All localities are urged to tighten their bail practices and to review their sentencing and parole procedures.

Gun Control. We support the right of citizens to keep and bear arms. We oppose federal registration of firearms. Mandatory sentences for crimes committed with a lethal weapon are the only effective solution to this problem.

Education. We believe that segregated schools are morally wrong and unconstitutional. However, we oppose forced busing to achieve racial balances in our schools. We believe there are educational advantages for children in attending schools in their own neighborhoods and that the Democrat-controlled Congress has failed to enact legislation to protect this concept.

If Congress continues to fail to act, we would favor consideration of an amendment to the Constitution forbidding the assignment of children to schools on the basis of race.

Local communities wishing to conduct non-sectarian prayers in their public schools should be able to do so. We favor a constitutional amendment to achieve this end.

Health. We support extension of catastrophic illness protection to all who cannot obtain it. We should utilize our private health insurance system to assure adequate protection for those who do not have it. Such an approach will eliminate the red tape and high bureaucratic costs inevitable in a comprehensive national program.

The Republican Party opposes compulsory national health insurance.

Civil Rights and Liberties. The Republican Party reaffirms its support for ratification of the Equal Rights Amendment. Our Party was the first national party to endorse the E.R.A. in 1940. We continue to believe its ratification is essential to insure equal rights for all Americans.

The Republican Party favors a continuance of the public dialogue on abortion and supports the efforts of those who seek enactment of a constitutional amendment to restore protection of the right to life for unborn children.

Labor. Union membership as a condition of employment has been regulated by state law under Section 14(b) of the Taft-Hartley Act. This basic right should continue to be determined by the states. We oppose strikes by federal employees, the unionization of our military forces and the legalization of common-situs picketing.

Employees of the federal government should not engage in partisan politics. The Civil Service system must remain nonpartisan and nonpolitical. The Hatch Act now protects federal employees; we insist that it be uniformly administered.

Welfare Reform. We oppose federalizing the welfare system; local levels of government are most aware of the needs of their communities.

We also oppose the guaranteed annual income concept or any programs that reduce the incentive to work.

Those features of the present law, particularly the food stamp program, that draw into assistance programs people who are capable of paying for their own needs should be corrected. The humanitarian purpose of such programs must not be corrupted by eligibility loopholes.

Cities. The Republican programs of revenue sharing and block grants for community development and manpower have already immensely helped our cities and counties. We favor extension of revenue sharing and the orderly conversion of categorical grants into block grants.

Housing. To continue to encourage home ownership which now encompasses 64 per cent of our families, we support the deductibility of interest on home mortgages and property taxes.

Transportation. In keeping with the local goal setting in transportation, the Republican Party applauds the system under which state and local governments can divert funds from interstate highway mileage not essential to interstate commerce or national defense to other, more pressing community needs, such as urban mass transit.

Energy. One fact should now be clear: We must reduce sharply our dependence on other nations for energy and strive to achieve energy independence at the earliest possible date. We cannot allow the economic destiny and international policy of the United States to be dictated by the sovereign powers that control major portions of the world's petroleum supplies.

We must immediately eliminate price controls on oil and newly-discovered natural gas in order to increase supply, and to provide the capital that is needed to finance further exploration and development of domestic hydrocarbon reserves.

At this critical time, the Democrats have characteristically resorted to political demagoguery seeking short-term political gain at the expense of the long-term national interest. They object to the petroleum industry making any profit. The petroleum industry is an important segment of our economy and is entitled to reasonable profits to permit further exploration and development.

Now, the Democrats proposed to dismember the American oil industry. We vigorously oppose such divestiture of oil companies—a move which would surely result in higher energy costs, inefficiency and under-capitalization of the industry.

The uncertainties of governmental regulation regarding the mining, transportation and use of coal must be removed and a policy established which will assure that governmental restraints, other than proper environmental controls, do not prevent the use of coal. Mined lands must be returned to beneficial use.

Uranium offers the best intermediate solution to America's energy crisis. We support accelerated use of nuclear energy through processes that have been proven safe.

Environment. We are in complete accord with the recent Supreme Court decision on air pollution that allows the level of government closest to the problem and the solution to establish and apply appropriate air quality standards.

We are determined to preserve land use planning as a unique responsibility of state and local government.

Foreign Policy. We recognize and commend that great beacon of human courage and morality, Alexander Solzhenitsyn, for his compelling message that we must face the world with no illusions about the nature of tyranny. Ours will be a foreign policy that keeps this ever in mind.

Ours will be a foreign policy which recognizes that in international negotiations we must make no undue concessions; that in pursuing detente we must not grant unilateral favors with only the hope of getting future favors in return.

Agreements that are negotiated, such as the one signed in Helsinki, must not take from those who do not have freedom the hope of one day gaining it.

Finally, we are firmly committed to a foreign policy in which secret agreements, hidden from our people, will have no part.

National Defense. A superior national defense is the fundamental condition for a secure America and for peace and freedom for the world. Military strength is the path to peace. A sound foreign policy must be rooted in a superior defense capability, and both must be perceived as a deterrent to aggression and supportive of our national interests.

As a necessary component of our long-range strategy, we will produce and deploy the B-1 bomber in a timely manner, allowing us to retain air superiority.

Security assistance programs are important to our allies and we will continue to strengthen their efforts at self-defense.

Asia. The United States is indisputably a Pacific power. Japan will remain the main pillar of our Asian policy.

United States troops will be maintained in Korea so long as there exists the possibility of renewed aggression from North Korea.

We recognize that there is a wide divergence of opinion concerning Vietnam, but we pledge that American troops will never again be committed for the purpose of our own

defense, or the defense of those to whom we are committed by treaty or other solemn agreements, without the clear purpose of achieving our stated diplomatic and military objectives.

The United States will fulfill and keep its commitments, such as the mutual defense treaty with the Republic of China.

Latin America. By continuing its policies of exporting subversion and violence, Cuba remains outside the Inter-American family of nations. We condemn attempts by the Cuban dictatorship to intervene in the affairs of other nations; and, as long as such conduct continues, it shall remain ineligible for admission to the Organization of American States.

The United States intends that the Panama Canal be preserved as an international waterway for the ships of all nations. This secure access is enhanced by a relationship which commands the respect of Americans and Panamanians and benefits the people of both countries. In any talks with Panama, however, the United States negotiators should in no way cede, dilute, forfeit, negotiate or transfer any rights, power, authority, jurisdiction, territory or property that are necessary for the protection and security of the United States and the entire Western Hemisphere.

Middle East. Our policy must remain one of decisive support for the security and integrity of Israel.

At the same time, Republican Administrations have succeeded in reestablishing communication with the Arab countries, and have made extensive progress in our diplomatic and commercial relations with the more moderate Arab nations.

Because we have such fundamental interests in the Middle East, it will be our policy to continue our efforts to maintain the balance of power in the Mediterranean region.

Africa. The United States has always supported the process of self-determination in Africa.

Our policy is to strengthen the forces of moderation, recognizing that solutions to African problems will not come quickly.

The interests of peace and security in Africa are best served by the absence of arms and greater concentration on peaceful development. We reserve the right to maintain the balance by extending our support to nations facing a threat from Soviet-supplied states and from Soviet weapons.

Detente. American foreign policy must be based upon a realistic assessment of the Communist challenge in the world. It is clear that the perimeters of freedom continue to shrink throughout the world in the face of the Communist challenge.

Thus our relations with the Soviet Union will be guided by solid principles. We will maintain our strategic and conventional forces; we will oppose the deployment of Soviet power for unilateral advantages or political and territorial expansion; we will never tolerate a shift against us in the strategic balance; and we will remain firm in the face of pressure, while at the same time expressing our willingness to work on the basis of strict reciprocity toward new agreements which will help achieve peace and stability.

United Nations. The political character of the United Nations has become complex. With 144 sovereign members, the U.N. experiences problems associated with a large, sometimes cumbersome and diverse body.

The United States does not wish to dictate to the U.N., yet we do have every right to expect and insist that scrupulous care be given to the rights of all members. Steamroller techniques for advancing discriminatory actions will be opposed.

The United States will continue to be a firm supporter and defender of any nation subjected to such outrageous assaults. We will not accept ideological abuses in the United States.

—Convention Narrative by Rhodes Cook

1980 Conventions

Presidential Candidates

Jimmy Carter
Democrat

Ronald Reagan
Republican

John B. Anderson
Independent

Democrats

President Jimmy Carter emerged victorious from a deeply divided Democratic National Convention unsure whether his plea for unity to supporters of rival Sen. Edward M. Kennedy of Massachusetts had succeeded. Kennedy had been Carter's main opponent in his quest for renomination throughout the spring primary season. When it became apparent that Kennedy had not won in the primaries and caucuses the delegate support he needed, he turned his efforts to prying the nomination away from the president at the convention.

Kennedy's presence was strong throughout the convention week and expressions of support for the senator sometimes upstaged those for the incumbent president. Chants of "We want Ted" rocked off the walls of New York's Madison Square Garden during the convention's four days, Aug. 11-14. And their echo faintly followed the president as he left the podium following his acceptance speech. It was a stark reminder that although Carter had captured the nomination and engaged in a series of reconciliation gestures with his rival, he still faced the difficult task of rallying a divided party behind his candidacy.

Kennedy's efforts to wrest the nomination from Carter centered around a convention rule that bound delegates to vote on the first ballot for the candidates under whose banner they were elected. When the convention opened, Carter could count 315 more votes than he needed for the nomination — votes that he had won in nominating caucuses and presidential primaries. As a result, Kennedy's only chance to gain the nomination was to defeat the binding rule.

In the week before the convention, negotiators for Carter and Kennedy agreed to one hour of debate on the rules question to begin at 6:30 p.m. Monday, Aug. 11. Kennedy forces had wanted a Tuesday night rules vote, which would have given them an extra day to lobby delegates. But they settled instead for the Monday night debate, which enabled them to argue their case before a prime-time nationwide television audience.

Opponents of the binding rule tried to present a broad-based front. Arguing against the rule on the convention floor were a Carter delegate, two Kennedy backers and two leading uncommitted delegates — New York Gov. Hugh L. Carey and prominent Washington attorney Edward Bennett Williams, the chief spokesman of the Committee for an Open Convention.

They argued that political conditions had changed since the delegates were elected months earlier and that to bind them would break with a century and a half of Democratic tradition. "For the first time in 150 years, delegates to the national convention are being asked to deliver their final freedom of choice, and to vote themselves into bondage to a candidate," Williams contended. To adopt the binding rule, other speakers added, would make the delegates little more than robots.

But most Carter supporters scoffed at that contention, stressing that delegates were free to vote their conscience on all roll calls but the one for president. Passage of the rule was simply fair play, they added. It had been adopted in 1978 without opposition by the party's last rules review commission and the Democratic National Committee. Only when it was apparent that Carter was winning, claimed Atlanta Mayor Maynard Jackson, did the Kennedy camp want to change the rules to allow a "fifth ball, a fourth out or a tenth inning."

When the measure finally came to a vote, Carter forces turned back the attempt to overturn the proposed rule. The vote was 1,390.580 to 1,936.418 against Kennedy's position. *(Chart, p. 195)*

Shortly after the vote, Kennedy ended his nine-month challenge to the president by announcing that his name would not be placed in nomination Aug. 13. Passage of the binding rule assured Carter's renomination. *(Chart, p. 195)*

In addition to its binding-rule objection, the Kennedy camp filed four other minority rules reports, but all were withdrawn before the Aug. 11 session. Three originally had been filed in response to Carter efforts to streamline the convention schedule. At its July meeting in Washington, D.C., the convention rules committee approved proposals to increase the number of signatures required on nominating petitions for president, vice president and convention chairman; to limit to two the number of speakers on each side of each issue of debate; and to allow every roll call, except for president and vice president, to be conducted by telephone while convention business proceeded.

In return for Kennedy's withdrawal of the minority reports, the Carter camp did consent to raise the number of speakers on each issue to three. They also agreed to a Kennedy proposal to add a platform accountability rule that would require each presidential candidate to submit his written views on the party platform along with his pledge to carry it out. The statement would have to be presented shortly after convention consideration of the platform was completed. The Kennedy proposal also called for the candidates' statements to be distributed and read to the delegates.

Despite the loss on the binding rule, the Kennedy camp succeeded in molding the party platform more to their liking. The final document was filled with so many concessions to the Kennedy forces that it won only a half-hearted endorsement from the president. The platform battle, one of the longest in party history, filled 17 hours of debate and roll calls that stretched over two days, Aug. 12 and 13.

Most of Carter's concessions and outright defeats came on the economic and human needs sections of the 40,000-word document. It was these revisions that Carter rejected — as diplomatically as possible — in a statement issued several hours after the debate wound to a close.

In the debate on social issues, Carter lost two roll-call votes — one on adoption of Kennedy's plank calling for jobs to be "our single highest domestic priority," and the other supporting Medicaid funding for abortions. The president also lost a voice vote on a minority report to withhold all party funds and campaign assistance to candidates who did not support the then-pending Equal Rights Amendment to the Constitution.

The only victory posted by Carter in the human needs chapter was over a Kennedy minority report calling for a single, comprehensive national health insurance plan with gradually phased-in benefits. That report was defeated on a 1,409.9-to-1,623.8 vote that came at the start of the platform debate.

It had been clear since the platform was drafted in late June that the economic plank, which contained the major Carter-Kennedy differences, would be the focus of dispute. When the hour for debate arrived, it was evident that the control Carter had exercised the previous evening on the question of binding delegates had evaporated.

Before the convention began, Carter had yielded to Kennedy language on several issues, including one of the senator's four minority economic reports. That report asserted that a policy of high interest rates and unemployment should not be used to fight inflation. White House domestic affairs adviser Stuart E. Eizenstat announced Aug. 10 that Carter would go along with that amendment — but none of the others in the economy section — because it stated a broad goal while the others called for specific legislation.

The marathon platform debate reached its high point on Tuesday evening, Aug. 12, when Kennedy addressed the delegates on behalf of his minority report on the economic chapter. Kennedy's speech provided the Democratic convention with its most exciting moments. The address, which sparked a 40-minute emotional demonstration when it was over, called for Democratic unity and laced into the Republican nominee, Ronald Reagan.

Kennedy defended his liberal ideology, supporting national health insurance and federal spending to restore deteriorated urban areas. He lashed out at Reagan's proposal for a massive tax cut, labeling it as beneficial only to the wealthy. "For all those whose cares have been our concern the work goes on, the cause endures, the hope still lives and the dream shall never die," concluded Kennedy. Buoyed by the Kennedy oratory, the convention went on to pass by voice vote three liberal Kennedy platform planks on the economy, thereby rejecting the more moderate versions favored by Carter.

The first of the Kennedy-sponsored planks was a statement pledging that fairness would be the overriding principle of the Democrats' economic policy and that no actions would be taken that would "significantly increase" unemployment. The convention next approved a Kennedy plank seeking a $12 billion anti-recession jobs program, a $1 billion rail renewal plan and an expanded housing program for low- and moderate-income families. The final Kennedy economic plank was a statement of opposition to fighting inflation through a policy of high interest rates and unemployment. Carter had agreed to this plank the day before the convention opened.

Carter floor managers realized that it would be difficult to block passage of the Kennedy economic proposals. After the senator's emotion-filled speech, Carter advisers — realizing their position could not prevail — quickly sought to change from a roll call to a voice vote on the economic planks.

During the floor demonstration that followed Kennedy's speech, a series of telephone calls ricocheted between the podium and the senator's campaign trailer located off the convention floor. The negotiations involved how many elements of the Kennedy program would be accepted by voice vote. In the end, Carter prevailed on only one of Kennedy's economic minority reports, the call for an immediate wage and price freeze followed by controls.

Prior to the 1980 convention, Democratic presidential nominees had been able to gloss over their distaste for objectionable portions of the platform. But Kennedy made that difficult to do. In his carefully worded statement following the platform debate, Carter did not flatly reject any of Kennedy's amendments, but he did not embrace them either.

Of Kennedy's $12 billion anti-recession jobs program, Carter said he would "accept and support the intent" of the program but he refused to commit himself to a specific dollar amount. Responding to Kennedy language that placed a jobs program above all other domestic priorities, Carter wrote, "We must make it clear that to acheive full employment, we must also be successful in our fight against inflation."

Carter treated two women's issues the same way. Responding to adopted language that endorsed federal funding for abortion, the president repeated his personal opposition but said he would be guided by court decisions on the questions. He also reiterated his support for ratification of the Equal Rights Amendment but did not directly comment on the platform language adopted on the floor that prevented the Democratic Party from giving campaign funds to candidates who did not back the amendment.

Carter concluded his statement with the unity refrain that had become the hallmark of every official White House comment on the platform since the drafting process began: "The differences within our party on this platform are small in comparison with the differences between the Republican and Democratic Party platforms." Kennedy apparently agreed. And shortly after Carter's renomination Aug. 13, Kennedy issued a statement endorsing the platform and pledging his support for Carter. In the final moments before adjournment, Kennedy made a stiff and brief appearance on the platform with Carter, Mondale and a host of Democratic officeholders. But the coolness of his appearance — accompanied by the warmest reception of the night — left questionable the commitment of the senator and his supporters to work strenuously for Carter's re-election.

Carter won the Democratic nomination with 2,123 votes compared with Kennedy's 1,150.5. Other candidates split 54.5 votes. *(Chart, p. 195)*

In his acceptance speech, Carter alluded to the convention's divisions. He led off with praise for Kennedy's tough campaign, thanks for his concessions during the convention and an appeal for future help. "Ted, your party needs — and I need — you, and your idealism and dedication working for us." Carter spent much of the speech characterizing Reagan's programs as a disastrous "fantasy world" of easy answers. He avoided detailed comments on the economic issues over which he and Kennedy had split, confining himself to statements that he wanted jobs for all who needed them.

As expected, Walter F. Mondale was renominated for vice president. Two other party members had their names placed in nomination so they could raise the issues of homosexual rights and Carter's decision to reinstitute draft registration. Activist Patricia Simon of Newton, Mass., withdrew after delivering a plea that "we be known as a party of peace." The other candidate was Melvin Boozer of Washington, D.C. Boozer, a number of favorite sons and others received only a smattering of votes and Mondale was nominated by acclamation before that roll call had been completed.

The vice president's acceptance speech set delegates chanting "Not Ronald Reagan" as Mondale reeled off a list of liberal values and programs that, he said, most Americans agreed with. Mondale was one of the few speakers to unequivocally praise Carter's record, which he did at some length. The speech ended with a warning not to "let anyone make us less than what we can be."

Jimmy Carter lost the election to Ronald Reagan by more than eight million votes. Carter won 35,483,820 votes, 41.0 percent of the total. Since Carter carried just six states and the District of Columbia, he managed to win only 49 electoral votes.

Following are excerpts from the Democratic party platform of 1980:

Employment. We specifically reaffirm our commitment to achieve all the goals of the Humphrey-Hawkins Full Employment Act within the currently prescribed dates in the Act, especially those relating to a joint reduction in unemployment and inflation. Full employment is important to the achievement of a rising standard of living, to the pursuit of sound justice, and to the strength and vitality of America.

Anti-Recession Assistance. A Democratic anti-recession program must recognize that Blacks, Hispanics, other minorities, women, and older workers bear the brunt of recession. We pledge a $12 billion anti-recession jobs program, providing at least 800,000 additional jobs, including full funding of the counter-cyclical assistance program for the cities, a major expansion of the youth employment and training program to give young people in our inner cities new hope, expanded training programs for women and displaced homemakers to give these workers a fair chance in the workplace, and new opportunities for the elderly to contribute their talents and skills.

Tax Reductions. We commit ourselves to targeted tax reductions designed to stimulate production and combat recession as soon as it appears so that tax reductions will not have a disproportionately inflationary effect. We must avoid untargeted tax cuts which would increase inflation.

Federal Spending. Spending restraint must be sensitive to those who look to the federal government for aid and assistance, especially to our nation's workers in times of high unemployment. At the same time, as long as inflationary pressures remain strong, fiscal prudence is essential to avoid destroying the progress made to date in reducing the inflation rate.

Fiscal policy must remain a flexible economic tool. We oppose a Constitutional amendment requiring a balanced budget.

Interest Rates. . . . [W]e must continue to pursue a tough anti-inflationary policy which will lead to an across-the-board reduction in interest rates on loans.

In using monetary policy to fight inflation, the government should be sensitive to the special needs of areas of our economy most affected by high interest rates.

Expanding American Exports. To create new markets for American products and strengthen the dollar, we must seek out new opportunities for American exports; help establish stable, long-term commercial relationships between nations; offer technical assistance to firms competing in world markets; promote reciprocal trading terms for nations doing business here; and help ensure that America's domestic retooling is consistent with new opportunities in foreign trade.

We must intensify our efforts to promote American exports and to ensure that our domestic industries and workers are not affected adversely by unfair trade practices, such as dumping. . . . We must ensure that our efforts to lower tariff barriers are reciprocated by our trading partners. We recognize the superior productivity of American agriculture and the importance of agricultural exports to the balance of trade.

Worker Protection. The Democratic Party will not pursue a policy of high interest rates and unemployment as the means to fight inflation. We will take no action whose effect will be a significant increase in unemployment, no fiscal action, no monetary action, no budgetary action. The Democratic Party remains committed to policies that will not produce high interest rates or high unemployment.

OSHA protections should be properly administered, with the concern of the worker being the highest priority; legislative or administrative efforts to weaken OSHA's basic worker protection responsibilities are unacceptable.

We will continue to oppose a sub-minimum wage for youth and other workers and to support increases in the minimum wage so as to ensure an adequate income for all workers.

Small Business. . . . [T]he Democratic Party commits itself to the first comprehensive program for small business in American history. That program will include the following measures:

. . . Allocation of a fair percentage of federal research funds to small business.

Protection of small and independent businesses against takeover by giant conglomerates.

Continued efforts to end federal regulations which reinforce barriers to entry by new and small firms, and which thereby entrench the dominance of market leaders.

A review of regulations and requirements which impose unnecessary burdens upon smaller firms. We will adopt regulatory requirements to meet the needs of smaller firms, where such action will not interfere with the objectives of the regulation.

Minority Business. The Democratic Party pledges itself to advance minority businesses, including Black, Hispanic, Asian/Pacific Americans, Native Americans and other minorities to:

• Increase the overall level of support and the overall level of federal procurement so that minority groups will receive additional benefits and opportunities.

• Triple the 1980 level of federal procurement from minority-owned firms as we have tripled the 1977 levels in the past three years.

• Increase substantially the targeting of Small Business Administration loans to minority-owned businesses.

• Increase ownership of small businesses by minorities, especially in those areas which have traditionally been closed to minorities, such as communications and newspapers.

• Expand management, technical, and training assistance for minority firms, and strengthen minority capital development....

Women and The Economy. The Democratic Party ... commits itself to strong steps to close the wage gap between men and women, to expand child care opportunities for families with working parents, to end the tax discrimination that penalizes married working couples, and to ensure that women can retire in dignity.

We will strictly enforce existing anti-discrimination laws with respect to hiring, pay and promotions. We will adopt a full employment policy, with increased possibilities for part-time work.... [W]e will ensure that women in both the public and private sectors are not only paid equally for work which is identical to that performed by men, but are also paid equally for work which is of comparable value to that performed by men.

Consumer Protection. Over the next four years, we must continue to guarantee and enhance the basic consumer rights to safety, to information, to choice and to a fair hearing.

We must continue our support of basic health, safety, environmental and consumer protection regulatory programs....

Human Needs. While we recognize the need for fiscal restraint ... we pledge as Democrats that for the sole and primary purpose of fiscal restraint alone, we will *not* support reductions in the funding of any program whose purpose is to serve the basic human needs of the most needy in our society — programs such as unemployment, income maintenance, food stamps, and efforts to enhance the educational, nutritional or health needs of children.

Health. The answer to runaway medical costs is not, as Republicans propose, to pour money into a wasteful and inefficient system. The answer is not to cut back on benefits for the elderly and eligibility for the poor. The answer is to enact a comprehensive, universal national health insurance plan.

To meet the goals of a program that will control costs and provide health coverage to every American, the Democratic Party pledges to seek a national health insurance program....

Social Security. The Democratic Party will oppose any effort to tamper with the Social Security system by cutting or taxing benefits as a violation of the contract the American government has made with its people. We hereby make a covenant with the elderly of America that as we have kept the Social Security trust fund sound and solvent in the past, we shall keep it sound and solvent in the years ahead.... We oppose efforts to raise the age at which Social Security benefits will be provided.

Finally, the Democratic Party vehemently opposes all forms of age discrimination and commits itself to eliminating mandatory retirement.

Welfare Reform. As a means of providing immediate federal fiscal relief to state and local governments, the fed-eral government will assume the local government's burden of welfare costs. Further, there should be a phased reduction in the states' share of welfare costs in the immediate future.

We strongly reject the Republican Platform proposal to transfer the responsibility for funding welfare costs entirely to the states. Such a proposal would not only worsen the fiscal situation of state and local governments, but would also lead to reduced benefits and services to those dependent on welfare programs. The Democratic policy is exactly the opposite — to provide greater assistance to state and local governments for their welfare costs and to improve benefits and services....

Education. ... [W]e will continue to support the Department of Education and assist in its all-important educational enterprise....

... The federal government and the states should be encouraged to equalize or take over educational expenses, relieving the overburdened ... taxpayer.

The Democratic Party continues to support programs aimed at achieving communities integrated both in terms of race and economic class.... Mandatory transportation of students beyond their neighborhoods for the purpose of desegregation remains a judicial tool of last resort.

The Party reaffirms its support of public school education and would not support any program or legislation that would create or promote economic, sociological or racial segregation.

The Party accepts its commitment to the support of a constitutionally acceptable method of providing tax aid for the education of all pupils in schools which do not racially discriminate, and excluding so-called segregation academies.

The Democratic Party is committed to a federal scholarship program adequate to meet the needs of all the underprivileged who could benefit from a college education.

We support efforts to provide for the basic nutritional needs of students. We support the availability of nutritious school breakfast, milk and lunch programs.

Equal Rights Amendment. ... [T]he Democratic Party must ensure that ERA at last becomes the 27th Amendment to the Constitution. We oppose efforts to rescind ERA in states which have already ratified the amendment, and we shall insist that past rescissions are invalid.

Civil Rights and Liberties. We oppose efforts to undermine the Supreme Court's historic mandate of school desegregation, and we support affirmative action goals to overturn patterns of discrimination in education and employment.

Our commitment to civil rights embraces not only a commitment to legal equality, but a commitment to economic justice as well. It embraces a recognition of the right of every citizen ... to a fair share in our economy.

We call for passage of legislation to charter the purposes, prerogatives, and restraints on the Federal Bureau of Investigation, the Central Intelligence Agency, and other intelligence agencies of government with full protection for the civil rights and liberties of American citizens living at home or abroad. Under no circumstances should American citizens be investigated because of their beliefs.

Abortion. The Democratic Party recognizes reproductive freedom as a fundamental human right. We therefore oppose government interference in the reproductive decisions of Americans, especially those government programs or legislative restrictions that deny poor Americans their right to privacy by funding or advocating one or a limited number of reproductive choices only. Specifically, the Democratic Party opposes ... restrictions on funding for health services for the poor that deny poor women especially the right to exercise a constitutionally-guaranteed right to privacy.

Tax Reform. Capital formation is essential both to control inflation and to encourage growth. New tax reform efforts are needed to increase savings and investment, promote the principle of progressive taxation, close loopholes, and maintain adequate levels of federal revenue.

Gun Control. The Democratic Party affirms the right of sportsmen to possess guns for purely hunting and target-shooting purposes. However, handguns simplify and intensify violent crime. . . . The Democratic Party supports enactment of federal legislation to strengthen the presently inadequate regulations over the manufacture, assembly, distribution, and possession of handguns and to ban "Saturday night specials."

Energy. We must make energy conservation our highest priority, not only to reduce our dependence on foreign oil, but also to guarantee that our children and grandchildren have an adequate supply of energy.

Major new efforts must be launched to develop synthetic and alternative renewable energy sources.

The Democratic Party regards coal as our nation's greatest energy resource. It must play a decisive role in America's energy future.

Oil exploration on federal lands must be accelerated, consistent with environmental protections.

Offshore energy leasing and development should be conditioned on full protection of the environment and marine resources.

Solar energy use must be increased, and strong efforts, including continued financial support, must be undertaken to make certain that we achieve the goal of having solar energy account for 20% of our total energy by the year 2000.

A stand-by gasoline rationing plan must be adopted for use in the event of a serious energy supply interruption.

. . . Through the federal government's commitment to renewable energy sources and energy efficiency, and as alternative fuels become available in the future, we will retire nuclear power plants. . . .

We must give the highest priority to dealing with the nuclear waste disposal problem. . . . [E]fforts to develop a safe, environmentally sound nuclear waste disposal plan must be continued and intensified.

Environment. We must move decisively to protect our countryside and our coastline from overdevelopment and mismanagement. . . . [P]rotection must be balanced with the need to properly manage and utilize our land resources during the 1980s.

We must develop new and improved working relationships among federal, state, local, tribal, and territorial governments and private interests, to manage effectively our programs for increased domestic energy production and their impact on people, water, air, and the environment in general.

Grain Embargo. Recognizing the patriotic sacrifices made by the American farmer during the agricultural embargo protesting the invasion of Afghanistan, we commend the agricultural community's contribution in the field of foreign affairs. Except in time of war or grave threats to national security, the federal government should impose no future embargoes on agricultural products.

Foreign Policy. The Democratic Administration sought to reconcile . . . two requirements of American foreign policy — principle and strength. . . . We have tried to make clear the continuing importance of American strength in a world of change. Without such strength, there is a genuine risk that global change will deteriorate into anarchy to be exploited by our adversaries' military power. Thus, the revival of American strength has been a central pre-occupation of the Democratic Administration.

The use of American power is necessary as a means of shaping not only a more secure, but also a more decent world. . . . [W]e must pursue objectives that are moral, that make clear our support for the aspirations of mankind and that are rooted in the ideals of the American people.

That is why the Democrats have stressed human rights. That is why America once again has supported the aspirations of the vast majority of the world's population for greater human justice and freedom.

. . In meeting the dangers of the coming decade the United States will consult closely with our Allies to advance common security and political goals. As a result of annual summit meetings, coordinated economic policies and effective programs of international energy conservation have been fashioned.

. . . [W]e must continue to improve our relations with the Third World by being sensitive to their legitimate aspirations. The United States should be a positive force for peaceful change in responding to ferment in the Third World.

Our third objective must be peace in the Middle East. . . . Our nation feels a profound moral obligation to sustain and assure the security of Israel. . . . Israel is the single democracy, the most stable government, the most strategic asset and our closest ally in the region.

To fulfill this imperative, we must move towards peace in the Middle East. Without peace, there is a growing prospect, indeed inevitability, that this region will become radicalized, susceptible to foreign intrusion, and possibly involved in another war. Thus, peace in the Middle East also is vital for our national security interests. . . . Our goal is to make the Middle East an area of stability and progress in which the United States can play a full and constructive role.

National Security. Our fourth major objective is to strengthen the military security of the United States and our Allies at a time when trends in the military balance have become increasingly adverse. America is now, and will continue to be, the strongest power on earth. It was the Democratic Party's greatest hope that we could, in fact, reduce our military effort. But realities of the world situation, including the unremitting buildup of Soviet military forces, required that we begin early to reverse the decade-long decline in American defense efforts.

Arms Control. . . . [T]he Democrats have been and remain committed to arms control, especially to strategic arms limitations, and to maintain a firm and balanced relationship with the Soviet Union.

To avoid the danger to all mankind from an intensification of the strategic arms competition, and to curb a possible acceleration of the nuclear arms race while awaiting the ratification of the SALT II Treaty, we endorse the policy of continuing to take no action which would be inconsistent with its object and purpose, so long as the Soviet Union does likewise.

Arms control and strategic arms limitation are of crucial importance to us and to all other people. The SALT II Agreement is a major accomplishment of the Democratic Administration. It contributes directly to our national security, and we will seek its ratification at the earliest feasible time.

Republicans

Ronald Reagan, the 69-year-old former California governor, was installed as the Republican presidential nominee at the party's national convention in Detroit, but his moment of glory nearly was overshadowed by an unusual flap over the number-two spot. The choosing of Reagan's running mate provided the only suspense at the GOP convention, held July 14-17, 1980, in Detroit's Joe Louis Arena.

Who would fill the number-one spot had been determined long before when Reagan won 28 out of the 34 Republican presidential primaries and eliminated all of his major rivals. The last to withdraw — George Bush — was tapped by Reagan July 16 as his ticket mate in a dramatic post-midnight appearance before the delegates.

For most of the evening of July 16, it looked as though Gerald R. Ford would occupy the second spot on the ticket, which would have made him the first former president to run for vice president. Private polls reportedly had shown that Ford was the only Republican who would enhance Reagan's chances in November. And a number of Republicans had described the combination as a "dream ticket." Groups described as "friends of Ronald Reagan" and "friends of Gerald Ford" had met four times to "discuss" the possibility of forging a Reagan-Ford ticket.

The Ford group consisted of former Secretary of State Henry A. Kissinger, Alan Greenspan, former chairman of the Council of Economic Advisers, and Ford aides Robert Barnett and John Marsh. The Reagan group was the nucleus of his primary campaign staff: Edwin Meese, campaign director, and Richard Wirthlin, Reagan's pollster. Reagan and Ford first discussed Ford's joining the ticket at a meeting July 15, although no formal offer was made, according to a source close to Reagan. " 'I want you to think this over and then we'll discuss it tomorrow,' " the source quoted Reagan as telling Ford.

The pair met again the following day to continue their discussions, but nothing was resolved. When the convention reconvened at 6:30 p.m., reports began swirling about the floor, many of them spawned by Ford himself, who in two televised interviews gave strong indications that he would accept the second spot if certain conditions were met.

In an interview with Walter Cronkite of CBS about 7:30 p.m., Ford said, "I would not go to Washington and be a figurehead vice president. If I go to Washington I have to be there in the belief that I would play a meaningful role." Later, in an interview with Barbara Walters of ABC, Ford said he did not want the job unless his role would be "nonceremonial, constructive and responsive." Such an arrangement, he said, would require a "far different structure" from the duties performed by other vice presidents. Asked whether it would be difficult to be a vice president again after having had the top job, Ford said, "Not at all. I'd be more interested in substance than glamor."

Ford declined to spell out what his conditions for taking the job would be, but descriptions of his requirements would have made him in effect co-president with Reagan. The discussions reportedly centered around providing a role for Ford somewhat akin to the White House chief of staff's. In this kind of post he would have had responsibility for agencies such as the Office of Management and Budget, the National Security Council, the domestic policy staff and the Council of Economic Advisers.

Ford further fed the speculation, offering a simple solution to the temporary problem that would have been posed by the 12th Amendment to the Constitution. The amendment would have had the effect of prohibiting the members of the electoral college from California from voting for both Reagan and Ford because both were California residents. The amendment says that the electors from any state must vote for at least one person who is not from that state.

However, nothing in the Constitution would have excluded two residents of the same state from serving as president and vice president or prevented electors from states other than their home state from voting for those two individuals. Ford said Reagan's lawyers had researched

the residency question and determined that legally there would be no problem if the former president changed his residence to Michigan, which he represented in the House for 25 years, or to Colorado, where he owned a home.

But Ford expressed reservations about how such a move might be interpreted. "I think it could create in the minds of the American people that we're trying to do something a little cute," he said. "Well, I've never done that in politics. I've got a good reputation and I'm worried about it. . . . I think it would be construed to be to some extent a gimmick."

As the evening of July 16 wore on, the speculation heightened. "The expectation, as it is presently being reported is it's going through," Michigan Gov. William G. Milliken said of the Ford candidacy. "I have it on very reliable sources within the Ford camp that it is put together," said Gov. Pierre S. (Pete) du Pont of Delaware.

About 9:15 p.m. Reagan telephoned Ford to ask him to make up his mind whether he wanted the vice president's job. Meanwhile, convention officials proceeded to call the roll of the states. When Reagan received enough votes to become the official nominee, the arena erupted into a cheering, hornblowing, flag-waving, foot-stomping, bandplaying demonstration. The noise abated a bit while the roll call was finished, but continued for more than an hour.

But at about 11:15 p.m. the Reagan-Ford arrangement fell apart. Ford went to Reagan's suite in the Detroit Plaza Hotel and the two men agreed that it would be better for Ford to campaign for the GOP ticket rather than be a member of it. "His [Ford's] instinct told him it was not the thing to do," Reagan said later.

When it became apparent that efforts to persuade Ford to join the ticket had failed, Reagan turned to Bush, a moderate with proven vote-getting ability. The Reagan camp refused to acknowledge that Bush was the second choice, even though it was widely perceived that way. "There was everybody else and then the Ford option," Edwin Meese, Reagan's chief of staff, said later.

Bush had been Reagan's most persistent competitor through the long primary season, but he won only six primaries — Michigan, Massachusetts, Connecticut, Pennsylvania, the District of Columbia and Puerto Rico. Bush was one of the vice presidential possibilities favored by those in the party who believed that Reagan had to reach outside the GOP's conservative wing if he were to have broad appeal in November.

Bush supporters said that Bush's background would balance the ticket geographically and that his extensive government service would overcome criticism that Reagan did not have any Washington experience. Bush served from 1967 to 1971 in the U.S. House from Texas and had been ambassador to the United Nations, head of the U.S. liaison office in Peking and director of the Central Intelligence Agency.

Bush's first appearance at the convention earlier had produced a rousing demonstration from supporters throughout the hall, but his strongest support on the floor was in delegations from the Midwest and Northeast, such as New Jersey and the states where he won primary victories.

Reagan's choice of the moderate George Bush was viewed as his first major choice between political pragmatism and ideological purity. Throughout the primary season, Reagan had drawn a large measure of his support from the right wing of the Republican Party and had pledged himself to support conservative economic, social and defense policies. During the convention, Sen. Jesse Helms of North Carolina, the most vocal leader of the GOP's right wing, masterminded the rightward tilt of the party platform to reflect conservative viewpoints. Helms, concerned about the nomination of a moderate such as Bush, threatened to place his own name in nomination to put pressure on the GOP standardbearers to abide by conservative and "moral" principles. In the end, Helms supported the Reagan-Bush ticket, but warned that it had better support the party's conservative platform. Though Helms was not nominated for vice president, his supporters nonetheless gave him 54 votes. He finished second behind Bush, who got 1,832 votes.

The Republican Party's 1980 platform was more a blueprint for victory in November than a definitive statement of party views. Rather than slug it out over specifics, the party's moderate and conservative wings agreed to blur their differences to appear united, to broaden the party's appeal and to smooth Reagan's way to the White House.

Platform writers veered from traditional Republican positions on a few issues. On others they went out of their way to embrace policies that meshed with Reagan's views more than their own. For the most part, they managed to fashion a policy statement that pleased no party faction entirely but with which all could live reasonably.

Overwhelmingly, platform committee members agreed the document should be basically consistent with Reagan's positions. Thus, though one media poll found delegates overwhelmingly in favor of resuming a peacetime draft, the platform bowed to the view of its nominee and stated its opposition to a renewal of the draft "at this time." In the same manner, the party's platform took no position on ratification of the Equal Rights Amendment (ERA) to the Constitution. Since 1940 Republican platforms had supported an ERA amendment. Reagan, however, opposed ratification, and ERA opponents far outnumbered the amendment's supporters on the platform committee. Yet Reagan, in a gesture to moderates, suggested that the platform not take a position on the issue, and the committee agreed.

Most of the platform document consisted of policy statements on which most Republicans agreed. There were calls for tax cuts, pleas for less government regulation and harsh criticisms of the Carter administration. In two areas, however, the platform took a particularly hard-line position. The platform supported a constitutional amendment that would outlaw abortion and called on a Reagan administration to appoint federal judges who opposed abortion. On defense, platform writers took an already hard-line plank that had been drafted by party staff and moved it sharply to the right. The platform called for massive increases in defense spending and scoffed at the Carter administration's proposed strategic arms limitation treaty (SALT II).

On the other hand, to pick up votes from organized labor, blacks and the poor, the platform made some new overtures to those traditionally non-Republican groups. It pledged to strengthen enforcement of the civil rights laws, made overtures to U.S. workers put out of their jobs by competition from foreign imports and promised to save America's inner cities.

The platform was adopted by the convention July 15 without change, but not before an attempt was made to reopen on the floor one of its more controversial sections. Although party moderates such as Sens. Charles H. Percy, Ill., Charles McC. Mathias Jr., Md., and Jacob K. Javits,

N.Y., made little secret of their unhappiness with the platform's failure to reaffirm the party's support for ratification of the ERA, they were particularly chagrined by the section suggesting that Reagan appoint federal judges who oppose abortion. Percy called the section "the worst plank I have ever seen in any platform by the Republican Party." The moderates July 14 sought to round up support for reopening the platform on the floor, but their efforts failed. In caucuses held early July 15, a number of state delegations including New York and Illinois voted down motions to change the platform's position on abortion.

Nonetheless, as Chairman John J. Rhodes, Ariz., proposed that the convention adopt the platform, Hawaii delegate John Leopold leaped onto a chair to seek Rhodes' recognition. When Rhodes ordered the Hawaii delegation's microphone turned on, Leopold said the group unanimously proposed a motion to suspend the convention rules to permit delegates to "discuss" the platform on the floor. If the rules were suspended, Leopold told reporters, he intended to propose that the language on federal judges be deleted. Not to allow floor discussion of the platform, he said, would be to "railroad" the document through the convention.

Rhodes explained that under convention rules a majority of the members of six state delegations was required to bring a motion to suspend the rules to a vote. He asked if a majority of the delegates from any other state supported Leopold's motion. Only Rep. Silvio O. Conte, chairman of the Massachusetts delegation, rose. But rather than announce support for Leopold's motion, Conte stated only that a majority of his delegation supported a recorded vote on the platform, something Leopold had not proposed. To the applause of many of the delegates, Rhodes then declared that Leopold's motion had failed. The platform subsequently was approved by voice vote.

Ronald Reagan received the Republican nomination on the first ballot. *(Chart, p. 196.)*

In his acceptance speech, Reagan combined sharp jabs at the alleged shortcomings of the Carter administration with a reaffirmation of his own conservative credo. Reagan cited three grave threats to the nation's existence — "a disintegrating economy, a weakened defense and an energy policy based on the sharing of scarcity." The culprits, Reagan contended, were President Carter and the Democratic Congress. He said they had preached that the American people needed to tighten their belts. "I utterly reject that view," he declared. Reagan was especially critical of the Democratic administration's conduct of foreign policy. He ridiculed it as weak, vacillating and transparently hypocritical.

Reagan went on to win the presidential election in November with an absolute majority of the popular vote — 43,901,812 votes or 50.7 percent. His electoral victory over Carter was more pronounced. Reagan carried 44 states for a total of 489 electoral votes to just 49 for Carter, who carried only six states and the District of Columbia.

Following are excerpts from the Republican Party's platform of 1980:

Taxes. . . . [W]e believe it is essential to cut personal tax rates out of fairness to the individual. . . .

Therefore, the Republican Party supports across-the-board reductions in personal income tax rates, phased in over three years, which will reduce tax rates from the range of 14 to 70 percent to a range of from 10 to 50 percent.

. . . Republicans will move to end tax bracket creep caused by inflation. We support tax indexing to protect taxpayers from the automatic tax increases caused when cost-of-living wage increases move them into higher tax brackets.

Welfare. We pledge a system that will:

• provide adequate living standards for the truly needy;

• end welfare fraud by removing ineligibles from the welfare rolls, tightening food stamp eligibility requirements, and ending aid to illegal aliens and the voluntarily unemployed;

• strengthen work incentives, particularly directed at the productive involvement of able-bodied persons in useful community work projects;

• provide educational and vocational incentives to allow recipients to become self-supporting; and

• better coordinate federal efforts with local and state social welfare agencies and strengthen local and state administrative functions.

We oppose federalizing the welfare system; local levels of government are most aware of the needs in their communities. We support a block grant program that will help return control of welfare programs to the states.

Black Americans. During the next four years we are committed to policies that will:

• encourage local governments to designate specific enterprise zones within depressed areas that will promote new jobs, new and expanded businesses and new economic vitality;

• open new opportunities for black men and women to begin small businesses of their own by, among other steps, removing excessive regulations, disincentives for venture capital and other barriers erected by the government;

• bring strong, effective enforcement of federal civil rights statutes, especially those dealing with threats to physical safety and security which have recently been increasing; and

• ensure that the federal government follows a non-discriminatory system of appointments ... with a careful eye for qualified minority aspirants.

Women's Rights. We acknowledge the legitimate efforts of those who support or oppose ratification of the Equal Rights Amendment.

We reaffirm our Party's historic commitment to equal rights and equality for women.

We support equal rights and equal opportunities for women, without taking away traditional rights of women such as exemption from the military draft. We support the enforcement of all equal opportunity laws and urge the elimination of discrimination against women.

We reaffirm our belief in the traditional role and values of the family in our society.... The importance of support for the mother and homemaker in maintaining the values of this country cannot be over-emphasized.

Abortion. While we recognize differing views on this question among Americans in general — and in our own Party — we affirm our support of a constitutional amendment to restore protection of the right to life for unborn children. We also support the Congressional efforts to restrict the use of taxpayers' dollars for abortion.

Education. ... [T]he Republican Party supports deregulation by the federal government of public education, and encourages the elimination of the federal Department of Education.

We support Republican initiatives in the Congress to restore the right of individuals to participate in voluntary, non-denominational prayer in schools and other public facilities.

... [W]e condemn the forced busing of school children to achieve arbitrary racial quotas.... It [busing] has failed to improve the quality of education, while diverting funds from programs that could make the difference between success and failure for the poor, the disabled, and minority children.

[W]e reaffirm our support for a system of educational assistance based on tax credits that will in part compensate parents for their financial sacrifices in paying tuition at the elementary, secondary, and post-secondary level.

Health. Republicans unequivocally oppose socialized medicine, in whatever guise it is presented by the Democratic Party. We reject the creation of a national health service and all proposals for compulsory national health insurance.

Older Americans. Social Security is one of this nation's most vital commitments to our senior citizens. We commit the Republican Party to first save, and then strengthen, this fundamental contract between our government and its productive citizens.

... [W]e proudly reaffirm our opposition to mandatory retirement and our long-standing Republican commitment to end the Democrats' earnings limitation upon Social Security benefits. In addition, the Republican Party is strongly opposed to the taxation of Social Security benefits and we pledge to oppose any attempts to tax these benefits.

Crime. We believe that the death penalty serves as an effective deterrent to capital crime and should be applied by the federal government and by states which approve it as an appropriate penalty for certain major crimes.

We believe the right of citizens to keep and bear arms must be preserved. Accordingly, we oppose federal registration of firearms. Mandatory sentences for commission of armed felonies are the most effective means to deter abuse of this right.

Foreign Competition. The Republican Party recognizes the need to provide workers who have lost their jobs because of technological obsolescence or imports the opportunity to adjust to changing economic conditions. In particular, we will seek ways to assist workers threatened by foreign competition.

The Republican Party believes that protectionist tariffs and quotas are detrimental to our economic well-being. Nevertheless, we insist that our trading partners offer our nation the same level of equity, access, and fairness that we have shown them.

Training and Skills. ... [T]he success of federal employment efforts is dependent on private sector participation. It must be recognized as the ultimate location for unsubsidized jobs, as the provider of means to attain this end, and as an active participant in the formulation of employment and training policies on the local and national level.

We urge a reduction of payroll tax rates, a youth differential for the minimum wage, and alleviation of other costs of employment until a young person can be a productive employee.

Fairness to the Employer. The Republican Party declares war on government overregulation.

While we recognize the role of the federal government in establishing certain minimum standards designed to improve the quality of life in America, we reaffirm our conviction that these standards can best be attained through innovative efforts of American business without the federal government mandating the methods of attainment.

OSHA. OSHA should concentrate its resources on encouraging voluntary compliance by employers and monitoring situations where close federal supervision is needed and serious hazards are most likely to occur. OSHA should be required to consult with, advise, and assist businesses in coping with the regulatory burden before imposing any penalty for non-compliance. Small businesses and employers with good safety records should be exempt from safety inspections, and penalties should be increased for those with consistently poor performance.

Agriculture. Republicans will ensure that:

• international trade is conducted on the basis of fair and effective competition and that all imported agricultural products meet the same standards of quality that are required of American producers....

• the future of U.S. agricultural commodities is protected from the economic evils of predatory dumping by other producing nations and that the domestic production of these commodities ... is preserved.

...We believe that agricultural embargoes are only symbolic and are ineffective tools of foreign policy.... The Carter grain embargo should be terminated immediately.

Big Government. The Republican Party reaffirms its belief in the decentralization of the federal government and in the traditional American principle that the best government is the one closest to the people. There, it is less costly, more accountable, and more responsive to people's needs....

Energy. We are committed to ... a strategy of aggressively boosting the nation's energy supplies; stimulating new energy technology and more efficient energy use; restoring maximum feasible choice and freedom in the marketplace for energy consumers and producers alike; and eliminating energy shortages and disruptions....

Republicans support a comprehensive program of regulatory reform, improved incentives, and revision of cumbersome and overly stringent Clean Air Act regulations.

We support accelerated use of nuclear energy through technologies that have been proven efficient and safe.

We reject unequivocally punitive gasoline and other energy taxes designed to artificially suppress energy consumption.

A Republican policy of decontrol, development of our domestic energy resources, and incentives for new supply and conservation technologies will substantially reduce our dependence on imported oil.

Republicans will move toward making available all suitable federal lands for multiple use purposes including exploration and production of energy resources.

Environment. We believe that a healthy environment is essential to the present and future well-being of our people, and to sustainable national growth.

At the same time, we believe that it is imperative that environmental laws and regulations be reviewed, and where necessary, reformed to ensure that the benefits achieved justify the costs imposed.

Balanced Budget. If federal spending is reduced as tax cuts are phased in, there will be sufficient budget surpluses to fund the tax cuts, and allow for reasonable growth in necessary program spending.

...We believe a Republican President and a Republican Congress can balance the budget and reduce spending through legislative actions, eliminating the necessity for a Constitutional amendment to compel it. However, if necessary, the Republican Party will seek to adopt a Constitutional amendment to limit federal spending and balance the budget, except in time of national emergency as determined by a two-thirds vote of Congress.

Inflation. The Republican Party believes inflation can be controlled only by fiscal and monetary restraint, combined with sharp reductions in the tax and regulatory disincentives for savings, investments, and productivity. Therefore, the Republican Party opposes the imposition of wage and price controls and credit controls.

National Security. Republicans commit themselves to an immediate increase in defense spending to be applied judiciously to critically needed programs. We will build toward a sustained defense expenditure sufficient to close the gap with the Soviets. Republicans approve and endorse a national strategy of peace through strength.... The general principles and goals of this strategy would be:

• to inspire, focus, and unite the national will and determination to achieve peace and freedom;

• to achieve overall military and technological superiority over the Soviet Union;

• to create a strategic and civil defense which would protect the American people against nuclear war at least as well as the Soviet population is protected;

• to accept no arms control agreement which in any way jeopardizes the security of the United States or its allies, or which locks the United States into a position of military inferiority;

• to reestablish effective security and intelligence capabilities;

• to pursue positive nonmilitary means to roll back the growth of communism;

• to help our allies and other non-Communist countries defend themselves against Communist aggression; and

• to maintain a strong economy and protect our overseas sources of energy and ... raw materials.

Nuclear Forces. ...We reject the mutual-assured-destruction (MAD) strategy of the Carter Administration.... We propose, instead, a credible strategy which will deter a Soviet attack by the clear capability of our forces to survive and ultimately to destroy Soviet military targets.

A Republican Administration will strive for early modernization of our theater nuclear forces so that a seamless web of deterrence can be maintained against all levels of attack, and our credibility with our European allies is restored.

Defense Manpower and the Draft. The Republican Party is not prepared to accept a peacetime draft at this time.... We will not consider a peacetime draft unless a well-managed, Congressionally-funded, full-scale effort to improve the all-volunteer force does not meet expectations.

National Intelligence. A Republican Administration will seek adequate safeguards to ensure that past abuses will not recur, but we will seek the repeal of ill-considered restrictions sponsored by Democrats, which have debilitated U.S. intelligence capabilities while easing the intelligence collection and subversion efforts of our adversaries.

Arms Control The Republican approach to arms control has been ... based on three fundamental premises:

• first, before arms control negotiations may be undertaken, the security of the United States must be assured by the funding and deployment of strong military forces sufficient to deter conflict at any level or to prevail in battle should aggression occur;

• second, negotiations must be conducted on the basis of strict reciprocity of benefits — unilateral restraint by the U.S. has failed to bring reductions by the Soviet Union; and

• third, arms control negotiations, once entered, represent an important political and military undertaking that cannot be divorced from the broader political and military behavior of the parties.

U.S.-Soviet Relations. Republicans believe that the United States can only negotiate with the Soviet Union from a position of unquestioned principle and unquestioned strength.

A Republican Administration will continue to seek to negotiate arms reductions in Soviet strategic weapons, in Soviet bloc force levels in Central Europe, and in other areas that may be amenable to reductions or limitations. We will pursue hard bargaining for equitable, verifiable, and enforceable agreements.

We reaffirm our commitment to press the Soviet Union to implement the United Nations Declaration on Human Rights and the Helsinki Agreements which guarantee rights such as the free interchange of information and the right to emigrate.

NATO and Western Europe. A Republican Administration, as one of its highest priorities and in close concert with our NATO partners, will ... ensure that the United States leads a concerted effort to rebuild a strong, confident Alliance....

In pledging renewed United States leadership, cooperation, and consultation, Republicans assert their expectation that each of the allies will bear a fair share of the common defense effort and that they will work closely together in support of common Alliance goals.

Middle East, Persian Gulf. With respect to an ultimate peace settlement, Republicans reject any call for involvement of the PLO as not in keeping with the long-term interests of either Israel or the Palestinian Arabs. The imputation of legitimacy to organizations not yet willing to acknowledge the fundamental right to existence of the State of Israel is wrong.

The sovereignty, security, and integrity of the State of Israel is a moral imperative and serves the strategic interests of the United States. Republicans reaffirm our fundamental and enduring commitment to this principle.

While reemphasizing our commitment to Israel, a Republican Administration will pursue close ties and friendship with moderate Arab states.

The Americas. We deplore the Marxist Sandinista takeover of Nicaragua and the Marxist attempts to destabilize El Salvador, Guatemala, and Honduras. We do not support United States assistance to any Marxist government in this hemisphere and we oppose the Carter Administration aid program for the government of Nicaragua. However, we will support the efforts of the Nicaraguan people to establish a free and independent government.

Asia and the Pacific. A new Republican Administration will restore a strong American role in Asia and the Pacific. We will make it clear that any military action which threatens the independence of America's allies and friends will bring a response sufficient to make its cost prohibitive to potential adversaries.

China. We will strive for the creation of conditions that will foster the peaceful elaboration of our relationship with the People's Republic of China.

At the same time, we deplore the Carter Administration's treatment of Taiwan, our long-time ally and friend. We pledge that our concern for the safety and security of the 17 million people of Taiwan will be constant.

Africa. The Republican Party supports the principle and process of self-determination in Africa. We reaffirm our commitment to this principle and pledge our strong opposition to the effort of the Soviet Union ... to subvert this process.

Foreign Aid. No longer should American foreign assistance programs seek to force acceptance of American governmental forms. The principal consideration should be whether or not extending assistance to a nation or group of nations will advance America's interests and objectives.

Decisions to provide military assistance should be made on the basis of U.S. foreign policy objectives. Such assistance to any nation need not imply complete approval of a regime's domestic policy.

International Economic Policy. Under a Republican Administration, our international economic policy will be harmonized with our foreign and defense policies to leave no doubt as to the strategy and purpose of American policy.

Republicans will conduct international economic policy in a manner that will stabilize the value of the dollar at home and abroad.

The Republican Party believes the United States must adopt an aggressive export policy. Trade, especially exporting, must be high on our list of national priorities. The Republicans will ... promote trade to ensure the long-term health of the U.S. economy.

National Unity Campaign

Illinois Republican Rep. John B. Anderson declared himself an independent candidate for the presidency April 24, 1980 after it became clear that he could not obtain his party's presidential nomination. Anderson created the National Unity Campaign as the vehicle for his third-party candidacy. No party convention was held to select Anderson or to ratify the selection.

On Aug. 25 Anderson announced he had tapped former Wisconsin Gov. Patrick J. Lucey, a Democrat, to be his running mate. The selection of Lucey was seen as a move by Anderson to attract liberal Democrats disgruntled by President Jimmy Carter's renomination. Anderson's choice of a running mate and the Aug. 30 release of a National Unity Campaign platform helped establish him as a genuine contender in the presidential race.

The 317-page platform put forth specific proposals on a variety of national issues, emphasizing domestic questions. The positions taken generally were fiscally conservative and socially liberal, remaining true to Anderson's "wallet on the right, heart on the left" philosophy.

The platform made clear that Anderson's primary goal was to restore the nation's economic health by adopting fiscal and tax policies that would "generate a substantial pool of investment capital," which then would be used to increase productivity and create jobs. Anderson proposed countercyclical revenue sharing to direct federal funds to areas hardest hit by the election year recession. He rejected mandatory wage and price controls as a cure for inflation, proposing instead a program under which the government would encourage labor and management to work toward agreement on proper levels for wages and prices and use tax incentives to encourage compliance with the standards set. In contrast to both Carter and Reagan, Anderson opposed tax cuts for individuals. He also criticized constitutional amendments to balance the federal budget, saying that while the budget should be balanced "in ordinary times," it could be expected to run a deficit in times of "economic difficulty."

Anderson's energy policy made reducing oil imports the top priority. His platform proposed a 50-cent-a-gallon excise tax on gasoline to discourage consumption, with the revenue to be used to cut Social Security taxes. Anderson favored the decontrol of oil prices begun under Carter and proposed a 40-mile-per-gallon fuel economy standard for new autos.

For American cities, Anderson proposed using about 90 percent of alcohol and tobacco taxes to help build mass transit systems and fight deterioration of public facilities. He also favored offering tax incentives to encourage businesses to locate in blighted urban areas.

In foreign policy, Anderson emphasized strengthening alliances with Western Europe and Japan, resisting Soviet expansion while negotiating "whenever possible" and respecting the sovereignty of Third World nations. His platform supported human rights and humanitarian aid for refugees and disaster victims abroad. He pledged to support the Middle East peace process, but opposed the creation of a Palestinian state between Israel and Jordan or U.S. recognition of the Palestine Liberation Organization until the PLO recognized Israel's right to exist.

On defense issues, Anderson opposed development of the MX missile, B-1 bomber and neutron bomb, criticized the arms race and opposed a peacetime draft registration. He pledged to seek ratification of the SALT II treaty negotiated with the Soviet Union, saying that "essential equivalence" existed between U.S. and Soviet missile forces. He opposed a strategy of nuclear superiority, emphasizing instead the beefing up of conventional military forces.

Anderson finished the 1980 presidential race a distant third behind Jimmy Carter with 5,719,722 votes, 6.6 percent.

Following are excerpts from the National Unity Campaign Platform of 1980:

Economy. We will construct a Wage-Price Incentives Program. Our administration will invite labor and management leaders to agree upon fair and realistic guidelines and to determine appropriate tax-based incentives to encourage compliance....

In the absence of sharp and prolonged increases in the rate of inflation, we will oppose mandatory wage and price standards.

Youth Unemployment. To deal with the critical problem of youth unemployment, particularly among minorities, we propose: enactment of the proposed Youth Act of 1980 to provide over $2 billion a year for job training and state and local educational programs designed to improve the employability of disadvantaged and out-of-school youth; increased funding for youth career intern programs; a youth opportunity wage incentive that would exempt eligible youths and employers from Social Security taxes during the first months of employment.

Gasoline Tax. We would couple decontrol of oil and gas prices with an excise tax of 50 cents per gallon on gasoline, the full revenues of that tax being returned to individuals through reductions in payroll taxes and increased Social Security benefits.... We will employ tax credits and other incentives to promote substitution of non-petroleum energy for oil, adoption of energy-efficient systems in industry and elsewhere, improvements in transportation and energy production technologies, and development of less wasteful structures for home and commerce.

Nuclear Power. ... [W]e will act on the recommendations of the Rogovin and Kemeny Commissions to make certain that installation of any future plants is preceded by demonstration of satisfactory standards and action on the nuclear waste question. We will assess nuclear power in light of its dependence on public subsidy and of the possibility that slower growth in demand may enable us to phase in other energy supplies in preference to nuclear systems.

Cities. ... [A]n Anderson-Lucey Administration will propose an Urban Reinvestment Trust Fund. Funded through ... revenues from the Federal alcohol and tobacco excise taxes and phased in over three years, it will disburse approximately $3.9 billion annually. It will be used for upgrading, rapair and replacement of [urban] capital plant and equipment.

Within our distressed older cities, there are zones of devastation, blighted by crime, arson and population flight.... We favor legislation that would create "enterprise zones" in these areas, by lowering corporate, capital gains, payroll and property taxes and by furnishing new tax incentives....

Environment. We will guard and consolidate the achievements in every field of environmental protection and preservation. We will insist, however, that economic impact studies, assessing not only direct costs but employment and energy implications, accompany proposals for major changes in environmental standards.

Social Issues. We are committed to ratification of the Equal Rights Amendment. We oppose government intrusion in the most intimate of family decisions — the right to bear or not to bear children — and will fight against any constitutional amendment prohibiting abortion. We support public funding of family planning services and other efforts to enable women to find ... alternatives to abortion.

National Defense and Arms Control. In strategic forces, we will maintain a stable balance by preserving essential equivalence with the Soviet Union. To meet an evolving threat to our deterrent, we will modernize and diversify our strategic arsenal.

The growing concern over the threat to fixed, land-based missiles poses an urgent problem to both the United States and the Soviet Union. Economically, environmentally and strategically, the ... cure proposed by the Carter Administration — the MX system — is unsound.

Arms control agreements must enhance our basic security and must not compromise our ability to protect our national interests. Agreements must preserve and reinforce the stability of the strategic balance.... Arms control must be based on adequate, effective verification.

The Western alliance should proceed with its plans to modernize its theater nuclear arsenal; at the same time, we should keep open the possibility of negotiations with the Soviet Union to limit theater nuclear forces.

We favor ... a short-term ... nuclear test ban treaty between the United States, the Soviet Union and the United Kingdom....

For a more effective defense, we will rely heavily on collective security arrangements with our principal allies in NATO and Japan. We will work to reinforce and enhance our historic partnership with our Western European allies.

We will propose to Moscow supplementary measures that could make possible the ratification of the SALT II Treaty and the start of SALT III negotiations. These proposals will respond to concerns expressed in the U.S. Senate regarding such issues as verification and future force reductions.

Middle East. The establishment and maintenance of peace in the Middle East will be an urgent objective.... A lasting settlement must encompass the principles affirmed in the Camp David accords.

Our administration will support the recognition of Palestinian rights as embodied in the Camp David accords, but will oppose the creation of a Palestinian state between Israel and Jordan.

The United States will not recognize or negotiate with the Palestine Liberation Organization unless that organization repudiates terrorism, explicitly recognizes Israel's right to exist in peace and accepts U.N. Security Council Resolutions 242 and 338....

China. ... [T]he Anderson-Lucey Administration would work to discourage antagonism between Russia and China. We should not become an arms supplier to China. We should work for better understanding by China's leaders of the consequences of nuclear war, of measures that should be taken to guard against accidental war and of ways to make the nuclear balance more stable.

Finally, our administration would abide by both the letter and spirit of the Taiwan Relations Act. We would maintain our contacts with Taiwan but would not establish official relations with its government.

KEY CONVENTION
BALLOTS

Key Convention Ballots: Sources

This section (pages 141-196) presents the results of important balloting from the presidential nominating conventions of three major American political parties from 1835 to 1980. The balloting results are arranged in chronological order by convention year. Each table contains a reference indicating the page in the preceding section, "Convention Chronology," where brief descriptions of each convention and key balloting appear.

The source for the balloting results for the 1835-1972 conventions is *Convention Decisions and Voting Records,* Brookings Institution, Washington, D.C., 1973, by Richard C. Bain and Judith H. Parris. Permission to use this material was granted by the Brookings Institution, which holds the copyright. The sources for the 1976 and 1980 vote totals are *The Official Proceedings of the Democratic National Convention* and the Republican National Committee.

Convention Decisions and Voting Records contains ballots for three major parties in American History — the Democrats, the Whigs and the modern Republicans. This section includes ballots from conventions of these three parties alone.

In selecting ballots to include in *National Party Conventions,* Congressional Quarterly followed several criteria:

● To include all initial and deciding presidential nominating ballots and selected other critical presidential ballots. The Democratic Party conventions of 1832, 1840, 1888, 1916, 1936 and 1964 nominated presidential candidates by acclamation without balloting.

● To include key ballots on important procedural issues, credentials contests and platform disputes.

● To exclude all ballots for vice presidential candidates.

Vote Total Discrepancies

Bain and Parris note frequent discrepancies between totals given in the published proceedings of the party conventions and the totals reached by adding up the state-by-state delegation votes. They state: "Wherever the discrepancy was obvious and the correct figure could be clearly derived, the record has been printed in corrected form. When the added totals of detailed figures listed differ from the sums printed in the proceedings, both totals are given."

Congressional Quarterly has followed this same procedure. For example, on page 144, the 49th presidential ballot of the 1852 Democratic Party convention appears. Franklin Pierce is listed as receiving 279 votes, the sum of the column. A footnote, however, indicates that the convention proceedings recorded Pierce as receiving 283 votes. Similar examples appear on pages 147, 148, and 188.

1835 Democratic

(Narrative. p. 22)

Delegation	Total Votes	First Pres. Ballot Van Buren
Connecticut	8	8
Delaware	3	3
Georgia	11	11
Indiana	9	9
Kentucky	15	15
Louisiana	5	5
Maine	10	10
Maryland	10	10
Massachusetts	14	14
Mississippi	4	4
Missouri	4	4
New Hampshire	7	7
New Jersey	8	8
New York	42	42
North Carolina	15	15
Ohio	21	21
Pennsylvania	30	30
Rhode Island	4	4
Tennessee	15	15
Vermont	7	7
Virginia	23	23
Total	265	265

1844 Democratic

(Narrative. p. 26)

Delegation	Total Votes	Amendment Ratifying Two-Thirds Rule		First Pres. Ballot [1]		Fifth Pres. Ballot [2]		Ninth Pres. Ballot (Before shift) [3]		Ninth Pres. Ballot (After shift)
		Yea	Nay	Van Buren	Cass	Van Buren	Cass	Polk	Cass	Polk
Alabama	9	9	—	1	8	1	8	9	—	9
Arkansas	3	3	—	—	—	—	—	3	—	3
Connecticut	6	3	3	6	—	—	—	6	—	6
Delaware	3	3	—	—	3	—	3	3	—	3
Georgia	10	10	—	—	9	—	9	9	—	10
Illinois	9	9	—	5	2	2	4	9	—	9
Indiana	12	12	—	3	9	1	11	12	—	12
Kentucky	12	12	—	—	—	—	—	12	—	12
Louisiana	6	6	—	—	—	—	—	6	—	6
Maine	9	—	9	8	—	8	1	7	1	9
Maryland	8	6	2	2	4	2	6	7	1	8
Massachusetts	12	5	7	8	1	7	3	10	2	12
Michigan	5	5	—	1	4	—	5	—	5	5
Mississippi	6	6	—	—	6	—	6	6	—	6
Missouri	7	—	7	7	—	7	—	7	—	7
New Hampshire	6	—	6	6	—	2	—	6	—	6
New Jersey	7	7	—	3	2	—	4	2	5	7
New York	36	—	38	36	—	36	—	35	—	36
North Carolina	11	5	—	2	4	—	7	11	—	11
Ohio	23	—	23	23	—	20	3	18	2	23
Pennsylvania	26	12	13	26	—	16	—	19	7	26
Rhode Island	4	2	2	4	—	1	1	4	—	4
Tennessee	13	13	—	—	13	—	13	13	—	13
Vermont	6	3	3	5	1	—	6	—	6	6
Virginia	17	17	—	—	17	—	17	17	—	17
Total	266	148	118	146	83	103	107	231	29	266

1. Other candidates: Richard M. Johnson, 24; John C. Calhoun, 6; James Buchanan, 4; Levi Woodbury, 2; Commodore Stewart, 1.
2. Other candidates: Johnson, 29; Buchanan, 26, not voting, 1.
3. Not voting, 6.

1844 Whig
(Narrative, p. 25)

Delegation	Total Votes	First Pres. Ballot Clay		Delegation	Total Votes	First Pres. Ballot Clay
Alabama	9	9		Missouri	7	7
Arkansas	3	3		New Hampshire	6	6
Connecticut	6	6		New Jersey	7	7
Delaware	3	3		New York	36	36
Georgia	10	10		North Carolina	11	11
Illinois	9	9		Ohio	23	23
Indiana	12	12		Pennsylvania	26	26
Kentucky	12	12		Rhode Island	4	4
Louisiana	6	6		South Carolina	9	9
Maine	9	9		Tennessee	13	13
Maryland	8	8		Vermont	6	6
Massachusetts	12	12		Virginia	17	17
Michigan	5	5		**Total**	**275**	**275**
Mississippi	6	6				

1848 Democratic
(Narrative, p. 27)

Delegation	Total Votes	Adoption of Two-Thirds Rule			Amendment on N.Y. Credentials			First Pres. Ballot[1]			Fourth Pres. Ballot[2]		
		Yea	Nay	Not Voting	Yea	Nay	Not Voting	Cass	Buchanan	Woodbury	Cass	Buchanan	Woodbury
Alabama	9	9	—	—	—	9	—	—	4	5	—	4	5
Arkansas	3	3	—	—	—	3	—	3	—	—	3	—	—
Connecticut	6	6	—	—	6	—	—	—	—	6	—	—	6
Delaware	3	2	1	—	1	2	—	3	—	—	3	—	—
Florida	3	3	—	—	—	3	—	—	—	—	—	—	3
Georgia	10	10	—	—	—	10	—	—	2	5	10	—	—
Illinois	9	9	—	—	9	—	—	9	—	—	9	—	—
Indiana	12	3	9	—	7	5	—	12	—	—	12	—	—
Iowa	4	4	—	—	4	—	—	1	3	—	4	—	—
Kentucky	12	12	—	—	10	2	—	7	1	1	8	1	1
Louisiana	6	6	—	—	—	6	—	6	—	—	6	—	—
Maine	9	9	—	—	9	—	—	—	—	9	—	—	9
Maryland	8	7	1	—	2	5	1	6	—	2	6	—	2
Massachusetts	12	10	2	—	11	1	—	—	—	12	8	—	4
Michigan	5	5	—	—	—	5	—	5	—	—	5	—	—
Mississippi	6	6	—	—	—	6	—	6	—	—	6	—	—
Missouri	7	1	6	—	1	4	2	7	—	—	7	—	—
New Hampshire	6	6	—	—	6	—	—	—	—	6	—	—	6
New Jersey	7	7	—	—	7	—	—	—	7	—	7	—	—
New York	36	—	—	36	—	—	36	—	—	—	—	—	—
North Carolina	11	11	—	—	—	11	—	—	10	1	11	—	—
Ohio	23	—	23	—	14	9	—	23	—	—	23	—	—
Pennsylvania	26	—	26	—	19	7	—	—	26	—	—	26	—
Rhode Island	4	3	1	—	2	2	—	1	—	3	4	—	—
South Carolina	9	9	—	—	—	9	—	—	—	—	9	—	—
Tennessee	13	13	—	—	9	4	—	7	2	1	7	2	2
Texas	4	4	—	—	4	—	—	4	—	—	4	—	—
Vermont	6	1	5	—	5	1	—	4	—	2	6	—	—
Virginia	17	17	—	—	—	17	—	17	—	—	17	—	—
Wisconsin	4	—	4	—	—	4	—	4	—	—	4	—	—
Total	**290**	**176**	**78**	**36**	**126**	**125**	**39**	**125**	**55**	**53**	**179**	**33**	**38**

1. Other candidates: John C. Calhoun, 9; W. J. Worth, 6; George M. Dallas, 3; not voting, 39.

2. Other candidates: William O. Butler, 4; Worth, 1; not voting, 35.

1848 Whig

(Narrative. p. 28)

		First Pres. Ballot[1]			Fourth Pres. Ballot[2]		
Delegation	Total Votes	Taylor	Clay	Scott	Taylor	Clay	Scott
Alabama	7	6	1	—	6	1	—
Arkansas	3	3	—	—	3	—	—
Connecticut	6	—	6	—	3	3	—
Delaware	3	—	—	—	2	—	1
Florida	3	3	—	—	3	—	—
Georgia	10	10	—	—	10	—	—
Illinois	8	4	3	1	8	—	—
Indiana	12	1	2	9	7	1	4
Iowa	4	2	1	—	4	—	—
Kentucky	12	7	5	—	11	1	—
Louisiana	6	5	1	—	6	—	—
Maine	9	5	1	—	5	—	3
Maryland	8	—	8	—	8	—	—
Massachusetts	12	—	—	—	1	—	2
Michigan	5	—	3	2	2	—	3
Mississippi	6	6	—	—	6	—	—
Missouri	7	6	—	—	7	—	—
New Hampshire	6	—	—	—	2	—	—
New Jersey	7	3	4	—	4	3	—
New York	36	—	29	5	6	13	17
North Carolina	11	6	5	—	10	1	—
Ohio	23	1	1	20	1	1	21
Pennsylvania	26	8	12	6	12	4	10
Rhode Island	4	—	4	—	4	—	—
South Carolina	2	1	1	—	1	1	—
Tennessee	13	13	—	—	13	—	—
Texas	4	4	—	—	4	—	—
Vermont	6	1	5	—	2	2	2
Virginia	17	15	2	—	16	1	—
Wisconsin	4	1	3	—	4	—	—
Total	**280**	**111**	**97**	**43**	**171**	**32**	**63**

1. Other candidates: Daniel Webster, 22; John McLean, 2; John M. Clayton, 4.
2. Other candidate: Webster, 14.

1852 Democratic

(Narrative, p. 29)

Delegation	Total Votes	First Pres. Ballot[1]		Twentieth Pres. Ballot[2]			Thirtieth Pres. Ballot[3]			Thirty-Fifth Pres. Ballot[4]				Forty-Eighth Pres. Ballot[5]				Forty-ninth Pres. Ballot[6]
		Cass	Buchanan	Buchanan	Cass	Douglas	Douglas	Buchanan	Cass	Cass	Douglas	Marcy	Buchanan	Marcy	Cass	Pierce	Douglas	Pierce
Alabama	9	—	9	9	—	—	—	9	—	—	—	—	9	9	—	—	—	9
Arkansas	4	—	4	—	—	4	4	—	—	—	4	—	—	—	—	—	4	4
California	4	—	—	1	—	3	3	1	—	2	1	—	1	—	4	—	—	4
Connecticut	6	2	2	2	2	1	6	—	—	3	3	—	—	6	—	—	—	6
Delaware	3	3	—	—	3	—	—	—	—	3	—	—	—	—	3	—	—	3
Florida	3	—	—	—	—	2	2	—	—	—	2	—	—	—	—	—	2	3
Georgia	10	—	10	10	—	—	—	10	—	—	10	—	—	10	—	—	—	10
Illinois	11	—	—	—	11	11	11	—	—	—	11	—	—	—	—	—	11	11
Indiana	13	—	—	—	—	—	—	—	—	13	—	—	—	—	13	—	—	13
Iowa	4	2	—	—	1	3	4	—	—	2	2	—	—	—	2	—	2	4
Kentucky	12	12	—	—	12	—	—	—	—	12	—	—	—	—	—	12	—	12
Louisiana	6	6	—	—	6	—	6	—	—	6	—	—	—	—	6	—	—	6
Maine	8	5	3	1	4	3	5	2	—	2	5	—	1	—	—	8	—	8
Maryland	8	8	—	—	8	—	—	—	8	8	—	—	—	1	1	5	—	5
Massachusetts	13	9	—	—	1	7	7	—	1	7	1	5	—	6	—	6	1	13
Michigan	6	6	—	—	6	—	—	—	6	6	—	—	—	—	6	—	—	6
Mississippi	7	—	7	7	—	—	—	7	—	—	—	7	—	7	—	—	—	7
Missouri	9	9	—	—	—	9	9	—	—	9	—	—	—	—	9	—	—	9
New Hampshire	5	4	—	—	5	—	—	2	—	5	—	—	—	—	—	5	—	5
New Jersey	7	7	—	7	—	—	—	7	—	7	—	—	—	7	—	—	—	7
New York	35	11	—	—	12	—	1	—	11	12	1	22	—	24	10	—	1	35
North Carolina	10	—	10	9	—	1	4	6	—	—	—	10	—	10	—	—	—	10
Ohio	23	16	—	—	13	6	9	—	7	18	3	—	—	—	15	—	4	17
Pennsylvania	27	—	27	27	—	—	—	27	—	—	—	—	27	—	—	—	—	27
Rhode Island	4	3	—	—	—	4	4	—	—	4	—	—	—	—	—	4	—	4
Tennessee	12	6	6	4	5	3	7	5	—	9	2	—	1	9	—	—	1	12
Texas	4	—	—	—	—	—	—	—	—	—	—	—	—	—	—	—	—	4
Vermont	5	5	—	—	—	5	5	—	—	—	5	—	—	—	—	—	5	5
Virginia	15	—	15	15	—	—	—	15	—	—	—	—	—	—	—	15	—	15
Wisconsin	5	2	—	—	3	2	5	—	—	3	2	—	—	—	3	—	2	5
Total	288	116	93	92	81	64	92	91	33	131	52	44	39	89	72	55	33	279[a]

a. Sum of column; proceedings record 283.
1. Other candidates: William L. Marcy, 27; Stephen A. Douglas, 20; Joseph Lane, 13; Samuel Houston, 8; J. B. Weller, 4; Henry Dodge, 3; William O. Butler, 2; Daniel S. Dickinson, 1; not voting, 1.
2. Other candidates: Marcy, 26; Lane, 13; Houston, 10; Butler, 1; Dickinson, 1.
3. Other candidates: Marcy, 26; Butler, 20; Lane, 13; Houston, 12; Dickinson, 1.
4. Other candidates: Franklin Pierce, 15; Houston, 5; Butler, 1; Dickinson, 1.
5. Other candidates: Buchanan, 28; Houston, 6; Linn Boyd, 2; Butler, 1; R. J. Ingersoll, 1; Dickinson, 1.
6. Other candidates: Cass, 2; Douglas, 2; Butler, 1; Houston, 1; not voting, 3.

1852 Whig

(Narrative. p. 30)

Delegation	Total Votes	First Pres. Ballot			50th Pres. Ballot			52nd Pres. Ballot			53rd Pres. Ballot		
		Scott	Fillmore	Webster	Scott	Fillmore	Webster	Scott	Fillmore	Webster	Scott	Fillmore	Webster
Alabama	9	—	9	—	—	9	—	—	9	—	—	9	—
Arkansas	4	—	4	—	—	4	—	—	4	—	—	4	—
California	4	2	1	1	3	1	—	3	—	1	3	—	1
Connecticut	6	2	1	3	2	1	3	2	1	3	2	1	3
Delaware	3	3	—	—	3	—	—	3	—	—	3	—	—
Florida	3	—	3	—	—	3	—	—	3	—	—	3	—
Georgia	10	—	10	—	—	10	—	—	10	—	—	10	—
Illinois	11	11	—	—	11	—	—	11	—	—	11	—	—
Indiana	13	13	—	—	13	—	—	13	—	—	13	—	—
Iowa	4	—	4	—	1	3	—	1	3	—	1	3	—
Kentucky	12	—	12	—	—	12	—	—	12	—	—	11	—
Louisiana	6	—	6	—	—	6	—	—	6	—	—	6	—
Maine	8	8	—	—	8	—	—	8	—	—	8	—	—
Maryland	8	—	8	—	—	8	—	—	8	—	—	8	—
Massachusetts	13	2	—	11	2	—	11	2	—	11	2	—	11
Michigan	6	6	—	—	6	—	—	6	—	—	6	—	—
Mississippi	7	—	7	—	—	7	—	—	7	—	—	7	—
Missouri	9	—	9	—	3	6	—	1	6	—	3	6	—
New Hampshire	5	1	—	4	1	—	4	1	—	4	5	—	—
New Jersey	7	7	—	—	7	—	—	7	—	—	7	—	—
New York	35	24	7	2	25	7	1	25	7	1	25	7	1
North Carolina	10	—	10	—	—	10	—	—	10	—	—	10	—
Ohio	23	22	1	—	23	—	—	23	—	—	23	—	—
Pennsylvania	27	26	1	—	26	1	—	27	—	—	27	—	—
Rhode Island	4	1	1	2	2	—	2	2	—	2	3	—	1
South Carolina	8	—	8	—	—	8	—	—	8	—	—	8	—
Tennessee	12	—	12	—	—	12	—	4	8	—	3	9	—
Texas	4	—	4	—	—	4	—	—	4	—	—	4	—
Vermont	5	1	1	3	2	—	3	2	2	1	5	—	—
Virginia	15	1	13	—	3	10	—	3	10	—	8	6	—
Wisconsin	5	1	1	3	1	1	3	2	—	2	1	—	4
Total	296	132[a]	133	29	142	122[a]	27	148[a]	118	25	159	112	21

a. The sum of the column for Scott on the first ballot is 131 votes, for Fillmore on the 50th ballot 123 votes and for Scott on the 52nd ballot is 146 votes. The source for these discrepancies is the Baltimore Sun for June 19, 1852 and June 22, 1852. The Sun reported June 19, 1852, total votes for Scott on the first ballot as 132 votes; however, the column of figures for the state-by-state ballots reported in the Sun add up to 131 votes. Similarly, on June 22, 1852 the Sun reported 122 votes for Fillmore on the 50th ballot and 148 for Scott on the 52nd ballot, but the state-by-state ballots reported in the Sun add up to 123 votes and 146 votes, respectively. Bain's *Convention Decisions and Voting Records* used the Baltimore Sun as its source for the 1852 Whig convention ballots.

1856 Democratic

(Narrative. p. 33)

Delegation	Total Votes	First Pres. Ballot Buchanan	Pierce	Douglas	Other	Tenth Pres. Ballot Buchanan	Pierce	Douglas	Other	Fifteenth Pres. Ballot Buchanan	Douglas	Other	17th Pres. Ballot Buchanan
Alabama	9	—	9	—	—	—	9	—	—	—	9	—	9
Arkansas	4	—	4	—	—	—	—	4	—	—	4	—	4
California	4	—	—	—	4	—	—	—	4	—	—	4	4
Connecticut	3	6	—	—	—	6	—	—	—	6	—	—	6
Delaware	3	3	—	—	—	3	—	—	—	3	—	—	3
Florida	3	—	3	—	—	—	3	—	—	—	3	—	3
Georgia	10	—	10	—	—	3	—	7	—	3	7	—	10
Illinois	11	—	—	11	—	—	—	11	—	—	11	—	11
Indiana	13	13	—	—	—	13	—	—	—	13	—	—	13
Iowa	4	—	—	4	—	2	—	2	—	2	2	—	4
Kentucky	12	4	5	3	—	4½	—	7½	—	4	7	1	12
Louisiana	6	6	—	—	—	6	—	—	—	6	—	—	6
Maine	8	5	3	—	—	6	2	—	—	7	—	1	8
Maryland	8	6	2	—	—	7	1	—	—	8	—	—	8
Massachusetts	13	4	9	—	—	6	7	—	—	10	3	—	13
Michigan	6	6	—	—	—	6	—	—	—	6	—	—	6
Mississippi	7	—	7	—	—	—	7	—	—	—	7	—	7
Missouri	9	—	—	9	—	—	—	9	—	—	9	—	9
New Hampshire	5	—	5	—	—	—	5	—	—	—	5	—	5
New Jersey	7	7	—	—	—	7	—	—	—	7	—	—	7
New York	35	17	18	—	—	18	17	—	—	17	18	—	35
North Carolina	10	—	10	—	—	—	10	—	—	—	10	—	10
Ohio	23	13½	4½	4	1	13	3½	5	1½	13½	6½	3	23
Pennsylvania	27	27	—	—	—	27	—	—	—	27	—	—	27
Rhode Island	4	—	4	—	—	—	4	—	—	4	—	—	4
South Carolina	8	—	8	—	—	—	8	—	—	—	8	—	8
Tennessee	12	—	12	—	—	—	12	—	—	12	—	—	12
Texas	4	—	4	—	—	—	4	—	—	—	4	—	4
Vermont	5	—	5	—	—	—	5	—	—	—	5	—	5
Virginia	15	15	—	—	—	15	—	—	—	15	—	—	15
Wisconsin	5	3	—	2	—	5	—	—	—	5	—	—	5
Total	**296**	**135½**	**122½**	**33**	**5**[1]	**147½**	**80½**	**62½**	**5½**[2]	**168½**	**118½**	**9**[3]	**296**

1. Other candidate: Lewis Cass, 5.
2. Other candidate: Cass, 5½.
3. Other candidates: Cass, 4½; Pierce, 3½; not voting, 1.

1856 Republican

(Narrative. p. 32)

Delegation	Total Votes	Informal Pres. Ballot[1] Fremont	McLean	Formal Pres. Ballot[2] Fremont	Delegation	Total Votes	Informal Pres. Ballot[1] Fremont	McLean	Formal Pres. Ballot[2] Fremont
California	12	12	—	12	Minnesota	2	—	—	—
Connecticut	18	18	—	18	New Hampshire	15	15	—	15
Delaware	9	—	9	9	New Jersey	21	7	14	21
Illinois	34	14	19	33	New York	105	93	3	105
Indiana	39	18	21	39	Ohio	69	30	39	55
Iowa	12	12	—	12	Pennsylvania	81	10	71	57
Kansas	10	9	—	9	Rhode Island	12	12	—	12
Kentucky	5	5	—	5	Vermont	15	15	—	15
Maine	24	13	11	24	Wisconsin	15	15	—	15
Maryland	9	4	3	7	District of Columbia	3	—	—	—
Massachusetts	39	39	—	39	**Total**	**567**	**359**	**190**	**520**
Michigan	18	18	—	18					

1. Other candidates: Nathaniel Banks, 1; Charles Sumner, 2; William Seward, 1; absent or not voting, 14.
2. Other candidates: John McLean, 37; Seward, 1; absent or not voting, 9.

1860 Democratic

(Narrative, p. 35)

Charleston Convention · Baltimore Convention

Delegation	Total Votes	Butler Amend. on 1856 platform Yea	Nay	Minority Report on platform Yea	Nay	First Pres. Ballot[1] Douglas	Hunter	Guthrie	57th Pres. Ballot[2] Douglas	Guthrie	Minority Report on Credentials Yea	Nay	Not Voting	Reconsider Louisiana Credentials Yea	Nay	Not Voting	First Pres. Ballot[3] Douglas	Second Pres. Ballot[4] Douglas
Alabama	9	—	9	—	9	—	—	—	—	—	—	—	9	—	—	9	9	9
Arkansas	4	—	4	—	4	—	1	—	—	—	½	½	3	½	½	3	1	1½
California	4	—	4	—	4	—	—	—	—	—	4	—	—	—	4	—	—	—
Connecticut	6	2½	3½	6	—	3½	—	—	3½	2½	2½	3½	—	3½	2½	—	3½	3½
Delaware	3	3	—	—	3	—	2	—	—	—	2	—	1	—	2	1	—	—
Florida	3	—	3	—	3	—	—	—	—	—	—	—	3	—	—	3	—	—
Georgia	10	10	—	—	10	—	—	—	—	—	—	—	10	—	—	10	—	—
Illinois	11	—	11	11	—	11	—	—	11	—	—	11	—	11	—	—	11	11
Indiana	13	—	13	13	—	13	—	—	13	—	—	13	—	13	—	—	13	13
Iowa	4	—	4	4	—	4	—	—	4	—	—	4	—	4	—	—	4	4
Kentucky	12	9	3	2½	9½	—	—	12	—	12	10	2	—	2	10	—	—	3
Louisiana	6	—	6	—	6	—	—	—	—	—	—	—	6	—	—	6	6	6
Maine	8	3	5	8	—	5	—	3	5	3	2½	5½	—	5½	2½	—	5½	7
Maryland	8	5½	2½	3½	4½	2	5	—	4	4	5½	2	½	2	6	—	2½	2½
Massachusetts	13	8	5	7	6	5½	6	—	6	6	8	5	—	5	8	—	10	10
Michigan	6	—	6	6	—	6	—	—	6	—	—	6	—	6	—	—	6	6
Minnesota	4	1½	2½	4	—	4	—	—	3	—	1½	2½	—	2½	1½	—	2½	4
Mississippi	7	—	7	—	7	—	—	—	—	—	—	—	7	—	—	7	—	—
Missouri	9	4½	4½	4	5	4½	—	4½	4½	4½	5	4	—	4½	4½	—	4½	4½
New Hampshire	5	—	5	5	—	5	—	—	5	—	½	4½	—	4½	½	—	5	5
New Jersey	7	5	2	5	2	—	—	7	2	5	4	3	—	2½	4½	—	2½	2½
New York	35	—	35	35	—	35	—	—	35	—	—	35	—	35	—	—	35	35
North Carolina	10	10	—	—	10	1	9	—	1	—	9	1	—	1	8½	½	1	1
Ohio	23	—	23	23	—	23	—	—	23	—	—	23	—	23	—	—	23	23
Oregon	3	3	—	—	3	—	—	—	—	—	3	—	—	—	3	—	—	—
Pennsylvania	27	16½	10½	12	15	9	3	9	9½	17½	17	10	—	10	17	—	10	19
Rhode Island	4	—	4	4	—	4	—	—	4	—	—	4	—	4	—	—	4	4
South Carolina	8	—	8	—	8	—	1	—	—	—	—	—	8	—	—	8	—	—
Tennessee	12	11	1	1	11	—	—	—	1	11	10	1	1	2	10	—	3	3
Texas	4	—	4	—	4	—	—	—	—	—	—	—	4	—	—	4	—	—
Vermont	5	—	5	5	—	5	—	—	5	—	1½	3½	—	4½	½	—	5	5
Virginia	15	12½	2½	1	14	—	15	—	1	—	14	1	—	—	15	—	1½	3
Wisconsin	5	—	5	5	—	5	—	—	5	—	—	5	—	5	—	—	5	5
Total	**303**	**105**	**198**	**165**	**138**	**145½**	**42**	**35½[a]**	**151½**	**65½**	**100½**	**150**	**52½**	**151[b]**	**100½[c]**	**51½**	**173½**	**190½[d]**

a. Sum of column; proceedings record 35.
b. Sum of column; proceedings record 150½.
c. Sum of column, proceedings record 99.
d. Sum of column; proceedings record 181½.

1. Other candidates: Andrew Johnson, 12; Daniel S. Dickenson, 7; Joseph Lane, 6; Isaac Toucey, 2½; Jefferson Davis, 1½; James A. Pearce, 1; not voting, 50.

2. Other candidates: Robert M. T. Hunter, 16; Lane, 14; Dickinson, 4; Davis, 1; not voting, 51.

3. Other candidates: James Guthrie, 9; John C. Breckinridge, 5; Thomas S. Bocock, 1; Horatio Seymour, 1; Henry A. Wise, ½; Dickinson, ½; not voting 112½.

4. Other candidates: Breckinridge, 7½; Guthrie, 5½; not voting, 99½.

1860 Republican

(Narrative, p. 36)

Delegation	Total Votes	First Pres. Ballot [1]					Second Pres. Ballot [2]		Third Pres. Ballot [3] (Before shift)		Third Pres. Ballot [4] (After shift)	
		Seward	Lincoln	Cameron	Bates	Chase	Seward	Lincoln	Seward	Lincoln	Seward	Lincoln
California	8	8	—	—	—	—	8	—	8	—	3	5
Connecticut	12	—	2	—	7	2	—	4	1	4	1	8
Delaware	6	—	—	—	6	—	—	6	—	6	—	6
Illinois	22	—	22	—	—	—	—	22	—	22	—	22
Indiana	26	—	26	—	—	—	—	26	—	26	—	26
Iowa	8	2	2	1	1	1	2	5	2	5½	—	8
Kansas	6	6	—	—	—	—	6	—	6	—	—	6
Kentucky	23	5	6	—	—	8	7	9	6	13	—	23
Maine	16	10	6	—	—	—	10	6	10	6	—	16
Maryland	11	3	—	—	8	—	3	—	2	9	2	9
Massachusetts	26	21	4	—	—	—	22	4	18	8	18	8
Michigan	12	12	—	—	—	—	12	—	12	—	12	—
Minnesota	8	8	—	—	—	—	8	—	8	—	—	8
Missouri	18	—	—	—	18	—	—	—	—	—	—	18
Nebraska	6	2	1	1	—	2	3	1	3	1	—	6
New Hampshire	10	—	—	—	—	1	1	9	1	9	—	10
New Jersey	14	1	7	—	—	—	4	—	5	8	5	8
New York	70	70	—	—	—	—	70	—	70	—	70	—
Ohio	46	—	8	—	—	34	—	14	—	29	—	46
Oregon	5	—	—	—	5	—	—	—	1	4	—	5
Pennsylvania	54	1½	4	47½	—	—	2½	48	—	52	½	53
Rhode Island	8	—	—	—	1	1	—	3	1	5	—	8
Texas	6	4	—	—	2	—	6	—	6	—	—	6
Vermont	10	—	—	—	—	—	—	10	—	10	—	10
Virginia	23	8	14	1	—	—	8	14	8	14	—	23
Wisconsin	10	10	—	—	—	—	10	—	10	—	10	—
District of Columbia	2	2	—	—	—	—	2	—	2	—	—	2
Total	466	173½	102	50½	48	49	184½	181	180	231½	121½	340 [a]

a. *Sum of column; proceedings record 364.*
1. *Other candidates: Benjamin F. Wade, 3; John McLean, 12; John M. Reed, 1; William L. Dayton, 14; Charles Sumner, 1; John C. Fremont, 1; Jacob Collamer, 10; absent and not voting, 1.*
2. *Other candidates: Edward Bates, 35; Simon Cameron, 2; John McLean, 8; Salmon P. Chase, 42½; William L. Dayton, 10; Cassius M. Clay, 2; absent and not voting, 1.*
3. *Other candidates: Edward Bates, 22; Salmon P. Chase, 24½; John McLean, 5; William L. Dayton, 1; Cassius M. Clay, 1; absent and not voting, 1.*
4. *Other candidates: Salmon P. Chase, 2; Dayton, 1; Cassius M. Clay, 1; McLean, ½.*

1864 Democratic

(Narrative. p. 39)

Delegation	Total Votes	First Pres. Ballot[1] (Before shift)		First Pres. Ballot (After shift)	
		McClellan	Seymour	McClellan	Seymour
California	5	2½	2½	5	—
Connecticut	6	5½	—	6	—
Delaware	3	—	3	—	3
Illinois	16	16	—	16	—
Indiana	13	9½	3½	9½	3½
Iowa	8	3	—	8	—
Kansas	3	3	—	3	—
Kentucky	11	5½	5½	11	—
Maine	7	4	3	7	—
Maryland	7	—	7	—	7
Massachusetts	12	11½	—	12	—
Michigan	8	6½	—	8	—
Minnesota	4	4	—	4	—
Missouri	11	6½	—	7	4
New Hampshire	5	5	—	5	—
New Jersey	7	7	—	7	—
New York	33	33	—	33	—
Ohio	21	8½	10½	15	6
Oregon	3	2	1	3	—
Pennsylvania	26	26	—	26	—
Rhode Island	4	4	—	4	—
Vermont	5	4	1	5	—
Wisconsin	8	7	1	8	—
Total	226	174	38	202½	23½ [a]

1. Other candidates: Horatio Seymour, 12; Charles O'Connor, ½; blank, 1½.
a. Sum of column; proceedings record 28½.

1864 Republican

(Narrative. p. 38)

Delegation	Total Votes	First Pres. Ballot[1]	
		Lincoln	Grant
Arkansas	10	10	—
California	10	7	—
Colorado	6	6	—
Connecticut	12	12	—
Delaware	6	6	—
Illinois	32	32	—
Indiana	26	26	—
Iowa	16	16	—
Kansas	6	6	—
Kentucky	22	22	—
Louisiana	14	14	—
Maine	14	14	—
Maryland	14	14	—
Massachusetts	24	24	—
Michigan	16	16	—
Minnesota	8	8	—
Missouri	22	—	22
Nebraska	6	6	—
Nevada	6	6	—
New Hampshire	10	10	—
New Jersey	14	14	—
New York	66	66	—
Ohio	42	42	—
Oregon	6	6	—
Pennsylvania	52	52	—
Rhode Island	8	8	—
Tennessee	15	15	—
Vermont	10	10	—
West Virginia	10	10	—
Wisconsin	16	16	—
Total	519	494 [b]	22

1. Not voting, 3.
b. Sum of column; proceedings record 484.

1868 Democratic

(Narrative, p. 41)

Delegation	Total Votes	First Pres. Ballot[1]				22nd Pres. Ballot[2] (Before shift)		22nd Pres. Ballot (After shift)
		Pendleton	Hancock	Church	Johnson	Hancock	Hendricks	Seymour
Alabama	8	—	—	—	8	8	—	8
Arkansas	5	—	—	—	—	—	5	5
California	5	2	—	—	—	—	5	5
Connecticut	6	—	—	—	—	—	—	6
Delaware	3	3	—	—	—	3	—	3
Florida	3	—	—	—	3	—	3	3
Georgia	9	—	—	—	9	9	—	9
Illinois	16	16	—	—	—	—	16	16
Indiana	13	13	—	—	—	—	13	13
Iowa	8	8	—	—	—	—	8	8
Kansas	3	2	—	—	—	1	2	3
Kentucky	11	11	—	—	—	—	—	11
Louisiana	7	—	7	—	—	7	—	7
Maine	7	1½	4½	—	1	4½	2½	7
Maryland	7	4½	—	—	2½	6	1	7
Massachusetts	12	1	11	—	—	—	—	12
Michigan	8	—	—	—	—	—	8	8
Minnesota	4	4	—	—	—	—	4	4
Mississippi	7	—	7	—	—	7	—	7
Missouri	11	5	2	1	½	2	8	11
Nebraska	3	3	—	—	—	—	3	3
Nevada	3	—	—	—	—	—	3	3
New Hampshire	5	2	2	—	—	4½	½	5
New Jersey	7	—	—	—	—	—	7	7
New York	33	—	—	33	—	—	33	33
North Carolina	9	—	—	—	9	—	9	9
Ohio	21	21	—	—	—	—	—	21
Oregon	3	3	—	—	—	—	3	3
Pennsylvania	26	—	—	—	—	26	—	26
Rhode Island	4	—	—	—	—	—	—	4
South Carolina	6	—	—	—	6	6	—	6
Tennessee	10	—	—	—	10	3½	1½	10
Texas	6	—	—	—	6	6	—	6
Vermont	5	—	—	—	—	—	5	5
Virginia	10	—	—	—	10	10	—	10
West Virginia	5	5	—	—	—	—	5	5
Wisconsin	8	—	—	—	—	—	—	8
Total	317	105	33½	34	65	103½	145½	317

1. Other candidates: James E. English, 16; Joel Parker, 13; Asa Packer, 26; James R. Doolittle, 13; Thomas A. Hendricks, 2½; Frank P. Blair, ½; Reverdy Johnson, 8½.

2. Other candidates: Horatio Seymour, 22; English, 7; Doolittle, 4; Johnson, 4; not voting, 31.

1868 Republican

(Narrative, p. 40)

Delegation	Total Votes	First Pres. Ballot Grant	Delegation	Total Votes	First Pres. Ballot Grant	Delegation	Total Votes	First Pres Ballot Grant
Alabama	18	18	Maine	14	14	Ohio	42	42
Arkansas	10	10	Maryland	14	14	Oregon	6	6
California	10	10	Massachusetts	24	24	Pennsylvania	52	52
Colorado	6	6	Michigan	16	16	Rhode Island	8	8
Connecticut	12	12	Minnesota	8	8	South Carolina	12	12
Delaware	6	6	Mississippi	14	14	Tennessee	20	20
Florida	6	6	Missouri	22	22	Texas	12	12
Georgia	18	18	Montana	2	2	Vermont	10	10
Idaho	2	2	Nebraska	6	6	Virginia	20	20
Illinois	32	32	Nevada	6	6	West Virginia	10	10
Indiana	26	26	New Hampshire	10	10	Wisconsin	16	16
Iowa	16	16	New Jersey	14	14	District of Columbia	2	2
Kansas	6	6	New York	66	66			
Kentucky	22	22	North Carolina	18	18	Total	650	650
Louisiana	14	14	North Dakota[a]	2	2			

a. Dakota Territory, includes North and South Dakota.

1872 Democratic

(Narrative, p. 43)

Delegation	Total Votes	First Pres. Ballot[1] Greeley
Alabama	20	20
Arkansas	12	12
California	12	12
Connecticut	12	12
Delaware	6	—
Florida	8	6
Georgia	22	18
Illinois	42	42
Indiana	30	30
Iowa	22	22
Kansas	10	10
Kentucky	24	24
Louisiana	16	16
Maine	14	14
Maryland	16	16
Massachusetts	26	26
Michigan	22	22
Minnesota	10	10
Mississippi	16	16
Missouri	30	30
Nebraska	6	6
Nevada	6	6
New Hampshire	10	10
New Jersey	18	9
New York	70	70
North Carolina	20	20
Ohio	44	44
Oregon	6	6
Pennsylvania	58	35
Rhode Island	8	8
South Carolina	14	14
Tennessee	24	24
Texas	16	16
Vermont	10	10
Virginia	22	22
West Virginia	10	8
Wisconsin	20	20
Total	**732**	**686**

1. Other candidates: Thomas F. Bayard, 15; Jeremiah S. Black, 21; William S. Groesbeck, 2; blank, 8.

1872 Republican

(Narrative, p. 43)

Delegation	Total Votes	First Pres. Ballot Grant
Alabama	20	20
Arizona	2	2
Arkansas	12	12
California	12	12
Colorado	2	2
Connecticut	12	12
Delaware	6	6
Florida	8	8
Georgia	22	22
Idaho	2	2
Illinois	42	42
Indiana	30	30
Iowa	22	22
Kansas	10	10
Kentucky	24	24
Louisiana	16	16
Maine	14	14
Maryland	16	16
Massachusetts	26	26
Michigan	22	22
Minnesota	10	10
Mississippi	16	16
Missouri	30	30
Montana	2	2
Nebraska	6	6
Nevada	6	6
New Hampshire	10	10
New Jersey	18	18
New Mexico	2	2
New York	70	70
North Carolina	20	20
North Dakota [a]	2	2
Ohio	44	44
Oregon	6	6
Pennsylvania	58	58
Rhode Island	8	8
South Carolina	14	14
Tennessee	24	24
Texas	16	16
Utah	2	2
Vermont	10	10
Virginia	22	22
Washington	2	2
West Virginia	10	10
Wisconsin	20	20
Wyoming	2	2
District of Columbia	2	2
Total	**752**	**752**

a. Dakota Territory, includes North and South Dakota.

1876 Democratic

(Narrative. p. 45)

Delegation	Total Votes	First Pres. Ballot[1]			Second Pres. Ballot[2]	
		Tilden	Hendricks	Hancock	Tilden	Hendricks
Alabama	20	13	5	2	20	—
Arkansas	12	12	—	—	12	—
California	12	12	—	—	12	—
Colorado	6	—	6	—	6	—
Connecticut	12	12	—	—	12	—
Delaware	6	—	—	—	6	—
Florida	8	8	—	—	8	—
Georgia	22	5	—	1	22	—
Illinois	42	19	23	—	26	16
Indiana	30	—	30	—	—	30
Iowa	22	14	6	2	22	—
Kansas	10	—	10	—	2	8
Kentucky	24	24	—	5	24	—
Louisiana	16	9	—	5	16	—
Maine	14	14	—	—	14	—
Maryland	16	11	3	—	14	2
Massachusetts	26	26	—	—	26	—
Michigan	22	14	8	—	19	3
Minnesota	10	10	—	—	10	—
Mississippi	16	16	—	—	16	—
Missouri	30	—	14	—	30	—
Nebraska	6	6	—	—	6	—
Nevada	6	3	3	—	4	—
New Hampshire	10	10	—	—	10	—
New Jersey	18	—	—	—	18	—
New York	70	70	—	—	70	—
North Carolina	20	9	4	5	20	—
Ohio	44	—	—	—	—	—
Oregon	6	6	—	—	6	—
Pennsylvania	58	—	—	58	—	—
Rhode Island	8	8	—	—	8	—
South Carolina	14	14	—	—	14	—
Tennessee	24	—	24	—	—	24
Texas	16	10½	2½	2	16	—
Vermont	10	10	—	—	10	—
Virginia	22	17	1	—	17	1
West Virginia	10	—	—	—	—	—
Wisconsin	20	19	1	—	19	1
Total	738	401½ [a]	140½	75	535	85

a. Sum of column; proceedings record 404½.
1. Other candidates: William Allen, 54; Allen G. Thurman, 3; Thomas F. Bayard, 33; Joel Parker, 18; James O. Broadhead, 16.
2. Other candidates: Allen, 54; Bayard, 4; Hancock, 58; Thurman, 2.

1876 Republican

(Narrative. p. 44)

Delegation	Total Votes	First Pres. Ballot[1] Blaine	Morton	Conkling	Bristow	Abolish Unit Rule Yea	Nay	Not Voting	Fifth Pres. Ballot[2] Blaine	Bristow	Conkling	Hayes	Morton	Sixth Pres. Ballot[3] Blaine	Morton	Conkling	Bristow	Hayes	Seventh Pres. Ballot[4] Blaine	Hayes
Ala.	20	10	—	—	7	20	—	—	16	4	—	—	—	15	—	—	4	1	17	—
Ariz.	2	2	—	—	—	2	—	—	2	—	—	—	—	2	—	—	—	—	2	—
Ark.	12	—	12	—	—	4	8	—	1	—	—	—	11	1	11	—	—	—	11	1
Calif.	12	9	—	1	2	11	1	—	6	—	3	3	—	6	—	2	—	4	6	6
Colo.	6	6	—	—	—	6	—	—	6	—	—	—	—	6	—	—	—	—	6	—
Conn.	12	—	—	—	2	3	9	—	2	8	—	2	—	2	—	—	7	3	2	3
Del.	6	6	—	—	—	5	1	—	6	—	—	—	—	6	—	—	—	—	6	—
Fla.	8	1	4	3	—	4	4	—	2	—	—	—	3	4	4	—	—	—	8	—
Ga.	22	5	6	8	3	9	13	—	8	2	6	—	5	9	4	6	2	—	14	7
Idaho	2	2	—	—	—	2	—	—	2	—	—	—	—	2	—	—	—	—	2	—
Ill.	42	38	—	—	3	38	4	—	33	5	—	3	—	32	—	—	5	3	35	2
Ind.	30	—	30	—	—	1	29	—	—	—	—	—	30	—	30	—	—	—	—	25
Iowa	22	22	—	—	—	22	—	—	21	—	1	—	—	21	—	—	—	1	22	—
Kan.	10	10	—	—	—	10	—	—	10	—	—	—	—	10	—	—	—	—	10	—
Ky.	24	—	—	—	24	1	23	—	—	24	—	—	—	—	—	—	24	—	—	24
La.	16	2	14	—	—	6	10	—	5	—	—	—	11	6	10	—	—	—	14	2
Maine	14	14	—	—	—	14	—	—	14	—	—	—	—	14	—	—	—	—	14	—
Md.	16	16	—	—	—	16	—	—	16	—	—	—	—	16	—	—	—	—	16	—
Mass.	26	6	—	—	17	15	7	4	5	19	—	—	—	5	—	—	19	—	5	21
Mich.	22	8	—	1	9	3	19	—	—	—	—	22	—	—	—	—	—	22	—	22
Minn.	10	10	—	—	—	7	3	—	9	—	—	—	—	9	—	—	—	—	9	1
Miss.	16	—	11	1	3	9	6	1	—	8	2	2	4	1	5	2	4	4	—	16
Mo.	30	14	12	1	2	25	5	—	20	3	—	2	5	18	7	—	3	2	20	10
Mont.	2	2	—	—	—	2	—	—	1	—	—	1	—	1	—	—	—	1	—	2
Neb.	6	6	—	—	—	6	—	—	6	—	—	—	—	6	—	—	—	—	6	—
Nev.	6	—	—	2	3	—	6	—	—	1	2	1	—	—	—	2	2	1	—	6
N.H.	10	7	—	—	3	10	—	—	7	3	—	—	—	7	—	—	3	—	7	3
N.J.	18	13	—	—	—	15	3	—	12	—	—	6	—	12	—	—	—	6	12	6
N.M.	2	2	—	—	—	2	—	—	2	—	—	—	—	2	—	—	—	1	2	—
N.Y.	70	—	—	69	1	15	54	1	—	2	68	—	—	—	—	68	2	—	9	61
N.C.	20	9	2	7	1	6	13	1	—	—	—	12	1	12	1	—	—	1	—	20
N.D.ᵃ	2	2	—	—	—	2	—	—	2	—	—	—	—	2	—	—	—	—	2	—
Ohio	44	—	—	—	—	14	30	—	—	—	—	44	—	—	—	—	—	44	—	44
Oregon	6	6	—	—	—	6	—	—	6	—	—	—	—	6	—	—	—	—	6	—
Pa.	58	—	—	—	—	1	57	—	5	—	—	—	—	14	—	—	—	—	30	28
R.I.	8	2	—	—	6	1	7	—	2	6	—	—	—	2	—	—	6	—	2	6
S.C.	14	—	13	—	1	2	12	—	5	3	—	1	5	10	2	—	1	1	7	7
Tenn.	24	4	10	—	10	19	5	—	7	10	—	—	7	7	1	—	12	4	6	18
Texas	16	2	5	3	6	4	12	—	3	3	—	1	8	2	4	1	1	7	1	15
Utah	2	2	—	—	—	2	—	—	2	—	—	—	—	2	—	—	—	—	2	—
Vt.	10	1	—	—	8	5	5	—	—	8	—	2	—	—	—	—	8	2	—	10
Va.	22	16	3	3	—	19	2	1	16	—	—	—	3	13	4	—	3	2	14	8
Wash.	2	2	—	—	—	2	—	—	2	—	—	—	—	2	—	—	—	—	2	—
W.Va.	10	8	—	—	—	10	—	—	7	—	—	2	—	6	—	—	—	4	6	4
Wis.	20	20	—	—	—	17	3	—	16	3	—	—	1	16	1	—	3	—	16	4
Wyo.	2	—	—	—	2	—	2	—	—	2	—	—	—	—	—	—	2	—	—	2
D.C.	2	—	2	—	—	2	—	—	1	—	—	—	1	1	1	—	—	—	2	—
Total	756	285	124	99	113	395	353	8	286	114	82	104	95	308	85	81	111	113	351	384

1. Other candidates: Rutherford B. Hayes, 61; John F. Hartranft, 58; Marshall Jewell, 11; William A. Wheeler, 3; not voting, 2.

2. Other candidates: Hartranft, 69; Elihu B. Washburne, 3; Wheeler, 2; not voting, 2.

3. Other candidates: Hartranft, 50; Washburne, 4; Wheeler, 2; not voting, 2.

4. Other candidates: Benjamin H. Bristow, 21.

a. Dakota Territory, includes North and South Dakota.

1880 Democratic

(Narrative. p. 48)

Delegation	Total Vote	First Pres. Ballot[1]			Second Pres. Ballot[2] (Before shift)			Second Pres. Ballot[3] (After shift)
		Bayard	Hancock	Payne	Hancock	Bayard	Randall	Hancock
Alabama	20	7	7	—	11	5	—	20
Arkansas	12	—	—	—	—	—	—	12
California	12	—	—	—	5	—	—	12
Colorado	6	—	—	—	—	—	—	6
Connecticut	12	4	—	2	—	1	—	12
Delaware	6	6	—	—	—	6	—	6
Florida	8	8	—	—	—	8	—	8
Georgia	22	5	8	—	7	5	—	22
Illinois	42	—	—	—	42	—	—	42
Indiana	30	—	—	—	—	—	—	—
Iowa	22	3	7	2	9	1	12	21
Kansas	10	—	—	—	10	—	—	10
Kentucky	24	6	1	—	8	7	—	24
Louisiana	16	—	16	—	16	—	—	16
Maine	14	—	14	—	14	—	—	14
Maryland	16	16	—	—	—	16	—	14
Massachusetts	26	11½	6	—	11	7	3½	26
Michigan	22	2	5	1	14	4	1	22
Minnesota	10	—	10	—	10	—	—	10
Mississippi	16	8	5	—	6	8	—	16
Missouri	30	4	12	—	28	2	—	30
Nebraska	6	—	—	6	—	—	6	6
Nevada	6	—	—	—	—	—	1	6
New Hampshire	10	3	4	—	5	—	5	10
New Jersey	18	10	—	—	7	4	4	18
New York	70	—	—	70	—	—	70	70
North Carolina	20	7	9	—	20	—	—	20
Ohio	44	—	—	—	—	—	—	44
Oregon	6	—	—	—	—	—	—	6
Pennsylvania	58	7	28	—	32	—	25	58
Rhode Island	8	2	2	—	6	—	1	8
South Carolina	14	14	—	—	—	14	—	14
Tennessee	24	9	11	—	14	8	—	24
Texas	16	5	9	—	11	5	—	16
Vermont	10	—	10	—	10	—	—	10
Virginia	22	10	3	—	7	8	—	22
West Virginia	10	—	3	—	7	1	—	10
Wisconsin	20	6	1	—	10	2	—	20
Total	**738**	**153½**	**171**	**81**	**320**	**112**	**128½**	**705**

1. *Other candidates: Allen G. Thurman, 68½; Stephen J. Field, 65; William R. Morrison, 62; Thomas A. Hendricks, 49½; Samuel J. Tilden, 38; Horatio Seymour, 8; W. A. H. Loveland, 5; Samuel J. Randall, 6; Thomas Ewing, 10; Joseph E. McDonald, 3; George B. McClellan, 2; Joel Parker, 1; Jeremiah Black, 1; Hugh J. Jewett, 1; James E. English, 1; Lothrop, 1; not voting, 10½.*

2. *Other candidates: Hendricks, 31; English, 19; Tilden, 6; Thurman, 50; Parker, 2; Field, 65½; Jewett, 1; not voting, 3.*

3. *Other candidates: Hendricks, 30; Bayard, 2; Tilden, 1.*

1880 Republican

(Narrative, p. 46)

Delegation	Total Votes	Minority Report Illinois 1st Dist. Yea	Nay	Not Voting	First Pres. Ballot 1 Grant	Blaine	Sherman	Other	34th Pres. Ballot 2 Grant	Blaine	Sherman	Other	35th Pres. Ballot 3 Grant	Blaine	Sherman	Garfield	Other	36th Pres. Ballot 4 Grant	Blaine	Garfield	Other
Ala.	20	16	4	—	16	1	3	—	16	4	—	—	16	4	—	—	—	16	4	—	—
Ariz.	2	—	2	—	—	2	—	—	—	2	—	—	—	2	—	—	—	—	—	2	—
Ark.	12	12	—	—	12	—	—	—	12	—	—	—	12	—	—	—	—	12	—	—	—
Calif.	12	—	12	—	—	12	—	—	—	12	—	—	—	12	—	—	—	—	12	—	—
Colo.	6	6	—	—	6	—	—	—	6	—	—	—	6	—	—	—	—	6	—	—	—
Conn.	12	—	10	2	—	3	—	9	—	3	—	9	—	3	—	—	9	—	1	11	—
Del.	6	—	6	—	—	6	—	—	—	6	—	—	—	6	—	—	—	—	6	—	—
Fla.	8	8	—	—	8	—	—	—	8	—	—	—	8	—	—	—	—	8	—	—	—
Ga.	22	6	16	—	6	8	8	—	8	9	5	—	8	9	5	—	—	8	10	1	3
Idaho	2	—	2	—	—	2	—	—	—	2	—	—	—	2	—	—	—	—	—	2	—
Ill.	42	40	—	2	24	10	—	8	24	10	—	8	24	10	—	—	8	24	6	7	5
Ind.	30	5	25	—	1	26	2	1	2	20	2	6	1	2	—	27	—	1	—	29	—
Iowa	22	—	22	—	—	22	—	—	—	22	—	—	—	22	—	—	—	—	—	22	—
Kan.	10	—	—	10	4	6	—	—	4	6	—	—	4	6	—	—	—	4	—	6	—
Ky.	24	21	3	—	20	1	3	—	20	1	3	—	20	1	3	—	—	20	1	3	—
La.	16	8	8	—	8	2	6	—	8	4	4	—	8	4	4	—	—	8	—	8	—
Maine	14	—	14	—	—	14	—	—	—	14	—	—	—	14	—	—	—	—	—	14	—
Md.	16	8	8	—	7	7	2	—	7	2	7	—	7	3	2	4	—	6	—	10	—
Mass.	26	4	22	—	3	—	2	21	4	—	21	1	4	—	21	—	1	4	—	22	—
Mich.	22	1	21	—	1	21	—	—	1	21	—	—	1	21	—	—	—	1	—	21	—
Minn.	10	4	6	—	—	—	—	10	—	6	—	4	1	6	—	—	3	2	—	8	—
Miss.	16	11	5	—	6	4	6	—	8	4	3	1	8	4	3	1	—	7	—	9	—
Mo.	30	29	1	—	29	—	—	1	29	—	—	1	29	—	—	—	1	29	—	1	—
Mont.	2	—	2	—	—	2	—	—	—	2	—	—	—	2	—	—	—	—	—	2	—
Neb.	6	—	6	—	—	6	—	—	—	6	—	—	—	6	—	—	—	—	—	6	—
Nev.	6	—	6	—	—	6	—	—	—	6	—	—	—	6	—	—	—	2	1	3	—
N.H.	10	—	10	—	—	10	—	—	—	10	—	—	—	10	—	—	—	—	—	10	—
N.J.	18	—	18	—	—	16	—	2	—	14	2	2	—	14	2	—	2	—	—	18	—
N.M.	2	—	2	—	—	2	—	—	—	2	—	—	—	2	—	—	—	—	—	2	—
N.Y.	70	47	22	1	51	17	2	—	50	18	2	—	50	18	2	—	—	50	—	20	—
N.C.	20	19	1	—	6	—	14	—	6	—	14	—	6	—	13	1	—	5	—	15	—
N.D.a	2	1	1	—	1	1	—	—	1	1	—	—	1	1	—	—	—	—	—	2	—
Ohio	44	16	28	—	—	9	34	1	—	9	34	1	—	9	34	—	1	—	—	43	1
Ore.	6	—	6	—	—	6	—	—	—	6	—	—	—	6	—	—	—	—	—	6	—
Pa.	58	34	24	—	32	23	3	—	35	22	—	1	36	20	—	1	1	37	—	21	—
R.I.	8	—	8	—	—	8	—	—	—	8	—	—	—	8	—	—	—	—	—	8	—
S.C.	14	10	4	—	13	—	1	—	11	1	2	—	11	1	2	—	—	8	—	6	—
Tenn.	24	16	8	—	16	6	1	1	17	4	3	—	17	4	3	—	—	15	1	8	—
Texas	16	11	4	1	11	2	2	1	13	1	1	1	13	1	1	—	1	13	—	3	—
Utah	2	—	2	—	1	1	—	—	1	1	—	—	1	1	—	—	—	—	—	2	—
Vt.	10	4	6	—	—	—	—	10	—	—	—	10	—	—	—	—	10	—	—	10	—
Va.	22	13	9	—	18	3	1	—	16	3	3	—	16	3	3	—	—	19	—	3	—
Wash.	2	—	2	—	—	2	—	—	—	2	—	—	—	2	—	—	—	—	—	2	—
W.Va.	10	—	10	—	1	8	—	1	1	8	1	—	1	8	1	—	—	1	—	9	—
Wis.	20	1	19	—	1	7	3	9	2	1	—	17	2	2	—	16	—	—	—	20	—
Wyo.	2	1	1	—	1	1	—	—	1	1	—	—	1	1	—	—	—	—	—	2	—
D.C.	2	1	1	—	1	1	—	—	1	1	—	—	1	1	—	—	—	—	—	2	—
Total	**756**	**353**	**387**	**16**	**304**	**284**	**93**	**75**	**312**	**275**	**107**	**62**	**313**	**257**	**99**	**50**	**37**	**306**	**42**	**399**	**9**

1. Other candidates: George F. Edmunds, 34; Elihu B. Washburne, 30; William Windom, 10; not voting, 1.
2. Other candidates: Washburne, 30; James A. Garfield, 17; Edmunds, 11; Windom, 4.
3. Other candidates: Washburne, 23; Edmunds, 11; Windom, 3.
4. Other candidates: Washburne, 5; Sherman, 3; not voting, 1.
a. Dakota Territory, includes North and South Dakota.

1884 Democratic

(Narrative, p. 49)

Delegation	Total Votes	Unit Rule: Amendment to Permit Polling of Delegates			First Pres. Ballot[1]			Second Pres. Ballot[2] (Before shift)			Second Pres. Ballot[3] (After shift)	
		Yea	Nay	Not Voting	Cleveland	Bayard	Thurman	Cleveland	Bayard	Hendricks	Cleveland	Bayard
Alabama	20	15	5	—	4	14	1	5	14	—	5	14
Arizona	2	—	—	2	2	—	—	2	—	—	2	—
Arkansas	14	—	14	—	14	—	—	14	—	—	14	—
California	16	16	—	—	—	—	16	—	—	—	16	—
Colorado	6	4	2	—	—	—	1	6	—	—	6	—
Connecticut	12	2	10	—	12	—	—	12	—	—	12	—
Delaware	6	6	—	—	—	6	—	—	6	—	—	6
Florida	8	2	6	—	8	—	—	6	2	—	8	—
Georgia	24	12	12	—	10	12	—	14	10	—	22	2
Idaho	2	—	—	2	2	—	—	2	—	—	2	—
Illinois	44	22	22	—	28	2	1	38	3	1	43	—
Indiana	30	30	—	—	—	—	—	—	—	30	30	—
Iowa	26	6	20	—	23	1	1	22	—	4	26	—
Kansas	18	3	15	—	11	5	2	12	4	—	17	1
Kentucky	26	20	6	—	—	—	—	3	7	15	4	21
Louisiana	16	—	16	—	13	1	1	15	—	—	15	—
Maine	12	2	10	—	12	—	—	12	—	—	12	—
Maryland	16	—	16	—	6	10	—	10	6	—	16	—
Massachusetts	28	21	7	—	5	21	2	8	7½	12½	8	7½
Michigan	26	12	12	2	14	1	11	13	—	13	23	—
Minnesota	14	—	14	—	14	—	—	14	—	—	14	—
Mississippi	18	18	—	—	1	15	1	2	14	2	2	14
Missouri	32	8	24	—	15	10	3	21	5	6	32	—
Montana	2	—	—	2	2	—	—	2	—	—	2	—
Nebraska	10	5	5	—	8	1	1	9	1	—	9	1
Nevada	6	6	—	—	—	—	6	—	—	5	—	—
New Hampshire	8	—	8	—	8	—	—	8	—	—	8	—
New Jersey	18	14	4	—	4	3	—	5	2	11	5	2
New Mexico	2	—	—	2	2	—	—	1	—	—	2	—
New York	72	—	72	—	72	—	—	72	—	—	72	—
North Carolina	22	10	12	—	—	22	—	—	22	—	22	—
Dakota[a]	2	—	—	2	2	—	—	2	—	—	2	—
Ohio	46	25	21	—	21	—	23	21	—	1	46	—
Oregon	6	—	6	—	2	4	—	2	2	2	6	—
Pennsylvania	60	21	39	—	5	—	—	42	2	11	42	2
Rhode Island	8	—	8	—	6	2	—	6	2	—	7	1
South Carolina	18	3	14	1	8	10	—	8	9	1	10	8
Tennessee	24	17	7	—	2	8	9	2	10	1	24	—
Texas	26	12	10	4	11	10	4	12	12	1	26	—
Utah	2	—	—	2	—	—	—	1	—	1	2	—
Vermont	8	—	8	—	8	—	—	8	—	—	8	—
Virginia	24	6	18	—	13	9	1	13	8	2	23	—
Washington	2	—	—	2	1	—	—	2	—	—	2	—
West Virginia	12	9	3	—	7	2	2	6	3	—	10	2
Wisconsin	22	5	17	—	12	1	2	20	—	2	22	—
Wyoming	2	—	—	2	2	—	—	2	—	—	2	—
District of Columbia	2	—	—	2	2	—	—	—	—	2	2	—
Total	820	332	463	25	392	170	88	475	151½	123½	683	81½

a. Dakota Territory, includes North and South Dakota.

1. Other candidates: Joseph E. McDonald, 56; Samuel J. Randell, 78; John G. Carlisle, 27; George Hoadly, 3; Thomas A. Hendricks, 1; Samuel J. Tilden, 1; Roswell P. Flower, 4.

2. Other candidates: Allen G. Thurman, 60; Randell, 5; McDonald, 2; Tilden, 2; not voting, 1.

3. Other candidates: Hendricks, 45½; Thurman, 4; Randall, 4; McDonald, 2.

1884 Republican

(Narrative. p. 49)

Delegation	Total Vote	Temporary Chairman[1]		First Pres. Ballot[2]			Third Pres. Ballot[3]		Fourth Pres. Ballot[4]	
		Lynch	Clayton	Arthur	Blaine	Edmunds	Arthur	Blaine	Arthur	Blaine
Alabama	20	19	1	17	1	—	17	2	12	8
Arizona	2	—	2	—	2	—	—	2	—	2
Arkansas	14	1	13	4	8	2	3	11	3	11
California	16	—	16	—	16	—	—	16	—	16
Colorado	6	—	6	—	6	—	—	6	—	6
Connecticut	12	6	6	—	—	—	—	—	—	—
Delaware	6	1	5	1	5	—	1	5	1	5
Florida	8	7	1	7	1	—	7	1	5	3
Georgia	24	24	—	24	—	—	24	—	24	—
Idaho	2	2	—	2	—	—	1	1	—	2
Illinois	44	16	28	1	3	—	1	3	3	34
Indiana	30	10	20	9	18	1	10	18	—	30
Iowa	26	3	23	—	26	—	—	26	2	24
Kansas	18	4	14	4	12	—	—	15	—	18
Kentucky	26	20	6	16	5½	—	16	6	15	9
Louisiana	16	11	4	10	2	—	9	4	7	9
Maine	12	—	12	—	12	—	—	12	—	12
Maryland	16	6	10	6	10	—	4	12	1	15
Massachusetts	28	24	4	2	1	25	3	1	7	3
Michigan	26	12	14	2	15	7	4	18	—	26
Minnesota	14	6	8	1	7	6	2	7	—	14
Mississippi	18	16	2	17	1	—	16	1	16	2
Missouri	32	14	16	10	5	6	11	12	—	32
Montana	2	1	1	—	1	1	—	1	—	2
Nebraska	10	2	8	2	8	—	—	10	—	10
Nevada	6	—	6	—	6	—	—	6	—	6
New Hampshire	8	8	—	4	—	4	5	—	2	3
New Jersey	18	9	9	—	9	6	1	11	—	17
New Mexico	2	2	—	2	—	2	—	2	—
New York	72	46	26	31	28	12	32	28	30	29
North Carolina	22	17	3	19	2	—	18	4	12	8
Dakota[a]	2	—	2	—	2	—	—	2	—	2
Ohio	46	22	23	—	21	—	—	25	—	46
Oregon	6	—	6	—	6	—	—	6	—	6
Pennsylvania	60	13	45	11	47	1	8	50	8	51
Rhode Island	8	8	—	—	—	8	—	—	1	7
South Carolina	18	18	—	17	1	—	16	2	15	2
Tennessee	24	21	2	16	7	—	17	7	12	11
Texas	26	12	12	11	13	—	11	14	8	15
Utah	2	—	2	2	—	—	2	—	—	2
Vermont	8	8	—	—	—	8	—	—	—	—
Virginia	24	20	4	21	2	—	20	4	20	4
Washington	2	1	1	—	2	—	—	2	—	2
West Virginia	12	—	12	—	12	—	—	12	—	12
Wisconsin	22	11	10	6	10	6	10	11	—	22
Wyoming	2	2	—	2	—	—	2	—	—	2
District of Columbia	2	1	1	1	1	—	1	1	1	1
Total	**820**	**424**	**384**	**278**	**334½**	**93**	**274**	**375**	**207**	**541**

1. Not voting, 12.
2. Other candidates: John A. Logan, 63½; John Sherman, 30; Joseph R. Hawley, 13; Robert T. Lincoln, 4; William T. Sherman, 2; not voting, 2.
3. Other candidates: George F. Edmunds, 69; Logan, 53; John Sherman, 25; Hawley, 13; Lincoln, 8; William T. Sherman, 3; not voting, 1.
4. Other candidates: Edmunds, 41; Hawley, 15; Logan, 7; Lincoln, 2; not voting, 7.
a. Dakota Territory, includes North and South Dakota.

1888 Republican

(Narrative, p. 52)

Delegation	Total Votes	First Pres. Ballot[1]						Sixth Pres. Ballot[2]					Seventh Pres. Ballot[3]					Eighth Pres. Ballot[4]			
		Alger	Allison	Depew	Gresham	Harrison	Sherman	Alger	Allison	Gresham	Harrison	Sherman	Alger	Allison	Gresham	Harrison	Sherman	Alger	Gresham	Harrison	Sherman
Ala.	20	6	—	1	—	1	12	6	—	—	1	12	6	—	—	12	—	10	—	3	5
Ariz.	2	2	—	—	—	—	—	2	—	—	—	—	2	—	—	—	—	—	—	2	—
Ark.	14	—	—	—	1	1	2	14	—	—	—	—	14	—	—	—	—	14	—	—	—
Calif.	16	—	—	—	—	—	—	—	—	—	—	—	1	—	—	15	—	—	—	15	—
Colo.	6	—	1	—	3	2	—	—	—	—	—	5	—	6	—	—	—	—	—	6	—
Conn.	12	—	—	—	—	—	—	2	4	—	—	6	2	—	—	4	5	—	—	12	—
Del.	6	—	—	—	—	6	—	—	—	1	5	—	—	—	1	5	—	—	—	6	—
Fla.	8	—	—	—	—	1	4	5	—	—	1	1	3	—	—	4	1	4	—	2	2
Ga.	24	—	—	—	1	2	19	—	—	1	2	19	1	—	1	3	17	3	1	10	9
Idaho	2	—	1	—	1	—	—	—	—	2	—	—	—	—	2	—	—	—	—	2	—
Ill.	44	—	—	—	44	—	—	—	—	41	3	—	1	—	40	3	—	—	40	4	—
Ind.	30	—	—	—	1	29	—	—	—	1	29	—	—	—	1	29	—	—	1	29	—
Iowa	26	—	26	—	—	—	—	—	26	—	—	—	—	26	—	—	—	1	3	22	—
Kan.	18	—	—	—	—	—	—	2	3	3	6	1	1	3	—	12	1	1	—	16	—
Ky.	26	4	—	1	5	4	12	6	—	2	7	9	3	—	2	10	9	1	2	15	7
La.	16	2	3	1	1	—	9	3	2	2	—	9	3	2	2	—	9	4	—	9	3
Maine	12	3	2	3	1	2	1	2	1	2	1	3	1	2	2	2	1	—	1	5	3
Md.	16	—	2	1	1	5	5	—	1	—	6	6	—	—	—	9	6	—	—	11	4
Mass.	28	6	2	1	2	4	9	8	2	1	5	11	2	3	1	9	11	1	—	25	2
Mich.	26	26	—	—	—	—	—	26	—	—	—	—	26	—	—	—	—	26	—	—	—
Minn.	14	1	—	2	11	—	—	3	—	5	6	—	2	—	4	8	—	1	—	13	—
Miss.	18	—	—	1	3	—	14	—	—	3	—	14	—	—	3	—	14	—	3	4	11
Mo.	32	6	3	2	11	3	6	15	1	11	2	2	14	—	12	3	2	15	8	7	2
Mont.	2	—	1	—	1	—	—	—	—	1	1	—	—	1	1	—	—	—	—	2	—
Neb.	10	2	3	—	—	—	3	2	5	—	—	3	2	5	—	2	1	1	—	9	—
Nev.	6	3	3	—	—	—	—	5	—	—	—	—	—	6	—	—	—	2	—	4	—
N.H.	8	—	—	4	—	4	—	—	1	—	6	1	—	—	—	8	—	—	—	8	—
N.J.	18	—	—	—	—	—	—	—	—	1	14	—	1	—	1	10	1	—	—	18	—
N.M.	2	1	—	—	—	—	—	1	—	—	—	1	1	—	—	—	1	—	—	2	—
N.Y.	72	—	—	71	—	—	1	—	—	—	72	—	—	—	—	72	—	—	—	72	—
N.C.	22	2	—	1	2	1	15	9	—	—	2	11	7	—	—	3	12	3	—	8	11
N.D.a	10	1	1	2	1	1	1	—	—	—	10	—	—	—	—	10	—	—	—	10	—
Ohio	46	—	—	—	—	—	46	—	—	—	1	45	—	—	—	1	45	—	—	1	45
Ore.	6	—	—	—	4	1	—	—	—	5	—	—	—	—	6	—	—	—	—	6	—
Pa.	60	1	—	5	—	—	29	—	—	—	6	54	—	—	—	9	51	—	—	59	1
R.I.	8	—	8	—	—	—	—	—	8	—	—	—	—	6	—	2	—	—	—	8	—
S.C.	18	3	—	1	—	—	11	11	—	—	1	6	11	—	—	1	6	10	—	4	4
Tenn.	24	9	1	2	1	1	7	6	1	—	1	8	9	1	—	3	5	3	—	20	—
Texas	26	2	7	—	5	1	7	3	8	3	1	7	2	8	1	3	7	—	—	26	—
Utah	2	—	2	—	—	—	—	—	—	2	—	—	—	—	2	—	—	—	—	2	—
Vt.	8	—	—	—	—	8	—	—	—	—	8	—	—	—	—	8	—	—	—	8	—
Va.	24	3	3	—	1	5	11	3	5	—	6	10	3	5	—	6	10	—	—	15	9
Wash.	6	—	1	—	3	1	—	1	—	4	1	—	1	—	4	1	—	—	—	6	—
W.Va.	12	1	—	—	2	2	5	1	—	1	2	5	—	—	5	3	1	—	—	12	—
Wis.	22	—	—	—	—	—	—	—	—	1	21	—	—	—	2	20	—	—	—	22	—
Wyo.	2	—	2	—	—	—	—	—	—	2	—	—	—	—	—	2	—	—	—	2	—
D.C.	2	—	—	—	—	—	—	1	—	—	—	—	1	—	—	—	—	—	—	2	—
Total	832	84	72	99	107	85	229	137	73	91	231	244	120	76	91	279	230	100	59	544	118

1. Other candidates: James G. Blaine, 35; John J. Ingalls, 28; William W. Phelps, 25; Jeremiah M. Rusk, 25; Edwin H. Fitler, 24; Joseph R. Hawley, 13; Robert T. Lincoln, 3; William McKinley, 2; not voting, 1.

2. Other candidates: Blaine, 40; McKinley, 12; Foraker, 1; Frederick D. Grant, 1; not voting, 2.

3. Other candidates: McKinley, 16; Blaine, 15; Lincoln, 2; Foraker, 1; Creed Haymond, 1; not voting, 1.

4. Other candidates: Blaine, 5; McKinley, 4; not voting, 2.

a. Dakota Territory includes North and South Dakota.

1892 Democratic

(Narrative, p. 54)

First Pres. Ballot [1]

Delegation	Total Votes	Cleveland	Boies	Hill
Alabama	22	14	1	2
Arizona	6	5	—	—
Arkansas	16	16	—	—
California	18	18	—	—
Colorado	8	—	5	3
Connecticut	12	12	—	—
Delaware	6	6	—	—
Florida	8	5	—	—
Georgia	26	17	—	5
Idaho	6	—	6	—
Illinois	48	48	—	—
Indiana	30	30	—	—
Iowa	26	—	26	—
Kansas	20	20	—	—
Kentucky	26	18	2	—
Louisiana	16	3	11	1
Maine	12	9	—	1
Maryland	16	6	—	—
Massachusetts	30	24	1	4
Michigan	28	28	—	—
Minnesota	18	18	—	—
Mississippi	18	8	3	3
Missouri	34	34	—	—
Montana	6	—	6	—
Nebraska	16	15	—	—
Nevada	6	—	4	—
New Hampshire	8	8	—	—
New Jersey	20	20	—	—
New Mexico	6	4	1	1
New York	72	—	—	72
North Carolina	22	3 1/3	1	—
North Dakota	6	6	—	—
Ohio	46	14	16	6
Oklahoma [a]	4	4	—	—
Oregon	8	8	—	—
Pennsylvania	64	64	—	—
Rhode Island	8	8	—	—
South Carolina	18	2	13	3
South Dakota	8	7	1	—
Tennessee	24	24	—	—
Texas	30	23	6	1
Utah	2	2	—	—
Vermont	8	8	—	—
Virginia	24	12	—	11
Washington	8	8	—	—
West Virginia	12	7	—	1
Wisconsin	24	24	—	—
Wyoming	6	3	—	—
Alaska	2	2	—	—
District of Columbia	2	2	—	—
Total	**910**	**617 1/3**	**103**	**114**

a. Includes Indian territory, 2 votes.
1. Other candidates: Arthur P. Gorman, 36½; John G. Carlisle, 14; Adlai E. Stevenson, 16 2/3; James E. Campbell, 2; William R. Morrison, 3; William E. Russell, 1; William C. Whitney, 1; Robert E. Pattison, 1; not voting, ½.

1892 Republican [a]

(Narrative, p. 53)

First Pres. Ballot [1]

Delegation	Total Votes	Harrison	Blaine	McKinley
Alabama	22	15	—	7
Arizona	2	1	1	—
Arkansas	16	15	—	1
California	18	8	9	1
Colorado	8	—	8	—
Connecticut	12	4	—	8
Delaware	6	4	1	1
Florida	8	8	—	—
Georgia	26	26	—	—
Idaho	6	—	6	—
Illinois	48	34	14	—
Indiana	30	30	—	—
Iowa	26	20	5	1
Kansas	20	11	—	9
Kentucky	26	22	2	1
Louisiana	16	8	8	—
Maine	12	—	12	—
Maryland	16	14	—	2
Massachusetts	30	18	1	11
Michigan	28	7	2	19
Minnesota	18	8	9	1
Mississippi	18	13½	4½	—
Missouri	34	28	4	2
Montana	6	5	1	—
Nebraska	16	15	—	1
Nevada	6	—	6	—
New Hampshire	8	4	2	—
New Jersey	20	18	2	—
New Mexico	6	6	—	—
New York	72	27	35	10
North Carolina	22	17 2/3	2 2/3	1
North Dakota	6	2	4	—
Ohio	46	1	—	45
Oklahoma	2	2	—	—
Oregon	8	1	—	7
Pennsylvania	64	19	3	42
Rhode Island	8	5	1	1
South Carolina	18	13	3	2
South Dakota	8	8	—	—
Tennessee	24	17	4	3
Texas	30	22	6	—
Utah	2	2	—	—
Vermont	8	8	—	—
Virginia	24	9	13	2
Washington	8	1	6	1
West Virginia	12	12	—	—
Wisconsin	24	19	2	3
Wyoming	6	4	2	—
Alaska	2	2	—	—
District of Columbia	2	—	2	—
Indian Territory	2	1	1	—
Total	**906**	**535 1/6**	**182 1/6**	**182**

a. Source: Official Proceeding, 10th Republican Convention, p. 114.
1. Other candidates: Thomas B. Reed, 4; Robert T. Lincoln, 1; not voting, 1 2/3.

1896 Democratic

(Narrative, p. 57)

Delegation	Total Votes	Minority Gold Standard Plank			First Pres. Ballot 1			Fourth Pres. Ballot 2			Fifth Pres. Ballot 3	
		Yea	Nay	Not voting	Bryan	Bland	Pattison	Bryan	Bland	Pattison	Bryan	Pattison
Alabama	22	—	22	—	—	—	—	22	—	—	22	—
Arizona	6	—	6	—	—	6	—	—	6	—	6	—
Arkansas	16	—	16	—	—	16	—	—	16	—	16	—
California	18	—	18	—	4	—	—	12	2	—	18	—
Colorado	8	—	8	—	—	—	—	8	—	—	8	—
Connecticut	12	12	—	—	—	—	—	—	—	2	—	2
Delaware	6	5	1	—	1	—	3	1	—	3	1	3
Florida	8	3	5	—	1	2	1	5	—	—	8	—
Georgia	26	—	26	—	26	—	—	26	—	—	26	—
Idaho	6	—	6	—	—	6	—	6	—	—	6	—
Illinois	48	—	48	—	—	48	—	—	48	—	48	—
Indiana	30	—	30	—	—	—	—	—	—	—	30	—
Iowa	26	—	26	—	—	—	—	—	—	—	26	—
Kansas	20	—	20	—	—	20	—	20	—	—	20	—
Kentucky	26	—	26	—	—	—	—	—	—	—	26	—
Louisiana	16	—	16	—	16	—	—	16	—	—	16	—
Maine	12	10	2	—	2	2	5	2	2	5	4	4
Maryland	16	12	4	—	4	—	11	5	—	10	5	10
Massachusetts	30	27	3	—	1	2	3	1	2	3	6	3
Michigan	28	—	28	—	9	4	—	28	—	—	28	—
Minnesota	18	11	6	1	2	—	2	10	1	—	11	—
Mississippi	18	—	18	—	18	—	—	18	—	—	18	—
Missouri	34	—	34	—	—	34	—	—	34	—	34	—
Montana	6	—	6	—	—	4	—	—	6	—	6	—
Nebraska	16	—	16	—	16	—	—	16	—	—	16	—
Nevada	6	—	6	—	—	—	—	6	—	—	6	—
New Hampshire	8	8	—	—	—	—	1	—	—	1	—	1
New Jersey	20	20	—	—	—	—	—	—	—	2	—	2
New Mexico	6	—	6	—	—	6	—	—	6	—	6	—
New York	72	72	—	—	—	—	—	—	—	—	—	—
North Carolina	22	—	22	—	22	—	—	22	—	—	22	—
North Dakota	6	—	6	—	—	—	—	—	—	—	4	—
Ohio	46	—	46	—	—	—	—	—	—	—	46	—
Oklahoma	12	—	12	—	—	12	—	—	12	—	12	—
Oregon	8	—	8	—	—	—	—	8	—	—	8	—
Pennsylvania	64	64	—	—	—	—	64	—	—	64	—	64
Rhode Island	8	8	—	—	—	—	6	—	—	6	—	6
South Carolina	18	—	18	—	—	—	—	18	—	—	18	—
South Dakota	8	8	—	—	6	—	1	7	—	1	8	—
Tennessee	24	—	24	—	—	24	—	—	24	—	24	—
Texas	30	—	30	—	—	30	—	—	30	—	30	—
Utah	6	—	6	—	—	6	—	—	6	—	6	—
Vermont	8	8	—	—	4	—	—	4	—	—	4	—
Virginia	24	—	24	—	—	—	—	—	24	—	24	—
Washington	8	3	5	—	1	7	—	2	6	—	4	—
West Virginia	12	—	12	—	—	—	—	1	10	—	2	—
Wisconsin	24	24	—	—	—	4	—	—	5	—	5	—
Wyoming	6	—	6	—	—	—	—	6	—	—	6	—
Alaska	6	6	—	—	—	6	—	—	6	—	6	—
District of Columbia	6	2	4	—	—	—	—	—	5	—	6	—
Total	930	303	626	1	137	235	97	280	241	97	652	95

1. Other candidates: Horace Boies, 37; Claude Matthews, 37; John R. McLean, 54; Joseph S. C. Blackburn, 82; Adlai E. Stevenson, 6; Henry M. Teller, 8; William E. Russell, 2; Benjamin R. Tillman, 17; James E. Campbell, 1; Sylvester Pennoyer, 8; David B. Hill, 1; not voting, 178.

2. Other candidates: Boies, 33; Mathews, 36; Blackburn, 27; McLean, 46; Stevenson, 8; Hill, 1; not voting, 161.

3. Other candidates: Richard P. Bland, 11; Stevenson, 8; Hill, 1; David Turpie, 1; not voting, 162.

1896 Republican

(Narrative, p. 56)

Delegation	Total Votes	First Pres. Ballot [1] McKinley	Reed	Morton	Allison	Quay
Alabama	22	19	2	1	—	—
Arizona	6	6	—	—	—	—
Arkansas	16	16	—	—	—	—
California	18	18	—	—	—	—
Colorado	8	—	—	—	—	—
Connecticut	12	7	5	—	—	—
Delaware	6	6	—	—	—	—
Florida	8	6	—	2	—	—
Georgia	26	22	2	—	—	2
Idaho	6	—	—	—	—	—
Illinois	48	46	2	—	—	—
Indiana	30	30	—	—	—	—
Iowa	26	—	—	—	26	—
Kansas	20	20	—	—	—	—
Kentucky	26	26	—	—	—	—
Louisiana	16	11	4	—	½	½
Maine	12	—	12	—	—	—
Maryland	16	15	1	—	—	—
Massachusetts	30	1	29	—	—	—
Michigan	28	28	—	—	—	—
Minnesota	18	18	—	—	—	—
Mississippi	18	17	—	—	—	1
Missouri	34	34	—	—	—	—
Montana	6	1	—	—	—	—
Nebraska	16	16	—	—	—	—
Nevada	6	3	—	—	—	—
New Hampshire	8	—	8	—	—	—
New Jersey	20	19	1	—	—	—
New Mexico	6	5	—	—	1	—
New York	72	17	—	55	—	—
North Carolina	22	19½	2½	—	—	—
North Dakota	6	6	—	—	—	—
Ohio	46	46	—	—	—	—
Oklahoma	12 [a]	10	1	—	1	—
Oregon	8	8	—	—	—	—
Pennsylvania	64	6	—	—	—	58
Rhode Island	8	—	8	—	—	—
South Carolina	18	18	—	—	—	—
South Dakota	8	8	—	—	—	—
Tennessee	24	24	—	—	—	—
Texas	30	21	5	—	3	—
Utah	6	3	—	—	3	—
Vermont	8	8	—	—	—	—
Virginia	24	23	1	—	—	—
Washington	8	8	—	—	—	—
West Virginia	12	12	—	—	—	—
Wisconsin	24	24	—	—	—	—
Wyoming	6	6	—	—	—	—
Alaska	4	4	—	—	—	—
District of Columbia	2	—	1	—	1	—
Total	**924**	**661½**	**84½**	**58**	**35½**	**61½**

1. Other candidates: J. Donald Cameron, 1; not voting, 22.
a. Including Indian Territory, 6 votes.

1900 Democratic

(Narrative, p. 59)

Delegation	Total Votes	First Pres. Ballot Bryan
Alabama	22	22
Arizona	6	6
Arkansas	16	16
California	18	18
Colorado	8	8
Connecticut	12	12
Delaware	6	6
Florida	8	8
Georgia	26	26
Idaho	6	6
Illinois	48	48
Indiana	30	30
Iowa	26	26
Kansas	20	20
Kentucky	26	26
Louisiana	16	16
Maine	12	12
Maryland	16	16
Massachusetts	30	30
Michigan	28	28
Minnesota	18	18
Mississippi	18	18
Missouri	34	34
Montana	6	6
Nebraska	16	16
Nevada	6	6
New Hampshire	8	8
New Jersey	20	20
New Mexico	6	6
New York	72	72
North Carolina	22	22
North Dakota	6	6
Ohio	46	46
Oklahoma	12[a]	12
Oregon	8	8
Pennsylvania	64	64
Rhode Island	8	8
South Carolina	18	18
South Dakota	8	8
Tennessee	24	24
Texas	30	30
Utah	6	6
Vermont	8	8
Virginia	24	24
Washington	8	8
West Virginia	12	12
Wisconsin	24	24
Wyoming	6	6
Alaska	6	6
District of Columbia	6	6
Hawaii	6	6
Total	**936**	**936**

a. Including Indian Territory, 6 votes.

1900 Republican

(Narrative p. 58)

Delegation	Total Votes	First Pres. Ballot McKinley
Alabama	22	22
Arizona	6	6
Arkansas	16	16
California	18	18
Colorado	8	8
Connecticut	12	12
Delaware	6	6
Florida	8	8
Georgia	26	26
Idaho	6	6
Illinois	48	48
Indiana	30	30
Iowa	26	26
Kansas	20	20
Kentucky	26	26
Louisiana	16	16
Maine	12	12
Maryland	16	16
Massachusetts	30	30
Michigan	28	28
Minnesota	18	18
Mississippi	18	18
Missouri	34	34
Montana	6	6
Nebraska	16	16
Nevada	6	6
New Hampshire	8	8
New Jersey	20	20
New Mexico	6	6
New York	72	72
North Carolina	22	22
North Dakota	6	6
Ohio	46	46
Oklahoma	12[a]	12
Oregon	8	8
Pennsylvania	64	64
Rhode Island	8	8
South Carolina	18	18
South Dakota	8	8
Tennessee	24	24
Texas	30	30
Utah	6	6
Vermont	8	8
Virginia	24	24
Washington	8	8
West Virginia	12	12
Wisconsin	24	24
Wyoming	6	6
Alaska	4	4
District of Columbia	2	2
Hawaii	2	2
Total	**926**	**926**

a. Including Indian Territory, 6 votes.

1904 Democratic *(Narrative, p. 61)*

Delegation	Total Votes	First Pres. Ballot[1] (Before shift)		First Pres. Ballot[2] (After shift)		Sending Telegram to Parker		
		Parker	Hearst	Parker	Hearst	Yea	Nay	Not Voting
Alabama	22	22	—	22	—	22	—	—
Arizona	6	—	6	—	6	—	6	—
Arkansas	18	18	—	18	—	18	—	—
California	20	—	20	—	20	16	4	—
Colorado	10	4	5	4	5	4	6	—
Connecticut	14	14	—	14	—	14	—	—
Delaware	6	—	—	—	—	6	—	—
Florida	10	6	4	6	4	6	4	—
Georgia	26	26	—	26	—	26	—	—
Idaho	6	—	6	6	—	—	6	—
Illinois	54	—	54	—	54	54	—	—
Indiana	30	30	—	30	—	30	—	—
Iowa	26	—	26	—	26	—	26	—
Kansas	20	7	10	7	10	—	20	—
Kentucky	26	26	—	26	—	26	—	—
Louisiana	18	18	—	18	—	18	—	—
Maine	12	7	1	7	1	7	2	3
Maryland	16	16	—	16	—	16	—	—
Massachusetts	32	—	—	—	—	32	—	—
Michigan	28	28	—	28	—	28	—	—
Minnesota	22	9	9	9	9	9	13	—
Mississippi	20	20	—	20	—	20	—	—
Missouri	36	—	—	—	—	—	36	—
Montana	6	6	—	6	—	—	6	—
Nebraska	16	—	4	—	4	—	16	—
Nevada	6	—	6	2	4	2	4	—
New Hampshire	8	8	—	8	—	8	—	—
New Jersey	24	24	—	24	—	24	—	—
New Mexico	6	—	6	—	6	6	—	—
New York	78	78	—	78	—	78	—	—
North Carolina	24	24	—	24	—	24	—	—
North Dakota	8	—	—	—	—	—	8	—
Ohio	46	46	—	46	—	31	6	9
Oklahoma	12[a]	7	3	7	3	7	5	—
Oregon	8	4	2	4	2	4	4	—
Pennsylvania	68	68	—	68	—	68	—	—
Rhode Island	8	2	6	2	6	2	5	1
South Carolina	18	18	—	18	—	18	—	—
South Dakota	8	—	8	—	8	—	8	—
Tennessee	24	24	—	24	—	24	—	—
Texas	36	36	—	36	—	36	—	—
Utah	6	6	—	6	—	6	—	—
Vermont	8	8	—	8	—	8	—	—
Virginia	24	24	—	24	—	24	—	—
Washington	10	—	10	10	—	10	—	—
West Virginia	14	10	2	13	1	14	—	—
Wisconsin	26	—	—	—	—	26	—	—
Wyoming	6	—	6	—	6	2	2	2
Alaska	6	6	—	6	—	6	—	—
District of Columbia	6	6	—	6	—	6	—	—
Hawaii	6	—	6	—	6	2	4	—
Puerto Rico	6	2	—	2	—	6	—	—
Total	**1000**	**658**	**200**	**679**	**181**	**794**	**191**	**15**

a. Including Indian Territory, 6 votes.

1. Other candidates: George Gray, 12; Nelson A. Miles, 3; Francis M. Cockrell, 42; Richard Olney, 38; Edward C. Wall, 27; George B. McClellan, 3; Charles A. Towne, 2; Robert E. Pattison, 4; John S. Williams, 8; Bird S. Coler, 1; Arthur P. Gorman, 2.

2. Other candidates: Gray, 12; Miles, 3; Cockrell, 42; Olney, 38; Wall, 27; McClellan, 3; Towne, 2; Pattison, 4; Williams, 8; Coler, 1.

1904 Republican
(Narrative, p. 60)

1908 Democratic
(Narrative, p. 63)

Delegation	Total Votes	First Pres. Ballot — Roosevelt
Alabama	22	22
Arizona	6	6
Arkansas	18	18
California	20	20
Colorado	10	10
Connecticut	14	14
Delaware	6	6
Florida	10	10
Georgia	26	26
Idaho	6	6
Illinois	54	54
Indiana	30	30
Iowa	26	26
Kansas	20	20
Kentucky	26	26
Louisiana	18	18
Maine	12	12
Maryland	16	16
Massachusetts	32	32
Michigan	28	28
Minnesota	22	22
Mississippi	20	20
Missouri	36	36
Montana	6	6
Nebraska	16	16
Nevada	6	6
New Hampshire	8	8
New Jersey	24	24
New Mexico	6	6
New York	78	78
North Carolina	24	24
North Dakota	8	8
Ohio	46 [a]	46
Oklahoma	12	12
Oregon	8	8
Pennsylvania	68	68
Rhode Island	8	8
South Carolina	18	18
South Dakota	8	8
Tennessee	24	24
Texas	36	36
Utah	6	6
Vermont	8	8
Virginia	24	24
Washington	10	10
West Virginia	14	14
Wisconsin	26	26
Wyoming	6	6
Alaska	6	6
District of Columbia	2	2
Hawaii	6	6
Philippine Islands	2	2
Puerto Rico	2	2
Total	**994**	**994**

a. Including Indian Territory, 6 votes.

Delegation	Total Votes	First Pres. Ballot[1] — Bryan
Alabama	22	22
Arizona	6	6
Arkansas	18	18
California	20	20
Colorado	10	10
Connecticut	14	9
Delaware	6	—
Florida	10	10
Georgia	26	4
Idaho	6	6
Illinois	54	54
Indiana	30	30
Iowa	26	26
Kansas	20	20
Kentucky	26	26
Louisiana	18	18
Maine	12	10
Maryland	16	7
Massachusetts	32	32
Michigan	28	28
Minnesota	22	—
Mississippi	20	20
Missouri	36	36
Montana	6	6
Nebraska	16	16
Nevada	6	6
New Hampshire	8	7
New Jersey	24	—
New Mexico	6	6
New York	78	78
North Carolina	24	24
North Dakota	8	8
Ohio	46	46
Oklahoma	14	14
Oregon	8	8
Pennsylvania	68	49½
Rhode Island	8	5
South Carolina	18	18
South Dakota	8	8
Tennessee	24	24
Texas	36	36
Utah	6	6
Vermont	8	7
Virginia	24	24
Washington	10	10
West Virginia	14	14
Wisconsin	26	26
Wyoming	6	6
Alaska	6	6
District of Columbia	6	6
Hawaii	6	6
Puerto Rico	6	6
Total	**1002**	**888½**

1. Other candidates: John A. Johnson, 46; George Gray, 59½; not voting, 8.

1908 Republican

(Narrative, p. 62)

Delegation	Total Votes	Minority Report on Changing Delegate Apportionment Formula			Minority Plank for Direct Election of Senators		First Pres. Ballot [1]
		Yea	Nay	Not Voting	Yea	Nay	Taft
Alabama	22	—	22	—	—	22	22
Arizona	2	—	2	—	—	2	2
Arkansas	18	—	18	—	—	18	18
California	20	—	20	—	—	20	20
Colorado	10	10	—	—	—	10	10
Connecticut	14	14	—	—	—	14	14
Delaware	6	—	6	—	—	6	6
Florida	10	—	10	—	—	10	10
Georgia	26	—	26	—	—	26	17
Idaho	6	—	6	—	3	3	6
Illinois	54	54	—	—	1	53	3
Indiana	30	30	—	—	11	19	—
Iowa	26	6	20	—	1	25	26
Kansas	20	—	20	—	—	20	20
Kentucky	26	1	25	—	2	24	24
Louisiana	18	—	18	—	—	18	18
Maine	12	12	—	—	—	12	12
Maryland	16	—	16	—	1	15	16
Massachusetts	32	32	—	—	—	32	32
Michigan	28	18	10	—	5	23	27
Minnesota	22	10	11	1	—	22	22
Mississippi	20	—	20	—	—	20	20
Missouri	36	12	24	—	4	32	36
Montana	6	—	6	—	—	6	6
Nebraska	16	7	9	—	16	—	16
Nevada	6	—	6	—	—	6	6
New Hampshire	8	8	—	—	—	8	5
New Jersey	24	23	1	—	—	24	15
New Mexico	2	—	—	2	—	2	2
New York	78	78	—	—	—	78	10
North Carolina	24	—	24	—	—	24	24
North Dakota	8	—	8	—	—	8	8
Ohio	46	8	38	—	2	44	42
Oklahoma	14	—	14	—	14	—	14
Oregon	8	3	5	—	—	8	8
Pennsylvania	68	68	—	—	13	55	1
Rhode Island	8	8	—	—	—	8	8
South Carolina	18	—	18	—	—	18	13
South Dakota	8	8	—	—	8	—	8
Tennessee	24	—	24	—	—	24	24
Texas	36	—	36	—	—	36	36
Utah	6	6	—	—	2	4	6
Vermont	8	8	—	—	—	8	8
Virginia	24	—	24	—	—	24	21
Washington	10	4	6	—	—	10	10
West Virginia	14	14	—	—	5	9	14
Wisconsin	26	26	—	—	25	1	1
Wyoming	6	—	6	—	—	6	6
Alaska	2	2	—	—	—	2	2
District of Columbia	2	1	1	—	—	2	1
Hawaii	2	—	2	—	1	1	2
Philippine Islands	2	—	2	—	—	2	2
Puerto Rico	2	—	2	—	—	2	2
Total	**980**	**471**	**506**	**3**	**114**	**866**	**702**

1. Other candidates: Philander C. Knox, 68; Charles E. Hughes, 67; Joseph G. Cannon 58; Charles W. Fairbanks, 40; Robert M. LaFollette. 25; Joseph B. Foraker, 16; Theodore Roosevelt, 3; not voting, 1.

1912 Democratic (Narrative p. 65)

Delegation	Total Votes	Temporary Chairman[1]		First Pres. Ballot[2]				Tenth Pres. Ballot[3]			Thirtieth Pres. Ballot[4]			43rd Pres. Ballot[5]		45th Pres. Ballot[6]		46th Pres. Ballot[7]
		Bryan	Parker	Clark	Wilson	Harmon	Underwood	Clark	Wilson	Underwood	Clark	Wilson	Underwood	Clark	Wilson	Clark	Wilson	Wilson
Ala.	24	1½	22½	—	—	—	24	—	—	24	—	—	24	—	—	—	—	24
Ariz.	6	4	2	6	—	—	—	6	—	—	4	2	—	3	2	3	3	6
Ark.	18	—	18	18	—	—	—	18	—	—	18	—	—	18	—	18	—	18
Calif.	26	7	18	26	—	—	—	26	—	—	26	—	—	26	—	26	—	2
Colo.	12	6	6	12	—	—	—	12	—	—	12	—	—	11	1	2	10	12
Conn.	14	2	12	—	—	—	—	7	—	7	7	3	4	1	5	2	5	14
Del.	6	6	—	—	6	—	—	—	6	—	—	6	—	—	6	—	6	6
Fla.	12	1	11	—	—	—	12	—	—	12	—	—	12	—	2	—	3	7
Ga.	28	—	28	—	—	—	28	—	—	28	—	—	28	—	—	—	—	28
Idaho	8	8	—	8	—	—	—	8	—	—	2½	5½	—	1	7	1½	6½	8
Ill.	58	—	58	58	—	—	—	58	—	—	58	—	—	—	58	—	58	58
Ind.	30	8	21	—	—	—	—	—	—	—	1	28	—	1	28	—	30	30
Iowa	26	13	13	26	—	—	—	26	—	—	12	14	—	11½	14½	9	17	26
Kan.	20	20	—	20	—	—	—	20	—	—	—	20	—	—	20	—	20	20
Ky.	26	7½	17½	26	—	—	—	26	—	—	26	—	—	26	—	26	—	26
La.	20	10	10	11	9	—	—	10	10	—	7	12	—	6	14	5	15	18
Maine	12	1	11	1	9	—	2	1	11	—	1	9	2	1	11	1	11	12
Md.	16	1½	14½	16	—	—	—	16	—	—	11	4½	—	9	5½	8½	7	16
Mass.	36	18	15	36	—	—	—	33	1	2	—	7	—	—	9	—	9	36
Mich.	30	9	21	12	10	7	—	18	9	—	18	12	—	2	28	2	28	30
Minn.	24	24	—	—	24	—	—	—	24	—	—	24	—	—	24	—	24	24
Miss.	20	—	20	—	—	—	20	—	—	20	—	—	20	—	—	—	—	20
Mo.	36	14	22	36	—	—	—	36	—	—	36	—	—	36	—	36	—	—
Mont.	8	7	1	8	—	—	—	8	—	—	2	6	—	1	7	1	7	8
Neb.	16	13	3	12	—	4	—	13	3	—	3	13	—	3	13	3	13	16
Nev.	6	6	—	6	—	—	—	6	—	—	6	—	—	6	—	6	—	—
N.H.	8	5	3	8	—	—	—	5	3	—	3	5	—	3	5	3	5	8
N.J.	28	24	4	2	24	—	2	4	24	—	4	24	—	4	24	4	24	24
N.M.	8	8	—	8	—	—	—	8	—	—	8	—	—	8	—	8	—	8
N.Y.	90	—	90	—	—	90	—	90	—	—	90	—	—	90	—	90	—	90
N.C.	24	9	15	—	16½	½	7	—	18	6	—	17½	6½	—	22	—	22	24
N.D.	10	10	—	—	10	—	—	—	10	—	—	10	—	—	10	—	10	10
Ohio	48	19	29	1	10	35	—	6	11	—	—	19	10	—	20	—	23	33
Okla.	20	20	—	10	10	—	—	10	10	—	10	10	—	10	10	10	10	20
Ore.	10	9	1	—	10	—	—	—	10	—	—	10	—	—	10	—	10	10
Pa.	76	67	9	—	71	5	—	5	71	—	4	72	—	2	74	—	76	76
R.I.	10	—	10	10	—	—	—	10	—	—	10	—	—	10	—	10	—	10
S.C.	18	18	—	—	18	—	—	—	18	—	—	18	—	—	18	—	18	18
S.D.	10	10	—	—	10	—	—	—	10	—	—	10	—	—	10	—	10	10
Tenn.	24	7	17	6	6	6	6	13	7½	3½	13½	8	2½	10	8	8	10	24
Texas	40	40	—	—	40	—	—	—	40	—	—	40	—	—	40	—	40	40
Utah	8	4	4	1½	6	½	—	1½	6½	—	1½	6½	—	1½	6½	—	8	8
Vt.	8	—	8	—	—	—	—	—	8	—	—	8	—	—	8	—	8	8
Va.	24	10	14	—	9½	—	14½	½	9½	14	3	9½	11½	—	24	—	24	24
Wash.	14	14	—	14	—	—	—	14	—	—	14	—	—	14	—	14	—	14
W.Va.	16	4½	10½	16	—	—	—	16	—	—	16	—	—	—	16	—	16	16
Wis.	26	26	—	6	19	—	—	6	20	—	6	19	—	4	22	—	26	26
Wyo.	6	6	—	6	—	—	—	6	—	—	6	—	—	—	6	—	6	6
Alaska	6	2	4	4	—	—	—	3	3	—	6	—	—	1	5	—	6	6
D.C.	6	—	6	6	—	—	—	6	—	—	6	—	—	6	—	6	—	—
Hawaii	6	2	4	2	3	—	1	2	3	1	2	3	1	2	4	2	4	6
Phil. Is.	6	2	4	—	—	—	—	—	—	—	—	—	—	—	—	—	—	—
P.R.	6	4	2	2	3	—	1	2	4	—	1½	4½	—	1	4½	1	4½	6
Total	1094	508	579	440½	324	148	117½	556	350½	117½	455	460	121½	329	602	306	633	990

1. Other candidates: James A. O'Gorman, 4; John W. Kern, 1; not voting, 2.
2. Other candidates: Simeon E. Baldwin, 22; Thomas R. Marshall, 31; William J. Bryan, 1; William Sulzer, 2; not voting, 8.
3. Other candidates: Harmon, 31; Marshall, 31; Kern, 1; Bryan, 1; not voting, 6.
4. Other candidates: Foss, 30; Harmon, 19; Kern, 2; not voting, ½.
5. Other candidates: Underwood, 98½; Harmon, 28; Foss, 27; Bryan, 1; Kern, 1; not voting, 7½.
6. Other candidates: Underwood, 97; Foss, 27; Harmon, 25; not voting, 6.
7. Other candidates: Clark, 84; Harmon, 12; not voting, 8.

1912 Republican

(Narrative p. 64)

Delegation	Total Votes	Temporary Chairman[1]		Table Motion Prohibiting Challenged Taft Delegates from Voting			First Pres. Ballot[2]		
		Root	McGovern	Yea	Nay	Not voting	Taft	Roosevelt	Present, Not voting
Alabama	24	22	2	22	2	—	22	—	2
Arizona	6	6	—	6	—	—	6	—	—
Arkansas	18	17	1	17	1	—	17	—	1
California	26	2	24	2	24	—	2	—	24
Colorado	12	12	—	12	—	—	12	—	—
Connecticut	14	14	—	14	—	—	14	—	—
Delaware	6	6	—	6	—	—	6	—	—
Florida	12	12	—	12	—	—	12	—	—
Georgia	28	22	6	24	4	—	28	—	—
Idaho	8	—	8	—	8	—	1	—	—
Illinois	58	9	49	7	51	—	2	53	1
Indiana	30	20	10	20	9	1	20	3	7
Iowa	26	16	10	16	10	—	16	—	—
Kansas	20	2	18	2	18	—	2	—	18
Kentucky	26	23	3	24	2	—	24	2	—
Louisiana	20	20	—	20	—	—	20	—	—
Maine	12	—	12	—	12	—	—	—	12
Maryland	16	8	8	9	7	—	1	9	5
Massachusetts	36	18	18	18	18	—	15	—	21
Michigan	30	19	10	20	10	—	20	9	1
Minnesota	24	—	24	—	24	—	—	—	24
Mississippi	20	16	4	16	4	—	17	—	3
Missouri	36	16	20	16	20	—	16	—	20
Montana	8	8	—	8	—	—	8	—	—
Nebraska	16	—	16	—	16	—	—	2	14
Nevada	6	6	—	6	—	—	6	—	—
New Hampshire	8	8	—	8	—	—	8	—	—
New Jersey	28	—	28	—	28	—	—	2	26
New Mexico	8	6	2	7	1	—	7	1	—
New York	90	76	13	75	15	—	76	8	6
North Carolina	24	3	21	2	22	—	1	1	22
North Dakota	10	—	9	2	8	—	—	—	—
Ohio	48	14	34	14	34	—	14	—	34
Oklahoma	20	4	16	4	16	—	4	1	15
Oregon	10	3	6	5	5	—	—	8	2
Pennsylvania	76	12	64	12	64	—	9	2	62
Rhode Island	10	10	—	10	—	—	10	—	—
South Carolina	18	11	7	11	6	1	16	—	1
South Dakota	10	—	10	—	10	—	—	5	—
Tennessee	24	23	1	23	1	—	23	1	—
Texas	40	31	8	29	9	2	31	—	8
Utah	8	7	1	7	1	—	8	—	—
Vermont	8	6	2	6	2	—	6	—	2
Virginia	24	22	2	21	3	—	22	—	1
Washington	14	14	—	14	—	—	14	—	—
West Virginia	16	—	16	—	16	—	—	—	16
Wisconsin	26	—	12	—	26	—	—	—	—
Wyoming	6	6	—	6	—	—	6	—	—
Alaska	2	2	—	2	—	—	2	—	—
District of Columbia	2	2	—	2	—	—	2	—	—
Hawaii	6	—	6	6	—	—	6	—	—
Philippine Islands	2	2	—	2	—	—	2	—	—
Puerto Rico	2	2	—	2	—	—	2	—	—
Total	**1078**	**558**	**501**	**567**	**507**	**4**	**556**[a]	**107**	**348**[b]

a. Sum of column; proceedings record 561.
b. Sum of column; proceedings record 349.
1. Other candidates: W. S. Lauder, 12; Asle J. Gronna, 1; not voting, 6.
2. Other candidates: Robert M. La Follette, 41; Albert B. Cummins, 17; Charles E. Hughes, 2; absent and not voting, 7.

1916 Democratic

(Narrative p. 69)

Delegation	Total Votes	Minority Plank on Women's Suffrage		
		Yea	Nay	Not Voting
Alabama	24	1	23	—
Arizona	6	—	6	—
Arkansas	18	—	18	—
California	26	—	26	—
Colorado	12	—	12	—
Connecticut	14	1	13	—
Delaware	6	—	6	—
Florida	12	4	8	—
Georgia	28	23½	4½	—
Idaho	8	—	8	—
Illinois	58	1	57	—
Indiana	30	24	6	—
Iowa	26	—	26	—
Kansas	20	—	20	—
Kentucky	26	—	26	—
Louisiana	20	8	12	—
Maine	12	—	6	6
Maryland	16	16	—	—
Massachusetts	36	6	30	—
Michigan	30	—	30	—
Minnesota	24	9	15	—
Mississippi	20	—	20	—
Missouri	36	4	24	8
Montana	8	—	8	—
Nebraska	16	—	16	—
Nevada	6	—	6	—
New Hampshire	8	1	7	—
New Jersey	28	10	11	7
New Mexico	6	—	6	—
New York	90	—	90	—
North Carolina	24	11	13	—
North Dakota	10	—	10	—
Ohio	48	20	28	—
Oklahoma	20	—	20	—
Oregon	10	—	10	—
Pennsylvania	76	—	76	—
Rhode Island	10	1	9	—
South Carolina	18	—	18	—
South Dakota	10	—	10	—
Tennessee	24	—	24	—
Texas	40	32	8	—
Utah	8	—	8	—
Vermont	8	—	8	—
Virginia	24	—	24	—
Washington	14	—	14	—
West Virginia	16	8	8	—
Wisconsin	26	—	26	—
Wyoming	6	—	6	—
Alaska	6	—	6	—
District of Columbia	6	—	6	—
Hawaii	6	—	6	—
Philippine Islands	6	1	4	1
Puerto Rico	6	—	6	—
Total	1092	181½	888½	22

1916 Republican

(Narrative p. 68)

Delegation	Total Votes	First Pres. Ballot[1]			Second Pres. Ballot[2]		Third Pres. Ballot[3]
		Hughes	Root	Weeks	Hughes	Root	Hughes
Alabama	16	8	—	3	9	—	16
Arizona	6	4	—	—	4	—	6
Arkansas	15	1	3	3	—	2	15
California	26	9	8	3	11	12	26
Colorado	12	—	5	—	—	5	12
Connecticut	14	5	5	1	5	7	14
Delaware	6	—	—	—	—	—	6
Florida	8	8	—	—	8	—	8
Georgia	17	5	—	6	6	—	17
Idaho	8	4	—	—	4	1	8
Illinois	58	—	—	—	—	—	58
Indiana	30	—	—	—	—	—	30
Iowa	26	—	—	—	—	—	26
Kansas	20	10	2	3	10	2	20
Kentucky	26	10	—	—	11	—	26
Louisiana	12	4	1	3	6	1	12
Maine	12	6	1	3	8	1	12
Maryland	16	7	1	5	7	1	15
Massachusetts	36	4	—	28	12	—	32
Michigan	30	—	—	—	28	—	30
Minnesota	24	—	—	—	—	—	24
Mississippi	12	4	—	1½	4	—	8½
Missouri	36	18	—	8	22	—	34
Montana	8	—	—	—	—	—	7
Nebraska	16	—	—	—	2	—	16
Nevada	6	4	2	—	4	2	6
New Hampshire	8	—	—	8	3	3	8
New Jersey	28	12	12	1	16	3	27
New Mexico	6	2	—	2	2	—	5
New York	87	42	43	—	43	42	87
North Carolina	21	6	2	3	6	2	14
North Dakota	10	—	—	—	—	—	10
Ohio	48	—	—	—	—	—	48
Oklahoma	20	5	1	6	5	1	19
Oregon	10	10	—	—	10	—	10
Pennsylvania	76	2	—	—	8	1	72
Rhode Island	10	10	—	—	10	—	10
South Carolina	11	2	1	3	4	—	6
South Dakota	10	—	—	—	—	—	10
Tennessee	21	9	—	3½	8	½	18
Texas	26	1	1	1	3	3	26
Utah	8	4	3	—	5	2	7
Vermont	8	8	—	—	8	—	8
Virginia	15	5½	3	3	8½	5	15
Washington	14	5	8	—	5	—	14
West Virginia	16	1	—	5	4	1	16
Wisconsin	26	11	—	—	11	—	23
Wyoming	6	6	—	—	6	—	6
Alaska	2	1	—	1	1	—	2
Hawaii	2	—	—	1	1	—	2
Philippine Islands	2	—	1	—	—	1	2
Total	**987**	**253½**	**103**	**105**	**328½**	**98½**	**949½**

1. Other candidates: Albert B. Cummins, 85; Theodore E. Burton, 77½; Charles W. Fairbanks, 74½; Lawrence Y. Sherman, 66; Theodore Roosevelt, 65; Philander C. Knox, 36; Henry Ford, 32; Martin G. Brumbaugh, 29; Robert M. La Follette, 25; William H. Taft, 14; Coleman du Pont, 12; Frank B. Willis, 4; William E. Borah, 2; Samuel W. McCall, 1; not voting, 2½.
2. Other candidates: Fairbanks, 88½; Cummins, 85; Roosevelt, 81; Weeks, 79; Burton 76½; Sherman, 65; Knox, 36; La Follette, 25; du Pont, 13; John Wanamaker, 5; Willis, 1; Leonard Wood, 1; Warren G. Harding, 1; McCall, 1; not voting 2.
3. Other candidates: Roosevelt, 18½; La Follette, 3; du Pont, 5; Henry Cabot Lodge, 7; Weeks, 3; not voting, 1.

1920 Democratic (Narrative, p. 72)

Delegation	Total Votes	First Pres. Ballot[1]				Thirtieth Pres. Ballot[2]			39th Pres. Ballot[3]		44th Pres. Ballot[4]	
		McAdoo	Cox	Palmer	Smith	McAdoo	Cox	Palmer	McAdoo	Cox	McAdoo	Cox
Alabama	24	9	3	6	2	12	7	—	8	—	8	13
Arizona	6	4	1	—	—	3	2	—	4	2	2½	3½
Arkansas	18	3	7	2	—	3	14	1	4	14	—	18
California	26	10	4	3	1	10	13	1	14	12	13	13
Colorado	12	3	—	8	—	5	6	—	4	7	3	9
Connecticut	14	—	—	—	—	1	6	4	3	10	2	12
Delaware	6	4	—	—	—	4	2	—	4	2	3	3
Florida	12	1	—	8	—	3	9	—	3	9	—	12
Georgia	28	—	—	28	—	—	—	28	28	—	—	28
Idaho	8	8	—	—	—	8	—	—	8	—	8	—
Illinois	58	9	9	35	5	21	36	1	18	38	13	44
Indiana	30	—	—	—	—	29	—	—	11	19	—	30
Iowa	26	—	—	—	—	—	26	—	—	26	—	26
Kansas	20	20	—	—	—	20	—	—	20	—	20	—
Kentucky	26	3	23	—	—	5	20	—	5	20	—	26
Louisiana	20	5	2	2	—	4	14	—	7	12	—	20
Maine	12	5	—	5	—	7	—	5	12	—	5	5
Maryland	16	5½	5½	—	—	5½	8½	—	5½	8½	—	13½
Massachusetts	36	4	4	17	7	2	15	16	1	33	—	35
Michigan	30	15	—	12	—	15	6	9	14	12	—	—
Minnesota	24	10	2	7	—	14	4	4	16	7	15	8
Mississippi	20	—	—	—	—	—	20	—	—	20	—	20
Missouri	36	15½	2½	10	—	18	6	5	20½	11½	17	18
Montana	8	1	—	—	—	8	—	—	8	—	2	6
Nebraska	16	—	—	—	—	7	—	—	7	—	2	5
Nevada	6	—	6	—	—	—	6	—	—	6	—	6
New Hampshire	8	4	—	1	—	5	2	1	5	2	6	2
New Jersey	28	—	—	—	—	—	28	—	—	28	—	28
New Mexico	6	2	—	1	—	6	—	—	6	—	6	—
New York	90	—	—	—	90	20	70	—	20	70	20	70
North Carolina	24	—	—	—	—	24	—	—	24	—	24	—
North Dakota	10	6	1	2	—	8	2	—	9	1	4	2
Ohio	48	—	48	—	—	—	48	—	—	48	—	48
Oklahoma	20	—	—	—	—	—	—	—	—	—	—	—
Oregon	10	10	—	—	—	10	—	—	10	—	10	—
Pennsylvania	76	2	—	73	—	2	1	73	2	1	4	68
Rhode Island	10	2	—	5	2	3	4	3	1	7	1	9
South Carolina	18	18	—	—	—	18	—	—	18	—	18	—
South Dakota	10	—	—	—	—	6	4	—	6	3	3	5
Tennessee	24	2	8	9	—	—	—	—	—	—	—	—
Texas	40	40	—	—	—	40	—	—	40	—	40	—
Utah	8	8	—	—	—	8	—	—	8	—	7	1
Vermont	8	4	2	1	1	1	6	1	4	4	—	8
Virginia	24	—	—	—	—	—	—	—	10	11	2½	18½
Washington	14	10	—	—	—	14	—	—	11	2½	—	13
West Virginia	16	—	—	—	—	—	—	—	—	—	—	—
Wisconsin	26	11	5	3	1	19	7	—	19	7	3	23
Wyoming	6	6	—	—	—	6	—	—	6	—	3	3
Alaska	6	2	1	3	—	2	1	3	4	2	—	6
Canal Zone	2	1	—	1	—	1	—	1	2	—	2	—
District of Columbia	6	—	—	6	—	—	—	6	—	6	—	6
Hawaii	6	2	—	4	—	1	5	—	1	5	—	6
Philippine Islands	6	—	—	—	—	3	2	1	3	2	2	4
Puerto Rico	6	1	—	2	—	2	—	2	6	—	1	5
Total	1094	266	134	254[a]	109	403½	400½	165	440	468½	270	699½

a. Sum of column; proceedings record 256.

1. Other candidates: Homer S. Cummings, 25; James W. Gerard, 21; Robert L. Owen, 33; Gilbert M. Hitchcock, 18; Edwin T. Meredith, 27; Edward I. Edwards, 42; John W. Davis, 32; Carter Glass, 26½; Furnifold M. Simmons, 24; Francis B. Harrison, 6; John S. Williams, 20; Thomas R. Marshall, 37; Champ Clark, 9; Oscar W. Underwood, ½; William R. Hearst, 1; William J. Bryan, 1; Bainbridge Colby, 1; Josephus Daniels, 1; Wood, 4.

2. Other candidates: Cummings, 4; Owen, 33; Davis, 58; Glass, 24; Clark, 2; Underwood, 2; not voting, 2.

3. Other candidates: Palmer, 74; Davis, 71½; Owen, 32; Cummings, 2; Clark, 2; Colby, 1; not voting, 3.

4. Other candidates: Palmer, 1; Davis, 52; Owen, 34; Glass, 1½; Colby, 1; not voting, 36.

1920 Republican

(Narrative, p. 71)

Delegation	Total Votes	First Pres. Ballot[1]			Fourth Pres. Ballot[2]			Eighth Pres. Ballot[3]			Ninth Pres. Ballot[4]			Tenth Pres. Ballot[5] (Before shift)		Tenth Pres. Ballot[6] (After shift)	
		Wood	Lowden	Johnson	Wood	Lowden	Johnson	Wood	Lowden	Harding	Wood	Lowden	Harding	Wood	Harding	Wood	Harding
Alabama	14	4	6	3	4	6	4	4	6	4	4	6	4	3	8	3	8
Arizona	6	6	—	—	6	—	—	6	—	—	6	—	—	6	—	—	6
Arkansas	13	6	6	—	2½	10½	—	1½	11½	—	1½	10½	1	—	13	—	13
California	26	—	—	26	—	—	26	—	—	—	—	—	—	—	—	—	—
Colorado	12	9	2	—	9	2	—	6	3	3	6	1	5	6	5	—	12
Connecticut	14	—	14	—	—	13	1	1	11	—	—	—	13	—	13	—	13
Delaware	6	—	—	—	—	2	—	—	—	3	—	—	3	—	6	—	6
Florida	8	4½	2½	—	6½	1½	—	7	1	—	1	—	7	½	7½	½	7½
Georgia	17	8	9	—	8	9	—	8	9	—	8	8	1	7	10	7	10
Idaho	8	5	—	1	5	1	1	4	2	1	5	1	1	3	2	3	2
Illinois	58	14	41	3	—	41	17	—	41	—	—	41	—	—	22.2	—	38.2
Indiana	30	22	—	8	18	3	6	15	4	11	15	4	11	8	20	9	21
Iowa	26	—	26	—	—	26	—	—	26	—	—	26	—	—	26	—	26
Kansas	20	14	6	—	14	6	—	10	6	4	—	—	20	1	18	1	18
Kentucky	26	—	20	1	—	26	—	—	26	—	—	—	26	—	26	—	26
Louisiana	12	3	3	1	3	6	—	3	7	2	—	—	12	—	12	—	12
Maine	12	11	—	—	11	—	—	12	—	—	12	—	—	12	—	12	—
Maryland	16	16	—	—	16	—	—	16	—	—	16	—	—	10	5	10	5
Massachusetts	35	7	—	—	16	—	—	11	—	—	11	1	1	17	17	17	17
Michigan	30	—	—	30	—	—	30	13	7	—	15	6	1	1	25	1	25
Minnesota	24	19	3	2	17	5	2	16	5	—	17	5	—	21	2	21	2
Mississippi	12	4½	2	2	7½	2½	—	8½	1½	2	7½	—	4½	2½	9½	—	12
Missouri	36	4½	18	3	8½	19	1	2½	15½	17	—	—	36	—	36	—	36
Montana	8	—	—	8	—	—	8	—	—	—	—	—	—	—	—	—	—
Nebraska	16	3	—	13	6	—	10	14	—	—	16	—	—	5	4	5	4
Nevada	6	2	1½	2	2½	2	1½	1½	—	3½	1½	—	3½	—	3½	—	3½
New Hampshire	8	8	—	—	8	—	—	8	—	—	8	—	—	8	—	8	—
New Jersey	28	17	—	11	17	—	11	16	—	2	15	—	4	15	5	15	5
New Mexico	6	6	—	—	6	—	—	6	—	—	6	—	—	6	—	—	6
New York	88	10	2	—	20	32	5	23	45	8	5	4	66	6	68	6	68
North Carolina	22	—	—	1	3	15	2	2	16	4	3	—	18	2	20	2	20
North Dakota	10	2	—	8	3	1	6	3	4	—	3	4	—	1	9	—	10
Ohio	48	9	—	—	9	—	—	9	—	39	9	—	39	—	48	—	48
Oklahoma	20	1½	18½	—	2	18	—	2	18	—	½	—	18	½	18	½	18
Oregon	10	1	—	9	5	—	5	4	—	1	4	—	1	3	2	3	2
Pennsylvania	76	—	—	—	—	—	—	—	—	—	—	—	—	14	60	14	60
Rhode Island	10	10	—	—	10	—	—	10	—	—	10	—	—	—	10	—	10
South Carolina	11	—	8	—	—	11	—	—	11	—	—	—	11	—	11	—	11
South Dakota	10	10	—	—	10	—	—	10	—	—	10	—	—	6	4	6	4
Tennessee	20	20	—	—	19	1	—	10	7	3	6	1	13	—	20	—	20
Texas	23	8½	5	1½	8	9½	1	5	8½	8½	1	1	19½	—	23	—	23
Utah	8	5	2	—	5	2	—	4	2	2	2	2	4	1	5	1	5
Vermont	8	8	—	—	8	—	—	8	—	—	8	—	—	8	—	8	—
Virginia	15	3	12	—	3	12	—	3	10	2	4	—	11	1	14	1	14
Washington	14	—	—	—	—	—	—	—	—	—	—	—	—	5	6	—	14
West Virginia	16	—	—	—	8	—	1	9	—	7	8	—	7	—	16	—	16
Wisconsin	26	1	—	—	1	—	2	1	—	—	1	—	—	—	1	—	1
Wyoming	6	—	3	—	3	3	—	—	—	6	—	—	6	—	6	—	6
Alaska	2	—	—	—	1	—	—	1	—	—	1	—	1	—	2	—	2
District of Columbia	2	2	—	—	2	—	—	2	—	—	—	—	2	—	2	—	2
Hawaii	2	—	—	—	—	2	—	—	2	—	—	—	2	—	2	—	2
Philippine Islands	2	2	—	—	2	—	—	2	—	—	2	—	—	2	—	2	—
Puerto Rico	2	1	1	—	1	1	—	1	1	—	—	—	2	—	2	—	2
Total	**984**	**287½**	**211½**	**133½**	**314½**	**289**	**140½**	**299**	**307**	**133**[a]	**249**	**121½**	**374½**	**181½**	**644.7**	**156**	**692.2**

a. Sum of column; proceedings record 133½.

1. Other candidates: Warren G. Harding, 65½; William C. Sproul, 84; Calvin Coolidge, 34; Herbert Hoover, 5½; Coleman du Pont, 7; Jeter C. Pritchard, 21; Robert M. La Follette, 24; Howard Sutherland, 17; William E. Borah, 2; Charles B. Warren, 1; Miles Poindexter, 20; Nicholas M. Butler, 69½; not voting, 1.

2. Other candidates: Harding, 61½; Sproul, 79½; Coolidge, 25; Hoover, 5; du Pont, 2; La Follette, 22; Sutherland, 3; Borah, 1; Poindexter, 15; Butler, 20; James E. Watson, 4; Knox, 2.

3. Other candidates: Johnson, 87; Coolidge, 30; du Pont, 3; Kellogg, 1; La Follette, 24; Poindexter, 15; Irving L. Lenroot, 1; Hoover, 5; Butler, 2; Philander C. Knox, 1; Sproul, 76.

4. Other candidates: Johnson, 82; Sproul, 78; Coolidge, 28; Hoover, 6; Lenroot, 1; Butler, 2; Knox, 1; La Follette, 24; Poindexter, 14; Will H. Hays, 1; H. F. MacGregor, 1; not voting, 1.

5. Other candidates: Lowden, 28; Johnson 80 4/5; Hoover, 10½; Coolidge, 5; Butler, 2; Lenroot, 1; Hays, 1; Knox, 1; La Follette, 24; Poindexter, 1; not voting, 2½.

6. Other candidates: Lowden, 11; Johnson, 80 4/5; Hoover, 9½; Coolidge, 5; Butler, 2; Lenroot, 1; Hays, 1; Knox, 1; La Follette, 24; not voting, ½.

1924 Democratic

(Narrative, p. 75)

Delegation	Total Votes	Minority Report on League of Nations			Minority Report on Ku Klux Klan			First Pres. Ballot[1]		Fiftieth Pres. Ballot[2]		Ninetieth Pres. Ballot[3]		
		Yea	Nay	Not voting	Yea	Nay	Not voting	McAdoo	Smith	McAdoo	Smith	McAdoo	Smith	Ralston
Alabama	24	12½	11½	—	24	—	—	—	—	—	—	—	—	—
Arizona	6	1½	4½	—	1	5	—	4½	—	3½	—	3½	—	—
Arkansas	18	3	15	—	—	18	—	—	—	—	—	—	—	—
California	26	4	22	—	7	19	—	26	—	26	—	26	—	—
Colorado	12	9½	2½	—	6	6	—	—	—	4	3	1	3	½
Connecticut	14	5	9	—	13	1	—	—	6	4	10	2	12	—
Delaware	6	6	—	—	6	—	—	—	—	—	—	—	—	—
Florida	12	5	7	—	1	11	—	12	—	10	1	9	—	3
Georgia	28	—	28	—	1	19½	7½	28	—	28	—	28	—	—
Idaho	8	8	—	—	—	8	—	8	—	8	—	8	—	—
Illinois	58	10	48	—	45	13	—	12	15	13	20	12	36	6
Indiana	30	—	30	—	5	25	—	—	—	—	—	—	—	30
Iowa	26	—	26	—	13½	12½	—	26	—	26	—	—	—	—
Kansas	20	—	20	—	—	20	—	—	—	20	—	—	—	—
Kentucky	26	9½	16½	—	9½	16½	—	26	—	26	—	26	—	—
Louisiana	20	—	20	—	—	20	—	—	—	—	—	—	—	—
Maine	12	11	1	—	8	4	—	2	3½	2½	4½	1½	4½	—
Maryland	16	—	16	—	16	—	—	—	—	—	—	—	—	—
Massachusetts	36	8	28	—	35½	½	—	1½	33	2½	33½	2½	33½	—
Michigan	30	6	24	—	12½	16½	1	—	—	15	15	—	10	20
Minnesota	24	10	14	—	17	7	—	5	10	6	15	6	15	—
Mississippi	20	—	20	—	—	20	—	—	—	—	—	—	—	20
Missouri	36	2	34	—	10½	25½	—	36	—	36	—	—	—	36
Montana	8	—	8	—	1	7	—	7	1	7	—	7	1	—
Nebraska	16	—	16	—	3	13	—	1	—	13	3	1	—	—
Nevada	6	—	6	—	—	6	—	6	—	6	—	—	—	6
New Hampshire	8	8	—	—	2½	5½	—	—	—	4½	3½	3	3½	—
New Jersey	28	—	28	—	28	—	—	—	—	—	28	—	28	—
New Mexico	6	—	6	—	1	5	—	6	—	6	—	6	—	—
New York	90	35	55	—	90	—	—	—	90	2	88	2	88	—
North Carolina	24	6	18	—	3 17/20	20 3/20	—	24	—	17	—	3	—	—
North Dakota	10	1	9	—	10	—	—	10	—	5	5	5	5	—
Ohio	48	48	—	—	32½	15½	—	—	—	—	—	—	20½	17
Oklahoma	20	—	20	—	—	20	—	20	—	—	—	—	—	20
Oregon	10	1	9	—	—	10	—	10	—	10	—	10	—	—
Pennsylvania	76	52	22	2	49½	24½	2	25½	35½	25½	38½	25½	39½	—
Rhode Island	10	—	10	—	10	—	—	—	10	—	10	—	10	—
South Carolina	18	18	—	—	—	18	—	18	—	18	—	18	—	—
South Dakota	10	—	10	—	6	4	—	10	—	9	—	9	—	—
Tennessee	24	15	9	—	3	21	—	24	—	24	—	24	—	—
Texas	40	—	40	—	—	40	—	40	—	40	—	40	—	—
Utah	8	5½	2½	—	4	4	—	8	—	8	—	8	—	—
Vermont	8	2	6	—	8	—	—	1	7	1	7	—	8	—
Virginia	24	24	—	—	2½	21½	—	—	—	—	—	—	—	—
Washington	14	—	14	—	—	14	—	14	—	14	—	14	—	—
West Virginia	16	16	—	—	7	9	—	—	—	—	—	—	—	1
Wisconsin	26	4	22	—	25	1	—	3	23	3	23	1	23	—
Wyoming	6	3	3	—	2	4	—	—	—	1	4½	—	3	—
Alaska	6	—	5	—	6	—	—	1	3	1	3	1	5	—
Canal Zone	6	—	6	—	2	4	—	6	—	6	—	3	3	—
District of Columbia	6	—	6	—	6	—	—	6	—	6	—	6	—	—
Hawaii	6	—	6	—	4	2	—	1	1	1	1	1	—	—
Philippine Islands	6	2	4	—	2	2	2	3	3	3	3	2	2	—
Puerto Rico	6	1	5	—	2	4	—	—	—	—	—	—	1	—
Virgin Islands	—	—	—	—	—	—	—	—	—	—	—	—	—	—
Total	**1098**	**353½**	**742½**	**2**	**542 7/20**	**543 3/20**	**12½**	**431½**	**241**	**461½**	**320½**	**314**	**354½**	**159½**

1. Other candidates: Oscar W. Underwood, 42½; Joseph T. Robinson, 21; Willard Saulsbury, 7; Samuel M. Ralston, 30; Jonathan M. Davis, 20; Albert C. Ritchie, 22½; Woodbridge N. Ferris, 30; James M. Cox, 59; Charles W. Bryan, 18; Fred H. Brown, 17; George S. Silzer, 38; Carter Glass, 25; John W. Davis, 31; William E. Sweet, 12; Patrick Harrison, 43½; Houston Thompson, 1; John B. Kendrick, 6.

2. Other candidates: John W. Davis, 64; Ralston, 58; Underwood, 42½; Robinson, 44; Glass, 24; Cox, 54; Ritchie, 16½; Saulsbury, 6; Walsh, 1; Jonathan M. Davis, 2; Owen, 4.

3. Other candidates: Underwood, 42½; Robinson 20; John W. Davis, 65½; Glass, 30½; Ritchie, 16½; Saulsbury, 6; Walsh, 5; Bryan, 15; Jonathan M. Davis, 22; Daniels, 19; Meredith, 26; not voting, 2.

1924 Democratic

(Narrative p. 75)

Delegation	100th Pres. Ballot[4]			101st Pres. Ballot[5]				102nd Pres. Ballot[6]			103rd Pres. Ballot[7] (Before shift)		103rd Pres. Ballot[8] (After shift)	
	McAdoo	Smith	Davis	Underwood	Smith	Davis	Meredith	Underwood	Davis	Walsh	Underwood	Davis	Underwood	Davis
Alabama	—	—	—	24	—	—	—	24	—	—	24	—	—	24
Arizona	3	—	—	3	—	—	—	3	—	—	3	—	3	—
Arkansas	—	—	—	—	—	—	—	—	—	—	—	—	—	—
California	16½	—	—	—	1	—	3	—	—	26	2	2	—	26
Colorado	½	3½	1½	1	3	2½	1	6½	1½	—	5	3	5	3
Connecticut	2	12	—	11	—	1	—	11	—	3	11	—	—	14
Delaware	—	—	—	—	—	6	—	—	—	—	6	—	6	—
Florida	9	—	3	—	—	3	—	—	5	4	—	6	—	6
Georgia	28	—	—	—	—	5	12	1	13	—	—	27	—	27
Idaho	—	—	—	—	—	—	—	—	—	8	—	8	—	8
Illinois	—	35	6	20	—	4	13	20	3	13	19	19	—	58
Indiana	—	—	14	3	—	10	6	10	10	—	5	25	5	25
Iowa	—	—	—	—	—	—	26	—	—	—	—	—	—	26
Kansas	—	—	20	—	—	20	—	—	20	—	—	20	—	20
Kentucky	12	—	8½	1	1	9	½	1	9	6½	1	22½	—	26
Louisiana	—	—	20	—	—	20	—	—	20	—	—	20	—	20
Maine	1	2	8	5	—	6	—	8	4	—	10	2	10	2
Maryland	—	—	—	—	—	16	—	—	16	—	—	16	—	16
Massachusetts	2½	33½	—	—	33	—	—	8	½	2	23½	2	23½	2
Michigan	—	10	15	10	—	12	1	14	16	—	—	29½	—	29½
Minnesota	6	15	1	—	15	1	—	14	2	1	16	3	16	3
Mississippi	—	—	—	—	—	20	—	—	20	—	—	20	—	20
Missouri	—	—	36	—	—	36	—	—	36	—	—	36	—	36
Montana	1	—	—	—	—	—	—	—	—	8	—	—	—	—
Nebraska	—	2	—	—	1	—	11	2	—	4	2	1	2	1
Nevada	—	6	—	—	—	—	—	—	—	6	—	6	—	6
New Hampshire	—	1	2	—	1	1	1½	—	3½	4½	—	3½	—	3½
New Jersey	—	28	—	16	—	—	—	16	2	—	16	1	16	1
New Mexico	6	—	—	—	1½	1	1	—	2½	—	—	2	—	2
New York	2	88	—	86½	—	—	—	84	1	1	44	4	—	60
North Carolina	—	—	—	1	—	20	1	—	23	—	5½	18½	—	24
North Dakota	3	5	—	—	5	—	1	5	—	5	—	—	—	—
Ohio	—	15	23	5	10	23	5	7	25	—	4	41	1	46
Oklahoma	—	—	—	—	—	—	—	—	20	—	—	20	—	20
Oregon	10	—	—	1	—	2	1	1	2	—	1	5	1	5
Pennsylvania	17½	39½	9	6	36½	19½	1	32½	29½	4	31½	37½	—	76
Rhode Island	—	10	—	10	—	—	—	10	—	—	—	10	—	10
South Carolina	18	—	—	—	—	18	—	—	18	—	—	18	—	18
South Dakota	—	—	—	—	—	—	—	2	—	—	2	—	2	—
Tennessee	6	—	8	1	—	15	—	—	19	—	—	19	—	19
Texas	40	—	—	—	—	—	40	—	40	—	—	40	—	40
Utah	—	—	4	—	—	—	—	—	4	4	—	8	—	8
Vermont	—	8	—	4	—	4	—	4	4	—	—	8	—	8
Virginia	—	—	—	—	—	12	—	—	12	—	—	12	—	24
Washington	—	—	—	—	—	—	—	—	—	14	—	14	—	14
West Virginia	—	—	16	—	—	16	—	—	16	—	—	16	—	16
Wisconsin	—	22	—	8	9	—	1	11	—	9	8	1	1	22
Wyoming	—	3	½	—	3	3	—	—	6	—	—	6	—	6
Alaska	—	6	—	6	—	—	—	6	—	—	2	4	2	4
Canal Zone	3	3	—	—	—	1	3	3	3	—	—	6	—	6
District of Columbia	—	—	—	—	—	—	—	—	6	—	6	—	6	—
Hawaii	1	1	3	1	1	4	—	1	4	—	1	4	1	4
Philippine Islands	2	2	—	5	—	—	1	5	—	—	1	4	1	4
Puerto Rico	—	1	5	1	—	5	—	1	5	—	1	5	1	5
Virgin Islands	—	—	—	—	—	—	—	—	—	—	—	—	—	—
Total	190	351½	203½	229½	121	316	130	317	415½	123	250½	575½	102½	844

4. Other candidates: Underwood, 41½; Robinson 46; Bryan, 2; Saulsbury, 6; Walsh, 52½; Owen, 20; Ritchie, 17½; Meredith, 75½; David F. Houston, 9; Glass, 35; Daniels, 24; Baker, 4; Berry, 1; James W. Gerard, 10; not voting, 9.

5. Other candidates: Robinson, 22½; McAdoo, 52; Walsh, 98; Ritchie, ½; Berry, 1; A. A. Murphree, 4; Houston, 9; Owen, 23; Cummings, 9; Glass, 59; Gerard, 16; Baker, 1; Daniels, 1; Cordell Hull, 2; not voting, 3½.

6. Other candidates: Robinson, 21; McAdoo, 21; Smith, 44; Thompson, 1; Ritchie, ½; Bryan, 1; Gerard, 7; Glass, 67; Daniels, 2; Berry 1½; Meredith, 66½; Henry T. Allen, 1; Hull, 1; not voting, 8.

7. Other candidates: McAdoo, 14½; Robinson, 21; Meredith, 42½; Glass, 79; Hull, 1; Smith, 10½; Daniels, 1; Gerard, 8; Thompson, 1; Walsh, 84½; not voting, 9.

8. Other candidates: Robinson, 20; McAdoo, 11½; Smith, 7½; Walsh, 58; Meredith, 15½; Glass, 23; Gerard, 7; Hull, 1; not voting, 8.

1924 Republican

(Narrative, p. 74)

Delegation	Total Votes	First Pres. Ballot[1] Coolidge
Alabama	16	16
Arizona	9	9
Arkansas	14	14
California	29	29
Colorado	15	15
Connecticut	17	17
Delaware	9	9
Florida	10	10
Georgia	18	18
Idaho	11	11
Illinois	61	61
Indiana	33	33
Iowa	29	29
Kansas	23	23
Kentucky	26	26
Louisiana	13	13
Maine	15	15
Maryland	19	19
Massachusetts	39	39
Michigan	33	33
Minnesota	27	27
Mississippi	12	12
Missouri	39	39
Montana	11	11
Nebraska	19	19
Nevada	9	9
New Hampshire	11	11
New Jersey	31	31
New Mexico	9	9
New York	91	91
North Carolina	22	22
North Dakota	13	7
Ohio	51	51
Oklahoma	23	23
Oregon	13	13
Pennsylvania	79	79
Rhode Island	13	13
South Carolina	11	11
South Dakota	13	3
Tennessee	27	27
Texas	23	23
Utah	11	11
Vermont	11	11
Virginia	17	17
Washington	17	17
West Virginia	19	19
Wisconsin	29	1
Wyoming	9	9
Alaska	2	2
District of Columbia	2	2
Hawaii	2	2
Philippine Islands	2	2
Puerto Rico	2	2
Total	**1109**	**1065**

1. *Other candidates: Robert M. La Follette, 34; Hiram W. Johnson, 10.*

1928 Democratic
(Narrative. p. 78)

Delegation	Total Votes	First Pres. Ballot[1] (Before shift) Smith	First Pres. Ballot[2] (After shift) Smith
Alabama	24	1	1
Arizona	6	6	6
Arkansas	17	17	17
California	26	26	26
Colorado	12	12	12
Connecticut	14	14	14
Delaware	6	6	6
Florida	12	—	—
Georgia	28	—	—
Idaho	8	8	8
Illinois	58	56	56
Indiana	30	—	25
Iowa	26	26	26
Kansas	20	—	11½
Kentucky	26	26	26
Louisiana	20	20	20
Maine	12	12	12
Maryland	16	16	16
Massachusetts	36	36	36
Michigan	30	30	30
Minnesota	24	24	24
Mississippi	20	—	9½
Missouri	36	—	—
Montana	8	8	8
Nebraska	16	—	12
Nevada	6	6	6
New Hampshire	8	8	8
New Jersey	28	28	28
New Mexico	6	6	6
New York	90	90	90
North Carolina	24	4²/₃	4²/₃
North Dakota	10	10	10
Ohio	48	1	45
Oklahoma	20	10	10
Oregon	10	10	10
Pennsylvania	76	70½	70½
Rhode Island	10	10	10
South Carolina	18	—	—
South Dakota	10	10	10
Tennessee	24	—	23
Texas	40	—	—
Utah	8	8	8
Vermont	8	8	8
Virginia	24	6	6
Washington	14	14	14
West Virginia	16	10½	10½
Wisconsin	26	26	26
Wyoming	6	6	6
Alaska	6	6	6
Canal Zone	6	6	6
District of Columbia	6	6	6
Hawaii	6	6	6
Philippine Islands	6	6	6
Puerto Rico	6	6	6
Virgin Islands	2	2	2
Total	**1100**	**724²/₃**	**849¹/₆**

1. Other candidates: Cordell Hull, 71 and five-sixths; Walter F. George, 52½; James A. Reed, 48; Atlee Pomerene, 47; Jesse H. Jones, 43; Evans Woollen, 32; Patrick Harrison, 20; William A. Ayres, 20; Richard C. Watts, 18; Gilbert M. Hitchcock, 16; Vic Donahey, 5; Houston Thompson, 2.
2. Other candidates: George, 52½; Reed, 52; Hull, 50 and five-sixths; Jones, 43; Watts, 18; Harrison, 8½; Woollen, 7; Donahey, 5; Ayres, 3; Pomerene, 3; Hitchcock, 2; Thompson, 2; Theodore G. Bilbo, 1; not voting, 2½.

1928 Republican
(Narrative. p. 77)

Delegation	Total Votes	First Pres. Ballot[1] Hoover
Alabama	15	15
Arizona	9	9
Arkansas	11	11
California	29	29
Colorado	15	15
Connecticut	17	17
Delaware	9	9
Florida	10	9
Georgia	16	15
Idaho	11	11
Illinois	61	24
Indiana	33	—
Iowa	29	7
Kansas	23	—
Kentucky	29	29
Louisiana	12	11
Maine	15	15
Maryland	19	19
Massachusetts	39	39
Michigan	33	33
Minnesota	27	11
Mississippi	12	12
Missouri	39	28
Montana	11	10
Nebraska	19	11
Nevada	9	9
New Hampshire	11	11
New Jersey	31	31
New Mexico	9	7
New York	90	90
North Carolina	20	17
North Dakota	13	4
Ohio	51	36
Oklahoma	20	—
Oregon	13	13
Pennsylvania	79	79
Rhode Island	13	12
South Carolina	11	11
South Dakota	13	2
Tennessee	19	19
Texas	26	26
Utah	11	9
Vermont	11	11
Virginia	15	15
Washington	17	17
West Virginia	19	1
Wisconsin	26	9
Wyoming	9	9
Alaska	2	2
District of Columbia	2	2
Hawaii	2	2
Philippine Islands	2	2
Puerto Rico	2	2
Total	**1089**	**837**

1. Other candidates: Frank O. Lowden, 74; Charles Curtis, 64; James E. Watson, 45; George W. Norris, 24; Guy D. Goff, 18; Calvin Coolidge, 17; Charles G. Dawes, 4; Charles E. Hughes, 1; not voting, 5.

1932 Democratic
(Narrative, p. 80)

Delegation	Total Votes	Louisiana Credentials Yea	Nay	Not voting	Minnesota Credentials Yea	Nay	Not voting	Permanent Organization Yea	Nay	First Pres. Ballot[1] Roosevelt	Smith	Second Pres. Ballot[2] Roosevelt	Smith	Third Pres. Ballot[3] Roosevelt	Smith	Fourth Pres. Ballot[4] Roosevelt	Smith
Alabama	24	—	24	—	—	24	—	4½	19½	24	—	24	—	24	—	24	—
Arizona	6	—	6	—	—	6	—	—	6	6	—	6	—	6	—	6	—
Arkansas	18	—	18	—	—	18	—	—	18	18	—	18	—	18	—	18	—
California	44	44	—	—	44	—	—	44	—	—	—	—	—	—	—	44	—
Colorado	12	—	12	—	—	12	—	—	12	12	—	12	—	12	—	12	—
Connecticut	16	9½	6½	—	9¼	6¾	—	9½	6½	—	16	—	16	—	16	—	16
Delaware	6	1	5	—	—	6	—	1	5	6	—	6	—	6	—	6	—
Florida	14	3	11	—	—	14	—	—	14	14	—	14	—	14	—	14	—
Georgia	28	—	28	—	—	28	—	—	28	28	—	28	—	28	—	28	—
Idaho	8	—	8	—	—	8	—	—	8	8	—	8	—	8	—	8	—
Illinois	58	50¼	7¾	—	48	10	—	42	16	15¼	2¼	15¼	2¼	15¼	2¼	58	—
Indiana	30	30	—	—	30	—	—	30	—	14	2	16	2	16	2	30	—
Iowa	26	13	13	—	—	26	—	10	16	26	—	26	—	26	—	26	—
Kansas	20	—	20	—	—	20	—	6½	13½	20	—	20	—	20	—	20	—
Kentucky	26	—	26	—	—	26	—	—	26	26	—	26	—	26	—	26	—
Louisiana	20	—	20	—	—	20	—	—	20	20	—	20	—	20	—	20	—
Maine	12	6	6	—	6	6	—	7	5	12	—	12	—	12	—	12	—
Maryland	16	16	—	—	16	—	—	16	—	—	—	—	—	—	—	16	—
Massachusetts	36	36	—	—	36	—	—	36	—	—	36	—	36	—	36	—	36
Michigan	38	—	38	—	—	38	—	—	38	38	—	38	—	38	—	38	—
Minnesota	24	1	23	—	1	23	—	3	21	24	—	24	—	24	—	24	—
Mississippi	20	—	20	—	—	20	—	—	20	20	—	20	—	20	—	20	—
Missouri	36	19½	19½	—	16½	19½	—	16½	10½	12	—	18	—	20½	—	36	—
Montana	8	—	8	—	—	8	—	—	8	8	—	8	—	8	—	8	—
Nebraska	16	—	16	—	—	16	—	1	15	16	—	16	—	16	—	16	—
Nevada	6	—	6	—	—	6	—	—	6	6	—	6	—	6	—	6	—
New Hampshire	8	—	8	—	—	8	—	—	8	8	—	8	—	8	—	8	—
New Jersey	32	32	—	—	32	—	—	32	—	—	32	—	32	—	32	—	32
New Mexico	6	—	6	—	—	6	—	3	3	6	—	6	—	6	—	6	—
New York	94	65	29	—	65	29	—	67	27	28½	65½	29½	64½	31	63	31	63
North Carolina	26	20½	5½	—	—	26	—	4	22	26	—	26	—	25 4/100	—	26	—
North Dakota	10	—	10	—	2½	7½	—	1	9	9	—	10	—	9	—	10	—
Ohio	52	40	11	1	48½	2½	1	49½	2½	—	—	½	—	2½	—	29	17
Oklahoma	22	22	—	—	22	—	—	22	—	—	—	—	—	—	—	22	—
Oregon	10	—	10	—	—	10	—	1	9	10	—	10	—	10	—	10	—
Pennsylvania	76	20½	55½	—	25	49	2	27½	48½	44½	30	44½	23½	45½	21	49	14½
Rhode Island	10	10	—	—	10	—	—	10	—	—	10	—	10	—	10	—	10
South Carolina	18	—	18	—	—	18	—	—	18	18	—	18	—	18	—	18	—
South Dakota	10	—	10	—	—	10	—	—	10	10	—	10	—	10	—	10	—
Tennessee	24	—	24	—	—	24	—	—	24	24	—	24	—	24	—	24	—
Texas	46	46	—	—	46	—	—	46	—	—	—	—	—	—	—	46	—
Utah	8	—	8	—	—	8	—	—	8	8	—	8	—	8	—	8	—
Vermont	8	—	8	—	—	8	—	—	8	8	—	8	—	8	—	8	—
Virginia	24	24	—	—	24	—	—	24	—	—	—	—	—	—	—	24	—
Washington	16	—	16	—	—	16	—	—	16	16	—	16	—	16	—	16	—
West Virginia	16	—	16	—	3	13	—	—	16	16	—	16	—	16	—	16	—
Wisconsin	26	2	24	—	2	24	—	2	24	24	2	24	2	24	2	24	2
Wyoming	6	—	6	—	—	6	—	—	6	6	—	6	—	6	—	6	—
Alaska	6	—	6	—	—	6	—	6	—	5	—	6	—	6	—	6	—
Canal Zone	6	—	6	—	—	6	—	—	6	6	—	6	—	6	—	6	—
District of Columbia	6	—	6	—	—	6	—	—	6	6	—	6	—	6	—	6	—
Hawaii	6	—	6	—	—	6	—	—	6	6	—	6	—	6	—	6	—
Philippine Islands	6	6	—	—	6	—	—	6	—	—	6	—	6	—	6	6	—
Puerto Rico	6	—	6	—	—	6	—	—	6	6	—	6	—	6	—	6	—
Virgin Islands	2	—	2	—	—	2	—	—	2	2	—	2	—	2	—	2	—
Total	1154	514¼	638¾	1	492¾	658¼	3	528	626	666¼	201¾	677¾	194¼	682 79/100	190¼	945	190½

1. *Other candidates: John N. Garner, 90 and one-fourth; Harry F. Byrd, 25; Melvin A. Traylor, 42 and one-fourth; Albert C. Ritchie, 21; James A. Reed, 24; George White, 52; William H. Murray, 23; Newton D. Baker, 8½.*

2. *Other candidates: Garner, 90 and one-fourth; Byrd, 24; Traylor, 40 and one-fourth; Ritchie, 23½; Reed, 18; White, 50½; Baker, 8; Will Rogers, 22; not voting, 5½.*

3. *Other candidates: Garner, 101 and one-fourth; Byrd, 24 and ninety-six-hundredths; Traylor, 40 and one-fourth; Ritchie, 23½; Reed, 27½; White, 52½; Baker, 8½; not voting, 2½.*

4. *Other candidates: Ritchie, 3½; White, 3; Baker, 5½; James M. Cox, 1; not voting, 5½.*

1932 Republican

(Narrative. p. 79)

Delegation	Total Votes	Repeal of Prohibition Plank		First Pres. Ballot [1]
		Yea	Nay	Hoover
Alabama	19	—	19	19
Arizona	9	9	—	9
Arkansas	15	—	15	15
California	47	6	41	47
Colorado	15	1	14	15
Connecticut	19	19	—	19
Delaware	9	—	9	9
Florida	16	—	16	16
Georgia	16	2	14	16
Idaho	11	—	11	11
Illinois	61	45	15½	54½
Indiana	31	28	3	31
Iowa	25	3	22	25
Kansas	21	4	17	21
Kentucky	25	15	10	25
Louisiana	12	—	12	12
Maine	13	5	8	13
Maryland	19	—	19	19
Massachusetts	34	16	17	34
Michigan	41	25½	15½	41
Minnesota	25	—	25	25
Mississippi	11	11	—	11
Missouri	33	8½	23¾	33
Montana	11	—	11	11
Nebraska	17	1	16	17
Nevada	9	8	1	9
New Hampshire	11	—	11	11
New Jersey	35	35	—	35
New Mexico	9	2	7	8
New York	97	76	21	97
North Carolina	28	3	25	28
North Dakota	11	—	11	9
Ohio	55	12 2/9	42 2/9	55
Oklahoma	25	—	25	25
Oregon	13	3	10	9
Pennsylvania	75	51	23	73
Rhode Island	8	8	—	8
South Carolina	10	—	10	10
South Dakota	11	3	8	11
Tennessee	24	1	23	24
Texas	49	—	49	49
Utah	11	1	10	11
Vermont	9	9	—	9
Virginia	25	—	25	25
Washington	19	11	8	19
West Virginia	19	4	15	19
Wisconsin	27	22	5	15
Wyoming	9	9	—	9
Alaska	2	—	2	2
District of Columbia	2	—	2	2
Hawaii	2	2	—	2
Philippine Islands	2	1	1	2
Puerto Rico	2	—	2	2
Total	1154	460 2/9	690 19/36	1126½

1. Other candidates: John J. Blaine, 13; Calvin Coolidge, 4½; Joseph I. France, 4; Charles G. Dawes, 1; James W. Wadsworth, 1; not voting, 4.

1936 Republican

(Narrative, p. 82)

Delegation	Total Votes	First Pres. Ballot[1] Landon
Alabama	13	13
Arizona	6	6
Arkansas	11	11
California	44	44
Colorado	12	12
Connecticut	19	19
Delaware	9	9
Florida	12	12
Georgia	14	14
Idaho	8	8
Illinois	57	57
Indiana	28	28
Iowa	22	22
Kansas	18	18
Kentucky	22	22
Louisiana	12	12
Maine	13	13
Maryland	16	16
Massachusetts	33	33
Michigan	38	38
Minnesota	22	22
Mississippi	11	11
Missouri	30	30
Montana	8	8
Nebraska	14	14
Nevada	6	6
New Hampshire	11	11
New Jersey	32	32
New Mexico	6	6
New York	90	90
North Carolina	23	23
North Dakota	8	8
Ohio	52	52
Oklahoma	21	21
Oregon	10	10
Pennsylvania	75	75
Rhode Island	8	8
South Carolina	10	10
South Dakota	8	8
Tennessee	17	17
Texas	25	25
Utah	8	8
Vermont	9	9
Virginia	17	17
Washington	16	16
West Virginia	16	15
Wisconsin	24	6
Wyoming	6	6
Alaska	3	3
District of Columbia	3	3
Hawaii	3	3
Philippine Islands	2	2
Puerto Rico	2	2
Total	**1003**	**984**

1. Other candidates: William E. Borah, 19.

1940 Democratic

(Narrative, p. 85)

Delegation	Total Votes	First Pres. Ballot[1] Roosevelt
Alabama	22	20
Arizona	6	6
Arkansas	18	18
California	44	43
Colorado	12	12
Connecticut	16	16
Delaware	6	6
Florida	14	12½
Georgia	24	24
Idaho	8	8
Illinois	58	58
Indiana	28	28
Iowa	22	22
Kansas	18	18
Kentucky	22	22
Louisiana	20	20
Maine	10	10
Maryland	16	7½
Massachusetts	34	21½
Michigan	38	38
Minnesota	22	22
Mississippi	18	18
Missouri	30	26½
Montana	8	8
Nebraska	14	13
Nevada	6	2
New Hampshire	8	8
New Jersey	32	32
New Mexico	6	6
New York	94	64½
North Carolina	26	26
North Dakota	8	8
Ohio	52	52
Oklahoma	22	22
Oregon	10	10
Pennsylvania	72	72
Rhode Island	8	8
South Carolina	16	16
South Dakota	8	3
Tennessee	22	22
Texas	46	—
Utah	8	8
Vermont	6	6
Virginia	22	5 14/15
Washington	16	15
West Virginia	16	12
Wisconsin	24	21
Wyoming	6	6
Alaska	6	—
Canal Zone	6	—
District of Columbia	6	6
Hawaii	6	6
Philippine Islands	6	6
Puerto Rico	6	3
Virgin Islands	2	2
Total	**1100**	**946 13/30**

1. Other candidates: James A. Farley, 72 and nine-tenths; John N. Garner, 61; Millard E. Tydings, 9½; Cordell Hull, 5 and two-thirds; not voting, 4½.

1940 Republican

(Narrative, p. 85)

Delegation	Total Votes	First Pres. Ballot[1] Dewey	Taft	Willkie	Fourth Pres. Ballot[2] Dewey	Taft	Willkie	Fifth Pres. Ballot[3] Taft	Willkie	Sixth (before shift)[4] Taft	Willkie	Sixth (after shift)[5] Willkie
Alabama	13	7	6	—	7	5	1	7	5	7	6	13
Arizona	6	—	—	—	—	—	6	—	6	—	6	6
Arkansas	12	2	7	2	3	7	2	10	2	10	2	12
California	44	7	7	7	9	11	10	12	9	22	17	44
Colorado	12	1	4	3	1	4	3	4	4	6	5	12
Connecticut	16	—	—	16	—	—	16	—	16	—	16	16
Delaware	6	—	1	3	—	—	6	—	6	—	6	6
Florida	12	6	1	—	9	2	—	3	7	2	10	12
Georgia	14	7	3	—	6	3	2	7	6	7	6	14
Idaho	8	8	—	—	8	—	—	7	—	6	2	8
Illinois	58	52	2	4	17	27	10	30	17	33	24	58
Indiana	28	7	7	9	5	6	15	7	20	5	23	28
Iowa	22	—	—	—	2	—	—	13	7	15	7	22
Kansas	18	—	—	—	11	2	5	—	18	—	18	18
Kentucky	22	12	8	—	9	13	—	22	—	22	—	22
Louisiana	12	5	5	—	6	6	—	12	—	12	—	12
Maine	13	—	—	—	2	2	9	—	13	—	13	13
Maryland	16	16	—	—	—	—	14	1	14	1	15	16
Massachusetts	34	—	—	1	—	2	28	2	28	2	30	34
Michigan	38	—	—	—	2	—	—	—	—	2	35	38
Minnesota	22	3	4	6	2	9	9	12	9	11	10	22
Mississippi	11	3	8	—	2	9	—	11	—	9	2	11
Missouri	30	10	3	6	4	3	18	7	21	4	26	30
Montana	8	8	—	—	3	3	2	4	4	4	4	8
Nebraska	14	14	—	—	2	5	5	9	5	6	8	14
Nevada	6	—	2	2	—	1	4	2	4	2	4	6
New Hampshire	8	—	—	—	—	—	4	2	6	2	6	8
New Jersey	32	20	—	12	6	1	23	1	26	—	32	32
New Mexico	6	3	1	2	1	1	4	2	4	1	5	6
New York	92	61	—	8	48	5	35	10	75	7	78	92
North Carolina	23	9	7	2	6	6	9	11	12	8	15	23
North Dakota	8	2	1	1	2	1	3	4	4	4	4	8
Ohio	52	—	52	—	—	52	—	52	—	52	—	52
Oklahoma	22	22	—	—	10	6	3	18	4	5	17	22
Oregon	10	—	—	—	1	—	1	—	1	3	7	10
Pennsylvania	72	1	—	1	—	—	19	—	21	—	72	72
Rhode Island	8	1	3	3	—	4	4	4	4	3	5	8
South Carolina	10	10	—	—	8	—	2	—	9	—	10	10
South Dakota	8	—	—	—	4	1	—	7	1	2	6	8
Tennessee	18	8	3	2	5	6	5	9	6	5	10	17
Texas	26	—	26	—	—	26	—	26	—	26	—	26
Utah	8	2	2	1	2	2	1	3	5	1	7	8
Vermont	9	1	3	3	1	3	5	3	6	2	7	9
Virginia	18	2	9	5	—	7	11	7	11	2	16	18
Washington		13	3	—	12	3	—	16	—	4	10	16
West Virginia	16	8	5	3	6	3	7	9	6	—	15	15
Wisconsin	24	24	—	—	24	—	—	—	—	2	20	24
Wyoming	6	1	1	2	3	2	1	3	3	—	6	6
Alaska	3	1	2	—	—	2	1	3	—	1	2	3
District of Columbia	3	2	1	—	—	1	2	1	2	—	3	3
Hawaii	3	—	—	—	—	—	—	1	1	—	3	3
Philippine Islands	2	—	1	1	—	1	1	1	1	—	2	2
Puerto Rico	2	1	1	—	1	1	—	2	—	—	2	2
Total	1000	360	189	105	250	254	306	377	429	318	655	998

1. Other candidates: Arthur H. Vandenberg, 76; Arthur H. James, 74; Joseph W. Martin, 44; Hanford MacNider, 34; Frank E. Gannett, 33; Styles Bridges, 28; Arthur Capper, 18; Herbert Hoover, 17; Charles L. McNary, 13; Harlan F. Bushfield, 9.

2. Other candidates: Vandenberg, 61; James, 56; Hoover, 31; MacNider, 26; McNary, 8; Gannett, 4; Bridges, 1; not voting, 3.

3. Other candidates: James, 59; Dewey, 57; Vandenberg, 42; Hoover, 20; McNary, 9; MacNider, 4; Gannett, 1; not voting, 2.

4. Other candidates: Dewey, 11; Hoover, 10; Gannett, 1; McNary, 1; not voting, 4.

5. Not voting, 2.

1944 Democratic

(Narrative. p. 87)

Delegation	Total Votes	First Pres. Ballot [1] Roosevelt
Alabama	24	22
Arizona	10	10
Arkansas	20	20
California	52	52
Colorado	12	12
Connecticut	18	18
Delaware	8	8
Florida	18	14
Georgia	26	26
Idaho	10	10
Illinois	58	58
Indiana	26	26
Iowa	20	20
Kansas	16	16
Kentucky	24	24
Louisiana	22	—
Maine	10	10
Maryland	18	18
Massachusetts	34	34
Michigan	38	38
Minnesota	24	24
Mississippi	20	—
Missouri	32	32
Montana	10	10
Nebraska	12	12
Nevada	8	8
New Hampshire	10	10
New Jersey	34	34
New Mexico	10	10
New York	96	94½
North Carolina	30	30
North Dakota	8	8
Ohio	52	52
Oklahoma	22	22
Oregon	14	14
Pennsylvania	72	72
Rhode Island	10	10
South Carolina	18	14½
South Dakota	8	8
Tennessee	26	26
Texas	48	36
Utah	10	10
Vermont	6	6
Virginia	24	—
Washington	18	18
West Virginia	18	17
Wisconsin	26	26
Wyoming	8	8
Alaska	6	6
Canal Zone	6	6
District of Columbia	6	6
Hawaii	6	6
Philippine Islands	6	6
Puerto Rico	6	6
Virgin Islands	2	2
Total	**1176**	**1086**

1. Other candidates: Harry F. Byrd, 89; James A. Farley, 1.

1944 Republican

(Narrative. p. 86)

Delegation	Total Votes	First Pres. Ballot [1] Dewey
Alabama	14	14
Arizona	8	8
Arkansas	12	12
California	50	50
Colorado	15	15
Connecticut	16	16
Delaware	9	9
Florida	15	15
Georgia	14	14
Idaho	11	11
Illinois	59	59
Indiana	29	29
Iowa	23	23
Kansas	19	19
Kentucky	22	22
Louisiana	13	13
Maine	13	13
Maryland	16	16
Massachusetts	35	35
Michigan	41	41
Minnesota	25	25
Mississippi	6	6
Missouri	30	30
Montana	8	8
Nebraska	15	15
Nevada	6	6
New Hampshire	11	11
New Jersey	35	35
New Mexico	8	8
New York	93	93
North Carolina	25	25
North Dakota	11	11
Ohio	50	50
Oklahoma	23	23
Oregon	15	15
Pennsylvania	70	70
Rhode Island	8	8
South Carolina	4	4
South Dakota	11	11
Tennessee	19	19
Texas	33	33
Utah	8	8
Vermont	9	9
Virginia	19	19
Washington	16	16
West Virginia	19	19
Wisconsin	24	23
Wyoming	9	9
Alaska	3	3
District of Columbia	3	3
Hawaii	5	5
Philippine Islands	2	—
Puerto Rico	2	2
Total	**1059**	**1056**

1. Other candidates: Douglas MacArthur, 1; absent, 2.

1948 Democratic

(Narrative, p. 90)

Delegation	Total Votes	Pro-Southern Amendment to Civil Rights Plank		Plank Endorsing Truman's Civil Rights Policy		First Pres. Ballot[1] (Before shift)		First Pres. Ballot[2] (After shift)	
		Yea	Nay	Yea	Nay	Truman	Russell	Truman	Russell
Alabama	26	26	—	—	26	—	26	—	26
Arizona	12	—	12	—	12	12	—	12	—
Arkansas	22	22	—	—	22	—	22	—	22
California	54	1½	52½	53	1	53½	—	54	—
Colorado	12	3	9	10	2	12	—	12	—
Connecticut	20	—	20	20	—	20	—	20	—
Delaware	10	—	10	—	10	10	—	10	—
Florida	20	20	—	—	20	—	19	—	20
Georgia	28	28	—	—	28	—	28	—	28
Idaho	12	—	12	—	12	12	—	12	—
Illinois	60	—	60	60	—	60	—	60	—
Indiana	26	—	26	17	9	25	—	26	—
Iowa	20	—	20	18	2	20	—	20	—
Kansas	16	—	16	16	—	16	—	16	—
Kentucky	26	—	26	—	26	26	—	26	—
Louisiana	24	24	—	—	24	—	24	—	24
Maine	10	—	10	3	7	10	—	10	—
Maryland	20	—	20	—	20	20	—	20	—
Massachusetts	36	—	36	36	—	36	—	36	—
Michigan	42	—	42	42	—	42	—	42	—
Minnesota	26	—	26	26	—	26	—	26	—
Mississippi	22	22	—	—	22	—	—	—	—
Missouri	34	—	34	—	34	34	—	34	—
Montana	12	—	12	1½	10½	12	—	12	—
Nebraska	12	—	12	3	9	12	—	12	—
Nevada	10	—	10	—	10	10	—	10	—
New Hampshire	12	—	12	1	11	11	—	11	—
New Jersey	36	—	36	36	—	36	—	36	—
New Mexico	12	—	12	—	12	12	—	12	—
New York	98	—	98	98	—	83	—	98	—
North Carolina	32	32	—	—	32	13	19	13	19
North Dakota	8	—	8	—	8	8	—	8	—
Ohio	50	—	50	39	11	50	—	50	—
Oklahoma	24	—	24	—	24	24	—	24	—
Oregon	16	3	13	7	9	16	—	16	—
Pennsylvania	74	—	74	74	—	74	—	74	—
Rhode Island	12	—	12	—	12	12	—	12	—
South Carolina	20	20	—	—	20	—	20	—	20
South Dakota	8	—	8	8	—	8	—	8	—
Tennessee	28	28	—	—	28	—	28	—	28
Texas	50	50	—	—	50	—	50	—	50
Utah	12	—	12	—	12	12	—	12	—
Vermont	6	—	6	6	—	5½	—	5½	—
Virginia	26	26	—	—	26	—	26	—	26
Washington	20	—	20	20	—	20	—	20	—
West Virginia	20	—	20	7	13	15	4	20	—
Wisconsin	24	—	24	24	—	24	—	24	—
Wyoming	6	1½	4½	4	2	6	—	6	—
Alaska	6	3	3	2	4	6	—	6	—
Canal Zone	2	—	2	—	2	2	—	2	—
District of Columbia	6	—	6	6	—	6	—	6	—
Hawaii	6	—	6	6	—	6	—	6	—
Puerto Rico	6	—	6	6	—	6	—	6	—
Virgin Islands	2	—	2	2	—	2	—	2	—
Total	1234	310[a]	924[b]	651½	582½	926	266	947½	263

a. Sum of column; proceedings record 309.
b. Sum of column; proceedings record 925.
1. Other candidates: Paul V. McNutt; 2½; James A. Roe, 15; Alben W. Barkley, 1; not voting, 23½.
2. Other candidates: McNutt, ½; not voting, 23.

1948 Republican

(Narrative. p. 89)

Delegation	Total Votes	First Pres. Ballot[1]			Second Pres. Ballot[2]			Third Pres. Ballot
		Dewey	Stassen	Taft	Dewey	Stassen	Taft	Dewey
Alabama	14	9	—	5	9	—	5	14
Arizona	8	3	2	3	4	2	2	8
Arkansas	14	3	4	7	3	4	7	14
California	53	—	—	—	—	—	—	53
Colorado	15	3	5	7	3	8	4	15
Connecticut	19	—	—	—	—	—	—	19
Delaware	9	5	1	2	6	1	2	9
Florida	16	6	4	6	6	4	6	16
Georgia	16	12	1	—	13	1	—	16
Idaho	11	11	—	—	11	—	—	11
Illinois	56	—	—	—	5	—	50	56
Indiana	29	29	—	—	29	—	—	29
Iowa	23	3	13	5	13	7	2	23
Kansas	19	12	1	2	14	1	2	19
Kentucky	25	10	1	11	11	1	11	25
Louisiana	13	6	—	7	6	—	7	13
Maine	13	5	4	1	5	7	—	13
Maryland	16	8	3	5	13	—	3	16
Massachusetts	35	17	1	2	18	1	3	35
Michigan	41	—	—	—	—	—	—	41
Minnesota	25	—	25	—	—	25	—	25
Mississippi	8	—	—	8	—	—	8	8
Missouri	33	17	6	8	18	6	7	33
Montana	11	5	3	3	6	2	3	11
Nebraska	15	2	13	—	6	9	—	15
Nevada	9	6	1	2	6	1	2	9
New Hampshire	8	6	2	—	6	2	—	8
New Jersey	35	—	—	—	24	6	2	35
New Mexico	8	3	2	3	3	2	3	8
New York	97	96	—	1	96	—	1	97
North Carolina	26	16	2	5	17	2	4	26
North Dakota	11	—	11	—	—	11	—	11
Ohio	53	—	9	44	1	8	44	53
Oklahoma	20	18	—	1	19	—	1	20
Oregon	12	12	—	—	12	—	—	12
Pennsylvania	73	41	1	28	40	1	29	73
Rhode Island	8	1	—	1	4	—	2	8
South Carolina	6	—	—	6	—	—	6	6
South Dakota	11	3	8	—	7	4	—	11
Tennessee	22	6	—	—	8	—	13	22
Texas	33	2	1	30	2	2	29	33
Utah	11	5	2	4	6	2	3	11
Vermont	9	7	2	—	7	2	—	9
Virginia	21	10	—	10	13	—	7	21
Washington	19	14	2	1	14	2	3	19
West Virginia	16	11	5	—	13	3	—	16
Wisconsin	27	—	19	—	2	19	—	27
Wyoming	9	4	3	2	6	3	—	9
Alaska	3	2	—	1	3	—	—	3
District of Columbia	3	2	—	—	3	—	—	3
Hawaii	5	3	—	1	3	—	2	5
Puerto Rico	2	—	—	2	1	—	1	2
Total	**1094**	**434**	**157**	**224**	**515**	**149**	**274**	**1094**

1. *Other candidates: Arthur H. Vandenberg, 62; Earl Warren, 59; Dwight H. Green, 56; Alfred E. Driscoll, 35; Raymond E. Baldwin, 19; Joseph W. Martin, 18; B. Carroll Reece, 15; Douglas MacArthur, 11; Everett M. Dirksen, 1; not voting, 3.*
2. *Other candidates: Vandenberg, 62; Warren, 57; Baldwin, 19; Martin, 10; MacArthur, 7; Reece, 1.*

1952 Democratic

(Narrative. p. 94)

Delegation	Total Votes	Seating Virginia Delegation Yea	Nay	Not voting	Table Motion to Adjourn Yea	Nay	Not voting	First Pres. Ballot[1] Harriman	Kefauver	Russell	Stevenson	Second Pres. Ballot[2] Harriman	Kefauver	Russell	Stevenson	Third Pres. Ballot[3] Kefauver	Russell	Stevenson
Alabama	22	22	—	—	13½	8½	—	—	8	13	½	—	7½	14	½	7½	14	½
Arizona	12	12	—	—	12	—	—	—	—	12	—	—	—	12	—	—	12	—
Arkansas	22	22	—	—	19	3	—	—	—	—	—	1	1½	18	1½	1½	—	20½
California	68	4	61	3	—	68	—	—	68	—	—	—	68	—	—	68	—	—
Colorado	16	4½	11½	—	4	12	—	5	2	8½	½	5	5	2½	3½	4	3½	8½
Connecticut	16	—	16	—	16	—	—	—	—	—	16	—	—	—	16	—	—	16
Delaware	6	6	—	—	6	—	—	—	—	—	6	—	—	—	6	—	—	6
Florida	24	24	—	—	19	5	—	—	5	19	—	—	5	19	—	5	19	—
Georgia	28	28	—	—	28	—	—	—	—	28	—	—	—	28	—	—	28	—
Idaho	12	12	—	—	—	12	—	3½	3	1	1½	—	—	—	12	—	—	12
Illinois	60	52	8	—	53	7	—	1	3	—	53	—	3	—	54	3	—	54
Indiana	26	14½	6½	5	25	1	—	—	1	—	25	—	1	—	25	1	—	25
Iowa	24	17	7	—	8	15	1	½	8	2	8	½	8½	3	9½	8	3	10
Kansas	16	—	16	—	16	—	—	—	—	—	16	—	—	—	16	—	—	16
Kentucky	26	26	—	—	26	—	—	—	—	—	—	—	—	—	—	—	—	—
Louisiana	20	20	—	—	20	—	—	—	—	20	—	—	—	20	—	—	20	—
Maine	10	2½	7½	—	4½	5½	—	1½	1½	2½	3½	1	1	2½	4½	½	2½	7
Maryland	18	18	—	—	18	—	—	—	18	—	—	—	15½	2	—	8½	2½	6
Massachusetts	36	16	19	1	30	4½	1½	—	—	—	—	—	2½	—	—	5	1	25
Michigan	40	—	40	—	—	40	—	40	—	—	—	—	40	—	—	—	—	40
Minnesota	26	—	26	—	—	26	—	—	—	—	—	1½	17	—	7½	13	—	13
Mississippi	18	18	—	—	18	—	—	—	—	18	—	—	—	18	—	—	18	—
Missouri	34	34	—	—	29	5	—	1½	2	—	18	1½	2	—	19½	2	—	22
Montana	12	—	12	—	12	—	—	—	—	—	—	3	3	3	—	—	—	12
Nebraska	12	8	3	1	—	12	—	—	5	1	2	—	5	1	2	3	1	8
Nevada	10	10	—	—	9½	½	—	—	½	8	1	—	½	7½	2	½	7½	2
New Hampshire	8	1	7	—	—	8	—	—	8	—	—	—	8	—	—	8	—	—
New Jersey	32	—	32	—	24	8	—	1	3	—	28	—	4	—	28	4	—	28
New Mexico	12	12	—	—	12	—	—	1	1½	4	1	—	1½	6	4½	1½	3½	7
New York	94	7	87	—	5	89	—	83½	1	—	6½	84½	—	1	6½	4	—	86½
North Carolina	32	32	—	—	32	—	—	—	—	26	5½	—	—	24	7	—	24	7½
North Dakota	8	8	—	—	8	—	—	—	2	2	2	—	—	—	—	—	—	8
Ohio	54	33½	14½	6	26	28	—	1	29½	7	13	1	27½	8	17½	27	1	26
Oklahoma	24	24	—	—	24	—	—	—	—	—	—	—	—	—	—	—	—	—
Oregon	12	4	8	—	—	12	—	—	12	—	—	—	12	—	—	11	—	1
Pennsylvania	70	57	13	—	35	35	—	4½	22½	—	36	2½	21½	—	40	—	—	70
Rhode Island	12	10	2	—	10	2	—	1½	3½	—	5½	—	4	—	8	—	—	12
South Carolina	16	—	—	16	—	—	16	—	—	16	—	—	—	16	—	—	16	—
South Dakota	8	—	8	—	—	8	—	—	8	—	—	—	8	—	—	8	—	—
Tennessee	28	—	28	—	—	28	—	—	28	—	—	—	28	—	—	28	—	—
Texas	52	52	—	—	52	—	—	—	—	52	—	—	—	52	—	—	52	—
Utah	12	3	9	—	—	12	—	6½	½	2	½	9	1½	—	½	—	—	12
Vermont	6	—	6	—	6	—	—	—	½	—	5	—	½	½	5	—	½	5½
Virginia	28	—	—	28	28	—	—	—	—	28	—	—	—	28	—	—	28	—
Washington	22	12½	9½	—	3	10	—	—	12	½	6	2	12½	½	6	11	½	10½
West Virginia	20	13½	5	1½	10	9	1	—	5½	7	1	—	7½	6½	5½	7½	3½	9
Wisconsin	28	1	27	—	—	28	—	—	28	—	—	—	28	—	—	28	—	—
Wyoming	10	5½	4½	—	2½	7½	—	3½	1½	½	3	2½	3	—	4½	—	—	10
Alaska	6	—	6	—	—	6	—	—	6	—	—	—	6	—	—	6	—	—
Canal Zone	2	2	—	—	2	—	—	—	—	2	—	—	—	2	—	—	—	2
District of Columbia	6	—	6	—	—	6	—	6	—	—	—	6	—	—	—	—	—	6
Hawaii	6	—	6	—	4	2	—	1	1	—	2	—	1	—	5	1	—	5
Puerto Rico	6	2	4	—	1	5	—	—	—	—	6	—	—	—	6	—	—	6
Virgin Islands	2	—	2	—	—	2	—	—	1	—	1	—	1	—	1	—	—	2
Total	1230	650½	518	61½	671	539½ᵃ	19½	123½	340	268	273	121	362½	294	324½	275½	261	617½

a. Sum of column; proceedings record 534.
1. Other candidates: Alben W. Barkley, 48½; Robert S. Kerr, 65; J. William Fulbright, 22; Paul H. Douglas, 3; Oscar R. Ewing, 4; Paul A. Dever, 37½; Hubert H. Humphrey, 26; James E. Murray, 12; Harry S Truman, 6; William O. Douglas, ½; not voting, 1.
2. Other candidates: Barkley, 78½; Paul H. Douglas, 3; Kerr, 5½; Ewing, 3; Dever, 30½; Truman, 6; not voting, 1½.
3. Other candidates: Barkley, 67½; Paul H. Douglas, 3; Dever, ½; Ewing, 3; not voting, 2.

1952 Republican
(Narrative. p. 93)

Delegation	Total Votes	Pro-Taft Amendment on Louisiana Delegates		Pro-Eisenhower Report on Georgia Delegates		First Pres. Ballot[1] (Before shift)		First Pres. Ballot[2] (After shift)	
		Yea	Nay	Yea	Nay	Eisenhower	Taft	Eisenhower	Taft
Alabama	14	9	5	5	9	5	9	14	—
Arizona	14	12	2	3	11	4	10	4	10
Arkansas	11	11	—	3	8	4	6	11	—
California	70	—	70	62	8	—	—	—	—
Colorado	18	1	17	17	1	15	2	17	1
Connecticut	22	2	20	21	1	21	1	22	—
Delaware	12	5	7	8	4	7	5	12	—
Florida	18	15	3	5	13	6	12	18	—
Georgia	17	17	—	—	—	14	2	16	1
Idaho	14	14	—	—	14	—	14	14	—
Illinois	60	58	2	1	59	1	59	1	59
Indiana	32	31	1	3	29	2	30	2	30
Iowa	26	11	15	16	10	16	10	20	6
Kansas	22	2	20	20	2	20	2	22	—
Kentucky	20	18	2	2	18	1	19	13	7
Louisiana	15	13	2	—	2	13	2	15	—
Maine	16	5	11	11	5	11	5	15	1
Maryland	24	5	19	15	9	16	8	24	—
Massachusetts	38	5	33	33	5	34	4	38	—
Michigan	46	1	45	32	14	35	11	35	11
Minnesota	28	—	28	28	—	9	—	28	—
Mississippi	5	5	—	—	5	—	5	5	—
Missouri	26	4	22	21	5	21	5	26	—
Montana	8	7	1	1	7	1	7	1	7
Nebraska	18	13	5	7	11	4	13	7	11
Nevada	12	7	5	2	10	5	7	10	2
New Hampshire	14	—	14	14	—	14	—	14	—
New Jersey	38	5	33	32	6	33	5	38	—
New Mexico	14	8	6	5	9	6	8	6	8
New York	96	1	95	92	4	92	4	95	1
North Carolina	26	14	12	10	16	12	14	26	—
North Dakota	14	11	3	3	11	4	8	5	8
Ohio	56	56	—	—	56	—	56	—	56
Oklahoma	16	10	6	4	12	4	7	8	4
Oregon	18	—	18	18	—	18	—	18	—
Pennsylvania	70	13	57	52	18	53	15	70	—
Rhode Island	8	2	6	6	2	6	1	8	—
South Carolina	6	5	1	1	5	2	4	6	—
South Dakota	14	14	—	—	14	—	14	7	7
Tennessee	20	20	—	—	20	—	20	20	—
Texas	38	22	16	—	—	33	5	38	—
Utah	14	14	—	—	14	—	14	14	—
Vermont	12	—	12	12	—	12	—	12	—
Virginia	23	13	10	7	16	9	14	19	4
Washington	24	4	20	19	5	20	4	21	3
West Virginia	16	15	1	1	15	1	14	3	13
Wisconsin	30	24	6	6	24	—	24	—	24
Wyoming	12	8	4	4	8	6	6	12	—
Alaska	3	3	—	—	3	1	2	3	—
Canal Zone	—								
District of Columbia	6	6	—	—	6	—	6	6	—
Hawaii	8	7	1	3	5	3	4	4	4
Puerto Rico	3	2	1	1	2	—	3	1	2
Virgin Islands	1	—	1	1	—	1	—	1	—
Total	1206	548	658	607	531	595	500	845	280

1. Other candidates: Earl Warren, 81; Harold E. Stassen, 20; Douglas MacArthur, 10.
2. Other candidates: Warren, 77; MacArthur, 4.

1956 Democratic
(Narrative, p. 96)

Delegation	Total Votes	First Pres. Ballot[1]		
		Stevenson	Harriman	Other
Alabama	26	15½	—	10½
Arizona	16	16	—	—
Arkansas	26	26	—	—
California	68	68	—	—
Colorado	20	13½	6	½
Connecticut	20	20	—	—
Delaware	10	10	—	—
Florida	28	25	—	3
Georgia	32	—	—	32
Idaho	12	12	—	—
Illinois	64	53½	8½	2
Indiana	26	21½	3	1½
Iowa	24	16½	7	½
Kansas	16	16	—	—
Kentucky	30	—	—	30
Louisiana	24	24	—	—
Maine	14	10½	3½	—
Maryland	18	18	—	—
Massachusetts	40	32	7½	½
Michigan	44	39	5	—
Minnesota	30	19	11	—
Mississippi	22	—	—	22
Missouri	38	—	—	38
Montana	16	10	6	—
Nebraska	12	12	—	—
Nevada	14	5½	7	1½
New Hampshire	8	5½	1½	1
New Jersey	36	36	—	—
New Mexico	16	12	3½	½
New York	98	5½	92½	—
North Carolina	36	34½	1	½
North Dakota	8	8	—	—
Ohio	58	52	½	5½
Oklahoma	28	—	28	
Oregon	16	16	—	—
Pennsylvania	74	67	7	—
Rhode Island	16	16	—	—
South Carolina	20	2	—	18
South Dakota	8	8	—	—
Tennessee	32	32	—	—
Texas	56	—	—	56
Utah	12	12	—	—
Vermont	6	5½	½	—
Virginia	32	—	—	32
Washington	26	19½	6	½
West Virginia	24	24	—	—
Wisconsin	28	22½	5	½
Wyoming	14	14	—	—
Alaska	6	6	—	—
Canal Zone	3	3	—	—
District of Columbia	6	6	—	—
Hawaii	6	6	—	—
Puerto Rico	6	6	—	—
Virgin Islands	3	3	—	—
Total	**1372**	**905½**	**210**	**256½**

1956 Republican
(Narrative, p. 97)

Delegation	Total Votes	First Pres. Ballot Eisenhower
Alabama	21	21
Arizona	14	14
Arkansas	16	16
California	70	70
Colorado	18	18
Connecticut	22	22
Delaware	12	12
Florida	26	26
Georgia	23	23
Idaho	14	14
Illinois	60	60
Indiana	32	32
Iowa	26	26
Kansas	22	22
Kentucky	26	26
Louisiana	20	20
Maine	16	16
Maryland	24	24
Massachusetts	38	38
Michigan	46	46
Minnesota	28	28
Mississippi	15	15
Missouri	32	32
Montana	14	14
Nebraska	18	18
Nevada	12	12
New Hampshire	14	14
New Jersey	38	38
New Mexico	14	14
New York	96	96
North Carolina	28	28
North Dakota	14	14
Ohio	56	56
Oklahoma	22	22
Oregon	18	18
Pennsylvania	70	70
Rhode Island	14	14
South Carolina	16	16
South Dakota	14	14
Tennessee	28	28
Texas	54	54
Utah	14	14
Vermont	12	12
Virginia	30	30
Washington	24	24
West Virginia	16	16
Wisconsin	30	30
Wyoming	12	12
Alaska	4	4
District of Columbia	6	6
Hawaii	10	10
Puerto Rico	3	3
Virgin Islands	1	1
Total	**1323**	**1323**

1. Other candidates: Lyndon B. Johnson, 80; James C. Davis, 33; Albert B. Chandler, 36½; John S. Battle, 32½; George B. Timmerman, 23½; W. Stuart Symington, 45½; Frank Lausche, 5½.

1960 Democratic

(Narrative, p. 99)

Delegation	Total Votes	First Pres. Ballot[1]			
		Kennedy	Johnson	Stevenson	Symington
Alabama	29	3½	20	½	3½
Alaska	9	9	—	—	—
Arizona	17	17	—	—	—
Arkansas	27	—	27	—	—
California	81	33½	7½	31½	8
Colorado	21	13½	—	5½	2
Connecticut	21	21	—	—	—
Delaware	11	—	11	—	—
Florida	29	—	—	—	—
Georgia	33	—	33	—	—
Hawaii	9	1½	3	3½	1
Idaho	13	6	4½	½	2
Illinois	69	61½	—	2	5½
Indiana	34	34	—	—	—
Iowa	26	21½	½	2	½
Kansas	21	21	—	—	—
Kentucky	31	3½	25½	1½	½
Louisiana	26	—	26	—	—
Maine	15	15	—	—	—
Maryland	24	24	—	—	—
Massachusetts	41	41	—	—	—
Michigan	51	42½	—	2½	6
Minnesota	31	—	—	—	—
Mississippi	23	—	—	—	—
Missouri	39	—	—	—	39
Montana	17	10	2	2½	2½
Nebraska	16	11	½	—	4
Nevada	15	5½	6½	2½	½
New Hampshire	11	11	—	—	—
New Jersey	41	—	—	—	—
New Mexico	17	4	13	—	—
New York	114	104½	3½	3½	2½
North Carolina	37	6	27½	3	—
North Dakota	11	11	—	—	—
Ohio	64	64	—	—	—
Oklahoma	29	—	29	—	—
Oregon	17	16½	—	½	—
Pennsylvania	81	68	4	7½	—
Rhode Island	17	17	—	—	—
South Carolina	21	—	21	—	—
South Dakota	11	4	2	1	2½
Tennessee	33	—	33	—	—
Texas	61	—	61	—	—
Utah	13	8	3	—	1½
Vermont	9	9	—	—	—
Virginia	33	—	33	—	—
Washington	27	14½	2½	6½	3
West Virginia	25	15	5½	3	1½
Wisconsin	31	23	—	—	—
Wyoming	15	15	—	—	—
Canal Zone	4	—	4	—	—
District of Columbia	9	9	—	—	—
Puerto Rico	7	7	—	—	—
Virgin Islands	4	4	—	—	—
Total	1521	806	409	79½	86

1. Other candidates:
   Barnett, 23 (Mississippi); Smathers, 30 (29 in Florida, ½ in Alabama, ½ in North Carolina); Humphrey, 41½ (31 in Minnesota, 8 in Wisconsin, 1½ in South Dakota, ½ in Nebraska, ½ in Utah); Meyner, 43 (41 in New Jersey, 1½ in Pennsylvania, ½ in Alabama); Loveless, 1½ (Iowa); Faubus, ½ (Alabama); Brown, ½ (California); Rosellini, ½ (Washington).

1960 Republican

(Narrative, p. 100)

Delegation	Total Votes	First Pres. Ballot	
		Nixon	Goldwater
Alabama	22	22	—
Alaska	6	6	—
Arizona	14	14	—
Arkansas	16	16	—
California	70	70	—
Colorado	18	18	—
Connecticut	22	22	—
Delaware	12	12	—
Florida	26	26	—
Georgia	24	24	—
Hawaii	12	12	—
Idaho	14	14	—
Illinois	60	60	—
Indiana	32	32	—
Iowa	26	26	—
Kansas	22	22	—
Kentucky	26	26	—
Louisiana	26	16	10
Maine	16	16	—
Maryland	24	24	—
Massachusetts	38	38	—
Michigan	46	46	—
Minnesota	28	28	—
Mississippi	12	12	—
Missouri	26	26	—
Montana	14	14	—
Nebraska	18	18	—
Nevada	12	12	—
New Hampshire	14	14	—
New Jersey	38	38	—
New Mexico	14	14	—
New York	96	96	—
North Carolina	28	28	—
North Dakota	14	14	—
Ohio	56	56	—
Oklahoma	22	22	—
Oregon	18	18	—
Pennsylvania	70	70	—
Rhode Island	14	14	—
South Carolina	13	13	—
South Dakota	14	14	—
Tennessee	28	28	—
Texas	54	54	—
Utah	14	14	—
Vermont	12	12	—
Virginia	30	30	—
Washington	24	24	—
West Virginia	22	22	—
Wisconsin	30	30	—
Wyoming	12	12	—
District of Columbia	8	8	—
Puerto Rico	3	3	—
Virgin Islands	1	1	—
Total	1331	1321	10

1964 Republican

(Narrative, p. 103)

Delegation	Total Votes	Minority Amendment on Civil Rights[1]		First Pres. Ballot[2] (Before shift)			First Pres. Ballot[3] (After shift)		
		Yea	Nay	Goldwater	Rockefeller	Scranton	Goldwater	Rockefeller	Scranton
Alabama	20	—	20	20	—	—	20	—	—
Alaska	12	12	—	—	—	8	—	—	8
Arizona	16	—	16	16	—	—	16	—	—
Arkansas	12	—	12	9	1	2	12	—	—
California	86	—	86	86	—	—	86	—	—
Colorado	18	—	18	15	—	3	18	—	—
Connecticut	16	11	5	4	—	12	16	—	—
Delaware	12	11	1	7	—	5	10	—	2
Florida	34	—	34	32	—	2	34	—	—
Georgia	24	—	24	22	—	2	24	—	—
Hawaii	8	4	4	4	—	—	8	—	—
Idaho	14	—	14	14	—	—	14	—	—
Illinois	58	4	54	56	2	—	56	2	—
Indiana	32	—	32	32	—	—	32	—	—
Iowa	24	2	22	14	—	10	24	—	—
Kansas	20	2	18	18	—	1	18	—	1
Kentucky	24	1	23	21	—	3	22	—	2
Louisiana	20	—	20	20	—	—	20	—	—
Maine	14	11	3	—	—	—	—	—	—
Maryland	20	17	3	6	1	13	7	1	12
Massachusetts	34	27	7	5	—	26	34	—	—
Michigan	48	37	9	8	—	—	48	—	—
Minnesota	26	17	9	8	—	—	26	—	—
Mississippi	13	—	13	13	—	—	13	—	—
Missouri	24	1	23	23	—	1	24	—	—
Montana	14	—	14	14	—	—	14	—	—
Nebraska	16	—	16	16	—	—	16	—	—
Nevada	6	—	6	6	—	—	6	—	—
New Hampshire	14	14	—	—	—	14	—	—	14
New Jersey	40	40	—	20	—	20	38	—	2
New Mexico	14	—	14	14	—	—	14	—	—
New York	92	86	6	5	87	—	87	—	—
North Carolina	26	—	26	26	—	—	26	—	—
North Dakota	14	1	13	7	1	—	14	—	—
Ohio	58	—	58	57	—	—	58	—	—
Oklahoma	22	—	22	22	—	—	22	—	—
Oregon	18	10	8	—	18	—	16	—	—
Pennsylvania	64	62	2	4	—	60	64	—	—
Rhode Island	14	11	3	3	—	11	14	—	—
South Carolina	16	—	16	16	—	—	16	—	—
South Dakota	14	—	14	12	—	2	14	—	—
Tennessee	28	—	28	28	—	—	28	—	—
Texas	56	—	56	56	—	—	56	—	—
Utah	14	—	14	14	—	—	14	—	—
Vermont	12	8	4	3	2	2	3	2	2
Virginia	30	—	30	29	—	1	30	—	—
Washington	24	1	23	22	—	1	22	—	1
West Virginia	14	4	10	10	2	2	12	1	1
Wisconsin	30	—	30	30	—	—	30	—	—
Wyoming	12	—	12	12	—	—	12	—	—
District of Columbia	9	7	2	4	—	5	4	—	5
Puerto Rico	5	5	—	—	—	5	5	—	—
Virgin Islands	3	3	—	—	—	3	3	—	—
Total	**1308**	**409**	**897**	**883**	**114**	**214**	**1220**	**6**	**50**

1. Not voting, 2.

2. Other candidates: George Romney, 41 (40 in Michigan, 1 in Kansas); Margaret C. Smith, 27 (14 in Maine, 5 in Vermont, 3 in North Dakota, 2 in Alaska, 1 in Massachusetts, 1 in Ohio, 1 in Washington); Walter H. Judd, 22 (18 in Minnesota, 3 in North Dakota, 1 in Alaska); Hiram L. Fong, 5 (4 in Hawaii, 1 in Alaska); Henry C. Lodge, 2 (Massachusetts).

3. Other candidates: Smith, 22 (14 in Maine, 5 in Vermont, 2 in Alaska, 1 in Washington); Fong, 1 (Alaska); Judd, 1 (Alaska); Romney, 1 (Kansas); not voting, 7 (5 in New York, 2 in Oregon).

1968 Democratic
(Narrative. p. 109)

Delegation	Total Votes	Texas Credentials[1] Yea	Nay	Georgia Credentials[2] Yea	Nay	Alabama Credentials[3] Yea	Nay	End Unit Rule[4] Yea	Nay	Report on Vietnam[5] Yea	Nay	First Pres. Ballot[6] Humphrey	McCarthy	McGovern	Phillips
Alabama	32	32	—	10	22	—	—	5½	24½	1½	30½	23	—	—	—
Alaska	22	17	5	5	17	14	8	22	—	10	12	17	2	3	—
Arizona	19	1½	17	17	2	7½	11½	—	19	6½	12½	14½	2½	2	—
Arkansas	33	33	—	3	29	8	23	—	32	7	25	30	2	—	—
California	174	1	173	173	1	173	1	173	1	166	6	14	91	51	17
Colorado	35	—	35	30	5	34	1	35	—	21	14	16½	10	5½	3
Connecticut	44	30	12	13	27	21	21	9	30	13	30	35	8	—	1
Delaware	22	21	—	3	18	2	19	—	21	—	21	21	—	—	—
Florida	63	58	4	9	54	6	57	11	52	7	56	58	5	—	—
Georgia	43	—	—	—	—	25	17½	39	4	19½	23½	19½	13½	1	3
Hawaii	26	26	—	4	22	—	26	3	23	—	26	26	—	—	—
Idaho	25	22½	2½	4½	20½	2	23	1	24	10	15	21	3½	½	—
Illinois	118	114	4	12	83	18	100	3	115	13	105	112	3	3	—
Indiana	63	34	10	25	38	13	41½	63	—	15	47½	49	11	2	1
Iowa	46	37½	8½	32	12	24½	21½	46	—	36	10	18½	19½	5	—
Kansas	38	38	—	3½	34½	5½	31½	6	20	4½	33½	34	1	3	—
Kentucky	46	40½	5½	6	40	6½	39½	6½	39½	7	39	41	5	—	—
Louisiana	36	32	4	7	29	—	36	—	36	2½	33½	35	—	—	—
Maine	27	25	1	5	22	—	26	27	—	4½	22½	23	4	—	—
Maryland	49	46	3	3	46	2	47	49	—	12	37	45	2	2	—
Massachusetts	72	16	47	39	24	29	29	37	31	56	16	2	70	—	—
Michigan	96	70	23	35	58	26	67	43½	44½	52	44	72½	9½	7½	6½
Minnesota	52	34½	14½	16	33	23½	28½	16	33½	16½	34½	38	11½	—	2½
Mississippi	24	2	18½	18	2	12½	8½	21½	½	19½	2½	9½	6½	4	2
Missouri	60	48	12	12	48	8	52	60	—	10	50	56	3½	—	½
Montana	26	20	4	2½	21½	3½	22½	12½	12	6	20	23½	2½	—	—
Nebraska	30	12	16	11	18	13	15	26	2	19	11	15	6	9	—
Nevada	22	13	7	14	8	12½	9½	22	—	3½	18½	18½	2½	1	—
New Hampshire	26	6	20	23	2	25	—	23	3	23	3	6	20	—	—
New Jersey	82	43	25	22	51	21	61	21	61	24	57	62	19	—	1
New Mexico	26	13	13	11	15	11	15	11	15	11½	14½	15	11	—	—
New York	190	—	190	190	—	80e	82e	190	—	148	42	96½	87	1½	2
North Carolina	59	54½	4½	3½	55½	1	58	2	57	7	51	44½	2	½	—
North Dakota	25	17	5	5	17	7	18	17	5	6	19	18	7	—	—
Ohio	115	37½	27	21	80	30½	65	23	92	48	67	94	18	2	—
Oklahoma	41	40	1	1	40	6½	34	6	35	4	37	37½	2½	½	½
Oregon	35	10	23	32	—	31	3	31	—	29	6	—	35	—	—
Pennsylvania	130	80¾	42¼	31½	90½	22¼	100½	39¾	79½	35¼	92¼	103¾	21½	2½	1½
Rhode Island	27	24½	2½	12	11	2½	24½	3½	23½	5	22	23½	2½	—	—
South Carolina	28	28	—	4	22	—	28	4½	23½	1	27	28	—	—	—
South Dakota	26	1	25	26	—	24	2	26	—	26	—	2	—	24	—
Tennessee	51	48½	1	—	51	½	49½	2½	46½	2	49	49½	½	1	—
Texas	104	—	—	2.55	101.45	—	104	5	99	—	104	100½	2½	—	1
Utah	26	18	8	7	19	5	21	26	—	6	20	23	2	—	1
Vermont	22	5	13	17	4	14	7	22	—	17	5	8	6	7	—
Virginia	54	21½	22½	8½	35½	1	53	9½	43½	8	46	42½	5½	—	2
Washington	47	31½	15½	18	29	16	28	21½	25½	15½	31½	32½	8½	6	—
West Virginia	38	19	12	8	22	9	29	38	—	8	30	34	3	—	—
Wisconsin	59	5	54	52	7	54	4	58	1	52	7	8	49	1	1
Wyoming	22	18½	3½	2	20	6½	15½	3	19	3½	18½	18½	3½	—	—
Canal Zone	5	4	—	2	3	—	4	1	4	1½	3½	4	—	1	—
District of Columbia	23	—	22	22	—	23	—	23	—	21	2	2	—	—	21
Guam	5	4½	½	—	5	—	5	½	4½	½	4½	5	—	—	—
Puerto Rico	8	8	—	7½	—	—	8	1	7	—	8	8	—	—	—
Virgin Islands	5	5	—	2½	—	—	5	5	—	—	5	5	—	—	—
Total	**2622**	**1368¼a**	**956¾b**	**1043.55c**	**1415.45d**	**880¾f**	**1607g**	**1351¼h**	**1209i**	**1041¼**	**1567¾**	**1759¼j**	**601**	**146½**	**67½**

1. Not voting, 297.
2. Not voting, 163.
3. Not voting, 134½.
4. Not voting, 61¾.
5. Not voting, 13.
6. Other candidates: Moore, 17½ (12 in North Carolina, 3 in Virginia, 2 in Georgia, ½ in Alabama); Kennedy, 12¾ (proceedings record, 12½) (3½ Alabama, 3 in Iowa, 3 in New York, 1 in Ohio, 1 in West Virginia, ¾ in Pennsylvania, ½ in Georgia); Bryant, 1½ (Alabama); Wallace, ½ (Alabama); Gray, ½ (Georgia). Not voting, 15 (3 in Alabama, 3 in Georgia, 2 in Mississippi, 1 in Arkansas, 1 in California, 1 in Delaware, 1 in Louisiana, 1 in Rhode Island, 1 in Vermont, 1 in Virginia).

a. Sum of column; proceedings record, 1368.
b. Sum of column; proceedings record, 955.
c. Sum of column; proceedings record, 1041½.
d. Sum of column; proceedings record, 1413.
e. New York vote announced after outcome of roll call.
f. Sum of column; proceedings record (without New York vote), 801½.
g. Sum of column; proceedings record (without New York), 1525.
h. Sum of column; proceedings record, 1350.
i. Sum of column; proceedings record, 1206.
j. Sum of column; proceedings record, 1761¾.

1968 Republican

(Narrative. p. 107)

Delegation	Total Votes	First Pres. Ballot[1] (Before shift)			First Pres. Ballot (After shift)		
		Nixon	Rockefeller	Reagan	Nixon	Rockefeller	Reagan
Alabama	26	14	—	12	26	—	—
Alaska	12	11	1	—	12	—	—
Arizona	16	16	—	—	16	—	—
Arkansas	18	—	—	—	18	—	—
California	86	—	—	86	86	—	—
Colorado	18	14	3	1	18	—	—
Connecticut	16	4	12	—	16	—	—
Delaware	12	9	3	—	12	—	—
Florida	34	32	1	1	34	—	—
Georgia	30	21	2	7	30	—	—
Hawaii	14	—	—	—	14	—	—
Idaho	14	9	—	5	14	—	—
Illinois	58	50	5	3	58	—	—
Indiana	26	26	—	—	26	—	—
Iowa	24	13	8	3	24	—	—
Kansas	20	—	—	—	19	1	—
Kentucky	24	22	2	—	24	—	—
Louisiana	26	19	—	7	26	—	—
Maine	14	7	7	—	14	—	—
Maryland	26	18	8	—	26	—	—
Massachusetts	34	—	34	—	34	—	—
Michigan	48	4	—	—	48	—	—
Minnesota	26	9	15	—	26	—	—
Mississippi	20	20	—	—	20	—	—
Missouri	24	16	5	3	24	—	—
Montana	14	11	—	3	14	—	—
Nebraska	16	16	—	—	16	—	—
Nevada	12	9	3	—	12	—	—
New Hampshire	8	8	—	—	8	—	—
New Jersey	40	18	—	—	40	—	—
New Mexico	14	8	1	5	14	—	—
New York	92	4	88	—	4	88	—
North Carolina	26	9	1	16	26	—	—
North Dakota	8	5	2	1	8	—	—
Ohio	58	2	—	—	58	—	—
Oklahoma	22	14	1	7	22	—	—
Oregon	18	18	—	—	18	—	—
Pennsylvania	64	22	41	1	64	—	—
Rhode Island	14	—	14	—	14	—	—
South Carolina	22	22	—	—	22	—	—
South Dakota	14	14	—	—	14	—	—
Tennessee	28	28	—	—	28	—	—
Texas	56	41	—	15	54	—	2
Utah	8	2	—	—	8	—	—
Vermont	12	9	3	—	12	—	—
Virginia	24	22	2	—	24	—	—
Washington	24	15	3	6	24	—	—
West Virginia	14	11	3	—	13	1	—
Wisconsin	30	30	—	—	30	—	—
Wyoming	12	12	—	—	12	—	—
District of Columbia	9	6	3	—	6	3	—
Puerto Rico	5	—	5	—	5	—	—
Virgin Islands	3	2	1	—	3	—	—
Total	1333	692	277	182	1238	93	2

1. Other candidates: James A. Rhodes, 55 (Ohio); George Romney, 50 (44 in Michigan, 6 in Utah); Clifford P. Case, 22 (New Jersey); Frank Carlson, 20 (Kansas); Winthrop Rockefeller, 18 (Arkansas); Hiram L. Fong, 14 (Hawaii); Harold Stassen, 2 (1 in Minnesota, 1 in Ohio); John V. Lindsay, 1 (Minnesota).

1972 Democratic
(Narrative. p. 113)

Delegation[1]	Total Votes	Minority Report South Carolina Credentials			Minority Report California Credentials			Minority Report Illinois Credentials		
		Yea	Nay	Not voting	Yea	Nay	Not voting	Yea	Nay	Not voting
California	271	120	151	—	120	—	151	84	136	51
South Carolina	32	—	9	23	3	29	—	31	1	—
Ohio	153	63	87	3	75	78	—	69	70	14
Canal Zone	3	1.50	1.50	—	3	—	—	1	2	—
Utah	19	10	8	1	13	6	—	5	14	—
Delaware	13	5.85	7.15	—	6.50	6.50	—	6.50	6.50	—
Rhode Island	22	20	2	—	22	—	—	7.09	14.91	—
Texas	130	34	96	—	34	96	—	96	34	—
West Virginia	35	13	22	—	15	20	—	24	11	—
South Dakota	17	17	—	—	17	—	—	—	17	—
Kansas	35	17	18	—	18	17	—	18	17	—
New York	278	269	9	—	267	11	—	20	256	2
Virginia	53	34.50	18.50	—	38.50	14.50	—	16.50	35.50	1
Wyoming	11	2.20	8.80	—	4.40	6.60	—	7.70	3.30	—
Arkansas	27	13	14	—	8	19	—	13	14	—
Indiana	76	18	58	—	33	43	—	53	23	—
Puerto Rico	7	6.50	0.50	—	6.50	0.50	—	0.50	6.50	—
Tennessee	49	22	27	—	23	26	—	20	29	—
Pennsylvania	182	55.50	126	0.50	72	105	5	106.50	62	13.50
Mississippi	25	20	5	—	19	6	—	—	25	—
Wisconsin	67	39	28	—	55	12	—	12	55	—
Illinois	170	79	90	1	114.50	55.50	—	76	30	64
Maine	20	1	19	—	—	20	—	13	7	—
Florida	81	1	80	—	3	78	—	80	1	—
New Hampshire	18	13.50	4.50	—	9.90	8.10	—	9	8.10	0.90
Arizona	25	15	10	—	12	13	—	4	21	—
North Carolina	64	6	58	—	21	43	—	39	23	2
Massachusetts	102	97	5	—	97	5	—	11	91	—
Nebraska	24	14	9	1	20	4	—	13	11	—
Georgia	53	5.50	47.50	—	21.75	31.25	—	24	27.50	1.50
North Dakota	14	7	6.30	0.70	8.40	5.60	—	2.10	11.90	—
Maryland	53	24	29	—	27.83	25.17	—	28.67	24.33	—
New Jersey	109	79	29	1	85.50	22.50	1	30	75.50	3.50
Vermont	12	7	5	—	11	1	—	2	10	—
Nevada	11	5.75	5.25	—	5.75	5.25	—	6.75	4.25	—
Michigan	132	51	81	—	55	76	1	85	47	—
Iowa	46	23	23	—	27	19	—	20	26	—
Colorado	36	23	13	—	27	9	—	5	31	—
Alabama	37	1	36	—	1	36	—	32	5	—
Alaska	10	6.75	3.25	—	7.25	2.75	—	4.75	5.25	—
Hawaii	17	2	15	—	7	10	—	17	—	—
Washington	52	—	52	—	—	52	—	52	—	—
Minnesota	64	56	8	—	29	35	—	32	32	—
Louisiana	44	25	19	—	22.50	21.50	—	9.50	32.50	2
Idaho	17	12.50	4.50	—	11.50	5.50	—	4	13	—
Montana	17	10	7	—	14.50	1	1.50	2.50	14.50	—
Connecticut	51	8	43	—	21	30	—	40	11	—
District of Columbia	15	12	3	—	13.50	1.50	—	1.50	13.50	—
Virgin Islands	3	1	2	—	2.50	0.50	—	3	—	—
Kentucky	47	10	37	—	11	36	—	36	10	1
Missouri	73	13.50	59.50	—	22.50	50.50	—	59	13	1
New Mexico	18	10	8	—	10	8	—	8	10	—
Guam	3	1.50	1.50	—	1.50	1.50	—	—	3	—
Oregon	34	16	18	—	33	1	- -	2	32	—
Oklahoma	39	11	28	—	11	28	—	29	9	1
Total	**3016**	**1429.05**	**1555.75**	**31.20**	**1618.28**	**1238.22**	**159.50**	**1371.56**[a]	**1486.04**[b]	**158.40**

1. Delegations at this convention are listed in the order in which they voted. All fractional votes are expressed in decimals for consistency.
  a. Sum of column; proceedings record, 1371.55.
  b. Sum of column; proceedings record, 1486.05.

1972 Democratic

(Narrative p. 113)

Minority Report Guaranteed Income			First Presidential[2] (Before shift)					First Presidential[3] (After shift)				
Yea	Nay	Not voting	McGovern	Jackson	Wallace	Chisholm	Sanford	McGovern	Jackson	Wallace	Chisholm	Sanford
131	114	26	271	—	—	—	—	271	—	—	—	—
4	21	7	6	10	6	4	6	10	9	6	—	6
39	86	28	77	39	—	23	3	77	39	—	23	3
2.50	0.50	—	3	—	—	—	—	3	—	—	—	—
8	11	—	14	1	—	—	3	14	1	—	—	3
4.55	8.45	—	5.85	6.50	—	0.65	—	5.85	5.85	—	0.65	—
10.86	11.14	—	22	—	—	—	—	22	—	—	—	—
15	115	—	54	23	48	4	—	54	23	48	4	—
3	32	—	16	14	1	—	4	16	14	1	—	4
1	16	—	17	—	—	—	—	17	—	—	—	—
5	30	—	20	10	—	2	1	20	10	—	2	1
152	118	8	263	9	—	6	—	278	—	—	—	—
30	21	2	33.50	4	1	5.50	9	37	5	—	2.50	8.50
0.55	10.45	—	3.30	6.05	—	1.10	—	3.30	6.05	—	1.10	—
10	16	1	1	1	—	—	—	1	1	—	—	—
17	56	3	26	20	26	1	—	28	19	25	—	—
4	3	—	7	—	—	—	—	7	—	—	—	—
21	27	1	—	—	33	10	—	5	—	32	7	—
49.50	117.50	15	81	86.50	2	9.50	1	81	86.50	2	9.50	1
22	—	3	10	—	—	12	3	23	—	—	2	—
29	38	—	55	3	—	5	—	55	3	—	5	—
59	95	16	119	30.50	0.50	4.50	2	155	6	—	1	—
1	19	—	5	—	—	—	—	5	—	—	—	—
4	77	—	2	—	75	2	—	4	—	75	1	—
0.90	14.40	2.70	10.80	5.40	—	—	—	10.80	5.40	—	—	—
6	19	—	21	3	—	—	1	22	3	—	—	—
17	47	—	—	—	37	—	27	—	—	37	—	27
60	40	2	102	—	—	—	—	102	—	—	—	—
2	22	—	21	3	—	—	—	21	3	—	—	—
10.50	34	8.50	14.50	14.50	11	12	1	14.50	14.50	11	12	1
1.40	10.50	2.10	8.40	2.80	0.70	0.70	—	10.50	2.10	—	0.70	—
14.33	38.67	—	13	—	38	2	—	13	—	38	2	—
61.50	35.50	12	89	11.50	—	4	1.50	92.50	11	—	3.50	—
4	8	—	12	—	—	—	—	12	—	—	—	—
2.75	8.25	—	5.75	5.25	—	—	—	5.75	5.25	—	—	—
30.50	96.50	5	50.50	7	67.50	3	1	51.50	7	67.50	2	1
6	39	1	35	—	—	3	4	35	—	—	3	4
15	21	—	27	—	—	7	—	29	2	—	5	—
10	27	—	9	1	24	—	1	9	1	24	—	1
3	5.50	1.50	6.50	3.25	—	—	—	6.50	3.25	—	—	—
1.50	15.50	—	6.50	8.50	—	1	—	6.50	8.50	—	1	—
1	51	—	—	52	—	—	—	—	52	—	—	—
28	33	3	11	—	—	6	—	43	—	—	4	1
22	20	2	10.25	10.25	3	18.50	2	25.75	5.25	3	4	1
5	12	—	12.50	2.50	—	2	—	12.50	2.50	—	2	—
2	14	1	16	—	—	1	—	16	—	—	1	—
22	29	—	30	20	—	—	1	30	20	—	—	1
15	—	—	13.50	1.50	—	—	—	13.50	1.50	—	—	—
2.50	0.50	—	1	1.50	—	0.50	—	1	1.50	—	0.50	—
1	41	5	10	35	—	—	2	10	35	—	—	2
12	55	6	24.50	48.50	—	—	—	24.50	48.50	—	—	—
3	15	—	10	—	8	—	—	10	—	8	—	—
—	3	—	1.50	1.50	—	—	—	1.50	1.50	—	—	—
11	23	—	34	—	—	—	—	34	—	—	—	—
5.50	31.50	2	10.50	23.50	—	1	4	9.50	23.50	—	2	4
999.34	**1852.86**	**163.80**	**1728.35**	**525.00**	**381.70**	**151.95**	**77.50**	**1864.95**	**485.65**	**377.50**	**101.45**	**69.50**

2. Humphrey, 66.70 (46 in Minnesota, 4 in Ohio, 4 in Wisconsin, 3 in Michigan, 2 in Indiana, 2 in Pennsylvania, 2 in Florida, 1 in Utah, 1 in Colorado, 1 in Hawaii, 0.70 in North Dakota); Mills, 33.80 (25 in Arkansas, 3 in Illinois, 3 in New Jersey, 2 in Alabama, 0.55 in Wyoming, 0.25 in Alaska); Muskie, 24.30 (15 in Maine, 5.50 in Illinois, 1.80 in New Hampshire, 1 in Texas, 1 in Colorado); Kennedy, 12.70 (4 in Iowa, 3 in Illinois, 2 in Ohio, 1 in Kansas, 1 in Indiana, 1 in Tennessee, 0.70 in North Dakota); Hays, 5 (Ohio); McCarthy, 2 (Illinois); Mondale, 1 (Kansas); Clark, 1 (Minnesota); not voting, 5 (Tennessee).

3. Humphrey, 35 (16 in Minnesota, 4 in Ohio, 4 in Wisconsin, 3 in Indiana, 3 in Michigan, 2 in Pennsylvania, 1 in Utah, 1 in Florida, 1 in Hawaii); Mills, 32.80 (25 in Arkansas, 2 in Illinois, 2 in New Jersey, 2 in Alabama, 1 in South Carolina, 0.55 in Wyoming, 0.25 in Alaska); Muskie, 20.80 (15 in Maine, 3 in Illinois, 1.80 in New Hampshire, 1 in Texas); Kennedy, 10.65 (4 in Iowa, 2 in Ohio, 1 in Kansas, 1 in Indiana, 1 in Tennessee, 1 in Illinois, 0.65 in Delaware); Hays, 5 (Ohio); McCarthy, 2 (Illinois); Mondale, 1 (Kansas).

1972 Republican

(Narrative, p. 116)

Delegation	Total Votes	First Pres. Ballot	
		Nixon	McCloskey
Alabama	18	18	—
Alaska	12	12	—
Arizona	18	18	—
Arkansas	18	18	—
California	96	96	—
Colorado	20	20	—
Connecticut	22	22	—
Delaware	12	12	—
Florida	40	40	—
Georgia	24	24	—
Hawaii	14	14	—
Idaho	14	14	—
Illinois	58	58	—
Indiana	32	32	—
Iowa	22	22	—
Kansas	20	20	—
Kentucky	24	24	—
Louisiana	20	20	—
Maine	8	8	—
Maryland	26	26	—
Massachusetts	34	34	—
Michigan	48	48	—
Minnesota	26	26	—
Mississippi	14	14	—
Missouri	30	30	—
Montana	14	14	—
Nebraska	16	16	—
Nevada	12	12	—
New Hampshire	14	14	—
New Jersey	40	40	—
New Mexico	14	13	1
New York	88	88	—
North Carolina	32	32	—
North Dakota	12	12	—
Ohio	56	56	—
Oklahoma	22	22	—
Oregon	18	18	—
Pennsylvania	60	60	—
Rhode Island	8	8	—
South Carolina	22	22	—
South Dakota	14	14	—
Tennessee	26	26	—
Texas	52	52	—
Utah	14	14	—
Vermont	12	12	—
Virginia	30	30	—
Washington	24	24	—
West Virginia	18	18	—
Wisconsin	28	28	—
Wyoming	12	12	—
District of Columbia	9	9	—
Guam	3	3	—
Puerto Rico	5	5	—
Virgin Islands	3	3	—
Total	1348	1347	1

1976 Democratic

(Narrative, p. 119)

Delegation	Total Votes	First Presidential[1] (before shifts)[2]			
		Carter	Udall	Brown	Wallace
Alabama	35	30	--	--	5
Alaska	10	10	--	--	--
Arizona	25	6	19	--	--
Arkansas	26	25	1	--	--
California	280	73	2	205	--
Colorado	35	15	6	11	--
Connecticut	51	35	16	--	--
Delaware	12	10.50	--	1.50	--
Florida	81	70	--	1	10
Georgia	50	50	--	--	--
Hawaii	17	17	--	--	--
Idaho	16	16	--	--	--
Illinois	169	164	1	2	1
Indiana	75	72	--	--	3
Iowa	47	25	20	1	--
Kansas	34	32	2	--	--
Kentucky	46	39	2	--	5
Louisiana	41	18	--	18	5
Maine	20	15	5	--	--
Maryland	53	44	6	3	--
Massachusetts[3]	104	65	21	--	11
Michigan	133	75	58	--	--
Minnesota	65	37	2	1	--
Mississippi	24	23	--	--	--
Missouri	71	58	4	2	--
Montana	17	11	2	--	--
Nebraska	23	20	--	3	--
Nevada	11	3	--	6.50	--
New Hampshire	17	15	2	--	--
New Jersey	108	108	--	--	--
New Mexico	18	14	4	--	--
New York	274	209.50	56.50	4	--
North Carolina	61	56	--	--	3
North Dakota	13	13	--	--	--
Ohio	152	132	20	--	--
Oklahoma	37	32	1	--	--
Oregon	34	16	--	10	--
Pennsylvania	178	151	21	6	--
Rhode Island	22	14	--	8	--
South Carolina	31	28	--	1	2
South Dakota	17	11	5	--	--
Tennessee	46	45	--	--	1
Texas	130	124	--	4	1
Utah	18	10	--	5	--
Vermont	12	5	4	3	--
Virginia	54	48	6	--	--
Washington	53	36	11	3	--
West Virginia	33	30	1	--	--
Wisconsin	68	29	25	--	10
Wyoming	10	8	1	1	--
District of Columbia	17	12	5	--	--
Puerto Rico	22	22	--	--	--
Canal Zone	3	3	--	--	--
Guam	3	3	--	--	--
Virgin Islands	3	3	--	--	--
Democrats Abroad	3	2.50	--	0.50	--
Total	3,008	2,238.50	329.50	300.50	57.00

[1] Other candidates: Ellen McCormack, 22 (1 in Illinois, 2 in Massachusetts, 11 in Minnesota, 7 in Missouri, 1 in Wisconsin); Frank Church, 19 (3 in Colorado, 4 in Montana, 1 in Nevada, 8 in Oregon, 1 in Utah, 2 in Washington); Hubert H. Humphrey, 10 (9 in Minnesota, 1 in South Dakota); Henry M. Jackson, 10 (2 in Massachusetts, 4 in New York, 1 in Washington, 3 in Wisconsin); Fred Harris, 9 (2 in Massachusetts, 4 in Minnesota, 3 in Oklahoma); Milton J. Shapp, 2 (1 in Massachusetts, 1 in Utah); receiving one vote each: Robert C. Byrd (W.Va.); Cesar Chavez (Utah); Leon Jaworski (Texas); Barbara C. Jordon (Oklahoma); Edward M. Kennedy (Iowa); Jennings Randolph (W.Va.); Fred Stover (Minnesota); "nobody", (0.50 in Nevada); abstentions, 3 (1 in Mississippi, 2 in North Carolina).

[2] At the conclusion of the roll call California switched to 278 for Carter and 2 for Udall. Rhode Island switched to 22 for Carter. Louisiana switched to 35 for Carter, 5 for Wallace and 1 for Brown. Totals after switches: Carter 2,925.50; Udall 329.50; Brown 70.50; Wallace 57.00. The votes received by other candidates did not change. The rules were suspended after the Louisiana switches and Carter was nominated by acclamation.

[3] Massachusetts passed when originally called on and cast its votes at the end of the roll call, after vote switches in California and Rhode Island.

1976 Republican

(Narrative, p. 124)

Delegation	Total Votes	Rule 16C[1]		First Presidential[2]	
		Yea	Nay	Ford	Reagan
Alabama	37	37	--	--	37
Alaska	19	2	17	17	2
Arizona	29	25	4	2	27
Arkansas	27	17	10	10	17
California	167	166	1	--	167
Colorado	31	26	5	5	26
Connecticut	35	--	35	35	--
Delaware	17	1	16	15	2
Florida	66	28	38	43	23
Georgia	48	39	7	--	48
Hawaii	19	1	18	18	1
Idaho	21	17	4	4	17
Illinois	101	20	79	86	14
Indiana	54	27	27	9	45
Iowa	36	18	18	19	17
Kansas	34	4	30	30	4
Kentucky	37	26	10	19	18
Louisiana	41	34	6	5	36
Maine	20	5	15	15	5
Maryland	43	8	35	43	--
Massachusetts	43	15	28	28	15
Michigan	84	29	55	55	29
Minnesota	42	5	35	32	10
Mississippi	30	--	30	16	14
Missouri	49	30	18	18	31
Montana	20	20	--	--	20
Nebraska	25	18	7	7	18
Nevada	18	15	3	5	13
New Hampshire	21	3	18	18	3
New Jersey	67	4	62	63	4
New Mexico	21	20	1	--	21
New York	154	20	134	133	20
North Carolina	54	51	3	25	29
North Dakota	18	6	12	11	7
Ohio	97	7	90	91	6
Oklahoma	36	36	--	--	36
Oregon	30	14	16	16	14
Pennsylvania	103	14	89	93	10
Rhode Island	19	--	19	19	--
South Carolina	36	25	11	9	27
South Dakota	20	11	9	9	11
Tennessee	43	17	26	21	22
Texas	100	100	--	--	100
Utah	20	20	--	--	20
Vermont	18	--	18	18	--
Virginia	51	36	15	16	35
Washington	38	31	7	7	31
West Virginia	28	12	16	20	8
Wisconsin	45	--	45	45	--
Wyoming	17	9	8	7	10
District of Columbia	14	--	14	14	--
Puerto Rico	8	--	8	8	--
Guam	4	--	4	4	--
Virgin Islands	4	--	4	4	--
Total	2,259	1,069	1,180	1,187	1,070

[1] Not voting, 10.

[2] Other candidate: Elliot L. Richardson, 1 (New York); abstensions, 1 (Ill.). The nomination was made unanimous at the end of the balloting.

1980 Democratic

(Narrative p. 128)

| Delegation | Total Votes | Minority Rule #5 [1] | | First Presidential [2] | | |
		Yea	Nay	Carter	Kennedy	Others [3]
Alabama	45	3	42	43	2	—
Alaska	11	6.11	4.89	8.4	2.6	—
Arizona	29	16	13	13	16	—
Arkansas	33	9	24	25	6	2
California	306	171	132[4]	140	166	—
Colorado	40	24	16	27	10	3
Connecticut	54	28	26	26	28	—
Delaware	14	6.5	7.5	10	4	—
District of Columbia	19	12	7	12	5	2
Florida	100	25	75	75	25	—
Georgia	63	1	62	62	—	1
Hawaii	19	4	15	16	2	1
Idaho	17	9	8	9	7	1
Illinois	179	26	153	163	16	—
Indiana	80	27	53	53	27	—
Iowa	50	21	29	31	17	2
Kansas	37	17	20	23	14	—
Kentucky	50	12	38	45	5	—
Louisiana	51	15	36	50	1	—
Maine	22	12	10	11	11	—
Maryland	59	27	32	34	24	1
Massachusetts	111	81	30	34	77	—
Michigan	141	71	70	102	38	1
Minnesota	75	30	45	41	14	20
Mississippi	32	—	32	32	—	—
Missouri	77	20	57	58	19	—
Montana	19	9	10	13	6	—
Nebraska	24	11	13	14	10	—
Nevada	12	6.47	5.53	8.12	3.88	—
New Hampshire	19	9	10	10	9	—
New Jersey	113	68	45	45	68	—
New Mexico	20	11	9	10	10	—
New York	282	163	118	129	151	2
North Carolina	69	13	56	66	3	—
North Dakota	14	10	4	5	7	2
Ohio	161	81	80	89	72	—
Oklahoma	42	9	33	36	3	2
Oregon	39	14	25	26	13	—
Pennsylvania	185	102	83	95	90	—
Puerto Rico	41	20	21	21	20	—
Rhode Island	23	17	6	6	17	—
South Carolina	37	6	31	37	—	—
South Dakota	19	10	9	9	10	—
Tennessee	55	8	47	51	4	—
Texas	152	47	105	108	38	6
Utah	20	12	8	11	4	5
Vermont	12	7.5	4.5	5	7	—
Virginia	64	7	57	59	5	—
Washington	58	24	34	36	22	—
West Virginia	35	16	19	21	10	4
Wisconsin	75	26	49	48	26	1
Wyoming	11	3.5	7.5	8	3	—
Virgin Islands	4	—	4	4	—	—
Guam	4	—	4	4	—	—
Latin American	4	4	—	4	—	—
Democrats Abroad	4	2.5	1.5	1.5	2	0.5
Total	3,331	1,390.58	1,936.42	2,123	1,150.5	54.5 [5]

1. The vote was on a minority report by supporters of Sen. Edward M. Kennedy to overturn a proposed rule that would bind all delegates to vote on the first ballot for the presidential candidate under whose banner they were elected. A "yes" vote supported the Kennedy position while a "no" supported the Carter view that delegates should be bound.

2. Other votes: Uncommitted, 10 (3 in Texas, 3 in Colo., 2 in N.D., 1 in Ark., 1 in Md., 1 in Idaho); Sen. William Proxmire, 10 (all in Minn.); Gov. Scott M. Matheson, D-Utah, 5 (all in Utah); Koryne Horbal of Minn., U.S. representative on the U.N. Commission on the Status of Women, 5 (all in Minn.); abstentions, 4 (2 in D.C. , 1 in Hawaii, 1 in Mich.); Rep. Ronald V. Dellums, D-Calif., 2.5 (2 in N.Y., 0.5 from Democrats Abroad.)

Receiving 2 votes each were: Sen. John C. Culver, D-Iowa (Iowa); Minnesota Attorney General Warren Spannous (Minn.); Alice Tripp (Minn.); Rep. Kent Hance, D-Texas (Texas); Senate Majority Leader Robert C. Byrd, D-W.Va. (W.Va.).

Receiving one vote each were: Sen. Dale Bumpers, D-Ark. (Ark.) Secretary of State Edmund S. Muskie (Colo.); Vice President Walter F. Mondale (Minn.); Gov. Hugh L. Carey, D-N.Y. (Okla); Rep. Tom Steed, D-Okla. (Okla.); Gov. Edmund G. Brown Jr., D-Calif. (Wis.)

3. At the conclusion of the roll call Del. switched to 14 for Carter and none for Kennedy. Iowa switched to 33 for Carter and 17 for Kennedy. After the switches, Carter was nominated by acclamation following a motion to that effect by the Mass. delegation.

4. One abstention.

5. This figure does not include: asbsent, 2 (1 in Ga., 1 in Okla.); 1 not voting (Texas).

1980 Republican

(Narrative p. 132)

First Presidential

State	Total Votes	Reagan	Anderson	Bush	Other	Abstentions
Alabama	27	27	—	—	—	—
Alaska	19	19	—	—	—	—
Arizona	28	28	—	—	—	—
Arkansas	19	19	—	—	—	—
California	168	168	—	—	—	—
Colorado	31	31	—	—	—	—
Connecticut	35	35	—	—	—	—
Delaware	12	12	—	—	—	—
District of Columbia	14	14	—	—	—	—
Florida	51	51	—	—	—	—
Georgia	36	36	—	—	—	—
Guam	4	4	—	—	—	—
Hawaii	14	14	—	—	—	—
Idaho	21	21	—	—	—	—
Illinois	102	81	21	—	—	—
Indiana	54	54	—	—	—	—
Iowa	37	37	—	—	—	—
Kansas	32	32	—	—	—	—
Kentucky	27	27	—	—	—	—
Louisiana	31	31	—	—	—	—
Maine	21	21	—	—	—	—
Maryland	30	30	—	—	—	—
Massachusetts	42	33	9	—	—	—
Michigan	82	67	—	13	1[1]	1
Minnesota	34	33	—	—	—	1
Mississippi	22	22	—	—	—	—
Missouri	37	37	—	—	—	—
Montana	20	20	—	—	—	—
Nebraska	25	25	—	—	—	—
Nevada	17	17	—	—	—	—
New Hampshire	22	22	—	—	—	—
New Jersey	66	66	—	—	—	—
New Mexico	22	22	—	—	—	—
New York	123	121	—	—	—	2
North Carolina	40	40	—	—	—	—
North Dakota	17	17	—	—	—	—
Ohio	77	77	—	—	—	—
Oklahoma	34	34	—	—	—	—
Oregon	29	29	—	—	—	—
Pennsylvania	83	83	—	—	—	—
Puerto Rico	14	14	—	—	—	—
Rhode Island	13	13	—	—	—	—
South Carolina	25	25	—	—	—	—
South Dakota	22	22	—	—	—	—
Tennessee	32	32	—	—	—	—
Texas	80	80	—	—	—	—
Utah	21	21	—	—	—	—
Vermont	19	19	—	—	—	—
Virginia	51	51	—	—	—	—
Virgin Islands	4	4	—	—	—	—
Washington	37	36	1	—	—	—
West Virginia	18	18	—	—	—	—
Wisconsin	34	28	6	—	—	—
Wyoming	19	19	—	—	—	—
Total	**1,994**	**1,939**	**37**	**13**	**1**	**4**

1. One vote for Anne Armstrong. Four not voting.

PROFILES OF AMERICAN POLITICAL PARTIES

Historical Profiles of
American Political Parties

American Party (1968-) and
American Independent Party (1972-)

Both the American Party and the American Independent Party (AIP) descended from the American Independent Party which served as the vehicle for George C. Wallace's third party presidential candidacy in 1968.

Alabama Governor Wallace (1963-67; 1971-79) burst onto the national scene in 1964 as a Democratic presidential candidate opposed to the 1964 Civil Rights Act. Entering three northern primaries — Wisconsin, Indiana and Maryland — he surprised political observers by winning between 30 and 43 per cent of the popular vote in the three primaries. His unexpectedly strong showing brought the term "white backlash" into the political vocabulary, a description of the racial undertone of the Wallace vote.

In 1968, Wallace broke with the Democrats and embarked on his second presidential campaign as a third party candidate under the American Independent Party label. His candidacy capitalized on the bitter reactions of millions of voters, especially whites and blue-collar workers, to the civil rights activism, urban riots, antiwar demonstrations and heavy federal spending on Johnson administration "Great Society" programs that marked the mid-1960s. With the help of his Alabama advisers and volunteer groups, Wallace was able to get his party on the ballot in all 50 states.

The former governor did not hold a convention for his party, but in October announced his vice presidential running mate (retired Air Force General Curtis LeMay) and released a platform. In the November election the Wallace ticket received 9,901,151 votes (13.5 per cent of the popular vote), carried five southern states and won 46 electoral votes. The party's showing was the best by a third party since 1924, when Robert M. La Follette collected 16.6 per cent of the vote on the Progressive Party ticket.

After his defeat in that election, Wallace returned to the Democratic Party, competing in Democratic presidential primaries in 1972 and 1976. Wallace's American Independent Party began to break into factions after the 1968 election, but in 1972 united behind John G. Schmitz, a Republican U.S. representative from southern California (1970-73), as its presidential nominee. Thomas J. Anderson, a farm magazine and syndicated news features publisher from Tennessee, was the candidate for Vice President. In many states, the party shortened its name to American Party. In the November election, the Schmitz ticket won 1,090,673 votes (1.4 per cent of the popular vote) but failed to win any electoral votes.

In December 1972, a bitter fight occurred for the AIP chairmanship between Anderson and William K. Shearer, the California chairman of the party. Anderson defeated Shearer, retaining control of the AIP but renaming it the American Party. Shearer, over the next four years, expanded his California-based group into a new national party. He had kept the name American Independent Party in California, and made that the name of the new nationwide group.

Thus, by 1976, there were two distinct entities — the American Party headed by Anderson and the American Independent Party headed by Shearer.

The 1976 American Party convention was held in Salt Lake City, Utah, from June 17 to 20. Anderson was nominated for President and Rufus Shakleford of Florida for Vice President.

The party's nomination of Anderson followed the failure to enlist a prominent conservative to lead the ticket. Both New Hampshire Gov. Meldrim Thomson Jr. (R) and North Carolina Sen. Jesse Helms (R) were approached, but both decided to remain in the Republican Party. With well-known conservatives declining the party's overtures, the convention turned to Anderson. He easily won the nomination on the first ballot by defeating six party workers.

Anderson's campaign stressed the "permanent principles" of the party, augmented by the 1976 platform. These principles included opposition to foreign aid, U.S. withdrawal from the United Nations and an end to trade with or recognition of Communist nations. The platform included planks opposing abortion, gun control, the Equal Rights Amendment and government-sponsored health care and welfare programs. In general, the party favored limits on federal power, and was against budget deficits except in wartime.

The American Party was on the ballot in 18 states, including eight states where the American Independent Party was also on the ballot. In seven of those eight states, Anderson ran ahead of the AIP ticket. Anderson's strength was spread fairly evenly across the country. His best

---

Sources

Congressional Quarterly Weekly Report, Congressional Quarterly Inc., Washington, D.C. 1975-76, 1980.

Dictionary of American History, Charles Scribners' Sons, New York, 1946.

Encyclopedia Americana, Encyclopedia Americana Corp., New York, 1968.

Encyclopaedia Britannica, Encyclopaedia Britannica Corp., Chicago, 1973.

Schlesinger, Arthur M. Jr., *History of U.S. Political Parties*, Chelsea House, New York, 1973.

Stimpson, George W., *A Book About American Politics*, Harper, New York, 1952.

showings were in Utah (2.5 per cent of the vote) and Montana (1.8 per cent). He received more than 0.5 per cent of the vote in Virginia (1.0), Mississippi (0.9), Minnesota (0.7) and Kentucky (0.7). Anderson's total of 160,773 popular votes (0.2 per cent) placed him 9,756 votes behind the AIP candidate nationally.

The AIP convention met in Chicago, Aug. 24-27, 1976, and chose former Georgia Gov. Lester Maddox (1967-71), a Democrat, as its presidential nominee and former Madison, Wis., Mayor William Dyke, a Republican, as its vice presidential candidate. Maddox won a first ballot nomination over Dallas columnist Robert Morris and former Democratic U.S. Representative John R. Rarick of Louisiana (1967-75).

At the convention, a group of nationally-prominent conservatives made a bid to take over the party and use it as a vehicle for building a new conservative coalition. Richard Viguerie, a fund raiser for Wallace and a nationally-known direct mail expert, was the leader of the group. He was joined at the convention by two leading conservatives — William Rusher, publisher of the *National Review*, and Howard Phillips, the former head of the Office of Economic Opportunity (1973) and leader of the Conservative Caucus, an activist conservative group. Viguerie, Phillips and Rusher all argued that the AIP should be overhauled, changed from a fringe group to a philosophical home for believers in free enterprise and traditional moral values. They also hoped they could attract Sen. Helms or Gov. Thomson, or Rep. Philip M. Crane (R Ill.). When none of these men agreed to run on the AIP ticket, Viguerie and his allies found themselves unable successfully to promote Morris, a lesser-known substitute.

Many AIP members favored Maddox because they saw him as a colorful personality, one capable of drawing media attention and perhaps of picking up the five per cent of the national vote needed to qualify the party for federal funding. Maddox never came close to that goal however, achieving only 0.2 per cent of the national vote (170,531). It was 51,098 votes in California, where American Party nominee Anderson was not on the ballot, that enabled Maddox to run slightly ahead of Anderson nationally.

Despite the power struggle between Anderson and Shearer, there was little difference between their two party platforms. Like the American Party, the AIP opposed abortion, gun control, forced busing, foreign aid and membership in the United Nations.

By 1980 neither party was much of a force in American politics. Both retained the same basic platforms, but each was on the ballot in only a handful of states. The American Independent Party's nominee, former Democratic Rep. John R. Rarick of Louisiana (1967-75), ran in only eight states. Economist Percy L. Greaves Jr., the American Party candidate, was listed in just seven states.

American Party-'Know-Nothings' (1856)

The American Party politicized the nativist, anti-immigrant movement in the mid-1850s, a peak period of European immigration to the United States in the pre-Civil War years. In the preceding decade before the rise of a formal party, the movement took the form of local, secret organizations whose members were sworn to secrecy with the movement's elaborate rituals. To questions about their affiliation, they pleaded ignorance. Hence, the party's popular name: the Know-Nothings.

Since many of the millions of immigrants in the mid-19th century were Catholic, the Know-Nothings were hostile to Catholics. They advocated nominating only native American Protestants for political office and requiring a 21-year waiting period before naturalization.

In addition to the great waves of immigrants, the party's meteoric rise was spurred by the increasing polarization of the Democrats and Whigs over the volatile slavery issue. The Know-Nothings benefited from the political situation and attracted members from both of the older parties. In the party's peak years 1854 and 1855, the Know-Nothings elected governors in California, Connecticut, Delaware, Kentucky, Massachusetts, New Hampshire and Rhode Island, and elected five senators and 43 members of the House.

But as a national party, the Know-Nothings, like the Democrats and Whigs, were eventually split by the slavery issue. When a party convention in June 1855 adopted a pro-southern position on slavery, anti-slavery elements bolted, dividing the party and setting the stage for its downfall.

The Know-Nothings held their first and only national nominating convention in February 1856, and selected as their candidate the former Whig President, Millard Fillmore (1850-53). The anti-slavery wing of the party convened separately and endorsed the Republican nominee, John C. Fremont. Fillmore finished third in the three-way race, receiving 21.5 per cent of the popular vote and carrying only one state, Maryland.

Within a year, the bulk of the northern Know-Nothings had joined the Republican Party. By the end of the decade, the party existed only in the border states, where it formed the basis for the unsuccessful, antiwar Constitutional Union Party. *(Constitutional Union Party, p. 201)*

Anti-Federalists (1789-96)

Never a formal party, the Anti-Federalists were a loosely organized group opposed to ratification of the Constitution. With the adoption of the Constitution in 1788, the Anti-Federalists served as the opposition to the Federalists in the early years of Congress.

Anti-Federalists were primarily rural, agrarian interests from inland regions, who favored individual freedom and states' rights, which they felt would be jeopardized by the new Constitution. Although the Constitution was ratified, the efforts of the Anti-Federalists led to adoption of the first 10 amendments, the Bill of Rights, which spelled out the major limitations of federal power.

As the opposition faction in Congress during the formative years of the Republic, the Anti-Federalists basically held to a strict interpretation of the Constitution, particularly in regard to the various economic proposals of Treasury Secretary Alexander Hamilton to centralize more power in the federal government.

Although never the majority faction in Congress, the Anti-Federalists were a forerunner of Jefferson's Democratic-Republican Party, which came into existence in the 1790s and dominated American politics for the first quarter of the 19th century.

Anti-Masonic Party (1832-36)

Born in the late 1820s in upstate New York, the Anti-Masonic Party focused the strong, anti-elitist mood of the period on a conspicuous symbol of privilege, the Masons. The Masons were a secret, fraternal organization with membership drawn largely from the upper class. Conversely, the appeal of the Anti-Masonic movement was to the common man — poor farmers and laborers especially —

who resented the secrecy and privilege of the Masons.

The spark which created the party came in 1826, when William Morgan, a dissident Mason from Batavia, N.Y., allegedly on the verge of exposing the inner workings of the order, mysteriously disappeared and was never seen again. Refusal of Masonic leaders to cooperate in the inconclusive investigation of Morgan's disappearance led to suspicions that Masons had kidnapped and murdered him, and were suppressing the inquiry.

From 1828 through 1831, the new Anti-Masonic Party spread through New England and the Middle Atlantic states, in many places establishing itself as the primary opposition to the Democrats. In addition to its appeal to the working classes, particularly in northern rural areas, and its opposition to Masonry, the Anti-Masons displayed a fervor against immorality, as seen not only in secret societies, but also in slavery, intemperance and urban life.

In September 1831, the party held the first national nominating convention in American history. One hundred and sixteen delegates from 13 states gathered in Baltimore, Maryland, and nominated former Attorney General William Wirt of Maryland for the presidency. While Wirt received only 100,712 votes (7.8 per cent of the popular vote) and carried just one state, Vermont, the Anti-Masons did reasonably well at other levels: winning two governorships and 53 House seats.

But the decline of Masonry, especially in New York, where the number of lodges dropped from 507 in 1826 to 48 six years later, robbed the Anti-Masons of an emotional issue and hastened their decline. The 1832 election was the high point for the Anti-Masons as a national party. In the 1836 campaign the party endorsed Whig candidate William Henry Harrison. Subsequently, the bulk of the Anti-Masonic constituency moved into the Whig Party.

Citizens Party (1979-   )

Organized in 1979 as a coalition of dissident liberals and populists, the first Citizens Party convention chose author and environmental scientist Barry Commoner as its 1980 presidential candidate and La Donna Harris, wife of former Democratic Sen. Fred R. Harris of Oklahoma, as his running mate. The Citizens Party ticket ran on the central theme that major decisions in America were made to benefit corporations and not the average citizen. The party proposed public control of energy industries and multinational corporations, a halt to the use of nuclear power, a sharp cut in military spending and price controls on food, fuel, housing and health care.

Commoner ran in all of the large electoral vote states except Florida and Texas. He made his biggest push in California, Illinois, Michigan, New York and Pennsylvania, where party leaders believed they could tap a "sophisticated working-class population" and appeal to political activists who had been involved in the environmental and anti-nuclear movements that sprang up in the late 1970s.

The Commoner/Harris ticket was on the ballot in 29 states and the District of Columbia in 1980. Party leaders claimed that it was the largest number of ballot positions attained by any third party in its first campaign. In addition to its presidential ticket, the Citizens Party also fielded 22 candidates running for other offices, including two for the U.S. Senate and seven for the House.

The Citizens Party won 234,279 votes in the 1980 presidential election, or 0.3 percent of the vote.

Communist Party (1924-   )

In 1919, shortly after the Russian Revolution, Soviet Communists encouraged American left-wing groups to withdraw from the Socialist Party and to form a Communist Party in the United States. After several years of internal dissension, a new political organization, named the Workers' Party of America, was established in 1921 at the insistence of Moscow. The goal of the new party was revolutionary — to overthrow capitalism and to create a Communist state with rule by the working classes.

William Z. Foster, a labor organizer, was the party's first presidential candidate in 1924. National tickets were run every four years through 1940 and again in 1968, 1972, 1976 and 1980, but the party's peak year at the polls was 1932, when Foster received 102,221 votes (0.3 per cent of the popular vote).

The Communists have a distinctive place in American political history as the only party to have had international ties. In 1929 a party split brought the formal creation of the Communist Party of the United States, with acknowledged status as a part of the international Communist movement (the Communist International).

The Communist International terminated during World War II and in 1944 the party's leader in America, Earl Browder, dissolved the party and committed the movement to operate within the two-party system. In the 1944 campaign the Communists endorsed President Franklin D. Roosevelt, who repudiated their support.

However, with the breakup of the U.S.-Soviet alliance after World War II, the Communists reconstituted themselves as a political party, but did not run a national ticket again until 1968. The Communists supported Henry Wallace's Progressive Party candidacy in 1948, but in the 1950s were limited by restrictive legislation passed by federal and state governments during the Cold War period, which virtually outlawed the party.

With the gradual easing of restrictive measures, the Communist Party resumed electoral activities in the late 1960s. In a policy statement written in 1966, the party described itself as "a revolutionary party whose aim is the fundamental transformation of society." The party's success at the polls, however, continued to be minimal. Its presidential candidates in 1968, 1972, 1976 and 1980 each received less than one-tenth of 1 percent of the vote.

Constitutional Union Party (1860)

The short-lived Constitutional Union Party was formed in 1859 to promote national conciliation in the face of rampant sectionalism, that included southern threats of secession. The party's basic appeal was to conservative remnants of the American (Know-Nothing) and Whig parties, who viewed preservation of the Union as their primary goal.

The Constitutional Union Party held its first and only national convention in Baltimore in May 1860. For president the party nominated John Bell of Tennessee, a former senator and Speaker of the House of Representatives, who had previously been both a Democrat and a Whig. The convention adopted a short platform which intentionally avoided controversial subjects, most notably the divisive slavery issue. Instead, the platform simply urged support for "the Constitution, the Union and the Laws."

In the fall election, Bell received 590,901 votes (12.6 per cent of the popular vote) and won three states — Kentucky,

Tennessee and Virginia. However, the Bell ticket finished last in the four-way presidential race, and together with the sectional split in the Democratic Party, was a prominent factor in the victory of Republican Abraham Lincoln.

In the months after the 1860 election, the Constitutional Union Party continued to urge national conciliation, but with the outbreak of the Civil War, the party disappeared.

Democratic Party (1832-   )

There is no precise birth date for the Democratic Party. It developed as an outgrowth of Thomas Jefferson's Democratic-Republican Party, which splintered into factions in the 1820s. The faction led by Andrew Jackson took the name Democratic-Republican, but after 1830 dropped the last half of this label and became simply the Democratic Party. The new party encouraged and benefited from the increasing democratization of American politics that began in the 1820s. Andrew Jackson was a symbol of this mass democracy, and when elected in 1828, began a period of Democratic dominance that lasted until the Civil War.

The Democrats were a national party, with a particular appeal among workingmen, immigrants and settlers west of the Alleghenies. The success of the party in the pre-Civil War period was in part due to a national organization stronger than that of its rivals. In 1832 the Democrats were the first major party to hold a national nominating convention, and in 1848 became the first party to establish an ongoing national committee.

Between 1828 and 1860, the party held the White House for 24 of the 32 years, controlled the Senate for 26 years and the House of Representatives for two years less. Leadership in the party generally resided in Congress. The Democrats' two-thirds nominating rule, adopted at the 1832 convention and retained for a century, gave the South a veto power over the choice of a national ticket. The result, not only in the pre-Civil War years, but until the rule was eliminated in 1936, was the frequent selection of conservative candidates for president.

The early philosophy of the Democratic Party stressed a belief in a strict interpretation of the Constitution, states' rights, and limited spending by the federal government. While party members throughout the nation accepted these basic tenets, there was no national consensus on the volatile slavery issue, which strained the party in the mid-19th century and finally divided it geographically in 1860. Two separate Democratic tickets were run in the 1860 election — one northern, one southern. The party division aided the election of the candidate of the new anti-slavery Republican Party, Abraham Lincoln, who received less than 40 per cent of the popular vote.

During the Civil War, the northern wing of the party was factionalized, with one wing, the Copperheads, hostile to the Union war effort and favoring a negotiated peace with the Confederacy. The stance of the Copperheads, coupled with the involvement of many southern Democrats in the Confederate government, enabled the Republicans for a generation after the Civil War to denounce the reunified Democratic Party as the "party of treason."

The Democrats were a national party after the Civil War, but they were displaced as the majority party by the Republicans. The strength of the Democrats was in the South, which voted in large majorities for Democratic candidates. Party strength outside the South, however, was scattered, but most noticeable among urban ethnics and voters in the border states. The period of Republican dominance lasted for nearly three-quarters of a century, 1860 to 1932. The Democrats occupied the White House for 16 of the 72 years, controlled the House of Representatives for 26 years and the Senate for 10.

The Depression which began in 1929 dramatically altered American politics and provided the opportunity for the Democrats to re-emerge as the majority party. The Democrats swept to victory behind Franklin D. Roosevelt in 1932 and with widespread popular acceptance of his New Deal programs, a new coalition was formed that has remained largely intact, especially at the state and local level, in the 1970s. The new majority coalition combined the bulk of the black electorate, the academic community and organized labor with the party's core strength among urban ethnic and southern voters.

Between 1932 and 1978, the Democrats occupied the presidency 30 of 46 years, and controlled both houses of Congress for 42 years. The acceptance of Roosevelt's New Deal, coupled with the abolishment of the two-thirds rule for nominating candidates and decline of southern power, resulted in more liberal party leadership. The liberal stance of the party included the belief by most party leaders in a broad interpretation of the Constitution, increased use of federal power and government spending to combat the problems of society. This basic philosophy has been maintained by Democratic presidential candidates since 1932.

While the years since 1932 have been the longest period of Democratic control in American history, the party's unity has at times been threatened. The party includes diverse elements across the political spectrum, and its strength at the congressional level has frequently been undermined by a loose alliance of Republicans and southern Democrats. At the national level the party has been internally divided by explosive, controversial issues — most notably in the late 1960s and early 1970s — such as the war in Vietnam.

In spite of the impact of divisive issues and inroads in the conservative sector of the party by the Republicans, particularly in presidential elections, the Roosevelt coalition continued basically intact and the Democrats remained the majority party in the 1970s.

The balance of power shifted in 1980, however. The Republicans regained the presidency and took control of the Senate for the first time in 28 years. Republican gains in the House, combined with support from conservative Southern Democrats, enabled the Republican administration to pass wide-ranging economic packages during its first year. The 1982 elections, however, swept 26 new Democrats into the House. This influx of new, moderate-to-liberal Democratic blood, strengthened their control in the House and forced the Republicans to compromise more often in the 98th Congress.

Democratic-Republican Party (1796-1828)

There is no formal birth date for the Democratic-Republican Party. It developed in the early 1790s as the organized opposition to the incumbent Federalists and successor to the Anti-Federalists, who were a loose alliance of elements initially opposed to the ratification of the Constitution and subsequently the policies of the Washington administration designed to centralize power in the federal government.

Thomas Jefferson was the leader of the new party, which as early as 1792 referred to themselves as Republicans. This remained the party's primary name throughout its history, although in some states it became known as the Democratic-Republicans, the label used frequently by historians to refer to Jefferson's party to avoid confusing it with the later Republican Party, which began in 1854.

The Democratic-Republicans favored states' rights, a literal interpretation of the Constitution and expanded democracy through extension of suffrage and popular control of the government. The Democratic-Republicans were dominated by rural, agrarian interests, intent on maintaining their dominance over the growing commercial and industrial interests of the Northeast. The principal strength of the party was in the southern and Middle Atlantic states.

The Democratic-Republicans first gained control of the federal government in 1800, when Jefferson was elected president and the party won majorities in both houses of Congress. For the next 24 years the party controlled both the White House and Congress, the last eight years virtually without opposition. For all but four years during this 24-year period, there was a Virginia-New York alliance controlling the executive branch, with all three presidents from Virginia — Jefferson, James Madison and James Monroe — and three of the four vice presidents from New York. Lacking an opposition party, the Democratic-Republicans in the 1820s became increasingly divided in 1824, when four party leaders ran for president. John Quincy Adams won the election in the House of Representatives, although Andrew Jackson had received more popular votes.

The deep factionalism evident in the 1824 election doomed the Democratic-Republican Party and the two-party system revived shortly thereafter with the emergence of the National Republican Party, an outgrowth of the Adams faction, and the Democratic-Republican Party, the political organization of the Jackson faction. After 1830 the Jacksonians adopted the name, Democratic Party.

Federalist Party (1789-1816)

The Federalist Party grew out of the movement that drafted and worked for the ratification of the Constitution of 1787, which established a stronger national government than that in operation under the existing Articles of Confederation. Supporters of the new constitutional government were known as Federalists and in the formative first decade of the young republic, they controlled the national government. With President George Washington staying aloof from the development of political parties, leadership of the Federalists was exercised by Alexander Hamilton and John Adams. The party's basic strength was among urban, commercial interests, who were particularly drawn to the Federalists by the party's belief in a strong federal economic policy and the maintenance of domestic order — viewpoints based on a broad interpretation of the Constitution.

The Federalists were widely perceived as a party of the aristocracy, a decided liability in the late 18th and early 19th centuries when the right to vote was being widely extended to members of the middle and lower classes. Never as well organized as the Democratic-Republicans, the Federalists were unable to compete for support of the important rural, agrarian elements that composed a majority of the electorate.

The election of Jefferson in 1800 ended Federalist control of both the White House and Congress. After 1800 the Federalists did not elect a president or win a majority in either house of Congress. The party's strength was largely limited to commercial New England, where Federalists became an advocate of states' rights and were involved in threats of regional secession in 1808 and again during the War of 1812.

In 1812 the Federalists held their last meeting of party leaders to field a presidential ticket. Four years later there were no nominations, but Federalist electors were chosen in three states. Although this marked the last appearance of the party at the national level, the Federalists remained in existence at the local level until the mid-1820s.

Free Soil Party (1848-1852)

Born as a result of the anti-slavery movement's opposition to the extension of slavery into the newly acquired southwest territories, the Free Soil Party was formally launched at a convention in Buffalo, N.Y., in August 1848. The Free Soilers were composed of anti-slavery elements from the Democratic and Whig parties as well as remnants of the Liberal Party. Representatives from all the northern states and three border states attended the Buffalo convention, which adopted the slogan — "free soil, free speech, free labor and free men" — an expression of the anti-slavery sentiment of the Free Soilers as well as the desire for cheap western land.

Former Democratic President Martin Van Buren (1837-41) was selected by the convention as the party's presidential candidate and Charles Francis Adams, the son of President John Quincy Adams (1825-29), was chosen as his running mate.

In the 1848 election the Free Soil ticket received 291,501 votes (10.1 per cent of the popular vote), but was unable to carry a single state. The party did better at the congressional level, winning nine House seats and holding the balance of power in the organization of the closely divided new Congress.

The 1848 election marked the peak of the party's influence. With the passage of compromise legislation on slavery in 1850, the Free Soilers lost their basic issue and went into a period of rapid decline. The party ran its second and last national ticket in 1852, headed by John Hale, who received 155,210 votes (4.9 per cent of the popular vote). As in 1848, the Free Soil national ticket failed to carry a single state.

Although the party went out of existence shortly thereafter, its program and constituency were absorbed by the Republican Party, whose birth and growth dramatically paralleled the resurgence of the slavery issue in the mid-1850s.

Greenback Party (1876-1884)

The National Independent or Greenback-Labor Party, commonly known as the Greenback Party, was launched in Indianapolis, Ind., in November 1874 at a meeting organized by the Indiana Grange. The party grew out of the Panic of 1873, a post-Civil War economic depression, which was particularly hard-felt by farmers and industrial workers. Currency was the basic issue of the new party, which opposed return to the gold standard and favored retention of the inflationary paper money (known as greenbacks) that was first introduced as an emergency measure during the Civil War.

In the 1876 presidential election, the party ran Peter

Cooper, a New York philanthropist, and drafted a platform that focused entirely on the currency issue. Cooper received 75,973 votes (0.9 per cent of the popular vote), mainly from agrarian voters. Aided by the continuing depression, a Greenback national convention in 1878 effected the merger of the party with various labor reform groups and a platform was adopted that discussed issues of interest to labor as well as currency. Showing voting strength in the industrial East as well as the agrarian South and Midwest, the Greenbacks polled over 1,000,000 votes in the 1878 congressional races and won 14 seats in the House of Representatives. It marked the high point of the party's strength.

Returning prosperity, the prospect of fusion with one of the major parties and a split between the party's agrarian and labor leadership, served to undermine the Greenback Party. In the 1880 election the party elected only eight representatives and its presidential candidate, Rep. James B. Weaver of Iowa, received 305,997 votes (3.3 per cent of the popular vote), far less than party leaders expected.

The party slipped further four years later, when the Greenbacks' candidate for president, former Massachusetts Governor Benjamin F. Butler, received 175,096 votes (1.7 per cent of the popular vote). With the demise of the Greenbacks, most of the party's constituency moved into the Populist Party, the agrarian reform movement that swept the South and Midwest in the 1890s.

Liberal Republican Party (1872)

A faction of the Republican Party, dissatisfied with President Ulysses S. Grant's first term in office, withdrew from the party in 1872 to form their own party. Comprised of party reformers, as well as anti-Grant politicians and newspaper editors, the new party focused on the corruption of the Grant administration, the need for civil service reform and for an end to the Reconstruction policy in the South.

The call for the Liberal Republican national convention came from the state party in Missouri, the birthplace of the reform movement. The convention, meeting in Cincinnati, Ohio, in May 1872, nominated Horace Greeley, editor of *The New York Tribune,* for president and Missouri Gov. B. Gratz Brown as his running mate. Greeley, the choice of anti-Grant politicians but suspect among reformers, was not popular either among many Democrats, who recalled his longtime criticism of the Democratic Party.

However, with the hope of victory in the fall election, the Democratic national convention, meeting in July, endorsed the Liberal Republican ticket and platform. The coalition was an unsuccessful one, as many Democrats refused to vote for Greeley. He received 2,833,711 votes (43.8 per cent of the popular vote), but carried only six states and lost to Grant by over 750,000 votes out of nearly 6.5 million cast. Greeley died shortly after the election.

Underfinanced, poorly organized and dependent on the Democrats' for their success, the Liberal Republicans went out of existence after the 1872 election.

Libertarian Party (1971-   )

In the brief period of four years, the Libertarian Party leaped from a fledgling organization, on the presidential ballot in only two states, to the nation's largest third party.

Formed in Colorado in 1971, the party nominated John Hospers of California for President in 1972. On the ballot in only Colorado and Washington, Hospers received 3,671 votes. But he received a measure of national attention when a Republican presidential elector from Virginia, Roger MacBride, cast his electoral vote for the Libertarian presidential nominee.

MacBride's action made him a hero in Libertarian circles and the party chose him as its 1976 standard bearer at its August 1975 convention in New York City. MacBride had served in the Vermont legislature in the 1960s and was defeated for the Republican gubernatorial nomination in that state in 1964. In the 1970s, he settled on a farm near Charlottesville, Virginia, and devoted himself to writing and party affairs. He was also co-creator of the television series, "Little House on the Prairie."

The Libertarians made a major effort in 1976, getting on the ballot in 32 states, more than Independent candidate Eugene J. McCarthy, or any other third party. The reward was a vote of 173,019, more than any other minor party candidate, but far below McCarthy's total and only 0.2 per cent of the national vote. MacBride's strength was centered in the West, where he received 5.5 per cent of the vote in Alaska and 1.0 per cent or more in Arizona, Hawaii and Idaho. He also ran well ahead of his national average in California (0.7 per cent) and Nevada (0.8 per cent). His running mate was David P. Bergland, a California lawyer.

In 1980, the Libertarian Party appeared on the ballot in all 50 states and the District of Columbia for the first time. In addition, the party fielded about 550 candidates for other offices, a number that dwarfed other third-party efforts. The party nominees, Edward E. Clark of California for president and David Koch of New York for vice president, garnered 921,188 votes or 1.1 per cent of the vote nationwide. Again the Libertarians major support came from Western states.

Individual responsibility and minimal government interference hallmark the Libertarian philosophy. The party favored repeal of laws against so-called victimless crimes, such as those that involve pornography, drug use and homosexual activity, the abolition of all federal police agencies, and the elimination of all government subsidies to private enterprise. In foreign and military affairs, the Libertarians advocated the removal of U.S. troops from abroad, a cut in the defense budget and the emergence of the United States as a "giant Switzerland," with no international treaty obligations. MacBride commented that it was his party's intention to "reduce the Pentagon to a trigon."

Libertarians also favored repeal of legislation which they feel hinders individual or corporate action. They opposed gun control, civil rights laws, price controls on oil and gas, labor protection laws, federal welfare and poverty programs, forced busing, compulsory education, social security, national medical care, federal land use restrictions, and the 55-miles-per-hour speed limit.

Liberty Party (1840-48)

Born in 1839, the Liberty Party was the product of a split in the anti-slavery movement between a faction led by William Lloyd Garrison that favored action outside the political process, and a second led by James G. Birney that proposed action within the political system through the establishment of an independent, anti-slavery party. The Birney faction launched the Liberty Party in November 1839 and the following April a national convention with delegates from six states nominated Birney for the presidency.

Although the Liberty Party was the first political party to take an anti-slavery position, and the only one at the time to do so, most abolitionist voters in the 1840 election supported the Democratic or Whig presidential candidates. Birney received only 6,797 votes (0.3 per cent of the popular vote).

Aided by the controversy over the annexation of slave-holding Texas, the Liberty Party's popularity increased in 1844. Birney, again the party's presidential nominee, received 62,103 votes (2.3 per cent of the popular vote), but again as in 1840, carried no states. The peak strength of the party was reached two years later in 1846, when in various state elections, Liberty Party candidates received 74,017 votes.

In October 1847 the party nominated New Hampshire Sen. John P. Hale for the presidency, but his candidacy was withdrawn the following year when the Liberty Party joined the broader-based Free Soil Party. *(Free Soil Party, p. 203)*

National Democratic Party (1896)

The National Democrats were a conservative, pro-gold standard party faction, which bolted the Democratic Party after the 1896 convention adopted a pro-silver platform and nominated William Jennings Bryan, who opposed the gold standard.

With the nation in the midst of a depression and the Populist movement sweeping the agrarian Midwest and South demanding monetary reform, currency was the dominant issue of the 1896 campaign and produced a brief realignment in American politics.

The Republican Party was controlled by leaders who favored maintenance of the gold standard, a non-inflationary currency. Agrarian midwestern and southern Democrats, reflecting a Populist philosophy, gained control of the Democratic Party in 1896 and committed it to the free coinage of silver, an inflationary currency demanded by rural elements threatened by debts. The Democrats attracted pro-silver bolters from the Republican Party, but gold standard Democrats, opposed to the Republicans' protectionist position on the tariff issue, established an independent party.

Meeting in Indianapolis, Ind., in September 1896, the National Democrats adopted a platform favoring maintenance of the gold standard and selected a ticket headed by 79-year old Illinois Senator John M. Palmer.

Democratic President Grover Cleveland and leading members of his administration, repudiated by the convention that chose Bryan, supported the National Democrats. During the campaign the National Democrats encouraged conservative Democrats to either vote for the National Democratic ticket or for the Republican candidate, William McKinley. The Palmer ticket received 133,435 votes (1.0 per cent of the popular vote), and McKinley defeated Bryan.

With returning prosperity and the Spanish-American War in the late 1890s, the currency issue was overshadowed somewhat by other issues and the intense Democratic Party factionalism which produced the National Democratic Party ended.

National Republican Party (1828-32)

The Democratic-Republican Party splintered after the 1824 election into two factions — one headed by Andrew Jackson retained the name Democratic-Republican, eventually shortened to Democrats; the other faction headed by President John Quincy Adams assumed the name National Republicans. The new party reflected the belief of President Adams in the establishment of national policy by the federal government: supporting a protective tariff, the Bank of the United States, federal administration of public lands and a national program of internal improvements. However, Adams' belief in a strong national government contrasted with the period's prevailing mood of populism and states' rights.

The Adams' forces controlled Congress for two years, 1825 to 1827, but as party structures formalized, the National Republicans became a minority in Congress and suffered a decisive loss in the 1828 presidential election. Running for re-election, Adams was beaten by Jackson. Adams received 43.6 per cent of the popular vote and carried eight states, none in the South. Henry Clay, the party's candidate against Jackson four years later, had even less success. He received only 37.4 per cent of the popular vote and carried just six states, again none of which were in the South.

Poorly organized, with dwindling support and a heritage of defeat, the National Republicans went out of existence after the 1832 election, but its members provided the base for a new anti-Jackson party, the Whigs, which came into being in 1834. *(For more details on the Whig party see profile, p. 211.)*

National Unity Campaign (1980-)

Republican Rep. John B. Anderson of Illinois formed the National Unity Campaign as the vehicle for his independent presidential campaign in 1980. Anderson began his quest for the presidency by trying to win the Republican Party nomination. But as a liberal in a party coming under conservative control, he won no primaries and could claim only 57 convention delegates by April 1980. Anderson quit the Republican race and declared his independent candidacy.

Anderson focused his campaign on the need to establish a viable third party as an alternative to domination of the political scene by the Republican and Democratic parties. The National Unity Campaign platform touted the Anderson program as a "new public philosophy" —more innovative than that of the Democrats, who "cling to the policies of the New Deal," and more enlightened than that of the Republicans, who talk "incessantly about freedom, but hardly ever about justice." Generally the party took positions that were fiscally conservative and socially liberal. Anderson and his running mate, former Democratic Wisconsin Gov. Patrick J. Lucey, tried to appeal to Republican and Democratic voters disenchanted with their parties and to the growing bloc of voters who classified themselves as independents.

The National Unity Campaign ticket was on the ballot in all 50 states in 1980, though Anderson had to wage costly legal battles in some states to ensure that result. In the end, the party won 6.6 percent of the presidential vote, well over the 5 percent necessary to qualify for retroactive federal campaign funding.

People's Party (1971-)

Delegates from activist and peace groups established the People's Party at a convention held in Dallas, Texas, in

November 1971. The initial co-chairmen were pediatrician Dr. Benjamin Spock and author Gore Vidal.

The People's Party first ran a presidential candidate in 1972. They chose Dr. Spock for President and black activist Julius Hobson of Washington, D.C., for Vice President. Despite hopes for widespread backing from the poor and social activists, the ticket received only 78,751 votes, 0.1 per cent of the national total. A total of 55,167 of those votes came from California alone.

At its 1975 convention, held in St. Louis, Mo., Aug. 31, the People's Party chose black civil rights activist Margaret Wright of California for President and Maggie Kuhn of Pennsylvania, a leader in the Gray Panthers movement for rights for the elderly, for Vice President. Kuhn, however, declined the nomination and was replaced on the ticket by Spock.

The party platform focused on cutting the defense budget, closing tax loopholes and making that money available for social programs. Other planks included redistribution of land and wealth; unconditional amnesty for war objectors; and free health care. In her campaign, Wright stressed the necessity for active participation by citizens in the governmental process, so that institutions and programs could be run from the roots up rather than from the top down.

As in 1972, the party's main backing came in California, where it was supported by the state Peace and Freedom Party. Of Wright's total national vote of 49,024, 85.1 per cent (41,731 votes) came from California. The party did not field a presidential ticket in 1980.

People's Party-Populists (1892-1908)

The People's Party, commonly called the Populists, were organized at a convention in Cincinnati, Ohio, in May 1891, and climaxed several decades of farm protest against deteriorating economic conditions. Chronically depressed commodity prices, caused by over-production and world competition, had spurred the politicization of farmers.

Most of the Populist leaders came from the defunct Greenback movement and southern and midwestern farm cooperative associations. The Populists tended to blame their problems on the most visible causes, primarily the high railroad rates and shrinking currency supply, but the platform they adopted at their first national nominating convention in 1892 was a wide-reaching one. As well as advocating the government ownership of railroads and the free coinage of silver, the Populists proposed institution of a graduated income tax and the direct election of senators. Although the Populists proposed labor reforms, such as an eight-hour working day, the party never gained appreciable support among industrial workers.

The Populists ran James B. Weaver, the former Greenback candidate, as its presidential nominee in 1892. Weaver received 1,024,280 votes (8.5 per cent of the popular vote) and carried five states in the Midwest and Far West. Increasingly tied to the silver issue, the party showed growing strength in the 1894 congressional races. Especially strong west of the Mississippi River, party congressional candidates polled nearly 1.5 million votes. After the election the Populists had six senators and seven representatives in Congress.

The Democrats surprised Populist leaders in 1896 by writing a free silver platform and nominating a free silver candidate, William Jennings Bryan. The Populists were faced with the dilemma of either endorsing Bryan and losing their party identity or of running a separate ticket and splitting the free silver vote. The Populist convention endorsed Bryan but ran a separate candidate for vice president, Thomas E. Watson.

After this initial fusion with the Democrats, most Populists remained within the Democratic Party after the 1896 election. The Populist Party remained in existence, running presidential candidates until 1908, but never received over 0.8 per cent of the popular vote. The party did not expand its voter appeal beyond an agrarian reform movement, but many of its proposals, particularly in the areas of government and electoral reform, were espoused by progressive politicians in the early 20th century and enacted into law.

Progressive Party-Bull Moose (1912)

A split in Republican ranks, spurred by the bitter personal and ideological dispute between President William Howard Taft (1909-13) and former President Theodore Roosevelt (1901-09), resulted in the withdrawal of the Roosevelt forces from the Republican Party after the June 1912 convention and the creation of the Progressive Party two months later. The new party was popularly known as the Bull Moose Party, a name resulting from Roosevelt's assertion early in the campaign that he felt as fit as a bull moose. While the Taft-Roosevelt split was the immediate reason for the new party, the Bull Moosers were an outgrowth of the progressive movement that was a powerful force in both major parties in the early years of the 20th century.

Although in 1908 Roosevelt had hand-picked Taft as his successor, his disillusionment with Taft's conservative philosophy came quickly, and with the support of progressive Republicans, Roosevelt challenged the incumbent for the 1912 Republican presidential nomination. Roosevelt outpolled Taft in the presidential primary states, but Taft won the nomination with nearly solid support in the South and among party conservatives, giving the incumbent a narrow majority of delegates that enabled him to win the bulk of the key credentials challenges.

Although few Republican politicians followed Roosevelt in his bolt, the new party had a popular base that was evident in its convention in Chicago in August 1912. Thousands of delegates, basically middle and upper class reformers from small towns and cities, attended the convention that launched the party and nominated Roosevelt for President and California Governor Hiram Johnson as his running mate. Roosevelt personally appeared to deliver his "Confession of Faith," a speech detailing his nationalistic philosophy and progressive reform ideas. The Bull Moose platform reflected key tenets of the progressive movement, calling for more extensive government antitrust action and labor, social, government and electoral reform.

Roosevelt was the victim of an assassination attempt while campaigning in Milwaukee, Wis., in October. Although wounded, he finished the campaign. In the general election Roosevelt received 4,119,207 votes (27.4 per cent of the popular vote) and carried six states. His percentage of the vote was the highest ever received by a third party candidate in American history, but his candidacy split the Republican vote and enabled the Democrats' progressive nominee, Woodrow Wilson, to win the election. The Progressive Party had minimal success at the state and local level, winning approximately 13 House seats but electing no senators or governors.

Roosevelt declined the Progressive nomination in 1916 and endorsed the Republican candidate, Charles Evans Hughes. With the defection of its leader, the decline of the progressive movement, and the lack of an effective party organization to continue, the Progressive Party ceased to exist.

Progressive Party (1924)

Like the Bull Moose Party of Theodore Roosevelt, the Progressive Party of the mid-1920s was a reform effort led by a progressive Republican leader. Wisconsin Sen. Robert M. La Follette led the new Progressive Party, a separate entity from the Bull Moosers, which unlike the middle and upper class Roosevelt party of the previous decade, had its greatest appeal among farmers and organized labor.

The La Follette Progressive Party grew out of the Conference for Progressive Political Action (CPPA), a coalition of railway union leaders and a remnant of the Bull Moose effort, that was formed in 1922. The Socialist Party joined the coalition the following year. Throughout 1923 the Socialists and labor unions argued over whether their coalition should form a third party, with the Socialists in favor of such a move and the labor unions against it. It was finally decided to run an independent presidential candidate, La Follette, in the 1924 election, but not to field candidates at the state and local levels. La Follette was given the power to choose his own running mate and selected Montana Sen. Burton K. Wheeler, a Democrat.

Opposition to corporate monopolies was the major issue of the La Follette campaign, although the party advocated various other reforms, particularly aimed at farmers and workers, that were earlier proposed by either the Populists or Bull Moosers. But the Progressive Party itself was a major issue in the 1924 campaign, as the Republicans attacked the alleged radicalism of the party.

Although La Follette had the endorsement of the American Federation of Labor (AFL), the large labor organization provided minimal support and the Progressives' basic strength, like the Populists in the 1890s, was among agrarian voters west of the Mississippi River. La Follette received 4,814,000 votes (16.6 per cent of the popular vote), but carried just one state, his native Wisconsin. When La Follette died in 1925, the party collapsed as a national force, although it was revived by La Follette's sons on a statewide level in Wisconsin in the mid-1930s.

Progressive Party (Wallace) (1948)

Henry A. Wallace's Progressive Party resulted from the dissatisfaction of liberal elements in the Democratic Party with the leadership of President Harry S Truman, particularly in the realm of foreign policy. The Progressive Party was one of two bolting groups from the Democratic Party in 1948; conservative southern elements withdrew to form the States' Rights Party.

Henry Wallace, the founder of the Progressive Party, was secretary of agriculture, Vice President and finally secretary of commerce under President Franklin D. Roosevelt and had the reputation as one of the most liberal idealists in the Roosevelt administration. Fired from the Truman Cabinet in 1946 after breaking with administration policy and publicly advocating peaceful coexistence with the Soviet Union, Wallace began to consider the idea of a liberal third party candidacy. Supported by the American Labor Party, the Progressive Citizens of America and other progressive organizations in California and Illinois, Wallace announced his third party candidacy in December 1947.

The Progressive Party was formally launched the following July at a convention in Philadelphia, which ratified the selection of Wallace for President and Senator Glen H. Taylor (D Idaho) as his running mate. The party adopted a platform that emphasized foreign policy — opposing the cold war anti-Communism of the Truman administration and specifically urging abandonment of the Truman Doctrine and the Marshall Plan, measures designed to contain the spread of Communism and bolster non-Communist nations. On domestic issues the Progressives stressed humanitarian concerns and equal rights for different sexes and races.

Minority groups — women, youth, blacks, Jews, Spanish-Americans — were in evidence in organizational positions in the new party, but the openness of the Progressives brought Wallace a damaging endorsement from the Communist Party. Believing the two parties could work together. Wallace accepted the endorsement although he characterized his own philosophy as "progressive capitalism."

The Progressives appeared on the ballot in 45 states, but the Communist endorsement helped keep the party on the defensive the entire campaign. In the November election, Wallace received only 1,157,057 votes (2.4 per cent of the popular vote), with nearly half of the votes from one state, New York. Not only were the Progressives unable to carry a single state, but in spite of their defection from the Democratic Party, President Truman won re-election. The Progressives had equally poor results in the congressional races, failing to elect even one representative or senator.

The Progressive Party's opposition to the Korean War in 1950 drove many moderate elements out of the party, including Henry Wallace. The party ran a national ticket in 1952, but its presidential candidate received only 0.2 per cent of the popular vote. The party crumbled completely after the election.

Prohibition Party (1869-1976)

The Prohibition Party has been in existence longer than any third party in American history. It was formed in September 1869 at a convention in Chicago that attracted approximately 500 delegates from 20 states. For the first time in American politics, women had equal status with men as delegates. By a narrow majority, the convention decided to form an independent party and three years later the new party ran its first national ticket. Throughout its history the Prohibitionists' basic goal has been enactment of laws prohibiting the manufacture and sale of intoxicating liquor, but their platforms over the past century have included other reform proposals. The 1872 Prohibition Party platform included the first women's suffrage plank.

For all but one election between 1884 and 1916, the Prohibitionists' presidential candidate received at least one per cent of the popular vote. The party's best showing was in 1892, when its presidential nominee, John Bidwell, received 270,770 votes (2.2 per cent of the popular vote). The party has run a national ticket in every presidential election since 1872, but its candidates have never carried a single state. After the 1976 election, the party changed its name to the National Statesman Party. Since 1924, the party standard-bearers have not received over 0.2 per cent of the popular vote.

The temperance movement succeeded in gaining prohibition legislation in numerous states in the late 19th and early 20th centuries, and their efforts were capped in 1919 by passage of national prohibition legislation (the 18th amendment to the U.S. Constitution, repealed 14 years later by the 21st amendment). But as much as the Prohibition Party, which had limited success at the polls, the achievements of the temperance movement were due to independent organizations, such as the Women's Christian Temperance Union (WCTU) and the Anti-Saloon League. These organizations allowed active Democrats and Republicans to remain in their own parties while working for prohibition.

Republican Party (1854-   )

Born in 1854 in the upper Midwest, the Republican Party was a direct result of the bitter dissatisfaction of anti-slavery forces with the passage of the Kansas-Nebraska Act. The bill overturned earlier legislation (the Missouri Compromise of 1820 and the Compromise of 1850) that limited the extension of slavery into the territories, and replaced it with the concept of popular sovereignty, by which each territory decided its own position on slavery. While historians generally credit residents of Ripon, Wis., with holding the party's first organizational meeting in March 1854, and citizens of Jackson, Mich., with running the party's first electoral ticket in July 1854, the birth of the party was nearly simultaneous in many communities throughout the northern states. The volatile slavery issue was the catalyst that brought the party's birth, but the political vacuum caused by the decline of the Whigs and the failure of the Know-Nothing and Free Soil parties to gain a stable, national following, allowed the Republicans to grow with dramatic rapidity.

The constituency of the new party was limited to the northern states, since the basic issue of the Republicans was opposition to slavery. But the party did attract diverse elements in the political spectrum — former Whigs, Know-Nothings, Free Soilers and dissident Democrats unhappy with their party straddling the slavery issue.

The new party took the name Republican in its first year. Horace Greeley, in his paper the *New York Tribune,* is credited with initiating the name in a June 1854 publication. In pushing the name, he referred to the Jeffersonian Republicans of the early 19th century and Henry Clay's National Republican Party of the 1830s, which was an early rival of the Democrats.

The Republicans ran candidates throughout the North in 1854 and in combination with other candidates opposed to the Kansas-Nebraska Act, won a majority in the House of Representatives. Two years later the Republicans ran their first national ticket, and although their presidential candidate, John C. Freemont, did not win, he polled one-third of the vote in a three-man race and carried 11 states. The Republicans were established as a major party.

While the party was built on the slavery issue, the Republicans were far from a one-issue party. They presented a nationalistic platform with appeal to business and commercial interests as well as rural anti-slavery elements. The Republicans proposed legislation for homesteading (free land), internal improvements, the construction of a transcontinental railroad, and the institution of a protective tariff.

Firmly established by the late 1850s, the Republican Party benefited from the increasing sectional factionalism in the Democratic Party over the slavery issue. In 1858 the party won control of the House of Representatives and two years later with Abraham Lincoln as its candidate, won the White House in addition to retaining control of the House. Lincoln won an unusual four-way race, benefiting from a sectional split in the Democratic Party, and captured the presidency with 39.8 per cent of the popular vote.

Lincoln was a wartime president, and his success in preserving the Union benefited the party for the next generation. After the Civil War the Republicans projected a patriotic image, which coupled with the party's belief in national expansion and limited federal involvement in the free enterprise system, helped make it the dominant party over the next three-quarters of a century. For the bulk of the period between 1860 and 1932, the Republicans were the majority party: occupying the White House for 56 of the 72 years, controlling the Senate for 60 years and the House for 50. With the exception of the South, where the party was basically limited to the small number of black voters, the Republicans were strong throughout the nation.

The party's congressional leaders exercised the dominant power during this period of Republican hegemony. Republican executives had little success in challenging the authority wielded by the congressional leadership of the party.

Just as the party vaulted to power on the divisive slavery issue, its history was altered by another traumatic event — the Great Depression, which began in 1929. As the incumbent party during the economic collapse, the Republicans suffered the political blame, and their fall from power was rapid. In 1928 the Republican presidential candidate (Herbert Hoover) carried 40 states; in 1936, the party's nadir, the Republican standard-bearer (Alfred M. Landon) won just two states. In 1928 the party held a clear majority of seats in both the House and Senate, 267 and 56 respectively. Eight years later their numbers had shrunk dramatically, the Republicans holding only 89 seats in the House and 17 in the Senate.

The party made a comeback from this low point in the midst of Franklin D. Roosevelt's New Deal, but remained the minority party through the 1978 elections. Between 1932 and 1980 the Republicans won four of 11 presidential elections but controlled Congress for just four years.

While the Republicans struggled to find the formula for a new majority, the party's basic conservatism made it increasingly appealing, especially in presidential races, to segments of the electorate that were previously firm parts of the Democratic coalition — notably blue-collar workers and the once Democratic South. The party was able to attract a winning combination when it ran presidential candidates with a moderate image such as Dwight D. Eisenhower and Richard M. Nixon, and came close to winning with the candidacy of moderate Gerald R. Ford. However, while the party has been competitive since 1932, running moderate presidential candidates, it has enjoyed less success at the state and local levels where Democratic majorities established during the New Deal have largely remained intact. The Republican difficulties in establishing a new majority were compounded after the 1972 election by the Watergate scandal, which brought down the Nixon administration.

Gerald R. Ford, who became president after Nixon resigned Aug. 9, 1974, lost his 1976 election bid to former Georgia Gov. Jimmy Carter, as the Democrats took control of the White House and both houses of Congress.

Republican fortunes improved dramatically with the 1980 elections, however. The party regained the presidency in the person of former California Gov. Ronald Reagan, who won a landslide electoral vote victory over Carter. Republicans also took control of the Senate for the first time in 28 years and made substantial gains in the House. Republicans capitalized on their return to power by forming a coalition with Southern Democrats in the House to pass a series of economic reform measures early in the 97th Congress.

Although a resurgence of Democratic political strength in the 1982 elections swept more Democrats into the House, the Republicans retained control of the Senate and the White House.

Socialist Party (1901-   )

The Socialist Party was officially born in July 1901 at a convention in Indianapolis, Ind., that joined together former American Railway Union president Eugene V. Debs' Social Democratic Party with a moderate faction of the Socialist Labor Party. The two groups had begun discussions the year before and in the 1900 presidential campaign jointly supported a ticket headed by Debs that received 86,935 votes (0.6 per cent of the popular vote).

The 1901 unity convention identified the new Socialist Party with the working class and described the party's goal as "collective ownership . . . of the means of production and distribution." The party grew rapidly in the early 20th century, reaching a peak membership of approximately 118,000 in 1912. That year also proved to be the party's best at the polls. Debs, a presidential candidate five times between 1900 and 1920, received 900,369 votes (6.0 per cent of the popular vote). Additionally, the Socialists elected 1,200 candidates to local offices, including 79 candidates for mayor.

With the outbreak of World War I, the party became a vehicle for antiwar protest. In 1917, pacifist Socialists converted a number of mayoral elections into referenda on the war: winning 34 per cent of the vote in Chicago; over 25 per cent in Buffalo; and 22 per cent in New York City.

The following year Debs was convicted of sedition for making an antiwar speech and was sentenced to a term in the Atlanta federal penitentiary, from which he ran for president in 1920 and received 913,664 votes (3.4 per cent of the popular vote).

Four years later the Socialists endorsed Wisconsin Sen. Robert M. La Follette's presidential candidacy, an unsuccessful attempt to establish a farmer-labor coalition. In 1928 the Socialists resumed running their own presidential ticket.

With the death of Debs, the party selected a new candidate, Norman Thomas, a former minister and social worker, who was the party's standard-bearer for the next six elections. The Depression brought a brief surge for the Socialists in 1932, with Thomas polling 883,990 votes (2.2 per cent of the popular vote). But 1932 proved to be only a temporary revival for the Socialists.

Roosevelt's New Deal stole their thunder, and the Socialist Party failed to attract even one-half of one per cent of the vote in any succeeding presidential election. In 1976 the party ran its first presidential ticket in two decades. The candidates received 6,038 votes. .01 per cent of the popular vote.

Although Socialist Party candidates received more votes in the 1980 elections, 6,720, their percentage share of the total vote, dropped below one one hundredth of one percent.

Socialist Labor Party (1888-   )

The Socialist Labor Party, the first national Socialist party in the United States, ranks second only to the Prohibitionists among third parties in longevity. Formed in 1874 by elements of the Socialist International in New York, it was first known as the Social Democratic Workingmen's Party. In 1877 the group adopted the name, Socialist Labor Party. Throughout the 1880s the party worked in concert with other left-wing third parties: first the Greenbacks, then the United Labor Party.

The Socialist Labor Party ran its first national ticket in 1892 and since then has run candidates in every presidential election except in 1980. The party collected its highest proportion of the national vote in 1896, when its candidate received 36,356 votes (0.3 per cent of the popular vote).

Led by the autocratic Daniel DeLeon (1852-1914), a former Columbia University law lecturer, the Socialist Labor Party became increasingly militant and made its best showing in local races in 1898. But DeLeon's insistence on rigid party discipline and his opposition to the organized labor movement alienated many members. Moderate elements in the party bolted, eventually joining the Socialist Party of Eugene V. Debs, which formed in 1901.

The Socialist Labor Party has continued as a small, tightly organized far left group bound to DeLeon's uncompromising belief in revolution. As late as 1970 the party advocated direct worker action to take over control of production and claimed 5,000 members nationwide.

Socialist Workers Party (1938-   )

The Socialist Workers Party was formed in 1938 by followers of the Russian Communist Leon Trotsky. Originally a faction within the U.S. Communist Party, the Trotskyites were expelled on the instructions of Soviet leader Joseph Stalin in 1936. A brief Trotskyite coalition with the Socialist Party ended in 1938 when the dissidents decided to organize independently as the Socialist Workers Party.

Since 1948 the party has run a presidential candidate, but its entry has never received over 0.1 per cent of the popular vote. Advocating radical change in American society, the Socialist Workers through its youth arm, the Young Socialist Alliance, was active in the anti-Vietnam War movement and contributed activists to civil rights protests.

Southern Democrats (1860)

Agitation over the slavery issue, building for a generation, reached a climax in 1860 and produced a sectional split in the Democratic Party. Throughout the mid-19th century the Democrats had remained unified by supporting the various pieces of compromise legislation that both protected slavery in the southern states and endorsed the policy of popular sovereignty in the territories. But in 1860 southern Democrats wanted the Democratic convention (meeting in Charleston, South Carolina) to include a plank definitely protecting slavery in the territories. When their plank was defeated, delegates from most of the southern states walked out.

The Charleston convention stalemated over a presidential choice, and recessing for six weeks, reconvened in Baltimore where Illinois Senator Stephen A. Douglas was nominated. The bulk of the southern delegates, plus those from California and Oregon, bolted the Baltimore convention and nominated their own ticket in a rump convention held after Douglas' selection. Vice President John C. Breckinridge of Kentucky was chosen for president and Joseph Lane, a states' rights advocate from Oregon, was selected as his running mate. A platform was adopted that recognized the right of slavery to exist in the territories. After the formation of the two sectional tickets, two separate Democratic national committees operated in Washington, D.C., to oversee their campaigns.

Although in the 1860 election the combined Douglas-Breckinridge vote comprised a majority of the ballots cast, the split in Democratic ranks was a boon to the campaign of the Republican candidate, Abraham Lincoln, who won with a plurality of the vote. The Breckinridge ticket received 848,019 votes (18.1 per cent of the popular vote) and carried nine southern and border states.

During the Civil War the Southern Democrats provided much of the leadership for the Confederate government, including its president, Jefferson Davis. At the end of the conflict the Southern Democrats made no attempt to continue as a separate sectional entity and rejoined the national Democratic Party.

States' Rights Democratic Party (1948)

The States' Rights Democrats, popularly known as the Dixiecrats, were a conservative, southern faction of the Democratic Party that bolted in 1948 and formed their own party. The immediate reason for the new party was dissatisfaction with President Harry S Truman's civil rights program, although the Dixiecrat effort was as much an attempt to show the political power of the southern Democrats and re-establish their importance in the Democratic Party, as to maintain a segregated way of life.

The Mississippi Democratic state executive committee hosted a meeting in Jackson in May 1948 to set the groundwork for the Dixiecrat secession from the Democratic Party. The meeting called for a bolt by southern delegates from the Democratic national convention that summer if the national party endorsed Truman's civil rights program. When the convention did approve a strong civil rights plank in support of the Truman program, the entire Mississippi delegation and half of the Alabama delegation left the convention. Governor Fielding L. Wright of Mississippi invited all anti-Truman delegates to meet in Birmingham three days after the close of the Democratic convention to select a states' rights ticket.

Most southern Democrats with national prominence, and with seniority in Congress and patronage privileges to protect, shunned the new Dixiecrat Party. The party's leaders came from the ranks of southern governors and other state and local officials. The Birmingham convention chose two governors to lead the party: J. Strom Thurmond of South Carolina for President and Wright of Mississippi for Vice President.

Besides the presidential ticket, the Dixiecrats did not run candidates for any other office. Rather than attempting to develop an independent party organization, the Dixiecrats, whenever possible, used existing Democratic Party apparatus.

The party was on the ballot in only one state outside the South and in the November election received only 1,169,134 votes (2.4 per cent of the popular vote). The Thurmond ticket carried four Deep South states where it ran under the Democratic Party label, but failed in its basic objective to prevent the re-election of President Truman.

After the election, the party ceased to exist almost as abruptly as it had begun, with most of its members returning to the Democratic Party. In a statement upon re-entering the Democratic fold, Thurmond characterized the Dixiecrat episode as "a fight within our family."

Union Party (1936)

Advocating more radical economic measures than those favored by President Franklin D. Roosevelt, several of the President's early fringe group supporters broke with him and ran their own ticket in 1936 under the Union Party label. Largely an outgrowth of Father Charles E. Coughlin's National Union for Social Justice, the new party also had the support of Dr. Francis E. Townsend, leader of a movement for government-supported old-age pensions and Gerald L. K. Smith, self-appointed heir of the late Louisiana Senator Huey P. Long's share-the-wealth program.

Coughlin, though, was the keystone of the Union Party and was instrumental in choosing its presidential ticket in June 1936 — Rep. William Lemke (R N.D.) for President and Thomas O'Brien, a Massachusetts railroad union lawyer, for Vice President. The new party did not hold a convention. The party's platform was reportedly written by Coughlin, Lemke and O'Brien and was similar to the program espoused by Coughlin's National Union. Among the features of the Union Party platform were proposals for banking and currency reform, a guaranteed income for workers, restrictions on wealth and an isolationist foreign policy.

Lacking organization and finances during the campaign, the party further suffered from the increasingly violent and often anti-Semitic tone of the oratory of both Coughlin and Smith.

With a primary goal of defeating Roosevelt, the Union Party failed badly. Roosevelt won a landslide victory and the Lemke ticket received only 892,492 votes (2.0 per cent of the popular vote). The party standard-bearers were unable to carry a single state and the Union Party's candidates for the House and Senate were all defeated. The party continued on a local level until it was finally dissolved in 1939.

U.S. Labor Party (1973-)

Formed in 1973 as the political arm of the National Caucus of Labor Committees (NCLC), the U.S. Labor Party (USLP) made its debut in national politics in 1976. The NCLC was organized in 1968 from some of the splinters of the radical movements of the 1960s. It is a Marxist group and its chairman, Lyndon LaRouche of New York, became the 1976 USLP presidential nominee. Wayne Evans, a Detroit steelworker, was his running mate. LaRouche was a self-taught economist who worked in the management and computer fields.

The party directed much of its fire at the Rockefeller family. It charged that banks controlled by the Rockefellers were strangling the U.S. and world economies. In an apocalyptic vein, the party predicted a world monetary collapse by election day and the destruction of the country by thermonuclear war by the summer of 1977.

LaRouche's party developed a reputation for harassment because of its shouted interruptions and demonstrations against its political foes, including the Communist Party and the United Auto Workers. It accused some left-wing organizations and individuals such as Marcus Raskin and his Institute for Policy Studies and Noam Chomsky, the linguist and left-wing theoretician, of conspiring with the Rockefellers and the Central Intelligence Agency.

During the campaign, LaRouche was more critical of Carter than Ford. He depicted Ford as a well-meaning man out of his depth in the presidency, but Carter as a pawn of nuclear war advocates and a disgracefully unqualified presidential candidate.

LaRouche captured only 40,041 votes, less than 0.1 per cent of the national vote. He was on the ballot in 23 states and the District of Columbia. The U.S. Labor Party did not run presidential candidates in the 1980 election.

Whig Party (1834-1856)

Organized in 1834 during the administration of President Andrew Jackson, the Whig Party was an amalgam of forces opposed to Jackson administration policies.

Even the name Whig was symbolic of the intense anti-Jackson feeling among the party's adherents. The name was taken from the earlier British Whig Party, founded in the 17th century in opposition to the tyranny of the Stuart monarchs. Likewise, the term was popular during the American Revolution as the colonists opposed the "tyranny" of King George III.

The monarch the new Whig Party was opposing was "King Andrew," the Whig characterization of President Jackson and his strong executive actions.

Southerners, enraged over Jackson's stand against states' rights in the South Carolina nullification dispute were an early part of the coalition. Then came businessmen, merchants, and conservatives in general, shocked and fearful of Jackson's war on the Bank of the United States. This group, basically a remnant of the National Republican Party, largely espoused Henry Clay's American Plan, a program of federal action to aid the economy and tie the sections of the country together. The plan included tariff protection for business, a national bank, public works, and distribution to the states of money received for the sale of public lands. The Clay plan became the base for the Whigs' nationalistic economic program.

Another influential group joining the Whig coalition was the Anti-Masons, an egalitarian movement strong in parts of New England, New York and Pennsylvania.

Throughout its life, the Whig Party was plagued by factionalism and disunity. In 1836, the first presidential election in which the Whigs took part, they had no national presidential candidate. Rather, three different candidates ran in different parts of the country — Gen. William Henry Harrison, Hugh L. White and Daniel Webster — each hoping to carry Whig electors in states where they were popular. Then the Whig electors, if a majority, could combine in the electoral college on one candidate, or if that proved impossible, throw the election into the House. But Van Buren, the Democratic nominee, won a majority of the electors.

Befitting their lack of unity, the Whigs adopted no platform in 1840, and nominated a military hero, Gen. William Henry Harrison of Ohio, for the presidency. His campaign, emphasizing an apocryphal log cabin and hard cider home life, resulted in a landslide victory.

But Harrison died only a month after taking office (April 4, 1841). The new President, John Tyler of Virginia, proceeded to veto most elements of the Whig economic program, including the tariff and the re-establishment of the national bank. Given Tyler's well-known states' rights position — ignored by the Whigs in 1840 when they capitalized on his southern appeal — the vetoes were inevitable. Tyler's outraged Cabinet resigned and for the rest of his term he remained a President without a party. Since his first two years in office were the only ones in which the Whigs controlled the presidency and both houses of Congress, Tyler's vetoes spoiled the only chance the Whigs ever had of implementing their program.

The Whigs won the White House for the second and last time in 1848 by running another military hero, Gen. Zachary Taylor. Like Harrison, Taylor was a non-ideological candidate, who died in office. He was succeeded by Vice President Millard Fillmore.

The rise of the slavery question in the 1840s and its intensification in the 1850s proved to be the death knell for the Whig Party. A party containing anti-slavery New Englanders and southern plantation owners was simply unable to bridge the gap between them. The Compromise of 1850 forged by Clay only briefly allayed the controversy over extension of slavery into the western territories. Many southern Whigs gravitated towards the Democrats, who they believed more responsive to their interests. In the North, new parties specifically dedicated to opposing the expansion of slavery (Free Soilers, Anti-Nebraskans, Republicans) attracted Whig voters.

The last Whig national convention, in 1856, adopted a platform but endorsed former President Millard Fillmore, already the nominee of the Know-Nothing Party. The Whig platform deplored sectional strife and called for compromise to save the Union. But it was a futile campaign, with Fillmore carrying only Maryland and winning only 21 per cent of the national vote.

Presidents and Vice Presidents of the United States

President and Political Party	Born	Died	Age at inauguration	Native of—	Elected from—	Term of Service	Vice President
George Washington (F)*	1732	1799	57	Va.	Va.	April 30, 1789-March 4, 1793	John Adams
George Washington (F)			61			March 4, 1793-March 4, 1797	John Adams
John Adams (F)	1735	1826	61	Mass.	Mass.	March 4, 1797-March 4, 1801	Thomas Jefferson
Thomas Jefferson (D-R)	1743	1826	57	Va.	Va.	March 4, 1801-March 4, 1805	Aaron Burr
Thomas Jefferson (D-R)			61			March 4, 1805-March 4, 1809	George Clinton
James Madison (D-R)	1751	1836	57	Va.	Va.	March 4, 1809-March 4, 1813	George Clinton
James Madison (D-R)			61			March 4, 1813-March 4, 1817	Elbridge Gerry
James Monroe (D-R)	1758	1831	58	Va.	Va.	March 4, 1817-March 4, 1821	Daniel D. Tompkins
James Monroe (D-R)			62			March 4, 1821-March 4, 1825	Daniel D. Tompkins
John Q. Adams (N-R)	1767	1848	57	Mass.	Mass.	March 4, 1825-March 4, 1829	John C. Calhoun
Andrew Jackson (D)	1767	1845	61	S.C.	Tenn.	March 4, 1829-March 4, 1833	John C. Calhoun
Andrew Jackson (D)			65			March 4, 1833-March 4, 1837	Martin Van Buren
Martin Van Buren (D)	1782	1862	54	N.Y.	N.Y.	March 4, 1837-March 4, 1841	Richard M. Johnson
W. H. Harrison (W)	1773	1841	68	Va.	Ohio	March 4, 1841-April 4, 1841	John Tyler
John Tyler (W)	1790	1862	51	Va.	Va.	April 6, 1841-March 4, 1845	
James K. Polk (D)	1795	1849	49	N.C.	Tenn.	March 4, 1845-March 4, 1849	George M. Dallas
Zachary Taylor (W)	1784	1850	64	Va.	La.	March 4, 1849-July 9, 1850	Millard Fillmore
Millard Fillmore (W)	1800	1874	50	N.Y.	N.Y.	July 10, 1850-March 4, 1853	
Franklin Pierce (D)	1804	1869	48	N.H.	N.H.	March 4, 1853-March 4, 1857	William R. King
James Buchanan (D)	1791	1868	65	Pa.	Pa.	March 4, 1857-March 4, 1861	John C. Breckinridge
Abraham Lincoln (R)	1809	1865	52	Ky.	Ill.	March 4, 1861-March 4, 1865	Hannibal Hamlin
Abraham Lincoln (R)			56			March 4, 1865-April 15, 1865	Andrew Johnson
Andrew Johnson (R)	1808	1875	56	N.C.	Tenn.	April 15, 1865-March 4, 1869	
Ulysses S. Grant (R)	1822	1885	46	Ohio	Ill.	March 4, 1869-March 4, 1873	Schuyler Colfax
Ulysses S. Grant (R)			50			March 4, 1873-March 4, 1877	Henry Wilson
Rutherford B. Hayes (R)	1822	1893	54	Ohio	Ohio	March 4, 1877-March 4, 1881	William A. Wheeler
James A. Garfield (R)	1831	1881	49	Ohio	Ohio	March 4, 1881-Sept. 19, 1881	Chester A. Arthur
Chester A. Arthur (R)	1830	1886	50	Vt.	N.Y.	Sept. 20, 1881-March 4, 1885	
Grover Cleveland (D)	1837	1908	47	N.J.	N.Y.	March 4, 1885-March 4, 1889	Thomas A. Hendricks
Benjamin Harrison (R)	1833	1901	55	Ohio	Ind.	March 4, 1889-March 4, 1893	Levi P. Morton
Grover Cleveland (D)	1837	1908	55			March 4, 1893-March 4, 1897	Adlai E. Stevenson
William McKinley (R)	1843	1901	54	Ohio	Ohio	March 4, 1897-March 4, 1901	Garret A. Hobart
William McKinley (R)			58			March 4, 1901-Sept. 14, 1901	Theodore Roosevelt
Theodore Roosevelt (R)	1858	1919	42	N.Y.	N.Y.	Sept. 14, 1901-March 4, 1905	
Theodore Roosevelt (R)			46			March 4, 1905-March 4, 1909	Charles W. Fairbanks
William H. Taft (R)	1857	1930	51	Ohio	Ohio	March 4, 1909-March 4, 1913	James S. Sherman
Woodrow Wilson (D)	1856	1924	56	Va.	N.J.	March 4, 1913-March 4, 1917	Thomas R. Marshall
Woodrow Wilson (D)			60			March 4, 1917-March 4, 1921	Thomas R. Marshall
Warren G. Harding (R)	1865	1923	55	Ohio	Ohio	March 4, 1921-Aug. 2, 1923	Calvin Coolidge
Calvin Coolidge (R)	1872	1933	51	Vt.	Mass.	Aug. 3, 1923-March 4, 1925	
Calvin Coolidge (R)			52			March 4, 1925-March 4, 1929	Charles G. Dawes
Herbert Hoover (R)	1874	1964	54	Iowa	Calif.	March 4, 1929-March 4, 1933	Charles Curtis
Franklin D. Roosevelt (D)	1882	1945	51	N.Y.	N.Y.	March 4, 1933-Jan. 20, 1937	John N. Garner
Franklin D. Roosevelt (D)			55			Jan. 20, 1937-Jan. 20, 1941	John N. Garner
Franklin D. Roosevelt (D)			59			Jan. 20, 1941-Jan. 20, 1945	Henry A. Wallace
Franklin D. Roosevelt (D)			63			Jan. 20, 1945-April 12, 1945	Harry S Truman
Harry S Truman (D)	1884	1972	60	Mo.	Mo.	April 12, 1945-Jan. 20, 1949	
Harry S Truman (D)			64			Jan. 20, 1949-Jan. 20, 1953	Alben W. Barkley
Dwight D. Eisenhower (R)	1890	1969	62	Texas	N.Y.	Jan. 20, 1953-Jan. 20, 1957	Richard M. Nixon
Dwight D. Eisenhower (R)			66		Pa.	Jan. 20, 1957-Jan. 20, 1961	Richard M. Nixon
John F. Kennedy (D)	1917	1963	43	Mass.	Mass.	Jan. 20, 1961-Nov. 22, 1963	Lyndon B. Johnson
Lyndon B. Johnson (D)	1908	1973	55	Texas	Texas	Nov. 22, 1963-Jan. 20, 1965	
Lyndon B. Johnson (D)			56			Jan. 20, 1965-Jan. 20, 1969	Hubert H. Humphrey
Richard M. Nixon (R)	1913		56	Calif.	N.Y.	Jan. 20, 1969-Jan. 20, 1973	Spiro T. Agnew
Richard M. Nixon (R)			60		Calif.	Jan. 20, 1973-Aug. 9, 1974	Spiro T. Agnew / Gerald R. Ford
Gerald R. Ford (R)	1913		61	Neb.	Mich.	Aug. 9, 1974-Jan. 20, 1977	Nelson A. Rockefeller
Jimmy Carter (D)	1924		52	Ga.	Ga.	Jan. 20, 1977-Jan. 20, 1981	Walter F. Mondale
Ronald Reagan (R)	1911		69	Ill.	Calif.	Jan. 20, 1981-	George Bush

*Key to abbreviations: (D) Democrat, (D-R) Democrat-Republican, (F) Federalist, (N-R) National Republican, (R) Republican, (W) Whig

SOURCE: Joseph Nathan Kane, *Facts About the President*, revised edition, 1976

Biographical Directory of Presidential and Vice Presidential Candidates

The names in the directory include all persons who have received electoral votes for president or vice president since 1789. Also included are a number of prominent third party candidates who received popular votes but no electoral votes. The material is organized as follows: Name, state(s) in the year(s) the individual received electoral votes, party or parties with which the individual was identified at the time(s) they received electoral votes, dates of birth and death (where applicable), major offices held, and the year(s) in which the person received electoral votes. For third party candidates who received no electoral votes, the dates indicate the year(s) in which they were candidates.

For the elections of 1789, 1792, 1796 and 1800 presidential electors did not vote separately for president and vice president. It was, therefore, difficult in many cases to determine whether an individual receiving electoral votes in these elections was a candidate for president or vice president. Where no determination could be made from the sources consulted by Congressional Quarterly, the year(s) in which the individual received electoral votes is given with no specification as to whether the individual was a candidate for president or vice president.

The following sources were used: *Biographical Directory of the American Congress, 1774-1971,* U.S. Government Printing Office, 1971; *Dictionary of American Biography,* Charles Scribner's Sons, New York, 1928-36; *Encyclopedia of American Biography,* John A. Garraty editor, Harper and Row, New York, 1974; *Who's Who in American Politics,* 6th edition, 1977-78, edited by Jaques Cattell Press, R. R. Bowker Co., New York, 1977; *Who Was Who in America, 1607-1968,* Marquis Co., Chicago, 1943-68: Petersen, Svend, *A Statistical History of the American Presidential Elections,* Frederick Ungar Publishing Co., New York, 1968; Scammon, Richard M., *America Votes 10* (1972), Governmental Affairs Institute, Congressional Quarterly, Washington, 1973; *America Votes 12* (1976), Governmental Affairs Institute, Congressional Quarterly, Washington, 1977; *America Votes 14* (1980), Elections Research Center, Washington, 1981.

ADAMS, Charles Francis - Mass. (Free Soil) Aug. 18, 1807 - Nov. 21, 1886; House, 1859-61; Minister to Great Britain, 1861-68; Candidacy: VP - 1848.

ADAMS, John - Mass. (Federalist) Oct. 30, 1735 - July 4, 1826; Continental Congress, 1774; signer of Declaration of Independence, 1776; Minister to Great Britain, 1785; Vice President, 1789-97; President, 1797-1801; Candidacies: VP - 1789, 1792; P - 1796, 1800.

ADAMS, John Quincy - Mass. (Democratic-Republican, National Republican) July 11, 1767 - Feb. 23, 1848; Senate, 1803-08; Minister to Russia, 1809-14; Minister to Great Britain, 1815-17; Secretary of State, 1817-25; President, 1825-29; House, 1831-48; Candidacies: P - 1820, 1824, 1828.

ADAMS, Samuel - Mass. (Federalist) Sept. 27, 1722 - Oct. 2, 1803; Continental Congress, 1774-82; signer of Declaration of Independence; Governor, 1794-97; Candidacy: 1796.

AGNEW, Spiro Theodore - Md. (Republican) Nov. 9, 1918—; Governor, 1967-69; Vice President, 1969-73 (resigned Oct. 10, 1973); Candidacies: VP - 1968, 1972.

ANDERSON, John B. - Ill. (Republican, Independent) Feb. 15, 1922—; state's attorney, 1956-60; U.S. House, 1961-80. Candidacy: P - 1980.

ARMSTRONG, James - Pa. (Federalist) Aug. 29, 1748 - May 6, 1828; House, 1793-95; Candidacy: 1789.

ARTHUR, Chester Alan - N.Y. (Republican) Oct. 5, 1830 - Nov. 18, 1886; Collector, Port of N.Y., 1871-78; Vice President, 1881; President (succeeded James A. Garfield, who was assassinated) 1881-85; Candidacy: VP - 1880.

BANKS, Nathaniel Prentice - Mass. (Liberal Republican) Jan. 30, 1816 - Sept. 1, 1894; House, 1853-57, 1865-73, 1875-79, 1889-91; Governor, 1858-61; Candidacy: VP - 1872.

BARKLEY, Alben William - Ky. (Democratic) Nov. 24, 1877 - April 30, 1956; House, 1913-27; Senate, 1927-49, 1955-56; Senate majority leader, 1937-47; Senate minority leader, 1947-49; Vice President, 1949-53; Candidacy: VP - 1948.

BELL, John - Tenn. (Constitutional Union) Feb. 15, 1797 - Sept. 10, 1869; House, 1827-41; House Speaker, 1834-35; Secretary of War, 1841; Senate, 1847-59; Candidacy: P - 1860.

BENSON, Allan Louis - N.Y. (Socialist) Nov. 6, 1871 - Aug. 19, 1940; Writer, editor; founder of *Reconstruction Magazine,* 1918; Candidacy: P - 1916.

BIDWELL, John - Calif. (Prohibition) Aug. 5, 1819 - April 4, 1900; California pioneer; Major in Mexican War; House, 1865-67; Candidacy: P - 1892.

BIRNEY, James Gillespie - N.Y. (Liberty) Feb. 4, 1792 - Nov. 25, 1857; Kentucky state legislature, 1816-17; Alabama state legislature, 1819-20; Candidacies: P - 1840, 1844.

BLAINE, James Gillespie - Maine (Republican) Jan. 31, 1830 - Jan. 27, 1893; House, 1863-76; House speaker, 1869-75; Senate, 1876-81; Secretary of State, 1881, 1889-92; President, first Pan American Congress, 1889; Candidacy: P - 1884.

BLAIR, Francis Preston Jr. - Mo. (Democratic) Feb. 19, 1821 - July 8, 1875; House, 1857-59, 1860, 1861-62, 1863-64; Senate, 1871-73; Candidacy: VP - 1868.

BRECKINRIDGE, John Cabell - Ky. (Democratic, Southern Democratic) Jan. 21, 1821 - May 17, 1875; House, 1851-55; Vice President, 1857-61; Senate, 1861; major general, Confederacy, 1861-65; Secretary of War, Confederacy, 1865; Candidacies: VP - 1856; P - 1860.

BRICKER, John William - Ohio (Republican) Sept. 6, 1893—; Attorney General of Ohio, 1933-37; Governor, 1939-45; Senate, 1947-59; Candidacy: VP - 1944.

BROWN, Benjamin Gratz - Mo. (Democratic) May 28, 1826 - Dec. 13, 1885; Senate, 1863-67; Governor, 1871-73; Candidacy: VP - 1872.

BRYAN, Charles Wayland - Neb. (Democratic) Feb. 10, 1867 - March 4, 1945;

Governor, 1923-25, 1931-35; Candidacy: VP - 1924.

BRYAN, William Jennings - Neb. (Democratic, Populist) March 19, 1860 - July 26, 1925; House, 1891-95; Secretary of State, 1913-15; Candidacies: P - 1896, 1900, 1908.

BUCHANAN, James - Pa. (Democratic) April 23, 1791 - June 1, 1868; House, 1821-31; Minister to Russia, 1832-34; Senate, 1834-45; Secretary of State, 1845-49; Minister to Great Britain, 1853-56; President, 1857-61; Candidacy: P - 1856.

BURR, Aaron - N.Y. (Democratic-Republican) Feb. 6, 1756 - Sept. 14, 1836; Attorney General of N.Y., 1789-90; Senate, 1791-97; Vice President, 1801-05; Candidacies: 1792, 1796, 1800.

BUSH, George - Texas (Republican) June 12, 1924—; House, 1967-70; ambassador to the United Nations, 1971-73; chairman of the Republican National Committee, 1973-74; head of the U.S. Liaison office in Peking, 1974-75; director of the Central Intelligence Agency, 1976-77; Vice President, 1981—; Candidacy, VP - 1980.

BUTLER, Nicholas Murray - N.Y. (Republican) April 2, 1862 - Dec. 7, 1947; president, Columbia University, 1901-45; president, Carnegie Endowment for International Peace, 1925-45; Candidacy: VP - 1912 (Substituted as candidate after Oct. 30, 1912, death of nominee James S. Sherman.)

BUTLER, William Orlando - Ky. (Democratic) April 19, 1791 - Aug. 6, 1880; House, 1839-43; Candidacy: VP - 1848.

BYRD, Harry Flood - Va. (States' Rights Democratic, Independent Democratic) June 10, 1887 - Oct. 20, 1966; Governor, 1926-30; Senate, 1933-65; Candidacies: P - 1956, 1960.

CALHOUN, John Caldwell - S.C. (Democratic-Republican, Democratic) March 18, 1782-March 31, 1850; House, 1811-17; Secretary of War, 1817-25; Vice President, 1825-32; Senate, 1832-43; 1845-50; Secretary of State, 1844-45; Candidacies: VP - 1824, 1828.

CARTER, James Earl Jr. - Ga. (Democratic) Oct. 1, 1924—; state senate, 1963-67; Governor, 1971-75; President, 1977-81; Candidacy: P - 1976, 1980.

CASS, Lewis - Mich. (Democratic) Oct. 9, 1782 - June 17, 1866; Military and civil governor of Michigan Territory, 1813-31; Secretary of War, 1831-36; Minister to France, 1836-42; Senate, 1845-48; 1849-57; Secretary of State, 1857-60; Candidacy: P - 1848.

CLAY, Henry - Ky. (Democratic-Republican, National Republican, Whig) April 12, 1777-June 29, 1852;

Senate, 1806-07, 1810-11, 1831-42, 1849-52; House, 1811-14, 1815-21, 1823-25; House Speaker, 1811-14, 1815-20, 1823-25; Secretary of State, 1825-29; Candidacies: P - 1824, 1832, 1844.

CLEVELAND, Stephen Grover - N.Y. (Democratic) March 18, 1837 - June 24, 1908; Mayor of Buffalo, 1882; Governor, 1883-85; President, 1885-89, 1893-97; Candidacies: P - 1884, 1888, 1892.

CLINTON, De Witt - N.Y. (independent Democratic-Republican, Federalist) March 2, 1769 - Feb. 11, 1828; Senate, 1802-03; Mayor of New York, 1803-07, 1810, 1811, 1813, 1814; Governor, 1817-23, 1825-28; Candidacy: P - 1812.

CLINTON, George - N.Y. (Democratic-Republican) July 26, 1739 - April 20, 1812; Continental Congress, 1775-76; Governor, 1777-95, 1801-04; Vice President, 1805-12; Candidacies: VP-1789, 1792, 1796, 1804, 1808.

COLFAX, Schuyler - Ind. (Republican) March 23, 1823 - Jan. 13, 1885; House, 1855-69; Speaker of the House, 1863-69; Vice President, 1869-73; Candidacy: VP - 1868.

COLQUITT, Alfred Holt - Ga. (Democratic) April 20, 1824 - March 26, 1894; House, 1853-55; Governor, 1877-82; Senate, 1883-94; Candidacy: VP - 1872.

COOLIDGE, Calvin - Mass. (Republican) July 4, 1872 - Jan. 5, 1933; Governor, 1919-21; Vice President, 1921-23; President, 1923-29; Candidacies: VP - 1920; P - 1924.

COX, James Middleton - Ohio (Democratic) March 31, 1870 - July 15, 1957; House, 1909-13; Governor, 1913-15, 1917-21; Candidacy: P - 1920.

CRAWFORD, William Harris - Ga. (Democratic-Republican) Feb. 24, 1772 - Sept. 15, 1834; Senate, 1807-13; President pro tempore of the Senate, 1812-13; Secretary of War, 1815-16; Secretary of the Treasury, 1816-25; Candidacy: P - 1824.

CURTIS, Charles - Kan. (Republican) Jan. 25, 1860 - Feb. 8, 1936; House, 1893-1907; Senate, 1907-13, 1915-29; President pro tempore, 1911; Vice President, 1929-33; Candidacies: VP - 1928, 1932.

DALLAS, George Mifflin - Pa. (Democratic) July 10, 1792 - Dec. 31, 1864; Senate, 1831-33; Minister to Russia, 1837-39; Vice President, 1845-49; Minister to Great Britain, 1856-61; Candidacy: VP - 1844.

DAVIS, David - Ill. (Democratic) March 9, 1815 - June 26, 1886; Associate Justice

of the Supreme Court, 1862-77; Senate, 1877-83; Candidacy: P - 1872.

DAVIS, Henry Gassaway - W.Va. (Democratic) Nov. 16, 1823 - March 11, 1916; Senate, 1871-83; Chairman of Pan American Railway Committee, 1901-16; Candidacy: VP - 1904.

DAVIS, John William - W. Va. (Democratic) April 13, 1873 - March 24, 1955; House, 1911-13; Solicitor General, 1913-18; Ambassador to Great Britain, 1918-21; Candidacy: P - 1924.

DAWES, Charles Gates - Ill. (Republican) Aug. 27, 1865 - Apr. 23, 1951; U.S. Comptroller of the Currency, 1898-1901; first Director of the Bureau of the Budget, 1921-22; Vice President, 1925-29; Ambassador to Great Britain, 1929-32; Candidacy: VP - 1924.

DAYTON, William Lewis - N.J. (Republican) Feb. 17, 1807 - Dec. 1, 1864; Senate, 1842-51; Minister to France, 1861-64; Candidacy: VP - 1856.

DEBS, Eugene Victor - Ind. (Socialist) Nov. 5, 1855 - Oct. 20, 1926; Indiana legislature, 1885; president, American Railway Union, 1893-97; Candidacies: P - 1900, 1904, 1908, 1912, 1920.

DEWEY, Thomas Edmund - N.Y. (Republican) March 24, 1902 - March 16, 1971; District Attorney, New York County, 1937-41; Governor, 1943-55; Candidacies: P - 1944, 1948.

DOLE, Robert Joseph - Kan. (Republican) July 22, 1923—; House, 1961-69; Senate, 1969—; Candidacy: VP - 1976.

DONELSON, Andrew Jackson - Tenn. (American "Know-Nothing") Aug. 25, 1799 - June 26, 1871; Minister to Prussia, 1846-48; Minister to Germany, 1848-49; Candidacy: VP - 1856.

DOUGLAS, Stephen Arnold - Ill. (Democratic) April 23, 1813 - June 3, 1861; House, 1843-47; Senate, 1847-61; Candidacy: P - 1860.

EAGLETON, Thomas Francis - Mo. (Democratic) Sept. 4, 1929—; Attorney General of Missouri, 1961-65; Lieutenant Governor, 1965-68; Senate, 1968—; Candidacy: VP - 1972 (resigned from Democratic ticket July 31, replaced by R. Sargent Shriver Jr.)

EISENHOWER, Dwight David - N.Y., Pa. (Republican) Oct. 14, 1890 - March 28, 1969; General of U.S. Army, 1943-48; Army chief of staff, 1945-48; president of Columbia University, 1948-51; Commander of North Atlantic Treaty Organization, 1951-52; President, 1953-61; Candidacies: P - 1952, 1956.

ELLMAKER, Amos - Pa. (Anti-Masonic) Feb. 2, 1787 - Nov. 28, 1851; House, 1815; Attorney General of Pennsylvania, 1816-19, 1828-29; Candidacy: VP - 1832.

ELLSWORTH, Oliver - Conn. (Federalist) April 29, 1745 - Nov. 26, 1807; Continental Congress, 1777-84; Senate, 1789-96; Chief Justice of U.S. Supreme Court, 1796-1800; Minister to France, 1799; Candidacy: 1796.

ENGLISH, William Hayden - Ind. (Democratic) Aug. 27, 1822 - Feb. 7, 1896; House, 1853-61; Candidacy: VP - 1880.

EVERETT, Edward - Mass. (Constitutional Union) April 11, 1794 - Jan. 15, 1865; House, 1825-35; Governor, 1836-40; Minister to Great Britain, 1841-45; President of Harvard University, 1846-49; Secretary of State, 1852-53; Senate, 1853-54; Candidacy: VP- 1860.

FAIRBANKS, Charles Warren - Ind. (Republican) May 11, 1852 - June 4, 1918; Senate, 1897-1905; Vice President, 1905-09; Candidacies: VP - 1904, 1916.

FIELD, James Gaven - Va. (Populist) Feb. 24, 1826 - Oct. 12, 1901; major in the Confederate Army, 1861-65; Attorney General of Virginia, 1877-82; Candidacy: VP- 1892.

FILLMORE, Millard - N.Y. (Whig, (American "Know-Nothing") Jan. 7, 1800 - March 8, 1874; House, 1833-35, 1837-43; N.Y. Comptroller, 1847-49; Vice President, 1849-50; President, 1850-53; Candidates: VP - 1848; P - 1856.

FISK, Clinton Bowen - N.J. (Prohibition) Dec. 8, 1828 - July 9, 1890; Civil War brevet major general; founder Fisk University, 1866; member Board of Indian Commissioners, 1874, president, 1881-90; Candidacy: P - 1888.

FLOYD, John - Va. (Independent Democratic) April 24, 1783 - Aug. 17, 1837; House, 1817-29; Governor, 1830-34; Candidacy: P - 1832.

FORD, Gerald Rudolph Jr. - Mich. (Republican) July 14, 1913—; House, 1949-73; Vice President, 1973-74; President, 1974-77; Candidacy: P - 1976.

FRELINGHUYSEN, Theodore - N.J. (Whig) March 28, 1787 - April 12, 1862; Attorney General of New Jersey, 1817-29; Senate, 1829-35; president of Rutgers College, 1850-62; Candidacy: VP - 1844.

FREMONT, John Charles - Calif. (Republican) Jan. 21, 1813 - July 13, 1890; explorer and Army officer in West before 1847; Senate, 1850-51; Governor of Arizona Territory, 1878-81; Candidacy: P - 1856.

GARFIELD, James Abram - Ohio (Republican) Nov. 19, 1831 - Sept. 19, 1881; Major General in Union Army during Civil War; House, 1863-80; President, Mar. 4-Sept. 19, 1881; Candidacy: P - 1880.

GARNER, John Nance - Texas (Democratic) Nov. 22, 1868 - Nov. 7, 1967; House, 1903-33; Speaker of the House, 1931-33; Vice President, 1933-41; Candidacies: VP- 1932, 1936.

GERRY, Elbridge - Mass. (Democratic-Republican) July 17, 1744 - Nov. 23, 1814; Continental Congress, 1776-81, 1782-85; signer of Declaration of Independence; Constitutional Convention, 1787; House, 1789-93; Governor, 1810-12; Vice President, 1813-14; Candidacy: VP - 1812.

GOLDWATER, Barry Morris - Ariz. (Republican) Jan. 1, 1909—; Senate, 1953-65, 1969—; Candidacies: VP - 1960; P - 1964.

GRAHAM, William Alexander - N.C. (Whig) Sept. 5, 1804 - Aug. 11, 1875; Senate, 1840-43; Governor, 1845-49; Secretary of the Navy, 1850-52; Confederate Senate, 1864; Candidacy: VP - 1852.

GRANGER, Francis - N.Y. (Whig) Dec. 1, 1792 - Aug. 31, 1868; House, 1835-37, 1839-41, 1841-43; Postmaster General, 1841; Candidacy: VP - 1836.

GRANT, Ulysses Simpson - Ill. (Republican) April 27, 1822 - July 23, 1885; commander-in-chief, Union Army during Civil War; Secretary of War, 1867; President, 1869-77; Candidacies: P - 1868, 1872.

GREELEY, Horace - N.Y. (Liberal Republican, Democratic) Feb. 3, 1811 - Nov. 29, 1872; founder and editor, *New York Tribune,* 1841-72; House, 1848-49; Candidacy: P - 1872.

GRIFFIN, S. Marvin - Ga. (American Independent) Sept. 4, 1907—; Governor, 1955-59; Candidacy: VP - 1968.

GROESBECK, William Slocum - Ohio (Democratic) July 24, 1815 - July 7, 1897; House, 1857-59; delegate to International Monetary Conference in Paris, 1878; Candidacy: VP - 1872.

HALE, John Parker - N.H. (Free Soil) Mar. 31, 1806 - Nov. 19, 1873; House, 1843-45; Senate, 1847-53, 1855-65; Minister to Spain, 1865-69; Candidacy: P - 1852.

HAMLIN, Hannibal - Maine (Republican) Aug. 27, 1809 - July 4, 1891; House, 1843-47; Senate, 1848-57, 1857-61, 1869-81; Governor, Jan. 8-Feb. 20, 1857; Vice President, 1861-65; Candidacy: VP - 1860.

HANCOCK, John - Mass. (Federalist) Jan. 12, 1737 - Oct. 8, 1793; Continental Congress, 1775-80, 1785-86; president of Continental Congress, 1775-77; Governor, 1780-85, 1787-93; Candidacy: 1789.

HANCOCK, Winfield Scott - Pa. (Democratic) Feb. 14, 1824 - Feb. 9, 1886; Brigadier General, commander of II Army Corps, Civil War; Candidacy: P - 1880.

HARDING, Warren Gamaliel - Ohio (Republican) Nov. 2, 1865 - Aug. 2, 1923; Lieutenant Governor, 1904-05; Senate, 1915-21; President, 1921-23; Candidacy: P - 1920.

HARPER, Robert Goodloe - Md. (Federalist) Jan. 1765 - Jan. 14, 1825; House, 1795-1801; Senate, 1816; Candidacy: VP- 1816, 1820.

HARRISON, Benjamin - Ind. (Republican) Aug. 20, 1833-March 13, 1901; Union officer in Civil War; Senate, 1881-87; President, 1889-93; Candidacies: P - 1888, 1892.

HARRISON, Robert H. - Md. 1745 - 1790; chief justice General Court of Maryland, 1781; Candidacy: 1789.

HARRISON, William Henry - Ohio (Whig) Feb. 9, 1773 - April 4, 1841; delegate to Congress from the Northwest Territory, 1799-1800; Territorial Governor of Indiana, 1801-13; House, 1816-19; Senate, 1825-28; President, Mar. 4 - April 4, 1841; Candidacies: P - 1836, 1840.

HAYES, Rutherford Birchard - Ohio (Republican) Oct. 4, 1822 - Jan. 17, 1893; Major General in Union Army during Civil War; House, 1865-67; Governor, 1868-72, 1876-77; President, 1877-81; Candidacy: P - 1876.

HENDRICKS, Thomas Andrews - Ind. (Democratic) Sept. 7, 1819 - Nov. 25, 1885; House, 1851-55; Senate, 1863-69; Governor, 1873-77; Vice President, 1885; Candidacies: P - 1872; VP - 1876, 1884.

HENRY, John - Md. (Democratic-Republican) Nov. 1750 - Dec. 16, 1798; Continental Congress, 1778-81, 1784-87; Senate, 1789-97; Governor, 1797-98; Candidacy: 1796.

HOBART, Garret Augustus - N.J. (Republican) June 3, 1844 - Nov. 21, 1899; New Jersey senate, 1876-82; president of New Jersey senate, 1881-82; Republican National Committee, 1884-

96; Vice President, 1897-99; Candidacy: VP - 1896.

HOOVER, Herbert Clark - Calif. (Republican) Aug. 10, 1874 - Oct. 20, 1964; U.S. Food Administrator, 1917-19; Secretary of Commerce, 1921-28; President, 1929-33; chairman, Commission on Organization of the Executive Branch of Government, 1947-49, 1953-55; Candidacies: P - 1928, 1932.

HOSPERS, John - Calif. (Libertarian) June 9, 1918—; director of school of philosophy at University of Southern California; Candidacy: P - 1972.

HOWARD, John Eager - Md. (Federalist) June 4, 1752 - Oct. 12, 1827; Continental Congress, 1784-88; Governor, 1788-91; Senate, 1796-1803; Candidacy: VP-1816.

HUGHES, Charles Evans - N.Y. (Republican) April 11, 1862 - Aug. 27, 1948; Governor, 1907-10; Associate Justice of U.S. Supreme Court, 1910-16; Secretary of State, 1921-25; Chief Justice of U.S. Supreme Court, 1930-41; Candidacy: P - 1916.

HUMPHREY, Hubert Horatio Jr. - Minn. (Democratic) May 27, 1911 - Jan. 13, 1978; mayor of Minneapolis, 1945-48; Senate, 1949-64, 1971-78; Vice President, 1965-69; Candidacies: VP - 1964; P - 1968.

HUNTINGTON, Samuel - Conn., July 3, 1731 - Jan. 5, 1796; Continental Congress, 1776-84; president of Continental Congress, 1779-81, 1783; Governor, 1786-96; Candidacy: 1789.

INGERSOLL, Jared - Pa. (Federalist) Oct. 24, 1749 - Oct. 31, 1822; Continental Congress, 1780-81; Constitutional Convention, 1787; Candidacy: VP - 1812.

IREDELL, James - N.C. (Federalist) Oct. 5, 1751 - Oct. 20, 1799; Associate Justice of U.S. Supreme Court, 1790-99; Candidacy: 1796.

JACKSON, Andrew - Tenn. (Democratic-Republican, Democratic) March 15, 1767 - June 8, 1845; House, 1796-97; Senate, 1797-98; 1823-25; Territorial Governor of Florida, 1821; President, 1829-37; Candidacies: P - 1824, 1828, 1832.

JAY, John - N.Y.(Federalist) Dec. 12, 1745 - May 17, 1829; Continental Congress, 1774-77, 1778-79; president of Continental Congress, 1778-79; Minister to Spain, 1779; Chief Justice of U.S. Supreme Court, 1789-95; Governor, 1795-1801; Candidacies: 1789, 1796, 1800.

JEFFERSON, Thomas - Va. (Democratic-Republican) April 13, 1743 - July 4, 1826; Continental Congress, 1775-76, 1783-85; author and signer of Declaration of Independence, 1776; Governor, 1779-81; Minister to France, 1784-89; Secretary of State, 1789-93; Vice President, 1797-1801; President, 1801-09; Candidacies: VP - 1792; P - 1796, 1800, 1804.

JENKINS, Charles Jones - Ga. (Democratic) Jan. 6, 1805 - June 14, 1883; Governor, 1865-68; Candidacy: P - 1872.

JOHNSON, Andrew - Tenn. (Republican) Dec. 29, 1808 - July 31, 1875; House, 1843-53; Governor, 1853-57; Senate, 1857-62, 1875; Vice President, 1865; President, 1865-69; Candidacy: VP - 1864.

JOHNSON, Herschel Vespasian - Ga. (Democratic) Sept. 18, 1812 - Aug. 16, 1880; Senate, 1848-49; Governor, 1853-57; Senator in Confederate Congress, 1862-65; Candidacy: VP-1860.

JOHNSON, Hiram Warren - Calif. (Progressive) Sept. 2, 1866 - Aug. 6, 1945; Governor, 1911-17; Senate, 1917-45; Candidacy: VP- 1912.

JOHNSON, Lyndon Baines - Texas (Democratic) Aug. 27, 1908 - Jan. 22, 1973; House, 1937-49; Senate, 1949-61; Vice President, 1961-63; President, 1963-69; Candidacies: VP - 1960; P - 1964.

JOHNSON, Richard Mentor - Ky. (Democratic) Oct. 17, 1781 - Nov. 19, 1850; House, 1807-19, 1829-37; Senate, 1819-29; Vice President, 1837-41; Candidacies: VP - 1836, 1840.

JOHNSTON, Samuel - N.C. (Federalist) Dec. 15, 1733 - Aug. 18, 1816; Continental Congress, 1780-82; Senate, 1789-93; Candidacy: 1796.

JONES, Walter Burgwyn - Ala. (Independent Democratic) Oct. 16, 1888 - Aug. 1, 1963; Alabama legislature, 1919-20; Alabama circuit court judge, 1920-35; Presiding judge, 1935-63; Candidacy: P - 1956.

JULIAN, George Washington - Ind. (Free Soil, Liberal Republican) May 5, 1817 - July 7, 1899; House, 1849-51, 1861-71; Candidacies: VP - 1852, 1872.

KEFAUVER, Estes - Tenn. (Democratic) July 26, 1903 - Aug. 10, 1963; House, 1939-49; Senate, 1949-63; Candidacy: VP - 1956.

KENNEDY, John Fitzgerald - Mass. (Democratic) May 29, 1917 - Nov. 22, 1963; House, 1947-53; Senate, 1953-

60; President, 1961-63; Candidacy: P - 1960.

KERN, John Worth - Ind. (Democratic) Dec. 20, 1849 - Aug. 17, 1917; Senate, 1911-17; Candidacy: VP - 1908.

KING, Rufus - N.Y. (Federalist) March 24, 1755 - April 29, 1827; Continental Congress, 1784-87; Constitutional Convention, 1787; Senate, 1789-96, 1813-25; Minister to Great Britain, 1796-1803, 1825-26; Candidacies: VP - 1804, 1808; P - 1816.

KING, William Rufus de Vane - Ala. (Democratic) April 7, 1786 - April 18, 1853; House, 1811-16; Senate, 1819-44, 1848-52; Minister to France, 1844-46; Vice President, March 4 - April 18, 1853; Candidacy: VP - 1852.

KNOX, Franklin - Ill. (Republican) Jan. 1, 1874 - April 28, 1944; Secretary of Navy, 1940-44; Candidacy: VP - 1936.

LA FOLLETTE, Robert Marion - Wis. (Progressive) June 14, 1855 - June 18, 1925; House, 1885-91; Governor, 1901-06; Senate, 1906-25; Candidacy: P - 1924.

LANDON, Alfred Mossman - Kan. (Republican) Sept. 9, 1887—; Governor, 1933-37; Candidacy: P - 1936.

LANE, Joseph - Ore. (Southern Democratic) Dec. 14, 1801 - April 19, 1881; Governor of Oregon Territory, 1849-50, May 16-19, 1853; House (Territorial Delegate), 1851-59; Senate, 1859-61; Candidacy: VP - 1860.

LANGDON, John - N.H. (Democratic-Republican) June 25, 1741 - Sept. 18, 1819; Continental Congress, 1775-1776, 1783; Governor, 1788-89; 1805-09, 1810-12; Senate, 1789-1801; first president pro tempore of Senate, 1789; Candidacies: VP - 1808.

LEE, Henry - Mass. (Independent Democratic) Feb. 4, 1782 - Feb. 6, 1867; Merchant and publicist; Candidacy: VP - 1832.

LeMAY, Curtis Emerson - Ohio (American Independent) Nov. 15, 1906—; Air Force Chief of Staff, 1961-65; Candidacy: VP - 1968.

LEMKE, William - N.D. (Union) Aug. 13, 1878 - May 30, 1950; House, 1933-41, 1943-50; Candidacy: P - 1936.

LINCOLN, Abraham - Ill. (Republican) Feb. 12, 1809 - April 15, 1865; House, 1847-49; President, 1861-65; Candidacies: P - 1860, 1864.

LINCOLN, Benjamin - Mass. (Federalist) Jan. 24, 1733 - May 9, 1810; Major

General in Continental Army, 1777-81; Secretary of War, 1781-83; Candidacy: 1789.

LODGE, Henry Cabot Jr. - Mass. (Republican) July 5, 1902—; Senate, 1937-44, 1947-53; Ambassador to United Nations, 1953-60; Ambassador to Republic of Vietnam, 1963-64, 1965-67; Candidacy: VP - 1960.

LOGAN, John Alexander - Ill. (Republican) Feb. 9, 1826 - Dec. 26, 1886; House, 1859-62, 1867-71; Senate, 1871-77, 1879-86; Candidacy: VP- 1884.

MACHEN, Willis Benson - Ky. (Democratic) April 10, 1810 - Sept. 29, 1893; Confederate Congress, 1861-65; Senate, 1872-73; Candidacy: VP- 1872.

MACON, Nathaniel - N.C. (Democratic-Republican) Dec. 17, 1757 - June 29, 1837; House, 1791-1815; Speaker of the House, 1801-07; Senate, 1815-28; Candidacy: VP- 1824.

MADISON, James - Va. (Democratic-Republican) March 16, 1751 - June 28, 1836; Continental Congress, 1780-83, 1786-88; Constitutional Convention, 1787; House, 1789-97; Secretary of State, 1801-09; President, 1809-17; Candidacies: P - 1808, 1812.

MANGUM, Willie Person - N.C. (Independent Democrat) May 10, 1792 - Sept. 7, 1861; House, 1823-26; Senate, 1831-36, 1840-53; Candidacy: P - 1836.

MARSHALL, John - Va. (Federalist) Sept. 24, 1755 - July 6, 1835; House 1799-1800; Secretary of State, 1800-01; Chief Justice of U.S. Supreme Court, 1801-35; Candidacy: VP - 1816.

MARSHALL, Thomas Riley - Ind. (Democratic) March 14, 1854 - June 1, 1925; Governor, 1909-13; Vice President, 1913-21; Candidacies: VP - 1912, 1916.

McCARTHY, Eugene Joseph - Minn. (Independent) March 29, 1916—; House, 1949-59; Senate, 1959-71; Candidacy: P - 1976.

McCLELLAN, George Brinton - N.J. (Democratic) Dec. 3, 1826 - Oct. 29, 1885; General-in-Chief of Army of the Potomac, 1861; Governor, 1878-81; Candidacy: P - 1864.

McGOVERN, George Stanley - S.D. (Democratic) July 19, 1922—; House, 1957-61; Senate, 1963-81; Candidacy: p - 1972.

McKINLEY, William Jr. - Ohio (Republican) Jan. 29, 1843 - Sept. 14, 1901; House, 1877 - May 27, 1884, 1885-91; Governor, 1892-96; President, 1897 - Sept. 14, 1901; Candidacies: P - 1896, 1900.

McNARY, Charles Linza - Ore. (Republican) June 12, 1874 - Feb. 25, 1944; state supreme court judge, 1913-15; Senate, 1917 - Nov. 5, 1918, Dec. 18, 1918 - 1944; Candidacy: VP - 1940.

MILLER, William Edward - N.Y. (Republican) March 22, 1914—; House, 1951-65; chairman of Republican National Committee, 1961-64; Candidacy: VP- 1964.

MILTON, John - Ga. ca. 1740 - ca. 1804, Secretary of State, Georgia, ca. 1778, 1781, 1783; Candidacy: 1789.

MONDALE, Walter Frederick - Minn. (Democratic) Jan. 5, 1928—; Senate, 1964-76; Vice President, 1977-81; Candidacy: VP - 1976, 1980.

MONROE, James - Va. (Democratic-Republican) April 28, 1758 - July 4, 1831; Senate, 1790-94; Minister to France, 1794-96, 1803; Minister to England, 1803-07; Governor, 1799-1802, 1811; Secretary of State, 1811-17; President, 1817-25; Candidacies: VP - 1808; P - 1816, 1820.

MORTON, Levi Parsons - N.Y. (Republican) May 16, 1824 - May 16, 1920; House, 1879-81; Minister to France, 1881-85; Vice President, 1889-93; Governor, 1895-97; Candidacy: VP - 1888.

MUSKIE, Edmund Sixtus - Maine (Democratic) March 28, 1914—; Governor, 1955-59; Senate, 1959-80; Secretary of State, 1980-81; Candidacy: VP - 1968.

NATHAN, Theodora Nathalia - Ore. (Libertarian) Feb. 9, 1923—; Broadcast journalist; National Judiciary Committee, Libertarian Party, 1972-75; Vice-chairperson, Oregon state Libertarian party, 1974-75; Candidacy: VP- 1972.

NIXON, Richard Milhous - Calif., N.Y. (Republican) Jan. 9, 1913—; House, 1947-50; Senate, 1950-53; Vice President, 1953-61; President, 1969-74; Candidacies: VP - 1952, 1956; P - 1960, 1968, 1972.

PALMER, John McAuley - Ill. (Democratic, National Democratic) Sept. 13, 1817 - Sept. 25, 1900; Governor, 1869-73; Senate, 1891-97; Candidacies: VP- 1872; P - 1896.

PARKER, Alton Brooks - N.Y. (Democratic) May 14, 1852 - May 10, 1926; Chief Justice of N.Y. Court of Appeals, 1898-1904; Candidacy: P - 1904.

PENDLETON, George Hunt - Ohio (Democratic) July 19, 1825 - Nov. 24,

1889; House, 1857-65; Senate, 1879-85; Minister to Germany, 1885-89; Candidacy: VP - 1864.

PIERCE, Franklin - N.H. (Democratic) Nov. 23, 1804 - Oct. 8, 1869; House, 1833-37; Senate, 1837-42; President, 1853-57; Candidacy: P - 1852.

PINCKNEY, Charles Cotesworth - S.C. (Federalist) Feb. 25, 1746 - Aug. 16, 1825; president, state senate, 1779, Minister to France, 1796; Candidacies: VP - 1800; P - 1804, 1808.

PINCKNEY, Thomas - S.C. (Federalist) Oct. 23, 1750 - Nov. 2, 1828; Governor, 1787-89; Minister to Great Britain, 1792-96; Envoy to Spain, 1794-95; House, 1797-1801; Candidacy: 1796.

POLK, James Knox - Tenn. (Democratic) Nov. 2, 1795 - June 15, 1849; House, 1825-39; Speaker, 1835-39; Governor, 1839-41; President, 1845-49; Candidacies: VP - 1840; P - 1844.

REAGAN, Ronald Wilson - Calif. (Republican) Feb. 6, 1911—; Governor, 1967-75; President, 1981—; Candidacy: P - 1976, 1980.

REID, Whitelaw - N.Y. (Republican) Oct. 27, 1837 - Dec. 15, 1912; Minister to France, 1889-92; Editor-in-chief, *New York Tribune,* 1872-1905; Candidacy: VP - 1892.

ROBINSON, Joseph Taylor - Ark. (Democratic) Aug. 26, 1872 - July 14, 1937; House, 1903-13; Governor, Jan. 16 - March 8, 1913; Senate, 1913-37; Senate minority leader, 1923-33; Senate majority leader, 1933-37; Candidacy: VP - 1928.

RODNEY, Daniel - Del. (Federalist) Sept. 10, 1764 - Sept. 2, 1846; Governor, 1814-17; House, 1822-23; Senate, 1826-27; Candidacy: VP - 1820.

ROOSEVELT, Franklin Delano - N.Y. (Democratic) Jan. 30, 1882 - April 12, 1945; Assistant Secretary of Navy, 1913-20; Governor, 1929-33; President, 1933-45; Candidacies: VP - 1920; P - 1932, 1936, 1940, 1944.

ROOSEVELT, Theodore - N.Y. (Republican, Progressive) Oct. 27, 1858 - Jan. 6, 1919; Governor, 1899-1901; Assistant Secretary of Navy, 1897-98; Vice President, March 4 - Sept. 14, 1901; President, 1901-09; Candidacies: VP - 1900; P - 1904, 1912.

ROSS, James - Pa. (Federalist) July 12, 1762 - Nov. 27, 1847; Senate, 1794-1803; Candidacy: VP- 1816.

RUSH, Richard - Pa. (Democratic-Republican, National-Republican) Aug.

29, 1780 - July 30, 1859; Attorney General, 1814-17; Minister to Great Britain, 1817-24; Secretary of Treasury, 1825-28; Candidacy: VP- 1820, 1828.

RUTLEDGE, John - S.C. (Federalist) Sept. 1739 - July 23, 1800; Continental Congress, 1774-76, 1782-83; Governor, 1779-82; Constitutional Convention, 1787; Associate Justice of U.S. Supreme Court, 1789-91; Candidacy: 1789.

SANFORD, Nathan - N.Y.(Democratic-Republican) Nov. 5, 1777 - Oct. 17, 1838; Senate, 1815-21, 1826-31; Candidacy: VP- 1824.

SCHMITZ, John George - Calif. (American Independent) Aug. 12, 1930—; House, 1970-73; Candidacy: P - 1972.

SCOTT, Winfield - N.J. (Whig) June 13, 1786 - May 29, 1866; General-in-chief of U.S. Army, 1841-61; Candidacy: P- 1852.

SERGEANT, John - Pa. (National-Republican) Dec. 5, 1779 - Nov. 23, 1852; House, 1815-23, 1827-29, 1837-41; Candidacy: VP - 1832.

SEWALL, Arthur - Maine (Democratic) Nov. 25, 1835 - Sept. 5, 1900; Democratic National Committee member, 1888-96; Candidacy: VP - 1896.

SEYMOUR, Horatio - N.Y. (Democratic) May 31, 1810 - Feb. 12, 1886; Governor, 1853-55, 1863-65; Candidacy: P - 1868.

SHERMAN, James Schoolcraft - N.Y. (Republican) Oct. 24, 1855 - Oct. 30, 1912; House, 1887-91, 1893-1909; Vice President, 1909-12; Candidacies: VP - 1908, 1912 (Died during 1912 campaign; Nicholas Murray Butler replaced Sherman on the Republican ticket.)

SHRIVER, Robert Sargent Jr. - Md. (Democratic) Nov. 9, 1915—; Director, Peace Corps, 1961-66; Director, Office of Economic Opportunity, 1964-68; Ambassador to France, 1968-70; Candidacy: VP - 1972 (Replaced Thomas F. Eagleton on Democratic ticket Aug. 8.)

SMITH, Alfred Emanuel - N.Y. (Democratic) Dec. 30, 1873 - Oct. 4, 1944; Governor, 1919-21, 1923-29; Candidacy: P - 1928.

SMITH, William - S.C., Ala. (Independent Democratic-Republican) Sept. 6, 1762 - June 26, 1840; Senate, 1816-23; 1826-31; Candidacies: VP - 1828, 1836.

SPARKMAN, John Jackson - Ala. (Democratic) Dec. 20, 1899—; House, 1937-46; Senate, 1946-79; Candidacy: VP - 1952.

STEVENSON, Adlai Ewing - Ill. (Democratic) Oct. 23, 1835 - June 14, 1914; House, 1875-77, 1879-81; Assistant Postmaster General, 1885-89; Vice President, 1893-97; Candidacies: VP - 1892, 1900.

STEVENSON, Adlai Ewing II - Ill. (Democratic) Feb. 5, 1900 - July 14, 1965; Assistant to the Secretary of Navy, 1941-44; Assistant to the Secretary of State, 1945; Governor, 1949-53; Ambassador to United Nations, 1961-65; Candidacies: P - 1952, 1956.

STOCKTON, Richard (Federalist) - N.J. April 17, 1764 - March 7, 1828; Senate, 1796-99; House, 1813-15; Candidacy: VP- 1820.

TAFT, William Howard - Ohio (Republican) Sept. 15, 1857 - March 8, 1930; Secretary of War, 1904-08; President, 1909-13; Chief Justice of U.S. Supreme Court, 1921-30; Candidacies: P - 1908, 1912.

TALMADGE, Herman Eugene - Ga. (Independent Democratic) Aug. 9, 1913—; Governor, 1947, 1948-55; Senate, 1957-81; Candidacy: VP - 1956.

TAYLOR, Glen Hearst - Idaho (Progressive) April 12, 1904—; Senate, 1945-51; Candidacy: VP- 1948.

TAYLOR, Zachary - La. (Whig) Nov. 24, 1784 - July 9, 1850; Major General, U.S. Army; President, 1849-50; Candidacy: P - 1848.

TAZEWELL, Littleton Waller - Va. (Democratic) Dec. 17, 1774 - May 6, 1860; House, 1800-01; Senate, 1824-32; Governor, 1834-36; Candidacy: VP - 1840.

TELFAIR, Edward - Ga.; 1735 - Sept. 17, 1807; Continental Congress, 1778-82, 1784-85, 1788-89; Governor, 1786, 1790-93; Candidacy: 1789.

THOMAS, Norman Mattoon - N.Y. (Socialist) Nov. 20, 1884 - Dec. 19, 1968; Presbyterian minister, 1911-31; author and editor; Candidacies: P - 1928, 1932, 1936, 1940, 1944, 1948.

THURMAN, Allen Granberry - Ohio (Democratic) Nov. 13, 1813 - Dec. 12, 1895; House, 1845-47; Ohio state supreme court, 1851-56; Senate, 1869-81; Candidacy: VP - 1888.

THURMOND, James Strom - S.C. (States' Rights Democrat, Democratic) Dec. 5, 1902—; Governor, 1947-51; Senate, 1954-56, 1956—; Candidacies: P - 1948; VP - 1960.

TILDEN, Samuel Jones - N.Y.(Democratic) Feb. 9, 1814 - Aug. 4, 1886; Governor, 1875-77; Candidacy: P - 1876.

TOMPKINS, Daniel D. - N.Y.(Democratic-Republican) June 21, 1774 - June 11, 1825; Governor, 1807-17; Vice President, 1817-25; Candidacies: VP - 1816, 1820.

TRUMAN, Harry S - Mo. (Democratic) May 8, 1884 - Dec. 26, 1972; Senate, 1935-45; Vice President, Jan. 20 - April 12, 1945; President, 1945-53; Candidacies: VP - 1944; P - 1948.

TYLER, John - Va. (Whig) March 29, 1790 - Jan. 18, 1862; Governor, 1825-27; Senate, 1827-36; Vice President, March 4 - April 4, 1841; President, 1841-45; Candidacies: VP - 1836, 1840.

VAN BUREN, Martin - N.Y. (Democratic, Free Soil) Dec. 5, 1782 - July 24, 1862; Senate, 1821-28; Governor, Jan. - March, 1829; Secretary of State, 1829-31; Vice President, 1833-37; President, 1837-41; Candidacies: VP - 1824, 1832; P - 1836, 1840, 1848.

WALLACE, George Corley - Ala. (American Independent) Aug. 25, 1919—; Governor, 1963-67, 1971-79, 1983—; Candidacy: P - 1968.

WALLACE, Henry Agard - Iowa (Democratic, Progressive) Oct. 7, 1888 - Nov. 18, 1965; Secretary of Agriculture, 1933-40; Vice President, 1941-45; Secretary of Commerce, 1945-46; Candidacies: VP - 1940; P - 1948.

WARREN, Earl - Calif. (Republican) March 19, 1891 - July 9, 1974; Governor, 1943-53; Chief Justice of U.S. Supreme Court, 1953-69; Candidacy: VP- 1948.

WASHINGTON, George - Va. (Federalist) Feb. 22, 1732 - Dec. 14, 1799; First and Second Continental Congresses, 1774, 1775; Commander-in-chief of armed forces, 1775-83; president of Constitutional Convention, 1787; President, 1789-97; Candidacies: P - 1789, 1792, 1796.

WATSON, Thomas Edward - Ga. (Populist) Sept. 5, 1856 - Sept. 26, 1922; House, 1891-93; Senate, 1921-22; Candidacies: VP - 1896; P - 1904, 1908.

WEAVER, James Baird - Iowa (Greenback, Populist) June 12, 1833 - Feb. 6, 1912; House, 1879-81, 1885-89; Candidacies: P - 1880, 1892.

WEBSTER, Daniel - Mass. (Whig) Jan. 18, 1782 - Oct. 24, 1852; House, 1813-17, 1823-27; Senate, 1827-41, 1845-50; Secretary of State, 1841-43, 1850-52; Candidacy: P - 1836.

WHEELER, Burton Kendall - Mont. (Progressive) Feb. 27, 1882 - Jan. 6,

1975; Senate, 1923-47; Candidacy: VP-1924.

WHEELER, William Almon - N.Y. (Republican) June 19, 1819 - June 4, 1887; House, 1861-63, 1869-77; Vice President, 1877-81; Candidacy: VP - 1876.

WHITE, Hugh Lawson - Tenn. (Whig) Oct. 30, 1773 - April 10, 1840; Senate, 1825-March 3, 1835, Oct. 6, 1835-1840; Candidacy: P - 1836.

WILKINS, William - Pa. (Democratic) Dec. 20, 1779 - June 23, 1865; Senate, 1831-34; Minister to Russia, 1834-35; House, 1843-44; Secretary of War, 1844-45; Candidacy: VP - 1832.

WILLKIE, Wendell Lewis - N.Y. (Republican) Feb. 18, 1892 - Oct. 8, 1944; Utility executive, 1933-40; Candidacy: P - 1940.

WILSON, Henry - Mass. (Republican) Feb. 16, 1812 - Nov. 22, 1875; Senate, 1855-73; Vice President, 1873-75; Candidacy: VP - 1872.

WILSON, Woodrow - N.J. (Democratic) Dec. 28, 1856 - Feb. 3, 1924; Governor, 1911-13; President, 1913-21; Candidacies: P - 1912, 1916.

WIRT, William - Md. (Anti-Masonic) Nov. 8, 1772 - Feb. 18, 1834; Attorney General, 1817-29; Candidacy: P - 1832.

WRIGHT, Fielding Lewis - Miss. (States' Rights Democratic) May 16, 1895 - May 4, 1956; Governor, 1946-52; Candidacy: VP - 1948.

Political Party Nominees, 1831-1980

The following pages contain a comprehensive list of major and minor party nominees for president and vice president since 1831 when the first nominating convention was held by the Anti-Masonic Party.

In many cases, minor parties made only token efforts at a presidential campaign. Often, third party candidates declined to run after being nominated by the convention, or their names appeared on the ballots of only a few states. In some cases the names of minor candidates did not appear on any state ballots and they received only a scattering of write-in votes, if any.

The basic source used to compile the list was Joseph Nathan Kane's *Facts About the Presidents,* 3rd edition, The H. W. Wilson Co., New York, 1974. To verify the names appearing in Kane, Congressional Quarterly consulted the following additional sources: Richard M. Scammon's *America at the Polls,* University of Pittsburgh Press, 1965; *America Votes 8* (1968), Congressional Quarter-

ly, 1969; *America Votes 10* (1972), Congressional Quarterly, 1973; *Encyclopedia of American History,* edited by Richard B. Morris, Harper and Row, New York, 1965; *Dictionary of American Biography,* Charles Scribner's Sons, 1928-1936; *Facts on File,* Facts on File Inc., New York 1945-75; *History of U.S. Political Parties,* Vols. I-IV, edited by Arthur M. Schlesinger, Bowker, New York, 1973; *History of American Presidential Elections, 1789-1968,* edited by Arthur M. Schlesinger, McGraw Hill, New York, 1971; and *Who Was Who in America,* Vol. I-V (1607-1968), Marquis Who's Who, Chicago. The source for the 1976 and 1980 candidates was Richard M. Scammon's *America Votes 12* (1976), and *America Votes 14* (1981).

When these sources contained information in conflict with Kane, the conflicting information is included in a footnote. Where a candidate appears in Kane, *but could not be verified in another source,* an asterisk appears beside the candidate's name on the list.

Election of 1832

Democratic Party
President: Andrew Jackson, Tennessee
Vice President: Martin Van Buren, New York
National Republican Party
President: Henry Clay, Kentucky
Vice President: John Sergeant, Pennsylvania
Independent Party
President: John Floyd, Virginia
Vice President: Henry Lee, Massachusetts
Anti-Masonic Party
President: William Wirt, Maryland
Vice President: Amos Ellmaker, Pennsylvania

Election of 1836

Democratic Party
President: Martin Van Buren, New York
Vice President: Richard Mentor Johnson, Kentucky
Whig Party
President: William Henry Harrison, Hugh Lawson White, Daniel Webster
Vice President: Francis Granger, John Tyler

The Whigs nominated regional candidates in 1836 hoping that each candidate would carry his region and deny Democrat Van Buren an electoral vote majority. Webster was the Whig candidate in Massachusetts; Harrison in the rest of New England, the middle Atlantic states and the West; and White in the South.

Granger was the running mate of Harrison and Webster. Tyler was White's running mate.

Election of 1840

Whig Party
President: William Henry Harrison, Ohio
Vice President: John Tyler, Virginia
Democratic Party
President: Martin Van Buren, New York

The Democratic convention adopted a resolution which left the choice of vice presidential candidates to the states. Democratic electors divided their vice presidential votes among incumbent Richard M. Johnson (48 votes), Littleton W. Tazewell (11 votes) and James K. Polk (1 vote).
Liberty Party
President: James Gillespie Birney, New York
Vice President: Thomas Earle, Pennsylvania

Election of 1844

Democratic Party
President: James Knox Polk, Tennessee
Vice President: George Mifflin Dallas, Pennsylvania
Whig Party
President: Henry Clay, Kentucky
Vice President: Theodore Frelinghuysen, New Jersey
Liberty Party
President: James Gillespie Birney, New York
Vice President: Thomas Morris, Ohio
National Democratic
President: John Tyler, Virginia
Vice President: None
Tyler withdrew from the race in favor of the Democrat, Polk.

Election of 1848

Whig Party
President: Zachary Taylor, Louisiana
Vice President: Millard Fillmore, New York
Democratic Party
President: Lewis Cass, Michigan
Vice President: William Orlando Butler, Kentucky
Free Soil Party
President: Martin Van Buren, New York
Vice President: Charles Francis Adams, Massachusetts
Free Soil (Barnburners—Liberty Party)
President: John Parker Hale, New Hampshire
Vice President: Leicester King, Ohio
Later John Parker Hale relinquished the nomination.

National Liberty Party
President: Gerrit Smith, New York
Vice President: Charles C. Foote, Michigan

Election of 1852

Democratic Party
President: Franklin Pierce, New Hampshire
Vice President: William Rufus De Vane King, Alabama
Whig Party
President: Winfield Scott, New Jersey
Vice President: William Alexander Graham, North Carolina
Free Soil
President: John Parker Hale, New Hampshire
Vice President: George Washington Julian, Indiana

Election of 1856

Democratic Party
President: James Buchanan, Pennsylvania
Vice President: John Cabell Breckinridge, Kentucky
Republican Party
President: John Charles Fremont, California
Vice President: William Lewis Dayton, New Jersey
American (Know-Nothing) Party
President: Millard Fillmore, New York
Vice President: Andrew Jackson Donelson, Tennessee
Whig Party (the "Silver Grays")
President: Millard Fillmore, New York
Vice President: Andrew Jackson Donelson, Tennessee
North American Party
President: Nathaniel Prentice Banks, Massachusetts
Vice President: William Freame Johnson, Pennsylvania
    Banks and Johnson declined the nominations and gave their
support to the Republicans.

Election of 1860

Republican Party
President: Abraham Lincoln, Illinois
Vice President: Hannibal Hamlin, Maine
Democratic Party
President: Stephen Arnold Douglas, Illinois
Vice President: Herschel Vespasian Johnson, Georgia
Southern Democratic Party
President: John Cabell Breckinridge, Kentucky
Vice President: Joseph Lane, Oregon
Constitutional Union Party
President: John Bell, Tennessee
Vice President: Edward Everett, Massacusetts

Election of 1864

Republican Party
President: Abraham Lincoln, Illinois
Vice President: Andrew Johnson, Tennessee
Democratic Party
President: George Brinton McClellan, New York
Vice President: George Hunt Pendleton, Ohio
Independent Republican Party
President: John Charles Fremont, California
Vice President: John Cochrane, New York
    Fremont and Cochrane declined and gave their support to
the Republican Party nominees

Election of 1868

Republican Party
President: Ulysses Simpson Grant, Illinois
Vice President: Schuyler Colfax, Indiana
Democratic Party
President: Horatio Seymour, New York
Vice President: Francis Preston Blair, Jr., Missouri

Election of 1872

Republican Party
President: Ulysses Simpson Grant, Illinois
Vice President: Henry Wilson, Massachusetts

Liberal Republican Party
President: Horace Greeley, New York
Vice President: Benjamin Gratz Brown, Missouri
Independent Liberal Republican Party (Opposition Party)
President: William Slocum Groesbeck, Ohio
Vice President: Frederick Law Olmsted, New York
Democratic Party
President: Horace Greeley, New York
Vice President: Benjamin Gratz Brown, Missouri
Straight-out Democratic Party
President: Charles O'Conor, New York
Vice President: John Quincy Adams, Massachusetts
Prohibition Party
President: James Black, Pennsylvania
Vice President: John Russell, Michigan
People's Party (Equal Rights Party)
President: Victoria Claflin Woodhull, New York
Vice President: Frederick Douglass
Labor Reform Party
President: David Davis, Illinois
Vice President: Joel Parker, New Jersey
Liberal Republican Party of Colored Men
President: Horace Greeley, New York
Vice President: Benjamin Gratz Brown, Missouri
National Working Men's Party
President: Ulysses Simpson Grant, Illinois
Vice President: Henry Wilson, Massachusetts

Election of 1876

Republican Party
President: Rutherford Birchard Hayes, Ohio
Vice President: William Almon Wheeler, New York
Democratic Party
President: Samuel Jones Tilden, New York
Vice President: Thomas Andrews Hendricks, Indiana
Greenback Party
President: Peter Cooper, New York
Vice President: Samuel Fenton Cary, Ohio
Prohibition Party
President: Green Clay Smith, Kentucky
Vice President: Gideon Tabor Stewart, Ohio
American National Party
President: James B. Walker, Illinois
Vice President: Donald Kirkpatrick, New York*

Election of 1880

Republican Party
President: James Abram Garfield, Ohio
Vice President: Chester Alan Arthur, New York
Democratic Party
President: Winfield Scott Hancock, Pennsylvania
Vice President: William Hayden English, Indiana
Greenback Labor Party
President: James Baird Weaver, Iowa
Vice President: Benjamin J. Chambers, Texas
Prohibition Party
President: Neal Dow, Maine
Vice President: Henry Adams Thompson, Ohio
American Party
President: John Wolcott Phelps, Vermont
Vice President: Samuel Clarke Pomeroy, Kansas*

Election of 1884

Democratic Party
President: Grover Cleveland, New York
Vice President: Thomas Andrews Hendricks, Indiana
Republican Party
President: James Gillespie Blaine, Maine
Vice President: John Alexander Logan, Illinois
Anti-Monopoly Party
President: Benjamin Franklin Butler, Massachusetts
Vice President: Absolom Madden West, Mississippi
Greenback Party
President: Benjamin Franklin Butler, Massachusetts
Vice President: Absolom Madden West, Mississippi

Prohibition Party
President: John Pierce St. John, Kansas
Vice President: William Daniel, Maryland
American Prohibition Party
President: Samuel Clarke Pomeroy, Kansas
Vice President: John A. Conant, Connecticut
Equal Rights Party
President: Belva Ann Bennett Lockwood, District of Columbia
Vice President: Marietta Lizzie Bell Stow, California

Election of 1888

Republican Party
President: Benjamin Harrison, Indiana
Vice President: Levi Parsons Morton, New York
Democratic Party
President: Grover Cleveland, New York
Vice President: Allen Granberry Thurman, Ohio
Prohibition Party
President: Clinton Bowen Fisk, New Jersey
Vice President: John Anderson Brooks, Missouri*
Union Labor Party
President: Alson Jenness Streeter, Illinois
Vice President: Charles E. Cunningham, Arkansas*
United Labor Party
President: Robert Hall Cowdrey, Illinois
Vice President: William H. T. Wakefield, Kansas*
American Party
President: James Langdon Curtis, New York
Vice President: Peter Dinwiddie Wigginton, California*
Equal Rights Party
President: Belva Ann Bennett Lockwood, District of Columbia
Vice President: Alfred Henry Love, Pennsylvania*
Industrial Reform Party
President: Albert E. Redstone, California*
Vice President: John Colvin, Kansas*

Election of 1892

Democratic Party
President; Grover Cleveland, New York
Vice President: Adlai Ewing Stevenson, Illinois
Republican Party
President: Benjamin Harrison, Indiana
Vice President: Whitelaw Reid, New York
People's Party of America
President: James Baird Weaver, Iowa
Vice President: James Gaven Field, Virginia
Prohibition Party
President: John Bidwell, California
Vice President: James Britton Cranfill, Texas
Socialist Labor Party
President: Simon Wing, Massachusetts
Vice President: Charles Horatio Matchett, New York*

Election of 1896

Republican Party
President: William McKinley, Ohio
Vice President: Garret Augustus Hobart, New Jersey
Democratic Party
President: William Jennings Bryan, Nebraska
Vice President: Arthur Sewall, Maine
People's Party (Populist)
President: William Jennings Bryan, Nebraska
Vice President: Thomas Edward Watson, Georgia
National Democratic Party
President: John McAuley Palmer, Illinois
Vice President: Simon Bolivar Buckner, Kentucky
Prohibition Party
President: Joshua Levering, Maryland
Vice President: Hale Johnson, Illinois*
Socialist Labor Party
President: Charles Horatio Matchett, New York
Vice President: Matthew Maguire, New Jersey
National Party
President: Charles Eugene Bentley, Nebraska
Vice President: James Haywood Southgate, North Carolina*

National Silver Party (Bi-Metallic League)
President: William Jennings Bryan, Nebraska
Vice President: Arthur Sewall, Maine

Election of 1900

Republican Party
President: William McKinley, Ohio
Vice President: Theodore Roosevelt, New York
Democratic Party
President: William Jennings Bryan, Nebraska
Vice President: Adlai Ewing Stevenson, Illinois
Prohibition Party
President: John Granville Woolley, Illinois
Vice President: Henry Brewer Metcalf, Rhode Island
Social-Democratic Party
President: Eugene Victor Debs, Indiana
Vice President: Job Harriman, California
People's Party (Populist—Anti-Fusionist faction)
President: Wharton Barker; Pennsylvania
Vice President: Ignatius Donnelly, Minnesota
Socialist Labor Party
President: Joseph Francis Malloney, Massachusetts
Vice President: Valentine Remmel, Pennsylvania
Union Reform Party
President: Seth Hockett Ellis, Ohio
Vice President: Samuel T. Nicholson, Pennsylvania
United Christian Party
President: Jonah Fitz Randolph Leonard, Iowa
Vice President: David H. Martin, Pennsylvania
People's Party (Populist—Fusionist faction)
President: William Jennings Bryan, Nebraska
Vice President: Adlai Ewing Stevenson, Illinois
Silver Republican Party
President: William Jennings Bryan, Nebraska
Vice President: Adlai Ewing Stevenson, Illinois
National Party
President: Donelson Caffery, Louisiana
Vice President: Archibald Murray Howe, Massachusetts*

Election of 1904

Republican Party
President: Theodore Roosevelt, New York
Vice President: Charles Warren Fairbanks, Indiana
Democratic Party
President: Alton Brooks Parker, New York
Vice President: Henry Gassaway Davis, West Virginia
Socialist Party
President: Eugene Victor Debs, Indiana
Vice President: Benjamin Hanford, New York
Prohibition Party
President: Silas Comfort Swallow, Pennsylvania
Vice President: George W. Carroll, Texas
People's Party (Populists)
President: Thomas Edward Watson, Georgia
Vice President: Thomas Henry Tibbles, Nebraska
Socialist Labor Party
President: Charles Hunter Corregan, New York
Vice President: William Wesley Cox, Illinois
Continental Party
President: Austin Holcomb
Vice President: A. King, Missouri

Election of 1908

Republican Party
President: William Howard Taft, Ohio
Vice President: James Schoolcraft Sherman, New York
Democratic Party
President: William Jennings Bryan, Nebraska
Vice President: John Worth Kern, Indiana
Socialist Party
President: Eugene Victor Debs
Vice President: Benjamin Hanford
Prohibition Party
President: Eugene Wilder Chafin, Illinois
Vice President: Aaron Sherman Watkins, Ohio

Independence Party
President: Thomas Louis Hisgen, Massachusetts
Vice President: John Temple Graves, Georgia

People's Party (Populist)
President: Thomas Edward Watson, Georgia
Vice President: Samuel Williams, Indiana

Socialist Labor Party
President: August Gillhaus, New York
Vice President: Donald L. Munro, Virginia

United Christian Party
President: Daniel Braxton Turney, Illinois
Vice President: Lorenzo S. Coffin, Iowa

Election of 1912

Democratic Party
President: Woodrow Wilson, New Jersey
Vice President: Thomas Riley Marshall, Indiana

Progressive Party ("Bull Moose" Party)
President: Theodore Roosevelt, New York
Vice President: Hiram Warren Johnson, California

Republican Party
President: William Howard Taft, Ohio
Vice President: James Schoolcraft Sherman, New York
Sherman died Oct. 30; replaced by Nicholas Murray
Butler, New York

Socialist Party
President: Eugene Victor Debs, Indiana
Vice President: Emil Seidel, Wisconsin

Prohibition Party
President: Eugene Wilder Chafin, Illinois
Vice President: Aaron Sherman Watkins, Ohio

Socialist Labor Party
President: Arthur Elmer Reimer, Massachusetts
Vice President: August Gillhaus, New York[1]

Election of 1916

Democratic Party
President: Woodrow Wilson, New Jersey
Vice President: Thomas Riley Marshall, Indiana

Republican Party
President: Charles Evans Hughes, New York
Vice President: Charles Warren Fairbanks, Indiana

Socialist Party
President: Allan Louis Benson, New York
Vice President: George Ross Kirkpatrick, New Jersey

Prohibition Party
President: James Franklin Hanly, Indiana
Vice President: Ira Landrith, Tennessee

Socialist Labor Party
President: Arthur Elmer Reimer, Massachusetts*
Vice President: Caleb Harrison, Illinois*

Progressive Party
President: Theodore Roosevelt, New York
Vice President: John Milliken Parker, Louisiana

Election of 1920

Republican Party
President: Warren Gamaliel Harding, Ohio
Vice President: Calvin Coolidge, Massachusetts

Democratic Party
President: James Middleton Cox, Ohio
Vice President: Franklin Delano Roosevelt, New York

Socialist Party
President: Eugene Victor Debs, Indiana
Vice President: Seymour Stedman, Illinois

Farmer Labor Party
President: Parley Parker Christensen, Utah
Vice President: Maximilian Sebastian Hayes, Ohio

Prohibition Party
President: Aaron Sherman Watkins, Ohio
Vice President: David Leigh Colvin, New York

Socialist Labor Party
President: William Wesley Cox, Missouri
Vice President: August Gillhaus, New York

Single Tax Party
President: Robert Colvin Macauley, Pennsylvania
Vice President: R. G. Barnum, Ohio

American Party
President: James Edward Ferguson, Texas
Vice President: William J. Hough

Election of 1924

Republican Party
President: Calvin Coolidge, Massachusetts
Vice President: Charles Gates Dawes, Illinois

Democratic Party
President: John William Davis, West Virginia
Vice President: Charles Wayland Bryan, Nebraska

Progressive Party
President: Robert La Follette, Wisconsin
Vice President: Burton Kendall Wheeler, Montana

Prohibition Party
President: Herman Preston Faris, Missouri
Vice President: Marie Caroline Brehm, California

Socialist Labor Party
President: Frank T. Johns, Oregon
Vice President: Verne L. Reynolds, New York

Socialist Party
President: Robert La Follette, New York
Vice President: Burton Kendall Wheeler, Montana

Workers Party (Communist Party)
President: William Zebulon Foster, Illinois
Vice President: Benjamin Gitlow, New York

American Party
President: Gilbert Owen Nations, District of Columbia
Vice President: Charles Hiram Randall, California[2]

Commonwealth Land Party
President: William J. Wallace, New Jersey
Vice President: John Cromwell Lincoln, Ohio

Farmer Labor Party
President: Duncan McDonald, Illinois*
Vice President: William Bouck, Washington*

Greenback Party
President: John Zahnd, Indiana*
Vice President: Roy M. Harrop, Nebraska*

Election of 1928

Republican Party
President: Herbert Clark Hoover, California
Vice President: Charles Curtis, Kansas

Democratic Party
President: Alfred Emanuel Smith, New York
Vice President: Joseph Taylor Robinson, Arkansas

Socialist Party
President: Norman Mattoon Thomas, New York
Vice President: James Hudson Maurer, Pennsylvania

Workers Party (Communist Party)
President: William Zebulon Foster, Illinois
Vice President: Benjamin Gitlow, New York

Socialist Labor Party
President: Verne L. Reynolds, Michigan
Vice President: Jeremiah D. Crowley, New York

Prohibition Party
President: William Frederick Varney, New York
Vice President: James Arthur Edgerton, Virginia

Farmer Labor Party
President: Frank Elbridge Webb, California
Vice President: Will Vereen, Georgia[3]

Greenback Party
President: John Zahnd, Indiana*
Vice President: Wesley Henry Bennington, Ohio*

Election of 1932

Democratic Party
President: Franklin Delano Roosevelt, New York
Vice President: John Nance Garner, Texas

Republican Party
President: Herbert Clark Hoover, California
Vice President: Charles Curtis, Kansas

Socialist Party
President: Norman Mattoon Thomas, New York
Vice President: James Hudson Maurer, Pennsylvania

Communist Party
President: William Zebulon Foster, Illinois
Vice President: James William Ford, New York
Prohibition Party
President: William David Upshaw, Georgia
Vice President: Frank Stewart Regan, Illinois
Liberty Party
President: William Hope Harvey, Arkansas
Vice President: Frank B. Hemenway, Washington
Socialist Labor Party
President: Verne L. Reynolds, New York
Vice President: John W. Aiken, Massachusetts
Farmer Labor Party
President: Jacob Sechler Coxey, Ohio
Vice President: Julius J. Reiter, Minnesota
Jobless Party
President: James Renshaw Cox, Pennsylvania
Vice President: V. C. Tisdal, Oklahoma
National Party
President: Seymour E. Allen, Massachusetts

Election of 1936

Democratic Party
President: Franklin Delano Roosevelt, New York
Vice President: John Nance Garner, Texas
Republican Party
President: Alfred Mossman Landon, Kansas
Vice President: Frank Knox, Illinois
Union Party
President: William Lemke, North Dakota
Vice President: Thomas Charles O'Brien, Massachusetts
Socialist Party
President: Norman Mattoon Thomas, New York
Vice President: George A. Nelson, Wisconsin
Communist Party
President: Earl Russell Browder, Kansas
Vice President: James William Ford, New York
Prohibition Party
President: David Leigh Colvin, New York
Vice President: Alvin York, Tennessee
Socialist Labor Party
President: John W. Aikin, Massachusetts
Vice President: Emil F. Teichert, New York
National Greenback Party
President: John Zahnd, Indiana*
Vice President: Florence Garvin, Rhode Island*

Election of 1940

Democratic Party
President: Franklin Delano Roosevelt, New York
Vice President: Henry Agard Wallace, Iowa
Republican Party
President: Wendell Lewis Willkie, New York
Vice President: Charles Linza McNary, Oregon
Socialist Party
President: Norman Mattoon Thomas, New York
Vice President: Maynard C. Krueger, Illinois
Prohibition Party
President: Roger Ward Babson, Massachusetts
Vice President: Edgar V. Moorman, Illinois
Communist Party (Workers Party)
President: Earl Russell Browder, Kansas
Vice President: James William Ford, New York
Socialist Labor Party
President: John W. Aiken, Massachusetts
Vice President: Aaron M. Orange, New York
Greenback Party
President: John Zahnd, Indiana*
Vice President: James Elmer Yates, Arizona*

Election of 1944

Democratic Party
President: Franklin Delano Roosevelt, New York
Vice President: Harry S Truman, Missouri
Republican Party
President: Thomas Edmund Dewey, New York

Vice President: John William Bricker, Ohio
Socialist Party
President: Norman Mattoon Thomas, New York
Vice President: Darlington Hoopes, Pennsylvania
Prohibition Party
President: Claude A. Watson, California
Vice President: Andrew Johnson, Kentucky
Socialist Labor Party
President: Edward A. Teichert, Pennsylvania
Vice President: Arla A. Albaugh, Ohio
America First Party
President: Gerald Lyman Kenneth Smith, Michigan
Vice President: Henry A. Romer, Ohio

Election of 1948

Democratic Party
President: Harry S Truman, Missouri
Vice President: Alben William Barkley, Kentucky
Republican Party
President: Thomas Edmund Dewey, New York
Vice President: Earl Warren, California
States' Rights Democratic Party
President: James Strom Thurmond, South Carolina
Vice President: Fielding Lewis Wright, Mississippi
Progressive Party
President: Henry Agard Wallace, Iowa
Vice President: Glen Hearst Taylor, Idaho
Socialist Party
President: Norman Mattoon Thomas, New York
Vice President: Tucker Powell Smith, Michigan
Prohibition Party
President: Claude A. Watson, California
Vice President: Dale Learn, Pennsylvania
Socialist Labor Party
President: Edward A. Teichert, Pennsylvania
Vice President: Stephen Emery, New York
Socialist Workers Party
President: Farrell Dobbs, New York
Vice President: Grace Carlson, Minnesota
Christian Nationalist Party
President: Gerald Lyman Kenneth Smith, Missouri
Vice President: Henry A. Romer, Ohio
Greenback Party
President: John G. Scott, New York
Vice President: Granville B. Leeke, Indiana*
Vegetarian Party
President: John Maxwell, Illinois
Vice President: Symon Gould, New York*

Election of 1952

Republican Party
President: Dwight David Eisenhower, New York
Vice President: Richard Milhous Nixon, California
Democratic Party
President: Adlai Ewing Stevenson, Illinois
Vice President: John Jackson Sparkman, Alabama
Progressive Party
President: Vincent William Hallinan, California
Vice President: Charlotta A. Bass, New York
Prohibition Party
President: Stuart Hamblen, California
Vice President: Enoch Arden Holtwick, Illinois
Socialist Labor Party
President: Eric Hass, New York
Vice President: Stephen Emery, New York
Socialist Party
President: Darlington Hoopes, Pennsylvania
Vice President: Samuel Herman Friedman, New York
Socialist Workers Party
President: Farrell Dobbs, New York
Vice President: Myra Tanner Weiss, New York
America First Party
President: Douglas MacArthur, Wisconsin
Vice President: Harry Flood Byrd, Virginia

American Labor Party
President: Vincent William Hallinan, California
Vice President: Charlotta A. Bass, New York
American Vegetarian Party
President: Daniel J. Murphy, California
Vice President: Symon Gould, New York*
Church of God Party
President: Homer Aubrey Tomlinson, New York
Vice President: Willie Isaac Bass, North Carolina*
Constitution Party
President: Douglas MacArthur, Wisconsin
Vice President: Harry Flood Byrd, Virginia
Greenback Party
President: Frederick C. Proehl, Washington
Vice President: Edward J. Bedell, Indiana
Poor Man's Party
President: Henry B. Krajewski, New Jersey
Vice President: Frank Jenkins, New Jersey

Election of 1956

Republican Party
President: Dwight David Eisenhower, Pennsylvania
Vice President: Richard Milhous Nixon, California
Democratic Party
President: Adlai Ewing Stevenson, Illinois
Vice President: Estes Kefauver, Tennessee
States' Rights Party
President: Thomas Coleman Andrews, Virginia
Vice President: Thomas Harold Werdel, California
Ticket also favored by Constitution Party.
Prohibition Party
President: Enoch Arden Holtwick, Illinois
Vice President: Edward M. Cooper, California
Socialist Labor Party
President: Eric Hass, New York
Vice President: Georgia Cozzini, Wisconsin
Texas Constitution Party
President: William Ezra Jenner, Indiana*
Vice President: Joseph Bracken Lee, Utah*
Socialist Workers Party
President: Farrell Dobbs, New York
Vice President: Myra Tanner Weiss, New York
American Third Party
President: Henry Krajewski, New Jersey
Vice President: Ann Marie Yezo, New Jersey
Socialist Party
President: Darlington Hoopes, Pennsylvania
Vice President: Samuel Herman Friedman, New York
Pioneer Party
President: William Langer, North Dakota*
Vice President: Burr McCloskey, Illinois*
American Vegetarian Party
President: Herbert M. Shelton, California*
Vice President: Symon Gould, New York*
Greenback Party
President: Frederick C. Proehl, Washington
Vice President: Edward Kirby Meador, Massachusetts*
States' Rights Party of Kentucky
President: Harry Flood Byrd, Virginia
Vice President: William Ezra Jenner, Indiana
South Carolinians for Independent Electors
President: Harry Flood Byrd, Virginia
Christian National Party
President: Gerald Lyman Kenneth Smith
Vice President: Charles I. Robertson

Election of 1960

Democratic Party
President: John Fitzgerald Kennedy, Massachusetts
Vice President: Lyndon Baines Johnson, Texas

Republican Party
President: Richard Milhous Nixon, California
Vice President: Henry Cabot Lodge, Massachusetts
National States' Rights Party
President: Orval Eugene Faubus, Arkansas
Vice President: John Geraerdt Crommelin, Alabama
Socialist Labor Party
President: Eric Hass, New York
Vice President: Georgia Cozzini, Wisconsin
Prohibition Party
President: Rutherford Losey Decker, Missouri
Vice President: Earle Harold Munn, Michigan
Socialist Workers Party
President: Farrell Dobbs, New York
Vice President: Myra Tanner Weiss, New York
Conservative Party of New Jersey
President: Joseph Bracken Lee, Utah
Vice President: Kent H. Courtney, Louisiana
Conservative Party of Virginia
President: C. Benton Coiner, Virginia
Vice President: Edward M. Silverman, Virginia
Constitution Party (Texas)
President: Charles Loten Sullivan, Mississippi
Vice President: Merritt B. Curtis, District of Columbia
Constitution Party (Washington)
President: Merritt B. Curtis, District of Columbia
Vice President: B. N. Miller
Greenback Party
President: Whitney Hart Slocomb, California*
Vice President: Edward Kirby Meador, Massachusetts*
Independent Afro-American Party
President: Clennon King, Georgia
Vice President: Reginald Carter
Tax Cut Party (America First Party; American Party)
President: Lar Daly, Illinois
Vice President: Merritt Barton Curtis, District of Columbia
Theocratic Party
President: Homer Aubrey Tomlinson, New York
Vice President: Raymond L. Teague, Alaska*
Vegetarian Party
President: Symon Gould, New York
Vice President: Christopher Gian-Cursio, Florida

Election of 1964

Democratic Party
President: Lyndon Baines Johnson, Texas
Vice President: Hubert Horatio Humphrey, Minnesota
Republican Party
President: Barry Morris Goldwater, Arizona
Vice President: William Edward Miller, New York
Socialist Labor Party
President: Eric Hass, New York
Vice President: Henning A. Blomen, Massachusetts
Prohibition Party
President: Earle Harold Munn, Michigan
Vice President: Mark Shaw, Massachusetts
Socialist Workers Party
President: Clifton DeBerry, New York
Vice President: Edward Shaw, New York
National States' Rights Party
President: John Kasper, Tennessee
Vice President: J. B. Stoner, Georgia
Constitution Party
President: Joseph B. Lightburn, West Virginia
Vice President: Theodore C. Billings, Colorado
Independent States' Rights Party
President: Thomas Coleman Andrews, Virginia
Vice President: Thomas H. Werdel, California*
Theocratic Party
President: Homer Aubrey Tomlinson, New York
Vice President: William R. Rogers, Missouri*
Universal Party
President: Kirby James Hensley, California
Vice President: John O. Hopkins, Iowa

Election of 1968

Republican Party
President: Richard Milhous Nixon, New York
Vice President: Spiro Theodore Agnew, Maryland
Democratic Party
President: Hubert Horatio Humphrey, Minnesota
Vice President: Edmund Sixtus Muskie, Maine
American Independent Party
President: George Corley Wallace, Alabama
Vice President: Curtis Emerson LeMay, Ohio
LeMay replaced S. Marvin Griffin, who originally had been selected.
Peace and Freedom Party
President: Eldridge Cleaver
Vice President: Judith Mage, New York
Socialist Labor Party
President: Henning A. Blomen, Massachusetts
Vice President: George Sam Taylor, Pennsylvania
Socialist Workers Party
President: Fred Halstead, New York
Vice President: Paul Boutelle, New Jersey
Prohibition Party
President: Earle Harold Munn, Sr., Michigan
Vice President: Rolland E. Fisher, Kansas
Communist Party
President: Charlene Mitchell, California
Vice President: Michael Zagarell, New York
Constitution Party
President: Richard K. Troxell, Texas
Vice President: Merle Thayer, Iowa
Freedom and Peace Party
President: Dick Gregory (Richard Claxton Gregory), Illinois
Patriotic Party
President: George Corley Wallace, Alabama
Vice President: William Penn Patrick, California*
Theocratic Party
President: William R. Rogers, Missouri
Universal Party
President: Kirby James Hensley, California
Vice President: Rcscoe B. MacKenna

Election of 1972

Republican Party
President: Richard Milhous Nixon, California
Vice President: Spiro Theodore Agnew, Maryland
Democratic Party
President: George Stanley McGovern, South Dakota
Vice President: Thomas Francis Eagleton, Missouri
Eagleton resigned and was replaced on August 8, 1972, by Robert Sargent Shriver, Maryland, selected by the Democratic National Committee.
American Independent Party
President: John George Schmitz, California
Vice President: Thomas Jefferson Anderson, Tennessee
Socialist Workers Party
President: Louis Fisher, Illinois
Vice President: Genevieve Gunderson, Minnesota
Socialist Labor Party
President: Linda Jenness, Georgia
Vice President: Andrew Pulley, Illinois
Communist Party
President: Gus Hall, New York
Vice President: Jarvis Tyner
Prohibition Party
President: Earle Harold Munn, Sr., Michigan
Vice President: Marshall Uncapher
Libertarian Party
President: John Hospers, California
Vice President: Theodora Nathan, Oregon

People's Party
President: Benjamin McLane Spock
Vice President: Julius Hobson, District of Columbia
America First Party
President: John V. Mahalchik
Vice President: Irving Homer
Universal Party
President: Gabriel Green
Vice President: Daniel Fry

Election of 1976

Democratic Party
President: Jimmy Carter, Georgia
Vice President: Walter F. Mondale, Minnesota
Republican Party
President: Gerald R. Ford, Michigan
Vice President: Robert Dole, Kansas
Independent Candidate
President: Eugene J. McCarthy, Minnesota
Vice President: none ⁴
Libertarian Party
President: Roger MacBride, Virginia
Vice President: David P. Bergland, California
American Independent Party
President: Lester Maddox, Georgia
Vice President: William Dyke, Wisconsin
American Party
President: Thomas J. Anderson, Tennessee
Vice President: Rufus Shackleford, Florida
Socialist Workers Party
President: Peter Camejo, California
Vice President: Willie Mae Reid, California
Communist Party
President: Gus Hall, New York
Vice President: Jarvis Tyner, New York
People's Party
President: Margaret Wright, California
Vice President: Benjamin Spock, New York
U.S. Labor Party
President: Lyndon H. LaRouche, New York
Vice President: R.W. Evans, Michigan
Prohibition Party
President: Benjamin C. Bubar, Maine
Vice President: Earl F. Dodge, Colorado
Socialist Labor Party
President: Jules Levin, New Jersey
Vice President: Constance Blomen, Massachusetts
Socialist Party
President: Frank P. Zeidler, Wisconsin
Vice President: J. Quinn Brisben, Illinois
Restoration Party
President: Ernest L. Miller
Vice President: Roy N. Eddy
United American Party
President: Frank Taylor
Vice President: Henry Swan

Election of 1980⁵

Republican Party
President: Ronald Reagan, California
Vice President: George Bush, Texas

Democratic Party
President: Jimmy Carter, Georgia
Vice President: Walter F. Mondale, Minnesota

Independent Candidate
President: John B. Anderson, Illinois
Vice President: Patrick J. Lucey, Wisconsin

Libertarian Party
President: Edward E. Clark, California
Vice President: David Koch, New York

Citizens Party
President: Barry Commoner, New York
Vice President: LaDonna Harris, New Mexico

Communist Party
President: Gus Hall, New York
Vice President: Angela Davis, California

American Independent Party
President: John R. Rarick, Louisiana
Vice President: ·Matilde Zimmerman

Socialist Workers
President: Andrew Pulley, Illinois
Vice President: Frank L. Varnum, Calif.

President: Clifton DeBerry, California
Vice President: Matilde Zimmermann

President: Richard Congress, Ohio
Vice President: Matilde Zimmerman

Right to Life
President: Ellen McCormack, New York
Vice President: Carroll Driscoll, New Jersey

Peace and Freedom
President: Maureen Smith, California
Vice President: Elizabeth Barron

Workers World
President: Dierdre Griswold, New Jersey
Vice President: Larry Holmes, New York

Statesman
President: Benjamin C. Bubar, Maine
Vice President: Earl F. Dodge, Colorado

Socialist
President: David McReynolds, New York
Vice President: Diane Drufenbrock, Wisconsin

American
President: Percy L. Greaves, New York
Vice President: Frank L. Varnum, California

President: Frank W. Shelton, Utah
Vice President: George E. Jackson

Middle Class
President: Kurt Lynen, New Jersey
Vice President: Harry Kieve, New Jersey

Down With Lawyers
President: Bill Gahres, New Jersey
Vice President: J. F. Loghlin, New Jersey

Independent
President: Martin E. Wendelken
(no vice presidential candidate)

Natural Peoples
President: Harley McLain, North Dakota
Vice President: Jewelie Goeller, North Dakota

---

1. 1912: Schlesinger's History of Presidential Elections lists the Socialist Labor Party vice presidential candidates as Francis. No first name is given for Francis.

2. 1924: Scammon's America at the Polls lists the American Party vice presidential candidate as Leander L. Pickett.

3. 1928: America at the Polls lists the Farmer Labor Party vice presidential candidate as L. R. Tillman.

4. 1976: McCarthy, who ran as an independent with no party designation, had no national running mate, favoring the elimination of the office. But as various state laws required a running mate, he had different ones in different states, amounting to nearly two dozen, all political unknowns.

* Candidates appeared in Kane's Facts About the Presidents but could not be verified in another source: see text p. 221.

5. 1980: In several cases vice presidential nominees were different from those listed for most states, and the Socialist Workers and American party nominees for president varied from state to state. For example, because Pulley, the major standard bearer for the Socialist Workers Party was only 29 years old, his name was not allowed on the ballot on some states (the Constitution requires presidential candidates to be at least 35 years old). Hence, the party ran other candidates in those states. In a number of states candidates appeared on the ballot with variants of the party designations listed, without any party designation, or with entirely different party names.

Bibliographies

Pre-Convention Politics, 1789-1828

Binkley, Wilfred E. *American Political Parties: Their Natural History.* New York: Knopf, 1966.

Bonadia, F. H., ed. *Political Parties in American History, 1815-1890.* New York: Putnam, 1973.

Bryce, James. *The American Commonwealth.* "The Party System," pp. 3-246. New York: Macmillan, 1922.

Burnham, Walter D. *The American Party System: Stages of Political Development.* New York: Oxford University Press, 1967.

Chambers, William N., ed. *First Party System: Federalists and Republicans.* New York: Wiley, 1972.

Chambers, William N. *Political Parties in a New Nation: The American Experience, 1776-1809.* New York: Oxford University Press, 1963.

Charles, Joseph. *Origins of the American Party System.* Williamsburg, Virginia: Institute of Early American History and Culture, 1956.

Claflin, Alta B. *Political Parties in the United States, 1800-1914.* New York: B. Franklin, 1915.

Cunningham, Noble. *The Making of the American Party System, 1789-1809.* Englewood Cliffs, New Jersey: Prentice-Hall, 1965.

Duverger, Maurice. *Political Parties.* New York: Wiley, 1959.

Goodman, William. *The Two-Party System in the United States.* Princeton, New Jersey: Van Nostrand, 1960.

Hofstadter, Richard. *The Idea of a Party System: The Rise of Legitimate Opposition in the United States, 1780-1840.* Berkeley, California: University of California Press, 1969.

James, Judson L. *American Political Parties and Democratic Government.* New York: Pegasus Press, 1969.

Ladd, Everett. *American Political Parties.* New York: Norton, 1971.

La Palombara, Joseph. *Political Parties and Political Development.* Princeton, New Jersey: Princeton University Press, 1966.

McCormick, Richard P. *The Second American Party System: Party Formulation in the Jacksonian Era.* Chapel Hill, North Carolina: University of North Carolina Press, 1966.

Macy, Jesse. *Political Parties in the United States, 1846-1861.* New York: Arno Press, 1974.

Main, Jackson. *Political Parties Before the Constitution.* Chapel Hill, North Carolina: University of North Carolina Press, 1973.

Merriam, Charles E. *The American Party System: An Introduction to the Study of Political Parties in the United States.* New York: Macmillan, 1949.

Nichols, Roy F. *The Invention of the American Political Parties.* New York: Macmillan, 1967.

Ostrogorski, Moisei. *Democracy and the Organization of Political Parties: The United States.* Volume II, Garden City, New York: Doubleday, 1964.

Owens, John R. *The American Party System.* New York: Macmillan, 1965.

Penniman, Howard R. *Sait's American Parties and Elections.* New York: Appleton-Century-Croft, 1952.

Ray, P. O. *Introduction to Political Parties and Practical Politics.* New York: Scribner, 1922.

Risjord, Norman, ed. *The Early Party System.* New York: Harper & Row, 1969.

Robinson, Edgar E. *The Evolution of American Political Parties.* New York: Harcourt, Brace, 1924.

Roseboom, Eugene H. *A History of Presidential Elections.* New York: Macmillan, 1959.

Rossiter, Clinton. *Parties and Politics in America.* Ithaca, New York: Cornell University Press, 1960.

Sait, Edward M. *American Parties and Elections.* New York: Appleton-Century, 1939.

Schattschneider, E. E. *Party Government.* New York: Farrar & Rinehart, 1942.

Schlesinger, Arthur M. Jr., ed. *History of U.S. Political Parties.* 4 vols., New York: Bowker, 1973.

Sindler, Allan P. *Political Parties in the United States.* New York: St. Martin's Press, 1966.

Sorauf, Frank J. *Party Politics in America.* Boston, Massachusetts: Little, Brown, 1968.

Sorauf, Frank J. *Political Parties in the American System.* Boston, Massachusetts: Little, Brown, 1972.

Stanwood, Edward. *A History of the Presidency from 1788 to 1897.* Boston: Houghton Mifflin, 1898.

Stimpson, George William. *A Book about American Politics.* New York: Harper, 1952.

Tocqueville, Alexis de. *Democracy in the United States.* 2 vols., New York: Knopf, 1948.

Van Buren, Martin. *Inquiry into the Origin and Course of Political Parties in the United States.* New York: A. M. Kelley, 1867.

Vorees, Edith. *Political Parties in the United States.* New York: Pageant, 1960.

Nominating Conventions

Books

Aly, Bower, ed *Selecting the President.* 2 vols. Columbia, Missouri: Lucas Brothers, 1953.

Bain, Richard C. and Parris, Judith H. *Convention Decisions and Voting Records.* Washington, D.C.: Brookings Institution, 1973.

Bickel, Alexander M. *The New Age of Political Reform: The Electoral College, the Convention and the Party.* New York: Harper & Row, 1968.

Bickel, Alexander M. *Reform and Continuity: The Electoral College, the Convention and the Party System.* New York: Harper & Row, 1971.

Binkley, Wilfred E. *American Political Parties: Their Natural History.* New York: Knopf, 1963.

Bishop, J. B. *Presidential Nomination and Elections: A History of American Conventions.* New York: Scribner, 1916.

Bryan, William J. *A Tale of Two Conventions.* New York: Funk and Wagnalls, 1912.

Chase, James S. *Emergence of the Presidential Nominating Conventions, 1789-1832.* Urbana, Illinois: University of Illinois Press, 1973.

David, Paul T. *The Politics of National Party Conventions*. Washington, D.C.: Brookings Institution, 1960.

David, Paul T., ed *Presidential Nominating Politics in 1952*. 4 vols. Baltimore, Maryland: Johns Hopkins Press, 1954.

Eaton, Herbert. *Presidential Timber: A History of Nominating Conventions*. New York: Free Press of Glencoe, 1964.

Farley, James A. *Behind the Ballots*. New York: Harcourt, Brace & World, 1938.

Halstead, Murat. *Caucuses of 1860: A History of the National Conventions of the Current Presidential Campaigns*. Columbus, Ohio: 1860.

Halstead, Murat. *Trimmers, Truckers and Temporizers: Notes of Murat Halstead from the Political Convention of 1856*. Madison, Wisconsin: Society Press, 1961.

Hart, William O. *The Democratic Conventions of 1908-1916, Republican Conventions 1912-1916, and Progressive Convention of 1912*. New Orleans, Louisiana: 1916.

Johnson, Walter. *How We Drafted Adlai Stevenson: Story of the Democratic Presidential Convention of 1952*. New York: Knopf, 1955.

Jones, Chester L. *Readings On Parties and Elections*, "National Conventions and Election of the President," pp. 80-124. Westport, Connecticut: Negro University Press, 1970.

Kane, Joseph Nathan. *Famous First Facts*. New York: H. W. Wilson Co., 1964.

Kent, Frank R. *The Democratic Party: A History*, "The First Party Convention," pp. 99-128. New York: Century, 1928.

McKee, Thomas H. *The National Conventions and Platforms of All Political Parties, 1789-1905: Convention, Popular and Electoral Vote*. New York: AMS Press, 1971.

Martin, Ralph G. *Ballots and Bandwagons*. Chicago, Illinois: Rand McNally, 1964.

Matthews, Donald R. *Perspectives on Presidential Selection*. Washington, D.C.: Brookings Institution, 1973.

Meyer, Ernst C. *Nominating Systems: Direct Primaries versus Conventions in the United States*. Madison, Wisconsin: 1902.

Morgan, H. Wayne. *From Hayes to McKinley: National Party Politics, 1877-1896*. Syracuse, New York: Syracuse University Press, 1969.

Official Proceedings of the Republican National Conventions, 1856-1976. Washington, D.C.: Republican National Committee.

Official Reports of the Proceedings of the Democratic National Conventions, 1856-1976. Washington, D.C.: Democratic National Committee.

O'Lessker, Karl. *The National Nominating Conventions*. New York: Robert A. Taft Institute of Government, 1968.

Ostrogorshi, Moisei. *Democracy and the Organization of Political Parties: The United States*, "The Establishment of the Convention," pp. 25-133, Volume II. Garden City, New York: Doubleday, 1964.

Parris, Judith H. *The Convention Problem: Issues in Reform of Presidential Procedures*. Washington, D.C.: Brookings Institution, 1972.

Pomper, Gerald M. *Nominating the President: The Politics of Convention Choice*. Evanston, Illinois: Northwestern University Press, 1963.

The Presidential Nominating Conventions, 1968. Washington, D.C.: Congressional Quarterly, 1968.

Sait, Edward M. *American Parties and Elections*, "The National Convention," pp. 529-596. New York: Appleton-Century, 1939.

Schlesinger, Arthur M. Jr., ed. *History of U.S. Political Parties*. 4 vols. New York: Bowker, 1973.

Stanwood, Edward. *A History of the Presidency from 1788 to 1897*, Volume I. Boston, Massachusetts: Houghton Mifflin, 1898.

Stoddard, H. L. *Presidential Sweepstakes: The Story of Political Conventions and Campaigns*. New York: Putnam, 1948.

Thompson, Charles S. *An Essay on the Rise and Fall of the Congressional Caucus as a Machine for Nominating Candidates for the Presidency*. New Haven, Connecticut: Yale University Press, 1902.

Tillett, Paul, ed. *Inside Politics: The National Conventions, 1960*. Dobbs Ferry, New York: Oceana, 1962.

Articles

Angle, Paul M. "The Republican Convention of 1860." *Chicago History*, Spring, 1960, p. 341.

"Bode vs. National Democratic Party: Apportionment of Delegates to National Political Conventions." *Harvard Law Review*, May 1972, pp. 1460-1477.

Carleton, William. "The Revolution in the Presidential Convention." *Political Science Quarterly*, June 1957, pp. 224-240.

Center, Judith A. "1972 Democratic Convention Reforms and Party Democracy." *Political Science Quarterly*, June 1974, pp. 325-350.

"Constitutional Safeguards in the Selection of Delegates to Presidential Nominating Conventions." *Yale Law Journal*, June 1969, pp. 1228-1252.

Cooke, Edward F. "Drafting the 1952 Platforms." *Western Political Quarterly*, September 1956, pp. 699-712.

Costain, Anne N. "An Analysis of Voting in American National Nominating Conventions, 1940-1976." *American Politics Quarterly*, January 1978, pp. 95-120.

David, Paul T. "Party Platforms As National Plans." *Public Administration Review*, May/June 1971, pp. 305-315.

"Exploring the 1976 Republican Convention: Five Perspectives." *Political Science Quarterly*, Winter 1977/1978.

Goldman, Ralph M. "Presidential Nominating Patterns." *Western Political Quarterly*, September 1955, pp. 465-80.

Hitlin, Robert. "Support for Changes in the Convention System — 1968." *Western Political Quarterly*, December 1973, pp. 686-701.

Jackson, John S. "Recruitment, Representation, and Political Values: The 1976 Democratic National Convention Delegates." *American Politics Quarterly*, April 1978, pp. 187-212.

McGrath, Wilma E. and Soule, John W. "Rocking the Cradle or Rocking the Boat: Women at the 1972 Democratic National Convention." *Social Science Quarterly*, June 1974, pp. 141-150.

Marshall, Thomas R. "Delegate Selection in 1976: Evaluating Causes and Primaries." *National Civic Review*, September 1977, pp. 391-396.

Marshall, Thomas R. "Delegate Selection in Nonprimary States: The Question of Representation." *National Civic Review*, September 1976, pp. 390-393.

Nicholas, H. G. "American Political Conventions." *Fort-*

nightly, September 1948, pp. 154-60.

Noyes, Charles. "Selection of Nominees for the Presidency." *Editorial Research Reports,* Volume I, 1939, pp. 419-431.

Patch, Buel W. "Open Conventions." *Editorial Research Reports,* May 9, Volume I, 1952, pp. 353-70.

Polsby, Nelson W. "Decision Making at the National Conventions." *Western Political Quarterly,* September 1960, pp. 609-19.

Potts, C. S. "The Convention System and the Presidential Primary." *American Review of Reviews,* May 1912, pp. 561-566.

Pressman, Jeffrey L. and Sullivan, Denis G. "Convention Reform and Conventional Wisdom: An Empirical Assessment of Democratic Party Reforms." *Political Science Quarterly,* Fall 1974, pp. 539-562.

Quinn, John M. "Presidential Nominating Conventions: Party Rules, State Laws, and the Constitution." *Georgetown Law Journal,* July 1974, pp. 1621-1622.

Raymar, Robert S. "Judicial Review of Credentials Contests: The Experience of the 1972 Democratic National Convention." *George Washington Law Review,* November 1973, pp. 1-39.

Roback, Thomas H. "Amateurs and Professionals: Delegates to the 1972 Republican National Convention." *Journal of Politics,* May 1975, pp. 436-468.

Soule, John W., and Clarke, James W. "Amateurs and Professionals: A Study of Delegates to the 1968 Democratic National Convention." *American Political Science Review,* September 1970, pp. 888-898.

"The United States Presidential Elections: Procedures and Prospects, the Primaries and Conventions." *World Today,* July 1952, pp. 278-287.

Walton, Hanes Jr. "Black Politics at the National Republican and Democratic Conventions, 1868-1972." *Phylon,* September 1975, pp. 269-278.

Wildavsky, Aaron B. "On the Superiority of National Conventions." *Review of Politics,* July 1962, p. 307.

Williams, D. C. "Choosing the Presidential Candidates." *Political Quarterly,* October 1952, pp. 368-79.

Wise, Sidney. "Choosing the Presidential Candidates." *Current History,* August 1974, pp. 52-57.

Convention Chronology

Adams, James Truslow, editor-in-chief. *Dictionary of American History.* New York: Charles Scribner's Sons, 1946. Five volumes.

Bain, Richard C. and Parris, Judith H. *Convention Decisions and Voting Records.* Washington, D.C.: The Brookings Institution, 1973.

Barber, James D., ed. *Choosing the President.* Englewood Cliffs, N.J.: Prentice-Hall, 1974.

Bennett, David H. *Demagogues in the Depression.* New Brunswick, N.J.: Rutgers University Press, 1969.

Bishop, Jim. *FDR's Last Year: April 1944-April 1945.* New York: William Morrow and Co., 1974.

Boyett, Joseph H. *Background Characteristics of Delegates to the 1972 Conventions: A Summary Report of Findings from a National Sample.* Athens, Ga.: Institute of Government, University of Georgia, 1973.

Burns, James MacGregor. *Roosevelt: The Soldier of Freedom.* New York: Harcourt Brace Jovanovich, 1970.

Byrne, Gary and Marx, Paul. *The Great American Convention: A Political History of Presidential Elections.* Palo Alto, Calif.: Pacific Books, 1977.

Chester, Edward E. *A Guide to Political Platforms.* Hamden, Conn.: Archon Books, 1977.

Congressional Quarterly Almanac (1960, 1964, 1968, 1972). Washington, D.C.: Congressional Quarterly Inc.

David, Paul T. *The Role of the Governor at the National Party Conventions, 1868-1960.* Washington, D.C.: Brookings Institution, 1960.

David, Paul T., Goldman, Ralph, and Bain, Richard C. *The Politics of National Party Conventions.* Washington, D.C.: The Brookings Institution, 1960.

Donahoe, Bernard F. *Private Plans and Public Dangers: The Story of FDR's Third Nomination.* Notre Dame, Ind.: University of Notre Dame Press, 1965.

Fleischman, Harry. *Norman Thomas: A Biography.* New York: W. W. Norton and Co., 1964.

Hesseltine, William B. *Third-Party Movements in the United States.* Princeton, N.J.: D. Van Nostrand, 1962.

Johnson, Allen and Malone, Dumas, eds. *Dictionary of American Biography.* New York: Charles Scribner's Sons, 1931. Twenty-two volumes.

Johnson, Donald B. *National Party Platforms.* 2 vols. Urbana, Ill.: University of Illinois Press, 1978.

Judah, Charles and Smith, George W. *The Unchosen.* New York. Coward, McCann & Geoghegan, 1962.

Keech, William R. and Matthews, Donald R. *The Party's Choice: With an Epilogue on the 1976 Nominations.* Washington, D.C.: Brookings Institution, 1976.

Kirkpatrick, Jeane. *The New Presidential Elite: Men and Women in National Politics.* New York: Basic Books, 1976.

Lorant, Stefan. *The Glorious Burden: The American Presidency.* New York: Harper and Row, 1969.

Lorant, Stefan. *The Presidency.* New York: Macmillan, 1951.

Lurie, Leonard. *The King Makers.* New York: Coward, McCann and Geoghegan, 1971.

McGovern, George and Fraser, Donald. *Mandate for Change: Report of the Commission on Party Structure and Delegate Selection to the Democratic National Convention.* Washington, D.C.: Democratic National Committee, 1969.

McNitt, Virgil B., ed. *A Tale of Two Conventions: An Account of the Republican and Democratic Conventions of June 1912.* New York: Arno Press, 1974.

Mailer, Norman. *Some Honorable Men: Political Conventions, 1960-1972.* New York: Little, Brown, 1976.

Moos, Malcolm C. *Hats in the Ring.* New York: Random House, 1960.

Morris, Richard B., ed. *Encyclopedia of American History.* New York: Harper and Row, 1965.

Murray, Robert K. *The One Hundred and Third Ballot: The Democrats and the Disaster in Madison Square Garden.* New York: Harper & Row, 1976.

Novak, Michael. *Choosing Our King: Powerful Symbols In Presidential Politics.* New York: Macmillan, 1974.

Parmet, Herbert S. *Eisenhower and the American Crusader.* New York: Macmillan, 1972.

Porter, Kirk H. and Johnson, Donald Bruce (compilers). *National Party Platforms, 1840-1968.* Urbana, Ill.: University of Illinois Press, 1972.

Reeves, Richard. *Convention.* New York: Harcourt Brace Jovanovich, 1977.

Roseboom, Eugene H. *A History of Presidential Elections.* New York: Macmillan, 1959.

Schlesinger, Arthur M. Jr. *The Age of Roosevelt: The Crisis of the Old Order, 1919-1933*. Boston, Mass.: Houghton Mifflin, 1956.

Schlesinger, Arthur M. Jr. *The Age of Roosevelt: The Politics of Upheavel*. Boston, Mass.: Houghton Mifflin, 1960.

Schlesinger, Arthur M. Jr., editor. *History of U.S. Political Parties*. New York: Chelsea House, 1973. Four volumes.

Schlesinger, Arthur M. Jr., editor. *The Coming to Power: Critical Presidential Elections in American History*. New York: Chelsea House, 1972.

Sullivan, Denis, et al. *Explorations in Convention Decision Making: The Democratic Party in the 1970s*. San Francisco, Calif.: W. H. Freeman, 1976.

White, Theodore H. *The Making of the President*, (1960, 1964, 1968, 1972). New York: Atheneum Publishers.

Historical Profiles of American Political Parties

Books

Ader, Emile B. *The Dixiecrat Movement: Its Role in Third Party Politics*. Wash., D.C.: Public Affairs Press, 1965. 1955.

Agar, Herbert. *The Price of Union*. Boston, Mass.: Houghton Mifflin, 1950.

Anspach, F. R. *Sons of the Sires: History of the Rise, Progress and Destiny of the American Party*. New York: A. M. Kelley, 1855.

Arnett, A. M. *The Populist Movement in Georgia*. New York: Columbia University Press, 1922.

Bartlett, R. J. *John C. Fremont and the Republican Party*. Columbus, Ohio: Ohio State University Press, 1931.

Bennett, David H. *Demagogues in the Depression. American Radicals and the Union Party, 1932-36*. New Brunswick, N.J.: Rutgers University Press, 1969.

Bernhard, Winfred E. and Borden, Morton, eds. *Political Parties in American History, 1789-1828*. 2 vols. New York: Putnam, 1974.

Bittleman, Alexander. *Milestones in the History of the Communist Party*. New York: Workers Library Publishers, 1937.

Blue, Frederick J. *The Free Soilers: Third Party Politics 1848-1854,*. Urbana, Ill.: University of Illinois Press, 1973.

Brown, Stuart G. *First Republicans: Political Philosophy and Public Policy in the Party of Jefferson and Madison*. Syracuse, N.Y.: Syracuse University Press, 1954.

Buck, Solon J. *The Agrarian Crusade: A Chronicle of the Farmer in Politics*. New Haven, Conn.: Yale University Press, 1921.

Budge, Ian et al, eds. *Party Identification and Beyond: Representations of Voting and Party Competition*. London: John Wiley, 1976.

Burdette, Franklin. *The Republican Party*. New York: Van Nostrand Reinhold, 1972.

Burner, David. *The Politics of Provincialism: The Democratic Party in Transition, 1918-1932*. New York: Knopf, 1968.

Burnham, Walter D. *Critical Elections and the Mainsprings of American Politics*. New York: Norton, 1970.

Burns, James M. *The Deadlock of Democracy: Four-Party Politics in America*. Englewood Cliffs, N.J.: Prentice-Hall, 1963.

Cannon, James P. *The History of American Trotskyism*

from Its Origin in 1928 to the Founding of the Socialist Labor Workers Party. New York: Pathfinders Press, 1972.

Carroll, E. Malcolm. *Origins of the Whig Party*. Durham, N.C.: Duke University Press, 1925.

Chambers, William N. and Burnham, Walter D., eds. *The American Party Systems*. New York: Oxford University Press, 1967.

Cole, Arthur C. *The Whig Party in the South*. Washington, D.C.: American Historical Association, 1914.

Colvin, David L. *Prohibition in the United States: A History of the Prohibition Party and the Prohibition Movement*. New York: Doran, 1926.

Converse, Philip E. *The Dynamics of Party Support: Cohort-Analyzing Party Identification*. Beverly Hills, Calif.: Sage Library of Social Research, 1976.

Cox, Edward F. *Voting in Postwar Federal Elections: A Statistical Analysis of Party Strengths Since 1945*. Dayton, Ohio: Wright State University Press, 1968.

Crandall, Andrew. *Early History of the Republican Party, 1854-1856*. Gloucester, Mass.: P. Smith, 1960.

Crotty, William J. *Decision for the Democrats: Reforming the Party Structure*. Baltimore, Md.: Johns Hopkins University Press, 1978.

Cunningham, Noble E. *The Jeffersonian Republicans in Power: Party Operations, 1801-1809*. Chapel Hill, N.C.: University of North Carolina Press, 1963.

Cunningham, Noble E. *Jeffersonian Republicans, 1789-1801*. Chapel Hill, N.C.: University of North Carolina Press, 1967.

Curtis, Francis. *The Republican Party: A History of Its Fifty Years Existence*. 2 vols. New York: AMS Press, 1976.

Davis, Lanny J. *The Emerging Democratic Majority: Lessons and Legacies from the New Politics*. New York: Stein & Day, 1974.

Desmond, Humphrey J. *The Know-Nothing Party*. Washington, D.C.: New Century Press, 1905.

Duncan-Clark, Samuel J. *The Progressive Movement: Its Principles and Its Programs*. New York: AMS Press, 1972.

Durden, Robert F. *The Climax of Populism: The Election of 1896*. Lexington: University of Kentucky Press, 1965.

Dutton, Frederick G. *Changing Sources of Power: American Politics in the 1970's*. New York: McGraw-Hill, 1971.

Fairlie, Henry. *The Parties: Republicans and Democrats in This Century*. New York: St. Martin's Press, 1978.

Fine, Nathan. *Labor and Farmer Parties in the United States, 1829-1928*. New York: Russell & Russell, 1961.

Fischer, David H. *The Revolution of American Conservatism: The Federalist Party in the Era of Jeffersonian Democracy*. New York: Harper & Row, 1965.

Foner, Eric. *Free Soil, Free Labor, Free Men: The Ideology of the Republican Party Before the Civil War*. New York: Oxford University Press, 1970.

Foster, William Z. *The Crisis in the Socialist Party*. Westport, Conn.: Greenwood Press, 1968.

Goldman, Ralph M. *The Democratic Party in American Politics*. New York: Macmillan, 1966.

Haynes, Fred E. *Third Party Movements Since the Civil War*. New York: Russell & Russell, 1966.

Hesseltine, William B. *Rise and Fall of Third Parties: From Anti-Masonry to Wallace*. Gloucester, Mass.: P. Smith, 1973.

Hesseltine, William B. *Third Party Movements in the United States*. New York: Van Nostrand, 1962.

Hicks, John D. *The Populist Revolt: A History of the Farmer's Alliance in the People's Party.* Minneapolis, Minn.: University of Minnesota Press, 1931.

Holcombe, Arthur M. *Political Parties of Today: A Study in Republican and Democratic Politics.* New York: Harper, 1924.

Isely, J. A. *Horace Greeley and the Republican Party, 1853-1861.* Princeton, N.J.: Princeton University Press, 1947.

Jones, Charles O. *The Republican Party in American Politics.* New York: Macmillan, 1965.

Kent, Frank R. *The Democratic Party: A History.* New York: Century, 1928.

Kenyon, Cecelia. *The Anti-Federalists.* Indianapolis, Ind.: Bobbs-Merrill, 1966.

Kipnis, Ira. *American Socialist Movement, 1897-1912.* Westport, Conn.: Greenwood Press, 1968.

Kleeberg, Gordon S. *Formation of the Republican Party As a National Political Organization.* New York: Burt Franklin, 1970.

Kuhn, Henry. *The Socialist Party During Four Decades, 1890-1930.* New York: Labor News Company, 1931.

Ladd, Everett. *American Political Parties: Social Change and Political Response.* New York: Norton, 1971.

Lee, John H. *The Origin and Progress of the American Party in Politics: Embracing a Complete History of the Philadelphia Riots in May and July, 1841.* Freeport, N.Y.: Books for Libraries, 1970.

Livermore, Shaw Jr. *Twilight of Federalism: The Disintegration of the Federalist Party 1815-1830.* Princeton, N.J.: Princeton University Press, 1962.

Long, John D. *The Republican Party: Its History, Principles and Policies.* New York: M. W. Hazen, 1888.

McCarthy, Charles. *The Antimasonic Party: A Study of Political Anti-Masonry in the United States, 1827-1840.* Washington, D.C.: Government Printing Office, 1903.

McKay, Kenneth. *The Progressive Movement of 1924.* New York: Octagon Books, 1966.

McKenna, George, ed. *American Populism.* New York: Putnam, 1975.

Maisel, Louis and Cooper, Joseph, eds. *Development of Political Parties.* Beverly Hills, Calif.: Sage Publications, 1978.

Mann, Arthur, ed. *The Progressive Era: Liberal Renaissance or Liberal Failure?* New York: Holt, Rinehart and Winston, 1963.

Marcus, Robert. *Grand Old Party: Political Structure in the Gilded Age, 1880-1896.* New York: Oxford University Press, 1971.

Martin, Roscoe C. *The People's Party in Texas: A Study in Third Party Politics.* Austin: University of Texas, Bulletin no. 3308, February 22, 1933.

Mayer, George H. *The Republican Party, 1854-1964.* New York, Oxford University Press, 1964.

Merrill, Horace S. *Bourbon Leader: Grover Cleveland and the Democratic Party.* Boston: Little, Brown, 1957.

Moos, Malcolm. *The Republicans: A History of Their Party.* New York: Random House, 1956.

Mowry, George. *Theodore Roosevelt and the Progressive Movement.* New York: Hill & Wang, 1960.

Murphy, Paul. *Political Parties in American History, 1890 to Present.* 3 vols. New York: Putnam, 1974.

Myers, William S. *Republican Party: A History.* New York: Johnson Reprint, 1968.

Nash, Howard P. Jr. *Third Parties in American Politics.* Washington, D.C.: Public Affairs Press, 1959.

Ormsby, Robert M. *A History of the Whig Party or Some of Its Main Features.* New York: H. Dexer, 1860.

Overdyke, William. *The Know-Nothing Party in the South.* Gloucester, Mass.: P. Smith, 1968.

Phillips, Kevin P. *The Emerging Republican Majority.* New Rochelle, N.Y.: Arlington House, 1969.

Pinchot, Amos R. E. *History of the Progressive Party, 1912-1916.* New York: New York University Press, 1958.

Plunkett, Margaret L. *A History of the Liberty Party With Emphasis Upon Its Activities in the Northwestern States.* Ithaca, N.Y. 1930.

Poage, George. *Henry Clay and the Whig Party.* New York: Peter Smith, 1965.

Ratner, Lorman. *Antimasonry: The Crusade and the Party.* Englewood Cliffs, N.J.: Prentice-Hall, 1969.

Rayback, Joseph G. *Free Soil: The Election of 1848.* Lexington, Ky.: University Press of Kentucky, 1970.

Remini, Robert V. *Martin Van Buren and the Making of the Democratic Party.* New York: Columbia University Press, 1959.

Rochester, Anna. *The Populist Movement in the United States.* New York: International Publishers, 1944.

Rose, Leslie A. *Prologue to Democracy: The Federalists in the South, 1789-1800.* Lexington, Ky.: University Press of Kentucky, 1968.

Ross, Earle D. *The Liberal Republican Movement.* Seattle: University of Washington Press, 1970.

Sait, Edward M. *American Parties and Elections.* New York: Appleton-Century, 1939.

Schnapper, Morris B. *Grand Old Party: The First One Hundred Years of the Republican Party.* Washington, D.C.: Public Affairs Press, 1955.

Shannon, David A. *The Decline of American Communism: A History of the Communist Party in the United States Since 1945.* Chatham, N.J.: Chatham Booksellers, 1971.

Shannon, David A. *The Socialist Party of America: A History.* Cleveland, Ohio: Quadrangle Books, 1967.

Sherman, John. "Birth of the Republican Party," *Recollections of Forty Years in the House, Senate and the Cabinet,* pp. 106-122. New York: Werner Company, 1895.

Schlesinger, Arthur M. Jr., ed. *History of U.S. Political Parties.* 4 vols. New York: Bowker, 1973.

Smith, Theodore C. *Liberty and Free Soil Parties in the Northwest.* New York: Arno Press, 1969.

Socialist Labor Party of America. Madison, Wis.: State Historical Society of Wisconsin, 1970.

Soule, Leon C. *Know-Nothing Party in New Orleans: A Reappraisal.* Baton Rouge, Louisiana: State University Press, 1961.

Southgate, D. *Passing of the Whigs.* New York: St. Martin's Press, 1962.

Stedman, Murray S., Jr. and Stedman, Susan W. *Discontent at the Polls: A Study of Farmer and Labor Parties, 1827-1948.* New York: Russell, 1967.

Stewart, John G. *One Last Chance: The Democratic Party, 1974-1976.* New York: Praeger, 1974.

Sundquist, James L. *Dynamics of the Party System: Alignment and Realignment of Political Parties in the United States.* Washington, D.C.: Brookings Institution, 1973.

Thomas, Harrison C. *The Return of the Democratic Party to Power in 1884.* New York: Columbia University Press, 1919.

Timberlake, James H. *Prohibition and the Progressive Movement, 1900-1920.* New York: Atheneum, 1970.

Walton, Hanes, Jr. *Black Political Parties: An Historical and Political Analysis.* New York: Free Press, 1972.

Weinstein, James. *The Decline of Socialism in America, 1912-1925.* New York: Random House, 1969.

Wilson, George. *The Greenbacks and Their Doctrine.* Lexington, Mo.: Intelligenser News, 1878.

Zieger, Robert H. *Republicans and Labor, 1919-1929.* Lexington, Ky.: University Press of Kentucky, 1969.

Articles

"The American Two-Party System." *Current History*, July 1974.

Black, Merle. "Republican Party Development in the South: The Rise of the Contested Primary." *Social Science Quarterly*, December 1976, pp. 566-578.

Burnham, Walter D. "The End of American Party Politics." *Transaction*, December 1969, pp. 12-22.

Converse, Philip E. et al. "Continuity and Change in American Politics: Parties and Issues in the 1968 Elections." *American Political Science Review*, December 1969, pp. 1097-1098.

Fotheringham, Peter. "Changes in the American Party System, 1948-1972." *Government and Opposition*, Spring 1973, pp. 217-241.

Ginsberg, Benjamin. "Critical Elections and the Substance of Party Conflict: 1844-1968." *Midwest Journal of Political Science*, November 1972, pp. 603-625.

Kester, John G. "Constitutional Restrictions on Political Parties." *Virginia Law Review*, May 1974, pp. 735-784.

Ladd, Everett C. Jr. et al. "A New Political Realignment?" *Public Interest*, Spring 1971, pp. 46-63.

McClellan, Jim. "The Bipartisan Ballot Monopoly: The Election Laws of Most States are Designed to Keep New Parties Out in the Cold." *Progressive*, March 1975, pp. 18-21.

Mitau, G. Theodore. "The Democratic-Farmer-Labor Party Schism of 1948." *Minnesota History*, Spring 1955, pp. 187-194.

Pomper, Gerald M. "The Decline of the Party in American Elections." *Political Science Quarterly*, Spring 1977, pp. 21-41.

Index